To Tove and Erik

STIGUM, & STIGUM

Bernt P

ADDISON-WESLEY PUBLISHING COMPANY

ECONOMICS

READING, MASSACHUSETTS · MENLO PARK · LONDON · DON MILLS, ONTARIO

ABOUT THE AUTHORS

Bernt P. Stigum is an associate professor in the department of economics, Northwestern University. He received his B.A. degree from Dartmouth College and his Ph.D. degree from Harvard University. He was previously an associate professor at Cornell University. His teaching interests include: mathematical economics, econometrics, economic theory, and statistics. He is a frequent contributor to journals in the fields of mathematical statistics and economics.

Marcia L. Stigum (Mrs. Bernt P. Stigum) received her B.A. degree from Middlebury College and her Ph.D. degree from the Massachusetts Institute of Technology. She has held academic posts at Cornell University, at Wellesley College, and at Northeastern University. Her primary fields of interest are economic theory and international trade.

PREFACE

Economists, as Walter Heller has pointed out in his *New Dimensions of Political Economy,* have in recent years come to play a much more influential role in government, and the government for its part has gradually begun to be more and more willing to consciously carry out bold economic policies. This means that today more than ever it's important for a person to understand the economic problems of the day and to be able to evaluate the different policies proposed to deal with them. But to do so a person needs a firm grasp of the tools of economic analysis and needs to be familiar with a wide range of economic institutions. Giving the student this grasp and this familiarity has been our objective throughout this book.

Writing a text that would give the student a firmer grasp of economic theory than he gets from the usual introductory book called, we thought, for doing two things: The first was to present a more comprehensive survey of the theory than most texts do, one that would have no missing links and would tie together the different strands of the theory into a single coherent whole. The second was to introduce the student to the theory in a way that would make it easier for him to thoroughly master it. To accomplish the first of these goals, we have covered a number of new theoretical topics that most texts do not: the consumer's investment decision, the firm's production function, the firm's investment decision, and the role of financial intermediaries in funds flows. We have also placed greater stress than most texts do on other theoretical topics, such as general equilibrium, monetary policy, and balance-of-payments adjustment. To accomplish our second goal—making it easier for the student to master the theory—we have sought to organize the book so that each chapter builds logically on the material presented in preceding chapters. Thus, for example, instead of introducing supply and demand curves out of the blue in an early chapter and then deriving them later on, we start out by talking about the consumer and the firm and we derive demand and supply curves there; then we go on to discuss price determination in a perfectly competitive market. Also, by not placing a chapter on supply and demand early in the book, we avoid giving the student the misleading impression that price is determined by supply and demand in all markets. Thus he doesn't stumble on monopoly and oligopoly, chapters later, as confusing afterthoughts that require him to unlearn the misconception he has acquired about supply and demand. As another aid to mastering the theory, we have repeatedly provided examples and data that point up the relevance of the theory we develop to the economic world in which the student lives. Finally, the problems at the end of each chapter and the study guide that Ronald Olsen has written offer the student an opportunity to work with the theoretical tools developed in the text. This we think is important, because the only way the student can master an analytic discipline like economics is to use it to solve problems.

Although theory has been an important concern throughout the book, it hasn't been our only concern. In addition we have tried to give the student the background information on economic institutions that he will need to apply the theory that this text presents to everyday economic problems. For this reason we have added to our discussion a number of institutional topics not usually dealt with in elementary texts, and given others more stress than they usually receive. Thus, for example, in addition to the usual chapters on unions, antitrust measures, and public finance, we have added a description of financial intermediaries and financial markets. This addition makes it possible for us to get away from the usual *IS-LM*-curve approach to monetary policy and to talk about monetary policy in terms of its effect on the cost and availability of credit. This we think is a real plus for the student, since this approach to monetary policy is an easy one for him to connect intuitively with real-life events. The student who has read parts 5 and 6 of our text will know what is going on when he reads on the front page of the *New York Times* (as he might have in November 1967) that a rise in the discount rate has led to a rise in the mortgage rates charged by savings and loan associations and to a rise in the commercial paper rate. He won't find himself asking: What's a savings and loan association? What's commercial paper? Or, worse still, what's a Treasury bill?

We hope that, besides writing a book that offers the student the opportunity to get a good grasp of economic theory and economic institutions, we have also written a book that the instructor will find it fun to teach from and that the student will find challenging and interesting to read. From our own experience in the classroom this book meets these criteria. But of course we're the authors, so we're a biased sample.

January 1968   Bernt P. Stigum
Ithaca, New York   Marcia L. Stigum

ACKNOWLEDGMENTS

This text charts a rather novel course, and for this the authors must take some of the credit and all of the blame. We have, however, had a lot of help and useful criticism. In particular, we wish to thank Morris Adelman, W. H. Locke Anderson, William J. Breen, Neil Chamberlain, Jon Cunnyngham, Richard Day, Peter Diamond, Duane Evans, Louis M. Falkson, Charles P. Kindleberger, Jerome La Pittus, Ronald R. Olsen, Jerome Rothenberg, Lars Sandberg, Dennis Starleaf, and James Tobin, all of whom have read parts of the manuscript. Their comments in many instances led us to make substantial revisions in the material. Special thanks must also go to Carolyn S. Bell, who read all the manuscript and who provided us with perceptive and invaluable suggestions throughout.

Also we want to thank Alan Deardorff, who did a manful job working on problems, Bob Kilpatrick, who time and again gave us the clue we needed when we were hunting up data, Tazu Warner and Carol Adomiak, who helped us out with typing, and most especially Margaret Tetor, who has been taking care of our children ever since we decided *four* years ago to spend *a* year writing a textbook.

Finally we would like to thank everyone at Addison-Wesley—from the copy editor, who translated the book from what she quaintly calls econ-English into people's English, to the designer, who did the diagrams—for the wonderful job they have done in turning the raw material we gave them into a book.

WHAT'S IN THE BOOK

MICROECONOMICS

MACROECONOMICS

SUGGESTED COURSE OUTLINES

The outline of this book reflects the authors' belief that microeconomics provides so many useful building blocks for macroeconomics that it ought to be studied before macroeconomics. However, we are aware that many people who teach economics prefer, for as good or better reasons, to take the opposite approach. So in writing our book we have made a conscious effort to keep its presentation as flexible as possible. As a result the book as it stands can easily be used in three different ways: (1) As a basis for a two-semester course that deals first with micro and then with macroeconomics, (2) as a basis for a two-semester course that deals first with macro and then with microeconomics, and (3) as a basis for a one-semester course that surveys the highlights of both.

1. A TWO-SEMESTER MICRO-MACRO SEQUENCE

Using the book for a two-semester micro-macro sequence presents no special problems, since this approach follows the natural outline of the book. Some instructors, however, may feel that the book contains a bit much for their purposes. If so, they may omit all appendixes and any of the following chapters without losing continuity:

2. A TWO-SEMESTER MACRO-MICRO SEQUENCE

Although the book begins with micro and goes on to macroeconomics, the instructor who chooses to can easily reverse the chapter sequence and deal with macroeconomics first. A natural way to do so would be to start out with Chapters 1, 2, and 6, which introduce the consumer and the firm; next to discuss supply and demand; and then to skip on to the macro section, beginning with Part 5, Chapter 26. The discussion of supply and demand could be handled either by a brief class lecture or by having the student read Chapters 12 and 13; in these chapters we introduce the topic of markets and talk about the way price is determined in a perfectly competitive market. The instructor who assigns Chapters 12 and 13 should explain briefly to the students what the consumer's demand curves and the firm's supply curve are, since these two concepts are used in Chapter 13 but are derived in earlier chapters.

Suggested Course Outline

First Semester

Chapter 1   Introduction
Chapter 2   The Consumer
Chapter 6   The Firm
Chapter 12   Markets
Chapter 13   Price Determination in a Perfectly Competitive Market

PART 5   Financial Markets
PART 6   Macro Models and Macro Policy
PART 7   International Economics

Second Semester

PART 1   The Consumer
PART 2   The Firm
PART 3   Perfectly Competitive Markets
PART 4   Imperfectly Competitive Markets

If this outline seems too full, the instructor may, as we have said, omit a number of chapters, in both the micro and macro sections, without losing continuity.

On the following page is the suggested outline for a one-semester course.

3. A ONE-SEMESTER SURVEY COURSE

The book can easily be used as a basis for a one-semester course in either micro or macroeconomics. To use it as a basis for a one-semester course that covers the highlights of both calls for some judicious skipping. This can be done in different ways, depending on the interests of the instructor. One possibility would be to use the following set of chapters, which cover the key topics in microeconomics but puts slightly more emphasis on macro than micro.

Suggested Course Outline

Chapter   1   Introduction
Chapter   2   The Consumer
Chapter   3   The Savings Decision
Chapter   4   The Consumption Decision
Chapter   6   The Firm
Chapter   7   The Production Function
Chapter   8   Cost Minimization
Chapter   9   Profit Maximization over the Short Run
Chapter 12   Markets
Chapter 13   Price Determination in a Perfectly Competitive Market
Chapter 19   Introduction to Imperfectly Competitive Markets
Chapter 20   Monopoly
Chapter 22   Oligopoly
Chapter 26   Funds Flows and Financial Assets
Chapter 27   The Role of Financial Intermediaries
Chapter 28   Money and Banks
Chapter 29   The Central Bank
Chapter 31   The Money Market
Chapter 32   Other Financial Markets
Chapter 33   Macro Models and Macro Policy
Chapter 34   The National Income Accounts
Chapter 35   Income Determination: A Short-Run Model
Chapter 37   The Public Sector
Chapter 38   Fiscal Policy
Chapter 39   Monetary Policy
Chapter 42   Introduction to International Economics
Chapter 43   The Balance-of-Payments Account
Chapter 44   The Theory of International Trade
Chapter 46   The International Payments Mechanism
Chapter 47   Balance-of-Payments Adjustment

This suggested material is shorter than it seems because it includes a number of brief introductory chapters.

CONTENTS

CHAPTER 1

INTRODUCTION

Between 1955 and 1967 the Dow Jones average of industrial stock prices rose by 450 points, corporate profits almost doubled, and employment on U.S. farms fell by over 2 million persons. Simultaneously—as indicated in Fig. 1.1 —national income rose dramatically, the number of families living in poverty fell by one-fifth, steel prices edged upward, steel imports soared, the Treasury-bill rate rose sharply, U.S. gold stock plummeted, and the unemployment rate fluctuated erratically around a downward trend.

Why did these key economic indicators move along the paths they did? In particular, why did the Dow Jones average advance while U.S. gold stock plummeted? Why did farm employment decline while national income rose? Why did the Treasury-bill rate rise while the unemployment rate fell? Were some of these changes interrelated? Specifically, did the steep rise in national income lead to the decline in the number of families living in poverty? Did the increase in steel prices lead to the increase in steel imports, and did this increase have something to do with U.S. gold losses? Were gold losses related to the post-1960 rise in the Treasury-bill rate? If so, how?

To answer these questions and hundreds of similar ones that we might ask, we must begin by observing that all these specific questions have general counterparts such as: How are the price and quantity sold of a particular commodity established? What determines the rates of return yielded by different financial assets such as common stock and Treasury bills? What determines the level of corporate profits? How is the level of national income in an economy established? Why does the structure of national output shift over time? Why does national output grow over time? And what determines the goods a nation imports and exports? These general questions all concern different aspects of the functioning of a market economy. Therefore, to answer these general questions first and then our more specific ones, we must develop a theory to "explain" how a market economy functions.

1

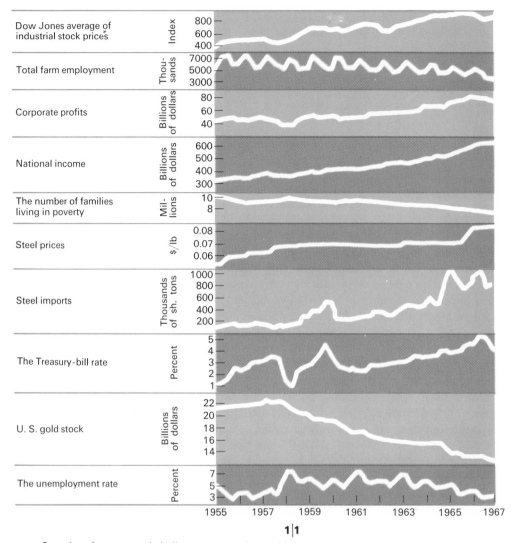

Dow Jones average of industrial stock prices	Index
Total farm employment	Thousands
Corporate profits	Billions of dollars
National income	Billions of dollars
The number of families living in poverty	Millions
Steel prices	$/lb
Steel imports	Thousands of sh. tons
The Treasury-bill rate	Percent
U. S. gold stock	Billions of dollars
The unemployment rate	Percent

1|1

Over time, key economic indicators move along widely divergent paths. (Source: U.S. Department of Commerce)

A THUMBNAIL SKETCH OF ECONOMIC THEORY

Fortunately our task will not prove too difficult, since economists have developed a broad body of theory that answers almost all the questions we might ask about how a market economy functions. Before we begin, however, we should pause to take a close look at the nature of economic activity and to note the different levels on which it can be studied.

Microeconomics

Any economic society is made up of two fundamental units: *consumers* and *producers*. Both play a dual role. Consumers supply productive inputs: land, labor, and capital. They also demand final outputs in the form of goods and services. Producers, on the other hand, demand inputs and supply outputs. Thus in any economy in which goods are actively produced and consumed, consumers and producers are linked by a circular flow of inputs and outputs like the one pictured in Fig. 1.2.

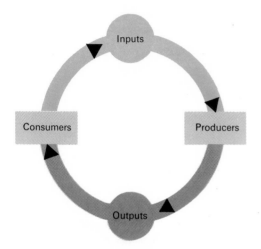

1|2

In an active economy, inputs constantly flow from consumers to producers, while outputs flow in the reverse direction.

If consumers' wants were small relative to society's resources, society could produce all the outputs that consumers desired and the circular flow in Fig. 1.2 would take place without creating any economic problems. In actual practice, however, life never happens this way. In real life, consumers have unlimited wants but society has limited resources.

Therefore society faces the difficult question: *How shall available resources be used to satisfy the unlimited wants of citizens?* In other words, how shall the composition and allocation of final output be determined?

This is the classic central problem of every economic society. In some it is solved by fiat, in others by tradition, and in still others by government planning boards. In a market economy, it is solved by the interaction of consumers and producers in the marketplace.

How, in a market economy, do consumers and producers interact to determine the composition and allocation of final output? This is the question that the student of *micro*economics seeks to solve. He starts by observing that producers and consumers generally trade inputs and outputs for money. Thus they are linked—as indicated in Fig. 1.3—not only by a circular flow of inputs and outputs, but also by an offsetting flow of money payments.

Next he observes that consumers and producers, in deciding what inputs and outputs to buy and sell, respond to the money prices established for these goods. This means that to explain how the composition and allocation of final output are determined, the microtheorist has to construct models that explain how price and quantity sold are determined in different markets. Thus the microtheorist is concerned primarily with studying the way consumers and producers behave in the marketplace, and with setting up theoretical models that show the different ways in which consumers and producers interact to determine market price.

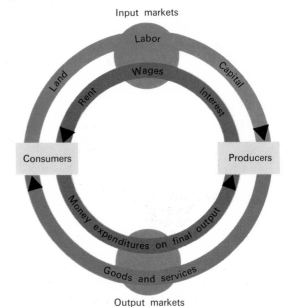

1│3

In a modern market economy, producers trade money for inputs, and final output for money; consumers, on the other hand, trade inputs for money income, and money income for final outputs.

Once he has his various models in hand, the microtheorist can answer a number of the questions we posed at the beginning of this chapter. In particular he can explain what determines the prices at which steel and other goods are sold, the rates of return that Treasury bills, common stock, and other financial assets yield, and the way labor is allocated between farm and factory.

Macroeconomics

Although micro models are fine for studying price determination and resource allocation, they are too unwieldy for answering questions such as: How is the level of national output established? How is the unemployment rate established? What determines whether the economy will experience inflation or deflation? What determines the growth rate of national output?

To answer questions of this sort the economist must set up macro models: that is, models in which the key variables are not the inputs and outputs demanded and supplied by individual consumers and producers, but aggregate economic quantities such as national income, total investments, total consumption, and total government expenditures.

Because of the inherent complexity of economic activity, developing such models might at first glance seem difficult if not impossible. This, however, has not proved to be the case. In practice, economists have been able to come up with simple macro models that explain quite accurately how and why the aggregate economy behaves as it does. These macro models, as we shall see, have been successfully used to explain how unemployment can occur as a result of inadequate aggregate demand, to determine what conditions are likely to induce rising prices, and to identify the forces that stimulate economic growth.

NORMATIVE VERSUS POSITIVE ECONOMICS

The micro and macro models we have described try to explain how a market economy functions in practice; in other words, they explain *what is*. If economics, like astronomy, dealt solely with phenomena that could not be changed by means of policy action, our study of economics would end here. However, the values of most economic variables can be changed. People who live in an economic society can, by means of conscious policy action, control (at least to some degree) the values assumed by output, prices, employment, and other key economic variables.

Thus the practicing economist is inevitably concerned not only with *what is*, i.e., with *positive* economics, but also with how the economy can best achieve *what ought to be*, i.e., with *normative* economics.

Any statement about what ought to be in the economy must inevitably rest on a value judgment, and the making of such judgments is outside the province of the economist. However, whenever society (Congress, the President, or some outside source) lays down general prescriptions as to what ought to be, the economist responds. Because of his knowledge of positive economics, he is the person best qualified to translate these prescriptions into specific policies and to identify alternative policies that might be used to pursue the given aims. Thus, in any modern, policy-oriented economy such as our own, professional economists do not just observe and interpret the economic scene. They also actively participate in the formation of government policy.

In the chapters that follow, we shall frequently focus on aspects of normative economics and on the targets pursued by—and the instruments available to—the government policy maker. What are some of these targets and instruments?

In microeconomics a principal aim of government policy is to allocate resources "efficiently"; that is, to allocate resources in such a way that no feasible reallocation would increase the welfare of one person without simultaneously decreasing the welfare of someone else. In macroeconomics, the principal aims of government policy are full employment, price stability, rapid economic growth, and balance-of-payments equilibrium. To pursue these aims the government has, as we shall see, an impressive array of policy instruments. It can impose new taxes or abolish old ones; it can raise or lower tax rates; it can modify the composition of its expenditures; it can raise or lower the level of these expenditures; it can alter the cost and availability of credit; and it can impose direct controls on particular prices and outputs.

This profusion of targets and instruments raises questions: How does the government, in designing its policies, match targets to instruments? How effective are the government's instruments in achieving the ends to which they are put? Do some of the government's major targets conflict? These are important questions, and we shall consider them carefully in the chapters that follow.

A PREVIEW OF WHAT'S TO COME

Since we shall be concerned with both theory and policy, we have lots of ground to cover. Where shall we begin our discussion?

As we have seen, consumers and producers are the fundamental decision makers in a market economy. Therefore the logical place for us to start is by developing theories that predict the way consumers and producers will behave in the marketplace. As indicated in Fig. 1.4, this will take up Parts 1 and 2 of our book.

Once we have these theories in hand, we can develop models to explain how price is determined in different markets. Part 3 focuses on perfectly competitive markets, that is, on markets in which buyers and sellers are many in number and the product sold is homogeneous. In this part we answer such questions as: How is price determined in a perfectly competitive market? What sorts of markets are perfectly competitive? In what sense can perfectly competitive markets be said to allocate resources efficiently? Part 4 talks about imperfectly competitive markets, that is, markets which fail to meet one or more of the conditions of perfect competition. Here we shall discuss questions such as: How is price determined in an imperfectly competitive market? How prevalent are imperfectly competitive markets in real life? Why do imperfectly competitive markets allocate resources inefficiently? What policies can the government use to improve the performance of such markets?

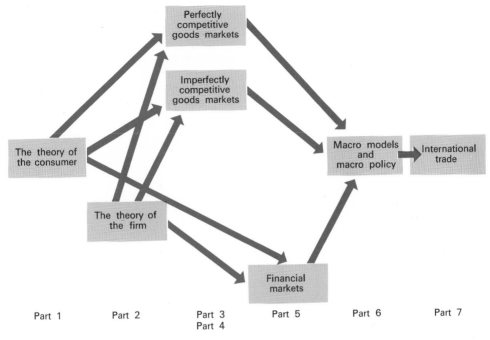

Part 1   Part 2   Part 3   Part 5   Part 6   Part 7
                                Part 4

1|4 A schematic outline of the chapters that follow.

In addition to goods markets, there are also financial markets, that is, markets in which capital funds and financial assets (i.e., stocks, bonds, and money) are traded. How are prices determined in these markets? How is money created? What is the role of that mysterious institution known as a central bank? These are the questions that will concern us in Part 5.

Once we know how goods and financial markets operate and how money is created, we'll have the tools we need to develop a macro model that describes the way the economy as a whole behaves. By means of this model we can study the ups and downs of the business cycle, the pros and cons of fiscal and monetary policy, and the factors that determine economic growth.

Finally, in the last section of our book, we shall discuss international economics. Why do nations trade with each other? Why do capital and other inputs flow between nations? What does balance of payments equilibrium mean? And how can such equilibrium be achieved?

Part 1
THE CONSUMER

CHAPTER 2

THE CONSUMER

How does the consumer make the economic choices that face him in each period? This question, as we have suggested, is an important one. In the chapters that follow we shall give it a careful answer.

WHO IS THE CONSUMER?

First let us ask just who "the consumer" is. Our observation that the consumer in a market economy plays a dual role suggests that we define a consumer as an economic unit that supplies productive inputs and demands final outputs. However, we need not think of the consumer as being an individual or to put it the other way round we need not consider every individual as a consumer. Instead we should think of the consumer as a *decision-making spending unit,* although this may seem a rather bloodless way of putting it. Who are these spending units? It is hard to say precisely, but a good approximation (and one on which almost all consumer statistics are based) is that spending units consist of (a) single adults living alone and (b) families living together.

WHAT SORTS OF ECONOMIC CHOICES DOES THE CONSUMER FACE?

Let us now list the principal economic choices the consumer faces. For any consumer we can set up two financial accounts, an income statement and a balance sheet, which, taken together, summarize all the economic choices he makes. Thus the easiest way to arrive at a list of choices is to examine these two accounts. What do they suggest concerning the kinds of economic choices the consumer must make during each period?

The Consumer's Income Statement

A consumer's income during any period equals the total payments he receives during that period for supplying productive inputs to producers.

Unless his income for the period is very low, he will have to pay taxes on this income. Therefore his after-tax or *disposable* income will be smaller than his total income.

The consumer usually spends most of his disposable income on *current consumption expenditures,* that is, the expenditures he makes for goods and services consumed during the current period. Although most of the services he consumes are supplied by outside sources, some may be supplied by *durable goods* such as a house, a car, or a washing machine that he himself owns. The cost of such self-provided services equals all the current expenses he incurs in operating them, plus whatever *depreciation* (i.e., loss in value) these goods undergo as a result of wear, tear, and aging during the current period. It follows that the current-consumption entry on the consumer's income statement should include his expenditures for *nondurable goods,* his expenditures for services purchased from outside sources, and the cost of the current-period services provided to him by his own durable goods. His current-consumption entry should not, however, include his current-period expenditures on new *durable* goods. His expenditures during a given period may be less than or greater than his disposable income. The difference between the two equals his current period *savings* (or in the jargon of economists, *dissavings,* if the figure is negative).

The above relationship among the consumer's income, consumption, and savings is summarized in his income statement.

The consumer's income statement is a listing of his total sources of income for a given time period, and of his allocation of this income among taxes, consumption, and saving.

TABLE 2|1

Income Statement: John Jones
January 1, 1970–December 31, 1970

Wages	$15,000
Rent	600
Interest and dividends	800
Total pretax income	$16,400
Less taxes on income	1,300
Disposable income	$15,100
Less consumption expenditures	14,000
Savings	$ 1,100

As an illustration of an income statement, we present in Table 2.1 a 1970 income statement for a man with the unusual name of John Jones. The first three entries on this statement record Jones's total sources of income during 1970. Jones's savings, a residual item, are obtained by subtracting from his 1970 income all taxes he paid and all consumption expenditures he made during this year.

The Consumer's Balance Sheet

Almost any consumer, regardless of income level, has at least some assets and liabilities. A consumer's *assets*—things he owns that are of value—fall into two principal categories: *real* ones and *financial* ones. Real assets are physical goods such as houses, automobiles, and other durable equipment which provide him with shelter, transportation, and other services over a period of time.

A consumer's financial assets, on the other hand, all constitute claims against other spending units. Most of these claims are ones that the consumer obtains in exchange for capital inputs which he supplies to producers in the business sector. Suppose, for example, that Jones owns a corporate bond. This is a debt claim which Jones obtains by supplying *debt capital* (i.e., by making a loan) to the issuing corporation; this claim obligates the issuer to pay Jones fixed amounts of interest during the life of the bond and to redeem the bond for cash at maturity. A share of common stock, on the other hand, is an *equity* (i.e., ownership) claim which Jones obtains by supplying equity capital to the issuing firm. This claim, which makes Jones a part owner in the issuing corporation, entitles him to a portion of this corporation's profits and to a voice in the management.

TABLE 2|2

Balance Sheet: John Jones, December 31, 1970

Assets			Liabilities and net worth		
Cash		$ 300	Short-term debt	$ 400	
Bank deposits		2,100	Mortgage	15,000	
Corporate stock and bonds		4,600			
Own home: cost	$25,000		*Total liabilities*		$15,400
Less depreciation	2,000				
		23,000			
Automobile: cost	$ 2,000		*Net worth*		15,100
Less depreciation	1,500				
		500			
Total assets		$30,500	*Liabilities plus net worth*		$30,500

All a consumer's *liabilities* are debts of one form or another. Some—in particular debts incurred through installment or credit purchases—are short-term. But if he has a mortgage on his home, it is likely to be a long-term debt, since mortgages are often written for 20- or even 30-year periods.

If we add up a consumer's assets and subtract his total liabilities, the resulting figure (which may be positive or negative) is a measure of his wealth or *net worth*. We can summarize this important relationship by setting up a *balance sheet* for the consumer; that is, *a statement which lists the value, at a given point in time, of the consumer's assets, liabilities, and residual net worth.*

Table 2.2 shows a balance sheet for John Jones; most of the entries on it are self-explanatory. Jones, as of Dec. 31, 1970, had $30,500 of assets, $15,400 of liabilities, and a net worth equal to $15,100. Since net worth is a *residual* item, Jones's balance sheet (and that of any other consumer) must by definition always be in balance.

The Consumer's Economic Choices

Let us examine Jones's income statement and balance sheet to see what they tell us about the different economic choices he faces.

The first and largest entry on his income statement is *wages.* Since a consumer obtains wage income by supplying labor inputs to producers, one important economic choice he has to make in each period is *to decide what kinds and quantity of labor services he will supply to the business sector.*

Wages, however, are not Jones's only source of income. He also receives rental income because he supplies producers with physical inputs (land or buildings), and he obtains interest and dividends by supplying capital inputs to the business sector. Moreover, if we look at any consumer's balance sheet, it is evident that the division of his nonwage income between rent, interest, and dividends depends on the kinds of assets he chooses to hold. Thus the consumer has to make a second important economic choice: selecting the kinds of assets in which he will hold his wealth. However, he can finance the purchase of assets not only with wealth but also with debt (i.e., by in-curring liabilities). Therefore his problem of asset selection is just one part (albeit an important one) of a larger economic choice: *deciding what compo-sition he will give to his overall balance sheet.*

If we continue our examination of Jones's income statement, we see that in each period he allocates his total income among taxes, consumption, and savings. Moreover, although the taxes he pays are certainly a nondiscretion-ary item (in other words, he has no choice in the matter), the division of his disposable income between consumption and savings is not. Thus a third economic choice he faces is *to decide what fraction of his disposable income he will devote to consumption and what fraction to savings.*

We might assume, at this point, that we had succeeded in listing all of a consumer's principal economic choices, but we'd be wrong, because consum-ers do not make generalized consumption expenditures. They buy specific consumption goods, such as food, clothing, shelter, transportation, and so forth. Thus the consumer faces a fourth and final economic choice: *deciding how to allocate the funds he has budgeted for consumption among the differ-ent consumption goods available to him.*

A THEORY OF THE CONSUMER

Now we are ready for the key task of Part 1: to develop a theory that explains how the consumer makes all those economic choices that confront him.

When an economist wants to develop theories that explain certain phenomena, he tackles the problem in the same way that a scientist in any other field does. First he makes certain fundamental assumptions, then he figures out the implications of these assumptions and organizes them into a coherent theory that explains the phenomena. Finally, to check the validity of his theory, he uses it to make predictions. Do the predictions agree with observed reality? If not, he rejects his theory and seeks out a better one. But if his predictions do jibe with experience, then his theory is confirmed, and he can, tentatively at least, accept it as valid.

Therefore, in order to construct a theory of the consumer, let us begin by making several *fundamental assumptions* as to his character and motivation. What assumptions shall we make? If you stop to think about how consumers behave and in particular how you yourself behave, two observations are likely to occur to you. The first is that consumers experience both satisfaction and dissatisfaction (in the language of the economist, *utility* and *disutility*), as a result of the economic decisions they make. Thus people have quite definite preferences as to the outcomes of their economic decisions. That is, they have definite preferences with respect to whether they eat hot dogs or steak, work long hours or short, and put their money in savings accounts or common stock. The second observation you are likely to make is that most consumers (including yourself), when faced with an economic decision, select from all feasible outcomes the one outcome they most prefer. If these two observations hold true, we can make the following assumptions:

1) *Every consumer has definite preferences with respect to the outcomes of all the economic choices he must make.*
2) *Every consumer, when he makes economic choices, tries to maximize the satisfaction (or utility) that he derives from the outcomes of these choices.*

Armed with these two assumptions, we can construct models that will enable us to explain how the consumer makes each of the principal choices that face him. In fact, this is precisely what we intend to do in the next three chapters. But first let us pause to think about three important points that lead up to the subject.

Point one is that all the different economic choices the consumer makes are interrelated, so that, practically speaking, he has to make all his economic choices not one-by-one, but *simultaneously*. However, we can't attempt to analyze all his economic choices simultaneously. If we did, we would have an awkward, multidimensional problem that we could solve in a general way, but only at the cost of losing our insight into the nature of the consumer's decision process and the character of his equilibrium position (this is a term we'll get to in a moment).

Therefore we shall examine each of the consumer's principal economic choices separately: How does he divide his current income between consumption and savings? How does he allocate funds budgeted for current consumption among available goods? How does he divide his time between labor, which yields income, and leisure, which yields immediate pleasure? And finally, how does he decide which assets to hold and which liabilities to incur?

Our second important point is that all the principal choices the consumer makes have the same basic character; they all force him to make a choice within limits set by a certain *constraint*. Jones, for example, when he decides how much to consume and how much to save in the current period, has to respect the constraint set by his limited income. Similarly, when he chooses the goods he will consume in the current period, he has to face the constraint set by the limited funds he has budgeted for current consumption. Finally, when he chooses the structure and composition of his balance sheet, he faces the constraint set by his net worth.

Third, let us explain a term we are going to use often. Throughout this discussion we shall refer to the consumer's resolution of each of the principal choices that confront him as his *equilibrium choice* or *equilibrium position*. A consumer who succeeds in making choices that maximize his satisfaction will presumably have neither reason nor inclination to alter his choices; in other words, he will be in *equilibrium*.

PROBLEMS

1   Set up a balance sheet for consumer Y, whose assets and liabilities are as follows: installment debt $2,450, government bonds $1,200, durable goods plus house $20,000, cash $100, unpaid charge accounts $150, other unpaid bills $200, common stock $1,000, depreciation on durable goods and house from date of purchase to the present $2,000, mortgage $10,000, and bank deposits $3,000.

2   a) During the current year a man earns $10,000 in salary and receives $300 in dividends and interest. He has to pay $1,000 in taxes, and his expenditure on nondurable goods equals $7,700. He incurs no depreciation because his only physical assets are works of art, which we assume do not depreciate. Construct his income statement for the year.

   b) A man buys a $2,700 painting which he finances by selling $1,200 worth of common stock, by drawing down his bank balance by $800, and by incurring $700 of short-term debt. Which entries on his balance sheet will change as a result of these transactions, and by how much will they change? In particular, how will his net worth be altered by this purchase?

3   James Phibete, a senior at Atlantis University, decides to compute his own net worth. He has $25 on hand, $50 in his checking account, and a bond worth $25 that someone gave him years ago. He has just bought a used car for $1,000 by borrowing $500 from the bank and using a gift of $500 from his father. Looking around his room, he sees that he has clothes on which he spent an estimated $300, a five-year-old typewriter for which he paid $50, and a collection of 100 comic books which he bought for 15¢ each. What is his net worth?

4   A man's income during a given period equals $6,000. During this period he sells $500 worth of common stock for cash, his car depreciates by $400, the balance in his checking account falls by $100, and his expenditures for current consumption (excluding depreciation) equal $5,500. Out of his current income he must pay $300 in taxes. What will be his net savings over the period? What will be the change in his net worth over the period?

5   Miss Adams reasons that if she charges a $50 dress she is buying, she will not have to pay for it until next month and her savings in the current month will therefore be $50 greater. Do you agree with her reasoning? How does charging, as opposed to paying in cash for a purchase, affect (a) a consumer's saving during the period in which he makes the purchase and (b) his net worth at the end of this period?

6   When Jones woke up this morning, he thought that his net worth was $20,000, as it had been the night before when he went to bed. Then his son came in to report that, in attempting to pass through a telephone pole, he had completely demolished the Thunderbird which Jones had purchased a week before at a cost of $5,000, and on which Jones unfortunately carried no collision insurance. How does this accident affect Jones's balance sheet? To answer this question do you need to know whether Jones paid for his new car with cash or financed it with debt? Explain your answer.

7   Suppose that you bought a used Bearcub three years ago for $1,050. At the time, on the basis of your knowledge of that make of car, you estimated that it would last five years before it would break down completely. The junk value of the car is $50. Yesterday a friend offered you $400 for it, and so far as you know that is the highest offer you are likely to receive. Explain how you would record the value of this car on your balance sheet as of today, giving your reasons for the amount of depreciation you assign.

CHAPTER 3

THE SAVINGS DECISION

When you look at the data on income, savings, and consumption in Fig. 3.1, you will immediately be struck by the wide divergences between the proportions of total income that consumers in different income classes allocate to savings. Comparisons based on criteria other than income also show marked differences between the proportions of total income that consumers in different groups allocate to savings. If you were to look at data on the income and savings patterns of large versus small families, of self-employed workers versus salaried professionals, and of renters versus homeowners, you would find that at any income level the proportion of income devoted to savings tends to be larger for small families than for large ones, larger for self-employed people than for salaried professionals, and larger for homeowners than for renters.

These marked differences in the *savings–consumption decisions* of different consumers raise two questions: How do people decide how to allocate their total disposable income between consumption and savings? And why are there such pronounced differences in the decisions of different individuals?

THE CONSUMER'S PREFERENCES

To understand the way the consumer makes his savings–consumption decision, we must begin by making certain fundamental assumptions about him. As we said in Chapter 2, the natural first assumption to make is that he has definite preferences as to how he allocates his current income between consumption and savings.*

---

* Since the main reason why a person saves is so that he can consume future goods, his choice between consumption and saving is in effect a choice between current and future goods. Thus his preferences for consumption and saving will obviously be *derived* from (i.e., depend on) his preferences with respect to current versus future goods.

17

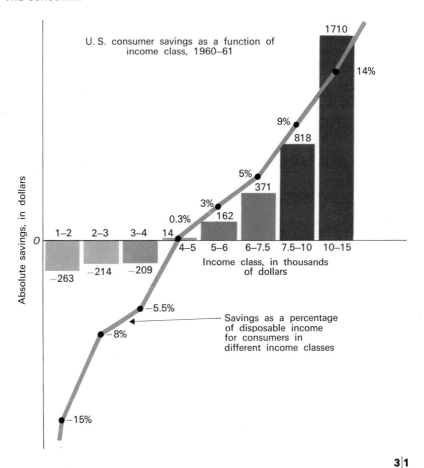

U. S. consumer savings as a function of
income class, 1960–61

Absolute savings, in dollars

Income class, in thousands
of dollars

Savings as a percentage
of disposable income
for consumers in
different income classes

3|1

The average *absolute* and *percentage* amounts of disposable income that consumers in different income classes devote to saving. The greater the consumer's income, the more
likely he is to be a positive saver and the greater his savings (measured either absolutely or as a
percentage of his income) are likely to be. (Source: U.S. Department of Labor)

The Consumer's Motives

What sort of saving–consumption preferences shall we attribute to the consumer? To answer this question, we must know a little about the consumer's
motives both for saving and consumption.

A person consumes things for a variety of reasons. First there are the
goods and services he has to consume in order to survive: food, clothing, and
shelter. Then there are other goods which he consumes because they add to
his enjoyment or enrich his life. Finally there are still other goods which he
consumes primarily because they add to his prestige and status; "conspicuous

consumption" of this sort may of course also add to his enjoyment of life. The important point is that, since the consumer desires goods not only for subsistence, but also for pleasure and prestige, we can assume that *his desires for consumption are unlimited.*

A person also saves for a variety of reasons. The strongest motive is the wish to finance predictable long-term needs. An economist describes this motive as the desire to arrange a lifetime expenditure time path that is optimal with respect to present and anticipated wants and with respect to present and expected income.

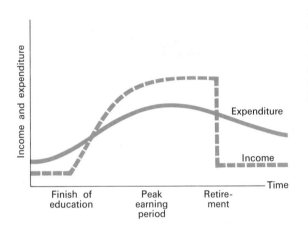

3|2

The income and expenditure time paths of a consumer who dissaves during his early low-income years, saves during his high-income work years, and then dissaves again during his low-income retirement years.

To illustrate, let's consider a typical middle-class consumer, Ernest Smith. Generally Smith will dissave during his early low-income years—particularly if his education is lengthy—save during his high-income work years, and then dissave again during his low-income retirement years. In doing so, he will establish income and expenditure time paths similar to those in Fig. 3.2. Note here that Smith's freedom to arrange an expenditure time path that differs from his income time path is limited by two factors. (1) His basic needs must be met in every period. (2) His initial dissaving will probably have to be financed by debt. Presumably he will be able to borrow only as much as lenders believe he can reasonably be expected to repay.

Although the desire to meet predictable long-term needs (such as retirement and the education of children) may be the single strongest motive for saving, most people save for other reasons as well. Consumers, especially young ones, save in order either to finance the purchase of durable goods or to make a down payment on a home. They also save in order to establish an estate, to obtain funds to invest in their personal business ventures, and to acquire financial independence.

Table 3.1 shows data selected from a recent U.S. survey of the saving objectives of consumers. These data support what we said about the motives consumers have for saving, especially the fact that the desire to meet predictable needs such as retirement and the education of children is an important saving motive for almost all consumers, regardless of wealth, income, or age.

TABLE 3|1

Consumer Saving Objectives, December 31, 1962*

Group characteristic	Build own business	Provide for			Provide estate	Buy home	Buy durable goods	Acquire financial independence
		Old age	Emergencies	Children's education				
			Percent mentioning specified objectives					
All units	3	41	32	29	3	18	7	11
Size of wealth:								
$5,000–9,999	3	31	33	34	4	21	10	11
$25,000–49,999	6	67	29	22	4	9	1	18
$500,000 and over	6	48	14	16	33	14	0	19
1962 income:								
$5,000–7,499	3	39	31	35	3	23	10	11
$15,000–24,999	5	62	32	43	10	11	7	20
$100,000 and over	2	62	5	13	71	1	1	10
Age of head:								
Under 35	5	17	27	39	1	40	13	12
45–54	3	53	31	32	3	15	6	11
65 and over	2	47	34	4	4	4	2	7

* Source: Dorothy S. Projector and Gertrude S. Weiss, *Survey of Financial Characteristics of Consumers*, Board of Governors of the Federal Reserve System, 1966.

The Consumer's Preference Map

What does what we have said about Smith's motives for saving and consumption imply about his preferences for one versus the other? The best way to answer this question is to graph his saving–consumption preferences and then see what our observations imply about the shape of the curves in the graph.

Whenever we say that the consumer has preferences with respect to consumption and saving, we mean that if he were faced with a number of alternative combinations of savings and consumption, he could rank or order these combinations from least to most preferred. Some combinations of saving and consumption, of course, offer Smith an identical amount of satisfaction, and these combinations are said to be *equally preferred*. That is, he is *"indifferent between"* them. ("Indifferent between" is admittedly not good grammar, but it is part of the lingo of economists, and we shall use it often.)

To illustrate: suppose that Smith were confronted with three different saving–consumption combinations: (1) $9,000 of consumption and $1,000 of saving, (2) $8,000 of consumption and $2,000 of saving, and (3) $9,000 of consumption and $500 of saving. If his needs for consumption are strong relative to his motives for saving, he might well say that he prefers combination (1) to combination (2), but that he is indifferent between combinations (2) and (3).

Now that we have defined what we mean by the consumer's preferences with respect to saving and consumption, let us graph these preferences. First we arbitrarily select a saving–consumption combination (point *A* in Fig. 3.3), then we try to draw through this point a line that connects all savings and consumption combinations the consumer would *prefer equally* to combination *A*. This line, for obvious reasons, is called an *indifference curve*.

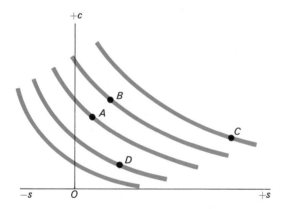

3|3

Graph of a consumer's preferences with respect to the allocation of current income between consumption and saving. Dollars of consumption (*c*) are measured along the vertical axis and dollars of saving (*s*) are measured along the horizontal axis.

What will its slope be? Our discussion of Smith's savings and consumption motives gives us a clue. Suppose that we offer him the combination of consumption and savings indicated by point *A* in Fig. 3.3. Then, since his desires for both consumption and saving are essentially unlimited, he would presumably prefer point *A* to any other point that offered him (1) the same saving, but less consumption, (2) the same consumption, but less saving, or (3) less of both consumption and saving. On the other hand, he would presumably prefer another point to point *A*, if the other point offered him: (1) the same saving, but more consumption, (2) the same consumption, but more saving, or (3) more of both consumption and saving. If this is true, then, as you should verify,* Smith's indifference curve through the point *A* must *slope downward*.

---

* See Problem 4 at the end of the chapter.

Suppose that now we move him along this indifference curve by offering him less consumption, but at the same time enough additional saving so that his level of satisfaction is unchanged. Presumably the increases in saving required to compensate him for successive and equal decreases in consumption will at some point begin to rise, either because the progressive substitution of saving for consumption would force him to leave more and more pressing desires for consumption unfulfilled (poor Smith wouldn't even be able to have his hair cut) or because the motives for saving which he could fulfill become weaker and weaker. If this happens, however, his indifference curve through *A* will not only slope downward but also be convex to the origin, like the curves in Fig. 3.3.

If he can rank all possible combinations of saving and consumption, he must have many indifference curves, one of which will pass through each point in Fig. 3.3. Moreover, we would expect each of these curves, like the indifference curve through *A*, to slope downward and to be convex to the origin. Any collection of several indifference curves (such as that in Fig. 3.3) is called an *indifference map* or a *preference map*.

Each curve in a consumer's indifference map corresponds to a different level of satisfaction; "higher" indifference curves (as you can easily verify) always correspond to higher levels of satisfaction. It follows that, although Smith will be indifferent between point *A* and any point along the indifference curve through *A*, he will clearly prefer points *B* and *C*, in Fig. 3.3, to point *A*, since *B* and *C* both lie on higher indifference curves than *A*. Even without knowing his indifference map, we could have predicted that Smith would prefer *B* to *A*, since *B* offers him more of both consumption and saving than *A*. We could not, however, have predicted that he would prefer *C* to *A*, since *C* offers him more saving but less consumption than *A*. We also could not have predicted that he would prefer *A* to *D*, since *A* offers him more consumption but less saving than *D*.

In practice, a consumer's saving in any period may be *positive* or *negative*. (See page 11 for an explanation of negative savings.) Thus the consumer has to rank not only combinations of positive consumption and positive saving, but also combinations of positive consumption and negative saving. If he does this, however, then at least some of the indifference curves in his preference map must cross the vertical axis, as several do in Fig. 3.3. Presumably he determines his preferences with respect to points to the left of the vertical axis (those corresponding to positive consumption and negative saving) by weighing the disutility of the dissaving associated with each such point against the utility of the consumption associated with the point.

THE CONSUMER'S BUDGET CONSTRAINT

So far in our discussion of the consumer's saving–consumption choice, we have concentrated on his preferences. But we must also take into account a crucial factor: the level of his income.

Let's suppose that a consumer named Bert Brown, during the current period, receives a fixed income equal to $\bar{y}$. Then, since saving is defined as income minus consumption, his allocation of current income between consumption and saving must (regardless of the form it takes) satisfy the condition

$$\bar{y} = c + s,$$

in which $\bar{y}$, c, and s denote his current income, current consumption, and current saving, respectively.

Next let's rewrite this condition, which is known as the consumer's *budget constraint* or *budget line,* in the form

$$c = -s + \bar{y}$$

and plot it. What position and slope will the resulting line have? Obviously this budget line must intersect the consumption axis at point $\bar{y}$, since, if Brown saves nothing, his consumption will precisely equal his fixed income. This budget line must also intersect the saving axis at point $\bar{y}$, since, if he consumes nothing, his saving will precisely equal his total income. Finally this budget line must have a slope equal to minus one, since each $1 increase in Brown's saving must (recall that his income is fixed) be matched by a $1 decrease in his consumption, and vice versa.

In Fig. 3.4 we have plotted Brown's budget constraint and labeled it *yy*. Since a consumer's budget constraint contains all points that are attainable by him (i.e., feasible to him), *the consumer must during each period attain equilibrium at some point along yy.* Moreover, if he attains equilibrium at a point on *yy* that lies to the right of the vertical axis, his consumption will be smaller than his income and his saving for the period will be *positive*. Conversely, if he attains equilibrium at a point on *yy* that lies to the left of the vertical axis, his consumption will exceed his income and his saving for the period will be *negative*. Note that, from Brown's point of view, *yy* does not extend indefinitely to the left because his ability to move to the left along this curve will be limited by his ability to finance dissavings in the current period, either by decreasing his assets or by increasing his liabilities (i.e., by borrowing).

EQUILIBRIUM DIVISION OF INCOME BETWEEN CONSUMPTION AND SAVINGS

The key question we've been building up to is: At what point along the budget line *yy* will Brown attain equilibrium? To answer it we recall the second fundamental assumption which we made in Chapter 2, namely that the consumer, in making his saving–consumption choice, consistently seeks to maximize his satisfaction (utility). Now we can easily locate Brown's equilibrium (i.e., satisfaction-maximizing) allocation of current income

between consumption and savings. Let's suppose that Brown, whose preference map and budget constraint are illustrated in Fig. 3.4, were to choose the
consumption–saving combination represented by the point E. Then let's
ask: Could he do better? Yes. If he moved to F, his satisfaction would increase, since F is on a higher indifference curve than E. Moreover, if he
moved from F to G, his satisfaction would increase still further, since G is on
a still higher indifference curve than F. However, no point along yy is on a
higher indifference curve than G. The point G thus represents Brown's equilibrium allocation of current income between consumption and savings.

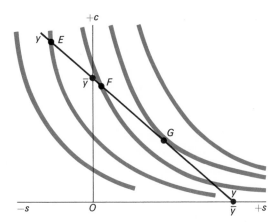

3|4

Locating the consumer's equilibrium
division of income between saving and
consumption.

How can we characterize the consumer's equilibrium position? Looking
at Fig. 3.4, we can sum the situation up as follows:

*The consumer—given the convexity of his indifference curves and his goal of
satisfaction maximization—will attain equilibrium by moving to a point
along his budget line yy at which this line is just tangent to one of the indifference curves in his preference map. In other words, he will attain equilibrium by moving to a point at which*

1) *his budget constraint is satisfied and*
2) *the slope of his indifference curve equals the slope of his budget constraint.*

THE SHORT-RUN CONSUMPTION FUNCTION OF A SINGLE CONSUMER

In order to analyze many macroeconomic problems and especially to figure
out how the level of national income is determined, we need to answer the
following question: How will a consumer alter his current consumption in
response to a change in his current income? Using the model of consumer

choice obtained above, we can suggest an answer to this question. We can determine the probable shape of a schedule that summarizes the relationship between the consumer's current income and the level of his current consumption. We shall refer to this schedule, which can be represented by the expression

$$c = c(y),$$

as the consumer's short-run *consumption function*.

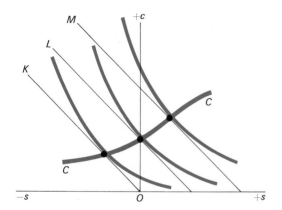

3|5

To derive the consumption function of an individual consumer, we determine how much he would consume at each possible level of income; i.e., we must locate the points of tangency between each budget line and one of the indifference curves in his saving–consumption preference map. All such points above are located along the line *CC*.

Suppose that Bert Brown has a consumption–saving preference map like the one illustrated in Fig. 3.5, and that we want to derive his consumption function. We must begin by generating a series of budget lines, each corresponding to a different level of current income for Brown. Since the slope of each of these lines will equal −1, they will of course all be parallel; higher budget lines correspond to higher levels of income (Brown's raises).

Now that we have several budget lines for Brown, let us find the point on each budget line at which that line is just tangent to one of the indifference curves in his preference map. This gives us several points. Each point tells us what Brown's equilibrium consumption (and savings) would be at a particular income level. This collection of points (represented by the line *CC* in Fig. 3.5) contains all the information we need to set up Brown's consumption function.

What shape and slope should we expect this curve to have? Well, logically enough, Brown's *CC* curve slopes upward, which indicates that he will respond to increases in his income by increasing his consumption. Then, too, his *CC* curve slopes to the right, which indicates that he will also respond to increases in his income by increasing his saving. Finally, Brown's *CC* curve begins in an area of *negative* saving and moves into an area of *positive* saving.

This shows that at low income levels he is a *dissaver,* while at high income levels he is a *positive saver.*

Taken together, these three observations imply that Brown's consumption function will assume the general form illustrated in Fig. 3.6. The 45° line represents all points at which Brown's current consumption just equals his current income. Thus at any point above the 45° line, consumption exceeds income and saving is negative; while at any point below the 45° line, income exceeds consumption and saving is positive. Brown's break-even income, y_b, thus corresponds to the income level at which his consumption function crosses the 45° line. In Fig. 3.5 this income level was represented by the budget line L.

So much for Bert Brown's consumption function. Will the consumption function of a *typical* consumer also look like the curve in Fig. 3.6? How would Mr. Typical Consumer respond to different levels of income?

3|6

The short-run consumption function of a typical consumer. Note that the 45° line contains all points at which consumption precisely equals income. The income level y_b thus represents the consumer's break-even income.

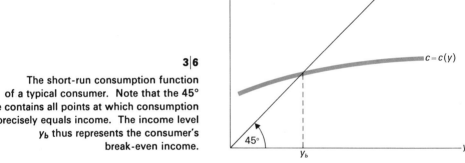

Presumably any typical consumer who "enjoyed" a zero income (this would correspond to budget line K in Fig. 3.5) would dissave an amount at least equal to that needed to finance a subsistence level of consumption. If he were accustomed to a high standard of living or if he anticipated high future income, he might dissave even more. Suppose now that his income were to start out at zero and then gradually increase. Presumably he would respond both by increasing his consumption and by decreasing his dissaving. Moreover, if his income continued to increase, he would probably eventually reach a *break-even point;* that is, a point at which his current consumption would just equal his current income. Just how high this point would be would depend on varied factors: his net worth, the liquidity and structure of his assets, the level of income he is used to, his expectations concerning future income, and his long-range planning goals. Since, as we have already pointed out, a typical consumer has strong motives both for saving and consumption, we would expect that, once he passed his break-even point, he would respond to further increases in his income by increasing both his consumption and his saving. But if this is the case, then a chart of the consumption function of a typical consumer—like Brown, whose preferences are pictured in Fig. 3.5— will look like Fig. 3.6.

Checking Our Derived Consumption Function Against Data

When we determined the probable shape of Bert Brown's consumption function, we relied on our knowledge of the saving and consumption motives of the typical consumer. This, however, is not all we know about the typical consumer. Economists also have data on the average *absolute* saving and average *percentage* of total income devoted to saving by U.S. consumers in different income classes. (By absolute saving, we mean actual saving in dollars, rather than the percentage rate.) Do these data (which we presented in Fig. 3.1) support our contention that the consumption function of the typical consumer resembles the shape and slope of the curve in Fig. 3.6?

Naturally, each person's consumption function is different. When we set up the theoretical consumption function in Fig. 3.6, we allowed for the possibility that some consumers would have steeper consumption functions and that some would have *higher* break-even points. Therefore the reader should not infer from Fig. 3.6 that some income classes contain only dissavers while other income classes contain only savers. Figure 3.6 implies that the proportion of dissavers in any income class should decline as income increases; by the same token, the proportion of savers in any income group should increase as income increases. It also implies that the average absolute saving of savers in any income class should increase as income increases. But if these two implications hold, then we would expect the average *absolute* saving and the average *percentage* of total income devoted to saving by people in different income classes to rise with income. This, however, is precisely what the data in Fig. 3.1 show. Thus our data on the saving–consumption decisions consumers make at different income levels support our contention that the consumption function of the typical consumer resembles in shape and slope the curve in Fig. 3.6.

*EDUCATION AND THE HEIGHT OF THE CONSUMPTION FUNCTION

When we derived Bert Brown's consumption function, we said that the slope and position of this curve depends on a consumer's preferences with respect to saving and consumption, and that these preferences in turn depend on the consumer's motives for saving and consumption. This implies that, if groups of people differ in some important characteristic such as age, level of

---

* The reader may skip sections which are starred without losing continuity.

education, or family size, then there are likely to be differences in the shapes of the curves of their savings–consumption preferences, and thus in the positions of their consumption functions.

The analytic tools we have developed in this chapter are very useful. To show just how useful, let's take an example that shows how differences in the characteristics of individual consumers can lead to pronounced differences in the positions of their consumption functions. For example, how are differences in one important consumer characteristic, *level of education,* likely to affect the heights of the consumption functions of different people?

We would expect that the more education a person has, the more income he's likely to earn relative to other people of the same age and circumstances. This supposition is, moreover, supported by the data in Fig. 3.7; the greater the number of years of education people in different age brackets have, the higher their average earnings.

3|7

The greater the number of years of schooling people in different age groups have completed, the greater their average earnings. (Source: H. S. Houthakker, "Education and Income," *The Review of Economics and Statistics,* Volume XLI, 1959, page 26. Houthakker's data are adapted from a Census Bureau study of the income tax returns filed by U.S. males in 1949.)

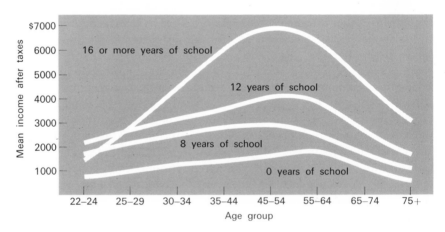

Since education enhances one's earnings potential, we would expect that the more education a person had, the more income he would anticipate earning in the future. The more income he anticipates earning, however, the less intense is his wish to provide for future needs. Suppose that two men were identical in all respects, except that one of them (Jack Learnwell) had more education and therefore anticipated earning more future income than the other (Bob Flunkout). We'd expect that Learnwell would be less willing to trade current-consumption dollars for additional-savings dollars than Flunkout would. Therefore Learnwell's indifference curves would at any point tend to be *flatter* than Flunkout's.

What effect would this difference in the slopes of their indifference curves have on the relative positions of the consumption functions of these two men? Figure 3.8 shows an indifference curve labeled I and a budget line labeled *yy* to portray Flunkout's equilibrium position. Let's draw through this equilibrium point a second *flatter* line, II, which portrays one indifference curve in Learnwell's preference map. Now if we compare curves I and II, we immediately observe that Learnwell cannot attain equilibrium at the same point at which Flunkout does. He must attain it at some other point, where a second indifference curve in his preference map, such as curve II', is tangent to *yy*. Moreover, since Learnwell's indifference curves are flatter than Flunkout's, it is obvious from Fig. 3.8 that Learnwell must attain equilibrium at a point along *yy* that lies to the left of the point at which Flunkout attains equilibrium. But if this is the case, then Learnwell, because he anticipates higher future earnings, will always tend to spend more out of a given level of income than Flunkout would, and as a result Learnwell's consumption function will tend to lie above (i.e., to be higher than) Flunkout's.

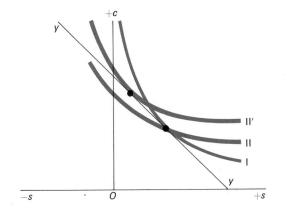

3|8

If Learnwell has *flatter* indifference curves than Flunkout, he will spend greater proportion of his income, and save a smaller proportion, than Flunkout does.

We have predicted that people with more education tend (other things being constant) to have higher consumption functions than people with less education. Figure 3.9 plots data from the Department of Labor on the relationship between disposable income and consumption expenditures for three different categories of consumers: those with 8 years or less of school, those with 9–12 years, and those with 13–16 years. These data show that people with more education spend more out of a given level of income than those with less education do, and thus our prediction is a valid one.

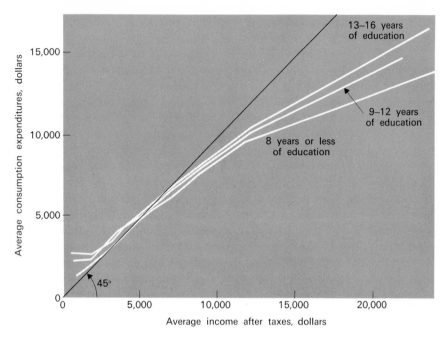

3|9 People with more education tend to spend more out of a given level of income than those with less education do, and thus have higher consumption functions. (Data, supplied by U.S. Department of Labor, apply to consumer expenditures in the U.S., 1960–61.)

SHIFTS IN AND MOVEMENTS ALONG THE CONSUMPTION FUNCTION

When we construct a person's consumption function, we are trying to isolate the relationship between his consumption and one other variable, his income. As we have seen, however, a person's current consumption depends, not only on his current income, but also on other factors such as current needs, future needs, and anticipated future income; these all determine the shape of his saving–consumption preferences. Therefore, in order to construct a person's consumption function, we must assume that all the many factors other than income that influence his current consumption are fixed. This assumption that *all other things are constant* is a crucial one in economic analysis, since it underlies not only the consumption function but also all the other schedules we shall derive.

All right, we've granted that a person's consumption function must be based on the idea that all other things are constant. Then we have to agree that a change in any variable other than his income, will, by altering the shape of his preferences between saving and consumption, induce a *shift in* his consumption function. The kind of changes we're talking about are changes in his current needs, in his expectations as to future needs, in the

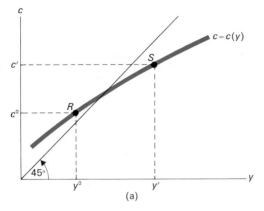

(a)

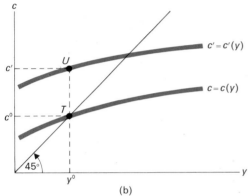

(b)

3|10

An increase in a person's current consumption may reflect either an increase in his current income or an upward shift in his consumption function.

a) An increase in his current income from y^0 to y' will shift his equilibrium from R to S and raise his current consumption from c^0 to c'.

b) An upward shift in his consumption function from $c = c(y)$ to $c' + c'(y)$ will shift his equilibrium from T to U and raise his current consumption from c^0 to c'.

size of his assets, in the investment opportunities open to him, or in his expectations concerning future goods prices. Things like that.

This means that a person may alter his current consumption not only because of

1) a change in his current income, but also because of
2) a change in one of the variables that-determine the shape of his saving–consumption preference map, and thus the position of his consumption function.

To show what we mean by (1), look at part (a) of Fig. 3.10. If the consumer's income increases from y^0 to y', all other things being constant, he will *move along* his consumption function from R to S, and by doing this he will increase his expenditures for current consumption from c^0 to c'.

To show what we mean by (2), look at part (b) of Fig. 3.10. If the consumer's consumption function shifts upward (maybe his wife has a baby, and his current needs increase), or maybe his anticipations of future needs decrease (his child graduates from college), his equilibrium position (assuming that no change occurs in his income) shifts from T to U. As a result, his expenditures for current consumption increase from c^0 to c'.

The distinction we have just made between *shifts in* and *movements along* a schedule seems to be hard for students to grasp. Nevertheless it is an extremely important one in all areas of economic analysis. Therefore, before you go on, go back over the last few paragraphs to make sure that you understand fully the distinction portrayed in Fig. 3.10 between these two kinds of change. Any time you spend now learning this distinction will save you much needless confusion later!

PROBLEMS

1 a) The data below refer to saving–consumption pairs; thus, for example, the pair (S1, C5) denotes one unit of saving and five units of consumption. Use these data, which show a consumer's preferences between saving and consumption, to draw up a preference map that has the general characteristics described in the text.

S1,C5	indifferent to	S2,C4
S − 1,C4$\frac{1}{2}$	indifferent to	S4$\frac{1}{2}$,C1
S1,C5	indifferent to	S8,C1
S − 1,C4$\frac{1}{2}$	indifferent to	S1,C2$\frac{1}{2}$
S1,C2$\frac{1}{2}$	preferred to	S − 3$\frac{1}{2}$,C5

   b) From the preference map drawn in part (a), determine which of the following pairs would be preferred.

S − 1,C4$\frac{1}{2}$	or	S5,C2
S1,C6	or	S7,C1
S5,C3	or	S1,C5

2 In drawing the indifference maps in this chapter, we have implicitly assumed that a consumer's preferences are *consistent*, i.e. that his indifference curves cannot cross. Comment on the following assertion: "A neurotic is someone whose indifference curves cross."

3 The following preference samples use the notation of Problem 1. Plot them and explain how each violates certain characteristics mentioned in the text.

a)

S1,C1	indifferent to	S0,C2
S − 1,C4	indifferent to	S2,C2
S1,C1	preferred to	S − 1,C4

b)

S1,C1	indifferent to	S4,C2
S2,C3	indifferent to	S5,C4
S5,C4	preferred to	S1,C1

c)

S0,C2	indifferent to	S1,C1
S − 1,C4	indifferent to	S0,C2
S2,C2	indifferent to	S − 1,C4
S2,C2	preferred to	S1,C1

d)

S1,C4	indifferent to	S3,C3
S3,C3	indifferent to	S4,C1
S4,C1	preferred to	S1,C3

4   a) Using the argument suggested in the text, show that the consumer's indiffer-
       ence curve through point A in Fig. 3.3 must *slope downward*. Can this same
       argument be applied to any savings–consumption point? In other words,
       can we be sure that the consumer's savings–consumption indifference curves
       will slope downward everywhere?

   b) Show that higher indifference curves must always be preferred to lower in-
       difference curves.

5   a) Suppose some generous person were to offer you $1,000 with the stipulation
       that you must spend $700 of it and save $300 of it. What other offers of this
       form would you consider equally desirable? In other words, determine your
       own indifference curve through the point described.

   b) By introspection, estimate your own preference map between savings and
       consumption. Then draw in budget lines corresponding to several different
       values of income. Are these budget lines parallel? Why?

   c) From your answer to part (b), derive your own consumption function.

6   Draw preference maps for the following consumers and number the indifference
       curves to indicate the order of preference.

   a) A consumer who does not care how much he saves so long as he does not
       dissave, and if he must dissave does not care how much he consumes.

   b) A consumer who is concerned only with the *sum* of the amount he saves and
       the amount he consumes.

   c) A consumer who is concerned only with the minimum of the two: savings
       and consumption.

   d) A consumer who is concerned only with consumption.

7   a) Determine the consumption function for the consumers described in parts
       (a) and (c) of Problem 6.

   b) What can you say about the consumption functions of the consumers de-
       scribed in parts (b) and (d) of Problem 6?

8   What effect would you expect the following changes to have, first on a con-
       sumer's indifference curves, and second on his consumption function?

   a) An increase in the interest rate paid by banks on savings deposits.

   b) A general fall in food prices.

9   Are the following changes of individual behavior the result of movement along
       the consumption function, shifts of the function itself, neither, or both? Ex-
       plain and illustrate graphically where possible.

   a) Jones increases his consumption by buying a new floor wax which he has
       seen advertised.

   b) Smith increases his consumption immediately after he learns that he is going
       to get a raise in salary one year from now.

   c) Brown sells his car so that he can use the money to buy stocks.

   d) Robinson increases his savings after he changes to a new job which pays the
       same as the old job but in addition provides free housing.

10   a) Discuss the differences you would expect to find in the consumption functions of: (i) large families versus small families, (ii) self-employed persons
versus salaried professionals, and (iii) homeowners versus renters.

b) Graph the consumption functions of the above groups from the following
data and compare the results with your predictions from part (a). Try to
explain any unusual features of these curves.

Group Consumption Patterns*

Homeowners		Renters		Salaried professionals and officials		Self-employed persons	
Dis. inc.	Cons. exp.	Dis. inc.	Cons. exp.	Dis. inc.	Cons. exp.	Dis. inc.	Cons. exp.
1,755	2,070	1,754	1,958	2,222	3,092	1,701	2,271
2,718	2,903	2,728	2,941	2,839	3,328	2,726	3,297
3,690	3,814	3,762	3,994	3,978	4,334	3,762	4,222
4,770	4,651	4,797	4,824	4,894	4,914	4,732	4,905
5,803	4,596	5,734	5,664	5,869	5,885	5,739	5,478
6,992	6,505	6,929	6,670	7,037	6,616	6,953	6,196
8,838	7,909	8,713	8,058	8,905	8,316	8,916	7,108
12,073	10,205	12,190	10,917	12,250	10,592	12,347	9,459
22,477	16,125	21,965	16,953	21,497	16,615	24,418	15,499

2-Person families		3-Person families		4-Person families		5-Person families	
Dis. inc.	Cons. exp.	Dis. inc.	Cons. exp.	Dis. inc.	Cons. exp.	Dis. inc.	Cons. exp.
1,882	2,177	1,815	2,295	1,916	2,447	1,850	2,404
2,686	2,888	2,741	3,031	2,869	3,509	2,946	3,379
3,728	3,833	3,794	4,028	3,825	4,335	3,847	4,541
4,815	4,569	4,817	4,960	4,888	5,058	4,758	5,011
5,777	5,217	5,773	5,629	5,818	5,900	5,784	5,904
6,952	6,259	7,002	6,723	7,019	6,784	7,047	6,930
8,754	7,529	8,866	7,951	8,835	8,051	8,846	8,282
12,014	9,453	12,026	10,300	12,281	10,805	11,937	10,528
23,392	16,696	22,773	14,919	23,186	15,644	22,143	16,986

*Adapted from statistics issued by the U.S. Bureau of Labor. Values given are average disposable income and average
expenditure for current consumption, measured in dollars, for one year, 1960–61.

CHAPTER 4

THE CONSUMPTION DECISION

In Chapter 3 we talked about the way the consumer allocates his current income between savings and current consumption. This decision, however, is only one economic choice he must make. He has to make a second important decision during each period: how is he going to allocate the funds he has budgeted for current consumption among all the available goods and services?

Figure 4.1 shows how U.S. consumers as a group allocated their total 1966 consumption expenditures among different categories of goods. This figure illustrates the fact that consumers purchase not only goods, but also services, such as housing, transportation, dry cleaning, telephone service, and education. Part (a) shows that consumers in 1966 spent almost as much of their income on services as on nondurable goods. It also shows that depreciation of consumer durables constitutes a high percentage of the total expenditure for personal consumption. Part (b) breaks down expenditures for personal consumption according to major categories of products. It shows that during 1966 consumers allocated roughly 25% of their total consumption expenditures to food and beverages, 20% to housing and household operation, 12% to transportation services (public and self-provided), 9% to clothing and shoes, and the remainder to miscellaneous goods.

Although the data in Fig. 4.1 are interesting, bear in mind that they picture only how consumers on the average allocate their consumption dollars. If you were to look behind these data for the average person, you would find that different consumers allocate their total consumption expenditures in strikingly different ways. For example, Fig. 4.2 presents data on a cross section of consumers, arranged according to level of income. Here we see that low-income consumers devote a significantly higher percentage of their total consumption expenditures to shelter and food than high-income ones do, while high-income consumers spend a higher percentage of their consumption expenditures on clothing, luxury food, and education than low-

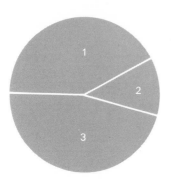

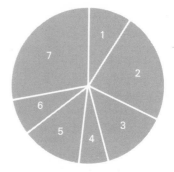

	%
1. Nondurable goods	46
2. Estimated depreciation on consumer durables	12
3. Services	42

	%
1. Clothing and shoes	9
2. Food and beverages	24
3. Housing	15
4. Household operation	6
5. Automobile parts, gas and oil, and transportation	12
6. Depreciation on other durable goods	7
7. All other	27

4|1

Distribution of expenditures for personal consumption in 1966. (Adapted from data issued by the U.S. Department of Commerce)

4|2

Percentages of their total consumption expenditures which consumers at different income levels devote to several types of consumption goods. (Source: U.S. Department of Labor. Data are for 1960–61.)

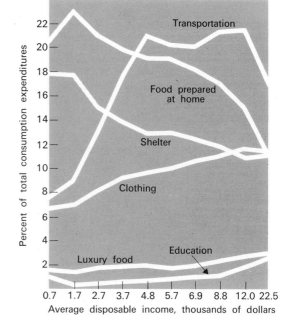

income ones do. If you were to look at other cross-sectional groupings of consumers, you would find that at every income level large families tend to devote a higher percentage of their total consumption expenditures to clothing than small families do, that homeowners devote a higher percentage to food consumed at home than renters do, and that skilled workers devote a higher percentage to recreation than unskilled workers do.

The fact that every consumer faces a consumption-allocation problem and that each solves it differently raises two questions that are similar to those posed at the beginning of the preceding chapter: How do individual consumers decide how to allocate their total consumption expenditures among available goods? And why is it that they resolve this choice in such widely differing ways?

THE CONSUMER'S CHOICE OF AN EQUILIBRIUM COMMODITY BUNDLE

Determining how the consumer allocates the funds he has budgeted for current consumption turns out to be—for us at least—a quite simple task, because we can analyze this new problem by using a model of consumer choice identical in general structure to the one we worked out in Chapter 3.

Let's begin by making a simplifying assumption: our consumer, Ernest Smith, can purchase only two sorts of goods: q_1 and q_2. At first glance we might think that this assumption is an extremely limiting one. In reality, however, it is not, because we can always think of q_1 as being one good (say oranges) and q_2 as being a composite commodity composed of all goods other than q_1.

The Consumer's Preferences

Next let's assume that Smith has definite preferences with respect to his consumption of q_1 and q_2. That is, he can rank alternative bundles of q_1 and q_2 from least to most preferred. What will the general shape of his (q_1, q_2)-indifference map be? If we make the natural supposition that Smith derives satisfaction from consuming both q_1 and q_2, then by appealing to experience, we can obtain a limited, but useful, answer. Experience suggests first that, if we were to decrease the quantity of q_1 available to Smith, we would have to increase the quantity of q_2 available to him in order to keep him at the same level of satisfaction or indifference; and conversely. But if this is the case, then Smith's indifference curves with respect to q_1 and q_2 must slope downward.

Experience also tells us that if we were to move Smith along one of his indifference curves by taking q_1 away from him while we simultaneously gave him just enough additional q_2 so that his level of satisfaction was unchanged, eventually the quantity of q_2 required to compensate him for successive and equal decreases in the amount of q_1 would begin to *rise*. This observation, however, implies that Smith's indifference curves between q_1 and q_2 must not only slope downward but also be *convex*, as are those in Fig. 4.3.

Finally, as you should verify, higher indifference curves in Smith's indifference map must correspond to higher levels of satisfaction.

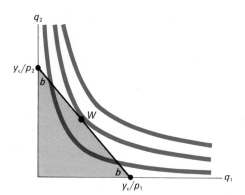

4|3

The consumer, faced with the budget constraint *bb*, will attain equilibrium by consuming at the point *W*.

The Consumer's Budget Constraint

To complete our new model of consumer choice, we must now introduce the budget constraint the consumer faces when he decides what goods to consume during the current period.

This budget constraint requires that the consumer's total expenditures on goods and services precisely equal the quantity of funds he has allocated for current consumption.

Recall that the consumer could not violate the budget constraint associated with his saving–consumption decision because this relationship, $y = c + s$, holds by definition. On the other hand, he *can* violate the second budget constraint we have just set up; if he does so, however, the amount he actually saves during the period will not be the amount he planned to save. Thus this second budget constraint may be said to require that the consumer, during each period, fulfill his planned allocation of current income between consumption and saving.

Let's continue our assumption that the consumer, Smith, can purchase only two commodities, q_1 and q_2. Let's also suppose that the prices of these goods, p_1 and p_2, are positive, and, from Smith's point of view, *fixed.* Then Smith's budget constraint for the period will be given by the expression

$$y_c = p_1 q_1 + p_2 q_2,$$

in which y_c represents funds Smith has budgeted for consumption during the period.* Note that y_c, p_1, and p_2 are all constants, while q_1 and q_2 are variables.

Solving Smith's budget constraint for q_2, we obtain a new expression,

$$q_2 = -(p_1/p_2)q_1 + y_c/p_2.$$

When we plot this budget line, what slope and position will it have? Obviously it must intersect the q_1-axis at the point y_c/p_1, like the budget line bb plotted in Fig. 4.3, since this point represents the maximum amount of q_1 that Smith could purchase if he spent all the funds he had budgeted for consumption on q_1. Similarly this line must intersect the q_2-axis at the point y_c/p_2, since this point represents the maximum amount of q_2 that Smith could purchase if he spent all the funds he had budgeted for consumption on q_2. Finally the slope of this line equals $-(p_1/p_2)$ and must therefore always be *negative*. The obvious interpretation of the fact that Smith's budget line has a negative slope is that, so long as he remains on this line (i.e., so long as he respects his period budget constraint), he cannot increase his consumption of one good without simultaneously decreasing his consumption of the other good.

The Consumer's Equilibrium Choice

The different points on Smith's budget line bb in Fig. 4.3 represent all the different *commodity bundles* (i.e., combinations of q_1 and q_2) that he might purchase with the funds he has budgeted for consumption. Which of these commodity bundles will he in fact choose to purchase?

Suppose that Smith has a preference map and budget constraint like that in Fig. 4.3. Let's also assume that he is a *satisfaction-maximizer* (recall our definition of this on page 14). Then he must attain equilibrium at the point W, since this point represents (as you should verify) the point along bb that will yield him maximum satisfaction. However, point W also represents the point at which Smith's budget line is just tangent to one of the indifference curves in his preference map. Therefore we can make a general conclusion as follows:

The consumer will maximize his satisfaction and thus attain equilibrium by moving to the point on his budget line at which this line is just tangent to one of the indifference curves in his preference map.

---

* Goods available in desired quantities at zero prices are called *free goods*. Air, for example, is a free good for most consumers, but not for mountain climbers, astronauts, or inhabitants of Los Angeles. Clearly free goods need not be included in the consumer's budget constraint.

THE CONSUMER'S DEMAND CURVE FOR A COMMODITY

In order to analyze a great many economic questions, we have to be able to answer the question: How will Mr. Typical Consumer alter his consumption of a given commodity if the price of that commodity changes?

Using the model of consumer choice presented above, we can easily answer this question. Let us say that we know how much a consumer has budgeted for current consumption and how much all other commodities cost. Then:

We can determine the probable shape of a schedule that summarizes the relationship between the price the consumer must pay for a given commodity and the quantity of it he will purchase.

Such a schedule is called a *demand curve.* To show how to derive one, let's assume that our consumer, Smith, has a preference map like that in Fig. 4.4. And let's derive his demand schedule for q_2.

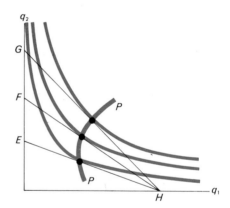

4|4

The information necessary to derive the consumer's demand schedule for q_2 is contained in the consumer's *price-versus-consumption curve, PP.*

We begin by constructing a series of budget lines for Smith, each of which corresponds to a different level of p_2. What relationship will these budget lines bear to each other? Well, note that decreasing p_2 increases the amount of q_2 that Smith would be able to buy if he devoted all his income to q_2; however, decreasing p_2 has no effect on the quantity of q_1 that he'd be able to buy if he devoted all his income to q_1. But if this is the case, then decreasing p_2 would shift Smith's budget line "upward," for example, from FH to GH; while increasing p_2 would (as you should verify) shift his budget line "downward," for example from FH to EH. We thus conclude that Smith's budget lines for different levels of p_2 will all begin at a single point, H, on the q_1-axis. Also higher budget lines will correspond to lower levels of p_2.

The next step in deriving Smith's demand curve for q_2 is to locate the point at which each of these budget lines is tangent to one of the indifference curves in his preference map. By so doing, we'll obtain a collection of points, each of which tells us how much q_2 Smith would purchase at a given level of p_2. This collection of points, which is represented by the *price–consumption curve PP* in Fig. 4.4, contains all the information we need to set up Smith's demand schedule for q_2.

Let's use this information to plot out Smith's demand schedule. The upward slope of his price–consumption curve *PP* tells us that, as the price of q_2 falls (i.e., as Smith's budget constraint is shifted upward from E toward G), his consumption of q_2 will increase. But if this is the case, then his demand curve for q_2 must therefore *slope downward,* as the demand curve in Fig. 4.5 slopes.

Although it is interesting to know that *our consumer's* demand curve for q_2 will slope downward, what we would really like to know is whether the *typical* consumer's demand curve for any commodity will slope downward. How would Mr. Typical Consumer respond to a decrease in the price of a given commodity?

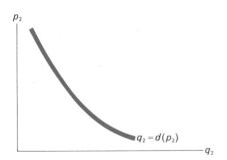

4|5

The consumer's demand curve for any commodity, q_2, will almost always be downward-sloping.

Whenever the price of a commodity decreases, two things happen:

1) the commodity will become cheaper relative to other commodities, and
2) the real income (i.e., the purchasing power) of every consumer who buys it will rise.

Presumably the typical consumer will always respond to change (1) (that is, to the change in relative prices) by substituting the commodity whose price has fallen for other commodities which are now relatively more expensive. Thus, for example, if the price of beef were to fall (to mention an unlikely circumstance), we would expect the consumer to substitute beef for fish and eggs.

How does Mr. Typical Consumer respond to change (2), that is, the induced increase in his real income? In most instances he would respond by consuming more of all commodities, including the one whose price has fallen.

Occasionally, however, a consumer may respond to the increase in his real income caused by a decline in the price of some commodity by consuming less of it. Take bread, for example. Suppose that the price of bread were to fall, and there happened to be a consumer who ate a lot of bread not because he liked bread but because he felt he could not afford other, more expensive goods. He might just respond to the increase in his real income induced by a decline in the price of bread by consuming more beef but less bread!

So long as the *income* and the *substitution effects* work in the same direction, the consumer will always respond to a *decrease* in the price of a commodity by *increasing* his consumption of it, and as a result his demand curve for it will slope downward. Even if the income effect works in a direction opposite to that of the substitution effect (i.e., even if increased real income leads the consumer to buy less of a thing in response to a fall in its price), his demand curve for it will still slope downward, unless the income effect is large enough to swamp the substitution effect. This, however, is not likely to occur, because the substitution effect associated with any price change is usually large, while the income effect is small (unless the commodity whose price has changed happens to be one on which the consumer spends a significant portion of his total income). Thus if the bottom fell out of the market in, say, turquoises, it wouldn't raise the real income of Mr. Typical Consumer very much.

Therefore it is safe to say that the consumer's demand curve for any commodity almost always slopes downward. We cannot say *always,* because there's the possibility that the income effect associated with a particular price change will not only work against, but even outweigh, the substitution effect generated by that price change. That this possibility is real is attested to by the English economist, Giffen, who observed that during the 1845 famine Irish families responded to the increase in the price of potatoes by *increasing* their consumption of potatoes.*

ELASTICITY OF DEMAND

People who are setting prices for things—whether they are government policy makers or people working for a business firm that is out to make a profit— often need to know how a certain change in the price of a commodity will influence the total amount consumers spend on it. An automobile manufacturer wants to know whether a change in the price of his automobiles would increase his profits. So he asks: how would consumers react to such a change? The city government wants to know whether an increase in bridge

---

* This oddity deserves an explanation: Poor families ate many potatoes because they could not afford meat. When the price of potatoes went up, these families had to spend more money on potatoes, which left them with less money to spend on meat than ever. Therefore, to stave off hunger, they had to increase their consumption of potatoes.

and tunnel tolls would keep commuter traffic out of New York City. So it asks: how would commuters respond to a rise in tolls? Similarly, the Federal government wants to know whether an increase in the price of fresh milk would increase the incomes of dairy farmers. So it asks: how would consumers react to such a price hike?

At first glance you might think that answering questions of this sort would present no problem. "After all," you might argue, "raising the price of a commodity will naturally lead consumers to spend more on it, while decreasing the price of it will naturally have the opposite effect." Superficially this argument is a plausible one. Unfortunately, however, it is also an incorrect one.

Why? Because the total amount a consumer spends on a commodity depends not only on the *price* of this commodity, but also on the *quantity* of it he buys. Therefore, when there is a change in the price of this commodity, the effect of the change on his spending will depend on two things:

1) the direction and magnitude of the price change, and
2) the way he alters his purchases of this commodity in response to the change in its price.

Suppose that the price of a given commodity were to decrease. Mr. Typical Consumer could respond in three ways.

1) He could decrease his spending on this commodity,
2) he could increase his spending on this commodity, or
3) he could leave his spending on this commodity unchanged.

This sounds pretty involved, so let's take a case in point: the price of Cokes in your friendly Coke machine. Let's say the price decreases.

Clearly the first effect of this change would be to *decrease* your spending on Cokes, since you can now buy the same quantity of them that you used to buy at the old price at a new *lower* price. But this will probably lead you to buy more of them, and buying more Cokes will tend to increase your spending on them. Thus what happens on balance to your spending on Cokes will depend on how responsive your consumption of them is to a change in their price. In the language of the economist,

it will depend on how large the percentage change in your consumption is relative to the percentage change that the seller makes in the price of his commodity.

This ratio, which is given by the expression

$$\epsilon = \left| \frac{\text{percentage change in } q}{\text{percentage change in } p} \right|,$$

is known as the *elasticity* of your demand.

If the elasticity of your demand for Cokes is greater than 1 (that is, if your consumption of them is very responsive to changes in price), you will respond to a decrease in their price by *increasing* your spending on them. Conversely, if the elasticity of your demand for Cokes is less than 1 (that is, if your consumption of them is not very responsive to changes in price), you will respond to a decrease in their price by *decreasing* your spending on them. Finally, in the borderline case of the elasticity of your demand being equal to 1, you will respond to a decrease in the price of Cokes by *making no change* in your spending on them.

Variation of Elasticity from Point to Point Along a Demand Curve

Is the elasticity of the consumer's demand for any commodity the *same* at all points along his demand curve for this commodity?

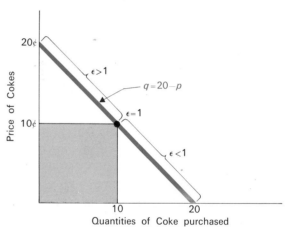

4|6

The elasticity ϵ of your demand curve for Cokes will be greater than 1 in the upper ranges of your demand curve for them, equal to 1 at some intermediate point, and less than 1 in the lower ranges of your demand curve.

To answer this question, let's suppose that your weekly demand for Cokes can be represented by the expression

$$q = 20 - p.$$

Suppose that the price were to be set at 19¢ per Coke. You would buy only one Coke a week, and your total spending on Cokes would be 19¢. If the price were instead set at the intermediate level of 10¢, you'd buy 10, and your total spending on Cokes would equal $1.00. Finally, if the price were to be set at the very low price of 1¢ per Coke, your consumption would soar to 19, but your spending on Cokes would equal only 19¢.

Therefore the elasticity of your demand for Cokes cannot be everywhere the same along your demand curve for them. Instead it must be greater than 1 in the upper ranges of your demand curve, equal to 1 at some intermediate point, and less than 1 in the lower ranges of your demand curve.

This result is shown graphically in Fig. 4.6. If Cokes are selling at 10¢ apiece, then you'll buy 10 a week, and your total expenditure on them can be represented by the area of the shaded "total expenditure" rectangle in Fig. 4.6. The area of this rectangle will, however, approach zero if the price is either raised to very high levels or brought down to very low levels. Therefore the elasticity of your demand for Cokes must begin high (i.e., be greater than 1) at the upper end of your demand curve for Cokes, and it must fall consistently as you move downward along this curve.

The observation that elasticity will fall consistently along a straight-line demand curve is an extremely important one, because, as we shall see in our discussion of profits and the firm, it provides a key to the relationship between the revenue curves of a company.

TABLE 4|1

Consumer Demand Elasticities for Selected Commodity Groups*

Commodity group	Estimated demand elasticity
Dairy products	0.381
Vegetables and fruits	0.350
Meats and meat products	0.337
Tobacco products	0.558
Drinks	0.459
Textiles	0.951
Footwear	0.354
Household articles	0.611
Other durable goods	0.935
Fuel and utilities	0.408

* A. P. Barten, "Consumer demand functions under conditions of almost additive preferences," *Econometrica* **32**, January–April 1964, pages 1–38. The above estimates refer to Dutch consumers. Similar data for U.S. consumers are given in Problem 13 at the end of this chapter.

Data on Demand Elasticities

Let's assume that we know the prices of certain goods. Let's also assume that we know the needs and tastes of the average consumer and the quantity of funds he has budgeted for consumption. How elastic will his demand for different goods be? To answer this question, economists have made studies of demand elasticities. Table 4.1 presents data from one such study, which show that the elasticity of demand of the average consumer for most groups of commodities is less than 1. As we might expect, however, demand elasticity is higher for durable goods such as cars and washing machines, which are frequently regarded as luxury items, than for necessities such as food and footwear.

SUBSTITUTES, COMPLEMENTS, AND INDEPENDENT GOODS

We can't determine either the shape or the position of John Q. Consumer's budget line without knowing both the size of his income and the prices of all commodities available to him. Thus, in order to construct his demand curve for any one commodity, we have to assume not only that his income is fixed, but also that the prices of all other commodities are fixed.* This assumption that all other things are constant may, of course, be violated. If it is, however, we must expect that the consumer's demand curve for the commodity in question will shift.

Sometimes the price of one commodity rises, and this makes the consumer's demand curve for some other commodity shift upward (as in Fig. 4.7). The two goods are then said to be *substitute* goods.† If two goods are substitutes, and one good rises in price, obviously the consumer will respond by using the other good, which is now relatively less expensive, in its place. Pairs of goods—such as dairy products and meat, fish and meat, and vegetables and other groceries—are substitute goods; this is confirmed by the Barten study cited in Table 4.1.

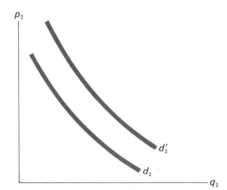

4|7

An increase in the price of q_1 may shift the consumer's demand curve for q_2 upward from d_2 to d_2'. If it does, then q_1 and q_2 are said to be substitute goods.

Sometimes when the price of one commodity rises, it makes the consumer's demand curve for some other commodity shift downward. Then the two goods are said to be *complements*. Complementarity implies that the consumer uses the two goods in question *together*. Therefore we would expect that pairs of goods such as tobacco and drinks, groceries and dairy products, and household articles and other durable goods would be complements. This supposition is also borne out by Barten's data.

---

* If this point is unclear to you, review our derivation of the consumer's demand curve for q_2 (pages 40–41).

† Our remarks on substitute, complementary, and independent goods are all based on the assumption that the income effects generated by the price changes in question are small.

Sometimes, however, an increase in the price of one commodity causes *no* shift in the consumer's demand for some other commodity. Then the two goods are said to be *independent*. If two goods are independent, this implies that they are neither consumed in place of each other nor consumed together. Thus it is not surprising that (again according to the Barten study) drinks and dairy products are close to being independent goods. So too are fish and footwear!

*THE CONSUMER'S DEMAND CURVE FOR EDUCATION: AN EXAMPLE

As we have seen, the consumer's demand curve for a commodity is partly determined by his preferences among different goods. Thus people who differ in some important characteristic such as education, occupation, or number of dependents display marked differences both in the shape of their "commodity preferences" and in the position of their demand curves. To review the results we have obtained in this chapter and to show their usefulness, let's work through an example which illustrates this point: What effect does a consumer's level of education have on the height of his demand curve for education?

It's logical to expect that the more education a person has, the more likely he is to appreciate the value of education and the stronger his preferences for education versus other commodities. If two people were identical in all respects except that one of them (Jack Learnwell—who else?) had more education than the other (Bob Flunkout), then probably Learnwell would place a greater value on education than Flunkout would. The more a person values education, however, the flatter his indifference curves between education and other goods will be.† (We are assuming here that education is plotted along the vertical axis.) Therefore we would expect that,‡ if Learnwell and Flunkout were both to budget the same number of dollars for current consumption, Learnwell, at each price that might be charged for education, would demand more education than Flunkout. In other words, Learnwell would have a *higher* demand curve for education than Flunkout!

We may venture a guess, then, that people with more education usually devote a greater proportion of their total consumption expenditure to education than people with less education.§ Is this hypothesis borne out by

---

* The reader may skip this starred example without loss of continuity.

† Note that the argument here is similar to that used in the preceding chapter to show that the indifference curves between consumption and savings of Learnwell are likely to be *flatter* than those of Flunkout. (See Fig. 3.8 and the related discussion.)

‡ See problem 11 at the end of this chapter.

§ The idea that people with more education tend to spend more on education than people with less was suggested to us by Richard Rosett. This topic is also discussed in *Consumer Choice in the American Economy,* by Carolyn Bell; New York: Random House, 1967.

experience? The data plotted in Fig. 4.8 indicate that it is: they show that at every expenditure level people with more education spend more on education than people with less education.

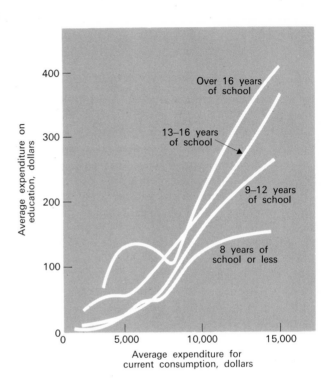

4|8

People with more education spend more on education (out of a given level of income) than people with less education do. (Source: U.S. Department of Labor. Data are for 1960–61.)

Average expenditure on education, dollars

400

300

200

100

0

0   5,000   10,000   15,000

Average expenditure for current consumption, dollars

Over 16 years of school

13–16 years of school

9–12 years of school

8 years of school or less

THE CONSUMER'S SUPPLY CURVE OF LABOR

So far in our analysis of the consumer, we have assumed that his current income is fixed. In reality, of course, his income is *not* fixed; it depends on how he divides his time between labor and leisure, on what sorts of labor services he supplies, on what kinds of investments he makes, on what risks he incurs. To put it in the jargon of economists, it depends on all the decisions he makes with respect to the *productive inputs* he supplies to the business sector.

How does the consumer decide how to allocate his scarce time between labor and leisure? And how does he decide how to allocate his limited capital among the wide range of alternative investment opportunities? We'll deal with the first (and simpler) of these questions in this section. The second is so complex that it merits a chapter to itself: Chapter 5.

The Consumer's Labor–Leisure Choice

Whenever the consumer works, he works in order to earn income. Therefore, when he chooses between leisure and labor, what he is really choosing between is *leisure* and *income*. Let's assume that the consumer has definite preferences with respect to leisure and income, and that these preferences can be represented by a preference map similar to the one in Fig. 4.9.

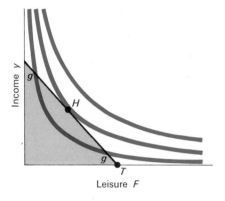

4|9

The consumer, faced with the budget constraint *gg*, will attain equilibrium by "consuming" the income–leisure combination *H*.

Under what constraint does the consumer operate when he chooses the combination of income and leisure he will "consume" in equilibrium? To answer this question, let's consider a consumer, Ernest Smith, who has T hours available each day and who devotes L of them to labor. If we denote Smith's remaining free or leisure hours by F, then we can represent the number of hours he works by the expression

$$L = T - F.$$

Moreover, if the *wage rate* equals w, then Smith's income, y, can be given by the equation

$$y = wL,$$

and the relationship between the maximum amounts of income and leisure that Smith can *simultaneously* enjoy, that is, the budget constraint under which he must make his income–leisure choice, can be given by the expression

$$y = wT - wF.$$

If we now assume that Smith's objective in making his income–leisure choice is to maximize his satisfaction, then obviously his equilibrium income–leisure choice will be represented by a point of tangency between his budget constraint and one of the indifference curves in his leisure–income preference map. Thus Smith, for example, whose preferences and budget constraint are shown in Fig. 4.9, will attain equilibrium at the point H at which his budget constraint, *gg*, is just tangent to one of the indifference curves in his leisure–income preference map.

The Consumer's Supply Curve of Labor

Suppose Smith gets a raise. Will this induce him to work longer hours? Or shorter hours? If the government taxes Smith's income in order to reduce the inequality of income distribution, will these taxes decrease his incentives to work? Or will they lead the heavily taxed Smith to work harder?

To answer these questions, we must derive the probable shape of a schedule that summarizes the relationship between the wage rate that Smith receives for his labor and the quantity of labor he is willing to supply. This schedule is known as the consumer's *supply curve of labor*.

First we generate a family of budget lines by varying the wage rate, w, that Smith receives. As you can easily verify, all the budget lines thus produced will intersect the leisure axis at the point T (recall that T represents the total number of hours Smith has available); steeper budget lines correspond to higher wage rates.

Since Smith is a satisfaction-maximizer, his equilibrium consumption of income and leisure at each wage rate will be indicated by the point at which the appropriate budget constraint is tangent to one of the indifference curves in his preference map. Look at Fig. 4.10. The line LL contains all such equilibrium points. From it we can easily read off what income Smith would earn, and thus how many hours of labor he would supply, at each wage rate. This information, when plotted, yields the consumer's supply curve of labor, which we can represent by the expression

$$s = s(w).$$

Intuition tells us that Smith would probably react to raises by offering to supply more labor. However, Fig. 4.10 indicates that Smith's preference map can easily be drawn so that successive increases in his wage rate will eventually lead him to reduce the number of hours he works. If so, then his supply curve of labor will (as the curve in Fig. 4.11 does) bend backward in its upper reaches. The portion of Smith's supply curve of labor that bends backward may at first puzzle you. But we can easily interpret it in terms of the income and substitution effects. Suppose that Smith's boss gives him a raise. Clearly Smith's leisure is going to be more expensive from now on, and he'll be induced to *substitute* income for leisure, i.e., to work longer hours.

A change in his wage rate, however, will also directly affect Smith's income; his income will be larger even if he does not choose to work longer hours. And this increase in his income will permit him to consume more of all of the goods he desires, including leisure. Thus the *income effect* will cause Smith to respond to an increase in his wage rate by working shorter hours.

It follows, therefore, that the substitution and income effects associated with an increase in the wage rate exert opposite influences on the slope of the consumer's supply curve of labor. Especially at high wage levels the income effect will be strong and might well outweigh the substitution effect.

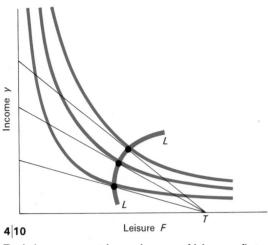

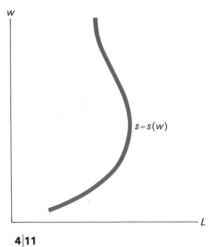

4|10   Leisure *F*

To derive a consumer's supply curve of labor, we first
determine how much labor he would supply at each
wage rate he might be offered. This information is
given by the line *LL*.

4|11

The consumer's supply curve of labor.

These two considerations explain why economists consider that a supply
curve of labor that bends backward is not only possible, but likely, while at
the same time they consider a demand curve that slopes upward to be
extremely unlikely.

Is it realistic to think of Mr. Typical Consumer as adjusting the number
of hours he works according to changes in the wage rate? Obviously he is not
completely free to vary the number of hours he works, so it must frequently
be the case that he can't work the precise number of hours he would like to,
given the wage rate he is paid. Data from a recent U.S. survey give some idea
of the incidence of such disequilibrium by showing that almost 50% of all
people who are (1) less than 25 years old, (2) who have less than a sixth-grade
education, or (3) who have annual incomes of less than $2,000 would "like
very much" to work additional hours at the wage rate they are paid. However, among workers who are older, better educated, and have higher incomes
few would prefer to work additional hours at their going wage rate.

The same survey also produced data indicating that consumers—especially if we interpret the term as meaning "spending units"—have more opportunities to vary the number of hours they work than might appear at first
glance. The survey reveals that many heads of households have the chance
to work overtime, that 14% of them "moonlight" (i.e., hold a second job),
and that 40% of all wives work on a full-time, part-time, or occasional basis.*

---

* George Katona, Eva Mueller, Jay Schmiedeskamp, John Sonquist, *1966 Survey of Consumer Finances.* Monograph No. 44, Survey Research Center, Institute for Social Research;
Ann Arbor, Mich.: The University of Michigan, 1967.

PROBLEMS

1 a) Suppose that at a meal you were given two hamburgers and one plate of French fried potatoes. For how many additional plates of French fries would you just be willing to give up one of the hamburgers? For how many additional hamburgers would you be willing to give up the plate of French fries? In this way, construct your own indifference map between the two foods.

   b) Using a similar technique construct your indifference curves with respect to the following pairs of goods: beer and books; laundry detergent and shoes; tennis shoes and shoelaces; staples and paper clips.

2 The Bureau of Labor Statistics and the Department of Commerce have done a study which predicts the patterns of consumption of United States consumers in 1970. In calculating these, they used 1954 prices and implicitly assumed that, if all prices and total expenditures were to rise in the same proportion, the pattern of consumption would not change. How valid is this assumption? What would happen to John Q. Consumer's budget line if all prices and his funds budgeted for consumption were to double? (The detailed results of this study are presented in H. S. Houthakker and L. D. Taylor, *Consumer Demand in the United States 1929–1970;* Cambridge, Mass.: Harvard University Press, 1966.)

3 H. S. Houthakker and S. J. Prais, in their study, *The Analysis of Family Budgets* (New York: Cambridge University Press, 1955), observed that the average price paid by the typical consumer for different products tends to increase with the consumer's income. They interpreted this fact as implying that consumers tend to shift their expenditures toward better-quality products as their incomes rise. Draw up the indifference map of a typical consumer for two different kinds of cheese, one of which is of better quality than the other. What would the observation of Houthakker and Prais imply about the shape of the indifference curves?

4 Show that, if an increase in a consumer's income causes him to consume more of a particular good, his demand curve for that good must slope downward.

   In this chapter, as in all of theoretical economics, we have started with certain assumptions and then reasoned from them to make predictions about behavior. These were not the only assumptions that could have been made, of course; they were not even the only assumptions that would have yielded the same results. Thus, though we may observe that our predictions are accurate, this does not mean that our assumptions were necessarily correct. The following three problems are intended · to help you to understand this relationship between assumptions and predictions.

*5 Explain the differences between the preference patterns of the following two consumers, and show that in spite of these differences they will behave exactly alike. *Consumer A:* Of any two commodity bundles, he always prefers the one with more of q_2. If they have the same amount of q_2, he is indifferent with respect to the choice between them. *Consumer B:* He also prefers a bundle with more of q_2 to one with less of q_2; but, if two bundles have the same amount of q_2, he prefers the one with more of q_1.

---

* An asterisk indicates a problem which is unusually difficult, and which may be omitted.

*6   Show that the following indifference maps, though quite abnormal, do lead to
     downward-sloping demand curves for q_1. In both graphs an increase in both
     q_1 and q_2 is always preferred. This is sufficient to determine the ordering of
     the indifference curves.

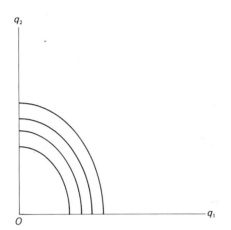

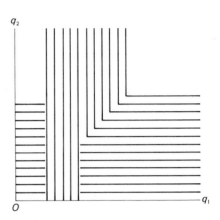

*7   Show that convexity of the indifference curves implies the following behavior:
     if a consumer does not buy a particular commodity bundle at one set of prices,
     even though he could afford it, then the set of prices at which he *would* buy
     this bundle must be one at which he cannot afford the bundle which he bought
     at the first set of prices. Would the two indifference maps of Problem 5 yield
     the same prediction about consumer behavior?

8   Discuss the way that knowledge of elasticities of demand would help you in
     answering the following questions:

     a) Would raising the tolls on the bridges into New York City help significantly
        to reduce traffic congestion in the city?

     b) Should the New Haven Railroad raise or lower its fares in order to increase
        its total revenue? (Houthakker and Taylor, *ibid.*, estimated that the elas-
        ticity of consumer demand for railway commuter service was 0.8121.)

     c) At what price should the government set milk prices in order to maximize
        the revenue received by dairy farmers from consumers?

9   Suppose that a student's demand curve for movies is a straight line, intersecting
     the price axis at $2.00 per movie and the quantity axis at 20 movies per year.

     a) Plot this demand curve.

     b) Investigate the way that demand elasticity changes along the demand curve.
        Use the formula,

$$\epsilon = \left| \frac{\text{percentage change in } q}{\text{percentage change in } p} \right|$$

     at several intervals along the curve.

c) Suppose that the current price of movies is $1. Show, with individual diagrams, the way that the student's demand for movies might reasonably be expected to change in response to each of the following changes: (i) A cut in his monthly allowance. (ii) A rise in movie prices to $1.25. (iii) A change in college regulations requiring all students to take an additional course. (iv) A rise in the price of basketball games. (v) A rise in the price of meals in the student dining hall.

10 Consider the following answers to the question, "How do you feel about spending money on movies?" What sort of demand curves for movies do these answers imply? Are the elasticities of demand for movies that these answers imply less than 1, greater than 1, or approximately equal to 1?

a) "I budget $10 a month for movies, and manage to stick pretty close to this budget. No more, no less."

b) "I go to a movie every Saturday night with my wife. That's all."

c) "I think $1.50 is too much to spend on a movie. At that price I would only go about once a month. But last year I found a place that only charges 75¢ and I've been going there every week since then."

d) "I don't believe in movies!"

11 a) Using the type of argument illustrated in Problem 1, show that highly educated persons have flatter indifference curves between education and all other consumption (when education is measured on the vertical axis) than less-well-educated persons.

b) Show that at any set of prices this will imply that the highly educated will spend a larger percentage of their incomes on education than will the less-well-educated.

12 a) Show graphically the effect of an income tax, stated as a fixed fraction of total income, on the amount of labor supplied and the incomes of laborers.

b) With the aid of indifference curves, show the way that an increase in income taxes could affect not only the total amount spent by consumers, but also the relative amounts of various products that they buy.

13 Assume that relative prices are roughly the same in the U.S. and in Holland and observe that on the average a U.S. consumer enjoys a higher standard of living than a Dutch consumer. Then use the analysis of this chapter to make an intelligent guess as to how the entries in Table 4.1 would change if we were to replace them with the corresponding demand elasticities for U.S. consumers. [Houthakker and Taylor, *ibid.*, obtained the following demand elasticities for U.S. consumers: footwear, 0.3878, kitchen and other household appliances, 0.6253, and household utility (electricity), 0.6502.]

*Appendix to Chapter 4

THE CONSUMPTION DECISION: A MATHEMATICAL TREATMENT

We have just stated, and solved graphically, the problem of how the consumer allocates the funds he has budgeted for consumption. This problem can also be solved mathematically as a problem of *constrained maximization*. In this appendix we shall use this alternative approach.

We can solve a problem of constrained maximization either by

1) substituting the constraint into the expression to be maximized, or by
2) introducing the Lagrange multiplier.

We shall use the technique of substitution (which proves satisfactory only in simple cases) to obtain conditions of consumer equilibrium in the two-good case, and the Lagrange multiplier, a more general technique, to obtain conditions of consumer equilibrium in the three-good case.

THE UTILITY FUNCTION

To state the problem of utility maximization mathematically, we need a new concept, the consumer's *utility function*.

Suppose that only two goods, q_1 and q_2, are available to the consumer. Then his utility function can be represented by the expression

$$U = f(q_1, q_2),$$

which states that his satisfaction or utility, U, is a function of his consumption of these two goods. When we plot this utility function, we get a three-dimensional surface like that in Fig. 4.12. Note that each point on this surface illustrates the relationship between the utility the consumer enjoys and the specific bundle of goods he consumes. Thus, for example, at point Z the consumer derives utility equal to U^0 by consuming the commodity bundle

---

* The reader may skip this appendix without loss of continuity.

(q_1^0, q_2^0). Note also in Fig. 4.12 that the shape of the utility surface is so drawn that utility is everywhere an *increasing* function of both goods (i.e., so that the consumer's utility always increases if he is given more of either good and not less of the other).

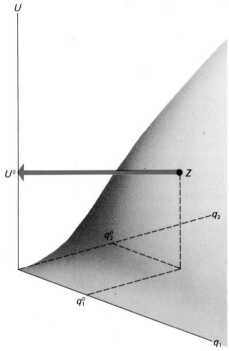

4|12

The consumer's utility function,
$U = f(q_1, q_2)$.

What is the relationship of the consumer's utility function to his preference map? Earlier we defined an indifference curve as a line linking all combinations of q_1 and q_2 that offer the consumer the same utility, so that he is indifferent between them. From this definition it follows that, if we take $\overline{U}$ to be a constant, then the equation $\overline{U} = f(q_1, q_2)$ represents an indifference curve. To locate the position of this indifference curve in the (q_1, q_2)-plane, we first solve the equation $\overline{U} = f(q_1, q_2)$ for all pairs of q_1 and q_2 that satisfy it; then we plot these points in the (q_1, q_2)-plane.

We can also, by an alternative procedure, derive the consumer's indifference curve $U = \overline{U}$ directly from his utility surface. First we find all points on the utility surface for which $U = \overline{U}$, then we project these points downward onto the (q_1, q_2)-plane to form the indifference curve corresponding to $U = \overline{U}$. We can think of this procedure intuitively as follows: first the utility surface is "sliced" in a direction *parallel* to the (q_1, q_2)-plane at a "height" corresponding to $U = \overline{U}$; then the outline of the resulting slice is projected downward onto the (q_1, q_2)-plane.

We can obtain our consumer's *indifference map* by simply repeating either procedure for different values of $\overline{U}$.

Interpreting the Utility Function

The main difficulty in using a utility function is interpreting the values assumed by U. Nineteenth-century economists assumed that the consumer had a *cardinal* measure of utility; in other words, that he could state precisely how many units of utility he got out of any commodity bundle. They also assumed that he could state, for example, that the utility he obtained by consuming commodity bundle A was x times greater than the utility he obtained from consuming some other commodity bundle B.

The modern theory of the consumer began to be formulated at the turn of the century. It is based on the assumption that the consumer's measure of utility is *ordinal,* which implies that if he is confronted with alternative commodity bundles, he can order them from least to most preferred. If a consumer's measure of utility is ordinal, the quantities of utility which consuming various commodity bundles will yield him are significant only as an index of his preferences among these bundles. Thus, for example, if our consumer's ordinal utility function were to yield values of 40 for bundle A and 10 for bundle B, we would know only that he preferred A to B, not that he liked A four times as much as B.

Since measures of ordinal utility are significant only as an index, any order-preserving (i.e., monotonic) transformation of an ordinal utility function is equivalent to that utility function. Suppose that a consumer claims to have the ordinal utility function $U = q_1 q_2$. This is a satisfactory utility function, but an economist would observe that other utility functions such as $U = 5q_1 q_2$, $U = q_1 q_2 + 10$, or $U = 2q_1^3 q_2^3 - 10$ would yield orderings identical to that yielded by $U = q_1 q_2$. Moreover, since an implied ordering is the only significant information yielded by an ordinal utility function, it makes no economic sense to ask which of these utility functions is the consumer's true one.

THE MEANING OF EQUILIBRIUM CONDITIONS

What do we mean when we say that we are solving for equilibrium conditions rather than for the values assumed by variables at the point of equilibrium? In elementary calculus we frequently seek the maximum point of a specific function, such as $y = 10 - x^2$. In economics, however, because we are searching for results that have general validity, we often work with general functional relationships, such as the utility function $U = f(q_1, q_2)$, and obtain as the solution to our problem of maximization (or minimization) not *values* assumed by functions at their maximum (or minimum) point, but rather *relationships* that must hold at the function's maximum (or minimum) point. When we are analyzing the consumer, we refer to such relationships as *equilibrium conditions,* because the consumer who has allocated his resources so that his utility is maximized presumably will have no reason to alter his consumption pattern; he will therefore be in equilibrium.

If we happen to know the specific form assumed by a consumer's utility function, then his equilibrium conditions can be solved to obtain his *demand curve* for each available good. Moreover, if we also know the resources he has budgeted for consumption during a given period and the prices of available goods, then we can also determine the composition of the bundle of goods he will consume in equilibrium.

CONSUMER EQUILIBRIUM IN THE TWO-GOOD CASE (SUBSTITUTION)

Let us now use mathematical means to solve the consumer's problem of utility maximization in a two-good world. Consider a consumer, Smith, whose utility function is given by the expression

$$U = f(q_1, q_2), \tag{4-1}$$

in which U represents utility and q_1 and q_2 are goods. To attain equilibrium, Smith must maximize the value of his utility function, subject to the budget constraint

$$y_c = p_1 q_1 + p_2 q_2, \tag{4-2}$$

in which y_c represents funds budgeted for consumption and p_1 and p_2 represent the prices of q_1 and q_2.

First we solve Smith's budget constraint for q_2 and substitute the resulting expression into his utility function. This yields the new equation

$$U = f\left(q_1, -\frac{p_1}{p_2} \cdot q_1 + \frac{y_c}{p_2}\right), \tag{4-3}$$

in which utility is a function of only one variable, q_1, since q_2 has been eliminated by substitution and p_1, p_2, and y_c are all constants.

To maximize Smith's utility subject to his budget constraint, we now take the derivative of Eq. (4–3) with respect to q_1 and set the resulting expression* equal to zero, as follows:

$$\frac{dU}{dq_1} = f_1 - \frac{p_1}{p_2} \cdot f_2 = 0. \tag{4-4}$$

Rewriting Eq. (4–4), we obtain the condition

$$f_1/f_2 = p_1/p_2, \tag{4-5}$$

which must hold whenever Smith's utility is maximized. Thus two conditions—Smith's budget constraint (4–2) and the condition we have just obtained (4–5)—must both hold at any point at which Smith allocates his fixed

---

* In this expression, f_1 represents the partial derivative of the function, $U = f(q_1, q_2)$, with respect to q_1, and f_2 represents the partial derivative of this same function with respect to q_2.

resources, y_c, between the goods q_1 and q_2 in a fashion that maximizes his satisfaction.

To interpret condition (4–5), we must ask ourselves the meaning of the term f_1/f_2. Let us take the *total differential* of the utility function, $U = f(q_1, q_2)$, to obtain the expression

$$dU = f_1\,dq_1 + f_2\,dq_2. \tag{4-6}$$

For movements along any indifference curve, $U = \overline{U}$, $dU = 0$, and f_1/f_2 is given by the expression

$$f_1/f_2 = -dq_2/dq_1, \tag{4-7}$$

in which dq_2/dq_1 equals the slope of the indifference curve $U = \overline{U}$. If we now substitute Eq. (4–7) into Eq. (4–5), we obtain the expression

$$dq_2/dq_1 = -p_1/p_2. \tag{4-8}$$

This expression tells us that Smith will maximize his satisfaction by moving to a point along his budget line at which the slope of this line, $-p_1/p_2$, just equals the slope of his indifference curve, dq_2/dq_1. In other words, Smith will attain equilibrium by moving to a point on his budget line at which that line is just tangent to one of the indifference curves in his preference map. This result, however, is just like the one we obtained by the graphic analysis presented above. Thus mathematics as well as geometry supports the conclusion that Smith's utility will be maximized—within the limits set by his budget constraint—at the point at which the conditions

$$y_c = p_1q_1 + p_2q_2 \quad \text{and} \quad dq_2/dq_1 = -p_1/p_2$$

are simultaneously satisfied.

In such mathematical analyses, the *negative* of the slope of the consumer's indifference curve, $-dq_2/dq_1$, is often defined as his *rate of commodity substitution*, RCS. When we take this approach, then

$$f_1/f_2 = \text{RCS} \tag{4-9}$$

and we can restate his equilibrium conditions in the somewhat simpler form

$$y_c = p_1q_1 + p_2q_2 \quad \text{and} \quad \text{RCS} = p_1/p_2.$$

In the two conditions of utility maximization we have just obtained, y_c, p_1, and p_2 are constants, while the value of RCS depends on q_1 and q_2. Our analysis has thus yielded two independent equations in two unknowns, q_1 and q_2. If, moreover, we knew the precise form of the functional relationship, $-dq_2/dq_1 = f_1/f_2$, we could, by solving these two equations, determine the precise quantities of q_1 and q_2 that Smith would buy in order to maximize his utility within the limits set by his budget constraint.

CONSUMER EQUILIBRIUM IN THE
THREE-GOOD CASE (LAGRANGE MULTIPLIER)

The reason we solved the consumer's problem of constrained maximization in the two-good case by the use of substitution is that this method is familiar and thus easy to follow. Substitution, however, constitutes an efficient approach only for solving simple problems. To solve more complex problems, we must use a *Lagrange multiplier.*

Consider the problem of utility maximization faced by a consumer, Brown, who has a choice among *three* different goods. Brown has a utility function

$$U = f(q_1, q_2, q_3),$$

in which q_1, q_2, and q_3 represent the three different goods. To attain equilibrium, Brown must maximize the value of this function subject to the budget constraint that

$$y_c = p_1 q_1 + p_2 q_2 + p_3 q_3.$$

To introduce a Lagrange multiplier, we first form a new function

$$U^* = f(q_1, q_2, q_3) + \lambda(y_c - p_1 q_1 - p_2 q_2 - p_3 q_3) \qquad (4\text{--}10)$$

by adding to the utility function a term, $\lambda(y_c - p_1 q_1 - p_2 q_2 - p_3 q_3)$, which equals zero for all values of q_1, q_2, and q_3 that satisfy the consumer's budget constraint. The new variable, λ, is the Lagrange multiplier.

The function U^* is a function of four variables, q_1, q_2, q_3, and λ. To obtain conditions that characterize the maximum point of this function, we take its partial derivatives with respect to each of these four variables and set the resulting expressions equal to zero, as follows:

$$
\begin{aligned}
\partial U^*/\partial q_1 &= f_1 - \lambda p_1 = 0, \\
\partial U^*/\partial q_2 &= f_2 - \lambda p_2 = 0, \\
\partial U^*/\partial q_3 &= f_3 - \lambda p_3 = 0, \\
\partial U^*/\partial \lambda &= y_c - p_1 q_1 - p_2 q_2 - p_3 q_3 = 0.
\end{aligned}
\qquad (4\text{--}11)
$$

At any (interior) point at which U^* attains a maximum, the last condition of (4–11) will hold, and U^* will be identically equal to U. Moreover, it is intuitively obvious that the conditions that characterize a maximum point of U^* also characterize a constrained-maximum point of U. Thus Eqs. (4–11) represent four conditions that must hold whenever Brown allocates his fixed resources, y_c, among the goods q_1, q_2, and q_3 in a fashion that maximizes his utility U.

We can reduce these four equations in four unknowns, q_1, q_2, q_3, and λ, to three equations in three unknowns by eliminating λ. To do this we rewrite the first three equations of (4–11) as follows:

$$f_1 = \lambda p_1, \qquad f_2 = \lambda p_2, \qquad f_3 = \lambda p_3.$$

If we now divide any two of these equations by the third, the λ's cancel out, and we obtain two conditions which—from our discussion of the two-good case—we recognize as "tangency conditions." These conditions, which might, for example, take the form

$$f_1/f_2 = p_1/p_2, \qquad f_3/f_2 = p_3/p_2,$$

must hold whenever Brown's utility function is maximized.

Thus the consumer who chooses among three available goods will maximize his utility within the limits set by his budget constraint by moving to the point at which the following three conditions are simultaneously satisfied:

$$f_1/f_2 = p_1/p_2,$$
$$f_3/f_2 = p_3/p_2,$$
$$y_c = p_1 q_1 + p_2 q_2 + p_3 q_3.$$

These equations state that at the point of maximization the following conditions must hold:

1) The slope of the consumer's indifference curve between q_1 and q_2 must equal the slope of his budget line between these two goods.
2) The slope of his indifference curve between q_2 and q_3 must equal the slope of his budget line between these two goods.
3) His budget constraint must be satisfied.

You may well ask at this point why we have excluded from the list of Brown's equilibrium conditions a third tangency condition, namely that

$$f_1/f_3 = p_1/p_3.$$

The answer is simple. Although this third tangency condition must in fact be satisfied whenever Brown attains equilibrium, we need not include it in our list of equilibrium conditions because it is implied by the other two tangency conditions. In fact, as you can verify, in the *three*-good case there are always only *two* independent tangency conditions.

Note that the set of equilibrium conditions we have just derived is obviously adequate to locate Brown's equilibrium position, since this set of conditions consists of three independent equations in the three unknowns, q_1, q_2, and q_3, whose equilibrium values we seek.

The *n*-Good Case

By using the Lagrange multiplier, we could easily solve the problem of utility maximization of the consumer who allocates his resources among n goods, where n is some positive integer. The conditions of consumer equilibrium thus obtained would include the consumer's budget constraint and $n - 1$ independent tangency conditions. Since these conditions are n in number, they would be enough to determine his equilibrium consumption of all n goods. The conditions of consumer equilibrium in the n-good case imply that the consumer will attain equilibrium at a point at which his budget constraint is satisfied and his rate of commodity substitution between any pair of goods equals the ratio of the prices of these goods.

Second-Order Conditions

A function of several variables may attain either a *maximum* or a *minimum* at the point at which its first derivatives equal zero. Therefore, whenever a function is maximized, second-order conditions, based on the second derivatives of this function, should be checked to verify that the point located is in fact a *maximum* and not a *minimum*. Unfortunately, the process of obtaining and interpreting second-order conditions for a function that contains more than one independent variable is too complex to take up here. We can note, however, that, when only two goods are available to the consumer, the second-order conditions for utility maximization (as opposed to utility minimization) require that the consumer's indifference curves between these goods be *convex* to the origin, at least at any point at which he attains equilibrium. But this, as you will recall, is precisely the point illustrated in Problem 6 at the end of Chapter 4. If more than two goods are available to the consumer, the second-order conditions for utility maximization can be interpreted as requiring that his indifference curves between each pair of these goods be convex to the origin, at least at any point at which he attains equilibrium.

PROBLEMS

1   Letting $y_c = p_1 = p_2 = 1$, find the equilibrium commodity bundle for a consumer whose utility function is:

     a) $f(q_1,q_2) = q_1 q_2$

     b) $f(q_1,q_2) = q_1 + 2q_2 + q_1 q_2$

2   For each of the two utility functions of Problem 1, derive the equation of the consumer's demand curve for q_1. Let $y_c = p_2 = 1$, and allow p_1 to vary.

3   From the demand curves you derived in Problem 2, find in each case the elasticity of demand as a function of q_1.

4   Consider an indifference map defined by*

$$U = \frac{q_1 - 1}{(q_2 - 2)^2}$$

---

* This example of an inferior good is due to H. Wold. For reference see H. Wold, *Demand Analysis;* New York: John Wiley, 1953, page 102.

in the region $q_1 > 1$, $q_2 \leqq 1.6$, and by vertical lines parallel to the q_2-axis everywhere else. Setting $p_2 = \frac{1}{3}$ and $y_c = 1$, find the quantity of q_1 demanded at prices $p_1 = \frac{2}{5}, \frac{1}{2}$, and $\frac{2}{3}$.

5   a) Show that the following two utility functions yield identical indifference maps:

$$f_1(q_1,q_2) = q_1 q_2 \quad\text{and}\quad f_2(q_1,q_2) = q_1{}^3 q_2{}^3.$$

     b) Show that the utility functions $f(q_1,q_2)$ and $U(f(q_1,q_2))$, where $U(\cdot)$ is a strictly increasing function of its argument, yield identical indifference maps.

6   Show that in each of the parts of Problem 5 the pairs of utility functions also yield identical demand curves, and hence give rise to the same market behavior.

7   Letting $y_c = p_1 = p_2 = p_3 = 1$, derive the equilibrium commodity bundle for a consumer with the following utility function:

$$f(q_1,q_2,q_3) = q_1 q_2 q_3.$$

8   For the utility function defined in Problem 7, let $y_c = p_2 = p_3 = 1$, and derive the consumer's demand function for q_1.

CHAPTER 5

*THE INVESTMENT DECISION

A consumer's saving must take the form either of an *increase* in his assets (including cash) or a *decrease* in his liabilities. How does he "allocate" his saving (or dissaving) among the different items on his balance sheet? Examining this problem inevitably raises more questions, because the consumer may always decide to make changes in the composition of his balance sheet that are independent of his current saving or dissaving. He might decide to take money out of his savings account and buy a car or some common stock with it. Or he might decide to buy a house with money obtained partly by dipping into his savings account and partly by assuming a mortgage (i.e., by incurring a liability). As these possibilities indicate, *the consumer can in each period substantially recompose his whole balance sheet.* Thus in each period he must choose not only the way he will dispose of his current saving, but also what his equilibrium balance sheet will be.

Since the consumer, in selecting this equilibrium balance sheet, must choose the composition of his assets, the composition of his liabilities, and the overall level of both, we cannot analyze simultaneously all the balance-sheet choices open to him; the problem would be too unwieldy. Therefore let us think of the consumer as making these choices one at a time, even though in practice he makes them all simultaneously.

We can analyze the way the consumer makes each of these three choices by setting up a decision model similar to the one we used in the preceding chapters. That is, a model based on the assumption that the consumer has definite preferences with respect to the outcome of each choice, and that when he makes this choice he attempts to maximize his satisfaction within the limits of his budget constraint. Our discussion here, however, will center not on the mechanics of locating his equilibrium position, but on the factors that determine his preferences, especially those that determine his preferences as to different assets.

---

* The reader may skip this chapter without loss of continuity.

ASSET SELECTION

When Ernest Smith selects his asset portfolio, he has to choose among a wide range of dissimilar assets. How does he come to a decision? Let's sketch the principal characteristics of the different assets that Smith might choose to hold. Then let's look at the principal factors that shape his asset preferences and that thus determine (within the limits set by his budget constraint) the composition of his equilibrium asset portfolio.

We must make a distinction between *physical* and *financial* assets, since their characteristics are quite different. Thus we shall deal first with physical and then with financial assets.

The Consumer's Choice of Physical Assets

Smith buys a physical asset, such as a house, a car, or a boat, so that he can enjoy the *services* (housing, transportation, or entertainment) that it provides. Therefore the aspects of a physical asset that most interest him are the type of service it provides, the quality of that service (e.g., a car, depending on its price, can be an elegant mode of transportation or just a way to get down the road), and in some instances the prestige that consumption of this asset will give him. Naturally the first of these three characteristics influences Smith most when he is deciding what kind of asset to purchase, while the last two influence his decision about how expensive an asset to purchase.

Because physical assets are durable goods, and because people's needs and tastes change over time, consumers frequently resell their physical assets. Therefore Smith's preferences with respect to physical assets are influenced not only by the services they offer him, but also by the opportunities for capital loss or gain to which their ownership would expose him, and by their liquidity.

An asset is said to be liquid if it can be sold rapidly without substantial loss in value.

Because of a number of factors, including the lack of organized markets in which they can be resold, consumer durables (with the possible exception of cars) are relatively illiquid assets whose resale value is typically small if not negligible in relation to their original purchase price. Therefore the ownership of consumer durables exposes the person who does not intend to keep these assets over their entire useful life to the possibility—even the probability—of substantial capital losses.

Houses, like consumer durables, are also relatively illiquid assets. Their resale value, however—because it reflects not only depreciation, but other factors such as changes in living patterns, population shifts, changes in the general price level, and changes in the cost of home construction—may go up as well as down. Therefore there is a real possibility, especially during periods of rising prices, that owning a home may give a person a chance to achieve substantial capital gains. The hope of such gains undoubtedly strengthens the consumer's preferences for home ownership.

Most of the services that consumers obtain through the ownership of durable goods can also be purchased "by the piece" from commercial sources. Thus, for example, a housewife faced with the weekly mound of laundry can obtain the washing services she requires not only by buying a washing machine, but also by relying on a commercial launderette or by sending her clothes to a commercial laundry. Similarly a person can obtain housing services not only by buying a house, but also by renting an apartment or a house. Because we can obtain most durable-goods services from commercial sources, our preferences for such goods are influenced not only by our needs for these services, but also by the convenience or inconvenience of using commercial facilities and by the cost of commercial services versus that of owning durable goods.

Financial Assets

The most important financial assets a person may hold are cash, money in checking accounts and in savings accounts, life insurance with a cash value,* corporate and government bonds, and corporate stocks. The investor who must decide among such dissimilar assets is chiefly interested in (a) their liquidity and (b) the return they yield.

As we noted above, an asset's liquidity depends on the ease and speed with which it can be converted into cash without substantial loss in value. Most financial assets are liquid in the sense that there are well-organized markets in which they can be traded for cash. However, *variable-price assets,* such as stocks and bonds, are somewhat illiquid, since their value fluctuates widely from period to period, and hence the timing of their sale affects the price they command. In contrast to variable-price assets, *fixed-price assets* (such as cash, checking account deposits, savings account deposits, and government savings bonds) are to all intents and purposes perfectly liquid. Technically a saver can be required to wait 30 days to withdraw funds from a savings account, but in practice he is always permitted to do so on demand.

The investor's overall return on any financial asset consists of two parts:

1) the current income payments (i.e., the dividends and interest) that the asset yields,
2) the capital gain or loss that he incurs by holding the asset.

---

* The premium paid by the consumer on a straight life insurance policy contains not only a payment for protection but also a savings element. Therefore, as such a policy matures (i.e., ages), savings accumulate. The amount of these savings is called the cash value of the policy, since it represents the amount of cash that would be refunded to the consumer if he discontinued his policy. Some low-premium life insurance, called *term insurance,* has no savings element and no cash value.

The character and size of the overall return of different assets vary widely. If we measure value in terms of money price, then fixed-price assets offer the investor no opportunity for capital gain. Most fixed-price assets (except cash) do, however, yield current income in the form of interest. Variable-price assets may offer the investor current income payments, or they may not (e.g., no dividends are paid on the common stock of many companies). But such assets all give him a chance at capital gain. And expose him to the danger of capital loss!

So far we've talked about the value of an asset just in terms of its money value. However, the sophisticated investor is interested not simply in the money value of his assets, but in the purchasing power represented by their money value, i.e., in their *real value*. If we measure in real as opposed to money terms, then fixed-price assets (like variable-price assets) also offer us the opportunity for capital gain and expose us to the danger of capital loss. From this point of view there is *no* asset whose value is not subject to unpredictable changes over time and therefore *no* asset that offers a *certain* return.* For the investor who fails (as many people do) to distinguish between real and money value, fixed-price assets "appear" to offer a certain return.

What Determines the Consumer's Asset Preferences?

A consumer's preferences as to the kind of financial assets he holds depend on his motives for holding them. When our friend Ernest Smith "invests" funds that he holds to satisfy short-term savings goals or to provide a reserve against unforeseen contingencies, he is primarily interested in liquidity. Therefore Smith chooses to hold such funds in the form of liquid assets: cash, checking account and savings account.

But when Smith is investing funds to satisfy long-term goals, such as accumulating wealth, financing retirement, or building up an estate, he's more interested in *return*. Now recall that overall return has two dimensions: current income payments and possibilities for capital gain (or loss). High current return will probably strike Smith as important for meeting some long-term goals, while he will feel that the opportunity for capital gain is important for meeting others. Different consumers, depending on the precise nature of their long-term investment goals, have different preferences with respect to assets held primarily for return. For example, Smith at

---

* If it chose to, the government could create an asset that offered a certain "real return." To do so it would issue a special bond that it would promise to redeem in the future for precisely the amount of cash necessary to provide the bondholder with the purchasing power he gave up when he originally bought the bond. The redemption value of such "purchasing-power bonds" would rise during a period of rising prices and fall during a period of falling prices, and the bond itself would constitute a perfect hedge against "real capital losses" due to a rising price level (and against "real capital gains" due to a falling price level).

28 is interested primarily in acquiring wealth, so he shops around for assets that offer opportunities for capital gain. But Jones, who is 56 and beginning to think about retirement, prefers assets that offer high current income and protection from capital loss.

In 1962 the Federal Reserve Board did a survey on the financial characteristics of consumers. They asked many people of varying ages, incomes, and wealth categories to list their principal investment objectives and their principal assets. It turned out that, oddly enough, people with investment objectives that were quite similar frequently held investment portfolios that were quite dissimilar.

Why should there be this lack of correlation? As we pointed out above, the real returns of any financial asset are uncertain. Therefore when we choose among alternative financial assets we are in effect choosing among alternative uncertain outcomes. So our preferences as to assets are really determined by our attitude toward uncertainty, that is, by our *risk preferences*. Although our risk preferences are obviously strongly influenced by our motives for holding assets (i.e., by our investment objectives), they also depend on personal psychology. And personal psychology, heaven knows, varies enormously from one person to another.

The Consumer's Risk Preferences

Bert Brown and Ernest Smith are both saving money to buy houses. Brown stashes away $20 every Saturday night in an old coffee can nailed to his closet wall, because he "doesn't trust banks." Smith sinks all his savings in the stock of a brand-new firm, the Blue Sky Uranium Hunters, Inc. Brown and Smith have different risk preferences.

An investor's expectations concerning the return he will earn by holding an asset may be *single-valued* or *multi-valued*. His expectations will be single-valued if he believes that the asset offers a certain, or sure-fire, return (Brown's coffee can will contain x dollars at the end of y years). His expectations will be multi-valued if he believes that the asset will yield one of a range of possible returns. (The Blue Sky Uranium Hunters may strike uranium, or they may find nothing, or they may just stumble across oil or gold while they are looking.) The investor whose expectations are multi-valued usually has some intuition or opinion as to the likelihood of his actually obtaining each rate of return that he considers possible. His expectations can be represented by

1) a range of possible returns, and
2) a set of associated probabilities.

In other words, his expectations can be represented by a *probability distribution* of possible returns or outcomes.*

Here is an example of a probability distribution: Smith took the plunge in Blue Sky this year; his expectations that his investment will yield a positive but uncertain return next year might take the form shown in Table 5.1. The figures indicate that Smith believes that there is one chance in eight that his investment will yield 1%, two chances in eight that it will yield 4%, three chances in eight that it will yield 6%, and two chances in eight that it will yield 20%. Taking a more intuitive approach, we could interpret these figures as implying that Smith considers it quite likely that the return on his investment will equal or exceed 6%, but rather unlikely that it will be less than 4%.

TABLE 5|1

Expectations as to the Rate of Return of an Uncertain Investment

Rates of return considered possible, %	Probability that each such rate will occur
1	1/8
4	2/8
6	3/8
20	2/8

Since a person's expectations about the return an asset will yield take the form of a probability distribution, to say that a person has risk preferences means that he has definite preferences among (i.e., that he can rank) alternative probability distributions. Moreover, to say that a person's asset preferences depend on his risk preferences means that

he ranks different assets on the basis of the way he ranks the probability distributions of the returns he associates with these assets.

The Character of the Consumer's Asset Preferences

What criteria does Mr. Typical Investor use to rank probability distributions? If we knew, we could make definite statements about the nature of a person's preferences among alternative uncertain investments. But alas, this question hasn't a simple answer, because a probability distribution has many characteristics, any one (or maybe several) of which might interest the investor. For example, suppose that a really keen investor with a head for

---

* The probability distribution associated with the outcome of any uncertain event consists of a list of all possible outcomes and a set of numbers (i.e., probabilities), one of which is associated with each such outcome. If the list of possible outcomes is complete, then one of the listed outcomes must occur. The probability that a certain event will occur is taken to be 1 and the sum of the probabilities associated with all possible outcomes equals 1.

mathematics is examining the probability distribution associated with a certain investment opportunity. He might be interested in the range of the distribution, in the concentration of the distribution, in the symmetry of the distribution, or in any one of a long list of the distribution's other attributes.

Bearing in mind the various factors that influence a person's asset preferences, what can we conclude about the probable shape of his indifference curves between any two assets? (1) Will these curves slope downward? (2) If so, will they be convex or concave? To answer question (1), note that, by repeating with a few modifications the argument we used to show that a person's indifference curves between any two goods will slope downward, we can show that

his indifference curves between any two assets will also slope downward.

We cannot, however, find any argument to show that the consumer's indifference curves between two assets will in general be convex rather than concave.

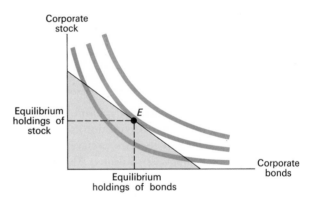

5|1

Only a consumer whose indifference curves between stocks and bonds are *convex* will hold both these assets in his equilibrium portfolio.

We can only observe that, if a consumer's equilibrium portfolio contains two uncertain assets, then his indifference curves between these particular assets must (like those shown in Fig. 5.1) be convex, at least in the neighborhood of his equilibrium point.*

RISK AND DIVERSIFICATION

Whenever an investor holds a variety of uncertain assets in his portfolio, we say, in the jargon of investors, that he is following a policy of *diversification.* Diversification is popular with investors, and those who follow this policy say that they do so in order to reduce the risks associated with their asset portfolios. In what sense does diversification reduce risk?

---

* To prove this result, refer back to Problem 6 at the end of Chapter 4. Although this problem concerns the consumer's selection of an equilibrium commodity bundle, it can as well be applied to his selection of an equilibrium asset portfolio. The problem shows that a consumer who has concave preference curves between two goods will in equilibrium always choose to purchase just one, not both, of these goods.

TABLE 5|2

Effect of Diversification on Range and Distribution of Possible Returns

Distribution of possible returns on asset I		Distribution of possible returns on asset II		Distribution of possible returns on a portfolio in which funds are divided equally between assets I and II	
Rate of return, %	Probability that it will occur	Rate of return, %	Probability that it will occur	Rate of return, %	Probability that it will occur
−10	1/3	−10	1/3	−10	1/9
10	1/3	10	1/3	0	2/9
30	1/3	30	1/3	10	3/9
				20	2/9
				30	1/9

Let's consider the case of John Q. Jones, who can invest in either one or both of two uncertain assets whose outcomes are independent and whose possible returns are represented by the probability distributions in Table 5.2. Obviously if Jones puts all his money in either of these assets, the distribution of the return on his total portfolio will be identical to the distribution of the return on this single asset.

Suppose, however, that instead of putting all his funds in one asset, Jones puts half into each. What will the distribution of the return on the resulting diversified portfolio be? Look at the probability tree shown in Fig. 5.2. The first stage of this tree represents Jones's return on the money he has invested in asset I, while the second stage is his return on the money he has invested in asset II. Each of the nine "paths" by which Jones might attain the second

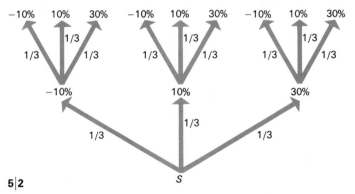

5|2

This probability tree illustrates the nine possible and equally probable outcomes of (or returns on) a diversified portfolio in which funds are divided equally between assets I and II, the possible yields of which are recorded in Table 5.2. The fractions along each line indicate the probability that the investor will move upward along this "path."

stage corresponds to one possible outcome of his investment in a diversified portfolio. Moreover, a *single* rate of return on his overall portfolio is associated with each outcome. For example, if Jones were to earn -10% on asset I and -10% on asset II, his portfolio as a whole would yield an average rate of return of -10%. But Jones could be lucky. Suppose he were to earn 30% on asset I and 10% on asset II. His portfolio as a whole would then yield an average rate of return of 20%. Thus the distribution of the returns that Jones might earn on his diversified portfolio must be that in the last two columns of Table 5.2.

When we compare the distributions of returns for a diversified versus an undiversified portfolio, we see that diversification reduces the chance that Jones will have to take an overall 10% loss from $\frac{1}{3}$ to $\frac{1}{9}$. But at the same time diversification reduces the chance that he will experience an overall gain of 30% from $\frac{1}{3}$ to $\frac{1}{9}$. Thus the effect of diversification is to concentrate the distribution of possible returns and thereby to decrease the probability that Jones will wind up with either an extreme loss or an extreme gain.

Investors always say that the reason they follow a policy of diversification is that they want to reduce risk. Therefore they must view a decrease in the probability of extreme loss—even if it is purchased at the expense of an equivalent decrease in the probability of extreme gain—as being a desirable reduction in risk.

SELECTION OF LIABILITIES

Naturally nobody wants to hold liabilities, since they are a source, not of utility, but of disutility. Nevertheless people do incur debts, especially when they go about financing assets whose possessions—like that of a house—will yield them considerable utility. There are many different forms of liabilities. What characteristics of alternative liabilities influence the consumer's choice of the kind of debts he will incur?

Presumably anyone's major consideration in the selection of liabilities is cost: We would expect a person to borrow from the lowest-cost source to which he has access. Another characteristic of any loan is the appropriateness of the loan's duration in relation to the kind of expense the person is financing and how quickly he will be able to repay this debt. Thus, for example, a short-term installment loan is appropriate when you are buying a car, while a longer-term mortgage is appropriate when you are buying a house.

With respect to debt shopping, note that just *how* cheaply a person is able to borrow money depends not only on the purpose of his loan (including the appropriateness of its duration), but also on his income, on the structure and size of his assets and other liabilities, and on his past record of debt and repayment. Thus someone like Ernest S. (for Solvent) Smith, who has a debtfree home or debtfree financial assets that he can use as collateral, can borrow from a bank on relatively favorable terms. But then along comes Jones, who has no unpledged collateral and who from other points of view appears to be a poor credit risk (he's a flashy dresser and bets on horses); Jones may be able to borrow (if indeed he can borrow at all) only from a finance company and then only on very unfavorable terms.

Interestingly enough, some consumers who as goods-shoppers are extremely conscious of the prices of alternative brands may as credit-shoppers display little knowledge of or interest in the relative costs of funds borrowed from alternative loan sources. Why this asymmetry in attitude? Perhaps when a person is going into debt in order to buy an asset, the cost of that debt appears to be a relatively insignificant and thus unimportant part of the asset's total cost. In fact, if he's buying a durable good such as a washing machine or a car *on time* (i.e., if he's financing his purchase by means of a short-term installment loan), he may be ignorant of both the rate of interest and the total dollar cost associated with this loan. Such ignorance is what the retailer is counting on when he advertises his credit terms as "no money down and just *x* dollars a month to pay."

Even if the consumer does try to compare the relative costs of funds borrowed from different lenders, he may be misled, because few lenders take the obviously reasonable approach of quoting the interest rates they charge for a particular kind of loan in terms of the *average unpaid balance* of that loan. Let's look at two consumers, Brown and Robinson; each borrows $120, supposedly at 10% per year. At the end of one year Brown, according to the terms of his loan, must pay back $132. That is, $120 of principal and $12 of interest. But Robinson, under the terms of *his* loan, has to pay back $11 per month each month for twelve months. That is, $10 of principal and $1 of interest. Which one is actually paying 10% on his loan? Obviously, in terms of an interest rate calculated on the average unpaid balance of the loan, Brown is paying 10%, since the average unpaid balance of his loan over the year is $120. But the average unpaid balance of Robinson's loan over the year is (as you should verify) not far above $60. Thus Robinson is paying an interest rate close to 20% per year! Note that, although both consumers pay interest charges of $12, Brown has clearly done better than Robinson, in the sense that, as the months pass, he continues to have the use of the whole $120 he has borrowed, while Robinson has the use of only a declining portion of his original loan.

OVERALL LEVEL OF A CONSUMER'S ASSETS AND LIABILITIES

So far in our discussion of the consumer's balance-sheet choices, we have dealt with his choices among alternative assets and alternative liabilities. However, when the consumer is selecting his end-of-period balance sheet, he has to make a third kind of choice as well. Should he, for example, buy a certain asset he wants, even if buying it will mean that he has to go into

debt? Similarly, should he pay off certain debts, even if to do so he must
liquidate some of his assets?

Smith has made up his mind to buy a house. Now he has to decide how
expensive a house. He has set aside for a down payment a certain portion of
the assets he currently holds. The relationship between the price of the
house he buys and the size of the mortgage he has to assume in order to
finance it will be fixed, and we can easily analyze his choice in terms of his
preferences and an appropriate budget constraint.

Let us first draw a graph to represent Smith's preferences with respect to
the house he buys and the mortgage he incurs (Fig. 5.3). Since he will derive
satisfaction (i.e., utility) from the house but disutility from a mortgage, he
is indifferent as to the choice between any two mortgage–house bundles only
if the bundle containing the larger mortgage also contains a more expensive
(and presumably more satisfying) house. Therefore indifference curves in
his mortgage–house preference map must slope upward, as in Fig. 5.3.

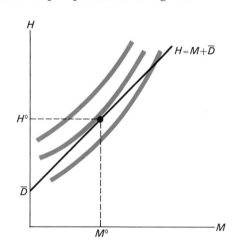

5│3

The consumer, given the limited quantity of
funds $\overline{D}$ that he has set aside for a down payment,
will maximize his satisfaction by buying a house
whose cost equals H^0 and by incurring a
mortgage equal to M^0.

When Smith is actually buying his house, he stands by his decision on the
size of the down payment he will make; so the mortgage he incurs will equal
the price of the house minus the fixed sum he has set aside for a down payment. We can thus represent his budget constraint by the expression

$$M = H - \overline{D},$$

in which M represents the amount of his mortgage, H is the price of the
house, and $\overline{D}$ is his fixed down payment.

When we plot this constraint, we get a budget line like that in Fig. 5.3.
Note that, from Smith's point of view, this line does not extend indefinitely
to the right, because his ability to move to the right along it is limited by his

ability to borrow, which in turn depends on his income, his general financial standing, and the kind of house he tries to finance.

Where along his budget line will Smith attain equilibrium? By repeating arguments used in preceding chapters, we can show that he will maximize his satisfaction (and thus attain equilibrium) by moving to the point on his budget line where that line is just tangent to one of the curves in his preference map. Thus Smith, whose preference map and budget constraint are shown in Fig. 5.3, will attain equilibrium by buying a house whose cost equals H^0 and by incurring a mortgage equal to M^0.

TABLE 5|3

Percentage Distribution of Total Assets Held by Consumers in Different Wealth Classes, December 31, 1962*

Wealth class	Total wealth	Own home	Auto-mobile	Portfolio of liquid and investment assets			Own business and misc. assets
				All	Liquid assets	Investment assets	
$1–999	100	10	48	37	33	4	4
$1,000–4,999	100	48	16	32	26	6	4
$5,000–9,999	100	59	8	23	17	6	10
$10,000–24,999	100	55	5	29	16	13	10
$25,000–49,999	100	37	3	39	18	21	21
$50,000–99,999	100	21	2	51	16	35	26
$100,000–199,999	100	17	2	62	14	48	18
$200,000–499,999	100	9	1	63	7	56	27
$500,000 and over	100	4	†	53	4	49	41

* Source: Dorothy S. Projector and Gertrude S. Weiss, *Survey of Financial Characteristics of Consumers,* Board of Governors of the Federal Reserve System, 1966.
† Less than ½ of 1%.

CONSUMER CHARACTERISTICS AND BALANCE-SHEET STRUCTURE

Table 5.3 presents data on the composition of wealth and assets of consumers who have varying amounts of wealth. Note that there are striking differences in the kinds of assets held by consumers in different wealth classes. Other cross sections of consumers would show equally striking differences in the composition of the assets held by different groups. For example, if you were to look at cross-sectional data on the composition of the asset portfolios of self-employed workers versus other workers and of females versus males, you would find that at every wealth level self-employed workers hold a lower proportion of their total wealth in liquid assets than other workers do, while women hold more of their wealth in common stock than men do!

Therefore, to wind up our discussion of the consumer's balance-sheet choices, let us ask the following question: Assuming that the typical consumer's indifference curves between any two assets are convex, can we—by combining the analytic model of consumer choice that we have developed with our knowledge of the characteristics and savings motives of consumers in different age, wealth, and income groups—make valid predictions as to the composition of the assets that different groups of consumers will hold?

Effect of Amount of Wealth on Diversification

Some of the differences in the composition of the assets held by different classes of people reflect not systematic differences in their preferences, but practical factors that limit the investment opportunities open to some classes of investors.

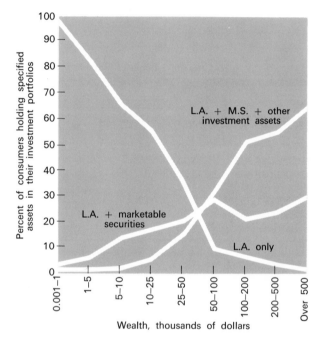

5|4

As wealth increases, the proportion of people who hold only liquid assets declines sharply, while the percentage of people who hold diversified asset portfolios rises sharply. (Source: D. S. Projector and G. S. Weiss, *op. cit.,* page 138)

Let's consider one important portfolio characteristic: *diversification*. Naturally the desire to reduce risk through diversification is as strong among people of modest wealth as among rich ones. A number of practical factors tend, however, to limit the opportunities for diversification that are open to low-wealth consumers: Many financial assets are available only in large indivisible units*; the cost of transactions on small purchases and sales of

---

* For example, a share of IBM—even when the stock market is depressed—generally runs well over $300, and any corporate bond is likely to cost the investor upwards of $1,000.

financial assets is high; and—very important—only a person with a good bit of money is likely to find it worth while to acquire the knowledge of markets and financial conditions that is necessary if one is to manage a diversified portfolio successfully.

Because these practical factors keep small investors from diversifying, we would expect diversification to rise markedly with amount of wealth. As we can see from the data plotted in Fig. 5.4, this in fact happens. Specifically, as wealth increases, the proportion of people who hold investment portfolios that contain only liquid assets (such as bank deposits and government savings bonds) decreases, while the percentage of people who hold a diversified asset portfolio (i.e., one that contains not only liquid assets but also marketable securities and other investment assets) rises sharply.

Effect of Amount of Wealth on Holdings of Liquid Assets

Our observations so far indicate that the less wealth a person has, the more likely it will be that he will hold only liquid assets. But what about the consumer who holds both liquid and nonliquid assets? Is the level of his wealth likely to influence in a systematic way the proportion of his total wealth that he holds in liquid assets?

As we said in Chapter 2, Mr. John Q. Consumer holds assets in order to protect himself against unforeseen contingencies and to provide for predictable future wants. Presumably the need he feels to provide for unpredictable contingencies and to provide for important future wants—such as financing his child's education, buying a house, or providing for retirement— is likely to be a pressing one. On the other hand, his drive toward future goals such as acquiring financial independence or building up an estate is likely to be less pressing.

Mr. John Q. Consumer wants to hold the wealth that is earmarked to meet pressing future needs in as certain an asset as possible, but he'll perhaps be willing to hold the wealth earmarked to meet less pressing future needs in less certain (i.e., riskier) assets. Given his expectations concerning the returns that different classes of assets are likely to yield over time, he'll probably view liquid assets as offering a more certain return than other investment assets (i.e., variable-price assets). Thus, to the extent that he feels a pressing need to provide for certain predictable and unpredictable future wants, his preferences for liquid versus other investment assets will be strengthened.

Considering the kinds of predictable and unpredictable future needs that probably appear most pressing to the consumer, it seems unlikely that the size of these needs will grow proportionately with his wealth. Therefore we would expect that the greater the consumer's wealth, the weaker his preferences for liquid versus other investment assets would be. More specifically, we would expect that if our friend Bert Brown were given the asset

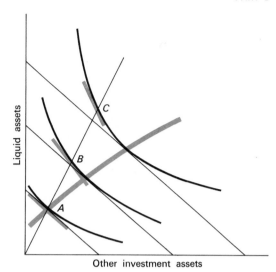

5|5

The consumer whose preference map is pictured here responds to increases in his wealth by holding a decreasing proportion of his total assets in the form of liquid assets.

Liquid assets

Other investment assets

bundle *A* in Fig. 5.5, he'd be less willing to trade liquid assets for other investment assets than he would be if he were given the asset bundle *B*, which combines liquid and other assets in the same proportion, but which corresponds to a higher level of wealth. If this expectation holds true, however, then the slope of Brown's indifference curve between liquid and other investment assets will be steeper at point *B* than at *A* and at point *C* than at *B*.

Let's suppose that our expectation concerning Brown's indifference curves between liquid and other investment assets holds true. What effect will this have on the way he allocates his wealth between liquid and other investment assets? From Fig. 5.5 it is obvious that (other things being equal) this tendency will lead him to respond to increases in his wealth by holding a decreasing proportion of it in the form of liquid assets.

This observation suggests in turn that, if we were to look at the kinds of assets held by consumers at different wealth levels, we would find that rich people tend to hold a lower proportion of their total wealth in liquid assets than people of modest means do. Before we check this expectation against experience, we should pause to note that our argument concerning the probable shape of the consumer's asset preferences does not rely on the practical factor that rich people have more opportunities for diversification than less-affluent people do. However, this factor does strengthen our grounds for expecting that consumers on the average will respond to an increase in their wealth by holding a decreasing proportion of their wealth in liquid assets. Is this expectation in fact borne out by experience? The data presented in Table 5.3 as well as the data depicted in Fig. 5.6 show that it is.

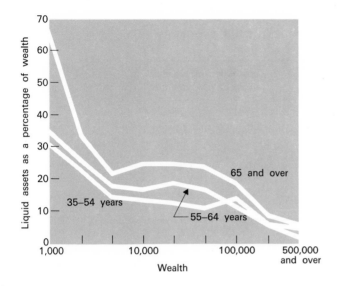

5|6
As their wealth increases, people tend to hold a lower proportion of their total wealth in liquid assets; the proportion increases, however, as their age increases. (Source: D. S. Projector and G. S. Weiss, *op. cit.,* page 32)

The data charted in Fig. 5.6 also show another feature: at each level of wealth, older people tend to hold a larger proportion of their total wealth in the form of liquid assets than younger people do. Why? Well, generally speaking, a person's need to hold funds as a reserve against unpredictable contingencies, and in particular against sickness and loss of work, increases with his age. And of course there are other reasons: people tend to get more conservative as they get older; they need current income when they retire; also they need estate liquidity. All these factors strengthen the preferences of older investors for liquid assets versus other investment assets. Therefore as a person gets older, his indifference curves between liquid assets and other investment assets* will presumably become flatter. And if this happens, then—as you can verify by means of the argument presented in the education example in Chapter 3—as time goes by he attains equilibrium by holding a growing proportion of his total wealth in liquid assets.

PROBLEMS

1   Consider a savings account which returns 5% interest. Suppose that the income tax rate on interest is 20%. Then what is the *real* rate of return if:

    a) prices remain constant,

    b) prices are falling by 10% per year,

    c) prices are rising by 3% per year?

---

* Assuming that liquid assets are plotted on the vertical axis.

2   Show that the indifference curves between any two assets will slope downward.

3   Consider the following two independent investments.

Distribution of possible returns on investment A		Distribution of possible returns on investment B	
Rate of return, %	Probability that it will occur	Rate of return, %	Probability that it will occur
−5	1/6	−10	1/6
10	1/3	15	1/2
15	1/3	20	1/3
30	1/6		

Set up a probability tree for these investments. Calculate the distribution of possible returns, first with funds divided equally between the two investments, and second with twice as much invested in B as in A.

4   A man needs to borrow \$240, and can do this by either of two methods. Method A is to pay back nothing for one year and then pay back \$264. Method B is to pay back \$11 at the end of each month for a total of 24 months. Basing your figures on average unpaid balance, determine which method charges the lower true interest. Discuss some of the factors, besides true interest, which should influence the man's decision as to which method to use.

5   "Businesses offering revolving credit accounts have argued that calling the monthly charge of 1½% an 18% yearly interest rate is misleading. They reason that customers do not generally pay this much because few of their debts remain unpaid for an entire year." [*New York Times*, August 9, 1967; © 1967 by The New York Times Company. Reprinted by permission.] Comment.

6   Estimate your own indifference maps between the following investments. Discuss the effect that obtaining more information about these investments would have on your preferences. Where could you get such information?

   a) Shares of stock issued by A.T. & T. and municipal bonds issued by New York City.

   b) Common stock in IBM and in the Nuclear Corporation of America.

7   Define a risk averter and a risk taker. Use your definition to show whether or not the following statements are true:

   a) The indifference curves of a risk averter between any two assets whose return *he* considers independent should be convex to the origin.

   b) The indifference curves of a risk taker between any two assets whose return *he* considers independent should be concave to the origin.

8   Assuming that consumer preferences for assets are convex to the origin, how would you expect a consumer's preferences for liquid versus other investment assets to be related to the following factors:

a) the size of his debt,

b) the expected level of his income from wages,

c) the variability of his income from wages?

9   Discuss the difficulties of representing preferences among durable goods by means of indifference maps in terms of the following two features: indivisibility (this might be solved by allowing consumers to share or rent the goods), and the varying lifetimes of durable goods (this might be solved by including lifetime in your definitions of the goods themselves). Does it really matter whether or not the indifference curves of durable goods are "accurate," so far as the predictions we seek (such as downward-sloping demand) are concerned?

10   The line separating individuals from firms is not always clear. Consider, for example, the student whose home is in Chicago, but who goes to school in California. Because of the difference in used-car prices between the two parts of the country, he finds it profitable to buy a car every time he is at home on vacation and resell it when he reaches the coast. Thus his preferences for cars are not motivated solely by their usefulness to him. Estimate what this student's indifference map between cars and all other goods would look like. Specify the relevant budget constraint. Compare your result with the indifference maps and budget constraints of students who do not have this option.

11   Ignoring the difficulties discussed in Problem 9, compare what you think would be the indifference maps of large families versus small ones, old people versus young ones, and educated people versus uneducated ones for the following pairs of durable goods:

a) Television sets and rocking chairs

b) Washing machines and automobiles

c) Desks and refrigerators

Specify also the relevant budget constraints.

12   In Fig. 5.3 the indifference curves have been drawn as convex and they slope upward. What does this imply about the consumer's attitude toward a mortgage? How would he choose his house and mortgage if these indifference curves were concave and sloped upward?

*13   Draw indifference curves between a revolving-credit loan (one which can be repeatedly renewed, and never needs to be paid off completely) and an installment loan. Specify the budget constraint and describe the equilibrium position. How do the entries on the asset side of the consumer's balance sheet affect the shape of his indifference curves between such loans?

* An asterisk indicates a problem which is unusually difficult, and which may be omitted.

Part 2
THE FIRM

CHAPTER 6

THE FIRM

Each year U.S. business firms buy billions of dollars worth of inputs, produce billions of dollars worth of output, make billions of dollars worth of investments, and earn billions of dollars worth of profits. How do these companies make the complex and varied economic choices that must lie behind all this activity? As we suggested in Chapter 1, this question is a crucial one, not only for understanding how firms operate, but also for explaining how the economy as a whole functions. Therefore in the chapters that follow we shall attempt to give it a careful answer.

In general terms, we can define a firm as follows:

A business firm is an economic unit that combines inputs which it buys to produce an output which it tries to sell at a profit.

This general view of the firm, although it is a valid one, tends to obscure the tremendous contrasts that exist among individual firms with respect to their form of organization, the complexity of their production processes, the structure of the markets in which they sell, the size and geographic distribution of their activities, and so forth.

To emphasize this point, let us contrast the General Motors Corporation and two boys selling lemonade on a street corner. The lemonade stand and G.M. are both business enterprises engaged in the production of goods and services. Both, moreover, engage in the same basic activities; i.e., both procure inputs, produce an output, and try to sell that output at a profit. Either enterprise may or may not be successful in its attempt to earn a profit.

The similarity, however, ends here. The life of the lemonade stand is likely to be ephemeral; the demise of General Motors is clearly not in sight. The lemonade stand does business on a single street corner, while the operations of G.M. are spread over much of the world. General Motors produces a variety of products, often by using very complex methods of production, while the lemonade stand carries out only one simple production process. The lemonade stand employs only two part-time workers, and may be lucky if it has total annual sales of $15 and a profit of $5. General Motors, on the other hand, employs thousands of workers, sells tens of billions of dollars worth of goods every year, and annually earns several billion dollars in profits!

CHARACTERISTICS OF THE FIRM

As we have suggested in our contrast between General Motors and the lemonade stand, the term "the firm" refers to an extremely heterogeneous group of decision units. Therefore, before we try to develop a theory of the firm, let us pause to look at some of the principal characteristics of U.S. firms.

Forms of Business Organization

One obvious way in which business firms differ is in their form of organization. Some are organized as sole proprietorships, others as partnerships, and still others as corporations. As the data in Table 6.1 show, sole proprietorships outnumber both corporations and partnerships, but corporations take in more receipts from sales and earn more profits than either proprietorships or partnerships.

TABLE 6|1

Numbers, Total Receipts, and Profits of U.S. Sole
Proprietorships, Partnerships, and Corporations*

	Number of firms, thousands	Total receipts, billions of dollars	Net profits, billions of dollars
Sole proprietorships	9,183	178.4	23.9
Partnerships	932	72.3	8.5
Corporations	1,267	893.5	49.6

*Source: U.S. Treasury Department, Internal Revenue Service, *Statistics of Income 1962, U.S. Business Tax Returns*, 1965.

Sole proprietorships: The sole proprietorship is the simplest form of business organization. Establishing a sole proprietorship requires no legal documents; in effect a proprietorship exists from the moment a person decides to go into business for himself. All the profits earned by a sole proprietorship, whether they are positive or negative, accrue to the owner. So too unfortunately do all of the debts incurred by the firm! This latter disadvantageous property of a sole proprietorship is referred to as *unlimited liability*.

In what line of business do we find sole proprietorships? Table 6.2 shows that they are concentrated in fields such as agriculture, retail trade, and services, where small operations are likely to be both feasible and profitable. There are relatively few sole proprietorships in manufacturing, but those that are earn a disproportionately large share of the total net profits earned by all sole proprietorships.

TABLE 6|2

Sole Proprietorships: Number and Net Profit, by Industry, 1962*

Industry	Number, thousands	Net profits, millions of dollars
Agriculture, forestry, and fisheries	3,444	3,696
Manufacturing	181	2,108
Wholesale and retail trade	1,887	5,837
Finance, insurance, and real estate	473	1,638
Services	2,133	9,289
All other	1,065	1,327
Total	9,183	23,895

*Scurce: U.S. Treasury Department, Internal Revenue Service, *Statistics of Income 1962, U.S. Business Tax Returns*, 1965.

Partnerships: Any group of people can establish a partnership simply by setting up an agreement that specifies the contribution that each will make to the partnership and the formula by which the partnership's profits will be shared. Typically such agreements are spelled out in a formal legal document.

In any given partnership, the contributions made by the individual partners and the share of profits they receive may vary. Suppose, for example, that two young engineers hit on an idea for making a new and better electric typewriter. They form a partnership with three other people to manufacture and sell it. Let's say that the engineers contribute to the partnership only their ideas and their services. Two of the other partners contribute only capital. The contribution of the final partner is to manage the newly formed firm. How are the partnership's profits to be divided among these five people? That depends on how they agreed in the beginning to view the relative importance of each person's contributions to the partnership.

In any case, all the partnership's profits and losses accrue wholly and solely to the partners. And any partner, regardless of how recently he has joined a partnership or how small his role in it, is *liable without limit* for the debts of the partnership.

A partnership is usually an awkward way to organize and run a large business, especially over long periods of time. One reason is that a large business will probably require substantial amounts of capital, and hence is likely to involve a number of partners. Also, whenever one partner dies or leaves the partnership, his share must be bought out by the other partners or by some new partner; and a new partnership agreement will have to be drawn up.

TABLE 6|3

Partnerships: Number and Net Profit, by Industry, 1962*

Industry	Number, thousands	Net profits, millions of dollars
Agriculture, forestry, and fisheries	133.7	655
Manufacturing	43.1	595
Wholesale and retail trade	267.5	2,199
Finance, insurance, and real estate	229.4	952
Services	166.7	3,394
All other	91.8	718
Total	932.2	8,513

*Source: U.S. Treasury Department, Internal Revenue Service, *Statistics of Income 1962, U.S. Business Tax Returns*, 1965.

Table 6.3, which presents data on the distribution of partnerships according to industry, shows that partnerships are most likely to be found in services, in wholesale and retail trade, and in finance, insurance and real estate, but not in manufacturing. We also see here that on the average the most profitable partnerships are those engaged in providing services.

Corporations: Although rules and procedures vary from state to state, people who want to form a corporation can generally do so by applying to a state for a corporation charter. Such charters, which render the firm a legal entity distinct from its owners, are automatically granted.

When a corporation is formed, a certain number of shares of *common stock* are issued. The number of shares issued may be large or small, according to the preferences of the founders of the corporation. With permission of the stockholders, additional shares may be issued in later periods. Each share represents part ownership in the corporation. Thus someone who owns 10 shares in a corporation that has 200 shares outstanding owns one-twentieth of that corporation. Common stock is fully negotiable (that means that you can sell it any time you want to to anyone willing to buy it) and the stocks of most large American corporations are listed and sold on major stock exchanges, such as the New York Stock Exchange and the American Stock Exchange.

All of a corporation's profits accrue to (i.e., are owned by) its stockholders. A corporation may distribute its profits to its stockholders by paying out a dividend of so many dollars or cents per share. A corporation need not, however, pay out all its profits in dividends. Frequently corporations, especially rapidly expanding ones, retain part or even all of their profits to provide capital for further expansion.

Although the corporate stockholder can share in the profits of the corporation, he cannot be held liable for its unpaid debts. Thus if a corporation goes bankrupt, the maximum loss which any stockholder will incur is the amount he paid for his stock. Therefore the corporate shareholder has what is called *limited liability*. This is one of the principal attractions of the corporate form of organization.

TABLE 6|4

Corporations: Number and Net Profit, by Industry, 1962*

Industry	Number, thousands	Net profits, millions of dollars
Agriculture, forestry, and fisheries	22.2	161
Manufacturing	182.9	25,249
Wholesale and retail trade	388.8	5,188
Finance, insurance and real estate	359.5	8,674
Services	149.8	843
All other	163.8	9,520
Total	1,267.0	49,635

*Source: U.S. Treasury Department, Internal Revenue Service, *Statistics of Income 1962, U.S. Business Tax Returns*, 1965.

Any growing firm can meet some of its needs for additional capital through retained earnings. But a corporation can raise long-term capital in two other ways: it can issue either bonds or additional stock, and put these up for sale. How successful it will be in doing so will of course depend on its credit standing, on its past profit performance, on its future profit perspectives, and on how well known it is to potential investors. The small, unknown, and untried corporation, like the typical proprietorship or the partnership, may have a hard time raising long-term capital.

The process by which a corporation raises capital through the sale of new stock is straightforward. First it may have to obtain the authorization of the current shareholders for an increase in the number of outstanding shares, and it must comply with any applicable government regulations. This done, it may issue the new shares and sell them directly, or sell them indirectly through an investment banker or brokerage house.

When a firm sells bonds, this is simply a special form of long-term borrowing. The firm can sell new bonds, like new stock, either directly, or indirectly through a banker or broker. The latter method is by far the more typical.

Table 6.4 shows that corporations are, as we might expect, relatively uncommon in agriculture, but quite common in manufacturing, in wholesale and retail trade, in finance, insurance and real estate, and even in the service trades. Although the corporations active in manufacturing are not as numerous as those in some other lines of business, corporations engaged in manufacturing earn the lion's share of total corporate profits.

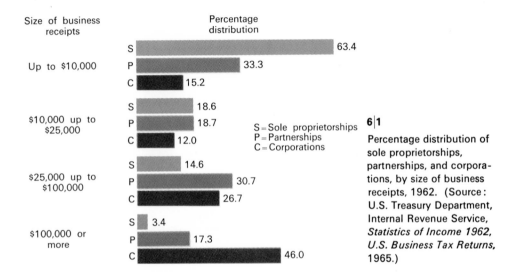

6|1

Percentage distribution of sole proprietorships, partnerships, and corporations, by size of business receipts, 1962. (Source: U.S. Treasury Department, Internal Revenue Service, *Statistics of Income 1962, U.S. Business Tax Returns,* 1965.)

Size Distribution of Firms by Form of Organization

When we think about the advantages and disadvantages of the different kinds of business organizations we have discussed, and the industries in which they predominate, we should expect that most sole proprietorships would be small firms, corporations large firms, and partnerships somewhere between the two. Figure 6.1 shows exactly that: most sole proprietorships have total annual receipts of less than $10,000, while almost half of all corporations have annual business receipts of over $100,000! Partnerships, on the other hand, are fairly evenly distributed through the different size classes.

Size Distribution of All Firms

The foregoing discussion about size differences in the average corporation, sole proprietorship, and partnership leads us to wonder: How important is the role of large versus small firms in the U.S. economy? Table 6.5, which presents data on the size distribution of U.S. firms, provides interesting insights into this question. Note that more than 50% of all firms have receipts of less than $10,000 a year, and that these firms together receive only 1.7% of total business receipts. Also note that more than 80% of all firms have receipts of less than $50,000 a year, and that these firms together receive less than 8% of total business receipts!

TABLE 6|5

Percentage Distribution of All Firms by Size of Business Receipts, 1962*

Size of business receipts, in thousands of dollars	Percent of all firms in this size class	Percent of total business receipts received by firms in this size class	Percent of total business profits earned by firms in this size class
Under 10	55.7	1.7	6.0
10–25	17.9	2.7	8.2
25–50	10.3	3.4	8.2
50–100	6.9	4.6	7.6
100–200	4.2	5.5	5.4
200–500	2.8	8.2	5.0
500–1,000	1.1	7.2	3.2
1,000–5,000	0.9	16.4	7.4
5,000–50,000	0.2	16.7	11.9
Over 50,000	(0.01)	33.6	37.1

*Source: U.S. Treasury Department, Internal Revenue Service, *Statistics of Income 1962, U.S. Business Tax Returns,* 1965.

Let's look at the other end of the size distribution: Firms with annual receipts of $5,000,000 or more account for only 0.2% of all firms, but they take in over 50% of all business receipts and earn almost 50% of all business profits. The most startling fact in Table 6.5 is that firms with annual receipts of over $50,000,000, although they represent only 0.01% of all firms, earn 37.1% of total business profits!

Thus Table 6.5 shows us that small firms are numerically strong but represent an insignificant portion of total business activity. On the other hand, large firms, though they are few in number, clearly carry on the bulk of business activity and earn a large share of total business profits. To quote two old sayings, "Money makes money," and "Them as has, gets."

Multi-Unit Versus Single-Unit Firms

In addition to size and form of business organization, another factor distinguishes some firms from others: the number of branches or units. Some firms have many; others operate only one. Figure 6.2 shows that most firms are single-unit ones, but that most *large* firms must have many branches, since multi-unit firms (although they represent only 2.9% of all firms) account for 53.8% of total business employment.

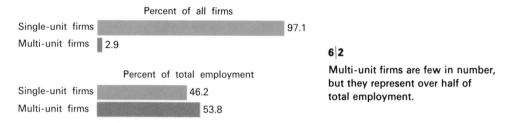

Percent of all firms

Single-unit firms   97.1

Multi-unit firms   2.9

6|2

Percent of total employment

Single-unit firms   46.2

Multi-unit firms   53.8

Multi-unit firms are few in number, but they represent over half of total employment.

Source: John C. Narver: *Conglomerate Mergers and Market Competition*, University of California Press, 1967. Narver's data were taken from U.S. Department of Commerce, Bureau of the Census, *Enterprise Statistics: 1958 Part I General Report*, 1963.

ECONOMIC CHOICES THE FIRM MUST MAKE

Regardless of its size, form of organization, or profitability, every firm, in each income period, has to make many complex and interrelated economic choices. To list these choices, we shall use the same approach that we used when we talked about the consumer's economic choices. We shall examine the firm's two principal financial accounts: its *income statement* and its *balance sheet*. These two accounts hold the clues to the economic choices (and economic strength) of any firm.

The Firm's Income Statement

As we have noted, the principal function of a firm is to combine inputs which it buys to produce an output which it sells. Thus during any income period the firms will incur *input costs,* and it will receive *revenue* (i.e., receipts) from the sale of output. The difference between the total revenue and the total cost of the goods the firm sells is equal to the firm's *profits*. Some of its profits go to pay corporate-profits taxes and some are distributed to the firm's stockholders in the form of dividends. The firm gets to keep the rest.

The above relationships can be summarized in a simple income statement.

A firm's income statement is a listing which tells how the firm's total revenue over a given period of time was allocated among costs, taxes, dividends, and retained profits.

Let us look, for example, at Table 6.6, which is a 1970 income statement for the Tectronics Corporation. (They're a fairly new company, and they make, let's say, light bulbs, out of a new kind of material called tectron. The bulbs can be folded flat.) The first entry records Tectronics' total revenue from sales during 1970. The next five entries all list Tectronics' major input costs during 1970. The first three of these are self-explanatory. The fourth, *depreciation,* refers to the decrease in the value of the firm's plant and equipment (i.e., capital stock) that occurred during the year as a result of wear, tear, and aging. The fifth cost entry, "taxes other than corporate-profits taxes," refers to local property and other taxes.

TABLE 6|6

Income Statement for the Tectronics Corporation, Jan. 1, 1970–Dec. 31, 1970

Total revenue from sales		$800,000
Goods and services purchased from other firms	$620,000	
Payroll	119,000	
Interest	1,900	
Depreciation	9,000	
Taxes other than corporate-profits taxes	9,100	
Total cost of goods produced during the year	$759,000	
Less: Change in inventories over the year		
(current level minus former level)	2,000	
Total cost of goods sold during the year	$757,000	757,000
Gross profits before corporate-profits taxes		$ 43,000
Less: Corporate-profits taxes		13,500
Net profits after taxes		$ 29,500
Less: Dividends		21,500
Retained profits		$ 8,000

A firm usually holds inventories of its output (Tectronics has half a million light bulbs in the basement) and during any income period some of the goods it sells may be drawn from its inventories (they bring cases of bulbs upstairs and ship them out), while some of the goods it produces may be added to its inventories. Therefore before we can calculate Tectronics' profits for any period, we must adjust its cost figure for the change, if any, in its inventories over the period. The "change in inventories" entry on Tectronics' income statement is designed to make this adjustment. (They had more light bulbs on hand at the end of this year than at the end of the year before.)

Once we have Tectronics cost-of-goods-*sold* figure in hand, we can calculate its profits simply by subtracting this cost figure from its total-revenue figure. The resulting profit figure is listed as "gross profits before taxes." The remaining four entries on Tectronics' income statement show how gross profits were allocated between corporate-profits taxes, dividends, and re-tained profits. Does the "retained-profits" entry remind us of something familiar? Yes. The Tectronics Company's *retained profits* constitute its savings for the year, just as the difference between John Q. Consumer's dis-posable income and his consumption constitutes *his* savings for the year.

The Accountant's Versus the Economist's Definition of Profits

The income statement of the Tectronics Corporation was set up on the basis of an accountant's definition of profits. From the economist's point of view this definition is an incomplete one, because it doesn't give the whole picture. There is the important—in fact, crucial—factor of *opportunity cost.*

The shareholders of Tectronics put their money into Tectronics stock instead of investing it in some alternative way (i.e., they had the opportunity to buy into Blue Sky Uranium Hunters, Inc., and didn't). Then there's John Jones, the founder and ex-president of Tectronics, who first thought of the idea of folding light bulbs 40 years ago. He often works in Tectronics' lab until midnight, but draws no salary from the company; also his wife de-votes all her spare time to getting out advertising ("Put a light bulb in your pocket") for which she charges the company only the cost of the postage. Both Jones and his wife are dedicated people, but they *could* choose to spend their time in some other way. They forgo the alternative opportunity.

Therefore the Tectronics Corporation has at its disposal certain inputs, such as the equity capital of the shareholders and the services of Jones and his wife, for which no explicit charges are made. When it uses these inputs, the Tectronics Company incurs an *opportunity cost* equal to the maximum amount that each such factor *could* have earned in an alternative employ-ment. Thus, for example, when Tectronics uses equity capital it incurs an opportunity cost equal to the return that this capital could reasonably be expected to have yielded if the shareholders had invested it in some other, equally risky activity. ("Let's look in the paper and see how Blue Sky is doing lately.") Similarly, when it uses the services of Jones and his wife, Tectronics incurs an opportunity cost equal to the maximum salaries that Jones and his wife could have commanded if they had gone to work for some other firm.

Because firms incur both explicit *and* opportunity costs, the economist argues that a firm's profits should be defined as the difference between its revenue and its explicit plus its opportunity costs. As we have already seen, however, the accountant defines a firm's profits as the difference between its total revenue and its total explicit costs, period. Therefore, from the econo-mist's point of view, the accountant's profit figure overstates the firm's true profits by an amount equal to the opportunity costs (if any) incurred by the firm.

A glance at the income statements that actual firms prepare and at the tax forms that governments issue is enough to show us that in practical matters the accountant's definition of profits has won the day. The economist's definition remains an important one, however, not only because it is the theoretically correct one, but also because it emphasizes opportunity cost, which as we shall see is a key concept that turns up again and again in the study of economics.

The Firm's Balance Sheet

Any going firm usually has both assets and liabilities. A firm's assets, like a consumer's, can be divided into two broad categories: financial and physical. A firm's *financial assets* include its cash and bank deposits, its accounts receivable (i.e., payments due to the firm for goods already sold), and its marketable securities. A firm's *physical assets* include its inventories of raw materials, of goods in process, and of finished output, plus of course its plant and equipment. In order not to overstate the value of its assets, a firm usually values its plant and equipment at cost minus accumulated depreciation. One final important note: a firm may possess valuable *intangible assets,* such as patents.

A firm's liabilities represent debt claims that consumers, as well as other business organizations, have acquired against the firm by supplying debt capital to it. Those debt claims which are payable within a year are referred to as *current liabilities,* while debt claims payable over longer periods are referred to as *long-term liabilities.*

The difference between the firm's assets and liabilities (like the difference between the consumer's assets and liabilities) is its *net worth.* We can summarize this important relationship by setting up a balance sheet for the firm.

A balance sheet is a statement which lists the value at a given point in time of the firm's assets, liabilities, and residual net worth.

Table 6.7 shows the Tectronics Corporation's balance sheet as of Dec. 31, 1970. Most of the entries in this account are self-explanatory, except perhaps for the entry "retained earnings." Let's take a closer look at that one. First we should realize that a firm's net worth represents the *ownership* interest that people who have invested equity capital in the firm have in the firm. At the moment that the Tectronics Corporation is founded, its net worth obviously equals the number of dollars that Tectronics' stockholders have invested in (i.e., paid for) whatever stock the firm has issued and sold. Now Tectronics starts turning out light bulbs, and it finds that business has its ups and downs. Some years it incurs losses and some years it earns and retains profits (i.e., it dissaves in some periods and saves in others). These changes affect Tectronics' net worth and thus the size of the ownership interest which its stockholders have in it. To take these changes into account, the accountant could continually alter the value he ascribes to Tectronics' outstanding common stock. Instead he adds to its balance sheet a residual balancing entry, *retained earnings*, which equals Tectronics' accumulated savings over time.

TABLE 6|7

Balance Sheet for the Tectronics Corporation, Dec. 31, 1970

Assets			Liabilities and net worth	
Current assets			*Current liabilities*	
Cash and bank deposits		$ 12,000	Accounts payable	$ 40,000
Accounts receivable		8,000	Notes payable	8,000
Government and other marketable securities		3,500		
Inventories		48,500	*Long-term liabilities*	
			Bonds payable	12,000
Fixed assets			Mortgages payable	27,200
Plant and equipment				
Cost	$60,000			
Less: Depreciation	15,000		*Net worth*	
		45,000	Common stock	19,900
Intangible assets			Retained earnings	11,400
Patents		1,500		
			Total liabilities plus net worth	
Total assets		$118,500		$118,500

The Firm's Economic Choices

As we said at the beginning of this chapter, a business organization has to make many complex economic choices. Now that we have set up a typical firm's income statement and balance sheet, let's examine these accounts to see what they tell us about these choices.

The first and (if the firm is profitable) largest entry on the firm's income statement is the total-revenue entry. As any child of ten knows, the total revenue of a business during any period equals the total output it sells times the price it charges for output. So this entry brings up two key economic choices a firm has to make:

What level of output should the firm produce?
What price should it charge for this output?

The next two entries—"goods and services" and "payroll"—both have to do with costs that the firm incurs in purchasing inputs that can be varied during the current production period. These are known as *variable inputs*. When we think about these entries, two more business choices occur to us:

What labor inputs should the firm demand from consumers?
What intermediate inputs (i.e., goods and services) should it demand from other producers?

Commonsense tells us that a firm uses more of some variable inputs than of others. So still another choice arises:

In what proportions should the firm combine the different variable inputs it uses?

Suppose the firm uses both raw materials and labor; it has to decide whether to combine a lot of raw materials with a little labor (as a steel mill would do) or combine a lot of labor with relatively little raw material (as a maker of precision instruments would do).

In addition to using variable inputs such as labor and raw materials to produce its output, the firm also uses capital inputs. Look at Tectronics' balance sheet and you'll see that a large proportion of the capital inputs it uses are in the form of plant and equipment. During any period a firm might decide to alter the character and size of its plant and equipment (Tectronics has its eye on a new filament-curling machine). Such changes, however, usually aren't completed in time to affect the firm's current operations. Therefore so far as the current period—or *short run*—is concerned the firm's inputs of plant and equipment are *fixed inputs*.

All right, now we've recognized the fact that any business firm uses both variable and fixed inputs. This means that during each current period the firm has to decide about not only its current operations but also its future ones; in particular it has to make an investment decision:

What kinds and quantity of plant and equipment should it acquire during the current period for use during future periods?

If the firm decides to acquire new plant and equipment during the current period (Tectronics decides to buy the new filament-curler and build a sub-basement to store more light bulbs), then it has to obtain additional funds to finance the acquisition of these assets. The firm can do this in three ways:

1) by incurring new debt,
2) by retaining profits, and/or
3) by selling new stock.

Thus another important economic choice is:

If the firm decides to make new investments, what sources of funds should it use to finance them?

This investment-financing choice is part of the larger economic choice that the firm faces in any given period: deciding what will be the composition of its overall balance sheet.

A THEORY OF THE FIRM

Now let's turn to the key task of this part of the book: we need a theory of the firm that will explain how any firm—whether it be a lemonade stand, a drugstore, a professional baseball team, or a giant like General Motors— makes the complex economic choices that it has to make. We shall again handle the firm as we did the consumer, and begin by making a fundamental assumption concerning its motivation, then figure out what this assumption implies. Finally we shall check the validity of our results by testing the predictions they yield against experience.

One way to arrive at a fundamental assumption is to examine the empirical evidence on how firms behave to see what clues it gives as to the underlying motivation of the firm. At first this may discourage us, since firms— superficially at least—seem to have more differences than similarities. But if we keep on looking for a unifying assumption, we'll soon find one. All firms —despite their apparent diversity—are trying to do the same thing: make the largest profit they can. So the natural assumption on which to base our theory of the firm is:

Any firm, when it makes the varied economic choices that confront it, always attempts to maximize its profits, both during the current period and in the foreseeable future.

Well, there we are. Now we can easily go on to develop a theory that explains the way the firm makes its varied economic choices. In order to maximize the profits it earns from the sale of current output, the firm obviously has to produce its output with an input combination that is not only feasible from a technical point of view but that will also minimize its cost of production. In addition any firm must always choose the output price and output level (i.e., the price–output combination) that will maximize its profits. So naturally we need to begin our discussion of the firm by asking:

1) How does the firm identify the feasible input combination that will minimize its cost of production during the short run (i.e., the current period)?
2) How does the firm choose the price–output combination that will maximize its profits during the short run?

After we know the answers to these questions, we can ask:

3) How does the firm choose the investment-financing option that will maximize its future profits?

PROBLEMS

1   Economists almost universally assume that firms attempt to maximize their profits. Though this assumption, as we shall see later, yields good predictions, economists have suggested that motives other than the profit motive are equally plausible. Discuss other goals that you think might guide a firm in its operations. What motives, other than profit, seem to be influencing the following firms?

   a) The owner of a small-town bookstore closes the store every Wednesday to play golf.

   b) A corporation pays its salesmen a percentage commission and allows them considerable freedom in the price they charge for the product.

   c) A law firm takes on the senior partner's son as a junior partner, even though he has a repellent personality and is known to be lazy.

   d) A corporation goes bankrupt because of its unwieldy personnel policy: The executives wanted to have as many people as possible under their control, and this wish was allowed to get out of hand.

2   Order the three forms of business organization discussed in the text according to their relative desirability from the following standpoints. Explain your ranking. Which factor is likely to be the most important in deciding what form of organization to use?

   a) Capital requirements

   b) Size of business

   c) Nature of product (goods versus services)

   d) Assets of the organizer

   e) Expected lifetime of the business

3   "The more you risk, the more you stand to gain." Discuss the validity of this statement as applied to the three forms of business organization and the various means of raising capital.

4   Consider a corporate bond which has a face value of $50 and which pays $3 yearly in interest. Suppose this bond is now selling for $50. What interest rate must other corporate bonds that are considered to be in the same risk class yield? If the interest rate were suddenly to double, what would happen to the price of this bond? Do you need more information about the bond to exactly determine the new price?

5   The Nuclear Orbit Corporation during 1970 received the following revenue, incurred the following costs, and disposed of its profits in the following ways (all figures are in thousands of dollars): Dividends on common stock 11, total sales 2,100, state and local taxes 9, inventory at the beginning of the year 168, goods and services purchased from other firms 1,600, interest paid 1, inventory at the end of the year 160, federal profits tax 19, payroll 263, depreciation 18. Set up an income statement for this company.

6   The Nuclear Orbit Corporation also has assets and liabilities as follows (all figures are in thousands of dollars): government and other securities 4, notes payable 21, mortgages payable 28, accounts receivable 162, original cost of plant and equipment 399, depreciation to date on plant and equipment 192, inventories 168, claims of common stockholders 90, bonds payable 86, bank deposits 23, accounts payable 73, intangible assets 0. Set up a balance sheet for this company.

7   We said in this chapter that retained profits for a firm are analogous to savings for a consumer. Do retained profits, like savings, have to equal the change in a firm's net worth over a given period of time?

8   How is the cost of plant and equipment entered in a firm's income statement?

9   Distinguish between bonds recorded on a corporation's balance sheet as assets and those recorded on its balance sheet as liabilities.

10 Can a firm which rents certain pieces of capital equipment from other firms rather than buying them (e.g., computers) regard them as assets? How would renting such equipment affect the income statement and balance sheet of the firm?

11 Several years ago, IBM sold a new issue of common stock. How must this transaction have affected IBM's balance sheet? Contrast this effect with that of the sale of outstanding shares by one stockholder to another. Does an individual who buys outstanding shares of stock actually supply capital to the firm?

CHAPTER 7

THE PRODUCTION FUNCTION

In order to figure out which combinations of inputs to employ to produce different levels of output at *minimum* cost, the firm has to begin by asking what maximum levels of output it can obtain by employing various input combinations, or alternatively what minimum input combinations will produce a specified level of output. The answer to this question lies in the firm's *production function*.

THE PRODUCTION FUNCTION: A GENERAL DESCRIPTION

The production function concerns the physical relationship between the inputs employed in the production process and the output yielded by this process. Therefore constructing a production function is an *engineering,* not an economic, problem. Also, since a production function summarizes what is possible given the current state of technical knowledge, it may undergo sudden and dramatic changes. For example, it used to be very hard to get aluminum out of bauxite ore by the old chemical-reaction process. Then in 1888 an American college boy, Charles Martin Hall, working in his woodshed, revolutionized the commercial production of aluminum by his discovery of the electrolytic process. More recently the invention of transistors and printed circuits revolutionized the production function for computers, while the harnessing of atomic power added a new dimension to the production function for electricity.

Returns to Scale

Once we know a firm's production function, we can ask questions concerning how the output of this firm would change if it were to change its inputs.

For example:

How would the output of this firm change if the firm were to increase, in equal proportions, all the inputs employed in its production process?

By all rights such a change should increase the firm's output. But by how much? The increase in output might be *more than proportionate, less than proportionate,* or *precisely proportionate* to the increase in inputs.

      Consider, for example, the Celery Improvement Company. They manufacture celery chips for dieters who want something to eat with their beer or their low-calorie soft drinks. Currently the Celery Improvement Company uses 100,000 bushels of celery, a ton of salt substitute, 500 people, and $50,000 of capital equipment to produce half a million bags of Celchips per month. If they were to increase their purchases of celery and salt substitute by 10%, if they were to hire 50 additional employees, and if they were to increase their capital stock by $5,000, this would constitute an *equi-proportionate* increase in their inputs. How would this change (that is, a 10% increase in all inputs) affect their output? Answer: It might increase output by more than 10%, by less than 10%, or by precisely 10%.

1) The first of these possibilities is referred to as *increasing returns to scale.*
2) The second is referred to as *decreasing returns to scale.*
3) The third is referred to as *constant returns to scale.*

      At first glance the possibility of *increasing returns to scale* might appear to controvert common sense. This phenomenon, however, can easily be explained once we observe that many inputs are available only in "lumpy," indivisible units. (For example, the Celery Improvement Company uses a giant automated freeze-dry machine. If the firm were to increase the amount of celery they process, they'd have to buy another of these expensive pieces of equipment. They couldn't buy *half* a machine.) Whenever a firm uses indivisible inputs, increases in the scale of its output are likely to *increase the efficiency* with which it can utilize its inputs, for two reasons:

1) An increase in the scale of its output may permit the firm to introduce new "lumpy" inputs into its production process or to utilize the "lumpy" inputs it already employs more fully. (Thus, for example, if the Celery Improvement Company doubles its output, it may be able to replace the calculating machines in its accounting department with a small computer. Another firm that already has a computer might, with greatly increased output, be able to up utilization of this computer from 12 to 20 hours a day.)

2) An increase in the scale of its output may permit a firm to establish a more complex division of labor among its workers. A complex division of labor that calls for individual workers to perform specialized tasks instead of functioning as jacks-of-all-trades usually raises the productivity of the workers, partly because some people are better suited to perform certain tasks than others, and partly because constant repetition of a single task increases a worker's skill in performing it.

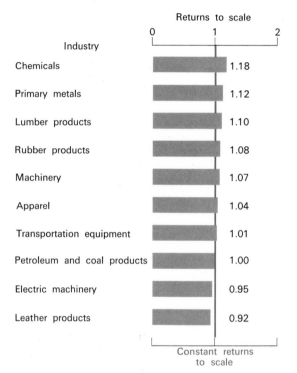

7|1

Estimated returns to scale in selected manufacturing industries. (Source: George H. Hildebrand and Ta-Chung Liu, *Manufacturing Production Functions in the United States;* Ithaca, N.Y.: The New York State School of Industrial and Labor Relations, Cornell University, 1965, pages 109–110.)

Industry	Returns to scale
Chemicals	1.18
Primary metals	1.12
Lumber products	1.10
Rubber products	1.08
Machinery	1.07
Apparel	1.04
Transportation equipment	1.01
Petroleum and coal products	1.00
Electric machinery	0.95
Leather products	0.92

Constant returns to scale

Decreasing returns to scale implies that increases in the firm's scale of output will decrease the efficiency with which it utilizes inputs. How and why might such a decrease occur? Presumably it wouldn't be due to the nature of the firm's physical production process, since a firm could always get around any diseconomies of scale associated with its production process by building a number of duplicate plants. As we saw in Table 6.6, most large U.S. firms do operate a number of plants. (The Celery Improvement Company is a Los Angeles outfit, but they have a branch plant in Connecticut.)

Decreasing returns to scale *may*, however, come about because the firm's growth severely complicates the problems associated with managing it. Often, as a firm grows, it reaches a point at which increasing difficulties of organization, coordination, and communication begin to outweigh the advantages of specialization usually associated with large-scale management.* Once this point is reached, further increases in the scale of the firm's operations will decrease the efficiency with which it utilizes inputs.

Constant returns to scale implies that changes in the scale of the firm's output will have *no* effect on the efficiency with which it utilizes inputs. Presumably only firms operating in industries in which the benefits of input specialization (i.e., a complex division of labor) are either small or can be fully realized at relatively modest levels of output would experience constant returns to scale over wide ranges of output.

Suppose that we could examine the returns to scale actually experienced by firms producing in real-life industries. With what relative frequency should we expect to observe increasing, decreasing, and constant returns to scale? What we have just said about the causes of these phenomena suggests that in most manufacturing industries firms probably operate within the range of increasing returns to scale. To test this proposition, Liu and Hildebrand have estimated the returns to scale experienced by firms in a wide range of different industries. Their results, some of which are presented in Fig. 7.1, indicate that increasing returns to scale are prevalent throughout manufacturing.

Input Substitution

So much for the effect on output of changing all inputs in *the same* proportion. Now let's consider a second sort of input change:

What will happen to the total output of a production process (such as the making of Celchips) if the quantity of one input employed in this process is decreased, while the quantity of some other input is simultaneously increased?

Naturally if you cut down on some really necessary input (such as celery), you're going to decrease your output; the effect of simultaneously increasing some other input is, however, more difficult to predict. If it so happens that this second input whose quantity is increased can be used to replace (i.e., perform the same task as) the first input, then you can maintain output in the face of a decrease in the first input by increasing the second one; and the two inputs are said to be *substitutes*. The Celery Improvement Company flavors its product with a certain ersatz salt, Slimsalt, which is said to be nonfattening because it does not help the body to retain fluids. A rival chemical company enters the market with a new salt substitute, Skin-ee, which they claim is just as non fattening as Slimsalt. So now the Celery Im-

---

* For a delightful, and wry, look at this subject, read *Parkinson's Law,* by C. Northcote Parkinson; Boston: Houghton Mifflin, 1957.

provement Company can use Skin-ee, Slimsalt, or both to flavor its chips. Slimsalt and Skin-ee are thus substitutes.

Whenever a production function employs many inputs, possibilities for substitution are greater between some inputs than between others. Thus for example, in a given production process, substitution may be possible between labor and capital equipment, but not between labor and raw materials. (You can hire ten extra people to scrape celery instead of buying a new automated celery-scraping machine. But no matter how many extra workmen you hire, your output will still drop if you can't get hold of the usual amount of celery.) Or, alternatively, substitution may be possible between different kinds of capital equipment, but not between capital and labor.

Let's look at a case in which substitution between two inputs *is* possible. As one input is substituted for the other, usually the successive increases in that input required to compensate for equal and successive decreases in the other input will grow progressively larger. The reason for this is that the two inputs are not equally well suited to performing all tasks involved in the production process. Therefore a point will eventually be reached at which the input being increased must be used to perform tasks for which it is less and less well suited in comparison with the input which it replaces.

Suppose that capital in the form of machines is substituted for labor. In a factory that uses much labor and little capital you can replace workers by introducing simple and inexpensive machines. But as you substitute more and more capital for labor, you have to introduce increasingly sophisticated and expensive machines. Thus as you substitute more and more capital for labor, the amount of capital required to replace a single worker rises, and the further you carry the substitution of capital for labor, the more steeply it is likely to rise.

The ease with which you can substitute one input for another frequently depends not only on the initial proportions in which you combine these inputs, but also on the *scale* of production. Since many kinds of capital equipment, from computers to assembly lines, are available only in big indivisible units (recall our earlier discussion of "lumpy" inputs), capital equipment often cannot be efficiently utilized (i.e., employed on a full-time basis) except when the operations are large-scale ones. Therefore the degree to which you can substitute capital for labor is especially likely to depend on the scale of output.

Possibilities for Input Substitution

How widespread are opportunities for input substitution in real-life production functions? Probably quite extensive, judging from experience, but let's seek out some data on this.

A good starting point would be to find out whether there are any significant variations in the ratios in which different producers operating in the same industry combine their various inputs. Let's take labor and capital, for example. What are the possibilities of substituting one for the other? One way to find out is to compare the ratio of capital to labor used by U.S. manufacturers with that used by foreign manufacturers *in the same industry.* Figure 7.2 makes precisely this comparison for a number of different industries; it shows the ratios of capital to labor used by producers in various industries in the United States and in Japan. These ratios turn out to be markedly different, so we conclude that opportunities for substitution between labor and capital must be widespread in all the industries studied. Figure 7.2 also suggests that Japanese producers consistently use lower capital-to-labor ratios than U.S. producers. Why? This is an interesting and important question that we'll get to in Chapter 8.

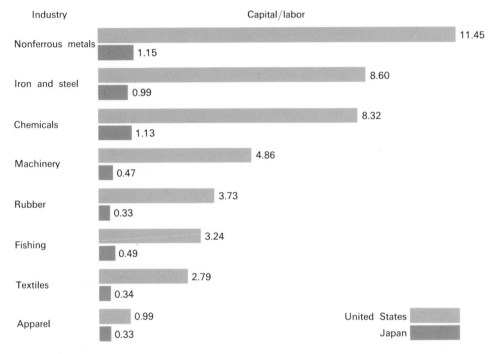

7|2

Ratios of capital to labor in selected industries in the U.S. and Japan. (Source: K. J. Arrow, H. B. Chenery, B. S. Minhas, and R. M. Solow, "Capital–Labor Substitution and Economic Efficiency," *The Review of Economics and Statistics* XLIII, August 1961, page 240)

A Graphic Representation of the Production Function

We have discussed the various properties of the production function; now let's graph such a function. We could simply plot up some imaginary production function which had the general properties we've talked about, but it would be more interesting to plot the production function of a firm operating in some real-life industry.

Although this approach is appealing, it presents certain problems, because we can graph the production function only if we stick to production functions that involve *two* inputs and a *single* output. Any real-life production function, however, is bound to involve at least *three* inputs: labor, capital, and raw materials. And any actual firm will typically produce, not a single homogeneous output, but a group of related outputs. How can we reduce the multi-input, multi-output production function of an actual firm to a simple three-variable relationship? Well, we could include only two inputs, capital and labor, in the firm's production function. And we could measure the firm's total output in terms of the market value of this output minus the cost of raw materials.

If we took this approach, we would obtain a production function that could be represented by

$$q = h(L,K),$$

in which q is the value of the total output produced jointly by labor, L, and capital, K. We could measure L (the firm's labor inputs) in terms of man-hours of labor employed, and K (its capital inputs) in terms of the dollar value recorded on its balance sheet for plant and equipment.*

Liu and Hildebrand† have estimated precisely this sort of production function for a number of industries, including rubber products.

The Production Surface

Suppose that we were to plot the production function of a certain firm in the rubber products industry, say the Snapback Rubber Company, Inc. According to Liu's and Hildebrand's results, we would obtain a three-dimensional *production surface* like the one in Fig. 7.3. Note that each point on the surface tells us the maximum quantity of output that the firm could produce by employing a specific combination of capital and labor inputs. Thus, for example, the point W tells us that, if Snapback were to employ L^0 labor inputs and K^0 capital inputs, the maximum quantity of output that it could produce would be q^0.

It follows that any point *above* the production surface is unattainable for the firm. Any point *on* the surface is not only attainable, but also optimal, in the sense that, if Snapback operates at such a point, it won't be able to increase its output even if it improves its utilization of inputs. This is the best it can do. Any point *below* the surface is attainable but suboptimal, be-

---

* See Problem 5 at the end of this chapter.
† George H. Hildebrand and Ta-Chung Liu, *ibid*.

cause if Snapback operates at such a point, it can increase output by utilizing its inputs more efficiently.

In Fig. 7.3, we see that the production surface slopes *upward* from both the capital axis and the labor axis. This upward slope indicates that, if the firm increases its labor inputs, its capital inputs, or both, then its total output will also increase.

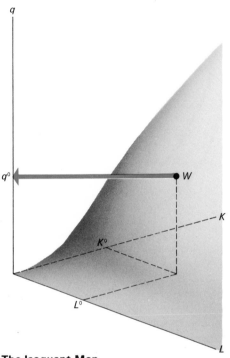

7|3

If we were to plot the production function of a firm producing rubber products, we would obtain a three-dimensional production surface like this one.

The Isoquant Map

When we examine the production function of the Snapback Rubber Company we can easily locate various input combinations that will yield the same level of output. In fact, we can see that a given amount of rubber products can be produced with almost any amount of labor, provided that this labor is combined with an appropriate amount of capital. Similarly a given amount of rubber products can be produced with almost any amount of capital, provided that this capital is combined with an appropriate amount of labor.

In order to graph the possibilities offered by Snapback's production function for substitution between labor and capital, we must introduce a new concept, the *isoquant*.

An isoquant is a curve which links all input combinations that yield the same level of output.

Suppose that Snapback's output is held constant at some positive level, $\bar{q}$. Then we can obtain the isoquant corresponding to this level of output by plotting all input combinations that satisfy the relationship

$$\bar{q} = h(L,K),$$

in which $h(L,K)$ is Snapback's production function. We can also obtain isoquants corresponding to other levels of output by repeating this procedure for additional values of $\bar{q}$.*

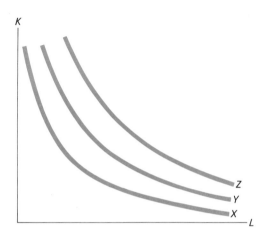

7|4

The isoquant map of the Snapback Rubber Company would consist of a set of convex curves like these. Since higher isoquants correspond to higher levels of output, input combinations along isoquant Y will yield *more* output than those along isoquant X but *less* output than those along isoquant Z.

Figure 7.4 shows a collection of isoquants for the Snapback Company. In interpreting this *isoquant map*,† note that the *downward slope* of the isoquants indicates that there are possibilities for Snapback, in the production of its rubber products, to substitute labor for capital and vice versa. The *convexity* of these curves implies that as Snapback keeps on substituting one factor for another in a single direction, they will have to put in more and more of the input being increased to compensate for equal and successive reductions in the input being decreased. The reader should verify that "higher" isoquants correspond to higher levels of output.

---

* We can also derive isoquants by another method: First the production surface is "sliced" in a direction parallel to the (L,K)-plane at various "heights," each of which corresponds to a particular level of output. Then all points of intersection (that is, all points at which the slicing edge cuts the production surface) are projected downward onto the (L,K)-plane. This procedure yields one isoquant for each slice.

† There is a strong similarity between the firm's isoquant map and the consumer's indifference map between two goods (recall Fig. 4.3). Note that each curve in the consumer's indifference map summarizes the opportunities the consumer has to substitute one consumption good for another while maintaining his satisfaction at a fixed level; similarly each curve in the firm's isoquant map indicates the possibilities the firm has to substitute one input for another while maintaining its output at a fixed level.

AN INPUT'S MARGINAL PRODUCTIVITY

Here's a definition to remember:

The change in total output that results from a small change in one input, all other inputs being constant, is known as that input's marginal productivity.

How will an input's marginal productivity change in response to successive increases in this input? Let's illustrate with a simple example.

You inherit a large area of land in Nebraska. It's standing idle, so you decide to farm it. In the interests of simplicity, let's say that the crop you plan to grow requires only two inputs, labor and land. You first hire a fellow named Zeke Smith to farm the place, thereby adding one farmer to the production process. Total output will now rise from zero to some positive amount, say 500 bushels of the crop. The full amount of this rise, 500 bushels of the crop, represents Zeke Smith's marginal productivity.

Now you hire a second farmer, Jed Jones, and add him to the production process. Total output will again rise, and the amount of the rise will equal the marginal productivity of Jed Jones. How will Jones's marginal productivity compare with Smith's? We have assumed that the tract of land is large, so the marginal productivity of the second farmer, Jones, will presumably be at least as large as that of the first, Smith; even larger if the two of them, by working together, are able to increase their efficiency through specialization. ("You plow and I'll weed.")

You're pleased with your rising output, so you hire still more farmers and add them to the production process. The marginal productivity of these added farmers will rise or remain constant so long as some vacant land is available. *But,* once all your land is under cultivation, if you keep on hiring more farmers, it will reduce the amount of land available per farmer; and this will lower the marginal productivity of each of the farmers.

The marginal productivity of the farmers will continue to fall as long as you keep on increasing the number of farmers. Eventually, in fact, your land would be used so intensively that a further increase in the number of farmers would have no impact at all on total output. In such a situation the marginal productivity of the additional farmers would be zero. Conceivably once the point of zero marginal productivity were reached, the addition of still more farmers to the production process might, by disrupting the organization of production, actually cause total output to fall. If this were to happen, the marginal productivity of an additional farmer would be negative.

Our example suggests the following valid generalization:

If one makes successive and equal additions of a variable factor to a production process that also utilizes another factor, the input of which is fixed, the marginal productivity of the variable factor will eventually fall.

This generalization is called *the law of diminishing returns*. Since the phenomenon of diminishing returns is fundamental to a number of important economic arguments, it is important that you understand precisely what it is and why it occurs.

In our Nebraska farm situation, as the input of the variable factor (labor) is progressively increased, each unit of that factor will have less and less of the fixed factor (land) to work with. It is this situation which can be regarded as the real cause of diminishing returns. Diminishing returns come about because we cannot continually increase total output by means of increases in a single variable factor alone, unless that factor is eventually used to perform tasks originally carried out by the fixed factor, and for which the fixed factor is better suited. It follows that diminishing returns result only when the fixed input is essential to the production process and when the variable factor and the fixed factor are not identical from the point of view of the production process. The ease with which the variable factor can be substituted for the fixed factor will determine both the speed with which diminishing returns set in and the severity of the phenomenon.

The relationship between the quantity of an input employed and the input's marginal productivity (*MP*) can be represented graphically by an *MP* curve. Your experience with your farm tells you that in general an input's *MP* curve will initially rise, since increases in the scale of output reflect a more efficient utilization of all inputs. Eventually, however, the problems associated with substituting the variable input for the fixed input will bring on diminishing returns, and when this happens the *MP* curve will turn down.

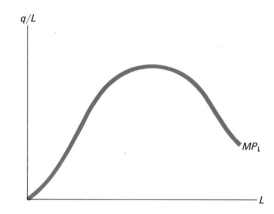

7|5

An input's marginal productivity curve generally rises and then falls, as does the *MP* curve of labor shown here.

Figure 7.5 shows an *MP* curve which displays these general properties. This curve is an important one because (as we shall see later) an input's marginal productivity plays a key role in determining how much of this input a profit-maximizing producer should use.

PROBLEMS

1   The following table presents data for a hypothetical production function for gizmos. Use these data to graph the isoquant map of this production function. Then graph the marginal productivity curve for labor with capital held constant, first at \$30,000 and then at \$70,000. Also graph the same curve for capital, with labor held constant at 100 workers. L = number of workers; K = thousands of dollars of capital; q = thousands of gizmos.

L	K	q	L	K	q	L	K	q	L	K	q
40	70	10	70	70	30	100	95	60	140	100	70
40	140	20	80	30	10	100	130	70	180	30	30
50	50	10	80	50	20	110	50	40	190	50	60
50	130	30	80	70	40	120	45	40	200	30	40
60	40	10	90	60	40	140	20	10	200	70	70
60	70	20	100	25	10	140	30	20	240	30	50
60	90	30	100	40	20	140	35	30	260	25	30
60	100	40	100	50	30	140	40	40	260	50	70
60	120	50	100	55	40	140	50	50	280	20	20
60	150	60	100	70	50	140	70	60	300	30	60

2   The Rialto Ratchet Corporation has only one production process: one worker together with one machine can produce 500 ratchets per day. The machine is useless without an operator and the operator is useless without a machine. One worker can operate only one machine. What will the isoquant map between machines and workers look like? Without having further information, what can you say about the advantages of large-scale production of ratchets?

3   In this chapter we compared the capital–labor ratios in the United States and Japan, in order to test the possibility of substitution between the two inputs. What assumptions were made implicitly in this test, and do you think they are valid? In other words, what relationships must hold between the efficiency of labor and capital in the two countries, and between the composition of outputs of similar industries in the two countries, in order that the test be valid?

4   a) Draw isoquant maps for two firms which use only two inputs, one firm showing increasing returns to scale and the other showing decreasing returns to scale.

    b) Assuming that labor and capital are the only inputs used in producing the gizmos of Problem 1, indicate the areas of increasing and decreasing returns to scale on the isoquant map that you drew for that problem.

5   Referring to a firm's balance sheet, which entries would you use in defining the firm's capital stock as it enters into its production function? Do you need more information than the balance sheet provides in order to define capital? [Arrow, Chenery, Minhas, and Solow measured capital by net fixed assets (including land) plus cash and working capital. Hildebrand and Liu found that they usu-

ally obtained the best fit if they measured capital by the gross book value of plant and equipment. They also experimented with a measure of capital that included not only gross book value of plant and equipment, but also an estimate of the value of rented plant and equipment.]

6   In Table 7.1 the terms "number employed" and "labor" refer to the total number of active proprietors, salaried personnel, and wage earners (monthly average), while "capital" refers to net fixed capital, cash, and working capital.

   a) What does this table tell you about returns to scale, opportunities for substituting labor for capital or vice versa, and labor productivity in the tobacco, leather, and motor-vehicle industries?

   b) What, if anything, do these data suggest about the appropriateness of measuring the size of a firm by using as a measure either "number employed" or the firm's total assets?

TABLE 7|1

Indexes of Selected Ratios: Number Employed, Capital, and Output, by Major U.S. Manufacturing Industries, Selected Years, 1900–1953 (1929 = 100)*

Ratio of	Index of Ratios						
	1900	1909	1919	1929	1937	1948	1953
Tobacco products							
1. Labor to output	292.1	259.6	178.1	100.0	65.8	32.9	31.5
2. Capital to labor	19.3	27.6	47.1	100.0	115.5	179.9	216.9
3. Capital to output	56.0	71.6	83.6	100.0	76.2	58.8	68.0
Leather and leather products							
1. Labor to output	96.7	78.9	100.9	100.0	117.4	94.8	92.1
2. Capital to labor	83.8	121.2	108.4	100.0	65.7	61.9	64.7
3. Capital to output	81.3	95.8	109.7	100.0	77.1	58.6	59.7
Motor vehicles							
1. Labor to output	964.9	598.2	162.3	100.0	96.5	82.5	63.9
2. Capital to labor	65.5	58.5	93.6	100.0	95.0	103.3	114.9
3. Capital to output	634.8	351.8	152.3	100.0	92.3	85.7	73.9

*Source: D. Creamer, S. P. Dobrovolsky, and J. Borenstein: *Capital in Manufacturing and Mining*; Princeton, N.J.: Princeton University Press, for National Bureau of Economic Research, 1960; pages 97–98.

7   What concepts are exemplified by the following comments? Explain and use diagrams where possible to illustrate.

   a) "That plant is too large to be run efficiently."

   b) "If you buy this machine you can cut your work force by 50%."

   c) "The Chinese rice paddies have so many people working in them that there isn't any room for rice."

   d) "I think we are big enough now to use a computer in our accounting department."

   e) "Two men working together can weave three times as many baskets as they could if each worked separately."

8 a) Illustrate the manner in which technological change might affect a firm's production function. Would such an effect necessarily be the same over the entire range of the production function?

b) Many devices are said to be "labor-saving." What, in your opinion, does this phrase mean? Illustrate your answer by using isoquant diagrams. Do you think any invention could be capital-saving? [In answering this question you might like to have at least one specific example in mind. If so, read Chapter 3 in R. G. Walsh and B. M. Evans, *Economics of Change in Market Structure, Conduct and Performance: the Baking Industry 1947–1958;* Lincoln, Nebr.: University of Nebraska Studies, New Series No. 28, 1963. This chapter contains an excellent discussion of technological change and returns to scale in bread production.]

9 The problem of measuring technological change is, as you might expect, very difficult. Discuss whether or not technological change would be reflected in the values of the two variables listed under (a) and (b). The last of these variables was used as a "proxy variable" for technological change by Hildebrand and Liu.

a) Changes in the ratio of the value of machinery and other equipment to the total value of plant plus equipment.

b) Changes in the ratio of the depreciated value of plant and equipment to the undepreciated value of plant and equipment. (This is intended as a measure of the age of fixed capital.)

*Appendix to Chapter 7

LABOR'S PRODUCTIVITY CURVES

We have constructed a marginal productivity curve for labor, but that is only one of three productivity curves we can set up for this input. The other two are labor's total productivity curve and its average productivity curve.

Labor's *total productivity* (*TP*) *curve* summarizes the relationship that exists (all other inputs being constant) between the quantity of labor used in the production process and the quantity of output yielded by this process. We can easily derive the general shape of labor's *TP* curve from its *MP* curve. We begin by observing that labor's total and marginal productivities can be represented by the expressions

$$TP_L = {}^{\bullet}q = h(L,\overline{K}), \qquad MP_L = \Delta q/\Delta L = \Delta h(L,\overline{K})/\Delta L,$$

where Δ stands for "change in," and the bar over the K indicates that capital inputs are held constant. From these expressions, it follows that labor's marginal productivity must equal the *slope* of labor's *TP* curve.

This being so, then labor's *TP* curve will rise at an increasing rate over the range for which the marginal productivity of labor is rising, and at a decreasing rate over the range for which the marginal productivity of labor is falling. It will reach a maximum at the point at which the marginal productivity of labor falls to zero, and it will decline over the range of labor inputs (if there are any) for which the marginal productivity of labor is negative.

Figure 7.6 shows a plot of labor's *TP* and *MP* curves. The dashed lines, L' and L'', indicate the points at which key relationships exist between labor's *TP* and *MP* curves: L' indicates the point at which labor's *MP* curve reaches a maximum and its *TP* curve ceases to rise at an increasing rate, while L'' indicates the point at which labor's *MP* curve falls to zero and its *TP* curve reaches a maximum.

---

* The reader may skip this appendix without loss of continuity.

Labor's *average productivity* (*AP*) *curve* summarizes the relationship that exists (all other inputs being held constant) between the quantity of labor used in the production process and the average output per unit of labor. Labor's *AP* curve can be represented by the expression

$$AP_L = q/L = h(L,\overline{K})/L.$$

We can figure out the shape of labor's *AP* curve by looking at its *TP* curve. First we note that the slope of a straight line drawn from the origin to any point on labor's *TP* curve equals q/L (that is, labor's average productivity). Next we sketch in straight lines from the origin to a number of points along labor's *TP* curve; from these lines we conclude two things about the shape and position of labor's *AP* curve.

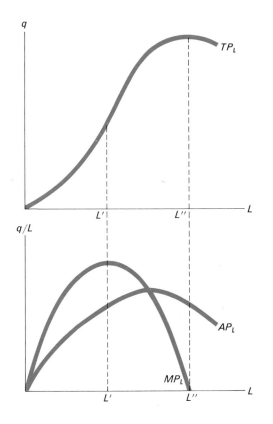

7|6

Labor's productivity curves: *AP* and *MP* curves.

1) Since the total productivity of labor is always positive, its *AP* curve must at all points lie above the labor axis.
2) As the quantity of labor used is progressively increased from zero upward, the average productivity of labor will first rise and then fall; therefore labor's *AP* curve must first rise, then reach a maximum, and finally fall.

Finally we note that labor's *MP* curve will intersect its *AP* curve from above at the point at which labor's *AP* curve reaches a maximum. To demonstrate this, let us select a point on labor's *AP* curve to the left of the point at which the *MP* curve crosses it. Let's say that one unit of labor is added to the production process. The resulting increase in output, which equals the marginal productivity of labor, will exceed labor's average productivity if labor's *MP* curve lies above its *AP* curve. But if this is the case (i.e., if the increase in output obtained from the last unit of labor added to the production process exceeds labor's average productivity), then increasing the input of labor will cause labor's average productivity to rise. Therefore if labor's *MP* curve lies above its *AP* curve, its *AP* curve must be rising. By an almost identical argument we can show that if labor's *MP* curve lies below its *AP* curve, then its *AP* curve must be falling. But if these two results hold, labor's *MP* curve must cross its *AP* curve when the latter attains a maximum.

PROBLEMS

1   Show that if the *MP* curve of an input lies below its *AP* curve, then its *AP* curve must be falling.

2   Given the following *TP* curves, construct the corresponding *AP* and *MP* curves.

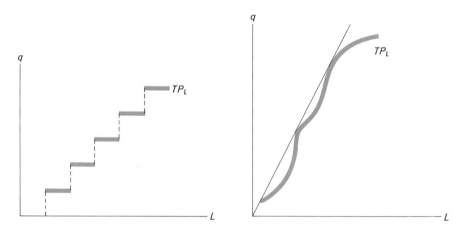

3   a) Consider a total productivity curve which slopes downward for large inputs. What does this imply about the *MP* curve? For this downward bending of the *TP* curve to occur, what shape must at least some of the isoquants assume?

    b) Economists sometimes assume "free disposal of inputs." That is, surplus inputs can always be stored out of the way without cost, if for some reason the firm does not want to use them. What restrictions would this assumption imply about the shapes of the isoquants and of the *TP* and *MP* curves?

CHAPTER 8

COST MINIMIZATION

To maximize its profits, any business firm must naturally begin by minimizing its costs of production. How shall the firm do this? Specifically:

What conditions must a firm fulfill in order to produce a specified level of output at minimum cost?

THE FIRM'S MINIMUM COST POSITION

To answer this question, let's again consider the Snapback Rubber Products Company, and let's suppose that this firm wants to produce the level of output $\bar{q}$. Starting from Snapback's production function, we can set up an isoquant which will portray all the alternative combinations of capital and labor that they might use to produce $\bar{q}$. Figure 8.1 shows this isoquant.

To analyze Snapback's problem of cost minimization, we must take into account not only its production possibilities but also the prices it must pay for its inputs. We'll talk about the way input prices are determined later on. For now, let's simply assume that Snapback is a *price taker* in input markets. This means that it cannot influence the level of input prices, and that it therefore regards the wage rate, w, and the cost of capital, r, as *given* or *fixed*.

Once we know the prices w and r that Snapback has to pay for inputs, we can set up a budget line that represents all the alternative input combinations that they could buy by spending a *fixed* number of dollars on inputs. Since, for simplicity, we are including only two inputs, labor and capital, in Snapback's production function, we can represent this budget line by the expression

$$\bar{c} = wL + rK,$$

in which $\bar{c}$ is a specified number of dollars spent on inputs. The expression $\bar{c} = wL + rK$ is known as an *isocost curve;* it is almost identical in concept and properties to the budget constraint, $y_c = p_1 q_1 + p_2 q_2$, that we set up when we analyzed the consumer's consumption decision.

Figure 8.1 shows a family of isocost curves for the Snapback Company. From these curves, we can determine the conditions that Snapback must fulfill in order to produce the output $\bar{q}$ at minimum cost. Obviously they must produce at some point along the isoquant, $q = \bar{q}$. To find their point of minimum cost, we need only determine which point along the isoquant $q = \bar{q}$ would involve the lowest total expenditure on the inputs K and L.

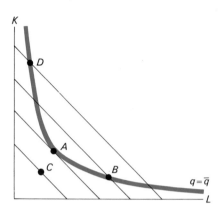

8|1

Snapback will minimize the cost of producing the output $\bar{q}$ by using the input combination indicated by the point A.

Suppose that Snapback were to choose the input combination D; this certainly would yield the required output. However, since higher isocost curves correspond to higher levels of total cost, Snapback could reduce costs without reducing output by moving to the point B, which lies on a lower isocost curve. Or better still by moving to the point A, which lies on a still-lower isocost curve. They could not, however, reduce costs still further by moving away from A because any combination of inputs indicated by a point such as C on a still-lower isocost curve would be insufficient to yield the required output, $\bar{q}$.

The point A represents not only Snapback's point of minimum cost, but also the point at which Snapback's isoquant is just tangent to an isocost curve. Therefore we can conclude that:

A firm will minimize the cost of producing a fixed level of output, $\bar{q}$, by moving to the point on the $\bar{q}$-isoquant where this curve is just tangent to an isocost curve.

Cost Minimization: An Example

Although this analysis of cost minimization is simple enough, it may appear somewhat abstract and theoretical to you. Therefore let's use this analysis to predict the way actual producers would behave under differing sets of circumstances, and then we shall see whether our prediction is borne out by experience.

Two companies are competitors: The Nuclear Orbit Corporation, of New York City, makes radioactive bedroom and terrace furniture which shines in the dark (they call their product Nucliture). The second firm, the Apex Fluorescent Fittings Corporation, of Dewey Rose, Georgia, also makes bedroom and terrace furniture which shines in the dark, although they achieve their shine by slightly less drastic means (they spray their furniture with luminous paint).

Both companies produce their furniture by combining two inputs, capital and labor. They don't, however, pay the same prices for these inputs. Nuclear Orbit is based in New York, and so it pays higher wages but lower rates of return to capital than Apex Fluorescent Fittings, down in Georgia. How does this affect the minimum cost positions of the two companies? Well, since they both combine capital and labor to produce output, they both have isocost curves of the form $\bar{c} = wL + rK$. Let's rewrite this equation as follows:

$$K = -(w/r)L + \bar{c}/r.$$

From this new expression we see that the slopes of the isocost curves of both firms must equal $-w/r$. But then, since Nuclear Orbit pays a higher w but a lower r than Apex, its isocost curves must be *steeper* than those of Apex. This contrast is illustrated in Fig. 8.2, where the line uu represents one of the isocost curves of the Nuclear Orbit Corporation (high w, low r), and the line jj represents one of the isocost curves of the Apex Fluorescent Fittings Corporation (low w, high r).

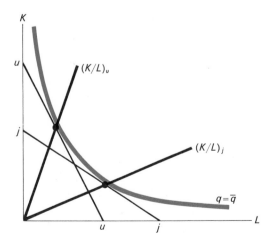

8|2

A firm that pays a high price for labor and a low price for capital will minimize costs by combining capital and labor in the proportion $(K/L)_u$, while a firm that pays a low price for labor and a high price for capital will minimize costs by combining capital and labor in the much lower proportion $(K/L)_j$.

Keeping this contrast in mind, let's next assume that both companies want to produce the output $\bar{q}$ (100 units of furniture that shines in the dark) at minimum cost. From Fig. 8.2 it follows that a manufacturer in the high-wage, low-capital-cost area (New York) will combine capital and labor in the proportion $(K/L)_u$, while a manufacturer in the low-wage, high-capital-cost area (Dewey Rose) will combine capital and labor in the much lower proportion, $(K/L)_j$. This observation suggests the following general prediction:

Whenever the ratio of wages to capital costs, w/r, is higher for one group of producers than for some other group of producers in the same industry, the producers faced with a high w/r will use a much higher proportion of capital to labor than the producers faced with a low w/r.

8|3

Each point labeled Japan represents the relationship between the relative factor costs Japanese producers must pay and the capital–labor ratio they use. The points labeled United States represent a similar relationship for U.S. producers. (Source: Arrow, Chenery, Minhas, and Solow, *ibid.*, page 241)

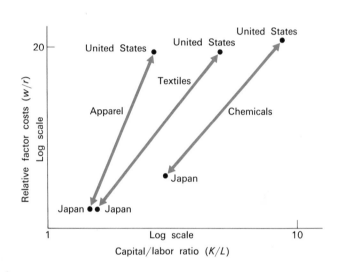

To test this prediction, let's compare the capital–labor ratios used by producers who operate in the same industry but who pay significantly different relative prices for capital and labor. Recall that in Chapter 7 we showed that Japanese producers use markedly lower capital–labor ratios than U.S. producers do. The same study from which this information was taken also contains data on the relative prices that U.S. and Japanese producers must pay for capital and labor. These figures (some of which are reproduced in Fig. 8.3) show that in every industry studied (w/r) was significantly lower for Japanese producers than for U.S. producers. Thus the fact that the Japanese use lower capital–labor ratios than U.S. manufacturers do bears out our prediction that producers will respond to low wages and high capital costs by combining a large amount of labor with relatively little capital, and conversely.

THE FIRM'S SHORT-RUN COST CURVES

As we have mentioned, the natural way to analyze the way a firm makes its economic choices is to analyze first the way it maximizes its profits during the current or short-run period and then the way it maximizes its profits over a period of time.

For our purposes here, we shall consider the short run to be a period long enough to permit the firm to produce an output but too short to permit the firm to change the size and character of its plant and equipment. Thus a firm's short-run economic choices are the following: (1) What combination of variable inputs should they employ? (2) What quantity of output should they produce? (3) What price should they charge for this output?

In Chapter 9 we shall analyze the way a firm makes these three choices. But first let us consider the following question:

How will the total costs incurred by the firm in the short run vary in response to changes in the level of its current output?

Fixed Versus Variable Costs

During any short-run period the total costs incurred by a firm will be of two sorts:

1) those associated with its *variable inputs,*
2) those associated with its *fixed inputs.*

The first are called variable costs, the latter fixed costs.

A firm's fixed costs include costs connected with the ownership of plant and equipment, some taxes such as local property taxes, payments made under long-term contracts, and the cost of management. The main fixed costs of the ownership of plant and equipment are (a) interest charges on invested capital and (b) depreciation. Recall that both of these cost items appeared on the income statement of the Tectronics Company in Table 6.6. The "taxes other than corporate-profits taxes" entry, which also appeared there, presumably represented mostly fixed costs. Contractual obligations that lead to fixed costs might include long-term leases of buildings and equipment (in some industries, such as the computer field, leasing equipment instead of buying it is standard practice) or long-term contracts to purchase raw materials. Thus the crucial characteristic of fixed costs is that *they do not vary in response to changes in the level of the firm's short-run output;* they will exist even if short-run output is reduced to zero.

A firm's variable costs in any short-run period equal the costs of all inputs whose use it can alter over the short run. The chief variable cost items on Tectronics' income statement in Table 6.6 were "goods and services purchased from other firms" and "payroll." A firm's variable costs (in contrast to its fixed costs) *depend directly on its level of output.* What happens if the firm's output drops to zero? Well, since the firm requires no variable inputs to produce a zero output, its total variable costs at zero output would be zero.

The Firm's Variable Cost Curve

If we assume as we did at the beginning of this chapter that all of a firm's inputs are variable, then the analysis of cost minimization presented there obviously applies to the firm's *long-run* cost problem. If, on the other hand, we assume that the firm's capital inputs (plant and equipment) are fixed, we can apply this same analysis to the firm's *short-run* cost problem (assuming, of course, that the firm uses more than one variable input).

By so doing, we can also determine the probable shape of a schedule that describes the way the variable costs (VC) of a cost-minimizing firm would change if it increased or decreased its short-run output. Such a schedule is called the firm's *variable cost curve,* and we can represent it by the expression

$$VC = c(q).$$

Let's derive a VC curve for the Nuclear Orbit Corporation, makers of the radioactive furniture called Nucliture. ("Prevent household accidents with Nucliture, the furniture you can see in the dark.") We shall now assume that Nuclear Orbit uses three inputs: labor (L), raw materials (R), and capital (K). The first two of these inputs are variable in the short run but the third is not. Thus we can express Nuclear Orbit's short-run production function by

$$q = h(L,R,\bar{K}),$$

in which the bar over the K indicates that it is *fixed.* Now we can derive its VC curve as follows: First we use the function $q = h(L,R,\bar{K})$ to draw up a set of isoquants like the ones in Fig. 8.4. Next we add a series of isocost curves; finally we locate the point at which each of the firm's isoquants is just tangent to an isocost curve. Since the Nuclear Orbit Corporation uses only two variable inputs (labor and raw materials), each of its isocost curves corresponds to a different level of total variable cost. Thus each point of tangency in Fig. 8.4 tells us the total variable costs that Nuclear Orbit would incur by producing a certain level of output during the short run. The collection of all such points (represented in Fig. 8.4 by the expansion path EE^*) contains all the information we need to plot Nuclear Orbit's variable cost curve.

---

* Note that the curved shape of *EE* indicates that cost minimization may require that variable inputs be combined in different proportions, depending on the scale of output.

What will be the shape and slope of this curve? The fact that "higher" isoquants will (as you should verify) be tangent to "higher" isocost curves indicates that Nuclear Orbit's *VC* curve must be an *increasing* function of its short-run output. This is a useful piece of information, but we'd like a more specific idea of the shape of the curve. Would an increase in Nuclear Orbit's short-run output induce a more-than-proportionate, less-than-proportionate, or exactly proportionate increase in its variable costs?

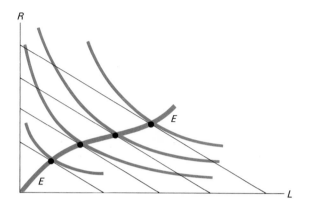

8|4

To construct a firm's *VC* curve, we must first determine the minimum amount it would cost the firm to produce each possible level of output. This is shown by the expansion path *EE*.

To illustrate the possibilities, let's work through a simple example. Suppose that Nuclear Orbit's reclining couches are not a very popular item. But then one day Jaycee Jones, the popular movie star, buys one. The item immediately becomes a hot seller, and Nuclear Orbit increases production from 10 to 100 units a month. In doing so Nuclear Orbit finds that they are able to increase the efficiency with which they organize production, and thus the marginal productivity of their variable inputs (labor and raw materials) rises. To the extent that this happens, increases in variable inputs yield *more than proportionate* increases in output, and so Nuclear Orbit's variable costs rise (initially at least) less rapidly than their output.

But suppose that Nuclear Orbit were to keep on increasing their scale of output (150 couches a month, perhaps even 200!). Then their variable inputs would have less and less of the fixed input capital to work with (Nuclear Orbit wouldn't have time to install a new assembly line during the short run), and the law of diminishing returns would eventually come into play. Once this happened, increases in Nuclear Orbit's variable inputs would yield *less than proportionate* increases in output, and as a result their variable costs would rise *more rapidly* than their output.

Our observations about Nuclear Orbit suggest that, if any firm increases its short-run output from zero upward, its variable costs first rise less rapidly and then more rapidly than its output. Therefore the firm's *VC* curve would resemble the curve in Fig. 8.5, which rises gradually in its initial stages but steeply in its later stages.

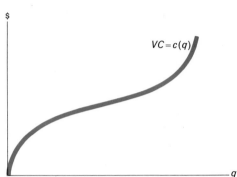

8|5

A firm's *VC* curve rises first gradually and then steeply.

The Firm's Total Cost Curve

Once we know the general shape of a firm's *VC* curve, we can easily sketch its total cost (*TC*) curve.

A firm's total cost (TC) curve describes the way its total costs vary in response to increases or decreases in its short-run output.

Recall that a firm's total short-run costs of production equal its variable costs plus its fixed costs. In symbols,

$$TC = FC + VC.$$

Since any firm's fixed costs are constant at all levels of output, we can repre-sent them by a *horizontal* curve like the line *FC* in Fig. 8.6. So if we sketch in a firm's *VC* curve "on top of" its *FC* curve, the resulting schedule will represent its *TC* curve.

A firm's TC curve will be identical in shape and slope to its VC curve, but "higher" in position.

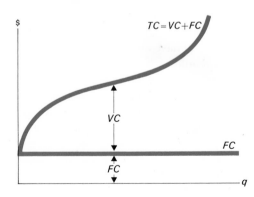

8|6

We can construct a firm's *TC* curve by "adding" its *FC* and *VC* curves

The Firm's Average and Marginal Cost Curves

So far, in talking about the relationship between a firm's costs and its output, we have focused on its *total* cost curves. In Chapter 9, however, we're going to look into the ways that a firm maximizes its short-run profits, and when we do so we shall find it convenient to work with its *marginal* and *average cost* curves.

A firm's marginal cost (MC) equals the change in its total costs that results from a small change in its total output.*

In symbols, we say that

$$MC = \Delta TC/\Delta q,$$

in which Δ stands for "change in." Obviously a firm's marginal cost must equal the slope of its TC curve, and since, as we already know, the slope of a firm's TC curve will first fall and then rise, the firm's MC curve must resemble in general shape the MC curve in Fig. 8.7.

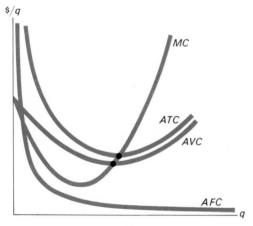

8|7

A firm's *MC, ATC, AVC,* and *AFC* curves. Note that the *MC* curve cuts the *ATC* and the *AVC* curves at their minimum points.

A firm's average total cost (ATC) equals its total cost divided by its total output.

In symbols we express this as

$$ATC = TC/q.$$

Since the firm's average total cost (like its marginal cost) depends on its total costs, the shapes of its ATC and MC curves naturally show a definite relationship. If the firm's MC curve falls and then rises as its output increases from zero upward, its ATC curve must also fall, reach a minimum, then rise.

---

* Note the similarity of the concept of marginal cost to that of marginal productivity, introduced in the preceding chapter.

Let's try this out on the Nuclear Orbit Corporation and its couches. Its ATC curve must be falling whenever the MC curve lies below it and rising whenever the MC curve lies above it. To show this, select a point on the firm's ATC curve to the left of the point at which the MC curve crosses it. Next suppose that Nuclear Orbit expands its output by one unit (one more couch per day). If Nuclear Orbit's MC curve lies below its ATC curve, the marginal cost of this additional couch will be less than the firm's average total cost per couch, and the assumed one-unit increase in output will cause Nuclear Orbit's average total cost per couch to fall. Therefore, whenever Nuclear Orbit's MC curve lies below its ATC curve, its ATC curve must be falling. By an almost identical argument you can show that, if its MC curve lies above its ATC curve, its ATC curve must be rising. This is the relationship shown in Fig. 8.7.

A firm's average fixed cost (AFC) equals its total fixed cost divided by its total output.

We can express this in another way as:

$$AFC = FC/q.$$

From the definition of average fixed costs, we know that the average fixed costs of any firm will fall continuously as its output increases. Therefore its AFC curve, like the one in Fig. 8.7, must fall continuously over its entire range.

A firm's average variable cost (AVC) is its total variable cost divided by its total output.

We can also express this in symbols:

$$AVC = VC/q.$$

Since any firm's average variable cost equals (as you should verify) the difference between its average total cost and its average fixed cost, its AVC curve at each level of output will lie below its ATC curve by an amount equal to its average fixed cost at that level of output. Also the firm's AVC curve must reach a minimum at the point at which the MC curve crosses it. These relationships are also shown in Fig. 8.7.

PROBLEMS

1   a) Find the minimum cost at which the firm described in Problem 1 of Chapter 7 can produce an output of 40,000 gizmos if the price of labor is $40 per week and the price of capital is $50 per thousand dollars' worth of capital.

b) At the same input prices, what is the maximum output that can be produced for a cost of $4,400?

2   Show graphically how a firm can find its minimum cost position by maximizing output for a given level of cost. Show that this approach gives the same result as the one discussed in the text, in which cost was minimized for a given output.

3   Using the same data as for Problem 1, fix capital at $50,000 and derive the total, average, and marginal cost curves for the firm.

4   Draw isoquant maps of 2-input production functions for which the following properties are true:

    a) The minimum cost position always involves equal amounts of both inputs, regardless of prices or quantity produced.

    b) The minimum cost position always has five units only of one of the inputs regardless of prices or quantity produced.

    c) The amount of one of the inputs used at the minimum cost position depends on the relative prices of the two inputs, but not on the quantity produced.

5   a) Prove that if an isoquant is concave to the origin, its point of tangency with an isocost curve will indicate a point of maximum cost relative to all other points along that isoquant.

    b) Show that cost minimization calls for a "corner solution" if isoquants are concave.

6   Describe the minimum cost position of a firm whose *isoquants* are all straight, downward-sloping, parallel lines. Interpret your result.

7   a) In the text we showed that a firm's VC curve first rises gradually and then steeply. Use this same argument to prove that the firm's MC curve will first fall and then rise.

    b) Prove that the MC curve intersects the AVC curve at the point at which the latter attains a minimum.

8   Discuss the classification of the following costs as variable or fixed. If they can be viewed either way, or if they do not fit either category, explain why.

    a) Cost of maintenance of plant and equipment

    b) Overtime wages to union workers

    c) Salaries to top-level management

    d) Depreciation allowances on equipment

    e) Cost of stationery for research department

    f) Cost of shipping product to customers

    g) Sales taxes on parts purchased from another firm

    h) Corporate-profits taxes

9   Describe the effects, if any, of the following changes on the production function, isocost curves, expansion path, and on the $TC, VC, AVC, ATC,$ and MC curves. Distinguish between shifts of and movements along the curves.

    a) An increase in the price of *one* variable input

    b) A proportionate increase in the prices of all variable inputs

    c) Discovery of a more efficient production technique

    d) A three-week production shutdown due to a strike

    e) A change to a cheaper means of plant maintenance

10   The data in Fig. 8.3 suggest that the difference between the relative costs paid by U.S. and Japanese manufacturers for various factors is roughly the same in the textile and apparel industries. However, the difference between the capital–labor ratios of manufacturers in the U.S. and in Japan is much more pronounced in the textile than in the apparel industry. What does this suggest about the nature of the production functions of manufacturers in the textile and apparel industries? Do you think that manufacturers in one of these industries have greater possibilities for substituting labor for capital than manufacturers in the other industry? If so, how would this show up in the shapes of the isoquants of manufacturers in the two industries? Illustrate with an appropriate diagram.

*11   When we analyzed the consumer, we distinguished two effects of a price change: the income effect and the substitution effect. Show whether analogous effects can be distinguished for a firm if we think of the firm (1) as maximizing output while keeping costs fixed, and (2) as minimizing cost with fixed output. Does your answer imply that the two approaches are truly equivalent? What is the significance of such income and substitution effects for a firm?

12   "If you measure the size of two plants in terms of the value of their plants and equipment, you will get a distorted comparison of plant sizes if the plants are in regions in which the relative prices of labor and capital differ." Comment.

---

* Starred problems are problems that are unusually difficult.

CHAPTER 9

PROFIT MAXIMIZATION
OVER THE SHORT RUN

During any period there exists a single combination of price and output that will maximize the firm's short-run profits. To identify this correct combination, we begin by deriving the firm's revenue curves; these summarize the relationship between the firm's revenue and the quantity of output it sells. Then we juxtapose these curves on the firm's cost curves. This will show us the firm's position of maximum profit.

DEMAND CURVES FOR THE FIRM'S OUTPUT

A definite relationship exists between the price a firm charges for its output and the quantity of output that buyers demand. This relationship is known as a *demand curve,* and it can be represented by

$$q = d(p)$$

in which q is the quantity of output demanded by buyers and p is the price the firm charges. Although the specific shape of a firm's demand curve depends on the nature of its product, in general we would expect this curve to slope downward, as the one in Fig. 9.1 does. This is so because consumers (as we have seen) almost always respond to a decrease in the price of a commodity by purchasing more of it.

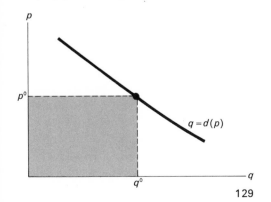

9|1

If a firm has a demand curve that slopes downward, sells the output q^0, and receives the price p^0, its total revenue will be the area of the shaded rectangle, p^0q^0.

The Firm's Revenue Concepts

A firm's demand curve gives us a basis from which to derive its revenue curves. Before we do so, however, we must introduce three different concepts of revenue.

1) *A firm's total revenue (TR) equals the total receipts it gets from the sale of output.*

We can represent this by the expression

$$TR = pq,$$

in which p is the price charged and q is the output sold.

2) *A firm's average revenue (AR) equals its total revenue divided by the number of units of output sold.*

We can represent this by the expression

$$AR = TR/q = p.$$

3) *A firm's marginal revenue (MR) equals the change in total revenue that results from a small increase or decrease in output sold.*

We can represent this by the expression

$$MR = \Delta TR/\Delta q,$$

in which Δ denotes "change in."

The Firm's Average Revenue Curve

A firm's average revenue (AR) curve *summarizes the relationship between average revenue (i.e., price) and quantity sold.* Since the demand curve for the firm's output represents the same relationship, these two curves must be identical. Therefore a firm with a downward-sloping demand curve like that in Fig. 9.1 will have an AR curve that slopes downward in an identical fashion.

The Firm's Total Revenue Curve

From a firm's demand curve, we can determine the *total revenue* it will obtain by selling any level of output. Suppose that a firm has the demand curve shown in Fig. 9.1 and that it sells the quantity of output q^0. Then the price it will obtain is p^0, and its total revenue equals p^0q^0, the area of the shaded rectangle.

The Stable Table Company makes tables with legs that can be adjusted individually to compensate for irregularities in the floor. It's a new company, and the management is jittery. They call in an economist for consultation. "How will our total revenue vary if we change the number of tables we sell?" they ask him. The economist estimates demand for their tables and finds that it slopes downward as the demand (AR) curve in Fig. 9.2 does. Then he pulls out pad and pencil and draws up total-revenue rectangles for different price–output combinations that fall along this demand curve. These rectangles show (check and see) that if Stable Table were to sell very large or very small numbers of tables (i.e., if they were to charge very small or very large prices for their tables), their total revenue would approach zero. Therefore their TR curve—*which summarizes the relationship between total revenue and quantity sold*—must, like the curve in Fig. 9.2, begin at the origin, rise to a maximum as quantity sold increases, and then fall back to zero. Also (as you can easily verify) Stable Table's TR curve must reach zero (i.e., intersect the quantity axis) at the same point at which its AR curve intersects this axis; in Fig. 9.2 this point is q''.

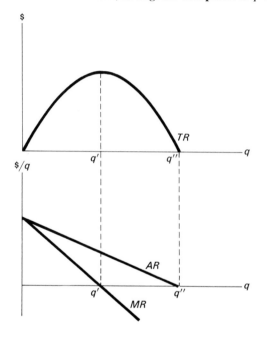

9|2

The demand (AR) curve for a firm's output and the TR and MR curves derived from it.

The conclusion that Stable Table's TR curve will rise from zero and then fall back to zero as the number of tables sold increases (and the price charged decreases) is just what we expect, because we know that Stable Table's total revenue from the sale of tables must equal the total expenditure made by the consumers for this product, and in Chapter 4, when we were talking about elasticity, we showed that the total expenditures consumers make on any product approach zero if the price charged for this product is raised to very high levels or reduced to very low levels.*

---

* This assumes, of course, that consumers have straight-line demand curves that slope downward, as the AR curve in Fig. 9.2 does.

The Firm's Marginal Revenue Curve

If the demand curve for Stable tables slopes downward, then the *marginal revenue* they will obtain by selling one additional table will always be less than the average revenue or price they get for this table. This is so because a *downward-sloping* demand curve implies that if a firm is to sell one more unit of output, it must decrease its price per unit; and, if it charges the same price to all buyers, it must lower the price not only on the last unit sold, but on all units sold. Therefore:

The marginal revenue a firm derives from the last unit sold equals the average revenue (price) it obtains for that unit minus the loss in total revenue which it incurs due to the decrease in the price at which it sells all other units.

Marginal revenue is thus the sum of two components, one *positive* and the other *negative*. The greater the quantity sold, the smaller the positive component and the larger the negative component. Therefore as quantity sold increases, marginal revenue falls, and it must fall more rapidly than average revenue falls.

With these ideas in mind, we can add to Fig. 9.2 the *MR curve* which corresponds to the *AR* curve shown there. Marginal and average revenue are identical for the first unit sold, but thereafter the *MR* curve falls more rapidly than the *AR* curve.

From the definition of marginal revenue (as $\Delta TR/\Delta q$), we know that a firm's marginal revenue equals the slope of its *TR* curve. Thus marginal revenue must be positive at all outputs at which total revenue is rising, and negative at all output levels at which total revenue is falling. And it must equal zero at the output level at which total revenue reaches a maximum. In other words, when the addition to total revenue that Stable Table earns by selling one more table equals zero, their total revenue will stop growing. This final relationship is indicated in Fig. 9.2 by the fact that the *TR* curve reaches a maximum at the same output, q', at which the *MR* curve reaches zero.

Elasticity and the Relationship Between the Firm's Revenue Curves

Consumers' total expenditures on any product equal the seller's total revenue. Our earlier discussion of elasticity suggests that, if elasticity of demand for a firm's output is greater than 1, the firm can increase its total revenue by decreasing its price per unit. But if elasticity of demand for a firm's output is less than 1, a decrease in its price will reduce its total revenue.

Thus, over the range of output for which demand for a firm's output is elastic, the firm's marginal revenue is positive and its *TR* curve *rises*. Similarly, over the range of output for which the firm's demand curve is inelastic, its marginal revenue is negative, and its *TR* curve *declines*. Applying these observations to Stable Table's revenue curves, pictured in Fig. 9.2, we conclude that the AR curve shown there must be *elastic* at all points to the left of q', *inelastic* at all points to the right of q', and that its elasticity must equal 1 at the point q'.

LOCATING THE FIRM'S MAXIMUM PROFIT POSITION

We said at the beginning of this chapter that by juxtaposing a firm's cost and revenue curves, we could determine the price–output combination that the firm should select in order to maximize its short-run profits. We're still going to do this. But first let's try to solve this problem in an alternative and more intuitive fashion.

The president of the Stable Table Company, Maximum ("Max") Smith, asks how it would affect their profits if they upped their output by one table per day. His economic consultant says that the net effect on the firm's profits of a one-unit increase in output will equal the difference between the marginal revenue and the marginal cost associated with this unit. If this difference is positive, the increase in output will *raise* the firm's profits; if it is negative, the increase in output will *lower* the firm's profits. Max Smith does some figuring and finds that a one-table increase would increase Stable Table's profits. So he telephones the workshop to make this increase. The minute he hangs up the telephone, however, he begins to worry again. "Should we increase our output by still another unit?" he asks.

"Of course," the consultant answers, "*if* you can show that the marginal revenue associated with this unit exceeds its marginal cost. In fact, you should keep on making successive small increases in output, so long as there is a positive difference between your marginal revenue and your marginal cost. If the difference is negative, however, you should decrease total output."

Max Smith looks at the consultant gratefully. "Could you put that in writing," he asks, "so I can keep it on my desk?"

"Certainly," the consultant says. "In fact, I'll put it in the form of two general rules."

1) Whenever marginal revenue *exceeds* marginal cost, in order to maximize its profits a firm should *expand* output, and continue to do so until the positive differential between marginal revenue and marginal cost disappears.

2) Whenever marginal revenue is *less than* marginal cost, in order to maximize its profits a firm should *decrease* output, and continue to do so until the negative differential between marginal revenue and marginal cost disappears.

From these two rules, it follows that *any firm, in order to maximize its profits and thus attain equilibrium, should produce the output level that precisely equates its marginal revenue with its marginal cost.* Thus the Stable Table Company, whose cost and revenue curves are illustrated in Fig. 9.3, will maximize its profits by producing the output q^0 and charging the price p^0, since this combination of price and output will make its marginal revenue just equal to its marginal cost.

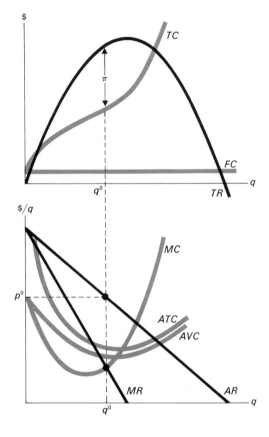

9|3

Two views of the maximum-profit position of a firm with a downward-sloping demand curve for its output.

a) The firm maximizes its profits at q^0, where the vertical distance between its *TR* and *TC* curves is greatest.

b) The firm maximizes its profits at q^0, where its *MR* and *MC* curves cross.

You can reach the same conclusion by examining the curves for Stable Table's total cost and total revenue, as shown in part (a) of Fig. 9.3. At any level of output the vertical distance between the firm's *TR* and *TC* curves represents the total profits (π) that Stable Table would earn by producing and selling this level of output. Their profits will be *positive* at any output level at which their *TR* curve lies *above* their *TC* curve and *negative* at any output level at which their *TR* curve lies *below* their *TC* curve.

So naturally Stable Table will be able to maximize their profits if they produce the output level at which the vertical distance between their *TR* and *TC* curves is greatest. "How can we characterize this maximum-profit point?" asks Max Smith. (Profits are the only thing he thinks about.)

His consultant suggests (and you should verify) that if any firm operates at a point where its TR curve is *less steep* than its TC curve, it can increase profits by *decreasing* output. Similarly, if it operates at a point where its TR curve is *steeper* than its TC curve, it can increase profits by *increasing* output. Therefore the Stable Table Company's maximum-profit position must be located at the point where the slope of their TR curve just equals the slope of their TC curve.

However, the slopes of any firm's TR and TC curves equal its marginal revenue and marginal cost, respectively. Therefore the conclusion we've just reached is equivalent to saying that Stable Table will maximize profits by producing the output that equates marginal revenue with marginal cost. This, however, is the same conclusion that we reached using the intuitive argument presented above.

The fact that a firm maximizes profits by equating marginal revenue with marginal cost suggests that only a firm's *variable* costs (as opposed to its fixed costs) will influence its short-run price–output decision. This is an important result and you should verify it by investigating, with the aid of a diagram, the effect on the firm's maximum-profit position of halving or doubling its fixed costs.

PROFIT MAXIMIZATION WITH A HORIZONTAL DEMAND CURVE

An auto manufacturer, in order to maximize his profits, has to make a conscious decision about the price he will charge for his output. A wheat farmer does not. The auto manufacturer is a *price setter*. The wheat farmer is not. There is a going market price for his product; he can sell nothing above this price, but as much as he wants to at this price. Thus he is invariably a *price taker*, because he has to take whatever price he can get. And wheat farmers aren't the only price takers in the economy. Most sellers of agricultural commodities, from soybeans to hogs, are price takers. So too are producers in a number of other industries.

All producers who are price takers (i.e., who are confronted with a going market price for their output) operate in markets that are described as *perfectly competitive*. How is the price they receive for their output determined? This is an important question, and we shall consider it carefully in Chapter 13. For the moment, let's just investigate the way a price-taking firm goes about maximizing its profits.

A good example of a price-taking firm is the Turngrass turnip farm. This firm is confronted with a going market price for its product. Therefore the demand for turnips can be represented by a horizontal demand curve like that in Fig. 9.4. (Yes, it's called a curve even though it's a straight line.) This curve indicates that, at the price p^0 or at any price below p^0, Turngrass can sell unlimited quantities of turnips. If they charge a price above p^0, however, their sales will drop to *zero*.

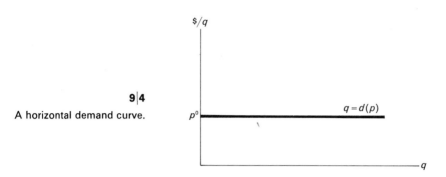

9|4

A horizontal demand curve.

The cost and revenue curves of a firm such as Turngrass, which faces a horizontal demand curve, are shown in Fig. 9.5. Although the cost curves of this firm do not differ from those in Fig. 9.3, the revenue curves do (compare the two). Note especially that, since the demand curve of Turngrass is horizontal, the quantity of turnips they sell will have no effect on the price they can get for them, and their *AR* curve will therefore be a horizontal line. Also their marginal revenue will obviously equal their average revenue at all levels of output, so their *MR* and *AR* curves will be identical. And their *TR* curve will be a straight line, too, like that in Fig. 9.5.

A firm with a horizontal demand curve, like a firm with a downward-sloping demand curve, will maximize its profits by producing the output that makes its marginal revenue just equal to its marginal cost.

Thus Turngrass, whose cost and revenue curves are shown in Fig. 9.5, can attain maximum profits by producing the quantity q^0 of turnips, and selling them at the price p^0.

"Not so fast," you may say. "Part (b) of Fig. 9.5 shows that Turngrass' *MC* curve intersects its *MR* curve not only at q^0, but also at the much smaller output q'. How can we be sure that q^0 and not q' is Turngrass' profit-maximizing output?" Answer: look at part (a) of Fig. 9.5. There you will see that q' corresponds to a position of *negative* profits, while q^0 corresponds to a position of maximum *positive* profits. Thus we were right in saying that q^0 corresponds to Turngrass' position of maximum profit.

However, you were right in suggesting that our rule that a profit-maximizing firm should equate marginal revenue with marginal cost is ambiguous in the present case. How shall we clear up this ambiguity? Figure 9.5 suggests that, whenever a firm's *MC* curve intersects its *MR* curve in more than one place (note that this didn't happen in Fig. 9.3, but it could have), a proper and unambiguous rule for a profit-maximizing firm to follow is that it should move to the point at which its *MC* curve cuts its *MR* curve *from below*.

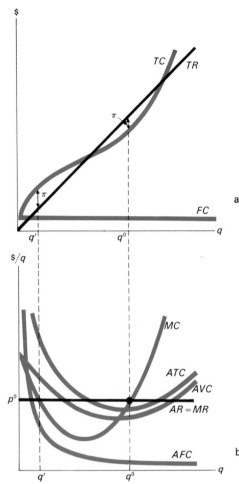

9|5

Two views of the maximum-profit position of a firm with a horizontal demand curve for its output.

a) The firm attains maximum profits at q^0, where the vertical distance between its TR and TC curves is greatest.

b) The firm attains maximum profits at q^0, where its MR and MC curves cross.

The Supply Curve of a Firm with a Horizontal Demand Curve

We can see from part (b) of Fig. 9.5 that a firm such as Turngrass, with a horizontal demand curve, will always sell its output at the price indicated by the intersection of their demand curve with the price axis. In other words, such a firm will (as we have mentioned) take the price as *given*. Therefore:

There is a unique relationship between the price at which a firm with a horizontal demand curve can sell its output and the quantity of output it will offer or supply.

This relationship is called a *supply curve,* and it is identical in concept to the consumer's supply curve of labor.

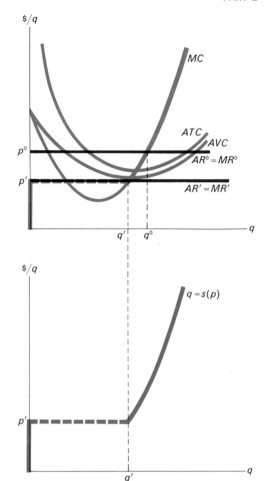

9|6

The supply curve of a firm with a horizontal demand curve. Note that for prices greater than minimum average variable cost, the firm's *MC* curve becomes its supply curve.

To illustrate how to derive the supply curve of a firm which has a horizontal demand curve, let's obtain Turngrass' supply curve for turnips. Their cost curves are shown in Fig. 9.6(a). Suppose that the demand (or AR) curve facing Turngrass is shifted upward and downward, but always remains parallel to the quantity axis, q. Then at each position of the AR curve (i.e., at each price Turngrass might get for turnips), this firm will supply the quantity of turnips indicated by the intersection of their AR ($= MR$) and MC curves. Thus, for example, if Turngrass gets the price p^0, they will supply the output q^0. But suppose that the bottom were to fall out of the turnip market, and the price Turngrass could get for turnips were to fall below their minimum average variable cost (i.e., below p'). Then Turngrass would be unable to cover even their variable costs. And to minimize their losses, they would cease production altogether. Of course this wouldn't reduce Turngrass' losses to zero, but it would reduce them to $-FC$, which is less than they would be if Turngrass kept on growing turnips.

Thus the short-run supply curve of Turngrass would assume the general shape of the supply curve, $q = s(p)$, shown in Fig. 9.6(b). This supply curve indicates that, whenever price falls below its minimum average variable cost, a firm will supply nothing. At prices higher than its minimum average variable cost, a firm will supply the quantity of output indicated by the intersection of its MR and MC curves. Thus for prices greater than p', a firm's MC curve becomes its supply curve. The dashed part of the supply curve indicates that the curve is discontinuous over this range of output, since at no price will the firm supply any quantity of output greater than zero but less than q'.

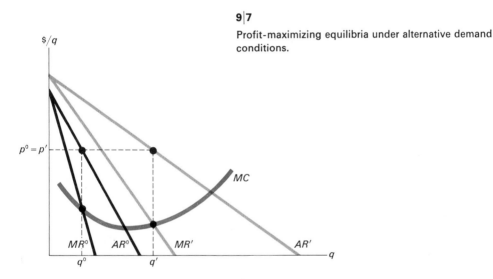

9|7

Profit-maximizing equilibria under alternative demand conditions.

No Supply Curve for a Firm with a Downward-Sloping Demand Curve

You may wonder why we failed to construct a supply curve for a firm with a *downward-sloping* demand curve for its output. The answer is simple: Such a firm has no supply curve as we've defined the term.

Figure 9.7 shows why. Here we see two pairs of AR and MR curves that might confront our old friend the Stable Table Company, plus their MC curve as well. Note that either set of revenue curves would lead Stable Table to charge the same price for its output, but the number of tables they would offer for sale in the two situations would differ. Figure 9.7 thus proves that, for a firm with a downward-sloping demand curve, the relationship between price charged and quantity supplied is *not* unique. But if not, then such a firm cannot have a supply curve.

PROFIT MAXIMIZATION AS A ONE-STEP PROCEDURE

In this chapter we have been talking about the firm's search for a position of maximum profit as a *two-step* procedure, in which the firm first calculates the minimum costs at which it can produce alternative levels of output and then selects the price–output combination that will maximize its short-run profits. But we can also treat this search as a *one-step* procedure, in which the firm locates its position of maximum profit by answering the following question:

Given its production function, the input prices it must pay, and the demand that exists for its output, how much of each variable input should the firm hire in order to attain maximum profits?

Let's work through a simple example. Consider a firm that produces output by combining *fixed* capital inputs with a single *variable* input, labor. The name of this firm is Renta Santa, Incorporated. They rent out Santa Clauses to department stores, children's parties, and community tree-lighting festivals. Renta Santa has its own modern brick building and owns several hundred Santa Claus suits, made of very durable materials, in all sizes; that is their fixed capital input. (For purposes of this example, we'll ignore such factors as maintenance on the building and repair of the suits.) Each year, about Labor Day, they hire 200 barrel-shaped men; that is their variable input, labor. Now, what effect would hiring one more Santa Claus have on Renta Santa's profits? Well, naturally a one-unit increase in labor inputs will raise Renta Santa's total costs by an amount equal to the cost of this unit of labor. Simultaneously, however, it will also change Renta Santa's total revenue by an amount equal to the marginal productivity of labor *times* the firm's marginal revenue. We can express this change in total revenue, which is referred to as labor's *marginal revenue product (MRP)* as

$$MRP_L = MR \cdot MP_L.$$

Thus a one-unit increase (one more Santa Claus) in the firm's labor input will alter its current profit by an amount equal to the difference between the cost of this Santa Claus and the marginal revenue product he yields.

Therefore whenever Renta Santa is producing Santa Clauses at a point at which the marginal revenue product of labor *exceeds* the price of labor, it should *increase* the number of men it employs. As it does this, however, eventually the marginal revenue product of labor will *fall* for one (or both) of two reasons.

1) If a firm uses any fixed inputs, diminishing returns will eventually set in, and thereafter any further increase in labor inputs will lower labor's marginal productivity.

2) If demand for a firm's output slopes downward, then the increase in output yielded by an additional unit of labor will lower the firm's marginal revenue.

Eventually, as Renta Santa employs increasing quantities of labor to produce current output (Santa Clauses), it will reach a point at which the marginal revenue product of the last Santa Claus it adds just equals the cost of this Santa Claus. If Renta Santa then adds still another Santa Claus, the marginal revenue product of this last unit of labor will be less than its cost; and the firm's profit will fall. Therefore:

*To maximize its profits, the firm should employ the quantity of labor that will make the marginal revenue product of labor just equal to the cost of labor.**

You probably think that it is oversimplification to talk about a company that uses only one variable input, labor, and in a way it is. All right then, let's talk about a firm that uses more than one variable input. Suppose that Renta Santa decides that they can improve their image if they have their Santa Clauses hand out giant lollipops to each child. This means that Renta Santa has to buy carloads and carloads of lollipops, which become raw materials (R). Then to maximize profits, Renta Santa should move to a point at which the marginal revenue product of each variable input just equals the price of this input. Thus Renta Santa, whose production function can be expressed by $q = h(L,R,\overline{K})$, can maximize its short-run profit by hiring the inputs L and R up to the point at which the marginal revenue product of each of these inputs just equals its price. Given that w is the price of input L and v is the price of input R, this means that Renta Santa will maximize its short-run profits by moving to the point at which

$$MRP_L = w \qquad \text{and} \qquad MRP_R = v.$$

At first glance you might think that these conditions identify only the quantities of inputs that Renta Santa should use. However, since the quantities of input that any firm employs determine the level of its output, and the level of its output in turn determines the price it can charge for its output, these conditions in fact determine the price–output combination that will maximize Renta Santa's short-run profits.

The one- and two-step procedures for profit maximization that we have described are alternative but equivalent ways of viewing the same process. Therefore the two sets of conditions which they yield are equivalent in the sense that, if one set holds, the other will necessarily also hold.

---

* If the marginal productivity of labor initially increases, its marginal revenue product may also increase initially, and there may be two points at which this condition is satisfied. In that case, the firm should choose the point at which MRP_L is declining.

THE FIRM'S INPUT DEMAND CURVES

Our discussion of profit maximization as being just a one-step procedure suggests two questions: Can we construct a demand schedule that will summarize the relationship between the price of a particular input and the quantity of this input demanded by the firm? If so, what slope will this input demand curve have?

Again we need, for our purposes, a firm that uses a single variable input, labor. So let's think back to the early days of Renta Santa, Inc., before they got so big and started handing out lollipops.

With every quantity of labor that Renta Santa might use, there is associated a specific level, not only of labor's marginal productivity, but also of total output and thus of marginal revenue. Therefore we can construct a marginal revenue product (MRP) curve that represents the relationship between the amount of labor employed by Renta Santa and labor's marginal revenue product. Since any profit-maximizing firm will always hire labor up to the point at which labor's marginal revenue product just equals the price of labor, Renta Santa's *demand curve for labor must correspond to labor's MRP curve.* Also, since the marginal revenue product of any input will eventually decrease whenever the quantity of that input is increased, the marginal revenue product curve of labor must eventually slope downward. But if so, then the demand curve of Renta Santa (and of any other profit-maximizing firm) for the input labor must also be a downward-sloping curve, like the one in Fig. 9.8.*

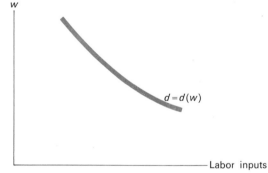

9|8
The firm's demand for labor inputs is a downward-sloping function of the wage rate, *w*.

Our conclusion that the firm's demand curve for labor will slope downward applies, strictly speaking, only to a firm that uses a single variable input. However, by an argument similar to (but somewhat more complex than) the one we have just presented, we could show that *if a firm uses many variable inputs its demand curves for all these inputs will slope downward.* This conclusion, as we shall see in Chapter 15, plays a key role in the analysis of price determination in input markets.

---

* See Problem 13 at the end of this chapter.

The Elasticity of the Firm's Input Demand Curves

How elastic or inelastic will a firm's input demand curves be? This question has a lot of sides, so let's look at a concrete example. Recall that at the beginning of Chapter 7 we introduced the Celery Improvement Company, makers of celery chips for dieters: Celchips.

(1) Now Celchips is a new product, and it might just develop a devoted band of snack eaters who think that there is absolutely *no* substitute for Celchips. In that case, demand for Celchips would become very inelastic (i.e., the Celery Improvement Company would sell about the same amount of chips no matter what price they charged for them). Suppose this were to happen. Then if the price of labor, of celery, or of salt substitute should rise, Celery Improvement's costs would rise and so too would the equilibrium price of Celchips. The quantity of Celchips produced and sold, however, would not change much; nor would the quantities of inputs used in the production of these chips. So we see that *the more inelastic demand for a firm's output is, the more inelastic its input demand curves will be.**

(2) Currently the Celery Improvement Company spends only about 1¢ out of every cost dollar on salt substitute. So even a big rise in the price of salt substitute, say a 10% hike, would not have much effect on their total costs (in fact it wouldn't raise their total costs by more than .01%). This means that changes in the price of salt substitute won't noticeably alter either the equilibrium output of Celchips or the quantity of salt substitute used in making them. Thus, regardless of whether demand for Celchips is elastic or inelastic, we can be sure that the Celery Improvement Company's demand curve for salt substitute will be inelastic. We can also be sure that *any firm's demand for a given input will be more inelastic the smaller the proportion of total costs it represents.*

(3) In contrast to salt substitute, celery represents an important part of the Celery Improvement Company's total costs. So we might be tempted to reason that this firm's demand for celery would be elastic. But there is one important factor working to make it inelastic: the fact that Celery Improvement has yet to find a vegetable they can use in place of celery. Celery Improvement is, however, constantly trying to find a way to substitute bleached carrots for celery without changing the taste and texture of their chips. If they succeed, they will of course be able to respond to a rise in the price of celery by substituting carrots for celery, and as a result their demand for celery will become a lot more elastic. Thus we see that *a firm's demand for any one input will be more elastic the greater the possibilities of substituting other inputs for it.*

---

* Check this result by investigating (1) what an inelastic demand curve for the firm's output implies about the shape of the firm's *MR* curve and (2) what this in turn implies about the shape of the firm's input demand schedules.

(4) Suppose Celery Improvement hits on a way to substitute bleached carrots for celery. By how much will this discovery increase the elasticity of their demand for celery? The answer depends on how elastic the supply of carrots is. If a small increase in demand shoots up the price of carrots, then Celery Improvement won't find it profitable to substitute carrots for celery on a very big scale, and being able to do so won't increase the elasticity of their demand for celery very much. On the other hand, of course, if the supply of carrots is very elastic, just the opposite will occur. So we conclude that *a firm's demand for any input will be less elastic the less elastic the supply of substitute inputs.*

*A TEST OF THE PROFIT-MAXIMIZATION HYPOTHESIS

In discussing what determines a firm's demand for labor, we concluded that a profit-maximizing firm will hire labor up to the point at which labor's marginal revenue product just equals the cost of labor. Do actual firms really do this?

Liu and Hildebrand attempted to answer this question by comparing, for 20 different industries, the estimated marginal revenue product of labor with the cost of labor. In each case, the marginal revenue product of labor was significantly *less than* the cost of labor. For example, they found that, in the rubber-products and leather-products industries, a dollar's worth of labor yielded only 95 cents' worth of marginal revenue product, while in the paper-products and fabricated-metals industries, a dollar's worth of labor yielded only 90 cents' worth of marginal revenue product.

At first glance these results might appear to disprove our fundamental assumption that firms are profit maximizers. As Liu and Hildebrand have pointed out, however, the constant development of new laborsaving technology, the existence of unions, and the danger of labor unrest all constitute valid reasons why real-life profit-maximizing firms may, during a given period, choose to employ "too much" labor.

Presumably a firm that is forced by circumstances to employ "too much" labor temporarily will try over a period of time to adjust its labor inputs to a level consistent with profit maximization. Presumably the more excessive the firm's labor force, the larger the adjustment it would try to make.

One way to test whether or not firms do in fact seek to adjust their labor inputs so that labor's marginal revenue product equals the cost of labor is to compare the *need* of these firms for adjustment with the *size* of the adjustments they actually make. To do this Liu and Hildebrand estimated the amount by which the labor force in each of the industries exceeded the labor force that the industry, if it wanted to maximize profits, should have em-

---

* The reader may skip this example without loss of continuity.

ployed. Using these figures and estimated feasible rates of adjustment, Liu and Hildebrand ranked all the industries according to the size of the adjustment in employment which they (if they wanted to make the greatest profit) should have made over the four-year period 1956–60.

Finally Liu and Hildebrand ranked these same industries again, this time according to the size of the adjustments in employment that they actually did make over this four-year period.*

TABLE 9|1

Required Versus Actual Changes in Employment, by Industry, 1956–60*

Industry	Percentage change in employment required to equate labor's *MRP* with the cost of labor (1956)	Ranking of industries according to size of required feasible adjustment in employment (1956–60)	Ranking of industries according to size of actual adjustment in employment (1956–60)
Apparel	− 20.4	1	1
Fabricated metals	− 17.7	2	4
Food products	− 23.2	3	2
Machinery	− 17.2	4	7
Electrical machinery	− 16.3	5	3
Rubber products	− 9.7	6	5
Paper products	− 16.5	7	6
Leather products	− 13.7	8	8

* Source: Liu and Hildebrand, *ibid.*, pages 117–118.

As indicated by the data in Table 9.1, which show the results for eight selected industries, the two rankings display a pronounced similarity. In fact this similarity is so strong that the chance that it would have occurred if the two rankings were independent is only 1 in 100. Thus these results suggest that firms in a wide range of industries do in fact try over a period of time to adjust their labor force to a level that will maximize their profits.

PROBLEMS

1   a) Draw a graph showing the total revenue curve for a firm with a downward-sloping, straight-line demand curve.

b) What would a demand curve have to look like in order for the TR curve to be a horizontal straight line? What is the TR curve for a firm with a horizontal demand curve?

---

* Doing so obviously called for adjusting total observed changes in employment for changes in employment attributable to changes in output over the period.

2   Show that the following assertion is true: "Over any range of output, the firm's profits will be positive if its AR curve lies above its ATC curve and negative if its AR curve lies below its ATC curve. Moreover, at any point at which these curves cross, the firm's profits will equal zero."

3   a) Show that the firm's profit is at a maximum when the slopes of the TR and TC curves are equal.

   b) Determine graphically the effects on profit earned, price charged, and quantity produced of first halving, then doubling, the fixed costs of a firm. Include the possibility of shutting down production.

4   Refer to the firm described in Problem 1 of Chapter 7. Let the price of labor be $50 and the price of capital be $100 per thousand dollars' worth of capital. Determine the profit-maximizing level of output and price, given the following demand curves for gizmos. Assume that labor and capital are the only inputs necessary, and that gizmos must be sold in batches of 10,000.

   a) A horizontal demand curve at a price of 30¢ per gizmo.

   b) A downward-sloping, straight-line demand curve intersecting the price axis at 60¢ per gizmo and the quantity axis at 180,000 gizmos.

   c) A downward-sloping, straight-line demand curve intersecting the price axis at 65¢ per gizmo and the quantity axis at 130,000 gizmos.

5   For the firm in Problem 4, hold the amount of capital constant at $50,000, and derive the firm's demand curve for labor under the three gizmo-demand conditions listed above.

6   Consider a firm with a downward-sloping demand curve and discuss the effects, if any, which the changes listed in Problem 9 of Chapter 8 would have on a firm's profit-maximizing price and output.

7   Starting with a firm whose cost and revenue curves are those shown in Fig. 9.6(a), describe the effects, if any, on those curves, the supply curve, the quantity supplied, and the price charged which would be caused by the following changes

   a) A uniform downward shift of the demand curve by 10%.

   b) An increase in the fixed costs of the firm.

   c) An increase by $5 in the variable cost of each unit produced.

   d) A shift in the demand curve so that it becomes downward-sloping.

   e) Introduction of an absolute capacity limitation on output, slightly to the right of the initial equilibrium output.

*8   a) Show that the one-step condition for profit maximization implies that the firm will operate at a point of tangency between one of its isocost curves and one of its isoquants. When you do so, use a result proved in the appendix: that the slope of an isoquant will at any point equal (-1) times the ratio of the marginal productivities of the firm's variable inputs at that point.

   b) Show that the one-step condition for profit maximization also implies the equality of MR and MC.

---

* Starred problems are problems that are unusually difficult.

9   Consider a firm whose production function gives rise to concave isoquants between two of its variable inputs. Discuss what effect, if any, such concave isoquants might have on our analysis of profit maximization.

10   Suppose that the government decided to levy a lump-sum tax on a firm. What is the maximum such tax that the firm would be willing to pay without shutting down production in the short run?

11   Illustrate graphically the effect of a tax of a fixed number of dollars *per unit of output* on the operations of a firm.

12   Suppose that the government were to impose a price ceiling on the product produced by a firm which has a downward-sloping demand curve, and that this ceiling were set at exactly the intersection of the demand curve with the firm's marginal cost curve. Show that this price ceiling will have the effect of raising the firm's output over what it would have been otherwise.

*13   In the text we introduced the concept of labor's marginal revenue product, *MRP*. We can also introduce a companion concept, labor's average revenue product (*ARP*). Labor's average revenue product equals its average productivity times average revenue, or, in symbols,

$$ARP_L = AP_L \cdot AR.$$

Consider a firm which uses a single variable input, labor, and which has a horizontal demand curve; that is, a firm for which $AR = MR = P$. (a) Show that, if labor's *MRP* and *ARP* curves are plotted together, its *MRP* curve must cut its *ARP* curve from above. [*Hint:* Look back at Fig. 7.6(b).] (b) Will this firm's demand curve for labor correspond to all of the downward-sloping portion of labor's *MRP* curve, or just to the portion of this curve that lies below the point at which it intersects labor's *ARP* curve? [*Hint:* Under what conditions will a firm choose to shut down in the short run?]

*Appendix to Chapter 9

PROFIT MAXIMIZATION
IN THE SHORT RUN: A MATHEMATICAL SOLUTION

We have solved the firm's problem of short-run profit maximization with the aid of diagrams, but we can do the same thing in terms of simple mathematics. This alternative method should increase your understanding of the results obtained in the chapter you have just read, and also permit us to prove several assertions we made there.

COST MINIMIZATION IN THE SHORT RUN

During any given period, a business firm has a problem of cost minimization; we can handle this as a problem of constrained minimization. Suppose that the firm's production function is given by

$$q = h(L,R,\overline{K}), \qquad (9\text{–}1)$$

in which L and R are variable inputs and $\overline{K}$ represents all inputs held constant during the current period. Then the total costs, c, incurred by the firm are given by the expression

$$c = wL + vR + \bar{r}, \qquad (9\text{–}2)$$

in which w and v are the prices of the inputs L and R, respectively, and $\bar{r}$ equals the costs associated with the firm's fixed inputs, $\overline{K}$. To minimize the cost of producing any specified output, $\bar{q}$, the firm must minimize the cost function (9–2), subject to the constraint that it operate within the limits set by its production function (9–I). The role of the production function as a constraint is obvious. If it were ignored, we would conclude that to minimize the cost of producing $\bar{q}$, the firm should operate using no inputs. And naturally that is impossible.

---

* The reader may skip this starred appendix without loss of continuity.

We shall solve this problem of constrained minimization by using the Lagrange multiplier, since it would be difficult, given the way the problem is stated, to substitute the constraint into the expression to be minimized. To introduce the Lagrange multiplier, we form a new function

$$c^* = wL + vR + \bar{r} + \lambda[\bar{q} - h(L,R,\overline{K})] \qquad (9\text{-}3)$$

by adding to the cost function (9–2) the term, $\lambda[\bar{q} - h(L,R,\overline{K})]$. This latter term equals zero for all values of L and R that satisfy the production constraint (9–1).

The variable c^* is a function of three variables, L, R, and λ; output $\bar{q}$ is a constant. To minimize c, the cost of producing $\bar{q}$, we take the partial derivatives of c^* with respect to L, R, and λ and set the resulting expressions† equal to zero as follows:

$$\partial c^*/\partial L = w - \lambda h_1 = 0, \qquad (9\text{-}4)$$

$$\partial c^*/\partial R = v - \lambda h_2 = 0, \qquad (9\text{-}5)$$

$$\partial c^*/\partial \lambda = \bar{q} - h(L,R,\overline{K}) = 0. \qquad (9\text{-}6)$$

Equations (9–4), (9–5), and (9–6) represent three conditions that must hold if the output $\bar{q}$ is to be produced at minimum cost. We can reduce these three conditions in three unknowns, L, R, and λ, to two conditions in two unknowns, L and R, by eliminating λ. To do so we rewrite (9–5) and (9–6) as follows: $w = \lambda h_1$ and $v = \lambda h_2$. Then, dividing the first of these equations by the second, we obtain

$$w/v = h_1/h_2. \qquad (9\text{-}7)$$

We have thus reduced the conditions that must be met if $\bar{q}$ is to be produced at minimum cost to the following:

$$\bar{q} = h(L,R,\overline{K}) \qquad \text{and} \qquad w/v = h_1/h_2.$$

The first equation simply states that, given the production function, inputs of L and R must be adequate to produce the output, $\bar{q}$.

To interpret the second condition, we must investigate the meaning of the term h_1/h_2. So we first take the *total differential* of the production function, $q = h(L,R,\overline{K})$, to obtain the expression

$$dq = h_1 \, dL + h_2 \, dR.$$

---

† In these expressions, h_1 represents the partial derivative of the function, $q = h(L,R,\overline{K})$, with respect to L, and h_2 represents the partial derivative of this same function with respect to R.

Next we observe that for movements along any isoquant, $q = \bar{q}$, $dq = 0$, and h_1/h_2 is given by the expression

$$h_1/h_2 = -dR/dL, \tag{9-8}$$

in which $-dR/dL$ equals the slope of the isoquant $q = \bar{q}$. Finally we substitute Eq. (9–8) into Eq. (9–7) to obtain the expression

$$dR/dL = -w/v. \tag{9-9}$$

This expression tells us that the firm can minimize its costs of production by moving to the point along an isocost curve at which the slope of this curve, dR/dL, just equals the slope of its isocost curves, $-w/v$. In other words the firm can attain equilibrium by moving to a point on the isoquant $q = \bar{q}$ at which this curve is just *tangent* to an isocost curve. Thus our mathematics as well as the intuitive argument presented in Chapter 8 support the conclusion that the firm can minimize its costs of production—within the limits set by its production function and input prices—at the point at which the conditions

$$\bar{q} = h(L,R,\overline{K}) \qquad \text{and} \qquad dR/dL = -w/v$$

are simultaneously fulfilled.

Frequently the *negative* of the slope of the firm's isoquant, $-dR/dL$, is defined as the firm's *rate of factor substitution* (*RFS*). In this case,

$$h_1/h_2 = RFS, \tag{9-10}$$

and the firm's conditions for cost minimization can be restated in the following form:

$$\bar{q} = h(L,R,\overline{K}) \qquad \text{and} \qquad RFS = w/v.$$

Cost Minimization and Input Productivities

We can give condition (9–7) an alternative and interesting interpretation if we begin by determining the meaning not of the ratio h_1/h_2, but of the partial derivatives h_1 and h_2 themselves. Since h_1 is the partial derivative of the production function with respect to L, it tells how output q will respond to a small change in the input of L when the input of R is held constant. This interpretation of the partial derivative of the production function with respect to L is, however, identical to our definition of the marginal productivity of L. Therefore h_1 must equal the marginal productivity of L. Similarly, h_2 must equal the marginal productivity of R, and

$$h_1/h_2 = MP_L/MP_R. \tag{9-11}$$

From (9–7) and (9–11), we see that our second condition of cost minimization, (9–7), can be restated as:

$$MP_L/MP_R = w/v.$$

We can grasp the intuitive meaning of this condition if we rewrite it as follows:

$$MP_L/w = MP_R/v.$$

In this form the condition in effect says that the firm can minimize its costs of producing any level of output only if it adjusts its purchases of both inputs so that the last dollar it spends on the input L yields the same addition to total output as the last dollar it spends on the input R. To illustrate: suppose that $w = \$10$, that $v = \$6$, and that the firm is producing at a point on its production function at which $MP_L = 10$ units of output and $MP_R = 3$ units of output. Then the last dollar's worth of L which the firm adds to the production process will yield one unit of output, while the last dollar's worth of R will yield only one-half a unit of output. Therefore the firm can reduce the cost of producing its current output by substituting L for R. It should continue to substitute L for R so long as $(MP_L/w) > (MP_R/v)$, that is, until it reaches the point at which $MP_L/w = MP_R/v$.

Solving for the Firm's Equilibrium Input Combination

In the two conditions of cost minimization (9–1) and (9–7), $\bar{q}$, $\bar{K}$, w, and v are constants, while the values of h_1 and h_2 depend on the amounts of L and R. Our mathematical analysis has thus yielded two independent conditions in two unknowns, L and R, and by solving these two equations we can determine the inputs of L and R that the firm should use in order to minimize the cost of producing $\bar{q}$.

Second-Order Conditions

Whenever we solve a problem of minimization, we should examine the second-order conditions to verify that the point located is in fact a minimum and not a maximum point. Unfortunately obtaining and interpreting second-order conditions for the above problem of cost minimization is too complex to take up here. However, we can note that when two inputs are variable, the second-order conditions for cost minimization require that all isoquants representing combinations of these two inputs must be *convex* to the origin. If the isoquant corresponding to the output $\bar{q}$ were concave instead, then the point of tangency between this isoquant and an isocost curve would represent a point of maximum cost relative to all other points along the isoquant. This is just the point suggested in Problem 5 at the end of Chapter 8. If many inputs are variable, the second-order conditions of cost minimization require that the isoquants relating combinations of any two inputs must be convex.

THE FIRM'S COST CURVES

We have suggested that there are several relationships which must exist between a firm's cost curves. Let us now test the validity of these relationships by mathematical means. We can represent the firm's variable cost by the expression

$$VC = c(q)$$

and its fixed cost by the expression

$$FC = \bar{r},$$

in which $\bar{r}$ represents the cost of the firm's fixed input, $\overline{K}$.

Since $TC = FC + VC$, it follows from these expressions that

$$TC = c(q) + \bar{r}, \tag{9-12}$$

that

$$MC = d(TC)/dq = c'(q), \tag{9-13}$$

and that the firm's average variable cost is

$$AVC = c(q)/q.$$

The firm's marginal cost equals the slope of its TC curve by definition. To show that the firm's MC curve must intersect its AVC curve at the point at which the AVC curve attains a *minimum,* we first take the derivative of the average variable cost with respect to q and set the resulting expression equal to zero, as follows:

$$d(AVC)/dq = c'(q)/q - c(q)/q^2 = 0.$$

We then multiply both sides of the resulting expression by q and move the second term to the right, so that we obtain

$$c'(q) = c(q)/q, \tag{9-14}$$

which must hold at the point at which average variable cost reaches a minimum. But $c'(q)$ equals marginal cost and $c(q)/q$ equals average variable cost. Therefore (9–14) indicates that at the point at which average variable cost reaches a minimum, marginal cost equals average variable cost, i.e., the MC curve must intersect the AVC curve at the point at which the latter attains a minimum. The second-order condition for average variable cost to reach a minimum requires that the MC curve cut the AVC curve *from below.**

---

* You can verify this result by noting that the second-order condition for average variable cost to reach a minimum requires that the second derivative of average variable cost with respect to quantity be positive. But this condition can easily be shown to imply that marginal cost must be rising at the point at which average variable cost attains a minimum.

PROFIT MAXIMIZATION

When we view profit maximization as a two-step procedure, the second step calls for the firm to utilize the information it has concerning its costs and its demand curve to select the price–output combination that will maximize its profits.

The Firm's Revenue Curves

Let us represent the demand for the firm's output by the expression

$$p = p(q), \tag{9-15}$$

which states that the price received by the firm for its output will be a function of the quantity of output it sells. If the demand curve slopes downward, price will be a decreasing function of quantity sold, and the derivative dp/dq will be *negative*.

Using the demand function (9–15), we can represent total, average, and marginal revenue as follows:

$$TR = pq = [p(q)]q, \tag{9-16}$$

$$AR = p = p(q), \tag{9-17}$$

$$MR = d(pq)/dq = p(q) + q[p'(q)] = p + q(dp/dq). \tag{9-18}$$

The derivative of total revenue with respect to quantity equals marginal revenue by definition. Therefore, if the demand curve slopes downward, total revenue will reach a maximum when quantity sold is increased to the point at which marginal revenue equals zero.

Equations (9–17) and (9–18) together imply that

$$MR = AR + q(dp/dq).$$

Marginal revenue, thus expressed, equals the sum of two terms. The first of these, AR, is always positive, but if the demand curve slopes downward, the second, $q(dp/dq)$, will be negative, and also (as you should verify) the greater the output the firm sells, the smaller AR will be and the larger the absolute value of $q(dp/dq)$ will be. Therefore, as the quantity sold increases, marginal revenue must decrease, and it must fall more rapidly than average revenue falls.

Locating the Firm's Maximum-Profit Position

To determine the output that will maximize the firm's profits (π), we begin with the defining equation

$$\pi = TR - TC. \tag{9-19}$$

Next we express profits as a function of quantity sold, by substituting Eqs. (9–16) and (9–12) into Eq. (9–19). The profit equation thus obtained is

$$\pi = [p(q)]q - [c(q) + \bar{r}]. \tag{9–20}$$

Finally we set the derivative of (9–20) with respect to quantity equal to zero:

$$d\pi/dq = p(q) + q[p'(q)] - c'(q) = 0.$$

Rewriting this expression, we obtain the equation

$$p(q) + q[p'(q)] = c'(q), \tag{9–21}$$

which must hold at the point at which the firm's profits are maximized. Now we note that, according to (9–18), the left-hand side of this equation, $p(q) + q[p'(q)]$, equals marginal revenue; while according to (9–13), the right-hand side of this equation, $c'(q)$, equals marginal cost. Thus (9–21) implies that profits will be maximized if the firm increases the quantity it sells until the marginal revenue it obtains for the last unit sold equals the marginal cost of that unit. The second-order condition of profit maximization requires that the MR curve cut the MC curve *from above*.*

Profit Maximization as a One-Step Procedure

As we suggested at the end of Chapter 9, the firm's search for a position of maximum profit can also be viewed as a one-step procedure, in which the firm attains its goal by answering the following question: Given its production function, the input prices it must pay, and the demand that exists for its output, how much of each variable input should it hire in order to attain maximum profits?

When we use this approach to a firm's problem of profit maximization, we shall assume that the firm is confronted with a horizontal demand curve like that in Fig. 9.4. If we make this assumption, the price at which the firm sells its output will not be a function of the quantity of output it sells, and we can thus avoid a rather involved process of substitution that would necessarily have arisen if we had assumed that the firm had a downward-sloping demand curve.

To solve the problem in a single step, we first obtain an expression for profits in terms of the inputs L, R, and $\bar{K}$. We can express the firm's total revenue in terms of the inputs it employs if we substitute the production

---

* To verify this result, note that the second-order condition of profit maximization requires that the second derivative of profit with respect to quantity be negative. This in turn implies that at the point of maximum profit the slope of the MR curve must exceed that of the MC curve, i.e., that the MR curve must cut the MC curve from above.

function, (9–1), into the total-revenue equation, (9–16), as follows:

$$TR = p[h(L,R,\overline{K})].\tag{9-22}$$

Now we substitute this expression for total revenue and the expression (9–2) for costs into the profit equation, (9–19), to obtain

$$\pi = p[h(L,R,\overline{K})] - (wL + vR + \overline{r}),\tag{9-23}$$

in which profits are expressed as a function of inputs used.

Since we assume that $\overline{K}$, p, w, v, and $\overline{r}$ are all constants, our new expression for profits, (9–23), is a function of two variables only, L and R. To determine the point at which profits reach a maximum, we take the partial derivatives of (9–23) with respect to L and R and set them equal to zero:

$$\partial\pi/\partial L = ph_1 - w = 0,\tag{9-24}$$

$$\partial\pi/\partial R = ph_2 - v = 0.\tag{9-25}$$

As noted above, h_1 and h_2 equal the marginal products of L and R, respectively. We can therefore rewrite Eqs. (9–24) and (9–25) in the final form:

$$p(MP_L) = w,\tag{9-26}$$

$$p(MP_R) = v.\tag{9-27}$$

If we had assumed that the demand curve sloped downward, we would have obtained the following two conditions of profit maximization. These are very similar to conditions (9–26) and (9–27), which of course we have obtained on the assumption that the demand curve is horizontal:

$$(MR)h_1 = w,\tag{9-28}$$

$$(MR)h_2 = v.\tag{9-29}$$

Alternatively we could write these two conditions as

$$MRP_L = w \quad \text{and} \quad MRP_R = v.$$

In this familiar form the conditions state that a firm will hire each variable input up to the point at which its marginal-revenue product equals its price. That is, it will hire additional factors up to the point at which the addition to cost due to the last unit hired just equals the addition to total revenue made by that unit. We can interpret conditions (9–26) and (9–27) similarly since, for a firm with a horizontal demand curve, price equals marginal revenue.

EQUIVALENCE OF THE
ONE- AND TWO-STEP PROCEDURES FOR PROFIT MAXIMIZATION

We have presented profit maximization first as a two-step and then as a one-step procedure; and each of these approaches yielded a different set of equilibrium conditions. Therefore, to prove that these two approaches are equivalent, we must show that these two sets of conditions are equivalent, i.e., that either one implies the other.

When we looked at profit maximization as a two-step procedure, we concluded that the following conditions must hold at the point of profit maximization:

$$q = h(L, R, \overline{K}), \tag{9-1}$$

$$w/v = h_1/h_2, \tag{9-7}$$

$$MR = MC. \tag{9-30}$$

When we looked at it as a one-step procedure, we obtained an alternative set of conditions, as follows:

$$q = h(L, R, \overline{K}), \tag{9-1}$$

$$MR \cdot h_1 = w, \tag{9-28}$$

$$MR \cdot h_2 = v. \tag{9-29}$$

When we were talking about profit maximization as a one-step procedure, we did not explicitly state that the production function was one of the conditions that must hold at the point of profit maximization, but we implied this by substituting the production function into the expression to be maximized.

Now we shall show that the conditions for profit maximization obtained using this second approach imply those obtained using the first approach. The converse is left to you to prove in a problem.

Since the production function (9-1) is included in both sets of conditions for profit maximization, our problem reduces to showing that Eqs. (9-28) and (9-29) together imply Eqs. (9-7) and (9-30). As you should verify, (9-7) can be obtained directly from (9-28) and (9-29) simply by dividing the first of these equations by the second.

We can show that Eqs. (9-28) and (9-29) imply Eq. (9-30) by the following argument. Suppose that the firm increases its output q by a small amount through additions of the variable input L. The marginal cost of this increase in output will equal the unit price of L, which is w, times the additional number of units of L needed. How much additional L will be required will in turn depend on the value assumed by the partial derivative, $\partial q / \partial L$, or more specifically on the value of its inverse. Thus the marginal cost of a unit increase in output obtained by increasing the input of L can be expressed as follows

$$MC = w \cdot \frac{1}{\partial q / \partial L} \cdot \tag{9-31}$$

The derivative $\partial q / \partial L$, however, equals h_1, the marginal product of L. Substituting h_1 for $\partial q / \partial L$ in Eq. (9–31), we obtain

$$MC = w / h_1.$$

If we now rewrite Eq. (9–28) as

$$MR = w / h_1,$$

this condition clearly implies that the input of L will be increased until the point is reached at which marginal revenue equals marginal cost; i.e., it implies the condition $MR = MC$. Alternatively, we could apply the same argument with regard to Eq. (9–29).

Now that we have shown that Eqs. (9–28) and (9–29) together imply Eqs. (9–7) and (9–30), we conclude that the one-step and the two-step procedures for profit maximization are equivalent.

PROBLEMS

1   Consider the following production function:

$$q = (L \cdot R \cdot K)^{1/2},$$

where L and R are variable inputs and K is fixed at unity. If $r_L = 1$, $r_R = 4$, and $r_K = 1$ are the wages paid to the inputs, what is the equation of the firm's expansion path? Let the demand function be

$$p = 10 - q.$$

Derive the price–output combination that will maximize the firm's profits.

2   Complete the proof of the equivalence of the one- and two-step procedures for maximizing profits by showing that Eqs. (9–7) and (9–30) together imply Eqs. (9–28) and (9–29).

3   Derive the short-run cost-minimization conditions for a firm with three variable inputs.

4   Let demand for a firm's output be represented by the function

$$q = 10 - p$$

and let its production function be defined by Eq. (9–1). Show that in equilibrium the firm will have chosen a price p and values of L and R such that

$$MR \cdot h_1 = r_L \quad \text{and} \quad MR \cdot h_2 = r_R.$$

5   Consider a production function $q = h(K,L)$, which has the following property:

$$\lambda h(K,L) = h(\lambda K, \lambda L)$$

for any positive number λ.

a) Show that this function has constant returns to scale.

b) Show that

$$K \cdot h_1(K,L) + L \cdot h_2(K,L) = h(K,L).$$

c) Show that if each input is paid a wage equal to the value of its marginal product, the firm will earn a profit of zero.

6   Verify that the second-order condition of profit maximization requires that at the point of maximum profit the slope of the MR curve must exceed that of the MC curve, i.e., that the MR curve must intersect the MC curve from above.

7   Show that, at the output which minimizes the average variable cost, the marginal cost must be rising. [*Hint:* Use the second-order condition for minimization of average variable cost.]

8   Let T denote the amount of tax per unit of output, and suppose that the firm's demand curve is that defined in Problem 4. Determine the sign of dp/dT at the optimum price level.

9   Repeat Problem 8, letting T be:

a) a percentage tax on total revenue.

b) a lump-sum tax.

10 Measured vertically, the curve of the total variable cost represents the minimum cost of producing a given output. Measured horizontally, the same curve represents the maximum output that can be produced at a given cost. Show how you would derive the TVC curve using the second approach.

CHAPTER 10

*THE FIRM'S INVESTMENT DECISION UNDER CERTAINTY

Usually, during any short-run period, a business firm has opportunities to install or introduce into the production process inputs that will contribute to its output and profits in future periods. Such opportunities arise for one or both of two reasons.

1) *Some inputs may provide services that it is technically impossible for the firm to exhaust or use up within a single period of time.*

The firm's plant and equipment for example fall in this category.

2) *The production process may require more than one period of time for completion.*

The firm, for example, may produce cheese that must be aged for months or trees that must grow for years.

We shall use the word *investment to refer to any expenditures which a firm makes in the current period in order to increase its profits in future periods.* This broad definition of investment takes in all forms of investment the firm might make, including the purchase of capital goods (plant and equipment), the utilization of goods in process, and the holding of inventories. Incidentally, that term "goods in process" is a very handy one; it refers to any inputs that are introduced into the production process in one period of time but which contribute to output in some later period of time.

During 1966 U.S. corporations made investments equal to $59.4 billion in plant and equipment and $10.9 billion in inventories. To finance these investments they sold $10.2 billion of bonds, incurred $26.0 billion of other debts, sold $1.2 billion of new stock, and retained $21.2 billion of earnings. When we look at such staggering figures as these, we wonder how business firms made all the complex investment and financing decisions that must

---

* The reader may skip this starred chapter without loss of continuity.

lie behind these aggregate figures. This fascinating subject will occupy us in this chapter and the next.

Analyzing the way a firm makes its investment and financing decisions turns out to be a difficult problem, and no wonder. Therefore, to simplify our discussion, we shall concentrate on how a firm makes choices with respect to one type of investment: fixed capital. Also we shall begin by considering the relatively easy case of a firm that knows exactly what is going to happen in the future, i.e., of a firm that has *certain knowledge of the future.** How does such a firm make its investment decision? Then, in Chapter 11, we shall talk about a firm whose knowledge of the future is *uncertain.* What effect does this *uncertainty* have on the firm's investment and financing decisions?

MAXIMIZING PROFITS OVER TIME

As we suggested in Chapter 6, the natural assumption to make when we analyze a firm's investment decision is that the firm always tries to maximize its profits over time (i.e., the profits it earns during current and future periods).

Although this assumption seems straightforward enough, if we attempt to apply it, we immediately run up against a problem. To see why, consider the Everwhite Reversible Collar Company. They are thinking about buying some new heavy-duty sewing machines. If they make this investment, they'll be able to produce more collars at lower cost, and as a result their profits will be higher during each of the next 3 years. Will this profit rise be enough to compensate Everwhite for the thousands of dollars it would have to invest to buy the new sewing machines? In other words, should Everwhite make the investment? At first glance the natural way to answer this question would seem to be to add up all the extra future profits that Everwhite would get from its investment and see whether or not they would be greater or less than the cost of the investment. Unfortunately, however, a dollar today is *not* the same thing as a dollar 3 years from now or even a dollar one year from now. So if we simply tote up Everwhite's extra profits over a 3-year period and then compare the resulting "total" with a current-cost figure, we'll be adding up "apples and oranges" and the answer we obtain won't mean a thing. (What's three apples plus two oranges minus one pear?)

---

* Naturally you're going to say to yourself that this is a rather unrealistic way of looking at things, because no one on earth really has certain knowledge of the future. And of course you are right. Nevertheless, studying the firm's investment decision under conditions of certainty is useful for several reasons: Studying the certainty case enables us to gain an insight into the firm's investment problem that we would have difficulty gaining if we studied the uncertainty case alone. Also, by contrasting the firm's investment decision under uncertainty with that under certainty, we can get a good idea of how the existence of uncertainty affects the firm's operations over time.

This dilemma leads to the realization that, if we are going to get anywhere in our discussion of investment, we shall have to begin by finding a way to compare dollars in different periods. The key to doing so is the concept of *present value*.

The present value of a dollar at a specified future date equals the value today of that future dollar.

Now let's find an expression for the present value of a future dollar. What is the maximum amount a rational person (you, perhaps?) would be willing to pay today for one dollar to be received today? Clearly the answer is anything up to, but not more than, one dollar. What is the maximum amount you'd be willing to pay for one dollar to be received a year from now? One dollar, you say? But think a moment. If the interest rate is positive, this implies that you can obtain a dollar one year from now by investing *less* than a dollar today. Therefore the present value (or worth) of a dollar one year from now must equal the amount (the principal) that you would have to invest today so that this principal plus accumulated interest would equal a dollar one year from now.

If you invest a principal, x, at the interest rate r, your principal plus your interest at the end of one year will equal $(1 + r)x$. Thus you can determine the principal that you must invest today to obtain one dollar a year from now by solving the equation

$$(1 + r)x = \$1.00$$

for x. Suppose that $r = 4\%$. This yields the solution

$$x = \$1.00/1.04 = \$0.96 \ldots$$

Assuming that the interest rate does not change in the next two years, the principal that you must invest today to yield one dollar two years from now can be found by solving the equation

$$(1 + r)[(1 + r)x] = (1 + r)^2 x = \$1.00$$

for x. So we again take $r = 4\%$, and find that the solution is

$$x = \$1.00/(1.04)^2 = \$0.92 \ldots$$

Thus if $r = 4\%$, the present value of one dollar is $0.96 if you are going to receive it a year from now and $0.92 if you are going to receive it two years from now. Here's a general formula that sums up the situation:

The present value of an amount R to be received n years from now equals $R/(1 + r)^n$.

Now we can give a precise meaning to the expression, "profit maximization over time" (or in the long run). Think of profits as flowing into the company in a steady stream over the years. Then, since dollars in different periods of time are directly comparable only if we measure them in terms of current dollars (i.e., in terms of their present value), the true measure of the value of any stream of profits which the firm gets over time must be its present value.

Therefore to say that a firm maximizes its profits over time means that it maximizes the present value of its profit stream over time.

THE FIRM'S CHOICE AMONG DIFFERENT TYPES OF FIXED CAPITAL

Suppose that a firm wants to increase its investment in fixed capital, say in machinery. Then it is likely to find that there are several *types* of machines available that will do the job it wants done. Some machines may have higher initial costs than others, some may have lower operating costs than others, some may be more durable than others, or they may differ in other characteristics. How shall the firm which has to choose among different machines decide which type to buy?

With every type and quantity of capital equipment the firm might buy, there will be associated a given profit stream, with a given present value; and we can calculate what the present value of this profit stream is. Example: Let us calculate the present value of the profit stream associated with the new sewing machines Everwhite is thinking of buying. Since the sewing machine companies demand cash, Everwhite will have to pay for its machines this year. However, shipping and installing these machines will take time, so Everwhite won't be able to use its machines to produce output until next year.

Once Everwhite gets its new machines into production, it will of course incur additional variable costs of production, and it will receive additional revenue from sales. So the simplest way for us to calculate the present value of the profit stream associated with the use of these machines is to calculate the net revenues these sewing machines will generate during each year of their useful life, and then to discount the resulting amounts back to the present.

This isn't as complicated as it sounds. Let's take it a step at a time. Suppose that Everwhite's machines will cost I_0, that they will last 3 years, and that during these 3 years they will generate net revenues equal to R_1, R_2, and R_3, respectively. (The numerical subscripts we shall use throughout our discussion of investment refer to periods of *time;* in this case years.) We let r equal the interest rate for one year. Then the present value of the net revenue which Everwhite will get at the end of the first year will equal $R_1/(1 + r)$. The present value of the net revenue they'll get at the end of the second year will equal $R_2/(1+r)^2$. The present value of the net revenue at the end of the third year will equal $R_3/(1+r)^3$. Therefore the present value of Everwhite's three-year profit stream, which we denote by $PV(\pi)$ (the π stands for profits), is given by the expression

$$PV(\pi) = R_1/(1+r) + R_2/(1+r)^2 + R_3/(1+r)^3 - I_0.$$

Note that the R_1, R_2, and R_3 are calculated on the assumption that in each short-run period (in this case, a year), Everwhite chooses the price–output combination that will maximize its profits for that period.

Now that we have figured out how a firm calculates the profit stream associated with investment in a single type of capital equipment, we can answer the question posed above: How does a firm choose between different types of capital equipment that will do the same job but that differ in their initial cost or operating characteristics?

The firm will choose the type of capital equipment that offers the profit stream of highest present value. Take Everwhite, for example. Increase Jones, the president of Everwhite, finds that the company can buy two different models of sewing machines. The first, Littlefinger, costs only $300. The second, Pachyderm, is more expensive (it costs $500), but it uses only half as much thread as Littlefinger does. Both machines have the same capacity and both will last 3 years. Which model should Everwhite buy? To answer this question, Increase Jones calls down to the accounting department to get estimates of the net revenues that both machines would yield over time. They tell him that 10 Pachyderms (which would cost $5,000 today) would yield net revenues of $2,000, $2,500, and $2,087 over the next 3 years. On the other hand, 10 Littlefingers (which would cost only $3,000 today) would yield net revenues of $1,200, $1,500, and $1,093 over the next 3 years. Increase Jones, who's awfully good at compound interest, makes a couple of mental calculations and declares with lightning speed to his amazed accountant, "We'll have to buy the Pachyderms. Admittedly they cost more today, but over time they'll offer us a profit stream with greater present value."*

---

* In case you are not as fast at figuring compound interest as Increase Jones is, note that the present value of the profit stream associated with 10 Pachyderms is

$$[\$2,000/(1.10)] + [\$2,500/(1.10)^2] + [\$2,087/(1.10)^3] - \$5,000,$$

and that this equals $451, while the present value of the profit stream associated with 10 Littlefingers is

$$[\$1,200/(1.10)] + [\$1,500/(1.10)^2] + [\$1,093/(1.10)^3] - \$3,000$$

which equals $150.

How did $r = 10\%$ get into the problem? The answer of course is that 10% is the going interest rate that Everwhite pays on funds it borrows and gets on funds it lends.

THE FIRM'S CHOICE AMONG DIFFERENT SCALES OF INVESTMENT

Whenever a firm increases its fixed capital, it must decide not only what kinds, but also what quantities of capital equipment to buy. In other words, it must choose not only the *type*, but also the *scale* of investment it will make. How does a firm figure out which scale of investment is its optimal one? To answer this question, we need two new concepts: the average rate of return and the marginal rate of return.

The average rate of return a firm earns on any investment equals the average rate of return it earns per time period per dollar invested.

Suppose that by investing $100 this year, a firm can earn $121 two years hence. Then we can find the average rate of return, ρ_a, which the firm earns on this investment by solving the expression

$$[\$100(1 + \rho_a)](1 + \rho_a) = \$100(1 + \rho_a)^2 = \$121$$

for ρ_a. As you should verify, in this expression $\rho_a = 10\%$.

The marginal rate of return (ρ_m) a firm earns on any investment equals the average rate of return it earns on the last or marginal dollar it invests.

Suppose that the firm finds that by investing one additional dollar it can increase the revenue it earns at the end of the two years by $1.10. Then, as you can easily verify, the marginal rate of return it earns on this investment will be about 5%.

There's a general formula we can use here too. Suppose that a firm, by increasing its current investment by an amount equal to ΔI_0, can increase its net revenue n years hence by an amount equal to ΔR_n. Then we can find the marginal rate of return ρ_m which the firm earns on this investment by solving, for ρ_m, the expression

$$\Delta I_0(1 + \rho_m)^n = \Delta R_n.$$

The n here stands for some positive integer, 3, 10, or whatever the length of the firm's investment period is.

Now let's backtrack to our original problem: How does a firm find out what its optimal scale of investment in fixed capital is?

First we need to know whether the marginal rate of return a firm earns on its investment changes as the firm increases its scale of investment, and if so, *how* it changes. Assume that a firm makes a small increase in its investment. The marginal rate of return yielded by this increase depends on:

1) the increase in the firm's future output that would be induced by a small increase in its current scale of investment (i.e., the *marginal productivity* of this investment),
2) the marginal revenue that the firm would obtain by selling this additional future output.

How will these two variables, marginal revenue and marginal productivity, change as the firm increases the scale of its investment from zero upward? Well, if demand for the firm's output slopes downward, we can be sure that, as the firm increases the scale of its investment, the marginal revenue it gets from future output will decline. The relationship between the scale of the firm's investment and the marginal productivity of this investment is likely to be more complex. Initially, as the firm increases the scale of its investment, the marginal productivity of this investment may rise because the firm, by operating on a larger scale, is able to organize production more efficiently. But suppose that the firm makes successive increases in the scale of its investment: what then? At some point diminishing returns, decreasing returns to scale,* or both will probably set in, and when this happens the marginal productivity of the firm's investment will level out and then decline.

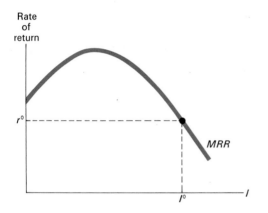

Rate
of
return

r^0

MRR

I^0

I

10|1

If the interest rate is r^0, the firm's optimal scale of investment is I^0.

Putting these observations together, we conclude that, as the firm increases the scale of its investment from zero upward, the marginal rate of return it earns on its investments is likely to rise initially and then fall, as the MRR curve in Fig. 10.1 does. With this in mind, we can characterize any firm's optimal scale of investment in fixed capital. Assume that the MRR curve for the firm's investment in plant and equipment has the form shown in Fig. 10.1, that the going interest rate is r^0, and that the firm can borrow as much as it wants to at that rate. Then, if the firm were to invest less than I^0, the marginal rate of return it would earn on a small increase in its scale of investment would exceed r^0, the cost of this investment; and any such small increase in its scale of investment would therefore increase the present value of its anticipated profit stream. Similarly, if the firm were to invest more than I^0, the marginal rate of return it would lose by making a small decrease in its scale

---

* The concepts of diminishing returns and decreasing returns to scale were introduced in Chapter 7, when we discussed the firm's production function.

of investment would be less than r^0, the cost of this investment; and any such decrease in its scale of investment would therefore increase the present value of its anticipated profit stream. It follows that the firm can maximize its profits over time only if its scale of investment is such that *the marginal rate of return it earns on its investment just equals the going interest rate, r^0*. For the firm whose marginal rate of return is shown in Fig. 10.1, this is obviously the scale of investment I^0.

Maybe all this sounds a bit complex. So let's boil it down to collars. Increase Jones, as we have seen, has just invested in 10 Pachyderms. Now he's wondering whether or not he should have invested in more. If 10 new machines would increase his profits, would 20 have been even better? And what about 30, or would that have been too many?

Increase Jones, who's a profit-maximizer at heart, decides to find out. First he calls up the production department. They tell him that if he buys more and more sewing machines without adding a new wing, his seamstresses are going to have to work closer and closer together, and as a result they'll sew slower and slower (that is, more sewing machines with no more floor space means diminishing returns).

The production department also suggests somewhat irreverently that if Increase goes on increasing plant size, the whole operation may get too big for him to manage efficiently (decreasing returns to scale may set in).

On that discouraging note Increase Jones hangs up and puts through a call to the people in market research. They tell him that, if he buys more machines and produces more collars, he'll have to lower the price of his collars in order to sell his total output. Demand for reversible collars is definitely downward-sloping. In fact, its elasticity is only 1.8.

Increase Jones, who as we have seen is a pretty alert fellow, concludes, from what the people in production and marketing have said, that the MRR curve for capital invested in Pachyderms must slope downward. What's its precise shape? Increase does some more rapid-fire mental calculations. These tell him that the marginal rate of return Everwhite earns on its investment in sewing machines will equal 15% if it buys 10 Pachyderms, 10% if it buys 20 Pachyderms, and a mere 7% if it buys 30 Pachyderms. Increase, even without consulting the accounting department, knows that the going interest rate equals 10%. So he's got the answer he was looking for: Twenty Pachyderms (that is, $10,000 of sewing machines) is his optimal scale of investment.

THE FIRM'S INVESTMENT DEMAND SCHEDULE

In the preceding section we showed the relationship between the scale of the firm's investment in plant and equipment and its marginal rate of return on this type of investment. Now we're going to talk about the relationship between the firm's *total* investment (including plant and equipment, inventories, and goods in process) and the marginal rate of return it earns on this total investment.

We can be pretty sure that any firm will maximize its profits over time by adjusting its total investment so that the marginal rate of return it earns on this investment just equals the going interest rate. Therefore the firm's *MRR* curve for total investment must show the relationship between the cost of capital and the total quantity of capital it will choose to invest in its operations. In other words such a curve must represent the firm's *demand schedule* for the input capital.* This schedule, which is frequently referred to as the firm's *investment demand schedule,* can be represented by

$$I = d(r),$$

in which I is the firm's optimal (i.e., profit-maximizing) scale of investment and r is the going interest rate.

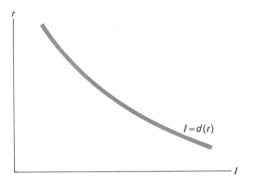

10|2
The firm's investment demand schedule, $I = d(r)$, is a downward-sloping function of the interest rate.

When we plot the firm's investment demand schedule, what will its slope be? By the same reasoning we used to show that the firm's *MRR* schedule for investment in fixed capital will eventually become a downward-sloping curve, we can show that, over some range of total investment, the firm's *MRR* schedule for *total* investment will also eventually slope downward. Moreover, since it is the downward-sloping portion of the firm's total *MRR* curve that is relevant to its investment decision, its investment-demand schedule must slope downward as the one in Fig. 10.2 does.

---

* Capital's *MRR* curve has a companion *ARR* (average rate of return) curve. Moreover, if the two are plotted together, the *MRR* curve will (as you can easily show) cut the *ARR* curve from above. Strictly speaking, the firm's demand curve for capital corresponds only to the portion of the *MRR* curve that lies below the *ARR* curve. To see why, refer back to Problem 13 at the end of Chapter 9; it illustrates the same point with respect to the firm's demand curve for labor.

THE FIRM'S REACTION TO CHANGE OVER A PERIOD OF TIME

How will a business firm react in the long run to any change in the conditions under which it operates: for example, to a shift in demand for its output, to a change in input prices, or to a change in technology?

Let's think back to the Everwhite Reversible Collar Company. Naturally a shift in demand for its output (reversible collars suddenly become all the rage in Paris) will shift its revenue curves, while a change in either input prices (cotton goes up a nickel a pound) or technology (someone invents an automatic sewing machine) will shift its cost curves. Therefore the firm's immediate reaction to any such change is to adjust its current output and price so as to maximize current profits. If the firm does not expect the change in question to last beyond the current period, it will do no more. However, if it expects this change to last over a number of periods, then, to maximize its profits over time, it will have to adjust, not only its current price and output, but also its capital stock, its plans as to its level of output, and the price it will charge in each future period.

For future reference, there is one aspect of this problem which is especially interesting. Suppose that a firm has a *horizontal* demand curve, and that there is a change in demand for its output, a change which it expects will last for a number of years. How will this firm respond over a period of time?

The Turngrass turnip farm, which we discussed in Chapter 9, is a good example of a firm with a horizontal demand curve, so we'll use them as an example. Let's say that Fig. 10.3 represents their cost and revenue curves. Initially Turngrass attains equilibrium at the point (p^0, q^0) where their MC curve intersects their demand curve D (which is also their MR curve). Suppose now that a quotable old country doctor comes out with a pronouncement that turnips prevent colds. Suddenly turnips catch on. The demand curve of Turngrass shifts upward to D'. Then Turngrass' immediate response will be to move to the point (p', q'), at which their MC curve cuts D', their new demand curve. In other words, Turngrass responds in the short run to an upward shift in demand for their turnips by increasing both the quantity of turnips they produce and the price at which they sell them.

The owners of Turngrass believe that the upward shift in demand for their turnips from D to D' will be permanent. They anticipate earning a greater marginal rate of return on their current investment, and so they increase the scale of their investment. They buy new tractors and an automated turnip harvester. Also they build an air-conditioned barn with automated facilities for washing, drying, sorting, and packing turnips. This increase in their capital stock enables them to produce greater outputs at lower variable cost; in other words, it shifts their short-run cost curves to the right. We can draw a neat conclusion from this: A firm which responds to

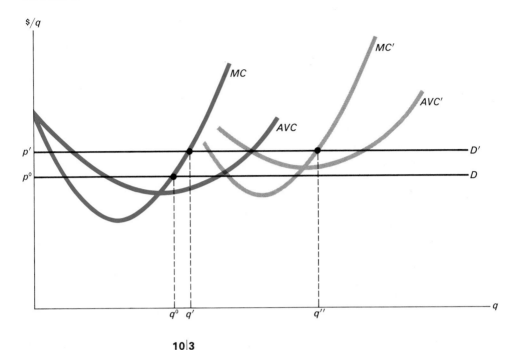

10|3

A firm's response, over time, to an upward shift in demand for its output from *D* to *D'*.

a rise in demand by immediately increasing its output will—when it has had time to adjust its capital stock—increase its output still further. Figure 10.3 shows such a chain of events graphically. Turngrass initially reacts to the shift in demand from *D* to *D'* by raising their output from q^0 to q' and by increasing their price from p^0 to p'. At the same time, however, they also invest in additional capital stock. And after this investment has had time to take effect, Turngrass' cost curves shift from *AVC* and *MC* to *AVC'* and *MC'*, respectively, and their equilibrium output rises from q' to q''.

So we may safely say that any firm with a horizontal demand curve will have, not only a short-run supply curve, but also a *long-run supply curve*. Remember that a firm's short-run supply curve shows the relationship between the price it receives for output and the quantity of output it will supply when it varies its output by adjusting its variable inputs, but *not* its capital stock. On the other hand:

A firm's long-run supply curve shows the relationship between the price it receives for output and the quantity of output it will supply when it has had time to respond to any price by adjusting its output, not only via changes in its variable inputs, but also via changes in its capital stock.

It stands to reason that a firm's long-run supply curve will be more elastic than its short-run supply curve, since, as we have just shown, the response the firm makes to any shift in the demand for (and the price of) its output will be larger in the long run when the firm is free to adjust its capital stock than in the short run when capital stock is fixed.

PROBLEMS

1 Determine the present value (to the nearest dollar) of the following:
   a) $150 five years from now at 5% interest.
   b) $25 one year from now, plus $25 two years from now, plus $25 three years from now, all at 5% interest.
   c) $700 three years from now at 4% interest.

2 Suppose that the interest rate in the current and in succeeding periods equals 10%.
   a) What is the present value of the following revenue stream? Initial cost incurred today, $100; revenue received today, 0; cost incurred one year from now, $200; revenue received one year from now, $50; cost incurred two years from now, $100; revenue received two years from now, $200; cost incurred three years from now, 0; revenue received three years from now, $600.
   b) Why will an individual who is rational, at least from an economic point of view, always discount future dollars?

3 Plot the average and marginal rates of return for the following investment schedule.

Initial investment	Return after one year	Initial investment	Return after one year
$100	$103	$ 600	$ 639
200	210	700	742
300	318	800	842
400	426	900	939
500	533	1000	1033

4 Suppose that you are given only a firm's income statement for a year and its balance sheet for the beginning of that year. Explain how you compute its average rate of return on capital. How do depreciation and the values of interest paid on borrowed funds enter your calculations? Do these two accounts contain enough information to determine the marginal rate of return on capital?

5 a) As an alternative to the definition given in the text, we can define the average rate of return on any investment as the rate at which the anticipated

profit stream must be discounted in order for its present value to equal zero. Show that this definition is equivalent to the one given in the text.

b) Similarly, we can define the marginal rate of return on any investment as the rate at which the change in the anticipated profit stream associated with a small change in the amount of this investment must be discounted in order that the change in the present value of the profit stream equal zero. Show that this definition is equivalent to the one given in the text for marginal rate of return.

6   Suppose that the manager of a firm objects to our use of the concept of the marginal rate of return. He says that his firm never computes such a value for an investment. Rather he just undertakes all investments whose future income streams, when discounted to the present, exceed their cost. How does this approach compare with the one used in the text? What advantage, from the economist's viewpoint, does the *MRR* approach offer?

7   a) Use the data from Problem 3 to determine the optimal scale of investment, given that the interest rate is 6%. At what rate of interest would this firm invest $800? Suppose that the firm has $1000 which it can divide between investment within the firm according to the schedule shown in Problem 3 and investment outside the firm at an interest rate of 7%. How would it allocate this $1000?

b) Derive the investment demand schedule for the firm in Problem 3.

8   The introduction of pneumatic conveyors to the baking industry in 1946 made possible bulk handling of ingredients from the rail siding to the mixing machines. According to a case study, this method of unloading flour into the plant increases man-hour output from 1,000 pounds for bagged delivery to 40,000 pounds for bulk delivery. By 1958, 70–90% of the medium to large bakery plants, but only 15% of the small bakery plants, had adopted the pneumatic-conveyor method (Walsh and Evans, *op. cit.*, page 48). On the basis of our discussion in this chapter and in Chapter 7, comment on the reaction of the small bakery plants.

9   Discuss various ways in which changes in the value of the future interest rate could influence the shape and position of the investment-demand curve for a firm. Describe as explicitly as you can the nature and direction of this influence.

10   In the text we traced the effect of a prolonged increase in demand for a firm's output. Use the same technique to discuss the effect of (a) a downward shift in the interest rate which is expected to last for some time, (b) a technological advance increasing the productivity of capital, and (c) an increase in the wage rate.

11   a) Consider a firm which displays increasing returns to scale. How would such a firm's short-run-cost curves shift as it expands its stock of fixed capital?

b) Suppose that such a firm has a horizontal demand curve. How would its profits be affected by an increase in all inputs, including fixed inputs? What is the theoretical limit on such a firm's expansion? What is the practical limit?

*12 Suppose that a man decides to plant a tree as an investment. The seedling costs him $5, and the value of the tree, as a source of lumber, grows over the years according to the following schedule.

Age of tree in years	Value of tree in dollars	Age of tree in years	Value of tree in dollars
1	$0.20	19	$20.00
2	0.50	20	22.00
3	0.90	21	24.10
4	1.40	22	26.30
5	2.00	23	28.60
6	2.70	24	31.00
7	3.50	25	33.40
8	4.40	26	35.60
9	5.40	27	37.50
10	6.50	28	39.00
11	7.60	29	40.20
12	8.80	30	41.10
13	10.10	31	41.70
14	11.50	32	42.00
15	13.00	33	42.20
16	14.60	34	42.30
17	16.30	35	42.35
18	18.10	36	42.35

a) Let the current interest rate be 5%. After how many years should he cut the tree and sell it at the value shown above in order to maximize the present value (today) of his investment? Assume that there are no costs involved in maintaining the tree.

b) After a number of years, the man probably does not care what the discounted value of the tree was initially. Show that the number of years which gives the maximum initial discounted value of the tree is also best from his point of view many years later.

c) Explain how you would determine whether this was a good investment (do not do the calculations).

d) How do the initial cost of the seedling and the interest rate affect the optimum cutting date? How do they affect his decision as to whether or not he should undertake this investment in the first place?

e) Compare the effects of the following on the desirability of the investment and the optimum cutting date: (i) a constant interest rate of 5%; (ii) an interest rate of 5% for the first 10 years followed by an interest rate of 6% thereafter; and (iii) a constant interest rate of 6%.

---

* Starred problems are problems that are unusually difficult.

CHAPTER 11

*THE FIRM'S INVESTMENT DECISION UNDER UNCERTAINTY

In the preceding chapter we talked about a firm's investment decision in an ideal situation in which it could see into the future with certainty. But the world we live in is full of *uncertainty*. No business organization made up of flesh-and-blood people can know for sure what price it will have to pay for inputs in the years to come, or what technological developments (i.e., changes in its production function) are in store for it. Any projections a firm makes as to future demand for its output (and thus as to future revenue) will be characterized by uncertainty, since these projections hinge on such difficult-to-predict factors as how the incomes and tastes of consumers will change over time, how competing firms will alter their level of output, what substitute products competing producers may introduce, and what prices they may charge for these products. Naturally, therefore, any real-life firm has to base its investment decision on uncertain projections about the future profitability of the alternative investment opportunities open to it.

The *degree* of uncertainty associated with each of the variables that enter into a firm's calculations of course differs markedly from firm to firm. In some industries, such as aircraft production, technology is advancing rapidly and unpredictably, while in others it is advancing slowly, if at all. For some firms, such as the electric utilities, demand grows in a steady predictable fashion, while for others, such as the automobile companies, demand fluctuates erratically around a long-term upward trend. For still other firms, all the variables that enter into their calculations are characterized by extreme uncertainty. For example, oil companies drilling in offshore waters do not know how much crude oil lies buried below these waters, how much of this oil can be extracted with currently available techniques, or what such extraction will cost. And they can't really predict what price crude oil will bring in future years, since this depends on such indeterminables as mideast politics, the degree of government protection granted to European coal pro-

---

* The reader may skip this starred chapter without loss of continuity.

ducers, the success of Russia in penetrating western oil markets, and even the success of General Electric in developing an *electric* auto.

Although business firms in an uncertain world do not all have identical levels or types of uncertainty, they do all face one problem: they cannot foresee with certainty the future consequences of their investment decisions. Thus a firm that operates in an uncertain world makes investment decisions very different in character from those made by a firm which operates in that ideal, certain world that we talked about in Chapter 10, and we are going to have to modify our analysis accordingly.

INVESTMENT FINANCING

Every firm has to finance its investments, and when it does so it relies on three principal kinds of funds:

1) funds obtained through loans and the sale of debt securities,
2) funds obtained through the sale of new equities, and
3) internally generated funds, including retained earnings and current depreciation.

For a firm that operates under uncertainty, the choice among alternative kinds of investment financing poses a much more complex problem than it does for a firm that operates under certainty. To see why, let's consider debt financing versus equity financing, first for firms that operate under certainty and then for firms that operate under uncertainty. (A thumbnail definition: "debt financing" means getting money by borrowing; "equity financing" means getting money by selling stock or by retaining earnings.)

Leverage: An Advantage of Debt Capital

When we were analyzing investment under certainty, we implicitly assumed that the firm, in order to finance new investment, would always borrow rather than sell new stock. Why? Well, if a firm finances an investment through the sale of additional stock, then the firm's initial stockholders have to share the profits yielded by this investment and *all the firm's other profits as well* with the people who buy this additional stock. In other words, equity financing always requires that the "profit pie" be divided into a larger number of slices. Debt financing has no such adverse effect.

There's another advantage of debt over equity financing: Whenever a firm invests debt capital at a rate of return that exceeds the interest rate (i.e., the cost of this capital), it raises the rate of return it earns on equity capital. For example, let's take a small new business firm: the Strangler Blue Jean Company, which makes super-tight blue jeans for teen-agers ("Wear Stranglers, the jeans with standing room only"). This firm has one asset: $10,000 of new fixed capital, invested in machinery to make jeans with. The Strangler Company raised the money to buy this machinery by selling $10,000 worth of stock. The machinery yields a rate of return equal to 10%, so the firm earns 10% on its equity capital. Now the president of Strangler, Elvis Smith, decides to put in a new line of jeans for teen-age girls only (to be called Miss-Fits), so it needs more machinery ($5000 worth) at once. Instead of selling more stock, Strangler borrows the $5000 of additional capital from a bank, at 5% interest. This new $5000 worth of machinery also yields a return of 10%. So Strangler's annual profits (check this yourself) rise from $1000 to $1250, and its rate of return on its equity capital rises from 10% to 12.5%. The power of debt capital to raise the rate of return on equity capital is referred to as *debt leverage,* or more simply as *leverage.*

So long as a firm can foresee the future with certainty, debt offers the advantage of leverage without entailing any offsetting disadvantage. Therefore in a world of certainty, we should always expect firms to make the maximum use of debt leverage.*

A Danger of Debt Capital: Risk

For a firm which operates under *uncertainty,* debt financing still offers the advantage of leverage, but it also offers the disadvantage of *risk.* When you use debt capital you of course have to pay a fixed interest charge in each period and maybe repay some of the principal too. This heightens the possibility that an unfavorable turn of events might bankrupt your firm or (less dramatically) might leave it with insufficient funds to meet semi-discretionary payments such as dividends and research and development expenses.

With this risk in mind, a firm which operates under uncertainty often chooses to finance new investments with equity rather than debt capital. To obtain new equity capital, the firm can:

1) retain current earnings instead of paying them out in dividends, and
2) sell new stock.

The first course of action offers the advantage of not diluting the earnings accruing to the firm's current stockholders, while the second offers the advantage of permitting the firm to maintain a higher and steadier rate of dividend payouts.

The Investment-Financing Choice Under Uncertainty

We have now seen that, for a firm which operates under uncertainty, the *way* the firm raises the money for needed investments is an important choice.

---

* This was implied by the rule for profit maximization over time which we derived in the last chapter. Recall that this rule said that the firm should continue to expand the scale of its investment until the rate of return on the last dollar it invests has fallen to the level of the going interest rate, i.e., until it has exhausted all possibilities for leverage!

This choice (like the choice of investments itself) affects the total profits which accrue to the firm's stockholders. Therefore:

A firm which operates under uncertainty can never choose among alternative investment opportunities without simultaneously considering how it will finance them.

So we shall think of such a firm as choosing not among alternative investment opportunities, but among alternative investment-financing options. (Note the similarity between a firm's investment-financing choice, which we are analyzing in this chapter, and a consumer's balance-sheet choice, which we analyzed in Chapter 5.)

PROFIT EXPECTATIONS UNDER UNCERTAINTY

Although naturally a firm which operates under uncertainty can never foresee with certainty what profit stream a given investment-financing option will yield over time, it's safe to say that the firm has fairly definite *expectations* as to the total size and time shape (i.e., timing) this profit stream will turn out to have.

The Formation of Expectations

Usually a firm's expectations about the future are influenced by its experiences during the recent past. Often these expectations are simply projections of recent experience, modified in light of whatever information the firm has about general economic trends and about other developments specifically related to its field.

Suppose that you are president and general manager of Laver Brothers, Inc., a small company which makes washing machines. You want to forecast your sales over the next five years. For a start, you might predict that your future sales will equal your current sales. Then you might modify this crude forecast by taking into account any general economic trends that would influence the demand for washing machines. For example, do the experts in, say, the *Wall Street Journal* predict an increase in consumer income, or in the rate of family formation? New families = new babies = *much* more laundry, so you raise your sales forecast. On the other hand, there's the growing rage for paper dresses; so you lower it a bit. Then you have to take into account data on the age and expected life of existing washing machines, the recent surveys of consumer buying intentions, and a government forecast of new housing starts in the next five years. And naturally you think to yourself: "What about our competitors? Will they make innovations? Will they change their prices? Certainly they aren't going to stand still. It's dog-eat-dog in the appliance field!"

The Nature of the Firm's Expectations

Obviously a producer who operates under uncertainty can forecast what future demand for his output will be, but he can never know with certainty. He can also forecast what his future costs of production will be, but again, never with certainty. Therefore it stands to reason that such a person's expectations about the earnings that an investment-financing option might yield over time would be *multi-valued* in character. In fact, the producer's expectations would very likely take the form of a *probability distribution* of possible earnings streams; i.e., of a range of possible earnings streams and a set of associated probabilities.

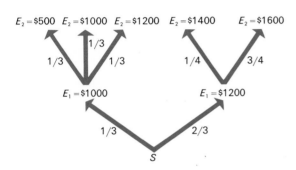

11│1

This probability tree represents a firm's expectations as to the earnings it would receive over time if it were to invest $10,000 of debt capital in a fixed-capital asset having an anticipated useful life of two years. The first stage = possible earnings during the first year; the second stage = possible earnings during the second year. The fractions along each line indicate the probability that the firm would move along this "path."

Let's suppose that your firm, Laver Brothers, is considering a $10,000 investment in fixed capital (to buy a new metal-stamping machine) which it intends to finance by debt. Let us represent your expectations as to the profits which this investment-financing option may yield over time by a probability tree* like that in Fig. 11.1. According to this "tree," you believe that during the first year the chances are one in three that Laver Brothers will earn $1000 on its $10,000 investment in the machine and two in three that it will earn $1200. You also anticipate that, if Laver Brothers earns only $1000 on its investment during the first year, it will have equal chances of earning $500, $1000, and $1200 during the second year; while, if it is lucky enough to earn $1200 during the first year, it will have one chance in four of earning $1400 and three chances in four of earning $1600 during the second year.

Another way to describe the expectations represented by the probability tree in Fig. 11.1 is to say that Laver Brothers believes that this investment-

---

* Note that this probability tree describes a firm's expectations as to the earnings which a *single* investment-financing option would yield over *several* periods, while the probability tree in Chapter 5 describes the consumer's expectations as to the average rate of return which a diversified portfolio composed of *several* investments would earn over a *single* period.

financing option may yield any one of *five different earnings streams* over a period of time. For example, Laver Brothers believes that the probability is $\frac{1}{9}$ (that is $\frac{1}{3} \times \frac{1}{3}$) that this investment-financing option will yield an earnings stream of $1000 the first year and $500 in the second year. It also believes, as you should verify, that the probabilities associated with the four remaining earnings streams are $\frac{1}{9}$, $\frac{1}{9}$, $\frac{1}{6}$, and $\frac{1}{2}$, respectively.

THE INVESTMENT-FINANCING DECISION UNDER UNCERTAINTY

In Chapter 10 we assumed that a firm, when it is choosing among alternative investments, will always choose the one that offers the profit stream of maximum present value. But remember that in Chapter 10 we were talking about a firm which operated in the ideal world of certainty, and now we are talking about a firm in the real world, a firm which invests under uncertainty. Such a firm has to choose not between investment options offering *known* profit streams, but between those offering probability distributions of possible profit streams. What assumptions shall we make about how it makes its investment choice? The following observations will help.

First: For a firm which operates under uncertainty, the maximization of profits over time may not—surprisingly enough—be in the best interests of the firm's stockholders. Because a firm which finances new investments by issuing additional stock may simultaneously *raise its total profits* but *lower its earnings per share.* So then the ultimate objective of such a firm must be defined not in terms of its *total profits over time,* but in terms of its *profits per share over time.*

Second: A big consideration is *how* decisions are made within the firm. Suppose that Laver Brothers is a young company which is still headed by the dynamic individual who founded it (you*). Decision-making in such a company is usually the responsibility of the founder-entrepreneur, so you have to do a lot of quick thinking. You are likely to have a considerable equity interest in the firm and thus you share personally both in the risks incurred by the firm and in the profits it earns. On the other hand, decision-making in an established corporation with many stockholders is typically the responsibility of a salaried, professional management group that is supposed to serve the interest of the firm's owners (i.e., stockholders) but which itself has only a negligible equity interest in the firm. The point we want to make is that whenever any firm makes a choice, the actual decision-making must be done by either one person or a group of people. For simplicity we shall refer to this person or group of people as *the entrepreneur.*

---

* Your brother's name is on the masthead, but he only put in capital to help start the business. He never does a lick of work.

Third: Since a firm which makes investment choices under uncertainty is in effect choosing among alternative uncertain outcomes, its investment decision is always determined by the attitude toward uncertainty (i.e., *risk preferences*) of the entrepreneur.*

These three observations lead to *two* assumptions about the firm's investment decision under uncertainty.

1) *The entrepreneur who directs the firm has a well-defined set of risk preferences that permits him to rank different investment-financing options.*
2) *In choosing among the investment-financing options open to his firm, the entrepreneur will always select the one that ranks highest in terms of his personal risk preferences.*

So now we have two assumptions about the entrepreneur, assumptions which apply whether the entrepreneur is a man or a board of directors. Using these assumptions, we could go on to show that the principal results we obtained in our discussion of investment under certainty hold in the uncertainty case as well: We could show that (1) a firm which operates under uncertainty has a well-defined demand schedule for input capital, a schedule which, like the one in Fig. 10.2, is a downward-sloping function of the interest rate;† and also that (2) the supply curve of a firm with a horizontal demand curve will—under uncertainty as under certainty—be more elastic in the long run than in the short run.‡

But the arguments needed to establish these results are similar to those used in previous chapters, so we shall relegate the proofs of these propositions to the problems in the appendix to this chapter, and focus instead on the *character* of the entrepreneur's risk preferences.

THE ENTREPRENEUR'S RISK PREFERENCES

Since the entrepreneur's risk preferences play a key role in the firm's investment-financing decision, we would like to generalize about the character of these preferences. But that's hard to do, because risk preference is a complex and personal phenomenon. We can, however, look at various responses business firms make to uncertainty and discuss what these responses indicate about the risk preferences of the firms that make them.

---

* As we pointed out in Chapter 5, to say that a person has risk preferences implies that he can rank from least to most preferred the probability distributions which represent his expectations as to the *returns* that alternative uncertain investments may yield over time. In the present context we take "returns" to be streams of earnings *per share.*

† See Problem 12 at the end of this chapter.

‡ See Problem 14 at the end of this chapter.

Size of Expected Earnings Versus Chance of Loss

Suppose that you are given a choice between two investments: one offers a small chance of loss and the other offers no chance of loss. If you are a *risk averter,* in the everyday sense of the term, you are likely to choose the second investment over the first, even when the first offers larger expected earnings per share.

One common response to uncertainty which indicates that a firm is a risk averter in this sense is *the substitution of equity capital for debt financing.* Figure 11.2 gives some idea of the frequency with which firms resort to equity versus debt financing. It shows that, during the period 1962–66, U.S. corporations increased their liabilities in the form of bonds, mortgages, loans from banks, and loans from other firms (that's what *trade credit* means) by over $125 billion. Simultaneously they obtained $88 billion of new equity financing, almost all of which came from retained earnings.

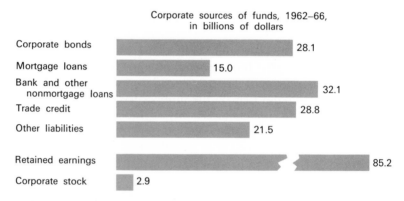

Corporate sources of funds, 1962–66, in billions of dollars

Corporate bonds	28.1
Mortgage loans	15.0
Bank and other nonmortgage loans	32.1
Trade credit	28.8
Other liabilities	21.5
Retained earnings	85.2
Corporate stock	2.9

11|2 Over the period 1962–66 U.S. corporations increased their liabilities by $125.5 billion and obtained $88.1 billion of additional equity capital, primarily through retained earnings. (Source: *Federal Reserve Bulletin*)

A second common response to uncertainty which indicates risk aversion of the sort we're talking about is the use of *a short pay-off period.* This means that a firm stipulates that any piece of fixed capital it invests in must pay for itself over a period much shorter than its expected useful life. For example, as president of Laver Brothers, you know that the $10,000 metal-stamping machine you are thinking of buying will probably last 15 years, but you won't buy it unless it will pay for itself in 3. In applying this short (3-year) pay-off period, you are in effect discounting by 100% all earnings which this machine might yield beyond the very near future. So your policy reduces to a negligible level the possibility that any investment Laver Brothers makes might lead to severe losses or, worse still, to bankruptcy. On

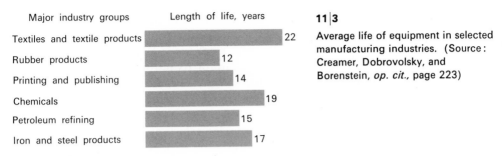

11|3

Average life of equipment in selected manufacturing industries. (Source: Creamer, Dobrovolsky, and Borenstein, *op. cit.,* page 223)

the other hand, however, your policy also keeps you from making a good many investments that would be profitable, so it tends to reduce your firm's expected earnings over time.

We can get some idea of the prevalence of short pay-off periods by comparing the average length of life of equipment in manufacturing industries with the length of the pay-off periods which firms apply when they buy equipment. Figure 11.3 shows that the average length of life of equipment in a wide range of manufacturing industries is at least 15 years. This figure contrasts sharply with those obtained in a Machine Institute survey, in which member firms were asked: "What pay-off period do your customers typically require on the investment in a replacement machine?" The surveyed firms replied that 60% of their customers expected new machines to pay for themselves within 2 to 3 years, while only 10% were willing to buy equipment with a pay-off period of over 5 years.*

Earnings Size Versus Earnings Variability

Often firms in the uncertain world of business reveal themselves to be risk averters in a second sense of the term. Whenever they have to choose between two investment options, one of which offers a distribution of possible earnings characterized by high variability and the other of which offers a distribution characterized by low variability, they choose the second option over the first, even if the first offers higher average earnings per period than the second.

One way that firms display this second sort of risk aversion is by making investments specifically designed to increase the flexibility of their operations and thus to decrease the variability of their profits over time. A firm that searches for *flexibility* this way is trying to create a capital stock that will enable it to adjust to widely varying circumstances. Of course, a capital stock that is satisfactory for each of a wide range of possible situations will probably be optimal for none, so following a policy of flexibility usually reduces

---

* George Terborgh, *Dynamic Equipment Policy;* New York: McGraw-Hill, 1949, page 191.

not only the variability of the firm's profits over time, but also its expected profits per period.

A firm can achieve flexibility in various ways. Which way will appeal to a given firm will depend on the nature of its output and the situation in which it operates. Let us hark back to the case of the Strangler Blue Jean Company, which we met earlier on in this chapter. Recall that they make super-tight jeans for teen-age girls. But they know that fashion is fickle, and next year teen-age girls may be wearing long skirts or, worse still, baggy pants. So Strangler is a firm that faces uncertainty with respect to future demand for its output. Strangler increases the flexibility of its operations by avoiding long-term purchase agreements for variable inputs (it never contracts for more than a two months' supply of blue denim at a time) and by avoiding long-term leases on fixed inputs such as buildings, land, or equipment (it makes its jeans in a dilapidated quonset hut down by the railroad tracks). Another firm might increase the flexibility of *its* operations by adopting less mechanized methods of production, by using obsolete equipment to meet peak demand, or by relying on subcontractors to perform certain tasks. Since the principal effect of such policies is to reduce a firm's investment in fixed capital, the main advantage they offer is that, by decreasing the firm's fixed costs, they protect it against losses during periods of slack demand. This advantage, however, can be purchased only at a price: lowering the firm's profits during periods of buoyant demand when more plant and equipment could profitably have been used.

Increasing the flexibility of its internal operations is not the only way a business firm can decrease the variability of its earnings. Another often-practiced method is the corporate merger. Mergers are a way in which a firm can, so to speak, hedge its bets. Mergers between firms fall into three classifications: *vertical, horizontal,* or *conglomerate.*

In a vertical merger, one firm buys out another firm that either supplies its inputs or buys its output.

As an investment technique, the vertical merger can be used in divers ways to reduce the variability of a firm's earnings over time. For example, the Strangler Blue Jean Company uses lots of blue denim and cotton thread. The prices of these raw materials are subject to wide fluctuations. So Strangler might buy out a small cotton mill, Ravel & Selvage, in order to reduce the uncertainty associated with its input prices. Or, alternatively, Ravel & Selvage might find that demand for their cotton cloth and thread is less stable than demand for the products in which it is used (such as blue jeans), so *they* might just buy out the Strangler Blue Jean Company in order to reduce the uncertainty associated with the demand for their cloth output. Vertical mergers work both ways.

In a horizontal merger, one firm buys out another firm that produces an identical or near-identical output.

In industries which sell in numerous, geographically distinct markets, horizontal mergers offer a firm a means of reducing risk through geographic diversification. The bakery industry is one example. As Walsh and Evans have noted, the primary basis for horizontal mergers between bakery producers in recent years has been ". . . to spread among many plants and markets the internal competitive risks of local markets such as price wars, active promotional campaigns of rivals, and bakery workers' strikes that cut off a plant's earnings capabilities."* We could make a similar comment about oil companies' incentives to establish retail outlets over a wide geographic area. Certainly geographic diversification was the principal professed objective of Union Oil, a company with retail outlets in the Far West, when it took over Pure Oil, a company with retail outlets throughout the Midwest and Southeast.

In a conglomerate merger, a firm in one industry buys out some other firm that manufactures a product totally unrelated to its own.

A firm can use this investment technique, which yields a diversified product line, to obtain protection against two basic sorts of risk.

First: A broadly diversified company benefits from a boom in almost any sector of the economy. Therefore business firms—particularly firms in industries subject to sharp cyclical fluctuations—can use diversification as a means of reducing the variability of their earnings over time.

Second: Diversification via conglomerate mergers can be used by firms with a narrow product base to obtain protection against obsolescence or any other threat to long-term demand for their product. This consideration undoubtedly explains why cigarette companies, whose product is clouded in a health controversy, have in recent years sought out mergers with companies whose products range from frozen chow mein to bourbon whiskey.

Conglomerate mergers are largely a postwar phenomenon. And in recent years they have become an increasingly important one, as indicated by the fact that in 1966, 60% of all mergers reported by the Federal Trade Commission were conglomerate mergers, i.e., mergers across broad industry lines. Currently the leading U.S. conglomerate is Textron, Inc., which produces a host of manufactured products—including bathroom accessories, rocket engines, electric golf carts, varnishes, cast-iron cookware, hearing aids, ball bearings, helicopters, brake drums, and cologne—and which is simultaneously one of the nation's 10 largest chicken farmers! Other recent examples

---

* Richard G. Walsh and Bert M. Evans, *op. cit.,* page 31.

of conglomerate mergers are General Mills' purchase of Playskool Manufacturing Co. (a toy producer), the Radio Corporation of America's purchase of Hertz Corp. (a car rental company), and International Telephone
and Telegraph's recent attempted merger with the American Broadcasting
Company.

Although a firm which engages in horizontal, vertical, or conglomerate
mergers in order to reduce the variability (and thus the risk) associated with
its earnings may realize a high rate of return on the funds it invests, some
such investments—like the other responses to uncertainty described above
—undoubtedly turn out to be purchases of additional certainty at the cost
of lower earnings per period. And to the extent that this is true, these investments illustrate the second sort of risk aversion described above.

OTHER INFLUENCES ON THE ENTREPRENEUR'S
ORDERING OF INVESTMENT-FINANCING OPTIONS

As we have been talking about the firm's investment decision under conditions of uncertainty, we have indicated that the entrepreneur's ordering of
alternative investment-financing options depends solely on the character of
his risk preferences. As a matter of fact, however, the entrepreneur's ranking
of investment-financing options is also influenced by other considerations.

Market Value of the Firm's Stock

If investors could always foresee the future with certainty, a share of common stock would always sell at a price precisely equal to the present value of
the profit stream which would accrue to the holder of that share over time.
Therefore, in a certain world, the effect on the firm's earnings of any investment it made would be immediately mirrored in the price of its stock. And
an entrepreneur who operated in a certain world would find that maximizing earnings per share over time would be equivalent to maximizing the
current market price of the firm's stock.

Any real-life entrepreneur, however, operates in an uncertain world.
And the way he evaluates the firm's earnings potential may differ from the
investors' way. So if he selects the investment-financing option that ranks
highest in terms of his own risk preferences, this may not be the selection
that would maximize the current market value of the firm's stock.

At first glance this possibility might appear to be a not-very-important
one, since it would seem that what the entrepreneur really ought to care
about is not the current market price of his firm's stock but its expected per-
share earnings over time. However, the entrepreneur who operates under
uncertainty may have good reasons for caring about whether or not the
current market value of his firm's stock is as high as it might be.

First: He might view maintaining a high market value for the firm's stock as an important part of his obligation to serve the interests of the firm's stockholders.

Second: He might regard the current market value of the firm's stock as an important objective measure of his personal success in managing the firm.

Third: He might be thinking of using a new stock issue to finance current or future investment. But, as we already know, whenever a firm finances an investment by issuing new stock, the profit pie must be sliced into more pieces, and that means that a cost is imposed on the firm's initial stockholders. The larger the number of shares that must be sold, the higher the cost to them. Therefore, the higher the price at which the firm's shares sell, the lower the "cost" of an equity issue will be.

Fourth: If the entrepreneur allows the market value of the firm's stock to fall to a level that is low relative to the firm's earnings per share, it may make the firm look like an attractive buy to other firms on the hunt for merger partners. If outsiders do buy up enough stock to gain control of the firm, they may fire all or most of the firm's top managers, a prospect hardly designed to appeal to the firm's officers. You might think that the management of a publicly held corporation can't really feel threatened by the possibility of a takeover by outsiders; such a threat might seem to be small and largely theoretical. However, the current flurry of corporate takeovers, voluntary and otherwise, indicates that there are plenty of corporate raiders around.

Therefore, when he makes his investment-financing decision, the entrepreneur who operates under uncertainty will be concerned not only with the way his decision will affect the firm's earnings over time but also with the way it affects the market value of the firm's stock. Thus he will rank different investment-financing options not only on the basis of his own risk preferences but also on the basis of how he thinks selection of each such option would influence the current market value of his firm's stock.

Dividend Policy

If the world were a *certain* place, a firm would have no real incentive to pursue a conscious dividend policy, because if investment returns could be foreseen with certainty, stockholders wouldn't care much one way or the other about dividends. If the firm retained current earnings and invested them profitably, this would be reflected by a rise in the market value of the firm's stock. Shareholders who preferred current to future income could convert retained earnings into current income simply by selling a small portion of their stock holdings.

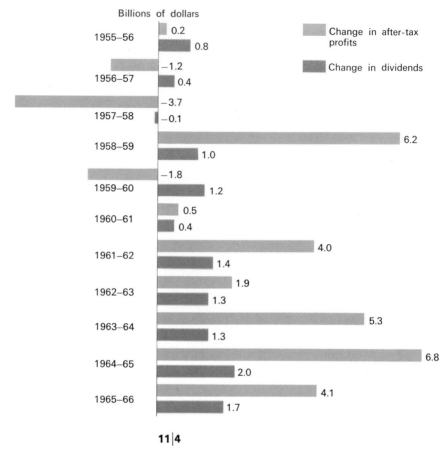

11|4

Corporations tend to maintain past dividend rates when
profits fall, but are slow to raise dividend rates when profits rise.
(Source: U.S. Department of Commerce)

In this uncertain world, however, a firm may be tempted to pay out regular dividends for several reasons.

First: Investors' risk preferences may be such that earnings retained and
profitably invested by the firm do not lead to a rise in the market value of
its stock, and stockholders who try to convert retained earnings into cash by
selling stock may therefore lose in the process.

Second: Investors are likely to view the stock of a firm with a good record of
dividend payments as a less risky investment than the stock of a company
which has paid dividends erratically or not at all; therefore dividend payments may do more than retained earnings to support the market value of
a firm's stock.

Third: An entrepreneur may, rightly or wrongly, view his firm's dividend record (like the market value of its stock) as an objective measure of his success in managing the firm.

Figure 11.4 records annual changes in corporate profits and dividend pay-outs from 1956 to the present. It suggests that corporations as a group follow a "no-retreat" dividend policy; i.e., they are loath to cut dividend pay-outs in the face of falling profits, and they are also wary about raising dividend pay-outs in a time of rising profits, unless they are pretty sure that they can sustain such increases over time.

Naturally a firm can pay out dividends only if it has money available for this purpose; whether or not it has depends on its profits during the preceding year. Thus the fact that firms tend to pursue a no-retreat dividend policy undoubtedly influences their ordering of alternative investment-financing options.

Therefore it seems likely that the investment-financing decisions made by an entrepreneur operating under uncertainty are influenced not only by his own risk preferences but also by the impact he thinks his decision will have on the current market value of his firm's stock and on the firm's ability to maintain its dividend policy.

Appendix to Chapter 11

The following problems have a special purpose: they are designed to familiarize you with the analysis developed in the chapter you have just read. In addition they are intended to show the usefulness of this analysis and to suggest how several important assertions made in the text can be proved.

So this is not just a problem section. It is a demonstration or proof-of-the-pudding section. Therefore, although it consists of problems, we have called it an appendix.

THE PRINCIPLE OF INCREASING RISK

1   a) In the example of leverage given on pages 174–175, verify that the Strangler Blue Jean Company's annual earnings increase by $1250 and that the resulting return on equity capital is 12.5%.

   b) A firm begins with $35,000 in new fixed equity-financed capital, on which it is earning a rate of return of 8%. It then borrows an additional $15,000 at 6% interest in order to buy more fixed capital. This new fixed capital yields a 7% return. Compute the firm's annual earnings and rate of return on equity capital, both before and after it takes on the $15,000 debt.

2   Suppose that a firm makes the investment whose possible returns are represented by the probability tree in Fig. 11.1. What are the probabilities of the following outcomes?

   a) The firm earns $1200 in the second year.

   b) The firm earns $1000 in both years.

   c) The firm earns more than $1000 in the second year.

   d) The firm earns $1200 in both years.

   e) The firm earns a total of $2600 in two years.

3 Point A in Fig. 11.5 represents the position of a firm that presently holds
   10,000 bushels of corn and $10,000 in cash. The price of corn is $2.00
   per bushel. By converting corn into cash, cash into corn, or borrowing
   cash to buy corn the firm can shift its position to any point along the
   line V_0P_0. For simplicity we assume that the interest rate is zero.

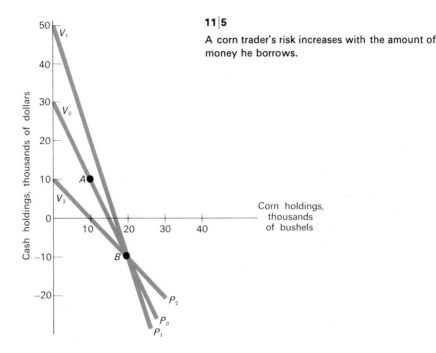

11|5

A corn trader's risk increases with the amount of
money he borrows.

a) Suppose that the firm expects that there is a $\frac{3}{4}$ probability that
   the price of corn in the next period will be $3.00, and that there is
   a $\frac{1}{4}$ probability that it will be $1.00. Then if the firm shifts to point
   B, there is a $\frac{3}{4}$ probability that its net worth in the next period will
   be V_1 and a $\frac{1}{4}$ probability that it will be V_2. Determine the maximum amount of corn that the firm could buy without incurring any
   risk of ending up in the next period with a negative net worth.

b) As the firm increases its corn holdings, what change occurs in the
   range of prices that would cause the firm's net worth in the next
   period to become negative?

4 A firm presently holds 20,000 bushels of soybeans and $5000 cash. Let
   the current price of soybeans be $2.00 per bushel and the interest rate
   be zero. The firm's expectations of what soybean prices will be in the
   next period are as follows: $3.00 per bushel with probability $\frac{2}{3}$, $1.50
   per bushel with probability $\frac{1}{6}$, $1.00 per bushel with probability $\frac{1}{6}$.

If these expectations are correct, what is the probability that the firm's net worth would be negative next period if it were to increase its soybean holdings to (a) 22,000 bushels, (b) 50,000 bushels, and (c) 100,000 bushels?

5   Sometimes a firm can choose between leasing capital equipment and borrowing funds to buy capital equipment. How would considerations of risk enter into its decision? [*Hint:* How would such a decision affect the risk of insolvency incurred by the firm? How would it affect the risk of equipment obsolescence incurred by the firm? Does your answer depend on whether the lease is a long-term or a short-term one? Note that, in actual practice, equipment leases of both sorts are frequently drawn up.]

THE FIRM'S ASSET STRUCTURE

6   a) Use the definition of investment in Chapter 10 to show that in an uncertain world all a firm's assets, whether financial or physical, are simply different forms of investment.

b) Would this result hold true in a world in which the future could be foreseen with certainty and in which debt capital were available in unlimited quantities? [*Hint:* In an uncertain world, liquid financial assets provide protection against cash inadequacy. Would they perform the same function in a certain world?]

Comment: Since all a firm's liabilities plus its net worth should be viewed as alternative forms of investment financing, it follows from Problem 6 that when a firm operates under uncertainty its investment-financing decision in each period involves choices with respect to every item on its balance sheet. Thus this decision can be described as the selection of an equilibrium balance sheet.

*7   If you look at the composition of the balance sheets of firms which are in the same industry but which have different asset sizes, you will see striking differences. Some of these differences are due to "indivisibilities." Consider for example liquid assets: Firms usually hold their liquid funds in the form of cash (i.e., currency and demand deposits†), treasury bills, certificates of deposit (a special form of commercial-bank time deposit), and commercial paper (short-term bonds issued by large corporations and finance companies). How would you expect the ratio of cash to other liquid assets to vary with the size of the firm? Statistics showing this relationship are given in the table at the top of the opposite page. [Think first, *before* you look at the statistics!]

---

* Starred problems are problems that are unusually difficult.

† *Demand deposit* is an economist's way of saying checking account.

Total manufacturing, 1961–62   Source: The U.S. Treasury Department

Asset size of firms, in thousands of dollars	Less than 1,000	1,000–2,500	2,500–5,000	5,000–10,000	10,000–25,000	25,000–50,000	More than or equal to 50,000
Cash/other liquid assets	3.93	2.25	1.83	1.49	1.24	1.23	0.60

*8   There are striking differences in the composition of the balance sheets of firms in different industries. Some reflect differences in the characteristics of the outputs these firms produce; some reflect differences in characteristics of the industries in which these firms operate. For instance, firms in the bakery industry produce a highly perishable product, while shoe manufacturers do not. Firms in the bakery industry buy their capital equipment, but shoe manufacturers rent much of theirs (from the United Shoe Machinery Corp.). How would you expect the structure of the assets held by firms in these two industries to differ? The relevant statistics are presented below, but think before you look.

Asset size of firms, in thousands of dollars	Less than 50	50–100	100–500	500–1,000	1,000–2,500	2,500–5,000	More than or equal to 5,000
Bakery products, 1963–64							
Inventories/total assets	0.13	0.15	0.12	0.09	0.11	0.12	0.14
Fixed assets/total assets	0.55	0.46	0.45	0.52	0.47	0.41	0.38
Cash/total assets	0.08	0.12	0.09	0.12	0.13	0.11	0.09
Footwear (except rubber), 1963–64							
Inventories/total assets	0.25	0.13	0.37	0.33	0.35	0.39	0.28
Fixed assets/total assets	0.30	0.22	0.16	0.15	0.12	0.9	0.13
Cash/total assets	0.05	0.25	0.07	0.06	0.07	0.07	0.07

Source: The U.S. Treasury Department

DERIVING THE FIRM'S INVESTMENT-DEMAND SCHEDULE

9   Consider bundles of goods involving different quantities of oranges, apples, and steaks. Show that if you can order all possible such bundles from least to most preferred, then you can also order bundles involving only oranges and apples. Would your ordering of oranges and apples depend on how many pounds of steak you have?

Comment: The results of Problems 9 and 6, together with our assumption about entrepreneurial risk preferences, imply that if we fix the level of all but two items in a firm's balance sheet, then the firm's entrepreneur will have well-defined preferences between these two remaining items. His preferences can, like those of the consumer, be represented by a set of indifference curves. In the problems that follow, we assume that the entrepreneur's indifference curves are: (a) convex and downward-sloping between any two assets, (b) convex and upward-sloping between an asset and a liability, if the asset is measured along the vertical axis, and (c) concave and downward-sloping between any two liabilities. Keep in mind that, other things being equal, the entrepreneur always prefers a low level of liabilities to a high level of liabilities.

10 If an entrepreneur's indifference curves between different pairs of assets and liabilities have the shapes we have assumed they do, would you consider the entrepreneur to be a risk averter? If so, in what sense are you using this term?

Note: In Problems 11 through 14, we assume that the firm under consideration does not sell any stock in the current period, and that it pays a fixed dividend. We make this assumption so that we can analyze the firm's investment decision with a graph. It does not affect the validity of our conclusions.

*11 Figure 11.6 shows a firm's indifference map for assets and liabilities. For simplicity we have assumed that all the firm's liabilities take the form of a single kind of bond. Initially the firm holds assets equal to OA and liabilities equal to OB. Thus, starting from the point O', any upward movement by the firm will represent an increase in its assets (i.e., positive investment), while any rightward movement will represent an increase in its outstanding bond liabilities.

For simplicity, assume that the firm pays no interest on its bonds, but sells them at a discount. Then the relationship between the investments the firm makes, the earnings it retains, and the additional bonds it sells can be represented by the budget line $CDEF$. The slope of this line depends on the going rate of interest. If this rate equals zero, the firm will be able to sell its bonds at face value, and the slope of the budget line $CDEF$ will equal 1. But if the market rate of interest is positive, the firm will have to sell its bonds at a discount (i.e., below face value), and the slope of its budget line will be less than 1.

   a) What is the significance of the distance $O'D$ (the amount of investment the firm can make without selling additional bonds)?

   b) Verify the assertions above concerning the relationship between the slope of the budget line $CDEF$ and the market rate of interest.

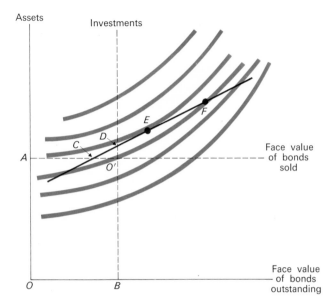

11|6 A firm which operates under uncertainty chooses
         its equilibrium balance sheet.

    c) What level of investment will the firm whose indifference map
and budget line are shown in Fig. 11.6 make in equilibrium?

    d) What would it mean if the firm were to attain equilibrium at a
point to the left of BO' but above AO'?

    e) Draw an arbitrary horizontal line starting from the investment
axis and going to the right. Then use the principle of increasing
risk, illustrated in Problem 3, to show that if the firm is a risk
averter the successive indifference curves which this horizontal
line intersects will become steeper and steeper.

*12 As we noted in Problem 11, the higher the going interest rate is, the
flatter the firm's budget line, $CDEF$, will be. Use this information to
generate a series of budget lines (each of which corresponds to a different interest rate) for the firm whose preferences and current investment position are shown in Fig. 11.6. Then use these budget lines to
derive this firm's investment demand schedule (i.e., a schedule that
shows the relationship between the going interest rate and the quantity
of investment the firm makes). Can you show that, if the firm is a risk
averter, then this curve will slope downward, as the investment demand
schedule in Fig. 10.1 does? [*Hint:* Use the result you obtained in Problem 11(e).]

*13 Use the results you obtained in Problems 11 and 12 to show that an increase in the firm's current profits will shift its investment-demand schedule to the right. [*Hint:* Use the result you obtained in Problem 11(e), and remember that the firm pays a fixed dividend.]

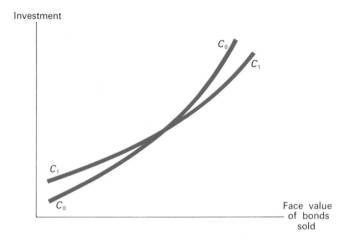

11|7 A permanent shift in a firm's demand curve changes
the slope of its indifference curves.

*14 A firm has a horizontal demand curve. The demand for its output shifts upward, and the change is expected to be permanent; this affects the shape of the firm's indifference curves for investment and liabilities. The increased demand lessens the risk associated with expansion and the firm is now willing to borrow more for a given increase in investment. Thus its indifference curves become flatter. This change is illustrated in Fig. 11.7, in which C_0C_0 is an indifference curve before the shift in demand and C_1C_1 is an indifference curve after the shift. Show that such a shift causes the firm's investment-demand curve to shift to the right. Then use this result to prove that, under uncertainty as under certainty, a firm's long-run supply curve will be more elastic than its short-run supply curve.

THE FIRM'S FINANCING STRUCTURE

*15 Since the cost of long-term borrowing compared with the cost of short-term borrowing is much higher for small firms than for large ones, we would expect the ratio of long-term debt to short-term debt to increase with the size of the firm. Verify this result with an appropriate diagram. Then check it against the data which are presented in the table at the top of the opposite page.

Total manufacturing, 1961–62   Source: The U.S. Treasury Department

Asset size of firms, in thousands of dollars	Less than 1,000	1,000–2,500	2,500–5,000	5,000–10,000	10,000–25,000	25,000–50,000	More than or equal to 50,000
Long-term liabilities/ short-term liabilities	0.37	0.39	0.48	0.59	0.65	0.90	1.00

*16 How do you think the variability of a firm's income would influence its preferences (i.e., the shape of its indifference curves) for long-term versus short-term debt? People buy bread every day, but they buy tables infrequently. Therefore the income streams of firms in the bakery industry are presumably more stable than those of firms in the furniture industry. If so, what does your answer to the above question imply about the relative ratios of long-term to short-term debt that firms in the bakery and furniture industries would maintain? Check your predictions against the data below.

Asset size of firms, in thousands of dollars	Less than 50	50–100	100–500	500–1,000	1,000–2,500	2,500–5,000	More than or equal to 5,000
Furniture (household), 1963–64							
Long-term liabilities /short-term liabilities	0.22	0.22	0.28	0.28	0.40	0.45	0.50
Bakery products, 1963–64							
Long-term liabilities /short-term liabilities	0.46	0.45	0.57	0.55	0.44	1.06	0.70

Source: The U.S. Treasury Department

*17 As indicated by the data below, the larger the size of the assets of a manufacturing firm, the lower its debt–equity ratio. What reasons can you think of that might explain this phenomenon?

Total manufacturing, 1961–62   Source: The U.S. Treasury Department

Asset size of firms, in thousands of dollars	Less than 1,000	1,000–2,500	2,500–5,000	5,000–10,000	10,000–25,000	25,000–50,000	More than or equal to 50,000
Debt/equity	0.95	0.70	0.60	0.53	0.49	0.53	0.51

Part 3
PERFECTLY COMPETITIVE
MARKETS

CHAPTER 12

MARKETS

As we said in Chapter 1, consumers have unlimited wants but society has limited resources. How are the scarce resources of an economy allocated? The microeconomist breaks this question down into three aspects:

1) What determines the composition of the bundle of goods and services that the economy produces?
2) What determines the proportions in which inputs are combined to produce these outputs?
3) What determines the way these outputs are allocated among consumers?

In a market economy resources are allocated by means of trading between buyers and sellers of inputs and outputs. Thus, to study resource allocation in such an economy, the microtheorist must analyze the way buyers and sellers of any good interact in the marketplace to determine the *quantity* that each buyer buys, the *quantity* that each seller sells, and the *price* at which trading occurs.

WHAT IS A MARKET?

A market is obviously a place where consumers and producers get together to trade inputs and outputs. But this country-fair picture of a market, although it may adequately describe some of the markets in a modern market economy, is too simplistic to describe all of them. Commodities are sold under richly varied sets of institutional arrangements, and the term "a market" may be applied to any one of these arrangements.

To gain some idea of the broad range of trading conditions, let's look at the different markets through which a single commodity, wheat, passes on its way from the farmer to the consumer. These markets all deal with some form of the same commodity, but they differ sharply in structure and in the fashion in which buyers and sellers interact within them to establish market price.

The Local and Terminal Wheat Markets

Farmers located over a wide geographic area produce wheat, and most of them sell the wheat they grow to one of the many small country grain elevators. Some of these elevators are operated by independent dealers, some by farmers' cooperatives, and some are "line" elevators, that is, elevators that form part of a chain of elevators operated by a grain company or a miller. Since country elevators are quite numerous in most areas, a farmer may have some choice as to which local elevator he will sell to, but typically he will be operating in a market in which there are many sellers but no more than 2 or 3 buyers at most.

The independent dealers and cooperatives who operate country elevators usually resell the wheat immediately in order to protect themselves against possible price fluctuations. The buyers to whom they sell are likely to be dealers who operate large elevators in terminal markets; or in some instances grain millers themselves. In any case these buyers are generally rather far away from the country elevator, and thus some sort of go-between is required to bring buyers and sellers "together." Typically this go-between is a cash commission merchant, who for a fixed price takes on the responsibility of selling the country elevator's wheat. Since country elevators number in the thousands and since terminal elevators and mills both number in the hundreds, the local grain-elevator operator usually resells the grain he has purchased in a market in which both buyers and sellers are numerous.

The terminal elevator operators who buy this wheat usually store it for months and then resell it, via brokers and cash commission merchants, mostly to domestic millers, but also in the export market. Because of the national (and international) scope of the wheat market, operators of terminal elevators have many potential buyers, but they also have to compete with many other sellers.

Now we come to an odd aspect of the situation: Most of the wheat that passes through the hands of local and terminal elevators is eventually resold to *domestic* millers to make into flour. Then why do there have to be all these intermediaries or middlemen between the farmer and the miller? Answer: Each of them performs important functions.

The operator of the local grain elevator does two things: (a) He accumulates small purchases of wheat into large lots that can be economically shipped to a central market and resold there to a large buyer. (b) He classifies the many kinds and qualities of wheat that farmers sell to him into standard grades; each grade is so nearly *homogeneous* that distant buyers can safely buy it sight unseen.

To understand the function of the terminal elevator operator, we must generalize for a moment. First: Almost all wheat is harvested between June and September, but all of us eat wheat in some form every day of the year.

Second: Because of the vagaries of the weather, the wheat harvest varies from year to year; however, people keep consuming wheat at the same rate year after year. Thus wheat production is both seasonal and erratic, while consumption remains almost constant. And this means that somewhere between the farmer and the ultimate consumer there have to be facilities for storing huge quantities of grain. The principal function of the terminal dealers is to provide such storage facilities. They have elevators capable of holding thousands or even millions of bushels of wheat.

Since operators of country elevators resell wheat in a terminal market, the prices these local operators offer farmers are geared to the prices commanded by different grades of wheat in the terminal market. These prices are in turn determined by trading between the buyers and sellers who participate in the terminal markets. Since these buyers and sellers are numerous, no one of them is able to exercise a perceptible influence on market price. Each buyer and seller has to accept the going market price.

The Wheat Exchange

The domestic millers who buy wheat in terminal markets produce (a) various grades of flour, which they sell to bakeries, and (b) millfeed, a waste byproduct which they sell as animal feed. Typically millers sell standard grades of flour to small bakers for immediate delivery. For larger bakeries, however, they frequently custom-produce special grades of flour; they sell this as much as 3 to 6 months before they deliver it. This timing raises a crucial problem.

Figure 12.1 gives a clue to the problem. It shows that the price of wheat is subject to enormous fluctuations. Therefore millers who contract to sell flour months hence at fixed prices obviously run a risk. What if the price of wheat soars upward? Millers are not the only buyers and sellers of wheat who run a risk because the price of wheat fluctuates; operators of country and terminal elevators do too. And even the farmer does, because the farmer inevitably ends up playing the dual role of producer and speculator in wheat unless he sells his wheat forward at the same time he plants it (that is, unless he contracts when he plants his wheat to sell this wheat at a fixed price at harvest time).

Naturally the primary interest of farmers, grain dealers, and millers is to carry out their business successfully and make a reasonable profit. Moreover, since the profits they earn are small at best, they are neither disposed to, nor are they financially capable of, bearing the immense aggregate risks posed by fluctuations in the market price of wheat. These risks must, however, be borne by someone.

The dilemma has been solved by the setting up of special wheat exchanges. A wheat exchange, like any other commodity exchange, is a market in which individuals, acting through brokers, buy and sell specified quantities of the commodity for delivery *at some future date*.

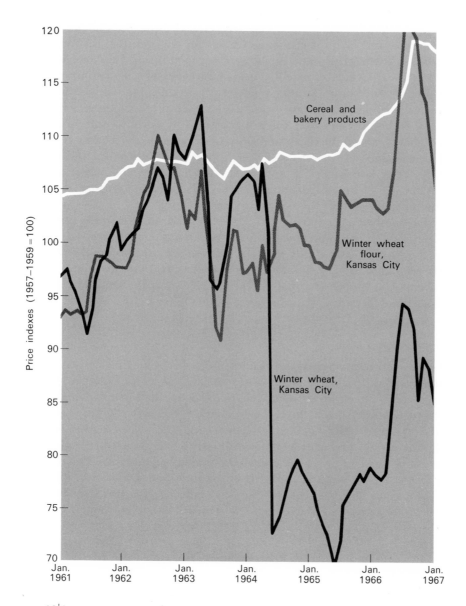

12|1

Over time, the prices of wheat and flour fluctuate sharply, while the price of bread goes steadily upward. (Source: U.S. Department of Commerce)

The primary function of a wheat exchange, however, is *not* to effect deliveries of actual wheat between buyers and sellers, but to permit the risks that would normally fall on wheat producers, dealers, and millers to be transferred to speculators who have the money and the inclination to bear these risks. On a wheat exchange, the farmer who produces wheat, the operator of a terminal elevator who stores it, and the miller who holds wheat inventories can all protect themselves against the risk that an unforeseen decline in the price of wheat might wipe out their normal business profits by selling wheat forward (i.e., selling it for future delivery) in amounts equal to the quantity of wheat that they are currently producing or selling. Similarly, the miller who sells flour for future delivery can protect himself against the risk of an unforeseen rise in the price of wheat by buying wheat forward.

These forward purchases and sales are frequently referred to as *hedges;* all are designed to protect the hedger from the risk of loss due to an unfavorable price movement. Of course, at the same time, the hedger also forgoes the possibility of gain due to favorable price movements; that's the other side of the coin.

Obviously if a commodity exchange is to function successfully there must be buyers willing to purchase the futures contracts offered by hedgers. Who are these buyers? Generally they are professional risk bearers (i.e., speculators) who are attracted by the hedger's contract because this contract offers not only the risk of loss that the hedger is trying to avoid, but also the opportunity for gain that the hedger is willing to forgo.

The Market for Flour

On the exchanges where wheat futures are traded among hedgers and speculators, as in the national market where wheat is traded for cash, participating buyers and sellers are so numerous that no one of them can perceptibly influence market price. In the flour market, however, the largest millers and the largest bakeries can and do perceptibly influence market price. In fact, the prices at which the major mills sell to the largest bakeries are the subject of active negotiation between these bakeries and mills. The prices set by means of such negotiations are crucially important throughout the industry, since they form the basis for the prices mills charge other large buyers as well as the prices at which they sell standard grades of flour to smaller bakeries.

The Market for Bread

Most bakeries of any size are wholesalers which sell their bread and other baked goods to independent grocers and grocery chains. Because bread must be transported rapidly from point of production to point of sale and because transportation costs rise sharply with distance traveled, most bread is sold within a 50-mile radius of its production point. Thus the market for bread is composed of many small local markets.

In the typical local bread market, several national or large regional bakeries and one or two local independents dominate supply. There is also frequently a fringe of smaller sellers, some of whom are able to survive only because they produce specialty products or provide special service functions.

Consumer demand for bread is notoriously price-inelastic. Therefore price competition doesn't appeal to bread producers, since it threatens the established price level but doesn't guarantee increased sales. So in local bread markets, price is frequently established not by competition among sellers, but by one of the big suppliers who acts as a price leader and whose prices are matched by all the other sellers in the market.

Although wholesale bakeries avoid price competition, they engage in extensive *nonprice competition.* This may assume the form of (a) advertising directed at the consumer, (b) product differentiation (e.g., a new low-calorie bread, a loaf which has a novel size, or an improved bread wrapper) designed to identify a bakery's products in the consumer's mind, and (c) special inducements to grocers, in the form of cash payments or building improvements in exchange for rack space in their stores.

The final market through which bread and other baked goods pass is the retail food market. Since consumers don't like to go very far to buy their food, this market, like the wholesale bread market, is composed of many small local markets, in which the number of buyers is large but the number of sellers varies from large to small, depending on the area. Food retailers usually sell bread at the retail price set by the wholesalers, but this doesn't mean that there is no price competition among grocers. Quite the contrary. Many chain stores engage in price competition by selling private-label breads at prices substantially below those of wholesale brand-name breads.

MARKET STRUCTURE

Our survey of the various markets through which a single commodity, wheat, passes on its way from producer to consumer has emphasized the fact that markets differ widely in their principal characteristics: Some markets, such as the terminal market for wheat, are worldwide in scope; some, like the market for flour, are national or regional in scope; and some, like the market for bread, are local in scope. In markets such as the wheat exchange, brokers, agents, and other go-betweens act to bring buyers and sellers together, while in other markets, such as the local retail food market, buyers and sellers meet face to face. In some markets many sellers operate; in others, sellers are few. Some markets are characterized by many buyers, others are dominated by a few large buyers and a fringe of smaller ones. In some markets a single homogeneous product (e.g., wheat) or a collection of homogeneous ones is sold; while in other markets product differentiation is rife and the product sold is heterogeneous.

The process by which price is determined must also vary considerably from market to market, as witnessed by our observation that in some markets (e.g., the wheat exchange) individual buyers and sellers cannot perceptibly influence market price, while in others (e.g., the market for flour) price is negotiated between major buyers and sellers, and in still others (e.g., the local market for wholesale bread), price is set by a single seller, the local price leader. The data in Fig. 12.1 give further evidence that the process of price determination varies from market to market. Note that the price of wheat and flour move through wide and erratic swings, while bread just follows a steady upward trend.

Does the fact that markets have such widely differing characteristics mean that in order to describe the way prices are determined in a modern market economy, we must make a market-by-market study? Fortunately, no. All we really need to know about a given market is its general structure; that is: (1) the numerousness of the buyers, (2) the numerousness of the sellers, and (3) the homogeneity or nonhomogeneity of the product.

When economists analyze the way prices are determined in a modern market economy, they begin by distinguishing between *perfectly competitive* and *imperfectly competitive* markets. As defined by an economist, a perfectly competitive market must meet three principal requirements:

First: The buyers and sellers who operate in this market must be so numerous that no buyer or seller will be able by his actions to perceptibly influence market price.

Second: The product sold in the market must be homogeneous; i.e., it must be impossible for buyers to distinguish among different units of that product according to their origin, terms of sale, or quality.

Third: All sellers and buyers in the market must have access to full and immediate knowledge of the price at which trading is currently taking place.

This last requirement ensures that any perfectly competitive market, even if it is geographically dispersed, will operate as a single whole instead of as many parts. It also ensures that at any instant all trading within a perfectly competitive market will take place at the same price. In many markets which fulfill the requirements of perfect competition, the function of brokers, agents, and other go-betweens is to provide the communication between geographically dispersed buyers and sellers so that each may have full knowledge of current market conditions.

Perfectly competitive markets represent one extreme in the broad range of possible market structures. They also provide a yardstick against which we can measure the efficiency with which different markets allocate resources. That is why we're going to begin our study of price determination with perfectly competitive markets. In Part 3 we shall analyze the way price and quantity sold are determined in perfectly competitive markets, and apply the perfectly competitive model to practical issues and situations. In Part 4 we shall talk about price determination in *imperfectly* competitive markets; that is, in markets which fail to meet the requirements of perfect competition.

PROBLEMS

1   Think of the markets in which you buy everyday commodities such as haircuts, milk, and other necessities. Do any of these markets meet the conditions of perfect competition? If not, why not? Are any of the markets in which you shop perfectly competitive?

2   Can you think of any market in which you might buy or sell in which there are active brokers or other go-betweens? If so, what functions do these people serve?

3   What homogeneous products, if any, are sold in a drugstore? In a grocery store? On the New York Stock Exchange?

4   On July 25, 1967, wheat was quoted on the Kansas City exchange at $1.59 per bushel for delivery in September, at $1.62 per bushel for delivery in December and at $1.65 per bushel for delivery in March. On the same day live hogs were quoted at $23.00 per hundred pounds for delivery in August and at $20.75 per hundred pounds for delivery in December. What factors do you think determine the relationship between the September, December, and March prices of wheat? Between the August and December price of hogs? Would you expect the price of wheat to move through a similar seasonal pattern every year? What about the price of hogs?

CHAPTER 13

PRICE DETERMINATION IN A PERFECTLY COMPETITIVE MARKET

In most markets we shall study in this part and the next, interaction between buyers and sellers establishes an easily identifiable *equilibrium* position. To say that the market for any commodity is in equilibrium implies that, if trading were to occur in this market during a number of consecutive periods, the price established and quantity traded would not change so long as all factors that influenced the behavior of buyers and sellers remained constant.

In this chapter we shall begin our survey of perfectly competitive markets by studying the way such markets attain equilibrium. Since competitive markets, like other markets, attain equilibrium through the interaction of buyers and sellers, we have to begin by analyzing the way buyers and sellers behave under conditions of perfect competition.

THE MARKET DEMAND CURVE

The first requirement of a perfectly competitive market is that buyers be so numerous that the purchases of each of them form an insignificant part of total market sales. Each buyer in such a market can purchase as much or as little as he chooses to at the going market price without fear or hope of altering that price. Thus the buyer who operates in a perfectly competitive market is a price taker. As we showed in Chapter 4, however, whenever the consumer operates in an output market as a price taker, his market behavior (i.e., his response to market price) can be represented by a demand curve that slopes downward, as the one in Fig. 4.5 does. Similarly in Chapter 9 we showed that, whenever a firm operates in an input market as a price taker, its market behavior can also be represented by a downward-sloping demand curve, like the one in Fig. 9.8.

What about the behavior of buyers *as a group* in a perfectly competitive market? Obviously if we can represent the behavior of each single buyer by a demand curve, then by adding the demand curves of all buyers, we can

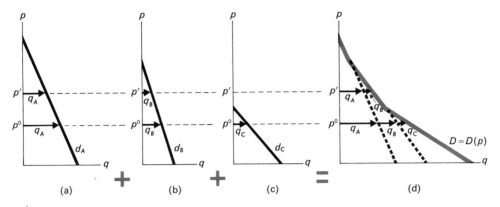

13|1

Adding the input demand curves of three firms. (a) The Ace Company's demand curve. (b) The Bullseye Company's demand curve. (c) The Chow Company's demand curve. (d) The combined demand curves of Ace, Bullseye, and Chow.

obtain a *market demand curve* that will tell us how these buyers behave as a group.

The market demand curve for any commodity, like the demand curves of individual consumers of this commodity, must slope downward. Example: Three frozen-food manufacturers make meat pies which they market under the brand names Ace, Bullseye, and Chow. All three companies use chicken as meat in their pies. They buy chickens by the ton. How would they respond to two prices, p' and a lower price p^0, that might be charged for chickens? If their demand curves slope downward, as we would expect them to, then (1) any one of these firms that was willing to buy some chickens at the price p' would be willing to buy more at a lower price such as p^0; also (2) any one of these firms that was *un*willing to buy chickens at the price p' might be willing to buy some at a lower price such as p^0. Possibility (1) is illustrated in Fig. 13.1 by the response of the Ace and Bullseye companies to a decrease in price from p' to p^0. Possibility (2) is illustrated by the response of the Chow Company to a similar decrease in price. Both responses to a decrease in price increase demand; thus we see that the market demand curve for any commodity will slope downward, as the curve in Fig. 13.1(d) does.

THE MARKET SUPPLY CURVE

The second requirement of a perfectly competitive market is that sellers be so numerous that no one seller can influence market price. Each seller in a perfectly competitive market is confronted with a going market price. He can sell nothing above this price but as much as he wants to at this price. Therefore the seller, like the buyer, is a *price taker*.

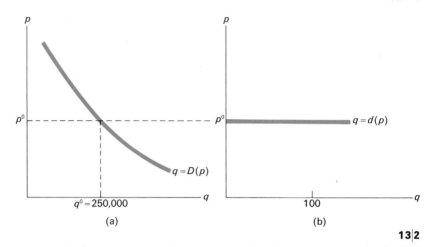

13|2

The relationship, in a perfectly competitive market, between market demand curve and the demand curve facing an individual seller. (a) The market demand curve for chickens. (b) The demand curve facing an individual seller of chickens when the going market price for them equals p^0.

In Chapter 9 we showed that the demand curve of a price-taking firm can be represented by a horizontal curve like that in Fig. 13.2(b). You may well wonder how a firm selling in a perfectly competitive market in which the market demand curve slopes downward always finds itself faced with a *horizontal* demand curve. We can explain this apparent paradox in terms of perspective.

Xtra Good Birds is a Georgia farm that produces and sells chickens. The market demand for chickens is shown in Fig. 13.2(a). The going price of chickens is p^0 and the quantity sold, q^0, equals 250,000 tons per month. Then potential demand for Xtra Good's chickens can be represented by the segment of the market demand curve lying to the right of q^0. However, not all this segment of the curve will be relevant to Xtra Good's decision about the quantity of chickens it will produce and sell; in fact, only a tiny portion of the curve lying directly to the right of the point (p^0, q^0) will be. We know that must be so because in a perfectly competitive market the maximum sales of each seller must be small relative to total market sales.

To illustrate what this requirement implies about the slope of the demand curve facing an individual seller, suppose that Xtra Good's *MC* curve begins to rise sharply after its monthly output reaches 50 tons, and that the price would never be high enough to induce it to produce and sell more than 100 tons per month. Then the portion of the market demand curve relevant to Xtra Good's decision will be the segment lying between the quantities 250,000 and 250,100. Any movement over this segment of the market demand curve would of course cause only an imperceptible price change. Moreover, if the tiny segment of the market demand curve lying between the quantities 250,000 and 250,100 is replotted on an axis in which the price scale is left unchanged but the quantity scale is vastly enlarged, the resulting curve will appear horizontal (like that in Fig. 13.2b), even though in fact it slopes imperceptibly downward.

This argument suggests that the firm which sells in a perfectly competitive market is like a person who stands on a curved earth and declares that what he sees is flat. Each sees too little of the whole to perceive its true shape.

How will our price-taking seller, Xtra Good, behave in the marketplace? As we showed in Chapter 9, whenever a firm takes price as given, its market behavior (i.e., its response to price) can be represented by a supply curve that slopes upward, as the one derived in Fig. 9.6 does.

We have said that every firm that sells in a perfectly competitive market is a price taker. Therefore, to obtain a single *market supply curve* that will represent the behavior of all sellers as a group, we must add their individual supply curves. It's a safe bet that this curve, like the supply curves of individual sellers, will slope upward.

To illustrate why, let's consider the chicken market again. Three farms —Xtra Good Birds, Yankee Poultry, and Zodiac Hens—all produce and sell chickens. How will they react to two different prices, p' and a lower price p^0, that they might get for their chickens? If their supply curves slope upward, as we'd expect them to, then (1) any one of these farmers who was willing to sell some chickens at the price p^0 would be willing to sell more at a higher price, such as p'; also (2) any one of these farmers who was *un*willing to sell chickens at the price p^0 might be willing to sell some at a higher price, such as p'. Possibility (1) is illustrated in Fig. 13.3 by the responses of Xtra Good

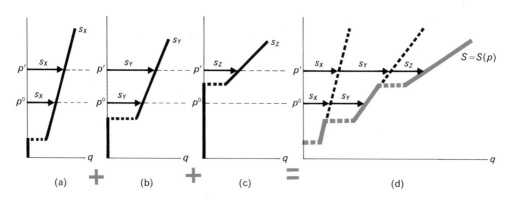

13|3

Adding the supply curves of three sellers. (a) The supply curve of Xtra Good Birds. (b) The supply curve of the Yankee Poultry Company. (c) The supply curve of Zodiac Hens. (d) The combined supply curves of the three.

Birds and Yankee Poultry to an increase in market price from p^0 to p'. Possibility (2) is illustrated by the response of Zodiac Hens to a similar increase in price. Since both responses increase market supply, we see that the market supply curve for any commodity must, like the supply curve in Fig. 13.3(d), slope upward.

PRICE DETERMINATION IN A PERFECTLY COMPETITIVE MARKET

Let us briefly summarize the results obtained so far in this chapter: (1) In any perfectly competitive market both buyers and sellers are *price takers* and *quantity setters;* that is, each regards price as given and responds to it by selecting the quantity he wishes to buy or sell at that price. (2) The quantity response to price of buyers as a group can be represented by a downward-sloping market demand curve, while the quantity response to price of sellers as a group can be represented by an upward-sloping market supply curve.

Now: How can we characterize the equilibrium price in a perfectly competitive market? From the definition of equilibrium we gave at the beginning of this chapter, it follows that:

An equilibrium price in a perfectly competitive market is one that, once established, will endure so long as the various factors that determine the positions of the market supply and demand curves do not change.

The only price that would fit this definition is *one that elicits mutually consistent quantity responses from both buyers and sellers.* If the price established in a perfectly competitive market did *not* elicit mutually consistent quantity responses from buyers and sellers (i.e., if it did not equate supply and demand), there would be either a group of unsatisfied sellers who could not sell as much as they would like to at that price or a group of unsatisfied buyers who could not purchase as much as they would like to at that price. The attempts of this *group* of unsatisfied individuals to increase either their purchases or their sales would inevitably alter market price.

What is the equilibrium position of the market in Fig. 13.4? Obviously at any price above p^0, the quantity offered by producers will exceed the quantity demanded by consumers. Suppose that price were set at p'. Then supply would exceed demand, and there would be *excess supply* equal to E_s, which indicates that, if the price p' reigned, some suppliers wouldn't be able to sell as much as they would like to. This group of unsatisfied sellers could be eliminated only by a fall in market price that would simultaneously increase demand and decrease supply.

At any price below p^0, the quantity demanded by buyers will exceed the supply offered by producers. Thus, for example, if price were set at p'', there would be *excess demand* equal to E_d, which would mean that there was a group of unsatisfied buyers who could be eliminated only by a rise in market price that would decrease demand and increase supply.

At the price p^0, however, demand equals supply (i.e., the quantity responses of buyers and sellers to price are mutually consistent), and no unsatisfied group of buyers or sellers exists. Hence p^0 must represent the equilibrium price. We thus conclude that:

In a perfectly competitive market, the equilibrium point is at the intersection of the market demand and supply curves, because this is the only point at which supply and demand are equal.

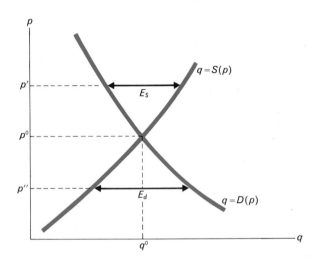

13|4

A perfectly competitive market attains equilibrium at the price p^0, since this is the price that equates market demand with market supply. The equilibrium quantity sold equals q^0.

Since both buyers and sellers in a perfectly competitive market set quantity in response to price, price in such a market plays the key role of an *equilibrating variable*. It is through upward and downward adjustments in price that the market attains equilibrium. Whenever market supply or demand shifts, price will change and there will be a new equilibrium.

Although we have been talking about the equilibrium price in a perfectly competitive market, we have simultaneously been characterizing the *equilibrium quantity sold*. If the market in Fig. 13.4 attains equilibrium at the price p^0, then obviously the quantity of output sold in equilibrium must equal q^0, since q^0 represents the quantity response that both buyers and sellers would make to the price p^0.

Once we know the equilibrium price, we can determine not only the quantity of output that will be traded, but also the amounts that all individuals in the market will buy and sell at that price. We can do this by looking at the individual demand and supply curves that were added to obtain the market supply and demand curves. Suppose for example that Figs. 13.1, 13.3, and 13.4 all refer to the same market: chickens. Then we can determine the quantity of chickens that the Ace Company will buy at the equilibrium price p^0 simply by consulting its demand schedule, which is shown in Fig. 13.1. Similarly we can determine the quantity of chickens that Yankee Poultry will sell at the equilibrium price, p^0, by consulting its supply schedule, shown in Fig. 13.3.

THE EFFECT ON EQUILIBRIUM OF SHIFTS IN MARKET DEMAND AND SUPPLY

We have defined the equilibrium values of price and quantity sold in a perfectly competitive market as values that will be maintained so long as the factors which determine the position and shape of the market demand and supply curves do not change. Over time, however, the *other-things-constant* assumption that underlies both the supply and the demand curve cannot be maintained. Whenever it is violated one or both of these curves will shift. What effect will such a shift have on market equilibrium?

A Shift in Market Demand

To take a concrete example, apples, we shall see how a shift in demand affects equilibrium in the apple market. Suppose that either a lot of people begin to prefer apples to other fruits, or the prices of oranges and bananas rise, or the incomes of apple-eating consumers increase. Any one of these changes would increase the amount of apples that consumers would demand at any given price. In other words, the demand curves of individual consumers for apples would shift upward and rightward, and thus the market demand curve for apples would also shift upward and rightward.

Figure 13.5 shows the impact on equilibrium in the apple market of such an upward and rightward shift. The initial market demand curve is the curve D; the market is initially in equilibrium at price p^0 and output q^0. As consumer demand for apples increases, the demand curve shifts upward from D to D', which creates excess demand at the old equilibrium price, p^0. This excess demand, E_d, forces price upward until a new equilibrium is established at price p' and output q', which correspond to the point of intersection between the new market demand curve D' and the market supply curve S.

All of which goes to prove that an upward shift in the market demand curve increases the equilibrium price and quantity sold. A downward shift in the market demand curve would have the opposite effect.

A Shift in Market Supply

Now let's see how a shift in supply alters market equilibrium. A fellow named Winesap Jones invents a new and revolutionary way to pick apples, which is a simple machine (it involves a vacuum-cleaner motor) with a long wand that operates by suction. He calls his machine the Applevac. Using

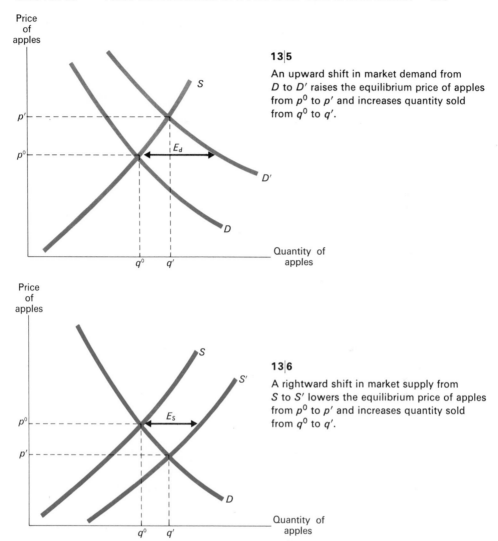

13|5

An upward shift in market demand from D to D' raises the equilibrium price of apples from p^0 to p' and increases quantity sold from q^0 to q'.

13|6

A rightward shift in market supply from S to S' lowers the equilibrium price of apples from p^0 to p' and increases quantity sold from q^0 to q'.

Applevac is a lot cheaper than using people to pick apples; also Applevac doesn't eat any apples, as workers always do. So Applevac lowers the cost curves of apple growers. As this happens, the supply curves of apple growers shift downward and rightward, and so too does the market supply curve for apples.

Figure 13.6 shows the effect on equilibrium of this downward and right-ward shift in the market supply curve (note that this corresponds to an *increase* in the supply of apples). The initial market supply curve is the curve S; the market is initially in equilibrium at price p^0 and output q^0. As the cost of producing apples decreases, however, the market supply curve for apples shifts rightward from S to S'. This shift, which creates excess supply equal to E_s at the old equilibrium price p^0, causes price to fall until a new equilibrium is established at the point (p', q') at which the market supply curve S' intersects the market demand curve D.

This example shows that a rightward shift in the market supply curve (i.e., an increase in the supply) lowers the equilibrium price and increases the equilibrium quantity sold. A leftward shift in the market supply curve (i.e., a decrease in supply) would have the opposite effect.

THE TANKSHIP MARKET: AN EXAMPLE

Textbooks usually turn to agriculture for examples of perfectly competitive markets, because the markets in which most agricultural products are sold contain thousands of small farmers on the supply side, hundreds of processors on the demand side, and to the delight of economists they deal in a homogeneous product. Examples: wheat, beef, eggs, soybeans, hogs, lard, and a host of other farm products. But for a change let's discuss the not-so-obvious example of tankships. Since oil companies are the principal users of tankship services, one would expect the tankship market to be controlled by the major oil companies and therefore to fit into the category of imperfectly competitive markets (which we shall talk about in Part 4). However, as Z. S. Zannetos showed in a recent study,* the tankship market turns out to be a highly competitive one, in which the price determined by the interaction of supply and demand is extremely volatile.

Tankship Services

Although the oil tankers now afloat range from World War II tankers with a capacity of 16,500 deadweight tons to modern supertankers of 100,000 DWT or more, they all provide basically the same service: transporting oil. Thus the service sold in this market is homogeneous. But, although the services they provide are homogeneous, tankers may be chartered in different ways: for a single voyage, for a number of consecutive voyages, or for a long-term period. The single-voyage market is referred to as the *spot* market; this is the market we shall talk about here.

The Demand for Tankship Services

Oil companies depend on their own ships, and on ships under long-term charter, to meet approximately 90% of their transport needs. For the remaining 10%, they depend on the spot tankship market. The number of

---

* Zenon S. Zannetos, *The Theory of Oil Tankship Rates;* Cambridge, Mass.: M.I.T. Press, 1966. Our discussion borrows heavily from Zannetos' description.

oil producers and refiners who are active bidders in this spot market is large. Therefore no one buyer is able to control or appreciably influence market price. All buyers are *price takers,* and their behavior can thus be represented by a market demand curve that slopes downward.

How elastic will this curve be? The answer hinges on three factors: *First,* tankship services constitute an input for which no substitute exists. *Second,* the cost of transport by tankship represents only a small fraction of the total cost of producing final petroleum products such as fuel oil and gasoline. *Third,* the demand for final petroleum products is highly inelastic, especially over the short run. We recall from Chapter 9 that each of these three factors—lack of substitutes, small role in total cost, and inelastic demand for output—tends to make demand for an input inelastic. Therefore the demand of oil companies for tankship services is extremely *inelastic.*

The Supply of Tankship Services

Since the oil companies are the principal users of tankers and since they also operate their own fleets, one would think that they would effectively control supply in the tankship market. But no. According to Zannetos,* there are more than 600 companies that own and operate tankships and no one of them controls more than 7% of the total number afloat. Even the largest independents, such as the fabled Greek shipowners Niarchos and Onassis, control fleets that are much smaller than those controlled by the big oil companies, and yet it is the independents and not the oil companies who are usually on the supply side of the tankship market. Therefore seller concentration in this market is probably much smaller than that 7% figure would indicate.

All this implies that sellers in the spot market must be *price takers* and that their market behavior can be represented by a single *market supply curve.* To envision the shape this supply curve will have in the short run, let's start from the top of the curve and work down. When *all* tankers are in operation, it is impossible, over the short run at least, for tankship owners to expand capacity in response to a rise in price. Therefore the top portion of the supply curve for tankers is almost vertical. We say almost because there is always the possibility that high rates in the oil-tanker market will bring about the transfer of ships from other uses, such as the transport of grain and molasses, into the transport of oil. However, it costs a lot to make such transfers, and the number of ships that could be transferred at a given moment represents only a fraction of total tankship capacity. Hence such transfers are unlikely to add much elasticity to the top portion of the supply curve for tankships.

---

* Zannetos, *op. cit.,* pages 174–175.

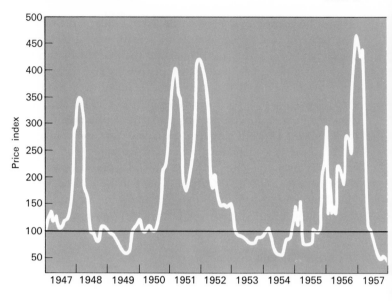

If tankship charter rates go down, there is initially little that tankship operators can do. They simply have to accept lower rates for the services they provide. However, if charter rates fall so far that operators can barely cover their variable costs of operation, they may respond by running their tankers more slowly to cut operating costs or by putting their tankers in for long repairs. However, the slowing down of vessels is limited by technical considerations and the number of repairs needed by the fleet at any moment is also limited. So neither action is likely to have much impact on total tankship capacity; that is, neither is likely to add much elasticity to the market supply curve for tankship services. However, should tankship rates fall below the variable costs of the fleet's *marginal* (i.e., most expensive to operate) ships, operators, in order to cut their losses, would begin to temporarily tie up (i.e., mothball) or even scrap these ships. Currently the marginal ships of the fleet are older tankers in the 16,500-ton class. Since there are many such ships, the short-run supply curve for tankship services probably turns, as the curve in Fig. 13.8(a) does, from almost vertical to almost horizontal at or just below the charter rate that corresponds to the cost of operating these marginal vessels.

Price Determination in the Tankship Market

There is no one route on which all tankers operate, but many routes between ports throughout the world. The same ship may travel from Maricaibo to Antwerp on one voyage and from the Persian Gulf to New York on another voyage. Thus the tankship market is geographically extremely disperse. In order for this market to be in equilibrium, it is necessary not only that the

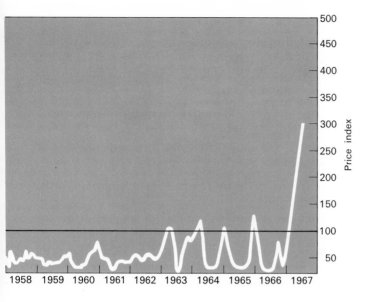

13|7

Over time the tankship charter rate fluctuates violently in response to shifts in market demand and supply. Note the sharp upswings in price caused by the Korean war and by the 1956 and 1967 closings of the Suez Canal. (Source: Conrad Boe Ltd., A/S, Oslo, Norway)

price be set at an appropriate level but also that vessels be appropriately allocated between different geographic sectors. How do the buyers and sellers of tankship services scattered throughout the world "get together" (i.e., interact) to establish a going market price for tankship services and an appropriate geographic distribution of tankers? The answer: *brokers.* These brokers try, through their worldwide connections, to get the highest possible prices for the sellers they serve and the lowest possible prices for the buyers they also serve. Brokers knit the scattered participants in the tankship market into a single competitive market. The price established in this market is one that equates market demand and supply.

The Response of the Tankship Market to Shifts in Demand and Supply

As you can easily verify with pencil and pad, the more inelastic market demand and supply are, the greater the fluctuations in price whenever either demand or supply shift. Since the demand for and supply of tankship services are both extremely inelastic, over a period of time wide fluctuations occur in the charter rate established in this market, as the time series data plotted in Fig. 13.7 show. Note in particular the humps in tankship rates brought about by the Korean war, the 1956–57 and the 1967 closings of the Suez Canal; that is, by events which caused sharp upward shifts in demand for tankship services.*

---

* It takes 44 days for a tanker traveling via Suez to make a round trip from the Persian Gulf to Northern Europe, but 70 days when the voyage is made around the southern tip of Africa (*The Wall Street Journal,* Aug. 24, 1967).

EQUILIBRIUM ADJUSTMENTS OVER TIME

Whenever demand shifts, any firm that operates in a perfectly competitive market will—if given sufficient time—respond to that shift by making appropriate adjustments in its capital stock. Since these adjustments will alter its equilibrium output, we must distinguish between

a) its *short-run* supply curve (which summarizes its quantity response to price when its capital stock is fixed), and
b) its *long-run* supply curve (which summarizes its quantity response to price when its capital stock is variable).

Since the supply curve in any perfectly competitive market equals the sum of the supply curves of all firms that participate in this market, we need to set up not only a short-run but also a long-run market supply curve; that is, a schedule showing the quantity response to price of all producers when their capital stock is variable. As we showed in Chapter 10, the long-run supply curves of individual producers are more elastic than their short-run supply curves. So the long-run market supply curve should be more elastic than the short-run one. Therefore, whenever market demand shifts, the longer the period of adjustment, the stronger the effect of this shift on output sold and the weaker its effect on price.

Adjustments Over Time in the Tankship Market

Whenever we analyze the pattern of adjustment that is likely to occur over time in a given market, we find that the specific time periods (i.e., the supply curves) that are interesting to consider depend on the peculiarities of the production process and on the length of time the producers in this market need to bring new plant and equipment into production. Take the market for fresh fish, for example: We can distinguish three different supply curves: the *momentary* supply curve which is established in the evening when the boats are in and output for the day is fixed: the *short-run* supply curves when man-hours are variable but fishing boats and equipment are fixed; and the *long-run* supply curve when all inputs including fixed capital in the form of boats and equipment are variable.

For the tankship market, in contrast to the fish market, these three supply curves would not be particularly interesting to study, since the momentary and short-run supply curves of tankship services are probably almost identical in position and shape. What supply curves should we set up for the tankship market?

Over the *short run*, tankship operators cannot increase the size of the fleet (i.e., their capital stock) and thus their output. Over the *intermediate run*, however (a few months to a year), they can, because (1) they will receive delivery on previously ordered ships, and (2) they can keep on running older ships that they would normally have scrapped. Over the *long run,* which we can take to be 20 months or more (since it takes 15 to 20 months to build a new ship), they can substantially increase the size of the fleet and thus the output of tankship services.

Thus in the tankship market we can distinguish three different supply curves: a very inelastic *short-run* supply curve (Fig. 13.8a), a slightly elastic *intermediate-run* supply curve (Fig. 13.8b) and a very elastic *long-run* supply curve (Fig. 13.8c). This figure indicates that over the short run an upward shift in demand for tankship services would have a sharp impact on price but little impact on output. Over the intermediate run, it would have a less-sharp impact on price and a greater impact on output. Over the long run, it would elicit a substantial increase in output but would have relatively little impact on price.

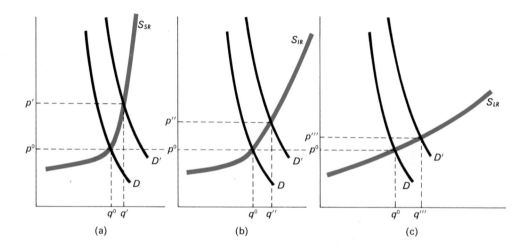

13|8

In the tankship market, an upward shift in demand is likely to have a sharp impact on price in the short run and on output in the long run. (a) Short-run adjustment. (b) Intermediate-run adjustment. (c) Long-run adjustment.

We would like to test the predictions yielded by our analysis against the time series plotted in Fig. 13.7. We can't, however, because the data plotted there show the effect on price not of a *single* shift in demand and the resulting adjustment in supply, but of *continued* shifts in both demand and supply. Thus the sharp rate dips that followed both the Korean and Suez crises reflected not only long-term increases in capacity brought on by high crisis rates, but also downturns in demand that occurred after each of these emergencies.

Expectations and Uncertainty

As we pointed out in Chapter 11, firms in this uncertain world must base their investment decisions on their expectations about the future. According to Zannetos, tankship owners have extremely *elastic* expectations about the future; that is, they expect price trends, once established, to continue. Therefore shipowners respond to periods of high demand and high spot rates by overbuilding. The result is that each upswing in demand is followed by a period in which rates are so depressed that shipowners can barely cover their variable costs of operation. All of which goes to prove that even under the "ideal" conditions of perfect competition, the producer's life in an uncertain world is risky, challenging, and far from dull.

PROBLEMS

1   To what extent do you think the following markets are perfectly competitive? Discuss specifically how well they fulfill the requirements of perfect competition.
   a) The automobile market
   b) The college textbook market
   c) The prescription drug market
   d) The retail gasoline market
   e) The market for General Motors' common stock

2   At what specific steps in our analysis of market equilibrium do the three conditions for perfectly competitive markets enter?

3   Trace the effects of the following changes on price and quantity sold in the relevant markets.
   a) Someone discovers a new use for soybean oil. Assume that cottonseed oil, which normally can be used as a substitute for soybean oil, cannot be used in this new way, and discuss the markets for both kinds of oil in both the short and long run.
   b) The wage that must be paid to migrant orange pickers increases. Discuss the market for oranges.

4   a) How will an increase in the fixed costs paid by the firms in an industry affect short-run equilibrium in the market for that industry's product?
   b) Repeat part (a), using an increase in variable costs rather than in fixed costs.

5   Show diagrammatically the role of elasticity of demand in determining the effects on market equilibrium of shifts of the supply and demand curves.

6   Why can we draw continuous supply and demand curves for markets? Recall that the supply curve of an individual firm is not continuous.

*7   Stated simply, an equilibrium point is stable if the market responds to disequilibrium by moving toward this equilibrium point. The stability of an equilibrium point may depend on the equilibrating mechanism.

Consider three markets for which the supply and demand curves are straight lines defined as follows:

Market I: Demand curve passes through $p = 5$, $q = 0$ and $p = 0$, $q = 5$
            Supply curve passes through $p = 0$, $q = 0$ and $p = 5$, $q = 4$

Market II: Demand curve passes through $p = 4$, $q = 0$ and $p = 0$, $q = 8$
            Supply curve passes through $p = 5$, $q = 1$ and $p = 0$, $q = 4$

Market III: Demand curve passes through $p = 5$, $q = 2$ and $p = 0$, $q = 5$
            Supply curve passes through $p = 4$, $q = 0$ and $p = 2$, $q = 7$

Will these markets be stable or unstable for the following adjustment processes?

a) *Walrasian adjustment process:* Starting from a given *price,* if supply is greater than demand, price will fall; if supply is less than demand, price will rise. (Note that here, as in the text, price is the equilibrating variable.)

b) *Marshallian adjustment process:* Starting from a given *quantity,* if the price at which this quantity would be demanded is greater than the price at which it would be supplied, then *quantity* will rise; if the opposite is true, quantity will fall. (Note that here, in contrast to the text, quantity has been taken to be the equilibrating variable.)

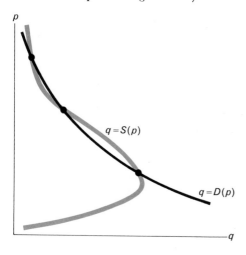

*8 Apply the definitions of stability given in Problem 7 to a market with the above supply and demand curves, testing each of the three points of equilibrium for stability under both the Walrasian and the Marshallian adjustment processes.

---

* Starred problems are problems that are unusually difficult.

CHAPTER 14

TAXES, SUBSIDIES, AND PRICE CONTROLS IN A PERFECTLY COMPETITIVE MARKET

Suppose that the government, in order to increase its revenue, imposes a tax on coffee, cocoa, or some other imported commodity that is produced and sold under highly competitive conditions. (A tax on imports is called a *tariff*.) How would this tax affect the price U.S. consumers would have to pay for the taxed commodity, the price foreign producers would receive for it, and the total tax revenues received by the government?

Or suppose that the government, in order to raise the incomes of farmers, subsidizes the production of beef and potatoes. How would such subsidies affect the prices U.S. consumers would have to pay for beef and potatoes and the prices U.S. producers would get for them? How much would such a program cost the government?

Or what if the government, in order to assure farmers a "just" price for their products, were to impose price floors in important agricultural markets? How would such a program affect the prices received by farmers and the quantities of output they would sell? Would the program prove workable without government purchases of agricultural commodities? To answer these and similar questions, we have to investigate the way taxes, subsidies, and price floors affect equilibrium in a perfectly competitive market.

TAXES IN A PERFECTLY COMPETITIVE MARKET

A tax on the sale or production of a particular commodity may be *specific, ad valorem,* or both. A specific tax requires that a fixed amount be paid on each physical unit of the taxed commodity. The federal tax of $10 per gallon on liquor is a good example of a specific tax. The tax per gallon is the same whether the liquor is a cheap gin or an expensive cognac. An ad valorem tax requires that a tax equal to a certain percent of the sales price of the taxed commodity be paid on each unit of that commodity. The 3% tariff imposed

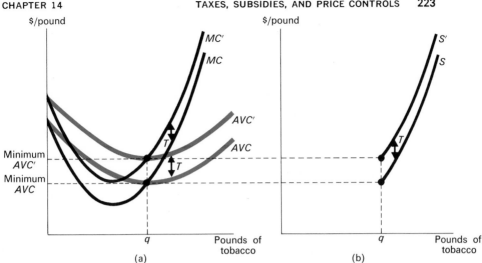

14|1

The effect on a tobacco grower's cost and supply curves of a specific tax T levied on each
pound of tobacco he produces and sells. (a) The tax T shifts the grower's cost curves upward
from MC and AC to MC' and AC'. (b) The tax T also shifts the grower's
supply curve upward from S to S'.

by the federal government on every foreign automobile imported into the
U.S. is thus an ad valorem tax. Clearly this tax falls harder on expensive
than inexpensive goods (compare the import duty on a $5500 Jaguar with
that on a $1500 Volkswagen).

Depending on the purpose for which a given tax is imposed, specific and
ad valorem taxes each offer certain advantages and disadvantages. Suppose
that the government wants to discourage consumption of a particular product. If this product is an inexpensive one like cigarettes, the government's
best choice is a high specific tax. The same effect could be achieved with an
ad valorem tax, but if the product is cheap, the rate might have to be set extremely high. One disadvantage of a specific tax, as opposed to an ad valorem
tax, is that during a period of rising prices a specific tax must be constantly
adjusted upward or its *real cost* to the consumer will fall and its power as
a deterrent will evaporate.

A Specific Tax Levied on the Seller

Suppose that the government in an attempt to discourage smoking imposes
a fixed tax on every pound of tobacco produced and sold. The imposition of
this tax will naturally shift the cost curves of each tobacco grower upward by
an amount exactly equal to the tax per unit. In Fig. 14.1(a), which illustrates
such an upward shift in the cost curves of an individual grower, the MC and

AC curves represent the grower's pre-tax marginal and average cost curves, while the MC' and AC' curves are his post-tax ones. Note that these curves are drawn so that at each output the vertical distance between the pre-tax and post-tax curves equals T, the tax per unit. Since imposition of the tax shifts the individual tobacco grower's MC curve upward by exactly T, it will also shift his supply curve upward by exactly T, as shown in Fig. 14.1(b).

Once we know how imposition of a specific tax will affect the cost and supply curves of the individual grower, we can determine how it will affect equilibrium in the tobacco market as a whole. Suppose that curves S and D in Fig. 14.2(a) represent the pre-tax market demand and supply curves for tobacco. Then initially the tobacco market will be in equilibrium at the price p^0, which corresponds to the intersection of these two curves.

Now the government imposes the specific tax. The market supply curve for tobacco, since it equals the sum of the supply curves of all tobacco growers, will shift upward from S to S'; and since the supply curve of each grower shifts upward by T, the vertical distance separating the S and S' curves must equal T.

The market's post-tax equilibrium position can no longer be located at the intersection of the S and D curves. Reason: The S curve now represents the response of growers to the *net* price paid by buyers, while the D curve represents the response of buyers to the *gross* price charged by growers. The market's post-tax equilibrium position must be at the intersection of the S' and D curves, both of which are functions of *gross* price. Thus after imposition of the tax, the growers will sell the quantity q' of tobacco; the buyers will pay the gross price p'; and the growers will receive the net price p''. The tax thus increases the gross price paid by buyers, but decreases both the net price received by growers and their equilibrium output. Once the tobacco market has attained its post-tax equilibrium position, the total revenue collected by the government will equal T, the tax per unit, times q', the number of units sold. In Fig. 14.2(a), this amount is represented by the shaded rectangle whose length equals q', whose width equals T, and whose area equals Tq', the total revenue generated by the tax.

A Specific Tax Levied on the Buyer

Suppose that no tax is levied on sellers of tobacco, but that a specific tax equal to T per unit is levied on buyers of tobacco. Think of the buyer as taking part of the gross price he pays and handing it directly over to the tax collector. Now the tobacco market's post-tax equilibrium position cannot be located at the intersection of the S and D curves in Fig. 14.2, for the same reasons given in the preceding paragraph.

The tobacco market's post-tax equilibrium position requires a new demand curve that shows the relationship between the net price growers receive

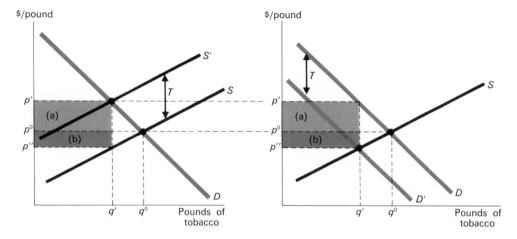

14|2

Alternative ways of representing the imposition of a specific tax *T* in a perfectly competitive market. (a) Tax levied on the grower. (b) Tax levied on the buyer.

and the quantity of tobacco buyers purchase. We can obtain such a net demand curve by shifting the original market demand curve downward by an amount exactly equal to T.

Figure 14.2(b) shows such a shift; the imposition of a specific tax T on buyers of tobacco is assumed to shift the market demand curve downward from D to D'. Obviously the imposition of a tax on buyers will shift equilibrium in the tobacco market from the point (p^0, q^0) where the supply and demand curves S and D intersect to the point (p'', q') where the supply curve S and the *net* demand curve D' intersect. Levying a specific tax T on buyers of tobacco thus decreases output from q^0 to q', increases the gross price buyers pay from p^0 to p', and decreases the net price growers receive from p^0 to p''. The revenue the government collects, $q'T$, is represented in Fig. 14.2(b) by the shaded rectangle whose length equals q' and whose width equals T.

The Incidence of a Specific Tax

When we compare parts (a) and (b) of Fig. 14.2 we see that when a specific tax T is imposed, its impact on the net price received by the producer, on the gross price paid by the buyer, and on the quantity of output sold will be the same whether the tax is levied on the buyer or on the seller. So we can draw two conclusions:

1) Legal stipulations as to what part of a tax buyers or sellers shall pay have *no* effect on the amount by which the tax actually raises the gross price

paid by the consumer and the amount by which it lowers the net price received by the producer.

2) When we are analyzing the effect on market equilibrium of any specific tax, we can use either of the approaches in Fig. 14.2; that is, we can represent any specific tax by either an upward shift in the market supply curve or a downward shift in the market demand curve.

Economists who are analyzing the consequences of a tax are often concerned with *who pays the tax;* i.e., with the *incidence* of the tax. In the tobacco case, above, a specific tax T caused the gross price paid by consumers to rise by an amount equal to $(p' - p^0)$ and the net price received by producers to fall by an amount equal to $(p^0 - p'')$. Thus, of the total receipts yielded by the tax, consumers paid $(p' - p^0)q'$, while producers paid $(p^0 - p'')q'$. As you should verify, the sum of these two amounts is Tq', the total revenue yielded by the tax. Figure 14.2(a) and (b) represents the total amount of taxes paid by consumers as area (a) and by producers as area (b) of the total tax rectangle.

What determines the incidence of a tax? Certainly not the wording of the tax laws [see conclusion (1) above], even though such laws frequently specify that a given tax is to be paid by producers, consumers, or both, according to some stated proportions.

In practice the incidence of a tax is determined solely by the elasticity of the market supply and demand curves. Figure 14.3(a) shows that, if market demand is completely inelastic, a specific tax T will cause the price consumers pay to rise by the full amount of the tax, but it will not alter the price producers receive. So in such a situation the burden of the tax falls wholly on consumers. Figure 14.3(b) illustrates precisely the opposite situation: Market supply is inelastic, and the burden of the tax falls wholly on suppliers. Note that in both these situations, the tax does not alter sales of the taxed commodity.

Impact on Market Equilibrium of an Ad Valorem Tax

We can analyze the economic consequences of an ad valorem tax in the same way we analyzed those of a specific tax. Under an ad valorem system, however, the tax due on each unit sold equals a percentage rate, t, times the price, p, at which that unit is sold. So naturally, the more expensive the unit is, the higher the amount of the tax. We can represent the effect of an ad valorem tax on market equilibrium in two ways, as in parts (a) and (b) of Fig. 14.4. These diagrams are like those in Fig. 14.2, except that the distance between the curves S and S' in Fig. 14.4(a) and between the curves D and D' in Fig. 14.4(b) is not constant; this distance increases as the price of the taxed commodity is increased.

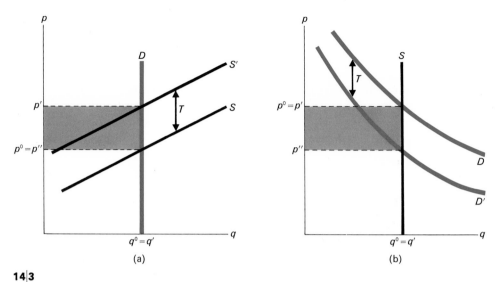

14|3

The incidence of a specific tax T depends on the elasticity of the market supply and demand curves. (a) If demand is inelastic, the burden of the tax falls wholly on buyers. (b) If supply is inelastic, the burden of the tax falls wholly on sellers.

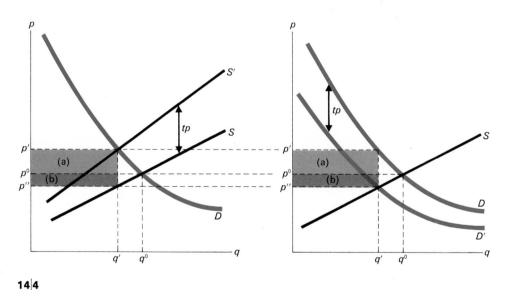

14|4

Alternative ways of representing the imposition of an ad valorem tax on a commodity sold in a perfectly competitive market. (a) Tax levied on the seller. (b) Tax levied on the buyer.

Impact on Market Equilibrium of a Subsidy

So far in this section we have been talking about taxes; however, a *subsidy* is simply a *negative tax*. So our analysis of the economic consequences of a tax will also serve us when we study the economic consequences of a subsidy. A subsidy usually lowers the price paid by consumers, increases the price received by suppliers, and increases the quantity produced and sold. Moreover, the way in which the benefits of a given subsidy are divided between buyers and sellers depends on the elasticity of the market supply and demand curves.

PRICE CONTROLS IN A PERFECTLY COMPETITIVE MARKET

Now we shall discuss price floors and price ceilings, and how they affect equilibrium in a perfectly competitive market. Consider the market for butter. We can represent the supply of and demand for butter by the curves S and D in Fig. 14.5. So long as the butter market is free from government control, the price of it will equal p^0, the price that equates market demand and supply. Let's say, however, that the government wants to assure dairy farmers a fair price for their product, so it imposes a price floor on butter. If this price floor (i.e., price minimum) is at or below p^0, equilibrium in the butter market will not be disturbed. But if it's above p^0, disequilibrium will result. Suppose that the government sets the price of butter at p'. Obviously at this price consumers will demand only q' of butter, while dairy farmers will supply q'' of butter. A price floor above the equilibrium price p^0 thus creates *excess supply* in the market. If this excess supply existed in a free market, it would be eliminated by a fall in price. But in this case it will persist, and in each period one of two things must happen: Either some dairy farmers will be unable to sell as much as they would like to at the established price p' or the government will have to step into the market and buy up the excess supply E_s. In the United States, the government follows the latter course. It buys the excess supply at the peg prices it sets for dairy products. This can of course turn out to be expensive for taxpayers; just how expensive is indicated by the fact that in the first half of 1967, U.S. government purchases of excess dairy products soared (in the wake of price floor hikes) to 8% of total dairy output!

Although most of the price controls the government imposes on commodity markets are floors rather than ceilings, the government during wartime has frequently resorted to price ceilings as a means of controlling inflation. For the effect of a price ceiling on equilibrium in a perfectly competitive market, consider the market in Fig. 14.6. Initially this market attains equilibrium at the price p^0 which equates market demand and supply. If the government now imposes a ceiling on the price established in this

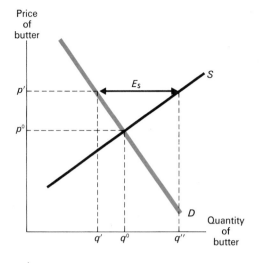

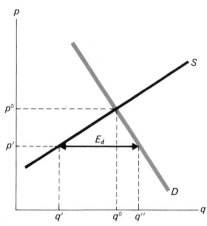

14|5

If the government establishes a price floor p' in the butter market, excess supply equal to E_s will result.

14|6

If the government establishes a price ceiling p' at a level below the equilibrium price p^0, excess demand equal to E_d will emerge.

market, market equilibrium will be undisturbed so long as the government sets this ceiling at or above p^0. However, if the government sets the price ceiling below p^0, for example at p', buyers will demand q'', while sellers will offer only q'. Excess demand equal to E_d will emerge, and will continue so long as the price ceiling is maintained.

Whenever a price ceiling creates persistent excess demand in a market, either (1) this market may be "cleared" on a first-come-first-served basis, or (2) the government may introduce a system of rationing to allocate available supply equitably. Under rationing, each ration coupon entitles the person to whom it is issued to buy a certain number of units of the rationed item. (This happened with such products as beef and sugar and liquor during World War II.) Suppose that rationing were introduced into the market in Fig. 14.6, and that the total supply of ration coupons issued entitled consumers to purchase q', the amount that would be supplied if price were set at p'. The introduction of rationing would mean that the initial downward-sloping market demand curve, derived on the basis of an *income* constraint, would be superseded by a new vertical demand curve, derived on the basis of a *coupon* constraint. This new vertical demand curve would obviously pass through the point (p', q'). Thus this rationing system would eliminate all excess demand at the price p'.

*COBWEB PATTERNS OF ADJUSTMENT

In our discussion of price determination in a perfectly competitive market, we have implicitly assumed that the production period is short and that a producer would determine his current output in response to current price. But suppose that the production process is a lengthy one, perhaps requiring *two* periods. Then the producer's current output reflects a production decision he made during the preceding period, a decision presumably made in response to the price that he *expected* to reign during the current period. How did he arrive at these expectations? Perhaps he decided that the best guess he could make was that the price that would be established during the current period would equal the price during the previous period. Suppose that he does take this approach. Then his current output, S_t, will be a response to the price, p_{t-1}, established during the previous period. Specifically:

$$S_t = S(p_{t-1}).$$

A Stable Cobweb

In any market in which producers' current supply is a response to the price during the previous period, equilibrium can be established only through a series of adjustments that take place over several consecutive periods. Take potato growers, for example. They produce only one crop a year. Suppose that they base their decision about how many potatoes they will grow this year on the assumption that the price of potatoes this year will equal the price the preceding year. Let the market demand and supply curves for potatoes be represented by the curves in Fig. 14.7. The price in the preceding year equaled the equilibrium price p^0, and producers intended to produce the equilibrium output q^0; but because of a blight their current harvest equals a smaller amount, q'. Given our assumptions about the market behavior of suppliers and demanders, what chain of price and quantity adjustments will this disturbance set in motion?

Clearly the price p' will be established this year, since this is the price at which demand for potatoes will equal current supply, q'. In the next or second year, however, potato growers will respond to the price p' by producing the quantity q''. This relatively large output will cause price in the second year to fall to p''. In the following or third year producers will respond to the fall in price from p' to p'' by decreasing their output from q'' to q'''. This decrease in output will cause price in the third year to rise to p'''.

Note that, when traced out, the series of adjustments we have just described produces a *cobweb* pattern like that in Fig. 14.7. This cobweb, which clearly converges toward the point of market equilibrium, will obviously continue until period-to-period changes in price and quantity have been reduced to zero; that is, until market equilibrium has been established.

---

* The reader may skip this starred section without loss of continuity.

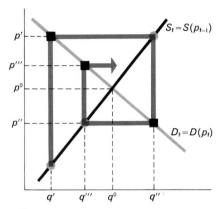

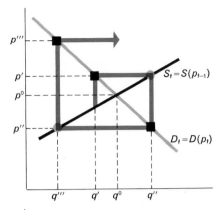

14|7

In a market in which current supply is a function of price in the preceding period, a temporary disturbance will set in motion a cobweb pattern of adjustment.

14|8

This market produces an *unstable* cobweb pattern of adjustment. Contrast it with the market in Fig. 14.7.

An Unstable Cobweb

In some markets equilibrium is *stable* and in others it is *unstable*.

A stable market is one in which the series of adjustments set in motion by a temporary disturbance is such that market equilibrium will eventually be restored.

The market in Fig. 14.7 fits this definition. However, the market in Fig. 14.8 is unstable, since a temporary disturbance in this market sets in motion a series of adjustments such that, in each succeeding period, price and quantity diverge by larger and larger amounts from their equilibrium values. Such a series of price and quantity adjustments is illustrated by the response of this market to a temporary disturbance that causes output to fall from its equilibrium value q^0 to a lower amount q'.

The contrast between the converging and diverging cobwebs in Figs. 14.7 and 14.8 leads us to wonder what characteristics of market demand and supply determine whether a market characterized by a cobweb pattern of adjustment will be stable or unstable. You can investigate the way changes in the slope, first of the demand curve and then of the supply curve, would affect the stability of these markets. Four or five drawings should suffice to show you that the less steep (i.e., more elastic) the demand curve and the steeper (i.e., less elastic) the supply curve, the more likely market equilibrium is to be stable. If it is, then the more elastic the demand and the less elastic the supply, the more rapidly the cobweb pattern of adjustment set in motion by a temporary disturbance will converge toward equilibrium.

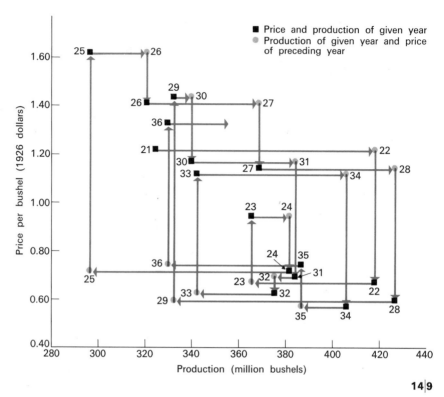

14|9

Over the years 1921–1936 the potato market traced out a cobweb pattern of adjustment, indicating that potato producers established current output in response to the price prevailing in the previous period. (Source: Mordecai Ezekiel, "The Cobweb Theorem," *Quarterly Journal of Economics* **LII**, February 1938, page 32)

The Potato Cobweb: An Example

Perhaps the idea of cobweb patterns of adjustment seems a bit esoteric at first glance. Therefore let's return to something concrete: the potato market. Figures 14.7 and 14.8, with their cobweb patterns of adjustment, indicate that if potato producers respond to the current price of potatoes with a lag, then—provided that (1) supply and demand in the potato market do not shift sharply over time, and (2) price is free to fluctuate—the price–output data of this market ought to display a cobweb pattern of adjustment.

These two conditions were met in the potato market over the years 1921 through 1936. In 1938, an economist named Mordecai Ezekiel, in a famous article, set out to see whether or not he could identify a cobweb pattern of adjustment in the way the potato market had acted during these years. He plotted points for the prices and outputs of potatoes in each of these years.

Figure 14.9 shows these points, dated according to year, as squares. Next Ezekiel plotted a series of points, each corresponding to one year's price and the succeeding year's output (i.e., to one year's price and to the supply produced in response to it). These points, dated by year of price, are represented by circles.

In Figs. 14.7 and 14.8, as in Fig. 14.9, realized price–output combinations are represented by squares, while outputs produced in response to the previous year's price are represented by circles. Obviously if potato producers over the years 1921–36 did respond with a one-year lag to current price, Ezekiel, by connecting in chronological order the points he had plotted, should have obtained either a converging cobweb like the one in Fig. 14.7 or a diverging cobweb like the one in Fig. 14.8. His result—Fig. 14.9—was indeed a cobweb, and a converging one; but not a "perfect" one. The deviations from the "perfect" cobweb pattern were caused by: (1) There are practical limits to the amount potato growers can expand output in a single year; so sharp price rises, such as the one in 1925, are likely to result in increases in output over several years. (2) There must have been some shifts in demand for and supply of potatoes over the period 1921–36, and each of these shifts would have marred the regularity of the cobweb pattern. (3) There are unpredictable year-to-year variations in yields; therefore the outputs actually produced in some of these years must have deviated from the outputs that growers intended to produce.

The data in Fig. 14.9 show only that a cobweb pattern of adjustment prevails in the potato market. But if we were to look at time series on prices and output for many other agricultural commodities, we would find similar cobweb patterns of adjustment.

PROBLEMS

1   Suppose that a property tax were levied on producers of a perfectly competitive commodity, so that they had to pay a set amount per dollar valuation of plant and equipment, regardless of quantity produced or profit earned. How would such a tax affect the market for that commodity in the short run and in the long run?

2   According to our analysis, how would the imposition of a tax on the profits earned by producers in a perfectly competitive market affect equilibrium in that market?

3   Discuss the effect that a specific tax on corn would have on the market price of hogs. (Hogs are fattened up on corn.) Both commodities are sold in competitive markets.

4   If a government wishes to impose a tax strictly for revenue purposes, what characteristics should it look for in the market for the commodity which it taxes?

5   What determines the effectiveness of a *sumptuary tax* (one which is intended solely to reduce the amount of a commodity consumed)? Be sure to include supply and demand elasticities in your answer. Can you think of any commodity which a government might wish to tax in this way, and which also is sold in a perfectly competitive market?

6   By means of a graph, analyze the effects of a subsidy in a perfectly competitive market. Determine the influence of supply and demand elasticities on the incidence of the benefits of the subsidy. Does it matter who gets the subsidy, consumers or producers?

7   Discuss the effect of imposing a quota (i.e., a restriction on output sold) in a perfectly competitive market. Is it possible for a quota, in the absence of any additional controls, to lower the price paid by consumers?

8   How could a government enforce a price floor that is above the equilibrium price? That is, how could it effectively prevent the emergence of a black market in which producers sold their output at illegally low prices? Illustrate your solution graphically. [*Hint:* Observe the U.S. government's farm policy.]

9   Use the concepts and techniques we have developed so far to analyze the effect of a policy of paying farmers not to produce. [*Hint:* When a farmer increases his output, he not only incurs the cost of additional labor and materials, but also incurs the opportunity cost of *not* receiving payment from the government.]

10   In Norway the government supports the incomes of dairy farmers by granting them subsidies. In the United States the government supports the incomes of dairy farmers by setting price floors for dairy products. Using appropriate diagrams, contrast the effects that these two different policies are likely to have on the price paid by the consumer, the total quantity of dairy products consumed, and the cost to the governments of maintaining each policy. From a social point of view, which type of program do you think is preferable?

11   Consider a system of rationing coffee in which the government purchases, at a price below the equilibrium price, all available coffee. Then it sells coupons for coffee at the same price, on a first-come-first-served basis. Suppose that a market is allowed to develop for the coupons themselves; determine graphically the price at which these coupons would sell.

CHAPTER 15

COMPETITIVE MARKETS FOR LABOR AND OTHER INPUTS

Many inputs, both primary and manufactured, are sold in perfectly competitive markets. And whenever they are, we can analyze the way their price is determined in terms of supply and demand.

In Chapter 13 we found that the market demand curve for any input is a downward-sloping curve that equals the sum of the demand curves of all firms that use this input. How steep will this curve be? If we use as a guide the factors that determine the elasticity of a single firm's input demands (remember the Celery Improvement Company back in Chapter 9), then we see that the *market* demand curve for any input will be less elastic:

1) the less elastic the demand for the goods in whose production it is used,
2) the smaller the proportion of total costs it represents for the firms that use it,
3) the more restricted the possibilities of substituting other inputs for it, and
4) the more inelastic the supply of such substitute inputs.

Although the market *demand* schedule for any input slopes downward, the market *supply* curve for any input slopes upward. Here are some examples: The market supply curve of labor initially slopes upward, since the individual supply curves from which it is obtained initially slope upward. The market supply curve of any *intermediate product* (i.e., any good produced by one firm and used as an input by another) also slopes upward, since the supply curve of any manufactured commodity typically slopes upward. And since the supply of land is more or less fixed by nature,* its supply curve will slope upward steeply, and in the limit may even be vertical.

Obviously, if in a perfectly competitive input market the supply curve slopes upward and the demand curve slopes downward, market equilibrium

---

* The late American humorist Will Rogers once said, "Buy land. They ain't making any more of it." However, people do "create" land by filling in bays, draining swamps, etc.

will be at the intersection of these two curves. In other words, any input sold in a perfectly competitive market will always be priced so that demand for this input just equals available supply.

PURE ECONOMIC RENT

Suppose that an input is nonreproducible; that is, it is *inelastically supplied.* How will its price be determined and what significance will this price have?

The price of any input in fixed supply will be determined by the intersection of a *vertical* market supply curve and a downward-sloping market demand curve. The primary function of price in such a market is to ration available supply among would-be users. If, however, market supply exceeds market demand at all prices, no rationing will be required, market price will fall to zero, and the input in question will become a *free good.*

The return earned by any factor of production whose supply is totally inelastic is referred to as a pure economic rent.

Note that this concept of rent has nothing to do with "rent" in the sense of payments for the use of buildings, equipment, or other physical assets.

The concept of economic rent can be applied not only to an input whose supply is everywhere inelastic, but also to an input whose supply becomes inelastic after its wage reaches some minimum level. Thus for example, any income earned by Picasso above the minimum necessary to induce him to paint *full time* can be classified as a pure economic rent. In such a situation, an alternative definition of economic rent is appropriate:

The surplus earned by a factor over and above the minimum necessary to induce it to do its work is pure economic rent.

Similar inputs frequently earn quite different rents. Some land, for example, is extremely valuable, and other land is worthless (i.e., it earns a zero rent). Reason: land is heterogeneous. Hence we must think of the land market as being broken up into a number of separate markets, within each of which a reasonably homogeneous category of land is traded and a different price established. Desert land with oil under it brings a high price, but desert land with no such redeeming feature brings a zero price, and green farming acres sell for an intermediate price. Note that the market demand curve for any one type of land represents the sum of the demand curves of many people who may want to use this land in different ways. Consider the various demand curves that go to make up the market demand curve for acreage around a lake. Some people would like to use it for a resort hotel, others would like to use it for summer cottages, and others would like to use it for farms, or for industrial sites. The use to which the land is finally put depends on the relationship between the prices that each of these groups is willing to pay and the final market price established for this land.

Shifts in Output Demand Alter Economic Rent

Suppose that an inelastically supplied input is used to produce a given output, and demand for that output shifts upward. Naturally this affects the size of the economic rent earned by this input.

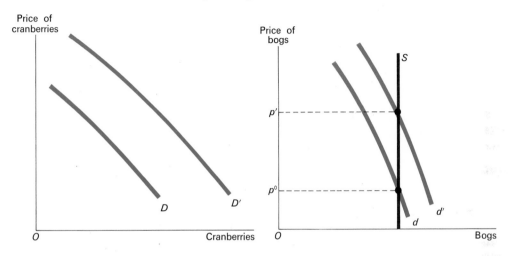

15|1

(a) The cranberry market.   (b) The bog market.

We shall illustrate with cranberries: If the demand for cranberries shifts upward, how would this affect the price of cranberry bogs?* Recall that in Chapter 9 we showed that the firm's input demand schedules depend partly on the demand for its output. Thus an upward shift in demand for the firm's output increases the quantity of output that the firm can profitably produce. And this shifts the firm's input demand schedules upward. Therefore an upward shift in the demand for cranberries will induce a corresponding upward shift in the *derived* demand of cranberry growers for bogs, and this in turn will raise the price of bogs. This chain of events is illustrated in Fig. 15.1: A rise in market demand for cranberries from D to D' causes the demand of growers for bogs to shift upward from d to d' and causes the equilibrium price of bogs to rise from p^0 to p'.

From our example it's clear that whenever demand shifts upward for an output in whose production an inelastically supplied input is used, the economic rent earned by this input will rise. Check and you'll see that a downward shift in demand for output would have precisely the opposite effect on the economic rent earned by such an input.

---

* Bogs are of course in inelastic supply, and they aren't good for anything but growing cranberries.

A Tax on Economic Rent

Whenever there is an input market in which supply is totally inelastic, and a tax* is levied on sales in that market, the total burden of the tax is borne by the suppliers of the input. The interpretation of this perhaps surprising result is simple: In the normal situation in which the supply curve of an input has a positive (but not vertical) slope, a tax decreases the net price sellers receive. This leads them to decrease the amount they supply. But this decrease in output will raise the gross price paid by the buyer, and the burden of the tax will therefore be divided between suppliers and buyers of the input. If an input's supply is totally inelastic, however, the same quantity of it will be supplied no matter how low price falls. Therefore taxing an inelastically supplied input does not increase the gross price paid by purchasers but instead reduces, by the full amount of the tax, the net price the suppliers receive.

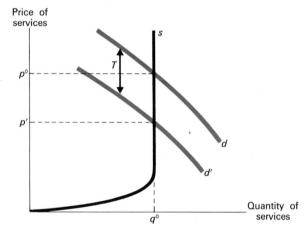

15|2

Imposing a tax T on the services provided by a person who earns an economic rent will lower the net price he receives for his services from p^0 to p', but will have no effect on the quantity, q^0, of services he provides.

Example: Suppose that a tax, T, is imposed on the professional services provided by Maria Callas, Cassius Clay, or any person you could name who, by virtue of his special talents, earns an economic rent. As indicated in Fig. 15.2, the net price the person receives for his services will fall from p^0 to p', but the quantity of services he supplies will remain unchanged at q^0.

Competitive Markets and Zero Profits

One interesting facet of the concept of economic rent is that it enables us to understand what economists mean when they assert, as some do, that the profits of any perfectly competitive firm in long-run equilibrium will always

---

* See Chapter 14 for an analysis of the effect of imposing a tax on a perfectly competitive market.

be zero. Suppose that there are two apple growers, Brown and Robinson, of equal efficiency. Brown owns good land and consequently has low costs. Robinson owns poor land and consequently has high costs. Initially the price of apples is at a level that just permits Brown to earn a zero profit, but then the price goes up to a point at which Robinson can just earn a zero profit. Clearly in this new situation Brown must be earning a positive profit. "Not so," says the zero-profit advocate, who then points out that, if Brown were to rent out his high-quality, profit-yielding land, the rent on this land would be bid up until it just equaled the maximum profit that the land would yield any grower who used it; thus Brown in reality earns no profit at all, because the apparent excess of his revenue over his cost is offset by the opportunity cost (i.e., implicit economic rent) that he incurs when he uses his land himself instead of renting it out to some other grower.

THE LABOR MARKET

So much for economic rent. Let's now focus on the labor market. To what extent can it be regarded as perfectly competitive?

Clearly the labor market will be perfectly competitive only if numerous employers and workers participate in it, and only if the commodity sold (labor) is homogeneous. The real-life labor market fails to meet these conditions on a number of counts. First, labor is not a homogeneous commodity; although of course we can always think of the labor market as being broken up into a number of separate markets in which different kinds of labor are sold: ditch diggers, bricklayers, or college professors. Even with this breakdown, however, there's a second difficulty: most workers, because of the expense of moving and because they lack information about jobs in faraway places, tend to be somewhat immobile, especially with respect to long moves.

But if labor is not only heterogeneous but also immobile, then we must view the labor market as a collection of regional markets for different kinds of labor. All these markets are interrelated to the extent that workers are willing to change jobs and to move from place to place, and to the extent that employers are willing to substitute one type of labor for another and to shop widely for workers.

Although the commodity traded in a regional market for a specific kind of labor is reasonably homogeneous, some such markets fail to meet the numerous-seller and numerous-buyer requirements. In a regional labor market for a given kind of labor, one or two employers may loom so large that their individual buying decisions do perceptibly influence market price. Similarly, workers in such a market may violate the numerous-seller condition by joining a union, i.e., by acting as a group.

Despite the fact that most labor markets have one or more imperfections, still, many regional markets for a particular grade of labor (e.g., the market for unskilled labor in a large city) at least approximate the conditions of perfect competition. Therefore let us think about how a perfectly competitive labor market would function: We know that the wage paid and the quantity of labor employed in equilibrium would be determined by the intersection of a market demand curve with the market supply curve of labor. And since "the" labor market is not a single market but a group of interrelated markets, a survey of wage rates within any region would presumably show that there is not a single equilibrium wage rate, but a set of equilibrium wage rates, and that differences in the wages of different workers would be *equalizing;* that is, they would reflect differences either in the skill of these workers or in the disutilities associated with their work. A chef would earn more than a short-order cook because he is more skilled. A coal miner would earn more than, say, a bus driver, since the miner's job involves the double disutilities of dirt and danger.

Income and Occupation

Table 15.1 presents data on the median incomes earned by family heads in different occupations, showing that professional and technical workers receive the highest incomes of any occupational group. Their high income reflects two factors:

1) Most professional and technical workers have valuable special skills which they have acquired through years of education and training.
2) Some of these people, such as the gifted surgeon or the brilliant trial lawyer, have innate and unreproducible talents for which they receive economic rent.

The high incomes of salaried proprietors and managers also reflect both payments received for acquired skills and economic rents received for innate talents. What is surprising about the incomes of managers and proprietors is not that salaried managers earn so much, but that self-employed proprietors earn so little. The typical independent proprietor is fairly well endowed with both acquired and innate skills. Yet he receives a median income lower than that of the typical skilled worker. The reason is probably that many self-employed proprietors who earn low incomes stay in business either because they value the independence that goes with being self-employed or because they hope (too often incorrectly) that next year their ship will come in.

The next three categories in Table 15.1 are *craftsmen, operatives,* and *laborers;* these correspond to skilled, semiskilled, and unskilled laborers. The marked income differences in these different occupational groups reflect the differences in their acquired job skills. Service workers, like unskilled workers in industry, receive a low median income, which reflects the low level of skills—acquired or innate—required for most of the tasks they carry out.

TABLE 15|1

Median Income of Family Heads, by Occupation, March 1965

Occupation	Median annual income
Professional and technical workers	
Salaried	$ 9,638
Self-employed	13,646
Proprietors, managers and officials	
Salaried	10,428
Self-employed	7,326
Craftsmen, foremen, and kindred workers	7,670
Operatives and kindred workers	6,542
Laborers, excluding farm and mine	5,086
Sales workers	8,170
Clerical workers	7,163
Service workers	5,525
Private household workers	2,367
Farmers and farm managers	3,329
Farm laborers and foremen	2,423
All family heads	6,569

Source: U.S. Department of Commerce, Bureau of the Census, *Current Population Reports*, Series P-60, September 1965.

And the extremely low median income of private household workers also reflects the low level of skills required to perform such work.

The last two entries in Table 15.1 are puzzling. Farmers really ought to fall in the category of highly skilled workers, yet their median income is less than half that of skilled workers in industry. And the median income of farm laborers is less than half that of laborers in industry. Why are farm incomes so low? Well, in the past few years, the productivity of farm labor has been rising much more rapidly than farm output, so that the demand for farm labor has actually declined rather than grown. This means that the incomes of farm workers would equal those of industrial workers (for whom demand has been increasing, *only* if the supply of farm workers had decreased faster than the demand for such workers (use a supply–demand diagram to check this). In practice the opposite has probably occurred: Farm workers, confronted with the problems inherent in moving from farm to city, have tended to leave agriculture more slowly than demand for their services has declined. Thus their incomes have fallen below those of workers in industry.

GOVERNMENT AND UNION POLICIES AFFECTING THE WAGE RATE

The fact that we view the labor market within the framework of supply and demand makes it possible for us to analyze the effect on labor-market equilibrium of a variety of government and union policies.

A Minimum Wage

Most people think that an economic society cannot be said to perform satis-factorily unless poverty is eliminated. Many people argue that a simple and efficient way to get rid of poverty is to set a high minimum wage, which will then guarantee that every employed individual will get a just living wage. Will a high minimum wage really do this? Suppose that the government imposes a minimum wage that raises the wage level of the most disadvan-taged and least skilled. How will this minimum wage affect the incomes of these people?

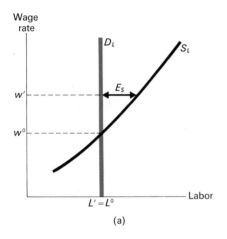
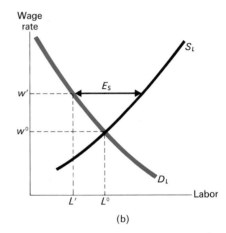

(a)   (b)

15|3

Whether or not a minimum wage will contribute to the elimination of poverty depends on how elastic the demand for labor is. (a) Inelastic demand for labor. (b) Elastic demand for labor.

Figure 15.3(a) shows that, if demand for unskilled labor is extremely in-elastic, then instituting a minimum wage equal to w' will help eliminate pov-erty because it will raise from w^0 to w' the wage earned by unskilled workers without decreasing the number of such workers who can find jobs. However, if demand for unskilled labor is elastic, then the contribution of a minimum wage to the elimination of poverty will be a mixed one (see Fig. 15.3b). On the one hand a minimum wage will decrease poverty by raising from w^0 to w' the wages of those unskilled workers who manage to keep their jobs. On the other hand it will increase poverty by decreasing the number of unskilled workers who can find work from L^0 to L'. The possibility that a high min-imum wage may create unemployment is not merely a hypothesis: In 1967 the Federal government instituted a $1-per-hour minimum wage for agri-cultural workers, which caused thousands of Southern farmhands and share-croppers to lose their jobs. Apparently their marginal worth to their employers was less than $1 an hour. So obviously the government cannot elim-inate poverty among unskilled workers simply by instituting a high minimum wage. What is needed are programs designed to increase the skills and geographic mobility of these people.

Since a high minimum wage will presumably elicit an increase in the quantity of labor offered in the market, it will create involuntary unemployment even if it does not eliminate jobs. In Fig. 15.3 the involuntary unemployment created by a minimum wage equal to w' is indicated by the arrows labeled E_s.

Union Policies Aimed at Increasing the General Level of Wages

Unions try to increase the level of wages not only by promoting continued increases in the minimum wage but also by following policies designed either to decrease the available supply of labor (i.e., to shift the market supply curve of labor leftward) or to increase demand for labor (i.e., to shift the market demand curve for labor upward). With respect to the supply side of the labor market, unions have promoted accelerated retirement programs and supported legislation restricting the immigration of foreign workers, raising the minimum work age, and shortening the standard work week.

With respect to the demand side of the labor market, unions have supported programs designed to promote full employment. They have also tried to maintain the demand for labor by preventing the substitution of other inputs for labor. Thus, for example, unions representing dockworkers, printers, steelworkers, and other groups have engaged in strenuous and sometimes successful attempts to block automation, that is, the substitution of capital (in the form of equipment) for labor. Another strategy labor organizations pursue in their attempts to bolster the demand for labor is featherbedding: forcing employers to use unneeded labor. Full-crew laws for trains, enforced in many states as a result of union pressures, are a case in point. A full-crew regulation may stipulate, for example, that a train must always have a fireman, as well as an engineer, in a locomotive; this in spite of the fact that locomotives nowadays run on diesel fuel and no longer need firemen to shovel coal.

Imposition of a Tax on the Labor Market

The equilibrium established in the labor market in any given period reflects the impact not only of policies designed to alter the wage level, but also of taxes imposed on the sale of labor. How will a tax on labor affect the gross wage paid by the employer, the net wage received by the worker, and the total quantity of labor sold in the market? Offhand we might think that a tax (such as the social security tax) imposed on the sale of labor would raise the gross wage, lower the net wage, and lower total employment. Certainly our analysis of commodity taxes (see Fig. 14.2) would lead us to think so. This is also the answer that must hold so long as the market demand curve for labor slopes downward and the market supply curve for labor slopes upward.

As we showed in Chapter 4, however, a person's supply curve of labor might well bend backward (i.e., slope negatively) in its upper reaches. And since the market supply curve of labor equals the sum of the supply curves of all individuals in the market, it too may bend backward. If so, then a tax on labor could actually cause total employment to rise and gross wage to fall!

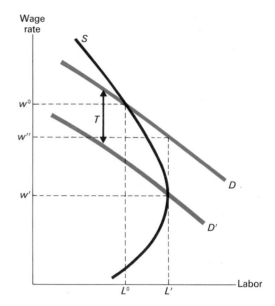

15|4

Imposing a specific tax T on the sale of labor.

Figure 15.4 shows this possibility: The imposition of a specific tax T on the sale of labor results in a downward shift from D to D' in *net* market demand for labor. Note that this shift causes the gross wage received by labor to fall from w^0 to w'' and total employment to rise from L^0 to L'. The interpretation of this somewhat surprising result is left to the reader.

PROBLEMS

1 Discuss the demand elasticity of the following factors of production with reference to the four considerations listed on page 143: (a) Spark plugs, (b) seed corn, (c) feed corn, (d) steel beams, (e) hearing-aid microphones, (f) vacuum tubes, (g) hops.

2 Using an appropriate diagram, show that the low-cost apple grower mentioned on page 239 will make a positive profit when the price of apples is bid up.

3 Using the techniques developed in Chapter 14, analyze the effect of imposing specific and ad valorem taxes on inputs sold in perfectly competitive markets. Who would bear most of the impact of specific taxes on the items in Problem 1, the buyer or the seller?

4 A special type of market restriction is often applied to land, in the form of zoning regulations. How would the price of land be affected by such regulations?

5 "The Florida groves are sagging with enough oranges to fill 140 million 90-pound boxes, a whopping 42% above last year's harvest. Orange growers, who last year received about $1.25 a box for on-tree fruit, now are selling at an average of 50 cents, with some prices as low as 35 cents. . . .

   "The glut is reflected in the prices of groves, too. They now go for $1,000 or less an acre, down from $2,000 a year ago and $4,000 to $6,000 four years ago, when the supply was reduced by a freeze.

   "The obvious solution to all these problems, say citrus officials, is to convince people to drink up." (*Wall Street Journal*, Feb. 2, 1967)

   Use diagrams to illustrate the causes of the decline in prices of orange groves described above. Also show how the solution mentioned in the last sentence would work to increase prices of groves.

6 The following table gives data on the average weekly wages paid to laborers in several different industries. Explain the evident differences in terms of the discussion in this chapter.

Average weekly wages

Retail sales persons	$ 70
Bank employees	82
Coal miners	152
Electrical workers	180
Sawmill workers	87
Cigar-production workers	65
Textile-mill workers	83

7 In the situation shown in Fig. 15.2, imposition of a specific tax T has no effect on the gross price p^0 paid by the buyer or on the amount of the input q^0 supplied by the seller. But if the tax were two or three times as large as T, then what effect would it have on the gross price paid by the buyer and on the quantity supplied by the seller? Illustrate your answer with an appropriate diagram.

8 Give an intuitive argument to show how the gross wage might fall and the level of employment rise in response to a tax on labor.

The level of training or education of a worker naturally has a strong influence on the wage he can earn. Gary S. Becker, an economist who has extensively studied the economic role of education, distinguishes between two types of training.* *Specific training* increases the productivity of a worker only in the performance of a specific job for a specific firm. Thus such training would not be of any value to him

* Gary S. Becker, *Human Capital;* New York: Columbia University Press, 1964.

if he were to change jobs or firms. *General training,* on the other hand, increases the worker's productivity in a variety of occupations, either doing different tasks, or doing the same task for different firms. Clearly, any training is likely to be a combination of these two categories, but the economic effects of training will depend in part on the extent to which it approximates one category or the other.

---

9   Classify the following forms of training as to the extent to which they are specific and the extent to which they are general:

   a) An undergraduate education in physics

   b) A company-familiarization program for new employees of an airline

   c) Astronaut training administered by the Air Force

   d) Study toward a Ph.D. in ancient history

   e) An apprenticeship in a cabinetmaking firm

   f) A course of study at a barber college

10   One of Becker's main points is that specific training tends to be paid for by employers, while general training tends to be paid for by the individuals receiving the training. Try to explain in economic terms why this should be so, and discuss evidence for and against this idea from real life. Keep in mind that a person who is receiving a smaller income while he is being trained than he could get elsewhere on the job market is actually paying an implicit cost for the training he receives.

11   Which type of training, specific or general, would you expect to be more effective in raising the wage rate of the trained person over that of the untrained person? [*Hint:* How much extra would an employer have to pay in order to attract and keep trained personnel of each type?]

CHAPTER 16

GENERAL EQUILIBRIUM

Recall that in Chapter 13 we introduced the topic of perfectly competitive markets. There we were primarily concerned with (a) how to characterize the equilibrium position of a *single* perfectly competitive market and (b) how such a market adjusts to change. In this chapter we shall talk about these same two processes for a competitive *multi-market* economy.

EQUILIBRIUM AND ADJUSTMENT IN TWO RELATED MARKETS

When we analyzed the way a single perfectly competitive market attains equilibrium and responds to change, we were doing what is known as *partial equilibrium analysis*. That is, we were disregarding the impact that the price in the market under study would have on the prices in other markets. Let's now enlarge our analysis of a single market and consider equilibrium and adjustment in two *related* markets.

Equilibrium in Two Related Markets

In Chapter 13 we defined market equilibrium as meaning that the values of price and quantity sold established in the market would endure so long as no factor underlying supply or demand were altered. This definition of equilibrium implies that a single market will attain equilibrium when one crucial condition holds: *supply must equal demand.* In the case of two related markets, one would naturally think that they would attain equilibrium simultaneously when supply equaled demand in each of them. This conclusion, though correct, is also incomplete. Recall that John Jones' demand for any output, say gizmos, depends not only on the price he must pay for gizmos, but also on the prices he receives for the inputs *he* supplies and on the prices he must pay for all other outputs. Similarly producer Ernest Smith's demand for any input, say labor, depends not only on the price he must pay for labor, but also on the prices he must pay for all other inputs and on the price he receives for his output. Therefore to construct the market *demand* curve for any commodity, be it input or output, we must assume that the prices of all other commodities are given and constant. For much the same reason, to construct the market *supply* curve for any one commodity, we must make a similar assumption.

Thus, in order for two markets to be simultaneously in equilibrium, it is not enough that demand equal supply in each. In addition, the demand and supply curves in each market must be based on the assumption that the price established in the other market equals the price at which that market attains equilibrium.

Adjustments in Two Related Input Markets

Now let's analyze the way that two related markets which are initially in equilibrium respond to a change that alters supply or demand, and thus price, in one of them. Consider the markets for two *substitute* inputs, rope and twine, which we shall abbreviate R and T. As a result of some outside disturbance such as bad weather which hurts the growing conditions of the hemp crop, the supply of R decreases. (The supply of T remains the same; we'll say that this twine is made of nylon.) Then the market supply curve for R (see Fig. 16.1a) shifts leftward from S_R to S'_R, and the equilibrium price of R rises from v^0 to v'.

This change in the price of R affects the price of T because, as the price of R increases from v^0 to v', cost-minimizing firms substitute T for R and the market demand curve for T shifts upward.* This upward shift, shown in Fig. 16.1(b) by the shift from D_T to D'_T, increases the quantity of T used in production from T^0 to T'. In addition it raises the price of T from u^0 to u'. How will this change in the price of T affect the price of R? Obviously as the price of T rises from u^0 to u', cost-minimizing firms will substitute R for T; market demand for R will shift upward from D_R to D'_R; and the market price of R will rise from v' to v''.

This secondary rise in the price of R does not of course mark the end of the adjustment process set in motion by the leftward shift in S_R. But we've described enough steps in this process to indicate that, if a change in supply or demand increases the price of one of two substitute inputs: (1) equilibrium will be disturbed in the markets in which both inputs are sold, and (2) these two markets will regain equilibrium only after a series of adjustments

---

* For simplicity we assume that the supply of T is not noticeably affected by a change in the price of R, and vice versa. In other words, we assume that from the point of view of supply, rope and twine are independent goods.

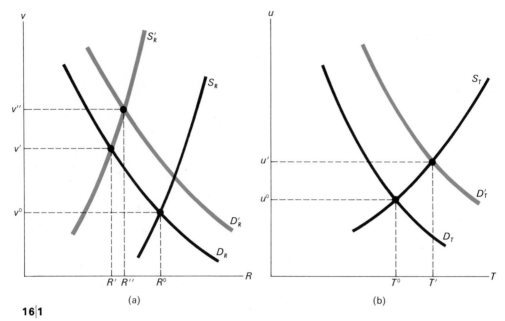

16|1

Adjustments in the markets for two substitute inputs, rope (*R*) and twine (*T*).
(a) Input *R*. (b) Input *T*.

and counteradjustments whose final effect will be to raise price in both markets.

So much for the effect of a change that *raises* the price of one of two substitute inputs. What will be the effect of a change in supply or demand that *lowers* the price of one of two substitute inputs? Check and you'll see that any such change will set off a chain of adjustments and counteradjustments whose final effect will be to lower the prices of both inputs.

Cottonseed Oil and Soybean Oil: An Example

The results we've just obtained suggest that the prices of substitute inputs sold in competitive markets ought to fluctuate together over time. For proof that they do, consider cottonseed oil and soybean oil. Both are sold in competitive markets, and both are used as inputs in shortening, margarine, cooking oil, salad oil, mayonnaise, and salad dressing. The proportion in which these two oils are combined in these different products can be varied considerably without altering the taste, odor, texture, color, or other qualities of the final outputs obtained. Therefore cottonseed oil and soybean oil are close substitutes; so, according to our theory, any price change occur-

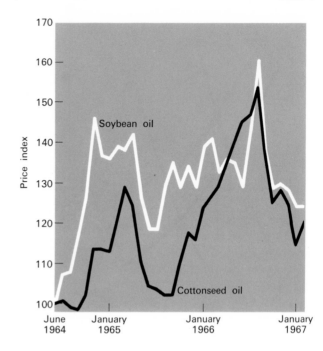

16|2

The prices of cottonseed oil and
soybean oil, two substitute
inputs, fluctuate together.
(Source: U.S. Department of
Commerce)

ring in the market for one of them ought to be immediately transmitted to
the market for the other. Does this in fact occur? Figure 16.2 shows that it
must, since the prices of these oils trace out very similar paths over time.

Adjustment in Any Two Related Markets

In studying how two related markets respond to change, we have focused on
the markets for two substitute inputs. We could of course go on to study
the way markets for other pairs of goods (such as complementary inputs,
complementary outputs, substitute outputs, or an input and an output)
respond to change. If we did we'd reach the following general conclusion:
So long as demand (or supply) in each of two markets depends on the price
in the other market, any change that disturbs equilibrium in one market
will set off a chain of adjustments and counteradjustments that will alter—
perhaps in the same direction or perhaps in different directions—the prices
established in both markets.

EQUILIBRIUM AND ADJUSTMENT IN A MULTI-MARKET ECONOMY

We have studied equilibrium and adjustment in two related markets; now
we shall enlarge our analysis still further, to include equilibrium and adjustment in a multi-market economy.

Equilibrium in a Multi-Market Economy

Whenever all markets in a competitive multi-market economy attain equilibrium simultaneously, the economy is said to be in general equilibrium.

From our discussion of equilibrium in two related markets, it follows that two conditions must hold in order for a competitive multi-market economy to attain general equilibrium.

1) Demand must equal supply in each market.
2) The demand and supply curves in each market must be based on the assumption that the prices established in *all* other markets equal the prices at which those markets attain equilibrium.

These two conditions are simple enough to state, but they imply that a complex set of relationships must be satisfied in order for an economy to attain general equilibrium. Can we be sure that a multi-market economy will have a position of general equilibrium? In other words, can we be sure that there is some set of prices that will simultaneously equate supply and demand in all markets in the economy?

When we studied equilibrium in a single perfectly competitive market, we were concerned with only two variables, price and quantity sold in the market under study. We were able to establish the existence of equilibrium in such a market by use of a simple diagram. When we study equilibrium in a *multi*-market economy, however, we are concerned with price and quantity sold in many markets. Therefore the question of whether or not such an economy has an equilibrium position turns out to be a multi-variable process that we cannot hope to solve with any single diagram or set of diagrams. We must turn to the economist's best friend, mathematics.

Using the tools of mathematics, economists have been able to show that an economy in which all markets are perfectly competitive will have a position of general equilibrium if certain conditions are met: There must be some upper limit on the quantity of output that the economy can produce during any one period. Consumers must have continuous, convex indifference curves; they must always want more goods; and there must be some upper limit on the quantity of labor services they can supply. Also the short-run production functions for all goods must be characterized everywhere by continuous, convex isoquants and by diminishing returns. These conditions are quite realistic. Also, as you'll note, our discussion throughout the preceding chapters implicitly assumed that all these conditions (with the exception of *everywhere* diminishing returns) were satisfied.

Adjustment in a Multi-Market Economy

We shall now talk about the way an economy in general equilibrium responds to a change that disturbs supply or demand in any one market. Let us again assume that the initial disturbance takes the form of a decrease in the supply of one input, R (rope). The first effect will of course be to raise the price of R. How will this affect the prices established in other markets? From our discussion above, it follows that a rise in the price of R will raise demand for and thus the price of not only the input T (twine), but also all other inputs that are substitutes for R.

What about inputs that are complements to R, that is, inputs that are used together with R? Obviously a rise in the price of R will lead cost-minimizing producers to substitute other inputs for R and for its complements. Thus a rise in the price of R would decrease demand for all inputs that are complements to R, and this decrease in demand would in turn lower the prices of these inputs.

So far we have focused on the effect that a change in the price of the input R will have on the prices of other *inputs*. What effect will such a change have on *output* prices? Whenever the price of an input rises, the cost curves of all firms that use that input shift upward, and their supply curves shift leftward. Therefore a rise in the price of R will lead to a decrease in the supply of (and thus to a rise in the price of) any output in whose production R is used as an input.

A change in the price of R will also affect the prices of other outputs in whose production R is not used at all. Why? Because consumers respond to hikes in the prices of those outputs in whose production R is an important input by increasing their demand for other substitute outputs in whose production R is not used. This will force up demand for (and thus price of) these other substitute outputs.

Example: cottonseed oil and lard. Lard does not compete directly with cottonseed oil as an input in food products, but it is a substitute for margarine and shortening made from cottonseed oil. Therefore any change in demand or supply that raised the price of cottonseed oil would, by raising the price of margarine and shortening, also raise the demand for (and thus the price of) lard. Similarly, any change in demand or supply that lowered the price of cottonseed oil would, by lowering the price of margarine and shortening, also lower the demand for (and thus the price of) lard. Therefore we'd expect the prices of lard and cottonseed oil to follow roughly similar patterns over time. Do they? Look at Fig. 13.6 and you'll see that they do.

We could go on to discuss the way a change in the price of R, by altering the incomes of consumers who supply R, also affects the quantities of different outputs they demand and thus the prices established for these outputs. But we have gone far enough to make three important points: *First,* in a multi-market economy, a change in the price of one input will affect the prices of a wide range of other inputs and outputs. *Second,* since all the price changes induced by the initial change in the price of R will themselves

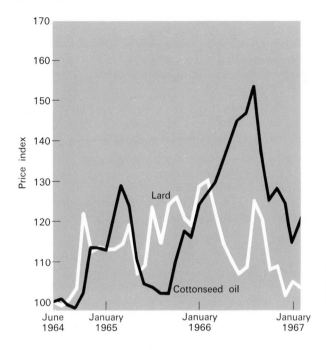

16|3

The prices of lard and cottonseed oil, two indirect substitutes, follow similar patterns over time. (Source: U.S. Department of Commerce)

affect supply and demand for R, a change in the price of R will set off a whole chain of adjustments and counteradjustments in the prices established in different markets. *Third,* the final effect of this adjustment process will be to raise price in some input and output markets and to lower price in others.

General Conclusions

We have been talking about how a competitive multi-market economy responds to a change whose initial effect is to alter supply or demand in a single *input* market. We could also have talked about how such an economy responds to a change whose initial effect is to alter supply or demand in a single *output* market. Both cases lead to the same conclusion:

Satisfaction-maximizing consumers and profit-maximizing firms respond to changes in the relative prices of different goods by altering their demand for and supply of individual inputs and outputs. Therefore, in a competitive multi-market economy, prices in different markets are closely interrelated. And any change that alters the price of one commodity will set off a complex and lengthy chain of adjustments and counteradjustments in the prices of both this commodity and a host of other commodities as well.

PROBLEMS

1   Using an appropriate pair of diagrams, show that a shift in demand that lowers the price of rope (swings go out of style), will set off a series of adjustments and counteradjustments whose final effect will be to lower the prices of both rope and twine.

2   Analyze the way that a perfectly competitive economy in equilibrium would respond to (a) a shift in consumer preferences from beef to turkey, and (b) a change in technology which halves the cost of producing computers.

3   A certain perfectly competitive economy has many goods and many consumers. Two of these goods, X and Y, are substitutes in consumption. Use diagrams to show the effect that a specific tax on X would have on the price and quantity sold of Y. Also compare the effect that such a change would have on the market for X under these assumptions to the effect it would have if *only* the market for X were allowed to adjust.

4   Repeat Problem 3, considering X and Y as complements in consumption.

5   Use diagrams to determine the effect of a government-enforced price ceiling applied to one good, X, on the price and quantity sold in the market for another good, Y, which is: (a) a close substitute for X in consumption, (b) complementary to X in consumption. Consider X and Y as only two of the many goods in a perfectly competitive economy.

6   Lard and margarine are close substitutes in many uses, and cottonseed oil is in turn one of the inputs used in producing margarine. Use diagrams to show how you would expect an increase in the demand for lard to affect the price of cottonseed oil.

7   Corn, like many other commodities, can be traded in any of several "futures" markets, i.e., commodity exchanges. As suggested in Chapter 12, the stock in trade of these markets consists of contracts between buyers and sellers for the sale of corn at some future date. For instance, a contract drawn up in January might state that, in May, the seller will deliver a specified quantity and quality of corn and the buyer will pay a specified price. At any moment you can find listed in the commodity quotations in the newspaper not only the cash price of corn (i.e., the price of corn delivered today), but also the prices of corn on a number of futures markets (i.e., corn for delivery in March, May, July, etc.). Ignoring here the influence of speculators, discuss and, where possible, illustrate with diagrams the way you would expect the prices of March corn and May corn to be related. The principal factors in this relationship are storage costs for corn and the market interest rate.

*Appendix to Chapter 16

LOCATING AN ECONOMY'S POSITION OF GENERAL EQUILIBRIUM

Suppose that we find an economy that satisfies all the conditions it must satisfy in order for it to have a position of general equilibrium. How could we determine the set of prices that would be established when this economy attains general equilibrium? Perhaps we could use the technique of examining one market at a time and of locating the price that equates supply and demand in that market (i.e., the price at which the supply and demand curves intersect in that market). For example, we might determine successively the equilibrium prices in the hog market, the house market, the labor market, the lard market, and so forth. But no, we couldn't use this market-by-market approach because we cannot establish the shape and position of the supply and demand curves in any one market until we know what prices will be established in *all* other markets. A market-by-market solution would be possible only if we *began* with full knowledge of the set of equilibrium prices that we were supposed to determine. Since such omniscience is unattainable, we must seek another solution.

Mathematics again comes to our rescue. We begin by collecting data on the "givens" of the problem; that is, on every consumer's preferences, his initial endowment of primary inputs, and the production functions of all outputs. Then for each consumer, on the basis of both his preferences and his initial input endowments, we compute schedules expressing his demand for every output and his willingness to supply every input as functions of all input and output prices. Similarly for each firm, on the basis of its production function, we construct schedules expressing its demand for every input and its willingness to supply output as functions of all input and output prices.

---

* The reader may skip this appendix without loss of continuity.

The conditions that characterize equilibrium in a perfectly competitive economy are those in which the set of prices in all input and output markets is such that:

1) The supply and demand schedules of all consumers and all firms in every market are satisfied.
2) All markets are cleared.*

We find the set of prices that satisfies these conditions by doing the following:

1) *We express these equilibrium conditions as a set of equations.*
2) *We solve these equations for the set of prices, quantities bought, and quantities sold that will simultaneously satisfy all of them.*

Solving our general equilibrium problem may sound complex, but it is identical in concept to solving the following simple problem: What values must x and y assume to satisfy simultaneously the requirements that

$$x + y = 3 \quad \text{and} \quad 2x - y = 0?$$

By using any of the familiar techniques for solving simultaneous equations, we can determine that both equations hold when $x = 1$ and $y = 2$.

Now we shall demonstrate our remarks by working through an example. Consider an economy in which there exist a large number n of consumers, each of whom has some endowment of society's two primary inputs, labor L and land (i.e., raw materials) R. In this economy there are a large number m of firms, each of which can transform the inputs L and R into one or both of two outputs, q_1 and q_2, according to certain rules embodied in the production functions for these outputs. These firms may earn profits in equilibrium. The profits of all m firms are divided among all n consumers according to some fixed proportions; i.e., each consumer receives a fixed percent of the total profits earned in the economy. Suppose that we have full knowledge of the preferences of consumers, their initial endowments of primary inputs, and the production functions for both outputs.

1) If equilibrium is established in this economy, what inputs will each consumer supply and what outputs will he buy?
2) What inputs will each firm buy and what outputs will it supply?
3) At what price will trading take place in each input and output market?

On the basis of our knowledge of each consumer's preferences, input endowment, and share of total profits, we construct his supply schedules for both inputs (L and R) as functions of all input and output prices. These

---

* This is an expression economists use to describe a state in which the total amount supplied equals the total amount demanded.

schedules can be represented as follows:

$$L_i^s = L_i(p_1, p_2, w, v, \overline{L}_i, \overline{R}_i, \alpha_i), \qquad i = 1, 2, \ldots, n,$$

$$R_i^s = R_i(p_1, p_2, w, v, \overline{L}_i, \overline{R}_i, \alpha_i), \qquad i = 1, 2, \ldots, n.$$

The first equation says that L_i^s, the amount of labor supplied by the ith consumer (who may be any consumer from the first to the nth) depends on: p_1 and p_2, the prices he must pay for both outputs; w and v, the prices he receives for both inputs; on $\overline{L}_i$ and $\overline{R}_i$, his initial endowments of both inputs; and α_i, his share in profits. The second equation says that R_i^s, the amount of R supplied by the ith consumer, depends on all input and output prices, on his initial endowments of both inputs, and on his share of profits.

Now we again use our knowledge of each consumer's preferences and input endowments to construct his demand schedules for both outputs, q_1 and q_2, as functions of all input and output prices, as follows:

$$q_{i1}^d = q_{i1}(p_1, p_2, w, v, \overline{L}_i, \overline{R}_i, \alpha_i), \qquad i = 1, 2, \ldots, n,$$

$$q_{i2}^d = q_{i2}(p_1, p_2, w, v, \overline{L}_i, \overline{R}_i, \alpha_i), \qquad i = 1, 2, \ldots, n.$$

These two sets of equations state that q_{i1}^d, the amount of q_1 demanded by the ith consumer, and q_{i2}^d, the amount of q_2 demanded by the ith consumer, both depend on all input and output prices, on the consumer's initial endowments of both inputs, and on his share of profits.

Next we turn to the firm. Using the production functions for both outputs, we construct each firm's demand schedule for each input as a function of all input and output prices, as follows:

$$L_j^d = L_j(p_1, p_2, w, v), \qquad j = 1, 2, \ldots, m,$$

$$R_j^d = R_j(p_1, p_2, w, v), \qquad j = 1, 2, \ldots, m.$$

This first equation says that L_j^d, the amount of labor L demanded by the jth firm, depends on the prices this firm must pay for both inputs and on the prices it receives for its outputs. The second equation says that R_j^d, the amount of the input R demanded by the jth firm, depends on prices of all inputs and outputs.

Using the production functions of both goods, we next construct each firm's supply schedules for each output as a function of all input and output prices, as follows:

$$q_{j1}^s = q_{j1}(p_1, w, v), \qquad j = 1, 2, \ldots, m,$$

$$q_{j2}^s = q_{j2}(p_2, w, v), \qquad j = 1, 2, \ldots, m,$$

in which q_{j1}^s and q_{j2}^s represent, respectively, the amounts of q_1 and q_2 that the jth firm is willing to supply as a function of the prices established in all markets.

We complete the set of equations describing equilibrium in our economy by adding to the demand and supply schedules we have obtained four additional equations which require that all input and output markets be cleared; i.e., that total amount supplied in each market equal total amount demanded in that market. For simplicity, (1) we denote the total quantities of L and R supplied by all n consumers by L^s and R^s, respectively, (2) we denote the total quantities of L and R demanded by all m producers by L^d and R^d, respectively, (3) we denote the total quantities of q_1 and q_2 demanded by all n consumers by q_1^d and q_2^d, respectively, and (4) we denote the total quantities of q_1 and q_2 supplied by all m producers by q_1^s and q_2^s, respectively. Then we can represent these four market-clearing conditions as follows:

$$L^s = L^d, \qquad R^s = R^d,$$
$$q_1^s = q_1^d, \qquad q_2^s = q_2^d.$$

To complete our model, let's introduce money into our economy as a *unit of account,* that is, as a unit in terms of which all prices are expressed. We arbitrarily set the price of one good as equal to a dollar. Suppose that we set the price of q_1 as equal to \$1. Then the final condition on equilibrium in our system will be given by the equation

$$p_1 = \$1.$$

We have now obtained a set of simultaneous equations that describes equilibrium in our system. Before solving it, we must check to see that we have enough equations to determine the values of all the unknowns. We recall from elementary algebra that, to solve for the numerical values of any number of unknowns, we need precisely the same number of independent equations. If we have *fewer* independent equations than unknowns, the system will be underdetermined, and there will exist infinitely many sets of numerical values that our unknowns could assume and still satisfy all equations in the system. If we have *more* independent equations than unknowns, our system will be overdetermined, and there will exist no set of values that our unknowns could assume and still satisfy simultaneously all equations in the system.*

---

*Illustration: Attempt to solve the following sets of equations, (a), (b), and (c) for *numerical* values of the two unknowns x and y. Note that system (a) is underdetermined, while system (c) is overdetermined.

(a) $x + y = 10$ (b) $x + y = 10$ (c) $x + y = 10$
                              $x - y = 6$ $x - y = 6$
                                                   $2x + y = 2$

TABLE 16|1

Determining the General Equilibrium Position of a Simple n-Consumer, m-Producer, Two-Input, Two-Output Economy

Variables whose values at the point of equilibrium are unknown	Number of such variables
The quantities of L and R supplied by each consumer	$2n$
The quantities of q_1 and q_2 demanded by each consumer	$2n$
The quantities of L and R demanded by each producer	$2m$
The quantities of q_1 and q_2 supplied by each producer	$2m$
Prices in the L, R, q_1, and q_2 markets	4
Total unknowns	$4(n + m + 1)$

Equations characterizing the economy's equilibrium position	Number of such equations
Each consumer's supply schedules for L and R	$2n$
Each consumer's demand schedules for q_1 and q_2	$2n$
Each producer's demand schedules for L and R	$2m$
Each producer's supply schedules for q_1 and q_2	$2m$
Supply equal to demand for each of the traded commodities: L, R, q_1, and q_2	4
The money price of q_1	1
Total equations	$4(n + m + 1) + 1$

Table 16.1 shows the number of variables in our general equilibrium system versus the number of conditions that characterize equilibrium in this system. At first glance we seem to have one equation too many. This difficulty, however, is only apparent, since only three of our four market-clearing equations are independent (i.e., any three of them taken together imply the fourth). Example: Consider a *two-good economy* in which apples are traded for pears. Clearly pears are paid for with apples and apples are paid for with pears. Therefore the demand for apples must represent the supply of pears, and the supply of apples must represent the demand for pears. Thus only one market, the pear–apple market, can exist in this economy. This one market, however, can be viewed either as the apple market (i.e., in terms of the market supply and demand curves for apples) or as the pear market (i.e., in terms of the market supply and demand curves for pears). Because these double viewpoints are possible, we say that the pear–apple economy is in equilibrium only if supply equals demand in both the pear and the apple markets. However, since these two markets are simply alternative ways of viewing the single pear–apple market, the apple market must be in equilibrium if the pear market is in equilibrium, and vice versa.

Thus, in a two-good economy, only one of the two apparent market-clearing conditions is independent. Similarly, as you can verify, in a three-good economy, only two of the three apparent market-clearing equations are independent; and in a four-good economy, like the one with which we are working, only three of the four market-clearing equations are independent.

Since this is so, we have precisely the right number of independent equations to solve our general equilibrium system. Thus, if we had a computer and were willing to go through the astronomical number of calculations that would be required to solve the system, we could obtain not only equilibrium prices of all inputs and outputs, but also equilibrium purchases and sales of every consumer and of every producer in the economy.

PROBLEMS

1   Consider the following approach to finding a solution to general equilibrium: First, set arbitrary values for all prices. Second, for each good find a new price, using the supply and demand functions based on this first set of prices. How would you know if the original arbitrary price structure happened to be that of equilibrium?

2   Consider a perfectly competitive economy in which *only two goods* are produced. Assume that *only two consumers* demand these goods and supply the one input used in producing them. Would it be possible for one of the two goods markets to be in disequilibrium while the other goods market and the input market were in equilibrium? Keep in mind the restrictions implied by the budget constraints of both consumers.

3   Expand Problem 2 to a perfectly competitive economy that still has only two outputs and one input, but now has a large number n of consumers.

4   Use the n equations that define the budget constraints of all consumers and the m equations that define the profits of all firms to show that only three of the four market-clearing equations in our economy are independent.

CHAPTER 17

*INPUT–OUTPUT ANALYSIS

By adding some restrictive assumptions to the general equilibrium model in Chapter 16, we can develop a modified model which we can apply to the world around us, and thus use to answer questions about our economy.

THE MODEL

We shall again consider equilibrium in a simple, perfectly competitive economy that produces only two outputs, q_1 and q_2. But the assumptions we shall now make about how these outputs are produced differ sharply from those we made in developing our original general equilibrium model in the appendix to Chapter 16. Here we shall assume that producers of q_1 and q_2 use only one primary input, labor, that this labor is supplied by the n consumers in the economy, and that its supply is inelastic. This inelasticity could reflect a variety of conditions; for example, laws might fix the standard work week at 40 hours and permit no deviations from that figure.

We shall also assume that each industry may use as inputs not only the primary input labor, but also its own output and the output of the other industry. We shall assume that the production functions for q_1 and q_2 are characterized by *fixed factor proportions;* i.e., in each industry there is only one set of proportions in which inputs can be efficiently combined, and factor (or input) substitution is therefore impossible in both industries. And we shall assume that the production functions for q_1 and q_2 display *constant returns to scale.*

Conditions of Consumer Equilibrium

We shall again begin with the consumer. Depending on the wage rate, each consumer will earn a certain income by selling labor to the productive sector,

---

* The reader may skip this chapter without losing continuity.

and will divide that income, according to his preferences, between purchases of q_1 and q_2. Since we assumed that the quantity of labor supplied by each consumer is fixed, we can dispense with individual supply schedules for labor, and simply represent the total amount of labor supplied by all consumers in the economy by the constant, $\overline{L}$.

On the other hand, each consumer's demand for the outputs q_1 and q_2 is variable. It depends on w, the wage rate, and on p_1 and p_2, the prices he must pay for q_1 and q_2. We shall construct our model by combining the demand schedules of individual consumers to obtain market demand schedules. Let q_1^d and q_2^d represent the total quantities of q_1 and q_2 demanded in the market. We can represent the market demand schedules for these goods by the equations

$$q_1^d = f(p_1,p_2,w), \qquad q_2^d = g(p_1,p_2,w),$$

which state that total demand for each good will depend on the price of that good, on the price of the other good, and on the wage rate.

Conditions of Producer Equilibrium

We shall next characterize equilibrium in the productive sector. First note that, if the production function of an output is characterized by fixed factor proportions and by constant returns to scale, then each unit of that output will be produced by combining the same bundle of inputs, and the output in question will be produced at *constant cost;* i.e., the marginal cost of every unit will be the same. But if marginal cost is a *constant,* then the average and marginal costs of every unit of output will be identical; and the MC and AC curves of a firm producing this output can be portrayed by a single straight line (see Fig. 17.1).

17|1

The marginal and average cost curves of a firm that produces under conditions of constant cost.

The fact that q_1 and q_2 will be produced at constant cost implies that producers will expand output of each of these goods until its price falls to the point at which it just equals average cost. Example: Suppose that the price of q_1 exceeded its average cost. Then, by producing and selling an additional unit of q_1, a producer could increase his profit by an amount equal to the difference between the price of q_1 and its average cost.* But this profit opportunity would induce producers to expand output of q_1; they would continue to do so until p_1 had fallen to the point at which it just equaled the average cost of a unit of q_1. At this point every profit-maximizing producer of q_1 would be in equilibrium, since his marginal revenue would equal his marginal cost.† Thus the equilibrium condition in each of our two industries is that price equal average cost or, alternatively, that profits equal zero.

To express these conditions more precisely, we must determine the average costs of producing q_1 and q_2. First we note that if the production function for any output is characterized by *fixed factor proportions* and *constant returns to scale,* then this function can be summarized by *a set of coefficients,* each of which states the number of units of a particular input needed to produce one unit of output. Table 17.1 gives such summary pro-

TABLE 17|1

Production Functions for Outputs q_1 and q_2

Input	Quantities of each input needed to produce one unit of q_1	Quantities of each input needed to produce one unit of q_2
q_1	a_{11}	a_{12}
q_2	a_{21}	a_{22}
L	a_{L1}	a_{L2}

duction functions for outputs q_1 and q_2 in our simple three-input, two-output economy. Each coefficient in the first column states the number of units of a particular input required to produce one unit of q_1; each coefficient in the second column states the number of units of a particular input required to produce one unit of q_2. Thus the coefficient a_{21} states the amount of q_2 required to produce one unit of q_1, while the coefficient a_{L2} states the number of units of labor L required to produce one unit of q_2. Clearly the average cost of one unit of q_1 will equal the total cost of all inputs used to produce it. The coefficients recorded in Table 17.1 thus indicate that the average (and

---

* Remember that our assumption of perfect competition implies that an individual producer of q_1 will always view his marginal and average revenue as identical, while our assumption of constant costs implies that his marginal and average costs will always be identical.

† In fact, because of our special assumptions, the producer would find that the values assumed at this point by his average cost, marginal cost, average revenue, and marginal revenue would all be equal.

marginal) cost of every unit of q_1 will equal $p_1a_{11} + p_2a_{21} + wa_{L1}$, while the average (and marginal) cost of every unit of q_2 will equal $p_1a_{12}+p_2a_{22}+wa_{L2}$.

With these expressions in hand, we can write the equilibrium conditions for each industry as follows:

$$p_1 = p_1a_{11} + p_2a_{21} + wa_{L1},$$

$$p_2 = p_1a_{12} + p_2a_{22} + wa_{L2}.$$

The first of these equations says that the price obtained by any producer of q_1 must equal his average cost of production: In other words, his profits must equal zero. The second equation states a similar requirement for producers of q_2.*

Market Clearing Equations

We have now obtained conditions that describe consumer and producer equilibrium. To complete our model we need only add three simple conditions. These state that, whenever our economy is in equilibrium, the markets in which labor and both outputs are sold must be cleared. These conditions can be represented by the following three equations, in which q_1^s and q_2^s represent the total outputs of q_1 and q_2, respectively:

$$a_{L1}q_1^s + a_{L2}q_2^s = \overline{L},$$

$$q_1^s - a_{11}q_1^s - a_{12}q_2^s = q_1^d,$$

$$q_2^s - a_{21}q_1^s - a_{22}q_2^s = q_2^d.$$

The first equation says that the total amount of labor used to produce q_1 and q_2 must equal the available supply of labor. The second equation says that the total output of q_1 minus inputs of q_1 used in the production of q_1 and q_2 must equal final demand for q_1. The third equation says that the total output of q_2 minus inputs of q_2 used in the production of q_1 and q_2 must equal final demand for q_2.

---

* Note that, although each industry's equilibrium output can easily be determined for any set of prices, the number of firms that will produce this output is indeterminate. Reason: Our assumption of constant costs refers to the costs incurred by the *individual producer*. Therefore each producer's marginal cost will be constant at all levels of output, and since each is a perfect competitor, his marginal revenue will also be constant at all levels of output. Thus, whenever the market in which he sells is in equilibrium, his marginal revenue will equal his marginal cost at any level of output. But if so, then his equilibrium output (normally the output that equates his marginal revenue and marginal cost) will be indeterminate. This indeterminacy reflects the fact that he will earn the same profit, zero, regardless of how much or how little he produces.

As you should verify, of the seven conditions that compose our model, only six are independent. The conditions we have imposed on equilibrium in our system are thus just sufficient in number to determine the equilibrium values of all unknowns in the system. These are the total outputs of q_1 and q_2, the amounts of these goods supplied to consumers (final demanders) and the *relative* prices at which goods and labor will be exchanged. Our model is thus complete, and we are now ready to apply it to practical problems.

PRACTICAL APPLICATIONS OF INPUT–OUTPUT ANALYSIS

Input–Output Tables

All activity in the productive sector of our simple economy could be summarized in an *input–output* table like Table 17.2. An input–output table provides two kinds of information:

1) It shows how available supplies of labor and other primary inputs used in production are allocated among industries in the economy.

2) It shows how the output of each industry is allocated among industries (including itself) that use it as an input and individuals who consume it.

TABLE 17|2

Input–Output Table for an Economy Producing
Two Outputs, q_1 and q_2, and Utilizing One Primary Input, Labor

	Inputs used in production of q_1	Inputs used in production of q_2	Final demand	Total output of each industry
q_1	30	70	200	300
q_2	20	80	350	450
L	50	40		

In Table 17.2 consumption is represented by the column labeled "final demand." This table is a schematic representation of the values assumed in equilibrium by all terms in the final three equations of our model. Tables 17.1 and 17.2 are closely related; in fact, by using Table 17.2, we can calculate all the input coefficients presented in Table 17.1. For example, Table 17.2 states that 70 units of q_1 are required to produce a total output of 450 units of q_2; this, however, tells us that a_{12}, the amount of q_1 needed to produce one unit of q_2, must equal approximately 0.15.

Because it refers to an economy that has only two outputs, Table 17.2 is extremely simple and artificial, but it does illustrate clearly the basic structure and properties of any input–output table.

Input–Output Table for the United States

Once we understand the fundamental idea of Table 17.2, the construction of an input–output table for an actual economy poses no conceptual difficulties, although it does pose practical ones.* The first step in constructing such a table is to select the industry groupings we wish to include. One major requirement is that each industry's output be as homogeneous as possible, in order that meaningful input coefficients can be computed from the table. Literal interpretation of this requirement would result in a table containing hundreds, if not thousands, of industries. Since it would be impossible to obtain the data necessary to fill in an input–output table involving so many industries, and since using such a large table for analytic purposes would pose insurmountable computational difficulties, input–output tables divide economic activity into a limited number of industries. The U.S. 1958 input–output table, for example, contains broad industry groupings such as "agriculture and fisheries," "iron and steel," "railroad transportation," and "eating and drinking places."

After one selects the industries to be included, one must collect data, for some base year, on the following four items:

1) The quantities of primary inputs used by each industry
2) The total output produced by each industry
3) The quantities of each industry's output that are used as inputs in every other industry
4) The quantity of each industry's output that goes to satisfy final demand

Following this general approach, accountants computing national income in many different countries have set up input–output tables for their domestic economies. The latest input–output table set up for the United States is based on 1958 data. It distinguishes 86 different productive sectors (i.e., broad industry groupings) and 5 final-demand sectors.

Such a detailed breakdown yields not only a lot of information but also a pretty unwieldy table. Therefore we present in Table 17.3 a condensed version of the 86-sector table for the United States, containing only 20 productive sectors (see pages 268–269). These range from "agricultural, forestry, and fishery products" to "government and government enterprises."

The first 20 *columns* in our table list the inputs used by each sector. Thus for example column 1 tells us that the "agricultural, forestry and fishery products" sector used as inputs over $1 billion of chemicals, plastics, and paints, over $1 billion of transportation and communication services, and

---

* For a detailed discussion of the practical problems involved in setting up an input–output table, see W. D. Evans and M. Hoffenberg: "The Interindustry Relations Study for 1947," *The Review of Economics and Statistics* **XXXIV**, No. 2, May 1952.

almost $6 billion of other services. The twenty-first entry is entitled "scrap and noncompetitive imports." It has to be added because domestic producers in every sector use as inputs goods, such as bananas and used railroad ties, that are neither primary inputs nor the current output of any domestic sector. The next-to-last entry in each column, "value added," records the total value of labor, capital, and other primary inputs used by the sector named at the head of the column. This entry corresponds to the final entry L for labor in the first two columns of Table 17.2. The final entry in each column in Table 17.3 records the total value of all outlays made by the sector named at the top of the column on primary inputs and on inputs purchased from other sectors.

The last 5 columns in Table 17.3 record the quantities of different outputs that went to satisfy each of the major components of final demand: personal consumption, business investment in fixed capital and inventories, net exports, and government purchases of goods and services.

Each *row* in Table 17.3 shows how the total output of the productive sector named at the left of the row was allocated among different uses. The first 21 entries in each row show how much of this sector's output was used as an input in other sectors. The five final entries show how much of this sector's output went to satisfy different segments of final demand. Thus for example row 1 of the table shows that over $14 billion of the total output produced by the "agricultural, forestry and fishery products" sector was used by this sector itself as inputs. Another $22 billion of this sector's output was used as inputs by manufacturers in the food and tobacco sector. Also $5 billion went directly to personal consumption expenditure and about $2 billion represented net exports.

An input-output table such as Table 17.3 is interesting because of the detailed picture it presents of the complex way in which the circular flow of goods described in Chapter 1 takes place in a modern industrial economy, and because it offers an analytic basis for answering practical questions about how the productive sector of an economy functions. The remainder of this chapter will deal with several such questions.

Consistent Forecasting

One practical use of input–output analysis is in forecasting. Suppose that the government wants to compare the long-run rate of growth in the labor force with the probable long-run rate of growth in demand for labor. Naturally the government will need projections of industry's future demand for labor inputs. It could obtain such estimates by simply projecting past trends in total employment. But such a crude method is likely to yield inaccurate results unless the series displays an unusually consistent pattern of change over time.

TABLE 17|3 Input–Output Table for the United States, 1958, Millions of Dollars

	Agricultural, forestry, and fishery products 1	Mining and quarrying 2	New construction and maintenance 3	Food and tobacco manufacturers 4	Textiles and textile products 5	Wood and paper products 6	Chemicals, plastics, and paints 7	Drugs and toilet preparations 8	Rubber products 9	Leather and footwear 10	Glass, stone, and clay products 11	Primary metals and metal products 12
Agricultural, forestry, and fishery products 1	14,806	*	237	22,467	1,502	998	28	*	7	53	4	*
Mining and quarrying 2	102	851	756	54	19	130	568	24	8	3	622	2,472
New construction and maintenance 3	613	7	8	234	16	72	33	7	2	*	4	145
Food and tobacco manufacturers 4	2,999	*	17	11,743	39	105	213	1	194	208	6	8
Textiles and textile products 5	106	4	6	148	11,964	391	45	625	6	142	21	82
Wood and paper products 6	146	55	4,607	1,506	317	7,826	478	91	265	100	484	471
Chemicals, plastics, and paints 7	1,181	135	1,513	351	1,689	699	4,280	1,304	860	66	336	629
Rubber products 8	187	59	377	154	169	376	164	207	63	192	86	190
Drugs and toilet preparations 9	29	*	*	220	27	36	217	6	413	24	49	57
Leather and footwear 10	5	*	*	*	58	9	*	13	*	1,033	1	5
Glass, stone, and clay products 11	30	115	4,800	609	29	213	76	68	144	16	1,079	511
Primary metals and metal products 12	121	194	10,754	1,846	46	868	647	130	189	29	176	14,317
Engines, machinery, and nonelectrical equipment 13	205	307	751	17	72	122	153	34	10	2	31	1,242
Electrical equipment and appliances 14	30	24	1,984	35	4	65	30	25	3	6	45	632
Transportation equipment 15	81	29	9	*	2	16	1	19	*	*	3	335
Scientific, photographic and misc. equipment 16	4	6	340	37	342	80	42	43	31	21	27	188
Transportation and communications 17	1,042	288	2,503	3,351	747	1,489	931	251	215	114	654	2,132
Energy 18	1,233	276	1,536	648	225	526	1,092	87	90	22	385	1,117
Services 19	5,889	586	10,055	5,439	1,962	1,989	1,175	536	1,303	287	697	3,044
Government and government enterprises 20	10	9	15	73	45	41	59	8	16	12	23	61
Scrap and noncompetitive imports 21	1,030	777	85	2,693	635	1,583	363	267	48	47	171	2,235
VALUE ADDED	22,110	3,744	28,937	19,485	9,431	9,940	7,044	3,131	2,768	1,655	4,900	18,739
TOTAL	51,960	7,465	69,291	71,109	29,341	27,575	17,641	6,876	6,636	4,033	9,805	48,612

*Less than $1 million.
Note: Each column shows what inputs were used by the sector listed at the top of the column. Each row shows what uses were made of the output produced by the sector listed at the left of the row.

	FINAL DEMAND				

Column headers (13–21):
- 13: Engines, machinery, and nonelectrical equipment
- 14: Electrical equipment and appliances
- 15: Transportation equipment
- 16: Scientific, photographic, and misc. equipment
- 17: Energy
- 18: Transportation and communications
- 19: Services
- 20: Government and government enterprises
- 21: Scrap and noncompetitive imports

13	14	15	16	17	18	19	20	21	Personal consumption expenditures	Gross private fixed capital formation	Net inventory change	Net exports	Government purchases
3	*	*	15	146	*	2,349	624	*	4,821	*	1,068	1,884	948
18	16	20	5	29	622	85	128	*	280	*	−75	455	272
25	24	103	17	1,594	581	7,765	1,206	*	*	36,957	*	2	19,877
1	*	*	20	2,205	12	785	260	3	50,009	*	222	1,734	325
27	37	336	196	81	9	792	6	92	13,720	45	−255	415	300
95	540	352	555	2,330	123	1,873	36	28	3,582	930	43	427	315
52	362	269	322	257	609	502	24	*	241	*	−72	1,043	990
224	388	880	242	281	46	844	7	5	1,309	52	−32	211	193
11	6	29	22	50	51	984	3	*	3,708	*	56	325	312
11	8	9	73	30	*	46	*	2	2,607	5	30	64	25
153	351	415	110	14	65	451	12	*	344	*	22	168	10
3,634	3,448	6,124	977	212	616	535	27	357	728	884	−339	1,371	720
2,427	545	1,941	134	179	153	809	2	120	184	7,589	−510	2,175	1,068
755	3,356	1,754	467	398	79	2,473	2	125	4,822	4,825	−420	1,142	2,300
577	398	10,430	239	589	11	4,342	22	166	10,112	5,112	−782	1,792	10,210
97	335	501	599	237	16	1,969	*	68	3,354	973	31	389	1,001
620	872	1,145	395	5,194	1,797	15,847	938	136	15,013	869	164	2,468	2,465
216	181	323	71	1,813	15,534	5,060	516	10	15,320	*	−226	717	1,942
1,448	2,214	2,482	1,104	8,087	3,537	38,721	489	3	152,778	4,956	91	2,212	8,741
25	60	65	19	928	2,988	3,170	12	*	945	*	*	64	39,272
274	175	671	438	1,613	1,672	483	184	807	6,192	−807	−509	−16,853	2,872
9,072	11,644	15,868	4,713	35,373	20,193	169,940	43,421	5,222					
19,764	24,962	43,715	10,733	61,641	48,714	259,824	47,918	7,146	290,066	62,391	−1,491	2,206	94,158

Source: This table has been condensed from the 86-sector table prepared by the National Economics Division of the U.S. Department of Commerce.

A better approach might be to forecast separately the level of output and demand for labor of *each* industry, then to add these projections to obtain an estimate of national demand for labor in the period in question. This approach might produce better results than simple trend projection, but if estimates of the final output of each industry are made independently, these estimates are likely to be inconsistent. The projected outputs of at least some industries will not equal the projected final demand, and the demand by other industries, for their outputs. To obtain better estimates of the outputs of all industries and thus of national demand for labor, we need to find a way to make mutually consistent forecasts of the total outputs of each of these industries.

By using the information in a national input–output table, we can do this. The steps we must carry out are simple in concept if not in computation.

1) We must make projections of final demand for each industry's output.
2) We must use input coefficients derived from the national input–output table (see the discussion of Table 17.2) to set up a system of simultaneous equations, one for each industry.

These equations in effect say that each industry's projected total output equals projected demand, both final and from other industries, for its output. The total outputs of all industries are thus the unknowns of the system, and their values can be obtained by solving the system.

TABLE 17|4

Production Functions for Steel and Coal

Inputs	Quantities of each input needed to produce one unit of steel	Quantities of each input needed to produce one unit of coal
Steel	0.1	0.3
Coal	0.2	0.1
Labor	0.4	0.2

Suppose for example that an economy produces only two goods, coal and steel, input coefficients for which are given in Table 17.4. We are required to estimate this economy's total labor requirements five years hence; and we want to base our projection of the economy's labor requirements on consistent estimates of total steel and coal output five years hence.

Our first step is to estimate final demand for coal and steel at that time. Suppose that these estimates are that five years hence 40 units of steel and 80 units of coal will be required to satisfy final demand. In order for this final demand to be met exactly, two conditions have to be satisfied: Each industry's total output will have to equal final demand for its output and demand from the other industry for its output. These two conditions can be expressed by the following equations, in which q_1^s and q_2^s represent total outputs of steel and coal, respectively:

$$q_1^s - 0.1q_1^s - 0.3q_2^s = 40, \qquad q_2^s - 0.2q_1^s - 0.1q_2^s = 80.$$

We solve these equations for q_1^s and q_2^s, and find that to satisfy final demand for 40 units of steel and 80 units of coal, the economy must produce 80 units of steel and 107 units of coal. How much labor will this require? According to Table 17.4, every unit of steel produced requires 0.4 units of labor, while every unit of coal produced requires 0.2 units of labor. Thus, by substituting $q_1^s = 80$ and $q_2^s = 107$ into the equation

$$0.4q_1^s + 0.2q_2^s = L,$$

we obtain our estimate: The total quantity of labor L that will be required by our economy five years hence will be approximately 53 units.

Feasibility and Size of Input Coefficients

In our discussion of consistent forecasting, we assumed that production of the final bundle of goods demanded by society would be *feasible*. In practice, however, feasibility is not guaranteed and must therefore be checked.

Let us check the conditions under which *positive* production of one commodity, steel, would be feasible in our simple two-output economy. First observe that Table 17.4 is simply a special case of Table 17.1, and thus each numerical coefficient in Table 17.4 corresponds to one of the general coefficients in Table 17.1. Next observe that, if production of one unit of steel required a *direct input* of steel that exceeded one unit, *net output* in the steel industry would always be negative, and steel "production" would in effect be a form of steel "consumption." Thus production will be "self-sustaining" in both of our industries only if the direct input coefficients, a_{11} and a_{22}, are both less than 1. To verify this, try to determine the total outputs of steel and coal that would have to be produced in order to satisfy a final demand for one unit of steel and one unit of coal if the coefficient a_{11} in Table 17.4 were set equal to 1.1 and all other input coefficients were unchanged.

So far we have discussed the viability of our economy simply in terms of the size of each industry's direct input requirement for its own output. However, an industry uses its own output as an input, not only directly, but also *indirectly*. Example: The total input of steel required to produce one unit of steel equals the steel used directly to make steel, plus the steel used to make the coal used in making steel, plus the steel used to make the steel used in making steel, plus the steel used to make the steel used to make the coal used in making steel, plus an infinite series of other terms. But if steel production requires both direct and indirect inputs of steel, then it will be feasible for the steel industry to produce a positive output only if *the sum of the direct and indirect inputs required to produce one unit of steel is less than 1*.

Let's try out a situation in which this condition is not met. See whether you can determine the total outputs of steel and coal that would have to be produced in order to make one unit of steel and one unit of coal available for final demand if the input coefficients in Table 17.4 were altered as follows: $a_{11} = 0.6$, $a_{12} = 0.8$, $a_{21} = 0.5$, and $a_{22} = 0.3$.

The solution of both these examples of nonfeasibility call for negative total outputs. In other words, in these situations, positive production goals can be met only if production is "subsidized" by running down stocks or inventories.

This result suggests an alternative way to view the problem of feasibility: The pair of total outputs, q_1^s and q_2^s, that must be produced in order to meet the pair of final demands, $\bar{q}_1^d$ and $\bar{q}_2^d$, will be identified by the intersection of the two lines obtained when the equations

$$(1 - a_{11})q_1^s - \qquad\qquad a_{12}q_2^s = \bar{q}_1^d,$$

$$- a_{21}q_1^s + (1 - a_{22})q_2^s = \bar{q}_2^d,$$

are plotted in the (q_1, q_2)-plane. Feasibility therefore requires that these two lines intersect in the positive quadrant of the (q_1, q_2)-plane. Such an intersection depends on their relative slopes, which in turn depend on the values of the input coefficients a_{11}, a_{12}, a_{22}, and a_{21}. Example: Assign any convenient pair of positive values to $\bar{q}_1^d$ and $\bar{q}_2^d$. Plot first the pair of curves obtained by using the input coefficients in Table 17.4 and then plot the pair of curves obtained by using the input coefficients in the nonfeasibility example given above.

Feasibility and Availability of Primary Inputs

So far we have discussed feasibility in terms of the technical characteristics of the input–output coefficients of the system. But suppose that society's supply of primary inputs is fixed. Then a given set of final demands is feasible only if sufficient quantities of primary inputs are available to produce the corresponding set of *total outputs*. Consider the manpower problem of a country at war. To win, the country needs both war materials and an army; yet the more men it puts into the army, the fewer it will have to produce war materials, and vice versa. A government can make rational decisions about manpower utilization only if it knows the relationship between the size of the army and the maximum amounts of war materials the economy can produce. Similarly, the government of a developing country needs to know the relationship between the quantity of goods it devotes to current consumption and the maximum amount of current investment it can sustain.

Input–output analysis can be used to answer such questions. Let us again talk about our two-good economy, whose input coefficients are given in Table 17.4. Suppose now that the total supply of available labor is fixed at 10 units, and that 15 units of steel are required to meet final demand. What is the maximum amount of coal that can be made available to meet final demand?

Obviously any solution requires that the inputs and outputs of each industry must be such that the production functions of both industries are satisfied, and that the total inputs of labor used in the coal and steel industries must equal the available supply of labor. If this were not the case, coal producers, by utilizing idle labor, could increase coal output without there being a concomitant decrease in steel output. These three conditions are expressed by the following equations, in which q_1^s represents total steel output, q_2^s represents total coal output, and q_2^d represents the amount of coal available for final demand:

$$q_1^s - 0.1q_1^s - 0.3q_2^s = 15,$$
$$q_2^s - 0.2q_1^s - 0.1q_2^s = q_2^d,$$
$$0.4q_1^s + 0.2q_2^s = 10.$$

Solving these three equations for q_2^d, we learn that the maximum amount of coal that can be made available for final consumption is 5 units. Final consumption of 5 units of coal and 15 units of steel implies that, in order for the input requirements of both industries to be met, total coal output must be 10 units, while total steel output must be 20 units.

Constructing a Production Possibility Curve

Given fixed primary inputs and technology, we can construct a *production possibility curve* that tells us the maximum final output combinations that an economy can produce. The problem we have just solved involved locating one point on our economy's production possibility curve between coal and steel; we could locate other points simply by varying the amount of steel to be included in the final bill of fare consumed.

If we were to locate enough points to draw up this curve, we would obtain a straight-line curve like the curve pp in Fig. 17.2. Assuming that 10 units of labor are available to our economy, this curve would intersect the coal axis at the output level 25 and the steel axis at the output level 18.75.

We could set up a second, outer frontier, $p'p'$. Unlike the inner frontier, pp, which describes the maximum combinations of coal and steel that can be made available for *final* consumption, $p'p'$ describes the maximum combinations of both goods that can be made available both for use in production (as inputs) and for final consumption. So long as steel inputs are required in coal production and coal inputs in steel production, it will be impossible to produce some of one good and none of the other; the outer frontier $p'p'$ can therefore never touch either axis. Similarly, so long as society's final consumption includes any amount of either good, something of both goods must be produced. Example: Suppose that society chose to consume as much steel as possible but no coal; in other words, suppose that society chose to consume at the point at which its inner production possibility curve intersected the q_1-axis. Then total coal output would equal, not zero, but an amount sufficient to cover all the coal inputs needed by the steel industry plus any coal inputs required by the coal industry itself in order to produce this output. Total steel output would equal 22.5 units; final consumption of steel would equal 18.75 units; and total coal output would equal 5 units, all of which would be used as inputs in the steel and coal industries.

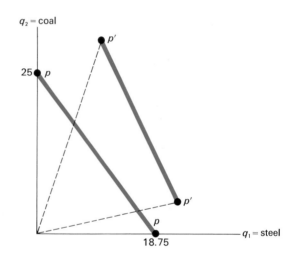

17|2

Production possibility
curve for coal and steel.

As this example indicates, there is a unique relationship between the position assumed by society on its inner and outer production possibility curves; in effect these two curves simply represent two different ways of viewing a single set of maximum output positions.

Other Applications of Input–Output Analysis

Our discussion of the applications of input–output analysis has touched on only a few of the many problems to which this technique of analysis can be applied. Economists have applied input–output analysis extensively not only to problems associated with the functioning of the national economy, but also to regional and interregional problems. Example: Interregional input–output tables have been used to study the effect of changes in demand for the outputs of one region on interregional trade flows. Regional input–output tables have been used to study problems that are regional analogs of the questions discussed above; for example, to study the effect of an expansion in the output of one key industry in a region on the outputs of other industries and on the total demand for labor in that region. If you would like to learn more about these applications, read *Input–Output Economics* (New York: Oxford University Press, 1966), by W. W. Leontief, who originated the idea of input–output analysis.

PROBLEMS

1   a) Use our 1958 input–output table (Table 17.3) to calculate the correct co-efficients in the first two rows of Table 17.4. (In answering this question and the one that follows, let industries 2 and 12 represent coal and steel, respectively.)

   b) If you substitute the real-life coefficients for our hypothetical coefficients in Table 17.4, what can you say about the feasibility of supplying one unit of both coal and steel for final demand?

2   Suppose that there is just enough labor in the economy to produce either $1 billion of coal or $2 billion of steel for final demand. Use the real-life coefficients you calculated in Problem 1 to determine the location and shape of the economy's outer production frontier, $p'p'$ (see Fig. 17.2). Use $L = 1,000,000$.

3   According to the 1958 input–output table, the sum of the direct and indirect demand for *coal* due to one dollar's worth of final demand for coal (steel) is $1.21 ($0.05). Similarly, the sum of the direct and indirect demand for *steel* due to one dollar's worth of final demand for coal (steel) is $0.04 ($1.32). Use this information to compute the true outer production frontier for the case considered in Problem 2.

4   As suggested on page 272, let $a_{11} = 0.6$, $a_{12} = 0.8$, $a_{21} = 0.5$, and $a_{22} = 0.3$, and determine the total outputs of steel and coal that would have to be produced in order to make one unit of steel and one unit of coal.

*5   Show that if the determinant

$$\begin{vmatrix} (1 - a_{11}) & -a_{12} \\ -a_{21} & (1 - a_{22}) \end{vmatrix}$$

is positive and if both a_{11} and a_{22} are less than 1, then any positive combination of q_1^d and q_2^d can be produced, provided there is enough labor available.

---

* Starred problems are problems that are unusually difficult.

*6   Suppose that $a_{11} = a_{22} = 0$ and that $a_{12}a_{21} < 1$. Show that

a) $\dfrac{1}{1 - a_{12}a_{21}} = \displaystyle\sum_{n=0}^{\infty} (a_{12}a_{21})^n$

and

b) $q_1^s = \dfrac{1}{1 - a_{12}a_{21}} \{q_1^d + a_{12}q_2^d\} = \{q_1^d + a_{12}q_2^d\} + a_{12}a_{21}\{q_1^d + a_{12}q_2^d\}$

$$+ \, a_{12}a_{21}\{a_{12}a_{21} \, \{q_1^d + a_{12}q_2^d\}\} + \cdots$$

Finally show that the results obtained under 3(b) illustrate mathematically the content of the last paragraph on page 271.

7   Show that the general equilibrium system developed in this chapter has only 6 independent equations.

8   a) Suppose that $a_{11} = 0 = a_{22}$ and that $a_{12}a_{21} < 1$. Let $w = 1$ and determine the equilibrium level of prices in our input–output economy.

b) Repeat the problem with $w = 4$.

c) Do the equilibrium prices of our input–output economy in any way depend on the availability of labor?

*9   Suppose that $a_{11} = 0 = a_{22}$, that $a_{12} = \frac{1}{2}$ and $a_{21} = \frac{2}{3}$, and that $a_{L1} = \frac{1}{3}$, $a_{L2} = \frac{1}{2}$. Moreover, suppose that $q_1^d = wL/2p_1$, and that $q_2^d = wL/2p_2$, where L denotes the supply of labor. Determine the equilibrium values of q_1^d, q_2^d, q_1^s, q_2^s as functions of L. What role does the equation

$$a_{L1}q_1^s + a_{L2}q_2^s = L$$

play in your calculations? Could you do without it?

*10   Show that the slope of the pp-line in Fig. 17.2 is equal to (-1) times the equilibrium value of (p_1/p_2) in any viable input–output economy.

*11   Write the equations for the two dashed lines in Fig. 17.2.

CHAPTER 18

ECONOMIC EFFICIENCY

In Chapter 1 we distinguished between *positive economics,* the study of what is, and *normative economics,* the study of what ought to be. Normative economists are always trying to think of ways for the economy to achieve an optimal economic state; that is, a state which would enable society to attain the maximum possible social welfare.

The normative economist's first problem is to define an optimal economic state, or to decide how social welfare should be measured. This calls for a value judgment, and the making of such judgments does not fall within the province of the economist. However, almost any definition of an optimal economic state would incorporate two premises:

1) The personal tastes of individual consumers should count (i.e., consumption patterns should not be dictated by a paternalistic autocrat).
2) Any change that increases the welfare of some people, without simultaneously decreasing the welfare of others, increases social welfare.

Whenever the economy allocates resources so that no feasible reallocation either of inputs or outputs would increase the welfare of at least one consumer without simultaneously decreasing the welfare of some other consumer, the economy is said to allocate resources *efficiently.* The concept of efficiency is an important one in economics because (see premises above) an optimal economic state—whatever its other attributes may be—must allocate resources efficiently. A society operating at an *inefficient* point can always reallocate its resources in a fashion that will increase the welfare of some people without simultaneously decreasing the welfare of others. But any such reallocation would, according to premise (2), increase society's welfare. Therefore an inefficient point cannot represent a social optimum.

Since any reasonable definition of optimality implies that an optimal economic state is also an efficient one, what is the likelihood that an economy operating in the real world will attain an efficient point? Well, *theoretically,*

277

if the government of a planned economy had data on the preferences of all consumers, on the production functions for all outputs, and on the initial quantities of all productive resources available, then it would be able to identify the efficient points and organize economic activity so that the economy operated at one of these points.

But what about a market economy that was able to operate free from government restrictions? Could it attain an efficient point? An imperfectly competitive economy will in general allocate resources inefficiently. On the other hand, however, a perfectly competitive economy can attain not only one efficient point, but many, because:

*Every point (and there are usually many of them) at which a perfectly competitive economy might attain general equilibrium corresponds to an efficient point.**

Whenever society moves from one efficient point to another, the welfare of some people will be increased, while that of others will be decreased. Our two premises are not an adequate basis for choosing among efficient points, since they do not tell us how we can compare the gains of the former with the losses of the latter. To choose among efficient points, we need a stronger value judgment than the two premises above.

Since democratic societies operate on the basis of majority rule, one way to select a single point that corresponds to the optimal economic state would be to say that the optimal economic state corresponds to the efficient state that society operating under majority rule would select.

If we adopt this stronger premise, will it suffice to single out one point that is optimal? Let us specify our problem in greater detail: Suppose that society *collectively orders* all the alternative efficient points open to it by the rule that any point A is preferred to some other point B whenever A is preferred to B by a majority of the community; will this collective ordering suffice to identify one point as the best of all points attainable by society? Yes. *But only if the collective ordering of these points is consistent* in the sense that, if society prefers X to Y and Y to Z, then it will also prefer X to Z.

We naturally assume that society's ordering would be consistent, at least if the preferences of all individuals in the society were consistent. However, before we make such an assumption, let's look at an example: Three people, A, B, and C, try to collectively order three possible outcomes, X, Y, and Z. Person A prefers X to Y and Y to Z, person B prefers Y to Z and Z to X, and person C prefers Z to X and X to Y. Then, if their preferences are *consistent*, a majority of these three people will prefer X to Y and Y to Z; therefore X is the collectively most preferred point. Or is it? As you should verify, a

---

* This result is proved in the appendix to this chapter.

majority will also prefer the apparently least preferred point, Z, to the apparently most preferred point, X. Our example thus shows that majority rule does not always identify a unique optimal choice.

Whenever it is inconsistent, perhaps the resulting dilemma should be solved by taking into consideration the *intensities* with which individuals prefer one alternative to another. This approach, however, might lead to a rule that the optimal economic state is one that maximizes the sum of the satisfactions (i.e., welfare) enjoyed by all individuals in a society. This rule has been supported by a number of distinguished economists, but it presents difficulties: *First,* it calls for us to make a new and arbitrary value judgment that, in calculating total social welfare, we should weigh *equally* every person's welfare. *Second,* it cannot provide a basis for practical decision-making, because to put it into operation we would have to make patently impossible comparisons of the welfare enjoyed by different people.

THE CONDITIONS NECESSARY FOR ECONOMIC EFFICIENCY

The fact that an optimal state must be an efficient state poses a problem for normative economists: how to derive the conditions that must hold in individual markets in order for an economy as a whole to allocate resources efficiently.

Think of the economy as composed of three large markets: In Market 1, consumers trade goods among themselves. In Market 2, producers trade inputs among themselves. In Market 3, producers and consumers trade inputs for outputs. Any trade that takes place in the economy must take place in one of these three markets. If we obtain a set of conditions that must hold in each of these markets in order for it to allocate resources efficiently, this will be the set of conditions that must hold if the economy *as a whole* is to do so.

Consider Market 1, in which consumers trade goods among themselves: This market will allocate resources efficiently only if the consumers continue to exchange goods until *they exhaust all feasible trades that would increase one consumer's satisfaction without simultaneously decreasing the satisfaction of some other consumer.*

Similarly, Market 2, in which producers trade inputs among themselves, will allocate resources efficiently only if the producers continue to exchange inputs until *they exhaust all feasible trades that would permit an increase in the output of one good without simultaneously forcing a decrease in the output of some other good.* If it were possible to reallocate a given bundle of inputs between producers of any two goods so as to increase the output of the first good without simultaneously decreasing the output of the second good, then by doing this we could increase the welfare of consumers of the first good without simultaneously decreasing the welfare of other consumers.

To derive conditions for efficiency in Market 3, in which producers and consumers trade inputs for outputs, we recall that the bundle of goods consumed by every individual will contain both primary inputs he retains (e.g., labor in the form of leisure) and final goods he obtains from the productive sector in return for the primary inputs he supplies. Thus Market 3 will allocate resources efficiently only if each consumer continues to adjust his trading pattern with goods producers until he reaches a point at which there *exists no feasible alteration of that pattern (no further trade with the productive sector) that would increase his welfare.* In other words, each consumer must adjust his pattern of trading with the productive sector so that *there exists no feasible change—either in the input mix he supplies, in the output mix he purchases, or in the overall volume of his trading—that would increase his welfare.*

These conditions* imply, among other things, that resource allocation in a market economy will be efficient *only if every final output is sold at a price that equals its marginal cost.* This result is an important one, and we shall use it frequently in Part 4, in which we shall discuss price determination in imperfectly competitive markets.

SOURCES OF INEFFICIENCY IN A MARKET ECONOMY

Although a perfectly competitive economy operating under ideal conditions always allocates resources efficiently, any real-life economy like our own is likely to allocate resources inefficiently. ("Real life" may sound like something out of a soap opera, but it is economists' jargon, meaning actual and practical, as opposed to theoretical.)

First: Some markets in the economy may not be perfectly competitive; and, as we shall see in Part 4, imperfectly competitive markets allocate resources inefficiently because output in such markets is sold at a price that exceeds its marginal cost.

Second: A market economy allocates resources inefficiently if any conditions or constraints (such as taxes) hinder the free operation of the system. Consider the effect on the efficiency of resource allocation in a perfectly competitive economy of a 5% tax imposed on the sale of all final outputs. The tax has no effect on efficiency in consumption or production. However, it violates our third condition for efficiency (i.e., that output must be sold at a price equal to its marginal cost). By reducing the volume of trading between consumers and producers, the tax creates a situation in which there exist feasible trades between these two groups that would increase consumer welfare but which cannot be carried out profitably unless the tax is removed.

---

* For a further discussion, see the appendix to this chapter.

The effect on efficiency of taxing the sale of inputs is similar to that of taxing the sale of outputs. An income tax, which is desirable from the points of view of social justice and ease of collection, nevertheless violates the conditions necessary for economic efficiency. The only way people might be taxed without violating these conditions would be for the government to impose on each income earner a *lump-sum tax,* the amount of which was totally independent of any economic activity in which he engaged.

Third: A perfectly competitive economy allocates resources inefficiently if price controls are imposed. Suppose that a minimum wage is imposed on the labor market, and that this wage is above the equilibrium wage rate. By reducing employment, this price floor creates a situation in which there exist feasible trades between consumers and producers (i.e., between workers and employers) that would increase consumer welfare but which cannot be carried out unless the wage rate is allowed to drop to its equilibrium level. A minimum wage is simply a law that prohibits individual consumers from trading a particular commodity (their labor) for other commodities (real income) at any price below a certain minimum, regardless of their preferences between leisure and the commodities that income buys.

External Economies and Diseconomies

In discussing perfectly competitive markets, we have assumed that a firm's total costs depend solely on the level of output it produces. Sometimes, however, the *position* of the firm's cost curves, and thus the cost it incurs in producing a given level of output, depend on the level of output of other firms.

1) A firm is said to experience *external economies* if increases in the output of other firms lower its cost curves.
2) A firm is said to experience *external diseconomies* if increases in the outputs of other firms raise its cost curves.*

External economies and diseconomies may link firms in the same industry or in different industries. For an example of external diseconomies linking producers in the same industry, consider the fishing industry. The more fishermen there are who fish in a given area, the scarcer fish become there. Thus the more fishermen there are who are active in the industry, the higher the cost curves of individual fishermen.

For an example of external diseconomies linking producers in different industries, consider this: Six factories dump wastes into a certain river that flows into a bay where oysters are grown. If pollution of the bay water be-

---

* Let c_i represent the costs incurred by the ith firm and q_i represent this firm's output. Also let q_j represent the output of some other firm. Then external economies or diseconomies link the ith and jth firms whenever $c_i = f(q_i, q_j)$ instead of $c_i = f(q_i)$.

comes serious, the oysters will cease to reproduce and new baby oysters will have to be brought in periodically. Hence the costs incurred by each oyster-man depend, not only on the level of his own output, but also on the level of output of the six firms who pollute the water he "farms."

For an example of external economies linking producers in different industries, consider a dam that is built primarily to produce water power, but which also prevents seasonal floods. By eliminating flood damage, the dam reduces the costs of downstream farmers. Thus the costs incurred by these farmers depend, not only on their own scale of output, but also on the scale of output and investment of the electric power industry.

Now: Recall that economic efficiency requires that every output be sold at a price equal to its marginal cost. But suppose that whenever one firm expands its output, this inflicts external diseconomies on other firms. Then the true marginal cost of a unit increase in this firm's output will equal the cost of the inputs used in producing this unit plus the costs that its produc-tion inflicts on other firms. Resource allocation will be efficient only if this unit is sold at a price equal to its total marginal cost to the firm that pro-duces it *and* to other firms as well, i.e., at a price equal to its marginal cost to society as a whole. However, a profit-maximizing firm operating in a per-fectly competitive economy will always sell its output at a price equal to its own private marginal cost. Therefore:

A perfectly competitive economy in which producers are linked by external diseconomies will always allocate resources inefficiently.

Using a similar argument, we could show that a perfectly competitive economy in which producers are linked by external *economies* will also allo-cate resources inefficiently.

Thus we see that external economies *or* diseconomies cause a system to deviate from an efficient pattern of resource allocation. Any firm that inflicts external diseconomies on other firms will produce *too much* output for resources to be allocated efficiently, and any firm that "inflicts" external eco-nomies on other firms will produce *too little* output for resources to be allocated efficiently.

Resource Immobility

Consider any real-life market economy. Such an economy is a changing, not a static, system. The conditions under which real-life producers operate are continually changing because unpredictable shifts occur in consumer de-mand (one year miniskirts are in, the next year they are out), because tech-nology changes (nuclear power plants are becoming cheaper to operate than fossil-fuel-powered ones), and because new goods are being born while old ones die out (battery-powered cars may "do in" gasoline-powered cars just as gasoline-powered cars "did in" the horse and buggy).

Therefore the kinds and quantities of inputs real-life producers demand also change constantly. Thus resources (especially workers) will earn the same rates of return in different industries and in different areas only if they are mobile enough to move rapidly out of industries and areas in which demand for them is slacking off into industries and areas in which demand for them is on the rise. But if resources are immobile, wide discrepancies arise between the returns earned by the same input in different industries or in different areas. In extreme cases factor immobility may even lead to factor unemployment. Instances of this in the United States are easy to find. Examples: the coal miners in West Virginia who were displaced by automated equipment and the textile workers in New England who were left behind when the mills moved South. Or consider the marked differential between the average income of laborers on the farm and that of laborers in industry (see Table 15.1).

Whenever differences exist in a competitive economy between the returns earned by the same factor in different areas or in different occupations, one can increase the value of this factor to society, and thus increase society's welfare, by moving this factor from low-wage, low-productivity uses into high-wage, high-productivity uses. Thus an efficient allocation of resources requires that a single input earn the *same* return in all uses. Therefore, in a dynamic real-life economy, resources will be allocated efficiently only if they are mobile enough to keep the wage rate earned by a single input identical in all industries and in all areas.

PROBLEMS

1   The economy of a new country begins from a position of perfectly competitive general equilibrium. Then a left-handed man becomes ruler. In an effort to discourage dextral deviation, he levies an annual lump-sum tax on all right-handed people and divides the proceeds among those who are left-handed. Since this change clearly benefits some people at the expense of others, can you say that the new equilibrium which obtains after the tax is imposed is economically inefficient?

2   Would you expect the principle of majority rule to lead to an efficient point? [*Hint:* Would you expect a bill to pass Congress if that bill benefited only one person and had no effect at all on anyone else?]

3   Consider the example of majority rule discussed in the text, in which it turned out that the majority preferred X to Y, Y to Z, and Z to X. If a person were to have such inconsistent preferences, we would consider him irrational. Does this mean that in this case more than half the people are irrational? Exactly who comprises the majority?

4   a) Smith has two sons, Johnny and Billy, and two lollipops to divide between
       them. The two boys naturally each prefer having two lollipops to having
       one, and prefer having one to having none. Neither is concerned about the
       number of lollipops his brother has. How can Smith dispose of the lollipops
       efficiently (in the sense defined in the text)? [Bear in mind that he is free to
       throw one or both of them away.]

    b) Jones also has two sons, Jimmy and Igor, and two lollipops to distribute.
       However, these boys are very much concerned with each other's welfare, in a
       negative sense. Their preferences may be ordered as follows, where the pairs
       of numbers represent how many lollipops Jimmy has/how many lollipops
       Igor has, and the ordering ranges from most preferred on top to least pre-
       ferred on the bottom:

Jimmy	Igor
(2,0)	(0,2)
(1,0)	(0,1)
(0,0)	(0,0)
(1,1)	(1,1)
(0,1)	(1,0)
(0,2)	(2,0)

    Which of the possible distributions of lollipops are efficient and which are
    not?

5   Explain how external economies which are internal to an industry would inter-
    fere with the efficiency of resource allocation. As an example, consider the coal
    industry. As output of coal increased, the railroads developed special cars for
    carrying coal and thus reduced the transportation costs of the coal producers.

6   Use diagrams to show that external economies cause firms to produce too little
    output for resource allocation to be efficient.

7   In this chapter we have suggested that efficiency of resource allocation is a neces-
    sary requirement for an optimal economic state, and we have pointed out a
    number of factors which cause our economy to be inefficient. However, several
    of these factors, such as external economies, seem to have improved the well-
    being of a large portion of the community. How can you reconcile this appar-
    ent paradox? When we say that external economies are a source of inefficiency,
    does this mean that if they could somehow be abolished, no one would be hurt?

8   Is every efficient point necessarily better than *every* inefficient point?

*Appendix to Chapter 18

A PERFECTLY COMPETITIVE ECONOMY ALLOCATES RESOURCES EFFICIENTLY

In a perfectly competitive economy the pattern of resource allocation is such that it meets every condition that must hold in order for resources to be allocated efficiently. We shall here take a market-by-market approach to prove that in a perfectly competitive economy (1) consumption will be efficient, (2) production will be efficient, and (3) the cross relationships between consumers and producers will be efficient.

Efficiency in Consumption

Point 1: In a perfectly competitive economy, consumption is efficient. To say this is to imply that trading between consumers is carried to the point at which there is no *feasible* trade among any group of people that would increase one person's satisfaction without simultaneously decreasing some other person's satisfaction.

Look at Fig. 18.1. Here we have a rectangle, whose height and width represent, respectively, the total amounts of two goods, q_1 and q_2, available to consumers A and B (Adams and Brown). The quantities of q_1 and q_2 available to Adams are measured along an axis whose origin is at the lower left-hand corner of the commodity box. The quantities of q_1 and q_2 available to Brown are measured along an axis whose origin is at the upper right-hand corner of the commodity box. Thus the curves labeled A represent Adams' preference map, and those labeled B represent Brown's preference map.

---

* The reader may omit this appendix without loss in continuity.

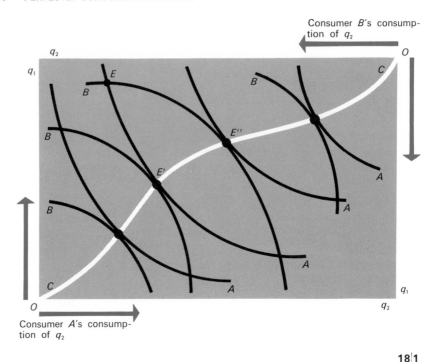

18|1
Derivation of the contract curve, *CC*,
between *A* and *B* (Adams and Brown), who trade and consume two goods, q_1 and q_2.

What conditions must hold in order that there exist no feasible trade between these two people that would increase the satisfaction of one of them without simultaneously decreasing the satisfaction of the other? The initial quantities of q_1 and q_2 available to both are indicated in Fig. 18.1 by point *E*. As indicated by the indifference curves that pass through *E*, consumption at this point would bring a certain satisfaction to both Adams and Brown. A trade between them that moved them from *E* to *E'* would increase Brown's satisfaction without decreasing Adams', while a trade that moved them from *E* to *E"* would increase Adams' satisfaction without decreasing Brown's. On the other hand, a trade that moved Adams and Brown to any point within the area enclosed by the two indifference curves that pass through *E* would increase the satisfaction of both of them. But if, by trading, they should reach any point such as *E'* or *E"* at which their indifference curves are *tangent*, there would exist no feasible trade that would increase the satisfaction of one of them without simultaneously decreasing the satisfaction of the other. (If they got to *E'*, any trade that put Adams on a higher indifference curve would put Brown on a lower one, and vice versa.)

In Fig. 18.1 all points at which Adams' and Brown's indifference curves are tangent are contained in the contract curve, CC.* Thus the allocation of goods between the two will be efficient if and only if Adams and Brown, by trading, reach a point along the contract curve.

The slope of a consumer's indifference curve between two goods is his *rate of commodity substitution.*

Thus in a two-person, two-commodity world, consumption will be efficient if and only if the rates of commodity substitution of both consumers are equal. In a many-person, many-commodity world, consumption will be efficient if and only if the rates of commodity substitution of all consumers between any two goods are equal. Recall that, in a perfectly competitive economy, each person attains equilibrium by consuming at a point on his budget line at which his rate of commodity substitution between any two goods equals the ratio of the prices of these two goods. However, if all consumers' rates of commodity substitution between any two goods are equal to the ratio of the prices of these two goods, then they are equal to each other; and consumption in a perfectly competitive economy must be efficient.

Efficiency in Production

Point 2: In a perfectly competitive economy, production is efficient. To say this is to imply that there exists no feasible reallocation of inputs among producers that would increase the output of one good without simultaneously decreasing the output of some other good.

Construct a diagram identical to Fig. 18.1, except that now two inputs, L and R (labor and raw materials), are measured along the sides of the rectangle and curves A and B represent isoquants in the production functions of two firms, the Able Company and the Baker Company. Label this new diagram. Now show, by reasoning identical to that used in our analysis of efficiency in consumption, that the allocation of the two inputs, L and R, between the Able Company and the Baker Company will be efficient if and only if these two firms, through trading, reach a point in the "input box" at which their isoquants between L and R are tangent†

The slope of a firm's isoquants is its *rate of factor substitution.*

---

* The name "contract" reflects the conviction held by some economists that the final trade or contract made between any two "rational" people would always bring them to some point along this curve.

† Key to the proof: At any point at which the isoquants of Able and Baker are not tangent, there will exist some feasible trade (i.e., reallocation of inputs) between these two firms that would permit one of them to increase output without simultaneously forcing the other to decrease output.

Thus in a two-firm, two-input world, production will be efficient if and only if the rates of factor substitution of both firms are equal. In a many-firm, many-input world, production will be efficient if and only if the rates of factor substitution of all firms between any two inputs are equal. Recall that, in a perfectly competitive economy, each firm will minimize its costs, maximize its profits, and thus attain equilibrium by producing at a point at which its rate of factor substitution between any two inputs equals the ratio of the prices of these two inputs. However, if all firms' rates of factor substitution between any two inputs are equal to the ratio of the prices of these two inputs, then they are equal to each other; and production in a perfectly competitive economy must be efficient.

Efficiency in the Cross Relationships Between Consumers and Producers

Point 3: In a perfectly competitive society, the cross relationships between consumers and producers will be efficient. This efficiency requires in effect that each consumer "spend" his initial endowment of primary inputs (including labor) so as to maximize his satisfaction.

Suppose that a consumer spends his endowment of some primary input, say labor L, to buy some final output, q. How much L should he spend on q in order to maximize his welfare? He should expand his purchases of q until he reaches a point at which his rate of commodity substitution between q and L just equals the rate of substitution between q and L in production (i.e., the *marginal productivity* of L in terms of q).

Here is an illustration: Satisfaction Brown has just built himself a patio where he and his wife can sit on hot summer evenings. Now he wants some deck chairs. A block away from Brown's home there is a small factory that just happens to make deck chairs: The Productive Chair Company. They are perfectly willing to let Brown come to work for them. Since they happen to be perfect competitors, they will pay Brown a wage equal to his marginal product; that is, they'll pay Brown the number of deck chairs that his presence on the production line adds to their total. Should Satisfaction Brown go to work for the Productive Chair Company? The answer depends on what Brown's rate of commodity substitution between labor and deck chairs is. Brown says that it equals 2/1; that is, he'd be indifferent between loafing for a day and working for a day to earn 2 chairs. If Brown's marginal productivity were to equal 3 chairs, then Brown would *add to* his satisfaction by working 1 day for the Productive Chair Company. If his marginal productivity were to equal only 1 chair, he would *decrease* his satisfaction by working for them. And if it were to equal precisely 2 chairs per day, Brown would be just as satisfied whether he went out to work and earned his chairs or stayed home and loafed.

This example suggests the following generalization:

In any economy in which consumers supply primary inputs in exchange for final outputs, efficiency obtains if and only if each consumer equates his rate of substitution between every input and every output with the marginal product of that input in terms of that output.

Recall that, in a perfectly competitive economy, a satisfaction-maximizing consumer will equate his rate of commodity substitution between any two goods to the ratio of the prices of these goods.* Thus the consumer who exchanges a primary input L for a final output q will attain equilibrium by fulfilling the condition

$$\Delta q/\Delta L = w/p,$$

where w is the price of L and p the price of q.

The profit-maximizing firm attains equilibrium by equating the marginal revenue product of any input it uses with the price of that input. For a perfect competitor, however, marginal revenue and average revenue (price) are identical, so the profit-maximizing perfect competitor attains equilibrium by fulfilling the condition $w = p(\Delta q/\Delta L)$. By rearranging terms, we can rewrite this as follows:

$$\Delta q/\Delta L = w/p.$$

We thus conclude that in a perfectly competitive economy both producers and consumers equate their rates of substitution between any output q and any input L with the ratio of the prices of these goods. However, if the rates of substitution between q and L in consumption and production both equal the same price ratio, they are obviously equal to each other. Thus, in a perfectly competitive economy, the pattern of resource allocation established by the trading of inputs and outputs between consumers and producers must be efficient.

We have shown that a perfectly competitive economy in equilibrium fulfills all the conditions that are sufficient for economic efficiency. In other words, that every point of general equilibrium is an efficient point. It can also be shown that, in a perfectly competitive economy, every efficient point corresponds to a point of general equilibrium. Thus, in a market economy,

---

* This condition must hold even if one of the goods is a *retained input*. Consider a consumer who sells an input L to obtain an output q, and think of his approach to equilibrium as follows: He sells his total supply of L to obtain income; then he allocates that income between purchases of q and L. He will carry out this allocation in such a way that he will maximize his satisfaction by consuming at a point at which his rate of commodity substitution between L and q equals the ratio of their prices (recall our analysis of consumer choice in Part 1).

resource allocation will be efficient only if each producer fulfills the condition $w/p = \Delta q/\Delta L$. We can rewrite this in a more useful form if we rearrange terms and substitute MP_L (marginal productivity of labor) for $\Delta q/\Delta L$. Thus we obtain $p = w/MP_L$. But the term w/MP_L equals the marginal cost of an additional unit of q,* and our efficiency condition thus requires that

$$P = MC.$$

In other words:

A market economy allocates resources efficiently only if each producer expands his output to the point at which his marginal cost just equals the price at which he sells his output.

PROBLEMS

1   Using an appropriate diagram, show that in a world in which two firms, A and B, combine two inputs, L and R, to produce a single output q, production will be efficient only if the rates of factor substitution of both firms are equal. Would your answer be different if firm A used L and R to produce an output q_1, while firm B used L and R to produce a different output q_2?

2   Suppose that two commodities, X and Y, are produced in a perfectly competitive economy; that a single primary input, labor, is used in their production; and that the economy is in general equilibrium (i.e., that resources are allocated efficiently). What does our characterization of an efficient allocation of resources tell you about the relationship that must exist between labor's marginal productivity in the production of X and its marginal productivity in the production of Y?

3   Does our condition for an efficient allocation of resources in Market 3 (i.e., in the cross relationships between consumers and producers) imply that producers will earn zero profits in their trading with consumers? Use an appropriate diagram and explain your answer carefully.

4   In the text we explored what the implications for majority rule would be if the preferences of three persons (A, B, and C) for three goods (X, Y, and Z) were as follows: A prefers X to Y and Y to Z; B prefers Y to Z and Z to X; C prefers Z to X and X to Y. We can represent these preferences graphically: To do so we first assign the numbers 1, 2, and 3 (which we measure along the horizontal axis) to X, Y, and Z, respectively. Next we assign the number 3 to the good which each person most prefers, 1 to the good he least prefers, and 2 to the remaining good; this second set of numbers is measured along the vertical axis.

a) Verify that the following pairs of points represent the preferences of persons A, B, and C:

A: (1,3), (2,2), (3,1)
B: (1,1), (2,3), (3,2)
C: (1,2), (2,1), (3,3)

---

* See Chapter 9.

b) Draw straight lines between the three points that represent A's preferences. This gives you a curve with a single peak. Obtain similar curves for B and C. Verify that the curve representing B's preferences has one peak, but the one representing C's preferences has two peaks.

c) The way we arranged X, Y, and Z along the horizontal axis was arbitrary. We could just as well have assigned the numbers 2, 1, and 3 to X, Y, and Z, respectively. Show that regardless of how we arrange X, Y, and Z along the horizontal axis, there will be at least one individual whose "preference curve" is not *single-peaked*.

5   Consider three individuals D, E, and F, whose preferences for X, Y, and Z are as follows: D prefers X to Y and Y to Z; E prefers Y to Z and Z to X; F prefers Z to Y and Y to X.

a) Check whether or not majority rule orders X, Y, and Z consistently.

b) Assign the value 1, 2, and 3 to X, Y, and Z, respectively; and show that D, E, and F all have single-peaked preferences for X, Y, and Z.

c) Assign the numbers 2, 1, and 3 to X, Y, and Z, respectively. Check whether or not the preference curves of D, E, and F are single peaked.

Comment: Consider an economy which contains many persons and which can attain many efficient points. Problems 4 and 5 suggest the following valid generalization:

If all attainable efficient points can be arranged along the horizontal axis in such a way that each and every person's preference curve is single peaked, majority rule will suffice to locate a single point that corresponds to society's optimal allocation of resources.

(For a more detailed discussion of this topic, read: Jerome Rothenberg, *The Measurement of Social Welfare;* Englewood Cliffs, N.J.: Prentice-Hall, 1962, Chapter 11.)

Part 4
IMPERFECTLY COMPETITIVE
MARKETS

CHAPTER 19

INTRODUCTION TO IMPERFECTLY COMPETITIVE MARKETS

In Part 3 we discussed price determination in *perfectly* competitive markets: markets in which both buyers and sellers are numerous and the product sold is homogeneous. Although some markets meet the conditions of perfect competition, many do not. Many are *imperfectly* competitive because they contain few buyers, few sellers, and/or because the product they deal in is nonhomogeneous.

In Part 4 we shall talk about the way price and quantity sold are determined in imperfectly competitive markets. Since a market may fail to meet the conditions of perfect competition in many ways, there exists a whole range of market *structures* that can be described as imperfectly competitive. Therefore we cannot discuss this subject in a general way; we must talk about it in terms of specific types of imperfectly competitive markets.

THE STRUCTURE OF THE AMERICAN ECONOMY

Our purpose in studying price determination in imperfectly competitive markets is to gain insight into how markets function. Therefore we shall now take a brief look at the overall structure of the American economy to get an idea of the relative importance of different types of imperfectly competitive markets on the American scene. Then we shall study those market structures that we have found to exist most often in practice.

Measuring Seller Fewness

We shall here begin to use two words: fewness and manyness. They may sound almost biblical in tone, but they are very useful words in the vocabulary of the economist, for they mean exactly what they imply.

Seller fewness is an important factor in the American economy. It would be useful if we could measure the degree of seller fewness industry by industry in each of the principal sectors of the economy. However, data that

TABLE 19|1

Concentration Ratios for Selected American Industries, 1963

Industry	Number of companies	Percentage of industry shipments accounted for by:		
		The 4 largest companies	The 8 largest companies	The 20 largest companies
Primary aluminum	7	na*	100	—
Motor vehicles and parts	1,655	79	83	90
Electric light bulbs	52	92	96	99
Telephone and telegraph equipment	65	92	96	99
Cereal breakfast foods	35	86	96	99+
Soap and detergents	641	72	80	88
Cigarettes	7	80	100	—
Beet sugar	11	66	97	100
Distilled liquor	70	58	74	92
Photographic equipment	499	63	76	86
Blast furnaces and steel mills	162	50	69	89
Household refrigerators	31	74	91	99+
Cigars	164	59	81	92
Watches and clocks	150	46	65	90
Cement	55	29	49	82
Fluid milk	4,030	23	30	40
Bread and related products	4,339	23	35	45
Fur goods	1,591	5	8	15

*na = not available.
Source: *Concentration Ratios in Manufacturing Industry, 1963.* Report prepared by the Bureau of the Census for the Sub-committee on Antitrust and Monopoly of the Committee on the Judiciary, U.S. Senate, 89th Congress, second session, 1966, Table 2.

are reasonably good are available only for the manufacturing sector, so we shall evaluate seller fewness mainly in the markets in which manufactured goods are sold.

We need some standard by which to measure this fewness. Perhaps, in order to measure seller fewness in any market, we should simply count the number of sellers active there. Unfortunately, this intuitively appealing approach will give a correct idea of seller fewness in only a limited number of situations.

Table 19.1 presents cases in point: Consider the data on the number and relative importance of individual producers in the aluminum and the soap industries. It takes 641 manufacturers to produce 100% of the soap that is made in this country, but only 7 to produce 100% of the aluminum. Anyone would think, then, that the aluminum industry is characterized by fewness of sellers but the soap industry is not. However, look again: 72% of the soap industry is accounted for by only 4 firms! Recall from our discussion of perfect competition that the significance of seller manyness, as opposed to seller fewness, is *the influence that a single seller can exert on market price.* If there are many sellers in a given market, then, presumably, the influence that any one seller can exert on market price will be small. But this holds only if all the firms in the market are roughly equal in size. If a few large sellers (out of many) have the lion's share of the market, then they will definitely be able to influence market price, even though their numerous small competitors cannot. Therefore:

A market is characterized by seller fewness not only when the number of sellers in it is small, but also when a few large sellers (out of many) dominate it.

Since seller fewness has this twofold character, we shall introduce a new term, *seller concentration,* to denote fewness of both sorts. To measure the degree of seller concentration in any market, we naturally would have to know both the number of sellers in that market and the size distribution of these sellers. This means that no single numerical measure can adequately represent the degree of seller concentration in any market. Therefore we must adopt some sort of compromise measure. One reasonably satisfactory one involves the use of *concentration ratios.* A concentration ratio tells us what percentage of total market sales (or of some other measure of total industry output) is controlled by the 4, 8 (or some other number) largest firms in the industry.

Seller Concentration in U. S. Manufacturing

The concentration ratios in Table 19.1 show, for a variety of U.S. manufacturing industries, the percentages of total shipments accounted for by the 4, 8, and 20 largest firms. The industries included in the table were selected, not to spotlight seller concentration in American manufacturing, but to show how widely concentration varies from industry to industry.

Although concentration ratios are a useful index of seller fewness, they can prove misleading unless we supplement them by other data. One reason is that concentration ratios overstate seller fewness in markets in which imports compete with domestic products. Example: Westinghouse and General Electric are the only American manufacturers of large steam-turbine generators, but whenever foreign producers try to sell such generators to U.S. buyers, seller concentration in the American market for such equipment is lessened.

Another problem with concentration ratios concerns the definition of "industry." In previous chapters we have used the word "industry" to mean a group of firms that produce a single well-defined output. Although this definition provides a good basis for theoretical analysis, it is a difficult one for the data collector to apply, for several reasons: First, if we were to consider producers of every different output produced in the economy as a separate industry, we would end up with an unmanageably long list of industries. Second, most firms do not in fact produce just a single output, but groups of related outputs. For example, a steel firm may produce stainless steel, steel plate, steel bars, and many other steel products.

Whenever firms in the same industry produce different outputs, they sell in different markets, and the degree of seller concentration in these various markets may vary significantly from that in the industry as a whole. For example, the cutlery industry as a whole displays only moderate seller concentration; but its single most important product is razor blades and razors, and 97% of these are produced by only 4 firms.

Firms in the same industry may sell in different markets not only because they produce different outputs, but also because they produce an output for which the market is strictly regional or even local. Whenever this occurs, concentration ratios for the national industry understate the actual degree of seller concentration in the regional and local markets in which the industry's output is sold. Take the bread industry, for example. As we pointed out in Chapter 12, bread is usually sold within a 50-mile radius of the bakery in which it is produced. Therefore "the market" for bread is really many local markets, so many that in most of them seller concentration is high, despite the fact that over 4000 different firms (see Table 19.1) produce bread and related products.

TABLE 19|2

Seller Concentration in American Manufacturing Industries

| | Market share of the 4 largest firms, % | | | |
	75–100	50–75	25–50	0–25
Number of industries in each concentration class	40	101	157	136
Percent of total industries in each concentration class	9.2	23.3	36.2	31.3
Percent of total manufacturing shipments made by industries in each concentration class	7.8	16.7	35.3	40.2

Source: *Concentration in American Industry*, Report of the Subcommittee on Antitrust and Monopoly, Committee of the Judiciary, U.S. Senate, 85th Congress, first session, 1957, Table 17.

Table 19.2 divides the 434 manufacturing industries listed in the U.S. census into 4 broad concentration classes. This division, which depends on a single concentration ratio—the market share of the four largest firms—is a very rough one, and probably understates seller concentration. But we have no way to correct this bias, so we must try to interpret the data in the form in which they are available. Inadequate as they are, they permit us to make one observation: In most American manufacturing industries, a large amount of total output is controlled by a limited number of dominant sellers.

Seller Concentration in Other Sectors

So far we have been talking about seller concentration only in manufacturing industries. Data are lacking on seller concentration in other sectors of the economy, so we shall have to limit ourselves to some general observations.

Consider *public utilities,* a sector which is close to manufacturing, and which includes three industries: transportation, communication, and power. Each produces many outputs or services that are sold in many geographically distinct markets. Thus each is a composite of many separate, smaller, industries. For example, the transportation industry contains producers who sell transportation by plane, trolley car, railroad, steamship, barge, truck, bus, or pipeline; all do so within specific geographic regions and between specific geographic points. Producers in the communications industry sell communications via radio, telephone, television, and telegraph; all do so within distinct geographic markets.

Since the transportation, communication, and power industries are each many industries in one, the public utility sector serves many markets, most of which are characterized by high seller concentration. This high degree of concentration is not accidental; it reflects government policies designed to limit entry into these areas of production. As we shall see in Chapter 24, such regulation is justified by the contention that excessive interfirm competition among public utility firms would lead to inefficient production and wasteful duplication of facilities.

The *mining and quarrying* sector is composed of several industries; seller concentration varies from industry to industry. In the mining of metallic ores (such as copper and iron), it is extremely high, since known deposits of these ores are in the hands of relatively few producers. In bituminous coal mining, on the other hand, producers are numerous; since none of them are large, seller concentration is low. In crude-oil extraction, there is an intermediate situation: producers are numerous but not all of them are small.

The *agricultural sector,* like others we have studied, contains many distinct industries. (Examples: wheat, beets, poultry, wool, eggs, potatoes, cotton, milk, citrus fruit.) But, as we've said before, since productive units in agriculture are numerous (over 2 billion) and typically small, most markets for agricultural products meet the many-seller requirement of perfect competition.

The allied industries of *forestry and fishery* are, like agriculture, mostly marked by relatively low seller concentration; although, depending on the product and the area, large sellers can be found even in these sectors.

The number of firms active in the *distributive and service trades* is extremely large. However, each of these sectors is composed of many distinct industries, each of which serves a vast quiltwork of regional and local markets. In order to measure seller concentration in the industries in these sectors, we must weigh the number of sellers against the number of markets. Since the number of markets is frequently large relative to the number of sellers, many sellers find that they have few rather than many direct competitors. Think about gas stations, grocery stores, and dry cleaning establishments. There are always many of these in any national or even regional area, but there may be few in any one of the many local markets in which they compete. In the distributive and service sectors there is also often a moderate concentration of sellers due to the large size of individual companies. Examples: The A and P (in food retailing) and Sears Roebuck and Montgomery Ward (in nonfood retailing).

Product Differentiation

The competitive character of markets is frequently marred, not only by seller concentration, but also by *product differentiation*.

A product is said to be differentiated if buyers can in any way distinguish it from other products designed to serve the same function.

Such distinctions are made on the following bases:

1) The outputs of various manufacturers may differ in physical characteristics (color, quality, design, or size), identifying characteristics (brand names or trademarks), or packaging. Think of the millions spent each year on product differentiation of this sort in the toothpaste, soap, clothing, and automobile industries alone!

2) The outputs of various manufacturers may differ in the conditions under which they are sold. Two steel mills producing the same grade of steel may promise different credit terms; or a person may distinguish among grocery stores that stock the same items on grounds such as the relative convenience of their locations, the hours they are open, the personality of their proprietors, or even their willingness to cash checks.

Because product differentiation has become so important in merchandising, it is present everywhere we turn in the American marketplace. Only graded agricultural commodities and certain industrial raw materials such as steel billets, scrap copper, lead, hides, or flasks of mercury can be classified as homogeneous (nondifferentiated) products. But the outputs of almost all manufacturing industries *are* differentiated, sometimes to an extreme degree. Even in the retailing and service trades, in which competing establishments perform identical services, the consumer distinguishes among establishments in the same business because of such trifling factors as the layout and attractiveness of the service facility, its reputation for efficiency and reliability, and the attitude of the salesclerks.

Summing Up and Looking Ahead

This brief survey of market structures in the American economy has shown that when markets deviate from conditions of perfect competition, it is usually because they contain few sellers or deal in a nonhomogeneous product. Among imperfectly competitive markets, three classifications are particularly important: monopoly, oligopoly, and monopolistic competition.

Monopoly refers to a market in which supply is controlled by a single seller.

Oligopoly refers to a market in which supply is controlled by a few rival sellers.

Monopolistic competition refers to a market in which sellers are numerous but the product sold is differentiated (nonhomogeneous).

In the chapters that follow, we shall analyze the way price is determined in each of these types of imperfectly competitive markets.

BARRIERS TO ENTRY OF NEW FIRMS INTO AN INDUSTRY

Whenever the number of sellers active in a certain market is limited, those who do sell in this market often earn sizable profits. Figure 19.1 shows this positive correlation between the degree of seller concentration in a market and the profit rate of firms operating in it. By all rights, the existence of such profits ought to attract to a market more manufacturers, whose entry would presumably increase the output sold in the market, force prices to fall, and thus diminish the high rate of profit attributable to seller fewness. The entry of new firms into a market often does work to reduce monopoly profits. However, in some industries, because of natural or artificial barriers that make it difficult for new firms to enter, abnormally large profits, attributable at least in part to seller fewness, persist for a long time.

Thus we come to a significant new dimension of market structure: the freedom and ease with which new sellers can enter a market.

The barriers to entry in an industry can be thought of as the advantages established firms have over potential entrants into that industry. One measure of the height of an industry's entry barriers is the percentage by which established firms in this industry could persistently elevate price over cost without inducing the entry of new firms.

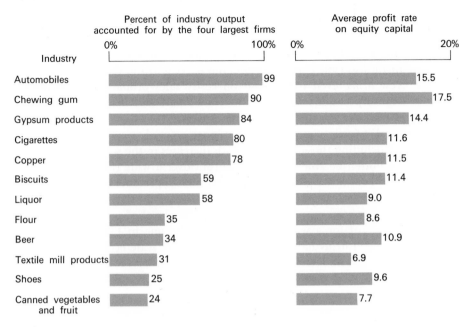

19|1

Concentration ratios and profit rates for selected U.S. industries. (Source: Concentration ratios are from the Census Bureau study cited in Table 19.1. Profit-rate figures are from: H. Michael Mann, "Seller Concentration, Barriers to Entry, and Rates of Return in Thirty Industries, 1950–60," *The Review of Economics and Statistics* **XLVIII**, 3, August 1966, page 299.)

Note the two key words, *could* and *persistently*. We say "could" instead of "do" because established firms may not choose to raise prices as high as entry barriers would permit, and "persistent" as opposed to "temporary," since only a persistent policy of high prices would induce new firms to enter, especially into industries in which a new manufacturer would have to spend a lot of money initially.

Barriers to entry fall into three broad categories:

1) *Economies of scale in production*
2) *Product differentiation*
3) *Absolute cost advantages*

In the rest of this chapter we shall discuss the way these three kinds of entry barriers work.

Economies of Scale in Production

One reason for the high degree of seller concentration in contemporary industry is that, in the production and distribution of many manufactured goods, the output range over which there are economies of scale is so large in relation to demand for these goods that their production can be carried out efficiently (i.e., at minimum average cost) only if the number of producers is limited. In other words, the economies of scale that established firms in an industry have are a formidable barrier to the entry of new producers. New firms, even if they put on costly sales promotion campaigns, have to begin operations with sales that are small and thus costs that are high in relation to those of established producers.

Empirical investigations suggest that, once a firm has exhausted all scale economies (including those associated with increases in the scale of its capital stock), it will often be able to increase output over a wide range at constant average cost. For such a firm, the AC curve that represents the relationship between the firm's level of output and the average cost it incurs when its capital stock has been optimally adjusted to that level of output will, after sloping downward for a way, flatten out like the one in Fig. 19.2. In any industry in which firms have this sort of AC curve, scale economies will set an upper limit, *but no lower limit,* on the number of firms that can efficiently produce the industry's total output.

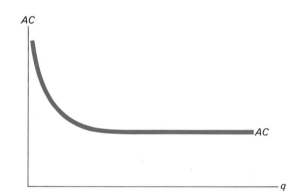

19|2

A firm's AC curve when the adjustment period is long and its capital stock is variable.

The importance of scale economies in discouraging the entry of new firms into an industry depends on (1) the size of these economies, and (2) the relationship between the range of output in which such economies occur and the total quantity of output the market demands. These variables are admittedly hard to measure, but there is one study* which evaluates the importance of scale economies in several American manufacturing industries. The results of this study (see Table 19.3) indicate that, although scale economies attainable in a *single plant* are sometimes significant when measured against total market sales, concentration often greatly exceeds that necessary to permit minimum-cost production.

---

* Joe Bain, *Barriers to New Competition;* Cambridge, Mass.: Harvard University Press, 1956.

TABLE 19|3

Efficient *Plant* Sizes Versus Observed *Firm* Sizes in
Selected American Manufacturing Industries, Early 1950's

Industry	Output of one efficient plant as a percentage of the national market	Average output of the four largest firms as a percentage of the national market
Copper	10.0	23.1
Cigarettes	5.5	22.6
Automobiles	7.5	22.5
Typewriters	20.0	19.9
Soap	5.0	19.8
Tires and tubes	2.1	19.2
Distilled liquor	1.5	18.7
Steel	1.8	11.2
Meatpacking	2.3	10.3
Petroleum refining	1.8	9.3
Cement	1.0	7.4
Flour	0.3	7.3

Source: Joe Bain, *Barriers to New Competition;* Cambridge, Mass.: Harvard University Press, 1956, page 84.

Seller concentration might possibly also be encouraged, and new entry discouraged, by the fact that large corporations have the advantage not only of significant single-plant economies in production, but also of multi-plant economies in purchasing, management, sales promotion, and distribution. Of course the importance of such multi-plant economies is hard to estimate; however, in the industries listed in Table 19.3, whenever producers could discern and were willing to estimate multi-plant economies, such economies were thought to be negligible or small. Given the varied nature of this sample of industries, we are left with the impression that there are probably few industries in which multi-plant economies are strong enough either to significantly encourage seller concentration or to discourage the entry of new firms.

Product Differentiation

Buyers' preferences based on product differentiation may constitute an additional barrier to entry of an industry by new firms. A new entrant into a brand-conscious market can attract consumers only by (1) selling his product at a price below that at which established brands are sold, or by (2) incurring formidable initial expenses for product design, packaging, advertising, sales representation, retail-dealer systems, and other forms of promotion designed to catch the consumer's eye and to establish the new brand as a known one.

The importance of product differentiation as a barrier to entry in an industry is large whenever the product is such that people's allegiances to certain brands can be established by means of variations in product quality or design, advertising, and/or distributor-service organization. Such allegiances are particularly strong in the case of complex, durable products which the person buys infrequently (e.g., home appliances) and in the purchase of which he is influenced by past experience, by the reputation of known brands, and by the availability of local sales and service facilities. A person's allegiances are also usually strong when it comes to products such as liquor and automobiles, in the purchase of which conspicuous consumption plays an important role. (Advertisers capitalize on this snob appeal, as witness such advertisements as: "Isn't it time you graduated to a Cadillac?")

One final and important note: Whenever every company in an industry relies for sales and service on extensive systems of exclusive dealers, the tremendous cost and practical difficulties of duplicating such a system constitute a formidable barrier to the entry of new firms into that industry.

So it isn't surprising that product differentiation is a substantial barrier to entry by new companies in the automobile, liquor, cigarette, and typewriter industries; a moderate barrier to entry in the soap, petroleum refining, and rubber tire industry; but only a negligible barrier to entry in the steel, meatpacking, cement, rayon, and copper industries.*

Absolute Cost Advantages

The other barriers that may impede entry of new firms into an industry all do one thing: they cause the entrant's costs to exceed those of the established producers at every level of output. Thus, whenever such barriers are present, the relationship between the cost curves of the entrant and those of the established producers assumes the form shown in Fig. 19.3. Whenever there are entry barriers which have this effect, the firms that benefit from them are said to have *absolute cost advantages*. Such barriers are usually associated with the control by established firms of raw materials or patents. A list of industries in which strategic patents have impeded the entry of new firms includes light bulbs, drugs, wallboard, and many other industries. Steel and copper are both examples of industries in which the unavailability of strategic materials effectively blocks the entry of new firms. In both these industries, established producers, through ownership or long-term contracts, control almost all known reserves of the basic ore.

Differences between the cost of capital to established firms and to entrant firms may also constitute an absolute cost barrier. In certain industries like steel or automobiles, if you tried to break into the field on a scale large

---

* Joe Bain, *op. cit.*, pages 127–129.

enough to have some hope of success, you'd have to have an enormous amount of capital. However, given the risk of such an investment, obviously debt capital in the required quantities would simply not be available (i.e., its price would be infinite). Raising such large quantities of equity capital might prove equally difficult even for a large, well-known corporation. Therefore entry into such industries is effectively blocked simply because no firm can *afford* such an entry.

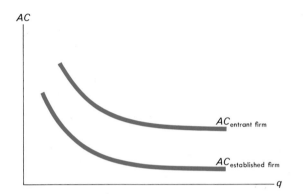

AC

$AC_{\text{entrant firm}}$

$AC_{\text{established firm}}$

q

19|3
Absolute
cost advantages as a barrier to entry.

One final point: entry into some industries may be accomplished rapidly, but entry into others (for example, aged liquors) requires years. Such a long entry period raises both the size and riskiness of the investment the entrant must make; thus it also raises the entry barriers that protect the established producers.

PROBLEMS

1 a) Consider a firm which has a long-run average cost curve such as that shown in Fig. 19.2. What does this firm's long-run marginal cost curve look like? If this firm were perfectly competitive, i.e., if the demand for its output were horizontal, could you determine its equilibrium long-run output?

   b) For an industry in which firms have long-run AC curves such as those in Fig. 19.2, why do economies of scale set an upper limit but not a lower limit on the number of firms that can efficiently produce the industry's output? Show that, in such a situation, a single firm could produce the industry's entire output as efficiently as several firms could.

2 Of the industries listed in Table 19.1, fluid milk is produced by almost the largest number of firms and has almost the lowest concentration ratios. However, in Ithaca, N.Y., for example, nearly all restaurants serve identical milk produced by a single local dairy. Discuss reasons why so many of the restaurants should buy their milk from the same firm when there appear to be 4029 other firms to choose from.

3 Innovations in packaging, storage, and transporation of meat products have caused great changes in the organiztion of the meat industry in the last 50 years. In what ways have these changes caused the meat market to become more nearly perfectly competitive, and in what ways have they had the opposite effect?

4 Firms retailing the same product or performing the same service often tend to locate their outlets in the same places. What reasons can you give for this phenomenon? What effect do you think this tendency to group together has on the degree of perfect competition in such industries?

5 Compare and contrast the following three forms of retailing from the standpoint of the degree of competition in each. Assume for simplicity that the citizens of a town must make all their purchases from retailers in that town.

   a) A town has only a single general store which sells everything available.

   b) A town has numerous small shopkeepers, each selling a different and relatively homogeneous product (one butcher, one baker, one shirt maker, one shoe store, etc.).

   c) A town has several large supermarkets and department stores, all selling a wide variety of products.

6 Is large size of businesses necessarily an indication of market imperfection? Explain.

7 When a firm wishes to diversify by entering a new industry of which it has not previously been a participant, it must choose whether to build an entirely new set of facilities or to buy up an existing firm in that industry. Discuss the manner in which barriers to entry would influence such a firm in its decision.

8 In the early 1960's a 100,000-ton oil tanker* was a "supertanker" and a boat a fraction of that size could profitably be operated in the spot charter market. Today 210,000-DWT tankers are afloat, 310,000-DWT tankers are under construction (one of these could haul away a whole day's crude-oil production from Kuwait), and 500,000-DWT tankers are on the drawing boards. According to *Fortune,* these big ships have alluring economies of scale.

"One of the most expensive parts of a tanker is its instrument-packed deckhouse and superstructure; but their size and cost remain largely unchanged as the size of the ship increases.

". . . Additional cost benefits arise from the fact that big ships are better able to withstand the battering of rough seas. . . . At no sacrifice in safety, therefore, their structure need not be made much stronger than that of smaller ships.

". . . Nowhere is the economics of big tankers more dramatic than in the engine rooms. Such are the principles of hydrodynamics that the longer the vessel, the more easily it moves through the water. Consequently, engine size increases only slightly with the size of the tanker. A 25,000-horsepower engine powers a 100,000-ton tanker at about 17 knots; the same engine can propel a ship double that size with a loss of speed of only 3 or 4 knots. With the addition of only a few hundred horsepower, the larger tanker can move along at 17 knots.

---

* Recall that we discussed the tankship market in Chapter 13.

"The shipyards also contribute to the economies of large tankers. . . . The Japanese have poured large sums into automated equipment that reduces labor costs and cuts construction time. All these savings bring down the cost of a tanker built in Japan from $200 per deadweight ton for a 25,000-ton vessel to $104 for a 50,000-tonner and $75 for tankers of 150,000 tons and up.

"Furthermore big ships are much more economical to operate. The thirty-man crew on a modern, automated 150,000-tonner is the same size as the crew required to man an older 25,000-tonner. And the big ships burn proportionately less fuel."*

How do you think these startling economies of scale will affect entry barriers into the tankship market? Traditionally these have been extremely low. In what way do you predict that these economies of scale will affect the competitive structure of the market for tankship services over time?

---

* Source: Gregory H. Wierzynski, "Tankers Move the Oil that Moves the World," *Fortune*, Sept. 1, 1967, pages 85 and 151.

CHAPTER 20

MONOPOLY

THE MEANING AND INCIDENCE OF MONOPOLY

Traditionally monopoly is defined as follows:

A monopoly is one-man or one-firm control over the supply of a commodity for which no close substitutes exist.

This definition seems straightforward enough, but when we try to use it to draw a line between monopoly and other market structures, we find that, since every good has at least some substitutes, the position of our line will hinge on how we interpret the word "close." Consider for example the deBeers diamond syndicate and the Ford Motor Company. In the non-communist world at least, deBeers controls the supply of newly mined diamonds, and although sapphires, rubies, and other precious stones may be used in place of diamonds, most women view such substitutes as inferior (recall Lorelei Lee's song in *Gentlemen Prefer Blondes:* "Diamonds Are A Girl's Best Friend"). Thus there is a gap in the chain of substitutes between diamonds and other goods. The control exercised by deBeers over the supply of newly mined diamonds therefore constitutes a true monopoly. On the other hand, Ford's control over the supply of Ford cars is not a monopoly in the same sense, because cars produced by General Motors, American Motors, and foreign firms are to most consumers satisfactory (if not perfect) substitutes for Fords.

If we wish to determine how prevalent monopoly is on the American scene, we must keep in mind our strict definition of monopoly, which emphasizes both (a) the seller's uniqueness and (b) the commodity's lack of close substitutes. Then even a cursory survey of markets will show that relatively few industrial products that are nationally marketed are controlled by a monopolist. On the other hand, many goods and services which have a market that is essentially local or regional in scope *are* under monopoly control. Thus the student who attends a small-town college may find that the local movie house and the college bookstore are both monopolies. Also, as we pointed out in Chapter 19, many firms in the public utility sector (which provides a range of services from cooking gas to TV cable hookups) are monopolists.

The fact that most monopolies are local or regional in scope and that so few basic industrial commodities are under monopoly control should not be taken to imply that monopoly is not an important subject. The absence of monopoly in the markets for major products such as aluminum, steel, and petroleum is due in large part to the efforts by the Justice Department to enforce the federal antitrust statutes. These statutes outlaw, among other things, the "monopolizing" of trade in any market. They were enacted because the concentration movement that began to sweep American industry toward the end of the nineteenth century led many people to fear that the emergence of widespread monopoly constituted a threat to free competition. Thus, when we examine the theory of monopoly, we find out about not only the way a few markets *do* function, but also the way many other markets *would* function if the government were to observe a laissez-faire policy toward business concentration. The theory of monopoly is also important because when there is any group of oligopolists who are few enough in number and one enough of mind to successfully (and collusively) maximize their joint profits, their behavior is like that of a monopolist.

ENTRY BARRIERS: A SOURCE OF MONOPOLY

In order for a profitable monopoly to continue to exist, it must be protected by some sort of entry barrier which deters other producers, to whom the monopolist's profits appear enticing, from entering his market. Thus one way to classify monopolies is according to the entry barriers that protect them.

1) *Patents and copyrights,* since they grant their holders the sole right to produce and sell a given commodity during a specified time span, constitute an entry barrier that is often a basis for monopoly. However, if we make a list of monopolies based on patents, we find that many patented goods, such as patented-formula toothpastes or soaps, have numerous close substitutes. Thus, although any patent may be a basis for a monopoly, most patents in fact are not. A patent that does provide the foundation for a significant monopoly* is one that confers on its holder the sole right to produce a commodity for which no close substitutes exist. The basic light-bulb patent, obtained by Edison in 1880 and later controlled by General Electric, fits this

---

* We use the adjective "significant" here to designate a monopoly for whose product there is a great demand and which makes a considerable profit, as opposed to one which is insignificant, i.e., one for whose product the demand is small, and which makes little profit.

definition; so too do the succeeding improvement patents which General Electric used to extend its control over light-bulb production. Du Pont's basic nylon patent can also be said to be the basis for a significant monopoly, since nylon has desirable characteristics that were possessed by no other fiber available at the time nylon was introduced. Du Pont's cellophane patent, however, poses a more difficult case. Cellophane, throughout the period during which du Pont controlled it, had close substitutes in some uses such as vegetable wrapping, but no substitutes in other uses such as wrappings for packs of cigarettes. The patent on the Xerox copying machine is another interesting (though perhaps borderline) case, since it provides its holder with the sole (and extremely profitable) right to produce a machine that does have substitutes, but none that are technologically equal to it.

2) *Control over a strategic raw material* is also the basis for certain monopolies. Thus deBeers' monopoly is based on its control of existing diamond fields. Similarly, Alcoa's pre-World War II monopoly of aluminum production in the United States was partly due to the control it obtained, first of domestic bauxite deposits, and later of high-grade foreign deposits.

3) *Extensive economies of scale in production* also form the bases of many monopolies. Most monopolies in this category are found in the public utility sector; that is, in the power, communication, and transportation industries. Many of these so-called "natural monopolies" reflect, not only the existence of substantial scale economies in production, but also the local or regional character of the markets in which the outputs of these industries are sold and the fact that interfirm competition in these industries would in many instances (e.g., the telephone, telegraph, and power industries) require an expensive and purposeless duplication of productive and distributive facilities.

Although the public utility sector does contain many examples of monopolies (albeit regulated ones), there are also many firms active in this sector that are not monopolists in the strict sense of the term. In some public utility markets (e.g., air transportation), firms selling products that are essentially identical compete with each other. In other public utility markets, interfirm competition may exist in a subtler form. A local power company usually has a true monopoly when it sells power for lighting purposes, but when it sells power for heating, its product runs into competition from other heat sources such as oil, gas, and even coal. Similarly a railroad that appears to hold a monopoly because it is the sole supplier of rail freight between two points may face competition from truckers, airlines, and other carriers. Thus in the public utility sector, as in other sectors, before we label any market as a monopoly, we should investigate the kind and closeness of all substitutes for the product that are sold in this market.

THE MONOPOLIST'S PRICE–OUTPUT POLICY

Our strict definition of monopoly (see page 308) enables us to determine what price the monopolist will charge in order to maximize his profits and what quantity of output he will produce. Since the monopolist controls the supply of a commodity for which there is no close substitute, demand for the monopolist's output is of course identical with market demand for this commodity. The downward-sloping market demand curve for the monopolist's output is in effect his AR curve, and from it we can construct his MR curve. Then we can determine what price–output policy he will adopt, since we know (from our analysis of profit maximization in Chapter 9) that the monopolist will maximize his profits by producing the output that equates his marginal revenue with his marginal cost. Thus the monopolist whose cost and revenue curves are shown in Fig. 20.1 will maximize his profits by selling the output q^0 at the price p^0.

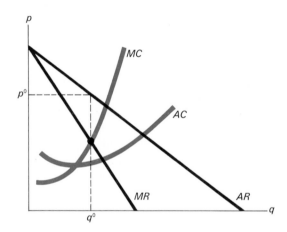

20|1

The equilibrium of a profit-maximizing monopolist who sells in a single market.

PRICE DISCRIMINATION

Price discrimination means charging different prices to different buyers.

Many monopolists operate in markets in which price discrimination is impracticable.* Sometimes, however, a monopolist may find that the market

---

* The assumption that price discrimination is impracticable holds widely. The taxi driver charges the same per-mile rate when he is driving the mink-coated woman to a bridge party as he does when he drives the handicapped child to school. The electric company charges the same rate for electricity whether it goes to the house of the millionaire industrialist or the apartment of the impoverished graduate student. Thus our original discussion of profit maximization in Chapter 9 was based on the assumption that the firm would charge the same price to all buyers, even though some buyers would, of course, be willing to pay higher prices than others.

for his product is composed of two or more markets which are *separate* or *separable,* because either due to (a) the nature of the good or service he sells or due to (b) trade barriers (that exist or that he can erect), no individual can purchase his output in one market and resell it in another. In such a situation price discrimination may prove both practicable and profitable. Examples: Many airlines, when they have planes that are about to take off with empty seats, offer to fly college students (if they are on hand at the airport) at lower rates than they do the general public. Many manufacturers sell their products in foreign countries more cheaply than they sell them on the home market.

The maximum-profit position of a monopolist who practices price discrimination has two aspects that we should consider: (1) If, in any market, his marginal revenue is more than his marginal cost, he can raise his total profits by increasing his sales in this market. (2) If, in any market, his marginal revenue is less than his marginal cost, he can raise his total profits by decreasing his sales in this market. Therefore:

To maximize profits, the price-discriminating monopolist who sells in several markets must adjust (a) the level of his output and (b) the allocation of his output between markets, so that his marginal revenue in each market just equals his marginal cost.

Let's use this result to locate the maximum-profit position of the monopolist whose MC curve is shown in part (c) of Fig. 20.2, and who faces the demand curves shown in parts (a) and (b). To locate his equilibrium position, we first add his MR_I and MR_{II} curves to obtain a *joint MR* curve. This curve summarizes the relationship between his output and his marginal revenue when he allocates output so that marginal revenue is equal in both markets. Next we observe that he will maximize his total profits by producing the output that equates his marginal cost with his joint marginal revenue* (i.e., the output indicated by the intersection of his MC curve with his joint MR curve). From part (c) of Fig. 20.2, we see that this output equals 15 units. Parts (a) and (b) show that the optimal allocation of this output will be 6 units to Market I and 9 units to Market II. Therefore this price-discriminating monopolist will maximize his profits by selling 6 units of output in Market I at $11 per unit and 9 units in Market II at $7 per unit.

To test your understanding of this result, prove that this monopolist cannot raise his total profits by shifting one unit of output from Market II to Market I. [*Hint:* Remember that the marginal revenue the producer derives from the last unit of output sold in any market equals the average

---

* This follows from our discussion of profit maximization in Chapter 9.

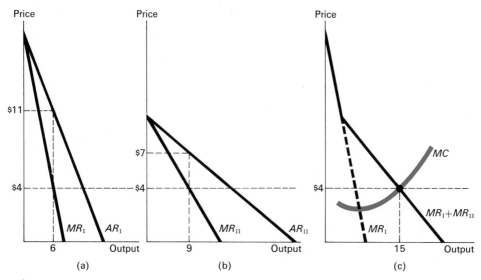

20|2

Locating the maximum-profit position of a price-discriminating monopolist who sells output in two markets at two different prices. (a) In Market I he sells 6 units at $11 per unit.
(b) In Market II he sells 9 units at $7 per unit. (c) To maximize his profits, he equates marginal cost with marginal revenue in *both* markets.

revenue or price he obtains for that unit *minus* the loss in total revenue he incurs due to the decrease in the price at which he sells all other units of output in this market.]

The above example of how price discrimination works brings us to realize two economic facts of life:

1) A monopolist who sells in two or more markets in which demand is not identical cannot maximize his profits *unless* he practices price discrimination.

Suppose that this monopolist started out by charging the same price in both markets. If demand in one market differed from that in the other, his marginal revenue would be higher in one market than in the other, and he would be able to increase profits by shifting sales from the low-marginal-revenue market to the high-marginal-revenue one. To do this, however, he would have to lower price in one market while raising it in the other, i.e., he would have to charge different prices in the two markets.

2) The price charged by a price-discriminating monopolist will be highest in the market in which demand is least elastic and lowest in the market in which demand is most elastic.

This result is a useful one to keep in mind when we are interpreting the examples of price discrimination discussed below. To prove it, look up the hint in Problem 4.

Price Discrimination in Practice

Opportunities for price discrimination often arise when a monopolist produces an output that is used as an input in several other industries. The reason is that firms in different industries have demands for the monopolist's output that differ in elasticity; and price discrimination, if practicable, will therefore seem enticing to the monopolist. Undertaking price discrimination for this reason usually proves difficult, however, because there are seldom any *natural* barriers that separate classes of buyers according to the use to which they intend to put the product. Suppose that a company that made chemicals tried to sell formaldehyde at a high price to undertakers (whose demand for it is inelastic) and at a low price to plastics firms (whose demand for it is more elastic). The chemicals company would soon find that undertakers were buying their formaldehyde from plastics manufacturers, or buying it indirectly through middlemen.

When natural barriers between different classes of buyers are lacking, the monopolist can of course always attempt to set up artificial barriers to wall off one class of buyers from another. One classic proposal for such a barrier involved the market for methyl methacrylate. In the late 1930's du Pont and Rohm & Haas, who were the only American manufacturers of methyl methacrylate, sold one form of this compound at 85¢ per pound to commercial plastics producers, a low-price, high-volume market, and another form of it at $22 per pound to denture manufacturers, a high-price, low-volume market. To separate the denture market from the plastics market, du Pont and Rohm & Haas required all plastics manufacturers who bought methyl methacrylate to agree not to resell it; at the same time, du Pont and Rohm & Haas refused to sell methyl methacrylate in any form to any other buyers. Nevertheless, because of the striking difference in prices between the two markets, bootleggers continuously tried, with some success, to obtain methyl methacrylate in the low-price market and to resell it in the high-price market. To stop such bootlegging, one licensee of Rohm & Haas suggested that methyl methacrylate destined for the low-price market be adulterated with a trace of arsenic or something else that would "make them rear up"!*

Another example along the same lines: du Pont and General Aniline, makers of a certain kind of coloring material trademarked Monastral, in-

---

* George Stocking and Myron Watkins, *Cartels in Action;* New York: The Twentieth Century Fund, 1946, pages 402–403.

vestigated the feasibility of separating the low-price paint and the high-price textile-dyeing markets for Monastral colors by contaminating Monastral colors destined for the paint market with some substance that would scratch textile printing rolls, deteriorate cotton, or irritate the skin and cause dermatitis.*

Although the above examples each involve more than one manufacturer, to the extent that these firms did not compete but instead pursued collusively established price, output, and contamination policies, these products were in effect under monopoly control.

The examples we have presented so far all involve price discrimination between different industrial buyers. Price discrimination, however, also touches the everyday life of the consumer. The price we pay to see a movie extravaganza depends on whether we see it in a Broadway reserved-seat theater just after it is released or in our home-town drive-in months later. The price we pay for electricity depends on whether we use it for general purposes or for heating hot water during the middle of the night. When we fly to Europe, the cartel-set price we pay for a ticket will depend on whether we are going for a three-week vacation, a summer, or a six-month sabbatical. Finally let us note that most ubiquitous form of price discrimination, the "student rate," which has encompassed everything from *Time* magazine to nights out on the town.

ENTRY BARRIERS AND ENTRY-FORESTALLING PRICES

In discussing monopoly pricing, we have implicitly assumed that the monopolist, when he maximizes his profits in the short run, does so without fear of attracting new competitors into the market in the long run, i.e., we have assumed that he thinks that entry into his market is effectively "blockaded." Although a few monopolists may feel this way, the typical monopolist probably views the barriers that protect his favored position as something less than impregnable. This position of his may be threatened over time not only by direct competition (new competitors may enter his market) but also by indirect competition (new substitute products may be developed or new possibilities may be discovered by which available products may be substituted for his output).

The threat posed by indirect competition is a very real one, as witness the experience of the American steel industry. During the first ten years after World War II, the steel companies in the United States raised both their wages and their prices. Then, during the late 1950's, they found that not only were they no longer able to compete actively in foreign markets, but they even faced direct competition from foreign producers in the home

---

* *Ibid.*, pages 403–404.

market. In addition, some of their apparently safe markets were being lost because of innovations: concrete, aluminum, plastics, and even glass were being substituted for steel.

The first reaction of the monopolist who considers the entry barriers that protect his position as tenuous is to try to shore up these barriers. He can do this in a number of ways:

1) He can manipulate patents.

For example, a monopolist whose top-dog position depended on control of a patented production process might try to defend his position by exploring and patenting as many feasible alternative production processes as possible. A case in point is du Pont, which defended its cellophane monopoly by developing and patenting a number of alternative production processes, not because it wanted to use them, but because it did not want any competitors to use them!

2) He can patent strategic improvements in his product or production process. (Xerox in recent years has used this ploy very effectively.)

3) He can avoid legal challenges to his patents and discourage the development of competitive products by licensing other producers to use his patents on a royalty basis.

One interesting point about licensing is that, if the monopolist's patent rights are interpreted as allowing him to fix, not only royalties, but also the prices and outputs of his licensees, then licensing may involve a much smaller surrender of monopoly power and profits than one might initially suppose.

If the threatened monopolist is successful in shoring up the entry barriers that protect his position, he can continue to maximize his profits without fear of potential competitors. But if his market cannot be fully protected, it may be impossible for him to maximize his profits without attracting competitors whose arrival would sharply diminish his profits. Faced with such a situation, the monopolist has two alternatives: (a) He can maximize his profits and run the risk that competitors will enter his market. (b) He can charge, not a profit-maximizing price, but a lower, *entry-forestalling* price. An entry-forestalling price is a price that is low enough to keep his profits from being alluring and to keep potential competitors out of his market.

The relationship between the monopolist's profit-maximizing price and his entry-forestalling price can be described as follows: The weaker the entry barriers that protect the monopolist's market, the farther apart these two prices will be.

TAXES AND PRICE CONTROLS

Taxing a Monopolist's Output

The imposition of a specific tax on the output of a monopolist affects his equilibrium output, his price, and his profits. Consider the monopolist whose cost and revenue curves are shown in Fig. 20.3. Initially he attains equilibrium by producing the output q^0, which he sells at the price p^0. Suppose now that a specific tax T is imposed on his output. Recalling our discussion of taxes in Chapter 14, we can represent this tax by a downward shift in the monopolist's average and marginal revenue curves from AR to AR' and from MR to MR'. Note that the revenue curves, AR' and MR', represent the relationship between the quantity of output the monopolist sells and the *net* (i.e., after-tax) revenue he receives.

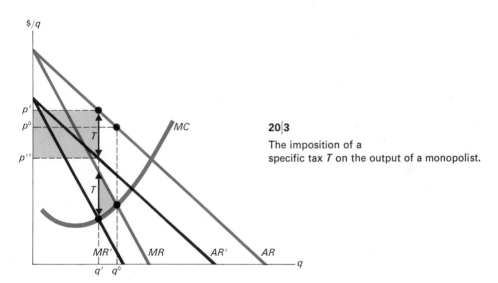

20|3

The imposition of a specific tax T on the output of a monopolist.

Once a specific tax T has been imposed on his output and sales, then the monopolist, to maximize his profits, must produce the output that equates his marginal revenue *net of the tax* with his marginal cost. In other words, he must produce the output indicated by the intersection of his MR' and MC curves. From Fig. 20.3 we see that after the tax has been imposed, the monopolist attains equilibrium by producing the output q' and selling it at the price p'. We also see that imposition of the tax causes him to reduce his output from q^0 to q'. This reduction constitutes a loss to both producer and consumer, but contributes nothing to the total tax collected. Imposition of the tax also raises the *gross price* paid by the consumer from p^0 to p', while reducing the *net price* received by the producer from p^0 to p''.

The total tax the government collects equals the unit tax T times the quantity sold q'. This amount is represented in Fig. 20.3 by the shaded rectangle $q'T$.

By how much does imposition of the tax reduce the monopolist's profit? At first glance, we might say his profit is reduced by $q'T$, the total amount of tax collected. But this represents only the profit he loses on the output q'. In addition he loses profit as a result of the reduction in his output from q^0 to q'. This loss in profit (check this yourself*) can be represented graphically by the triangular shaded area in Fig. 20.3 lying between his MR and MC curves, and over the output range q' to q^0.

This example shows that, unless demand for the monopolist's output is totally inelastic, a specific tax on his output always raises the price the consumer pays, lowers both the price received and the profits earned by the monopolist, and reduces the total output he produces.

Taxing a Monopolist's Profits

We have been talking about taxes on output, but a government has other taxes up its sleeve.

1) The government may require the monopolist to pay a fixed tax, the amount of which is independent of his equilibrium price and output.

Such a *lump-sum tax,* so long as it does not exceed his total profits, has no effect on his equilibrium price and output. (Figure that one out for yourself.) However, if the tax exceeded his equilibrium profits, his after-tax profits would become negative, and he would be forced to shut down.

2) The government may require the monopolist to pay a fixed percentage of his profits in taxes.

If the average and marginal rates of such a tax are set below 100%, the monopolist will maximize his after-tax profits by maximizing his before-tax profits! Thus a profits tax, like a lump-sum tax, has no effect on the monopolist's equilibrium price and output. However, taxes of both sorts can be used to limit the size of monopoly profits and thus to counter any inordinate inequalities in income distribution attributable to monopoly.

Imposing a Ceiling on the Monopolist's Price

The imposition of a ceiling on the monopolist's price affects both his equilibrium output and profits. Suppose that the government imposes a ceiling

---

* Recall the argument in Chapter 9 showing that a profit-maximizing firm should continue to expand output so long as marginal revenue exceeds marginal cost.

on the price which the monopolist whose cost and revenue curves are shown in Fig. 20.4 can charge. Since he initially attains equilibrium by selling the output q^0 at the price p^0, a price ceiling above p^0 would not affect either his price or his output. However, if a price ceiling were set between p^0 and p' (the price at which his MC curve crosses his AR curve), this would induce him not only to decrease his price, but also to *expand* his output! This result may surprise you, but check this out yourself: If the monopolist is forced to charge any price between p^0 and p', he would maximize his profits by fully satisfying market demand at that price;* and if the price ceiling were set at p', he would maximize his profits by producing the output q'.

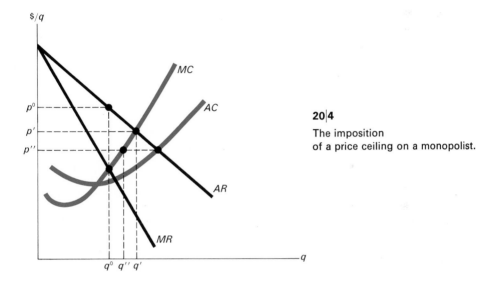

20|4

The imposition
of a price ceiling on a monopolist.

If the price ceiling were set below p', the profit-maximizing monopolist would respond to such a low price ceiling not only by decreasing his price but also by decreasing his output. Thus if the price ceiling were set at p'', the monopolist would choose to produce the output q''. Of course he could be *required* to satisfy total market demand at the price p'', but if he had to do this, his profit would be reduced to zero. This leads us to an important point: If the price ceiling were set below p'', the monopolist could be required to satisfy total market demand only if the government gave him a subsidy big enough to cover his inevitable losses.

---

* Think first about how the imposition of any price ceiling, high or low, would alter a monopolist's marginal and average revenue curves. [*Hint:* The new AR curve you get is going to have a kink at one point, and the new MR curve is going to be discontinuous at that point.]

PROBLEMS

1   Discuss instances of monopoly which you have yourself encountered. Remember that many products have a variety of uses (sources of demand). Thus a local newspaper may have many substitutes as a source of national news but may have a monopoly on such items as wedding announcements and want ads. To what extent are the following businesses likely to have monopoly positions?
a) A college bookstore
b) A small-town bowling alley
c) The rapid-transit system of a large city
d) A garbage disposal company

2   According to the *Wall Street Journal,* the trend toward long hair among college boys has led to a sharp decline in the demand for haircuts and to empty barber chairs, especially in college towns. The barbering trade has responded to this decrease in demand, according to the *Wall Street Journal,* by "raising prices in order to cover costs." What does this suggest to you about the competitive structure of this industry? Does your conclusion apply to barbers in your college town? [*Hint:* What would happen to price in a perfectly competitive market if demand shifted downward?]

3   In the example illustrated in Fig. 20.2, show that the monopolist could not increase his profits by shifting one unit of output from the low-price market to the high-price market.

4   Prove that a price-discriminating monopolist will charge a higher price in a market in which demand is inelastic than in a market in which demand is elastic. [*Hint:* Start by assuming the opposite and show the effect on profits of shifting output toward the elastic market.]

5   Relate the common practice of giving discounts to buyers of large quantities to the analysis of price discrimination given in the text. What other factors might account for quantity discounts?

6   Scandinavian Airlines System charges 25¢ for a beer served on trans-Atlantic flights, but only 15¢ for a beer served on intra-European flights. What reasons can you suggest for this price discrimination? What does it indicate about the elasticity of demand for beer on the two different flights?

7   Consider the (we hope hypothetical) case of a college which is run as a profit-maximizing firm selling education. Such a college could, if it wished, use price discrimination by charging different tuitions for freshmen, sophomores, juniors, and seniors. What pattern of prices would you expect the college to charge if it were interested only in maximizing its profits for the coming year? Would discrimination of this sort be practical as a long-run policy?

8   How would the output produced and the price charged by a price-discriminating monopolist be affected if you forced him to charge the same price to all buyers?

9   Why is it impossible to use a supply and demand analysis of the sort given in Chapter 12 for analyzing markets which have only a single seller?

10 Is it possible, by using a price ceiling alone, to ensure that a monopoly with an increasing AC curve will make zero profits?

11 Suppose that the government imposes a price ceiling on a commodity produced by a monopolist and that it sets the price ceiling at a level such that the public demands more of the commodity than the monopolist is willing to supply. Show that a subsidy equal to a set amount per unit of output could be used to induce the monopolist to increase his output. Determine, by means of graphs, the amount of subsidy that would be needed.

12 Show the manner in which a price ceiling changes the MR and AR curves of a firm. To what extent does a price ceiling transform a monopolist into a price taker?

13 A certain monopolist is forced to license its patents to other firms, but is also allowed to fix the outputs and prices of these other firms and the royalties they must pay. Show that this monopolist need not surrender very much of its monopoly profits.

14 In the text we analyzed the way that a specific tax affects a monopolist by shifting the firm's revenue curves. Show that the same results can be obtained by shifting the firm's cost curves.

15 a) What other factors, besides the height of entry barriers, would you expect to influence a monopolist in determining an entry-forestalling price? For example, would a firm ever charge a price that is so low that its profits as a monopolist are less than its profits would be if it allowed other firms to enter?

b) In the text we discussed the effect of a specific tax on a profit-maximizing monopolist. How would you expect the analysis to change if the monopolist were instead charging an entry-forestalling price?

CHAPTER 21

UNIONS, BILATERAL MONOPOLY, AND MONOPSONY

In Chapter 20 we analyzed the way price is determined in a market characterized by monopoly; that is, in a market which has a single seller and many buyers. In addition to monopoly, two other market structures depart radically from the many-buyer, many-seller structure of perfect competition. The first of these, *monopsony,* is a market in which there are many sellers but only one buyer. The second, *bilateral monopoly,* is a market in which there is only one seller and only one buyer.

MONOPSONY

Markets are more often characterized by fewness of sellers than by fewness of buyers. Occasionally, however, we encounter examples of *monopsony* (one buyer, many sellers). A buyer tends to become a monopsonist under the following circumstances:

1) Any monopolist who uses an input not used in the production of some other commodity will be a monopsonist (i.e., sole active buyer) in the market in which this input is sold.
2) Any large producer may find that, because of resource immobility, he is a monopsonist in certain local or regional input markets.

Monopsony power, like monopoly power, can be a source of considerable profit to the firm that exercises it. A fascinating example of monopsony power is the case of Standard Oil at the turn of the century. Standard Oil then held a near monopoly over the pipelines through which crude oil was gathered and shipped out of the Appalachian oil field. The company was willing to ship crude oil from independent sellers to independent seaboard refiners, but it charged a prohibitively high price for doing so. Consequently the oil that flowed through Standard's pipelines was oil purchased by Standard for use in Standard's seaboard refineries. What this meant was that

Standard, through its pipeline monopoly, was able to establish and maintain a near monopsony over purchases of crude oil in the Appalachian field, and a near monopoly over the refining of crude oil along the Atlantic seaboard. It would be difficult to estimate the profits yielded by these operations alone, but they certainly contributed substantially to Standard's total profits, which in this period averaged around $80,000,000 a year!

Price Determination Under Monopsony

To show how price is determined in a monopsonistic market, let's consider a concrete example: Ravel & Selvage is a textile mill that employs practically every able-bodied person willing to work in the little town of Loose Ends, Arkansas. In other words, Ravel & Selvage looms so large in the local labor market that it is for all intents and purposes a monopsonist. How much labor will it hire and what wage will it pay this labor?

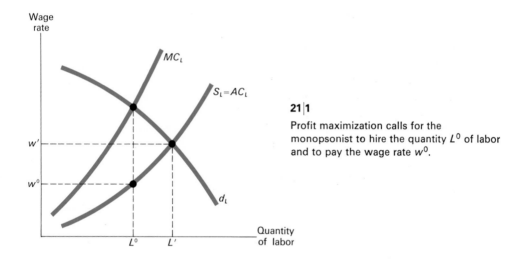

21|1

Profit maximization calls for the monopsonist to hire the quantity L^0 of labor and to pay the wage rate w^0.

In Chapter 9 we saw that the behavior of a profit-maximizing firm in an input market can be represented by a downward-sloping demand curve. Therefore we can represent Ravel & Selvage's behavior in the labor market by a downward-sloping demand schedule like the curve labeled d_L in Fig. 21.1. Now let's think about the opposite side of the market: labor. Would-be workers in Loose Ends are numerous, and so we can represent their market behavior by a positively sloped supply curve like the one labeled S_L in Fig. 21.1.

In a perfectly competitive market, the equilibrium price of a commodity is always indicated by the intersection of the market supply curve and the market demand curve. Therefore you might think that in the present situation the equilibrium wage rate would be the wage rate that corresponds to the intersection of the firm's demand curve for labor, d_L, and the market supply curve of labor, S_L. Actually, though, this is not the case.

To explain why not, we first observe that in a perfectly competitive market both buyers and sellers are price takers. This monopsonist, however, is definitely *not* a price taker. Old Genghis Jones, president of R & S, knows that workers would have to drive *many* miles to the nearest town to get any kind of a job doing anything else. Therefore his purchases of labor significantly influence (and in fact, set) the wage rate commanded by labor in Loose Ends. If Jones were to hire the quantity L^0 of labor, he would have to pay the wage rate w^0, while if he were to hire some larger quantity of labor, say L', he would have to pay a higher wage rate w'. But if Ravel & Selvage's purchases set the price of labor, then the equilibrium wage rate established in this market will depend on how much labor R & S must hire in order to maximize its profits.

How much will this be? Well, the monopsonist, Jones (or Ravel & Selvage) in this case, will always distinguish between the *marginal* and the *average* cost of each worker he hires. And the marginal cost to him of an additional worker will always *exceed* the wage rate received by (i.e., the average cost of) this worker. The reason is that the upward slope of the supply curve of labor means that Jones must offer a higher wage to attract an additional worker. If he pays all his workers the same wage, this higher wage will apply not only to the last worker he hires but to *all* workers he employs. Thus the marginal cost to Ravel & Selvage of hiring an additional worker will equal the new higher wage it must pay for that worker *plus* the rise in its total wage bill due to the higher wage it must now pay to all its workers.

We can show the relationship between the quantity of labor employed by the monopsonist and the average and marginal labor costs the monopsonist incurs by means of a graph (look at Fig. 21.1 again). The supply curve of labor S_L summarizes the relationship between the total number of workers the monopsonist employs and the wage rate he must pay them. Therefore this curve represents, from Jones's point of view, an average cost curve for labor, and so it is labeled $S_L = AC_L$. Then, since the marginal cost of each worker Ravel & Selvage hires will exceed the wage this worker receives, the marginal cost curve faced by R & S must, like the MC_L curve in Fig. 21.1, lie above and be steeper than the AC_L curve.

After we have located the MC_L curve faced by R & S, we can determine how much labor it will hire and thus what wage rate will be established for labor. To maximize its profits, R & S must continue to hire workers until the marginal revenue product yielded by the last worker it hires just equals the marginal cost of this worker.* As we showed in Chapter 9, the relationship between the number of workers employed by a firm and the marginal revenue product which an additional worker would yield the firm is summarized in the firm's demand curve for labor. Therefore this monopsonist, Ravel & Selvage, will maximize its profits by operating at the point at which its demand curve for labor, d_L, intersects its marginal cost curve for labor, MC_L; that is, by hiring L^0 workers and by paying the wage rate w^0.

UNIONS AND BILATERAL MONOPOLY

Now suppose that the demand curve in Fig. 21.1 represented not the demand curve of a single monopsonist for labor, but the sum of the demand curves of many small firms for labor (i.e., suppose that the labor market graphed in Fig. 21.1 were a perfectly competitive one). In that case, the wage rate established in the market would be w' and the quantity of labor employed would be L'. Thus Fig. 21.1 shows that the effect of monopsony on market equilibrium is to lower both the equilibrium wage rate paid and the equilibrium number of workers employed from what they would be under conditions of perfect competition.

From the point of view of workers, the wage–employment combination (w', L') is clearly superior to the combination (w^0, L^0). How might the workers who sell their services in the labor market increase their bargaining power vis-à-vis their monopsonistic employer and thus force him to move away from the position (w^0, L^0) toward the position (w', L')? Well, they could unite to form a *labor union,* an association which would represent all workers as a group in negotiations with their employer. If they did this, then the one-buyer, many-seller situation in Fig. 21.1 would reduce to a one-buyer, one-seller situation: a *bilateral monopoly.*

This would be a good time to say a few words about the history of unions, and about modern unionism.

A BRIEF INTRODUCTION TO UNIONS

Nowadays unions are a widely accepted institution on the American scene. Union members number over 18 million, and represent about a third of the total work force (outside agriculture). Their size and strength, however, are a recent development. Only a few decades ago unions were still struggling for their lives.

---

* This follows from our discussion in Chapter 9 of profit maximization as a one-step procedure.

History of American Unionism

The unions which appeared on the American scene in the nineteenth century were few in number and small in scale. They represented skilled workers almost exclusively, and were generally organized along craft lines. This meant that there was no organization to support unskilled workers in their relations with employers. It also meant that there was no broad union movement to act as spokesman for the laboring class as a whole.

In the 1870's an attempt was made to remedy this situation through the organization of the Knights of Labor. This group was national in scope, and its members included not only skilled workers in different trades but also unskilled workers and friends of labor. Although the Knights were definitely interested in improving wages and working conditions, they were even more dedicated to ideological causes and political reform. This orientation, together with the loose organization of the Knights of Labor and its failure to win a number of key strikes, doomed it to a fadeout at the end of the 1880's that was as rapid as had been its spectacular growth at the beginning of this decade.

In 1886 the Knights of Labor was joined on the national scene by the American Federation of Labor (AFL). This organization united in a single federation a wide variety of different craft unions, and its formation was a crucial turning point in the history of American unionism. The AFL, led by a man named Samuel Gompers (son of immigrant parents and himself a workingman), developed many of the key traits that today characterize the American labor movement. In particular the AFL under Gompers eschewed as unrealistic the goal of bringing about a socialist state in America. Instead it accepted capitalism as a fact of American life and it set out to obtain for American workers the highest wages and best working conditions that a flourishing capitalist society could provide. The AFL's commitment to "bread-and-butter" unionism as opposed to social and political revolution meant that the U.S. labor movement never developed (as many of its European counterparts did) into a national political party.* However, this is not to say that organized labor in the U.S. has not been active on the political scene. On the contrary, it has actively lobbied in favor of legislation that it views as vital to labor's interests, and union members have consistently voted for those legislators who work to further labor's interests.

As shown by the data plotted in Fig. 21.2, union membership in the U.S. grew steadily from the turn of the century through 1920. Then for over a decade it declined. This decline reflected not a retrenchment on the part of labor, but a stiffening of employer resistance to unions; it also reflected the general prosperity of the 1920's, which improved the lot of all workers.

---

* For a short, lively comparison of the labor movement in the U.S. with that in Britain, read *Left Luggage*, by C. Northcote Parkinson; Boston: Houghton Mifflin, 1967.

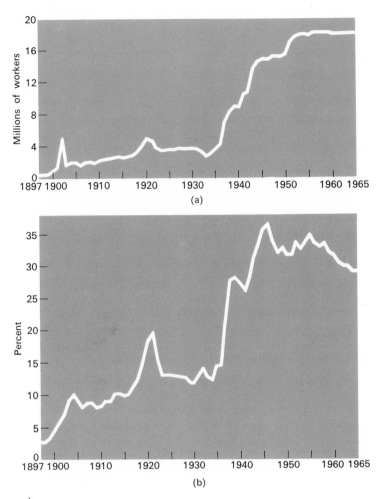

21|2
Union membership in the United States from 1900 to the present.
(a) Total union membership.   (b) Union membership as a percentage
of the nonagricultural labor force. (Source: U.S. Department of Labor)

With the onslaught of the Great Depression in 1929, wages fell, employment dropped off dramatically, and labor regained a sense of urgency about
the need to organize. Simultaneously public opinion shifted more in favor
of unions; and the courts (which had previously done much to block union
growth) began to adopt a more permissive attitude toward the unions' organizing activities. Finally Franklin Roosevelt's New Deal, with its stress on
higher wages and more jobs as a means to economic recovery, led to the
passage of a number of pro-labor laws. Of these the most important was the

Wagner Act in 1935. Previous legislation had guaranteed workers the right to organize, but employers fought the unions with every trick at their command. However, the Wagner Act forbade employers to engage in all these anti-union practices. In addition the Wagner Act made it possible for unions to gain employer recognition not only by striking, but also by using the ballot box. It specified that an employer had to recognize any union that could win a majority vote in a secret ballot conducted among the employer's workers; it also set up the National Labor Relations Board (NLRB) to enforce this and other provisions of the act. As a reading of the labor news in any newspaper will show, secret ballots conducted under the auspices of the NLRB remain today the chief way by which unions seek and obtain the right to represent previously unorganized workers.

As a result of pro-labor legislation and the change in public attitude, union membership shot up during the last half of the 1930's. Some of this growth in membership reflected increases in the size of the AFL craft unions. But these unions proved to be unsatisfactory vehicles for organizing workers in mass-production industries such as autos and steel, because these industries employed skilled workers not just from a single craft but from many crafts, and large numbers of *un*skilled workers as well. The gap left by the AFL led to the formation in 1935 of the Congress of Industrial Organizations (CIO) which, under the fiery leadership of John L. Lewis of the United Mine Workers, organized workers in the auto, steel, rubber, and many other industries.

Union membership continued to rise throughout World War II, and the attitude of the public as well as that of government remained generally sympathetic to labor. Immediately after the war, however, unions in key industries such as steel and railroads engaged in a number of large-scale and protracted strikes. These strikes, whose impact is clearly mirrored in the data which are plotted in Fig. 21.3, alienated the public and many legislators as well.

One result of this alienation was the passage in 1947 of the Taft-Hartley Act. This act prohibited unions from engaging in a variety of "unfair" labor practices in dealing with employers. It also set up special procedures for dealing with crippling strikes that created or threatened to create a national emergency (i.e., with strikes that "imperiled the national health or safety"). The Taft-Hartley Act banned also the *closed shop,* which requires that an employer may hire only union members, and it opened the door for states to ban the *union shop,* which requires that all employees who are represented by a union join that union. This last provision of the Taft-Hartley Act, which has led to the enactment of "right-to-work" laws in several states, particularly rankles labor unions, and they have bitterly but so far unsuccessfully fought for its repeal.

Throughout the 1950's union membership continued to grow, but this growth reflected increases solely in the size of the labor force, not in the relative importance of organized labor. Currently union members represent roughly 30% of all nonagricultural workers; that is about the same proportion that they represented during the early postwar period.

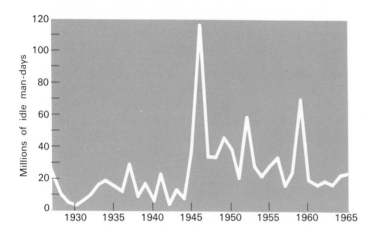

21|3

Working days lost through strikes in the United States, 1927–1965. (Source: U.S. Department of Labor)

During the 1960's union membership has showed signs of peaking out, and in some years it has even declined. The unions' drive for more members and a more influential role in American economic life seems to have faltered, partially because unions, in their attempts to organize new workers, face certain difficulties which are likely to continue to plague them for some time.

1) *Automation* (the replacement of workers with machines) has crimped the growth of and even reduced the size of union membership in some key industries, such as steel and autos.

2) *The expansion of white-collar jobs* offers small comfort to unions, since unions have traditionally had only limited success in organizing white-collar workers.

3) *Union attempts to organize Southern industry* (which is currently growing at a fast pace) *remain largely unsuccessful* because of the hostile attitude of the Southern public and of Southern state and local governments toward unions.

4) *Union progress in organizing agricultural workers has been* (and remains) *discouragingly slow.*

Collective Bargaining in Practice

The way that unions go about bargaining with management varies according to circumstances.

First: When an employer has no local competitors, he usually bargains directly with local union officials. The agreement they reach is strictly local in scope, although if the local union is a member of a large national union, the national union may help the local negotiate with the employer, and may even suggest the terms and concessions for which the local should bargain.

Second: If an employer has close geographic competitors, as for example a building contractor in a city, the union cannot force up the wage rates paid by this employer alone without threatening both his economic life and the jobs of his employees. Therefore in such cases wage rates and work conditions are typically established by means of bargaining between the union and an employers' association which represents all competing producers in the area.

Third: In some industries, and in particular in industries in which employers in different geographic areas tend to compete in a single national market, bargaining takes place between a national union and a national employers' association representing employers throughout the industry. For example, industry-wide bargaining occurs in such diverse industries as coal mining, clothing production, trucking, and merchant shipping.

Fourth: In other industries in which employers in different geographic areas sell in a single national market, a national union representing workers in the industry bargains with key employers one at a time. Usually the union hammers out a contract with one employer and then attempts to force a similar contract pattern on all other employers in the industry. "Pattern bargaining" is practiced in a number of industries, including of course the auto industry; in 1967, as in every contract year, the auto workers' union kept the companies and the country guessing as to whether Ford, General Motors, or Chrysler would be that year's strike target.

The prime issue over which labor and management bargain is the wage rate. Many other issues, however, are also the subject of active negotiation: (a) fringe benefits (such as paid holidays, sick leaves, health plans), supplemental unemployment benefits, and pension plans which the employer provides; (b) the hours, work speeds, and other conditions under which employees work; the employer's freedom to change work rules, hire out work, and introduce new automated equipment; (c) the conditions under which workers may be hired, fired, laid off, and promoted; and (d) the degree of recognition accorded to the union. (Will the employer enforce a union shop? Will he deduct union dues from the paychecks of union members?)

After the union and management have bargained over these and many other issues, the outcome is incorporated in a formal contract. Sometimes the contract may fail to be clear on some points, and the union and management may interpret its meaning differently. Therefore union contracts usually provide for a grievance procedure by which disputes between labor and management may be peaceably settled during the life of the contract.

Union contracts run for one or more years. Some time before the contract expires, management and labor get together to bargain over and hammer out a new contract. If all goes well, they can agree on the terms of such a contract; and, when the old contract expires, it will be immediately superseded by a new one. However, there's always the possibility that bargaining will not be successful. If not, the union, in order to get the employer to accept its demand, may resort to a strike; or the employer, in order to get labor to accept his offer, may resort to a lockout (i.e., he may close down his plant).

COLLECTIVE BARGAINING IN THEORY

Remembering that a market is called a *bilateral monopoly* if it contains only one buyer and one seller, let us now talk about the nature of the agreement that the union (the seller) and the employer (the buyer) reach through bargaining.

The Theory of Bilateral Monopoly

Bilateral monopoly has often been analyzed in a Robinson-Crusoe-Man-Friday framework: Two individuals, each having an initial endowment of one of two commodities, meet to decide whether to trade these commodities, and if so, in what quantities and on what terms.

A graph of this sort of situation was presented in Fig. 18.1. If you turn back to this diagram, you will see that it shows a rectangle whose height and width represent the total amounts of two goods, q_1 and q_2, available to two consumers, Adams and Brown (or A and B). The quantities of q_1 and q_2 available to Adams are measured along an axis whose origin is at the lower left-hand corner of the commodity box. The quantities available to Brown are measured along an axis whose origin is at the opposite corner of the commodity box. The curves labeled A represent Adams' preference map; those labeled B represent Brown's preference map.

To apply this to the Crusoe–Friday type of bilateral monopoly problem, suppose that the initial endowments of Crusoe and Friday place them at point E in the commodity box in Fig. 18.1. Will they trade? Presumably yes, since any trade that moves them to a point in the area enclosed by the two indifference curves that pass through E will increase the welfare of *both* (check this yourself). We cannot find out to what point in this area trading will bring them unless we know more about the character of the two and their relative bargaining strengths. We do know, however, that trading is likely to bring them to a point somewhere along the *contract curve CC* which links all points of tangency between their indifference curves. The reason for this is: If the two were to strike a bargain represented by a point *off* the contract curve, then they would be able through further trading to strike a new bargain that would simultaneously increase the welfare of each of them.

Bilateral Monopoly Applied to Collective Bargaining

We can apply the above model of a bilateral monopoly to a collective bargaining situation. Assume for simplicity that the employer and the union bargain over only two things: the wage rate that the employer must pay and the number of workers that he will hire. The latter condition is a shorthand way of representing the agreement to be reached concerning work rules, work speeds, and the use of automated equipment.

Assume also that the employer and the union have definite preferences among the different wage–employment packages that might be agreed upon. Presumably the employer will be indifferent between two wage–employment packages only if the wage–employment package with the higher wage is combined with work rules and work speeds that permit him to get along with fewer workers. Presumably the union will be indifferent between wage–employment packages only if the wage–employment package with the lower wage calls for the employment of more workers. If these two suppositions hold, then the employer's and the union's preferences among different wage–employment packages can be represented by a set of downward-sloping indifference curves, like the one we used to represent the consumer's preferences among different goods.

Figure 21.4 (which is similar in construction to the trading box in Fig. 18.1) denotes the employer's preferences with respect to the wage rate w that he must pay and the work force N that he will employ by the preference map M (for management). Note that the origin of management's preference map is at the lower left-hand corner of the trading box. The union's preferences with respect to the wage rate and the size of the work force are denoted by the preference map U, whose origin is at the upper right-hand corner of the trading box.

Suppose now that we represent last year's contract settlement by the point E in Fig. 21.4. We want to know to which point in the trading box (i.e., to what wage–employment settlement) collective bargaining will bring the employer and the union during the current year. Recall that in our Crusoe–Friday example we concluded that trading would bring the two parties to some point between (or along) the two indifference curves that passed through the initial point *E*. In the present situation, however, *E* represents a contract settlement that loses all force on the day it expires. There is no reason why the succeeding year's settlement should not make the employer or the union (but presumably not both of them) worse off. For example, employers who would like to automate often have to settle year after year for contracts that increase the wages they must pay but in no way liberalize their right to automate. Certainly the New York daily newspapers in their periodic tussles with the printers' union seem to come out worse and worse each year.

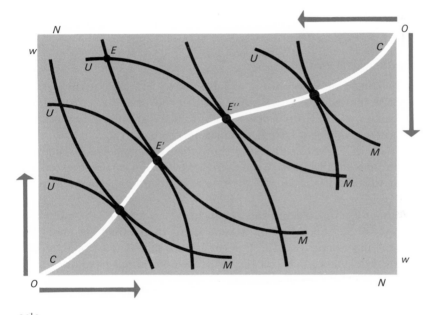

21|4

A problem in bilateral monopoly: bargaining between an employer with the preference map *M* and a union with the preference map *U* over the wage rate *w* and employment *N*.

Obviously when the initial position *E* represents the settlement reached in a previous contract that is due to expire, the range of indeterminacy in the solution of the bilateral monopoly problem at hand extends to the whole box (and even to the dimensions of the box). Thus the location of the new point of settlement will depend on the bargaining strengths of the two parties and on the skill with which each bargains.

In our discussion of the theory of bilateral monopoly, we suggested that probably Crusoe and Friday (who can sit from now to eternity trading in palm leaves and coconuts) would through a series of exchanges eventually reach a point on their mutual contract curve. How likely is it that a union and an employer would through collective bargaining reach a point on their contract curve? Not very likely, for the following reasons: (a) Union contracts are frequently negotiated under considerable time pressure. (b) In the negotiation of such a contract, each party attempts to strengthen his bargaining position by hiding his true preferences, and therefore neither the union or the employer ever knows whether a proposed settlement represents a point on the contract curve.

When a new contract is being negotiated, either union or management might view the "last offer" made by its opponent as unacceptable. Hence there is always the possibility that a stalemate will occur and that no settlement will be reached. When this happens, a strike or a lockout results.

DO UNIONS RAISE WAGES?

One of the chief aims of unions is to raise wages; let's look at the data on income shares plotted in Fig. 21.5 to see whether they have succeeded. These data show that over time the proportions of national income going to labor, business, interest, and rent have been amazingly stable. If we compare them with the data in Fig. 21.2, they also show that, although labor's share in national income has risen over time, there is little or no correlation between the *rate* at which it has risen and the rate at which union membership has risen.

We cannot use this observation as conclusive evidence of the effect that unions have or have not had on labor's share in national income. The changes that have occurred over time in labor's share of national income reflect a great deal more that just the influence that *unions* have had on the wage rate. Since the turn of the century, many factors have influenced the rate of labor's wages: (a) changes in labor's skills, (b) changes in factor (input) proportions, (c) changes in technology, (d) changes in the mix of final outputs produced by the economy, (e) changes in immigration laws, (f) the tendency of women to enter the work force, and (g) the tendency of youths to stay in school longer. All these factors have affected the demand for and supply of labor, and thus also the equilibrium wage rate. So, in order to evaluate the effect of unions on labor's share in national income, we would have to compare what actually happened to labor's share of national income over time with what *would* have happened to labor's share if there had been no unions.

Since the data at hand offer us little help in determining whether or not unions have bolstered labor's share in national income, we might turn to theory to seek the answer. From our discussion of the firm, we know that profit-maximizing producers respond to an increase in the wage rate by substituting capital for labor and by raising the prices of the goods they sell. Therefore each time the unions succeed in raising labor's money wage rate,

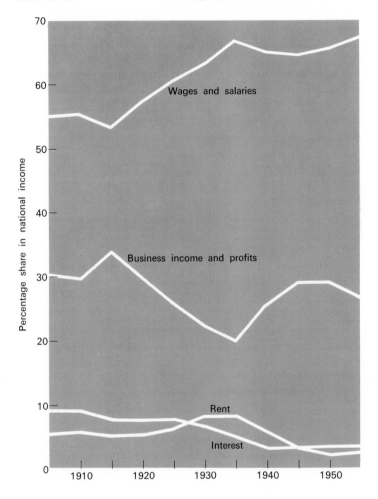

21|5

Relative shares in U.S. national income, 1900–1957. (Source: I. B. Kravis, "Relative Income Shares in Fact and Theory," *American Economic Review,* December 1959)

this gain will be partially offset by (1) a fall in employment, which lowers the total money income going to labor, and by (2) a rise in the prices of goods, which lowers labor's real income (i.e., purchasing power). Theory thus suggests that each time the unions succeed in raising wages, this rise will set off a complex chain of reactions. How will a hike in labor's wage affect labor's share in national income? We can't know the answer unless we know what the relative sizes of these reactions will be. The answer, in addition to the fact that it is difficult to ascertain, is also likely to change from year to year.

PROBLEMS

1   Show that a firm which is a monopsonist in several local labor markets will minimize its total cost by adjusting its purchases in each market so that the marginal cost of labor in each is the same. [*Hint:* Show that if the above condition were not satisfied, the monopsonist would decrease costs by shifting its purchases from one market to another.]

2   Skilled labor is usually paid a higher wage than unskilled labor. Is this an example of price discrimination in the sense defined in Chapter 20?

3   Construct a box diagram of the type discussed in Chapter 18 to illustrate the problem of trading between Robinson Crusoe and Friday. Give each of them initial endowments of bananas and coconuts, but be sure that this endowment point, *E,* does not lie on the contract curve.

   a) Show that any trade which moves Crusoe and Friday to a point in the area enclosed by the two indifference curves passing through *E* will be considered preferable to *E* by both of them.

   b) Show that any bargain which moved them to a point off the contract curve could be improved on by another bargain which would increase the satisfaction of at least one of them without simultaneously decreasing the satisfaction of the other.

4   Why is it an advantage to the automobile workers' union to bargain with and strike only one of the large automobile companies at a time? Why do you suppose that the companies do not get together and agree to bargain as a unit with the union? Why, specifically, do the companies not agree to all shut down production when one of them is struck?

5   Suppose that you were able to ascertain that increases in the wage rate induced by union activities during, say, the 1930's, raised labor's share of national income. Would this mean that increases in the wage rate induced by union activities in later periods must also have increased labor's share of national income? If not, why not? What conditions might have changed over time?

6   Discuss the effects of the following union objectives on the efficiency of resource allocation.

   a) Union shops

   b) Pension plans

   c) Seniority-pegged wage scales

7   We have suggested that, in the absence of any other effects, an increase in the wage rate will cause an increase in prices. However, this need not be the case if the productivity of labor also increases. Use diagrams to show that a wage increase, if accompanied by an increase in the productivity of labor, could result in prices staying the same, or even falling.

8   In studying both the firm and the consumer we were able to make clear-cut assumptions as to their objectives: Maximization of profit for the firms and maximization of satisfaction for consumers. Can you make any such clear-cut assumption as to the objectives of a union? For whose benefit do you think a

union usually works: all workers in its industry, only those workers which are members of the union, or just the officers of the union?

9   Consider a labor market which is perfectly competitive on the demand side. Would it be to the advantage of the workers in this market to organize, and, if so, what policies would the workers be likely to pursue? An example of such a market might be the market for typists in a large city.

10   Discuss the pros and cons of union shops from a social-welfare standpoint. If it were possible to completely abolish union shops without creating new problems (such as excessive government interference) in the process, would you be in favor of doing so?

CHAPTER 22

OLIGOPOLY

An *oligopoly* is a market situation in which a few rival producers control the supply of a commodity (which may or may not be homogeneous). The key characteristic of oligopolistic markets is thus *seller fewness*.

It is difficult to study price determination in an oligopolistic market because many outcomes are possible, and *which* outcome occurs depends not only on the price–output policies of the rival sellers but on how these sellers interact. Thus we cannot study "the" equilibrium of an oligopolistic market; we can only talk about the various possible outcomes of an oligopolistic situation, and these run the gamut from warfare to well-organized collusion. Throughout this chapter, we shall be concerned primarily with how oligopolistic rivals would behave *if* they were free to pursue, singly or jointly, their own self-interests. Later on, in Chapter 25, we shall discuss the restrictions government antitrust policy places on oligopolistic behavior.

ENTRY BARRIERS

As we said in Chapter 19, oligopoly is quite prevalent on the American scene, and it is often extremely profitable. If it is to continue for a long time, a profitable oligopoly, like a profitable monopoly, must be protected by barriers which deter producers that are attracted by the oligopolists' profits from entering their market. One way to characterize oligopolies is thus according to the entry barriers that protect them.

Economies of Scale

Economists have often said (usually on the basis of intuition rather than data) that economies of scale constitute an important entry barrier in many oligopolistic markets. It's very hard to judge just how important such economies really are. However, the data from the study by Joe S. Bain (see

Table 19.3) do offer some suggestions. In several of the industries studied by Bain, scale economies in production extended over such a large range of output that only a few firms could simultaneously produce on a scale adequate to attain minimum cost. For example, according to the data in this table, efficient production would have permitted not more than 5 producers in the typewriter industry, 8 in the tractor industry, 10 in the copper industry, 12 in the auto industry, and 20 each in the cigarette and soap industries. If these estimates are correct, then in each of these industries production can be efficient only if supply is controlled by a limited number of oligopolists.

However, if scale economies are to constitute an important entry barrier, it is not enough that they extend over a wide range of output; they must also be large in size. In many of the industries studied by Bain, a firm operating a plant as small as one-half optimal size had costs that were no more than a few percentage points higher than those of firms operating optimal-size plants. But this was not the case in either the auto or the typewriter industries, where scale economies were both extensive and important.

From the above rather limited data we may postulate that, although scale economies do constitute a barrier to entry in many oligopolistic markets, this barrier is a high one in relatively few of these markets.

Product Differentiation

Product differentiation is common in oligopolistic markets, but its effect on entry barriers is mixed. On the one hand, by distracting the consumer's attention from price, product differentiation reduces the importance of scale economies as an entry barrier. On the other hand, by building strong consumer allegiances for established products, product differentiation may itself constitute a formidable entry barrier. This is certainly true in the automobile, liquor, cigarette, and typewriter industries, all of which are oligopolies.

Absolute Cost Advantages

In several oligopolistic markets, the absolute cost advantage which established firms derive from their control over the supply of a strategic raw material constitutes an important entry barrier. For example, in the copper industry all known reserves of copper ore, both domestic and foreign, are controlled by established refiners and smelters. Therefore entry into the markets of this industry would be feasible only in the rather unlikely event that the entrant discovered new reserves of commercially exploitable ore. Similar, if somewhat less limiting, situations exist in the steel, nickel, and sulphur industries.

Patents, another absolute cost advantage, also constitute an entry barrier in many oligopolistic industries. The importance of patents as a barrier varies from industry to industry, of course, depending on factors such as the number, strength, and breadth of the patents held by established firms, how rapidly technology in the industry is changing, and how willing established firms are to make licensing agreements with each other and with new entrants.

In some oligopolistic industries, such as automobiles, aircraft, and electrical equipment, in which competing firms hold a lot of complementary product and process patents, *patent pools* have been formed to facilitate efficient production and to avoid continual patent litigation and licensing negotiations. These pools provide for cross-licensing between member firms on a no-royalty or moderate-royalty basis, and they have the obvious advantage of permitting unobstructed utilization of available technology by all member firms. However, if patent pools are *closed,* they have the obvious disadvantage of constituting an insurmountable entry barrier for newcomers to an industry. Cross-licensing agreements have also frequently been used as a basis for collusive price and output agreements.

MUTUAL DEPENDENCE AMONG RIVAL OLIGOPOLISTS

When we were talking about price determination under a monopoly, we assumed that an individual producer could change the price he charges for his output without shifting demand for that output. That assumption doesn't hold true for an oligopolistic market, because any change that an individual oligopolist makes in his price will shift demand for the outputs of his rivals,* and this will induce these rivals to make counteradjustments in their prices. These counteradjustments will in turn shift demand for the first oligopolist's output. Thus the demand curves facing any group of rival oligopolists are all mutually dependent, in the sense that the position and shape of the demand curve facing any one oligopolist depends on the price–output policies of each of his rivals.

Mutual Dependence: An Example

Suppose that two producers sell a homogeneous product, say aluminum ingots, for which we can construct a market demand curve. The name of the first company is Amalumco, and the name of the second is the Hall Processing Company. For simplicity suppose that the cost curves of both companies are identical and that each can expand output from zero upward at

---

* For example, a change in the price of Fords will obviously shift the demand for Chevrolets, and vice versa.

constant cost. Then their AC and MC curves will be single straight-line curves like the curve $MC = AC$ in Fig. 22.1.

Amalumco and Hall Processing both begin from a position of zero output. What chain of events will ensue if each firm attempts to maximize its profits on the assumption that the price set by its rival is constant? If Amalumco enters the market first, demand for its output will be identical with the market demand schedule for aluminum ingots (represented in Fig. 22.1 by the curve AR). Since Amalumco's cost curves are represented by the curve $MC = AC$, it will obviously maximize its profits by selling the output quantity q^0 at the price p^0.

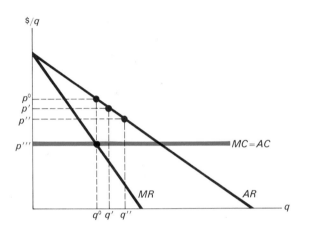

22|1

Two rival oligopolists who assume that each other's price is constant will drive market price down to the zero profit level, p'''.

Now Hall Processing enters the market. This company will be unable to sell any output at a price greater than p^0, the price at which Amalumco is selling. However, if Hall Processing assumes that the price set by Amalumco is fixed, then it will conclude that, although demand for its output is zero at any price *greater than* p^0, it is identical with market demand at any price *below* p^0. Therefore, in its attempt to maximize profits, Hall Processing will charge a price p', that is just under p^0, and sell a quantity q', that is slightly larger than q^0.

If Hall Processing follows this price–output policy, however, Amalumco will now find that *it* can sell nothing unless it charges a price lower than p'. But if Amalumco maintains its assumption that all prices, including the price set up by Hall Processing, are fixed, then it will conclude that to maximize its profits, it must charge a price such as p'', which lies just below p', the price charged by Hall Processing.

At this point a pattern emerges: So long as each views the other's price as fixed, each will respond to a reduction in the other's price by reducing its own price to a still lower level. However, if both manufacturers act this way, the price will eventually be driven down from the monopoly level, p^0, to the zero-profit level, p'''. It will be in the interest of neither firm to sell at a price below p''', since any sale made at such a low price would yield a negative profit. [To prove this, check the relationship between each firm's average cost and its average revenue for prices below p'''.]

This example of mutual dependence indicates the way we should go about analyzing price determination in an oligopolistic market: (1) We cannot analyze the equilibrium of a single oligopolist apart from that of his rivals. (2) Our analysis must be based on the assumption that rival oligopolists recognize their mutual dependence and take it into account in their profit calculations.

WARFARE

In an oligopolistic market in which rival sellers recognize their mutual dependence, price and quantity sold may be determined in various ways. One possibility is that through *warfare* the structure of the market will evolve from oligopoly to monopoly. Several strategies are open to the aggressive oligopolist who wants to eliminate his rivals and gain monopoly control over his market. One is *predatory price-cutting*. With this tactic (which used to be more common than it is now), the would-be monopolist sets his price so low that his competitors, in attempting to meet this price, incur substantial losses that force them out of business.* With his competitors thus eliminated, the predatory price cutter raises his price to the monopoly level and reaps monopoly profits.

To come out on top in price warfare, the predatory price cutter must enjoy some advantage over his rivals, such as lower costs or larger financial resources. One way an aggressive producer may get a decisive cost advantage over his rivals is by pressuring input suppliers into granting him discriminatory price concessions. Secret rail rebates, for example, played an important role in the early, phenomenal growth of the Standard Oil Trust, an organization that later gained monopoly control over the markets for gasoline and oil in many areas of the United States. Although price concessions made by sellers to large buyers may in part be justified by the fact that large orders cost less per unit to fill than small ones, such concessions also reflect the superior bargaining power that a large buyer is able to exert on individual sellers.

---

* If he sells in a number of geographic markets, the war-waging oligopolist need not take on all his competitors at once. Instead he can use *localized price cutting* (i.e., *predatory price discrimination*) to destroy his smaller competitors one by one, or at whatever rate his financial resources can bear.

In addition to waging overt price warfare, the aggressive producer who wants to gain monopoly control over his market may employ other less dramatic, but nevertheless effective, strategies. For example, he might engage in *preemptive buying* of inputs, transportation facilities, or sales outlets that would be needed by other firms if they were to compete in his market. In other words, he buys up or otherwise gains control not only of resources he needs, but also of resources that he wants to prevent competitors, present or potential, from using. A good example of preemption is Alcoa's acquisition of bauxite deposits and water power sites in quantities that, according to allegations made in a 1945 antitrust suit, far exceeded its foreseeable needs. Extensive systems of exclusive dealerships also constitute obvious attempts at preemption.

The aggressive oligopolist who wants to gain monopoly control might also attempt to do so by *securing a dominant patent position.* Even if this device failed, the monopolizing firm, if it were a large one, might be able to ruin smaller rivals or force them into undesired and perhaps unfavorable mergers simply by harassing them with patent infringement suits based on questionable patents or questionable instances of infringement. One fascinating case of such domination, in which a company attempted monopolization of an initially oligopolistic industry by means of patent abuses, is the case of the Hartford Empire Corporation. This company, during the interwar years, persistently accumulated patents on glassmaking machinery, and used these patents to secure near-monopoly control over the glass container industry.

Overt and aggressive monopolization was once a common occurrence on the American scene, but now it is infrequent, probably as a result of antitrust legislation, which forbids firms to use coercive, predatory, or other "unfair" tactics to monopolize markets. For our purposes the important point is that monopolization is, either for legal or economic reasons, an unacceptable and even an improbable solution to the problems of an oligopolistic situation.

PERFECT COLLUSION

Let us consider a group of rival oligopolists: They recognize their mutual dependence but reject internecine warfare. What price and output policies are they likely to pursue, individually and collectively? Under these circumstances (fewness of sellers, mutual dependence recognized, and warfare rejected) rivals that were rational would undoubtedly try to *maximize their joint profits.* The rivals could then presumably allocate (or reallocate) these profits among themselves according to some mutually agreed on "fair-share" formula.

To successfully maximize their joint profits, a group of rival oligopolists would have to engage in *perfect collusion*.

Perfect collusion means that a group of rival oligopolists enter into a clearly defined, strictly enforced agreement that fixes the prices and outputs of all firms in the group at levels that maximize the joint profits of the group.

Example: Three firms—Xcel Mines, York Metals Company, and Zonal Development, Inc.—control the *total* supply of a homogeneous commodity, q, for which no close substitutes exist. The commodity is elasticium, a metal discovered in the 1980's. Elasticium has the properties of both strength and elasticity, and is in demand both by itself and as an alloy. Figure 22.2 shows the MC curves of these three firms. What price and output policies will maximize the total (i.e., joint) profits these three firms earn?

In Chapter 9 we said that a single firm will maximize profits by producing the output that equates its marginal revenue with its marginal cost. This same argument can be used to show that a group of producers will maximize profits by producing the output that equates their *joint* marginal revenue with their *joint* marginal cost. (Here "joint marginal cost" refers to the extra cost that the group as a whole incurs by producing an extra unit of output, while "joint marginal revenue" refers to the extra revenue that the group receives by selling an extra unit of output.)

To locate the joint MR curve of Xcel Mines, York Metals, and Zonal Development, we first note that the market demand curve for q (elasticium) summarizes the relationship between the total amount of elasticium they produce and the price they receive for it; in other words, it is their joint AR curve. Therefore we can construct the joint MR curve of these three producers directly from the market demand curve D for their output.

To construct the joint MC curve of these three firms, we recall that a marginal cost curve states how much small additions to output will cost when total output is produced at *minimum* cost. Next we observe that, if one firm's marginal cost were higher than another's, the total production costs incurred by these firms as a group could be reduced by shifting output from the high-marginal-cost firm to the low-marginal-cost firm. Thus, to minimize the total cost of producing any level of joint output, Xcel Mines, York Metals, and Zonal Development must allocate this output among themselves so that each of them incurs the same marginal cost. This result is important because it implies that the joint MC curve of these three firms can be obtained simply by adding their individual MC curves.*

---

* If we assume for simplicity that the MC curves of these producers are nowhere downward sloping, then this adding process is identical to the one we used in Chapter 13 to obtain market supply and demand curves.

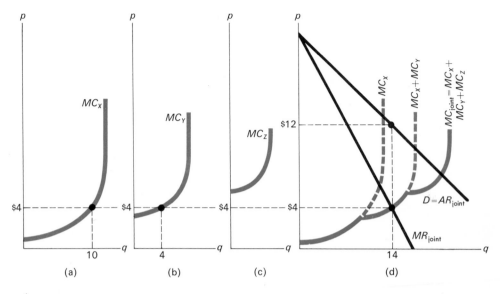

22|2

The solution of a one-market, three-seller problem in joint profit maximization.
a) Xcel Mines produces 10 tons of output q (elasticium).
b) York Metals Company produces 4 tons.
c) Zonal Development, Inc., produces zero tons.
d) The three firms produce 14 tons of the homogeneous product, elasticium, which they sell at a price of $12 per ton.

Part (d) of Fig. 22.2 shows the joint MR and MC curves of Xcel Mines, York Metals, and Zonal Development. From these curves we see that in equilibrium these colluding oligopolists produce 14 tons of elasticium which they sell at a price of $12 per ton. How will they allocate this total output among themselves? Looking back at parts (a), (b), and (c) of Fig. 22.2, we observe that cost minimization (and thus profit maximization) calls for Xcel Mines, a low-cost firm, to produce 10 tons of elasticium; for York Metals, a medium-cost firm, to produce 4 tons; and for Zonal Development, a high-cost firm, to produce nothing!

We can see from this example that if a group of firms with quite different cost structures try to maximize their joint profits, the outputs produced and profits earned by each of them in equilibrium will differ, perhaps quite sharply. In fact, a high-cost producer may end up producing zero output and earning zero profits, while a low-cost producer may end up producing a large output and earning large profits. But if so, then the collusion, to be successful, will probably require *interfirm compensation,* that is, payments from low-cost firms that produce a large share of output to high-cost firms that produce little or no output.

Perfect Collusion: An Example

A fascinating case history of oligopolistic collusion is Phoebus, the international light-bulb cartel.* This cartel was organized in 1924 and numbered among its members (indirectly in the case of General Electric) all major manufacturers of electric light bulbs in the world. Its principal purpose was to limit and control competition among these producers, particularly in international markets. Phoebus divided world markets into three categories (home territories, British overseas territories, and common territory), and it assigned member firms quotas in each of these market areas. Member firms were free to exceed their quotas; but if they did so, they had to pay penalties that were then distributed among those cartel members who failed to fill their quotas. Phoebus itself did not fix the prices of light bulbs. Participants in each market fixed prices within that market, but when they chose their price policy, they were advised by Phoebus. In addition to dividing markets and fixing prices, Phoebus also engaged in an extensive "standardization program," two interesting results of which were the deliberate reduction of bulb life and the elimination of quality competition among competing bulb manufacturers!†

One particularly noteworthy aspect of Phoebus was that it incorporated a patent pool that was virtually worldwide. To the extent that this pool facilitated the development of technology in the industry, its effect was undoubtedly beneficial. On the other hand, this patent pool constituted a formidable entry barrier that protected the prices and profits of cartel members.

IMPERFECT COLLUSION

Although perfect collusion *is* possible, a study of the literature concerning collusion and attempted collusion reveals that it is extremely difficult for a group of rival producers (1) to negotiate, and (2) to maintain the comprehensive kind of agreement needed for perfect collusion. The difficulties that beset attempts at collusion spring from many sources.

First: Unless all the colluding firms are identical with respect to both cost structure and size (a condition that is highly unlikely to exist in practice), it may be very hard to hammer out an agreement concerning the interfirm allocation of market shares and profits. Because the colluding firms usually hold conflicting aspirations, any agreement reached would probably, from the outset, be unsatisfactory to at least some parties.

---

* Thumbnail definition: A cartel is an agreement among business rivals whose aim is to limit or eliminate competition. Such an agreement may be loose and informal or detailed and strictly enforced. It may be open-and-above-board or highly secret. And, depending on the laws of the country or countries in which it operates, it may be legal or illegal.

† George Stocking and Myron Watkins, *op. cit.,* pages 304–362.

Second: In many oligopolistic industries, entry barriers are not high, and output is supplied by an oligopolistic core of major producers and a fringe of smaller competitors. In a case such as this, the numerousness of producers in the market renders industry-wide collusion difficult, if not impossible.

Third: Perfect collusion may be difficult for a group of firms to attain if some firms in the group believe that the long-run consequences of collusion might be unfavorable to them. Certainly a firm that is required by perfect collusion to shut down would have good reason to fear the effects of such action on its future bargaining power *vis-à-vis* its rivals. A rapidly expanding firm whose costs were low might fear that collusion would stunt its growth. Even among firms of approximately equal strength, perfect collusion may call for a degree of mutual disarmament that is hard to achieve so long as even a slight threat of renewed warfare remains. To agree on terms of collusion may also prove difficult because firms do not share similar views of the present and of the future, and therefore cannot agree on what price and output policies to pursue in order to maximize their profits both in the current period and over time. Unless all member firms in the group are strongly committed to cooperation (as opposed to competition), outside disturbances, such as a sharp slump in demand, may lead to a breakup of the agreement and to a resumption of price competition.

Fourth: The enforcement of antitrust legislation in the United States acts as a powerful deterrent to extensive and overt collusion. Although such legislation has not prevented all attempts at collusion, it has at least forced these attempts underground. And a covert agreement is likely to be more difficult to negotiate and to enforce than an overt one. Therefore, when restrictions are imposed on competition by covert agreements, these restrictions are probably not only incomplete but imperfectly observed as well.

Because it is so hard to establish *perfect* collusion, *imperfect* collusion is a situation that is more frequently observed, at least in the United States in mid-twentieth century. Collusion among a group of producers may be imperfect on a number of counts:

1) A collusive agreement may not include all producers in the industry.

2) The terms of the agreement may not be strictly enforced. For example, firms might engage in secret price shading, particularly in response to downward shifts in market demand.

3) The terms of agreement may be incomplete. An agreement might, for example, cover price but not shares of the market, or price and market shares but not expenditures for cost reduction, product differentiation, product development, advertising, or other forms of *nonprice competition.*

The kind of imperfect collusion that perhaps comes closest to perfect collusion is an agreement regulating price and relative shares of the market, but not nonprice competition. Since collusion on this scale violates U.S. antitrust laws, and since it would be difficult to set up and maintain covertly, it probably occurs infrequently. However, isolated instances of collusion do exist, as witnessed by the following account.

In 1959, the government proved that representatives of firms producing electrical apparatus (such as turbine generators, power transformers, and numerous other items) attended meetings during the 1950's at which market shares were allocated and prices were fixed. These firms allocated sealed-bid business among themselves, rigged bids, and decided which firm would be low man on any forthcoming bid. The prices these firms quoted both to commercial customers and to government customers were collusively rigged. However, to cover up their activities, these firms "rippled" prices and maintained inconsequential differentials between the prices they quoted to commercial buyers on any one item at any one time. (The ripples and differentials were created by the fantastic scheme of having each firm rotate its prices up and down according to the phase of the moon!) The eventual outcome of the government's case against the colluding firms was that several officials of these companies were sent to jail. Such examples have a chilling effect on other would-be transgressors.

Eliminating Price Competition

Although imperfectly collusive agreements in some markets may cover both price and market shares, such agreements often have a much more limited goal: eliminating price competition between the colluding firms. The reason why producers attach such importance to this one goal is probably that in many industries firms think of price competition as the one form of competition that (in the short run at least) threatens to lower, perhaps dramatically, the profits of all producers and to raise the profits of none. The consequences of price competition are especially feared in industries such as steel, cement, and electrical equipment, in which:

a) output is reasonably homogeneous,
b) fixed costs are high, but marginal cost is low, and
c) demand is both inelastic and subject to sharp cyclical fluctuations.

Business firms may try to eliminate price competition in a variety of ways, each of which requires the setting up of some sort of system to ensure that, at any point in time, all sellers in the market quote identical prices. The simplest way a group of rival sellers could maintain uniform prices would be to get together periodically and hold quiet price-rigging sessions. But this simple approach is a risky one, since it calls for an overt violation of antitrust laws.* Therefore, to assure that everyone in an industry gets at least some of the gravy, pragmatic business firms aim at price uniformity by means of covert and indirect approaches. Let us look at three of these in some detail.

Price leadership. One of the most common approaches to the problem is price leadership. Price leadership implies that all producers in a given industry quote prices identical to those quoted by the price leader, and that they match whatever price changes he initiates.

The functioning and results of price leadership vary considerably from industry to industry. In industries in which entry barriers are high and other circumstances favor successful collusion, there is likely to be a well-disciplined system of price leadership that significantly raises market price above the competitive level. In other industries, in which circumstances are less favorable to collusion, there is more likely to be *barometric price leadership*. In such a situation, the price leader usually just announces price changes that he regards as inevitable. He does this because his price followers are apt to act independently of him sometimes, especially during times when demand is weak. At such times, the followers are inclined to shade their prices.

Price leadership is a practice that is strongly entrenched in the steel industry, as should be obvious to anyone who reads the newspapers or listens to newscasts. Price changes posted by major steel mills are given widespread coverage in the press, and these changes invariably display a follow-the-leader pattern. Price leadership in the steel industry can have a certain dramatic quality, especially when (as happened in 1962) the president of a steel company defies the president of the United States. Roger Blough, president of U.S. Steel, raised the price of steel by $6 a ton, and other steel companies followed suit. President John F. Kennedy made a nationwide address denouncing this price rise, and the resulting fracas caused stocks to fall on Wall Street. Price leadership also touches our lives in more mundane and less obvious ways. In a large city the wholesale market for bread is usually characterized by strong price leadership,† a circumstance which can

---

* As we noted before, the U.S. airlines are an exception to the no-collusive-price-fixing laws. The airlines are regulated by the Federal Aviation Agency, a government department. The FAA permits the airlines to belong to an international price-fixing cartel, known as the International Air Transport Association, which sets prices on all international flights. IATA also tries to limit nonprice competition between these airlines; it has solemnly defined what constitutes the sandwich that a tourist-class passenger may be served (hot or cold? with a top or open-face?) and it has deliberated over whether such passengers may see in-flight movies without extra charge.

† The price and nonprice conduct of bread producers and retailers is discussed in Walsh and Evans, *op. cit.*, pages 82–114.

easily be explained. As we pointed out in Chapter 12, consumer demand for bread is notoriously inelastic, and hence price competition is unattractive to bread producers, since it threatens established price levels without offering the possibility of increased sales. Despite the fact that it is usually strictly observed, price leadership in the bread industry represents an *imperfect* mode of collusion, because wholesale bakeries engage in extensive nonprice competition, in the form of advertising and product differentiation (aimed at the consumer) and promotional programs (aimed at retail bread outlets).

Basing-point pricing. Some industries turn out a product that is sold in a local market (baked goods) or a product that is both high in price and cheap to ship (watches). In such industries a well-disciplined system of price leadership is enough to eliminate all but slight differences in the prices rival sellers quote to any one buyer; thus price competition is ruled out.

Many industries, however, produce an output that is low in price and costly to ship. In such industries freight charges are a significant part of the *delivered price* (i.e., factory FOB price* plus freight) that buyers of the output must pay, and a price-leadership system that equates producers' FOB prices does not mean that all producers will quote the same price to any one buyer. If producers are all to quote similar delivered prices to such a buyer, they must combine price leadership with a *basing-point system.*

Under the simplest basing-point system, the delivered price quoted by every seller—regardless of his location—equals his FOB price plus the freight charges he would incur if he shipped goods to the buyer from a specified geographic point, called the *base point,* by a specified mode of transportation, frequently rail. In other words, under a basing-point system, a buyer has to pay the same freight charges no matter which seller actually fills his order, no matter what distance the goods he buys actually move, and no matter what mode of transportation is used to move them. Thus under a basing-point-plus-price-leadership system, the delivered prices quoted by rival sellers to buyers at any one point are identical, and price competition among these sellers is precluded.

Under a basing-point system the freight charges a seller actually incurs in filling an order usually differ from the freight charges included in his delivered price. He "absorbs" freight on shipments to customers far away from his plant but close to the base point, and charges "phantom freight" to customers in the reverse position. Therefore, unless his mill is located at the base point, the seller receives a different net price (i.e., gross price minus freight) on shipments to different destinations. Thus a basing-point system is simply an elaborate form of *price discrimination* designed to equate the delivered prices quoted by rival sellers to any one buyer.

---

* A price quoted FOB (free on board) excludes freight; a price quoted CIF (cost, insurance, and freight) includes these items as well.

The history of pricing in the steel industry is a good example of price leadership combined with a basing-point system. The steel industry has characteristics that make such pricing policies attractive: (1) Many of its products are homogeneous; thus producers have to meet each other's prices. (2) Although the cost of shipping steel products is high relative to their value, they are nevertheless shipped great distances, because (a) economies of scale in production make large plants desirable and (b) the high cost of shipping coke and ore makes it uneconomical to locate plants far from sources of raw material.

By the turn of the century, U.S. Steel was established as the price leader in the steel industry, and Pittsburgh as the base point. Under the reign of the basing-point system that became known as "Pittsburgh-plus," every steel buyer, in *any* part of the country, had to pay a delivered price that included rail freight from Pittsburgh, even if his steel came from a local mill. In 1924 the Federal Trade Commission ordered U.S. Steel to increase the number of base points; but at the same time U.S. Steel created differentials among base-point FOB prices. These differentials in effect froze a certain amount of phantom freight into the price structure of the industry. Thus in actual fact Pittsburgh-plus endured until 1938, when these differentials were eliminated. After the war the Federal Trade Commission bore down on basing-point systems as an illegal form of collusion, and this forced the steel industry to abandon formal basing-point pricing. Currently steel mills price FOB, and phantom freight has thus been eliminated. Freight absorption, on the other hand, still goes on, especially when demand is weak.

Implicit bargaining. In some industries characterized by fewness of sellers, no explicit collusion takes place. Nevertheless each seller, when he evaluates the effect of a contemplated price adjustment, takes into account any counteradjustments that he believes his action may evoke from his rivals; thus he takes into account both the direct and indirect consequences of his actions. In that case, the market equilibrium established may be said to result from *implicit* as opposed to *explicit bargaining.*

The possibility of implicit bargaining brings us to a question that arises frequently in antitrust litigation: Where does collusion end and the prudent recognition of mutual dependence begin? Any distinction one made would presumably have to be based on actions rather than intent. At the one extreme, when rival business firms try to maximize profits by instituting clearly defined, well-enforced agreements among themselves, clearly this constitutes collusion. At the other extreme, it is only normal business practice (and commonsense) for rival sellers to take into account both the direct and indirect effects of their actions.

In addition to price leadership, basing-point pricing, and implicit bargaining, industries use two other methods to maintain price uniformity:

(1) Rival sellers may agree to use identical formulas both in calculating costs and in setting prices. (2) Rival sellers may agree to a rapid and continuous dissemination (via a trade association or other organization) of information about costs incurred and prices charged by all firms in the industry. The advantage of Method 1 is that producers arrive at identical prices through "independent" cost and price calculations. The advantage of Method 2 is that producers can easily keep their prices "in line with those set by other producers"; at the same time this method discourages price shading, at least of the overt type.

All the above practices, however one classifies them, are likely to result in a high degree of price uniformity in any oligopolistic market in which a homogeneous product is sold.

PROBLEMS

1   The demand curve for a certain commodity slopes downward. Initially there is only one firm, the Alpha Company, producing the commodity. The Alpha Company behaves exactly in accordance with our analysis of monopoly behavior in Chapter 20. Another firm, the Beta Company, is considering entering the market. With the following assumptions about Alpha's behavior, draw Beta's marginal revenue curve.

   a) Alpha will continue to charge the same price it charged before Beta entered the market.

   b) Alpha will respond to any price Beta charges by changing to a slightly lower price, so long as it is able to make a profit by doing so; otherwise Alpha will leave the market.

   c) Alpha will set its price to *equal* Beta's price.

2   a) What price will the Beta Company charge and what quantity, if any, will it produce under each of the three assumptions of Problem 1? Assume that Beta is concerned only with maximizing its profits in the short run.

   b) Under what circumstances, and under which of the assumptions in Problem 1, do you think the Beta Company would be wise to attempt predatory price cutting?

3   Discuss examples of oligopoly in your home town. To what extent do these businesses come under the heading of "small business," whose virtues politicians extol?

4   a) Show that the joint solution to the one-market, three-seller problem illustrated in Fig. 22.2 is unstable without some binding agreement or interfirm compensation. That is, show that any one of the firms could profit by breaking the agreement if it could be certain that the other firms would not break it.

   b) Which of the firms represented in Fig. 22.2 would be most likely to "win" a price war?

5   Can a market be perfectly competitive and at the same time include profit-maximizing firms which have horizontal cost curves? [*Hint:* What output would such a firm produce it it were faced with a horizontal demand curve?]

6   Some years ago, one large automobile maker raised prices on nearly all its models, giving as a reason "We're only trying to meet the competition." What kind of behavior in the automobile industry does this comment suggest?

7   Given an oligopolistic market composed of several firms of different sizes, would you expect the price leader (if there is one) to be a large or a small firm? Would your answer be different if you knew that one of the firms, though quite small in the local market, also operated in a number of other markets?

8   Do you think that product differentiation would work to weaken the bonds of mutual dependence that link rival oligopolists? How sensitive would your own purchases be to shifts in the prices of differentiated products produced by rival oligopolists?

9   Until recently the four theaters in Ithaca, N.Y., formed an oligopolistic market. Three were owned by one firm; the fourth was operated independently. Then the independent theater was purchased by the same firm which owned the other three, thus forming what was for all practical purposes a monopoly. Immediately thereafter the admission price at all of the theaters was raised from $1.00 to $1.50. What does this price increase suggest about the competitive solution that was attained in the original oligopolistic situation? Were the theaters maximizing profits as a group before the purchase of the independent theater?

10 Suppose that the Able Company operates as a price leader in a certain industry, and suppose that the following assumptions hold:

i) Every firm, including the Able Company, has increasing marginal costs beyond some level of output.

ii) Market demand for the industry's product is downward-sloping.

iii) All firms other than the Able Company will accept the price charged by Able and will act as price takers, so long as they are able to sell their entire output at that price.

iv) If the other firms are unable to sell their output at Able's price, a price war will develop, to the detriment of all involved.

Now answer the following questions.

a) Assuming that the Able Company wishes to maintain its leadership, when it is deciding what price to charge, it must take into account the outputs that the other firms in the industry would choose to produce at that price. Show that the effective demand curve facing the Able Company, and the curve that is consistent with maintaining its leadership, can be derived from the market demand curve by subtracting, at each price, the quantity that the other firms, as price takers, would supply.

b) Show that the effective demand curve derived in part (a) will be flatter (if price is measured on the vertical axis) than the market demand curve.

c) Show that if the Able Company uses this effective demand curve in determining its profit-maximizing output and price, then the market as a whole will be cleared.

d) How do price and quantity produced in the market as a whole compare in this situation with the corresponding results that would occur if the Able Company were a monopolist?

e) Do you think that the construction we have used here gives stable results? That is, would the Able Company and the other firms be likely to accept such a solution?

f) Does the Able Company, as a result of its position as price leader, have an advantage over the other firms in this situation?

CHAPTER 23

*MONOPOLISTIC COMPETITION

A monopolistically competitive market is one in which both buyers and sellers are numerous, but the output is differentiated.

As we pointed out in Chapter 19, *a product is said to be differentiated if buyers distinguish in any way the output of one seller from that of another.* In markets in which the output is a material *good,* such distinctions may be based on physical properties, such as color and design, or on identifying characteristics, such as brand names and trademarks. On the other hand, in markets in which the output is a *service* (for example, dry cleaning, repairs, or retailing) such distinctions may be based on store location, personality of the proprietor, convenience of his facilities, size of his stock, and so forth.

In a given market, two conditions must be met in order for monopolistic competition to develop:

1) The product must offer some basis, however slight, on which the output of one seller may be differentiated from that of another.
2) The range of output over which individual producers attain economies of scale must be small enough relative to total industry output so that seller manyness is possible.

There are many examples of monopolistic competition. Often, however, industries which produce a differentiated product are also characterized by seller fewness. In such a case, an industry must be classified under *differentiated oligopoly* rather than under *monopolistic competition.* The automobile, liquor, typewriter, and office-equipment industries are differentiated oligopolies because they exhibit product differentiation plus seller fewness. The

---

* This chapter may be omitted without losing continuity. The idea of monopolistic competition was originated by Edward Chamberlain in *The Theory of Monopolistic Competition,* Cambridge, Mass.: Harvard University Press, 1933.

garment, textile, and wood-products industries are examples of monopolistic competition because they exhibit product differentiation plus seller manyness.

The service industries often combine product differentiation with seller manyness, so they too provide examples of monopolistic competition. However, because each of these industries sells its products in many differently structured markets, each provides examples not only of monopolistic competition, but also of differentiated oligopoly and even of monopoly. Example: The gasoline retailing industry: (a) Many firms in this industry operate on the fringes of large cities and have numerous nearby competitors. Thus they are monopolistic competitors. (b) Many others operate in small towns and have few competitors. Thus they are differentiated oligopolists. (c) Finally, a few firms operate alone in isolated areas, and are for all intents and purposes local monopolists.

The incidence of monopolistic competition in the United States today is difficult to gauge, since any assessment of the relative importance of different market structures in the economy must be based on rough estimates. Our observations in Chapter 19 do, however, indicate that in practice relatively few industries meet the polar conditions of either monopoly or perfect competition. Most manufacturing industries could probably be classified as oligopolies, while monopolistic competition is probably more typical in the service trades.

THE EQUILIBRIUM OF AN INDIVIDUAL MONOPOLISTIC COMPETITOR

Our definition of a monopolistically competitive market (numerous buyers and sellers, a differentiated product) tells us several things about the position of an individual monopolistic competitor.

First: The fact that buyers and sellers are numerous tells us that each monopolistic competitor must face a definite demand curve for his output. *Second:* The fact that the monopolistic competitor's output is differentiated from that of his competitors tells us that this demand curve must slope downward. To prove this second and less obvious result, note that if a monopolistic competitor raises his price relative to the prices charged by his competitors, he'll lose some customers who are unwilling to pay a higher price, but he'll retain others who strongly prefer his output to that of his competitors. Similarly, if he lowers his price, he'll lure some customers away from his competitors, but only those who do not strongly prefer his competitors' outputs to his own.

In a market in which a homogeneous product is sold, *seller numerousness* (as we pointed out in Chapter 13) implies that a single seller is unable by his actions to perceptibly influence market price, and therefore *he takes market price as given.* In a market in which a differentiated product is sold, however, the fact that each seller faces a downward-sloping demand curve, means that he must *choose* the price at which he will sell his output. Therefore, in a monopolistically competitive market, seller numerousness means that each firm knows that its competitors are so numerous that any price change it makes will draw a negligible response from them, and that each seller views, the demand curve for his output as given, in the sense that no price change he initiates could cause this curve to shift position.*

Since the demand curve facing an individual monopolistic competitor slopes downward, it follows that his profit-maximizing output is determined by the intersection of a downward-sloping MR curve with his MC curve. Thus the equilibrium price and output of the monopolistic competitor whose cost and revenue curves are shown in Fig. 23.1 are p^0 and q^0, respectively.

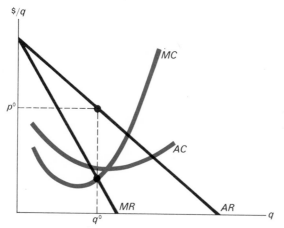

23|1

The equilibrium of an individual profit-maximizing monopolistic competitor.

THE EQUILIBRIUM OF A GROUP OF MONOPOLISTIC COMPETITORS

Whenever a group of monopolistic competitors attains equilibrium, the firms in this group usually charge different prices and produce different quantities of output. Why? The fact that their outputs differ indicates that the demand (or cost) curves facing the individual firms differ. Hence the price–output combinations that maximize the profits of these different producers also differ.

---

* Contrast the position of the monopolistic competitor with that of the oligopolist who (as we said in Chapter 22) knows that if he alters his price significantly his rivals will respond with significant price changes of their own, and hence demand for his own output will shift.

We can characterize the equilibrium output of a group of monopolistic competitors and the range of prices at which they will sell this output as follows: Consider a monopolistically competitive industry* in which there are no entry barriers.† Whenever profits in such an industry are widespread new firms will enter the industry, and industry output will rise. On the other hand, whenever losses in the industry are widespread, existing firms will leave, and industry output will fall. Therefore a monopolistically competitive industry in which exit and entry are free will attain an enduring or long-run equilibrium only when there is no tendency for firms to either enter or leave the industry.

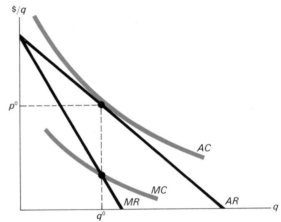

23|2

The zero-profit equilibrium of the *marginal firm* in a monopolistically competitive market.

This state will be attained whenever the *marginal* (i.e., least profitable) firm in that industry has profits precisely equal to zero. Since both the demand and the cost curves of producers in a monopolistically competitive industry may vary, the marginal producer in such an industry need not be the one with the highest costs; he might simply be a low-cost producer for whose output demand is weak. In any case his zero-profit equilibrium (see Fig. 23.2) is located at the point at which his AC curve is tangent to his AR curve.

Given that the number of firms has been adjusted as described above, we can (a) determine the industry's *equilibrium output* by summing up the equilibrium outputs of all firms that are active in the industry, and (b) determine the *range of equilibrium prices* at which this output will be sold by comparing the equilibrium prices charged by these firms.

---

*Here we use the word industry to refer to a group of competing firms that produce outputs that are close substitutes for one another and that sell these outputs in a single market. This market may be national, regional, or local in scope.

† To say that free entry exists in a monopolistically competitive industry implies that new firms are free to produce outputs that are *close substitutes* for, but not identical to, the outputs of firms already active in the industry.

How wide will this range of equilibrium prices be? The answer depends mostly on the degree to which individual producers in the industry succeed in differentiating their outputs. If consumers think that there's a lot of difference between the outputs of competing producers, the demand curves facing these producers will be relatively steep, and the range of prices at which they sell their outputs is likely to be wide. But if consumers consider the outputs of all producers in the industry as almost identical, the demand curves facing these producers will be relatively flat (i.e., almost horizontal), and the range of prices at which they sell their outputs is likely to be narrow.

NONPRICE COMPETITION AND THE
OVERALL EQUILIBRIUM OF A MONOPOLISTIC COMPETITOR

At the beginning of the chapter when we analyzed the way an individual monopolistic competitor maximizes his profits, we proceeded as if his profits depended solely on his price–output decision. The monopolistic competitor, however, is always free to vary his product, either by varying its physical characteristics or by altering the programs he undertakes to promote its sale. Whenever he does so, the demand curve for his output will shift; so will the cost curves associated with producing it. The size of the profit he can earn by producing the quantity of output that equates his marginal revenue with his marginal cost will also be altered. Therefore, to maximize his profits, the monopolistic competitor must make optimal adjustments, not only in the price he charges and the quantity of output he sells, but also in the design of his product and the fashion in which he promotes the sale of it.

Product Variation

*Product variation is any change that alters either the physical characteristics of a product or the conditions under which it is sold.**

How does the monopolistic competitor achieve the precise product variation that will maximize his profits, i.e., how does he attain *product equilibrium?* As we said above, whenever he alters the design of his product, his cost and revenue curves will shift. Therefore he attains product equilibrium as follows:

1) He determines the cost and revenue curves associated with each product he might produce.

---

* Lest you think that product differentiation has to do just with simple things like changing the color of a toothpaste tube, note the following quote from the *Wall Street Journal:* "Negligees [draped across a bed] . . . are becoming a standard gimmick in model-home decoration. 'They stimulate the imagination,' says one designer. 'Anything a builder can do to make people identify with his houses separates him from his competition!'" (*Wall Street Journal,* September 12, 1967, page 1.)

2) On the basis of this information, he determines the maximum profit he could earn by selling each.
3) He selects for actual production that product which will permit him to earn the largest total profit.

Profitable product variation may lead in many directions. A producer might find that a costly change in his product, because it would increase demand for his output, would prove profitable. Or he might find that downgrading his product, because it would lower his costs more than it would lower demand for his output, would increase his profits.

Examples of product variation are easily found: The dry cleaner that offers credit, free pickup and delivery, and free summer storage is trying to maximize its profits by making real but costly improvements in the basic service it offers. The gas station that moves from a cheap location to one that is more expensive, but also more convenient for its customers, is a similar example. An opposite case is the discounter who offers no credit and little sales help; he is a producer who tries to maximize his profits by cutting his prices and downgrading the service he supplies.

Sales Promotion

Sales promotion is comprised of all activities that a producer undertakes specifically to increase (i.e., shift upward) demand for his output.

Sales promotion is obviously closely tied to product variation, and at times it may be difficult to draw a line between the two. (For example, one might ask whether putting a product into a new eye-catching package constitutes product variation or sales promotion.) A monopolistic competitor who wants to find the sales promotion program that will maximize his profits tackles the problem in the same way he does product equilibrium:

1) He identifies the cost and revenue curves associated with each sales promotion program he might undertake.
2) On the basis of these curves, he determines the maximum profit he could earn from each.
3) He selects for actual use that program which will permit him to earn the highest possible profits.

Overall Equilibrium of the Monopolistic Competitor

In our discussion of the way a monopolistic competitor attains equilibrium (i.e., maximizes his profits), we have treated his product-design and sales-promotion decisions separately. In actual practice, of course, these two decisions are interdependent and must therefore be made simultaneously.

Because changes in product design and in sales promotion both shift a producer's cost and revenue curves, we can't show graphically the process by which a monopolistic competitor selects the product-design–sales-promotion combination that will maximize his profits. Instead let us think of him as examining the cost and revenue curves associated with each combination he might adopt, and then selecting the policy that will enable him to earn the largest possible profits.

PROFITS UNDER MONOPOLISTIC COMPETITION

When there is a group of monopolistic competitors, what factors determine how large their profits will be, and how widespread?

The average level of profits of producers in any monopolistically competitive industry depends on whether entry into that industry is free; if it is, then competition from new producers will always force down profits until the profits earned by the marginal firm just equal zero. If entry is *not* free, even the least favorably situated firm in the industry may earn substantial profits.

In a monopolistically competitive industry, as in a perfectly competitive one, some producers earn more profits than others because they enjoy some sort of cost advantage over the others,* and some earn more profits than others because of monopoly elements which make it impossible for their competitors to produce a perfect substitute for their outputs. These monopoly elements thus protect their profits from encroachment by rivals. Such elements include patents on products, patents on production processes, secret formulas, copyrighted brand names or trademarks, and (in the case of distribution outlets) location. But so long as producers in the industry are numerous, competition among them tends to eliminate all firm-to-firm differences in profits except for those caused by these cost differences or monopoly elements.

PROBLEMS

1 Automobile *manufacturers* form a highly concentrated national oligopoly. But what about automobile *dealers?* Are they monopolists, oligopolists, or monopolistic competitors? Does your answer depend on where the dealers are located? [*Hint:* Automobile manufacturers sell in a single national market. In what sorts of markets do automobile dealers sell?] Do competing dealers sell a homogeneous or a differentiated service? [*Hint:* If you wanted to buy a new Chevrolet and there were 5 Chevrolet dealers in town, what sorts of dealer characteristics would interest you when you chose which dealer to buy from?]

---

* Recall the example of the apple growers presented on page 239.

2   Why does the steepness of the demand curves facing individual monopolistic competitors depend on the degree of product differentiation? [*Hint:* Consider shampoo. What range of prices would consumers be willing to pay for a particular brand of shampoo if they thought all shampoos were alike? How would your answer change if consumers thought one brand of shampoo made hair more attractive?]

3   By looking at the prices charged by the various firms in a monopolistically competitive industry, can one determine which firm is the marginal firm? (The term "marginal" was defined in the text.)

4   Consider the sector of the economy consisting of all producers of beverages. Could our analysis of monopolistic competition be applied to this sector as a whole? Could it be applied to the various industries in this sector, i.e., to soft-drink producers, coffee producers, beer producers, and so on?

5   Show graphically the two different results of product variation mentioned in the text:
    a) The upgrading of a product to increase profits.
    b) The downgrading of a product to increase profits.

6   How would a stepped-up advertising program affect a firm's marginal cost curve?

7   Consider firms which sell beer directly to consumers.
    a) What factors do you think give rise to the differences in the prices charged by grocers, liquor stores, taverns, and restaurants for beer?
    b) How do you think legal restrictions on who can buy and sell beer affect the prices charged by different beer sellers?

8   At the time of the 1965 cut in federal excise taxes, there was considerable discussion in Congress as to whether or not these tax cuts would be passed on to the consumer. Do you think that Congress would need to have been concerned over whether or not a cut in excise taxes would be passed on to the consumer if:
    a) the taxed commodity were produced by a monopolist?
    b) the taxed commodity were produced by rival oligopolists?
    c) the taxed commodity were a homogeneous product produced by many firms?
    d) the taxed commodity were a differentiated product produced by many firms?

9   Under what conditions will all firms in a monopolistically competitive industry earn zero profits? If these conditions are fulfilled, will all firms in the industry charge identical prices and produce identical quantities of output? Explain your answer.

10 Note that, in Fig. 23.2, $MR = MC$ at the point at which the AR curve is tangent to the AC curve. Why must this relationship hold?

11 Is it conceivable that a monopolistic competitor would ever practice price discrimination? If so, try to dream up an example.

CHAPTER 24

ECONOMIC INEFFICIENCY
AND ANTITRUST

In Chapter 18 we showed that perfectly competitive markets allocate re-sources efficiently. We also said that imperfectly competitive markets allocate them inefficiently. We shall now talk about the way resource allocation in imperfectly competitive markets could be improved, and what steps the government is taking to achieve this goal.

MONOPOLISTIC RESTRICTION OF OUTPUT

As we have seen, seller fewness and product differentiation are two chief factors in an imperfectly competitive market. Therefore let's focus on the impact these factors have on resource allocation.

Recall that in Chapter 18 we said that, in order for resource allocation to be efficient, all producers must expand their individual outputs to the point

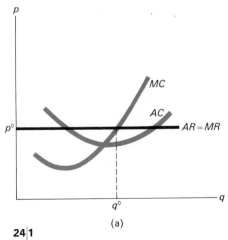

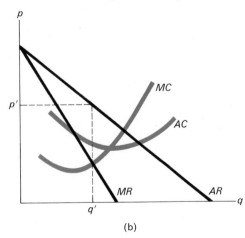

24|1

a) A perfect competitor.

b) An imperfect competitor.

at which the price they receive for their output just equals the marginal cost they incur in producing it. A perfect competitor, like the one whose cost and revenue curves are shown in Fig. 24.1(a), maximizes his profits by producing the output q^0 which equates his marginal cost with the price, p^0, that he receives for it. But monopolists, colluding oligopolists, and monopolistic competitors (see Fig. 24.1b) always maximize their profits by producing an output q' that is *too small* to equate their marginal cost with the price p' that they charge for it.

Thus in any market characterized by seller concentration, product differentiation, or both, output is less than it should be for an efficient allocation of resources. This source of inefficiency in imperfectly competitive markets is known as *monopolistic restriction of output.*

The Incidence of Monopolistic Restriction of Output

Since so many business firms in the United States today are either monopolies, oligopolies, or monopolistic competitors, monopolistic restriction of output is a common phenomenon, and it must cause extensive deviations from optimal output levels. Liu and Hildebrand, in the study cited in Chapter 9, have attempted to measure just how large these deviations are.

As a prelude to discussing their results, let us define the *value of labor's marginal product* (VMP_L) as labor's marginal product times the price obtained for this product. Then it can be shown that:

*Any firm that produces the output that equates marginal cost with price will hire labor up to the point at which the value of labor's marginal product just equals the wage rate.**

This condition, $VMP_L = w$, suggests a way to test for the presence of monopolistic output restriction in any industry: *First,* compute the value of labor's marginal product in that industry. *Second,* compare it with the going wage rate paid by the industry. If the ratio of these two figures (that is, VMP_L/w) equals 1, then the industry is hiring the precise quantity of labor consistent with an efficient allocation of resources. But if the ratio is

---

* Proof: Recall from Chapter 7 that labor's marginal product equals the increase we obtain in total output when we make a small increase in the quantity of labor employed. In symbols, $MP_L = \Delta q/\Delta L$. From this definition we see that the extra labor required to produce an additional unit of output equals $1/MP_L$. Thus, if the cost of hiring a unit of labor equals the wage rate w, the marginal cost of an extra unit of output is given by $MC = w \cdot (1/MP_L) = w/MP_L$.

Suppose now that the output in question is sold at a price equal to marginal cost; that is, that $MC = p$. Then from our two expressions for marginal cost, it follows that $p = w/MP_L$. If we now solve this equation for w, we find that $w = p \cdot MP_L = VMP_L$. This, of course, is the result we set out to prove.

TABLE 24|1

Gauging Monopolistic Restriction of Output in Selected Industries, 1957*

Industry	$\dfrac{VMP_L}{w}$	Required increase in employment to make $(VMP_L/w) = 1$
Food products	1.11	+13%
Apparel	1.14	+23%
Paper products	1.48	+49%
Rubber products	1.49	+72%
Leather products	1.32	+63%
Fabricated metal products	1.26	+77%
Machinery	1.17	+41%
Electrical machinery	1.13	+27%

*These data, except in the case of rubber and leather products, refer to production workers only. (Source: Liu and Hildebrand, op. cit., page 124)

greater than 1, the industry is hiring too little labor for resource allocation to be efficient, i.e., it is engaging in monopolistic restriction of output.

Liu and Hildebrand computed the ratio (VMP_L/w) for a number of industries. Their results (see the first column of Table 24.1) show that monopolistic restriction of output is common in manufacturing but varies in severity from industry to industry. Liu and Hildebrand also estimated the amount by which each industry would have to increase employment in order to eliminate monopolistic restriction of output [i.e., in order to make $(VMP_L/w) = 1$]. The resulting figures (see the second column of Table 24.1) tell a fascinating story: Some industries, in order for resource allocation to be efficient, would have to increase employment by over 70%!

An interesting sidelight to these figures is that all the industries shown here to be employing *too little* labor for resource allocation to be efficient were shown in Table 9.1 to be employing *too much* labor to maximize profits. Thus if any of these industries were to decrease its labor force to a level consistent with profit maximization, it would engage in monopolistic restriction of output to an even greater degree than indicated in Table 24.1.

EXCESS CAPACITY AND HIGH-COST PRODUCTION

Although monopolistic restriction of output is the chief source of inefficiency in imperfectly competitive markets, it is not the only one. A second source is that, in markets controlled by rival oligopolists, competition-limiting agreements (ranging from perfect collusion to some form of price leadership) often make it possible for firms that have excess capacity which they are not using, and firms that are otherwise inefficient, high-cost firms, to keep on producing, even though these firms would otherwise have been eliminated by competition.

A good example of this second sort of inefficiency is provided by the bread industry. As we pointed out earlier, bread (because it is highly perishable) is generally sold within a 50-mile radius of the plant where it is baked. Therefore the market for bread is not a single market, but is splintered into many small local markets, in most of which supply is controlled by a few rival oligopolists.

After World War II a number of changes were made in the technology of bread production. Wholesale bakeries altered their formula for making dough in a way that enabled them to halve baking time, a change which doubled the capacity of their ovens. To match this increase, many bakeries installed additional equipment to facilitate other steps in the breadmaking process. Many bakers who had previously used automated equipment to produce bread dough in batches switched over to continuous-mix equipment. This innovation too increased capacity, since most bakeries that installed continuous-mix equipment continued to keep their automated batch equipment in operation to produce specialty breads. The result of all these changes was a dramatic increase in the industry's *productive capacity*.

This increase, however, was not matched by an equal increase in output. On the contrary, after World War II, per capita consumption of bread actually declined, and the industry was able to maintain its previous output levels only because population increased. The inevitable result of these conflicting trends in capacity and output was the emergence of considerable excess capacity.

The way the bread industry responded to this excess capacity was dictated by several factors. First, bakers recognized that, because demand for their output was inelastic, price competition would not benefit them. Second, the high costs of shipping bread any distance and of the kind of advertising and in-store promotion required to substantially increase a firm's share of the market discouraged bakers from trying to eliminate their rivals. Third, the fact that the demand for bread was static created an entry barrier to the market, because no new producer could enter the industry without displacing an existing firm.

Given these considerations, the oligopolistic rivals who controlled the typical local bread markets responded to excess capacity not by vigorous price competition which by lowering prices and profits would have forced the needed decrease in the number of producers active in the industry—but by an imperfect form of collusion: price leadership. Although in general the firms that have become price leaders in local bread markets are large and efficient producers, they have nevertheless consistently set bread prices high enough to cover not only their own low costs, but also the high costs of small producers.

Thus many small, high-cost producers, who should have been eliminated by competition, have been permitted to survive. Also excess capacity (estimated to run as high as 40–60 percent*) has been perpetuated. As a result most firms are forced to operate at output levels below those at which they could attain minimum cost.

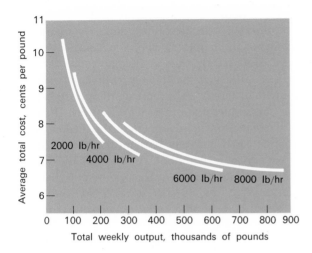

24|2

Average total cost curves for continuous-mix bread plants of different capacity, 1959. (Source: Evans and Walsh, *op. cit.*, page 56)

We can get some idea of the waste of resources caused by the survival of small-scale bakeries and by the forced underutilization of most bread plants from the four curves in Fig. 24.2. These show (1) that large-scale, fully utilized plants incur lower average costs than small-scale plants, and (2) that the costs of any plant, large or small, decrease as this plant's output is increased from zero up to full capacity.

PRODUCT DIFFERENTIATION

So far we have considered only the inefficiency that seller concentration introduces into resource allocation. Product differentiation, another market imperfection, also leads to such inefficiency.

A manufacturer, in order to differentiate his product from other products,† usually spends a lot of money on product design and sales promotion. Many economists argue that most product differentiation does not really widen the consumer's range of choice, that much advertising used to differentiate products is void of useful information or worse still misleading, and that product differentiation is therefore a waste of resources.

---

* Evans and Walsh, *op. cit.*, page 65.

† Sometimes the competing product he's trying to differentiate his product from is a thing he himself makes. Example: Proctor and Gamble makes several different brands of detergent, shampoo, etc.

Whether or not this indictment holds true depends not on the opinions of economists, of course, but on whether or not the availability of differentiated products does significantly widen the consumer's range of choice and on whether or not advertising of differentiated products does give consumers information that they regard as useful. For example, if Smith, who never rides anything more adventurous than the New York subway, enjoys his Marlboros more because rough, tough characters who ride horses over the prairie smoke Marlboros in TV commercials, then such commercials are not necessarily a waste of resources. Similarly, if the Joneses really enjoy getting a new car each year, even though half the time the most significant difference (advertising people call it the "just-noticeable difference") between the new car and the old is the curve of the fender or the placement of the chrome, then annual model changeover, though costly, may not be a waste of resources.

Although the economist who is concerned about public welfare cannot write off product differentiation as pure waste, he can point out that expenditures for differentiation are high, and he can ask: Would you really rather buy differentiated (as opposed to nondifferentiated) products if you knew the true cost of product differentiation? For example, if you knew that Bristol-Myers (makers of Ban deodorant, Ipana toothpaste, Bufferin, Clairol hair coloring, and Drano) spends almost 30% of its total revenue for advertising* (i.e., if you knew that 20¢ out of every dollar you spend on Bristol-Myers products goes to pay for advertising to make you like the product you have just bought and other Bristol-Myers products as well), would you still prefer differentiated products? Or would you rather settle for plain-Jane, undifferentiated products that could be sold at lower cost? Similarly, if you realized that 35% of the price you pay for name-brand bread goes to pay for advertising, in-store promotion, and high delivery cost (high because independent wholesalers deliver small quantities of bread to many markets), would you rather buy grocery-store private-label bread which can be retailed much more cheaply?

If the answers to these questions and similar ones are no, then product differentiation is useful. If they are yes, then product differentiation does waste resources.

GOALS AND POLICIES FOR THE REGULATION OF IMPERFECT COMPETITION

Since seller fewness and product differentiation both interfere with the efficiency of resource allocation, should the government try to improve the performance of markets characterized by these features? If so, what form should such regulation take?

---

* T. A. Wise, "Bristol-Myers' Hard Sell," *Fortune*, February 1967, page 118.

The Regulation of Product Differentiation

The inefficiencies associated with product differentiation are easy to define in theory, but difficult to identify in practice. It would be hard to distinguish between *useful* product differentiation that widens the consumer's range of choice and *wasteful* product differentiation that does not. Therefore *clearly defined, objective* criteria for regulating product differentiation cannot be derived; such regulation would be arbitrary and capricious at best. Prudence thus suggests that the government had better not try. Another factor that militates against regulating product differentiation is its widespread character. If the government were to try to regulate product differentiation, it would have to issue and enforce such a spate of rules that the regulatory program itself might be considered incompatible with a free market economy.

The Regulation of Seller Fewness

Seller fewness, on the other hand, is more susceptible to regulation, at least in the sense that the government (depending on what it wanted to achieve) might be able to regulate seller fewness on the basis of criteria that were objective and measurable.

Suppose that the government were to try to abolish monopolistic restriction of output by regulating seller fewness. A regulation to achieve this aim would have to take into account the cost structure of the industry to be regulated. In an industry in which scale economies were unimportant, the government could simply order large firms to be broken up into many smaller ones; in other words it could transform monopolies and oligopolies into competitive industries. However, in industries characterized by extensive scale economies (for example, the bread, steel, automobile, and many other industries), such a structural remedy would not do. In such industries the government would have to require every firm to produce and sell the quantity of output that would equate its marginal cost with its price.

The above two-pronged solution to the regulation of seller fewness is easily conceived of in theory, but difficulties would arise if one tried to put it into practice. *First,* in industries characterized by extensive economies of scale, some producers who were made to price their output at marginal cost might incur losses. Look at Fig. 24.3, which shows the cost and revenue curves of a certain firm. If there weren't any regulations, this firm would maximize profits by charging the price p^0 and selling the quantity q^0. Now the government steps in and says, "Price your output at marginal cost." The firm would then charge the price p' and sell the output q'; it would also incur a *negative profit* (loss) equal to the area of the shaded rectangle in Fig. 24.3. The possibility of negative profits is a real obstacle to marginal-cost pricing. The government could lick this, however, by redistributing these

losses among consumers and positive-profit firms. It could subsidize firms
which it required to take losses, and it could get the money to do this by
making consumers and positive-profit firms pay lump-sum taxes, determined
according to some equitable formula.

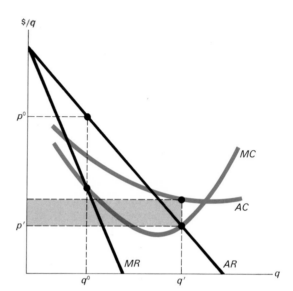

24|3

A producer who is forced to equate
price to marginal cost may incur a loss.

There is a *second* reason why regulation of seller concentration is likely
to prove difficult. Seller concentration is so widespread that any program
designed to regulate it would be incompatible with a free market economy.
This second difficulty is less tractable than the first, and it is therefore likely
to lead the government to adopt some sort of compromise policy. The U.S.
government has done just this: It has chosen to regulate certain industries
that are natural monopolies or oligopolies (we'll define what these are in the
next chapter), while simultaneously trying to limit (but not to eliminate)
seller fewness in other industries.

Other Policy Targets

As we have seen, regulating seller fewness is a potentially useful way to
promote economic efficiency. However, one has to consider its effect on
other targets as well. Of these targets, the most important is continuing
economic growth. We must measure an industry's performance not only in
terms of its contribution to economic efficiency, but also in terms of its
capability of developing new products, improving production processes,
investing in plant and equipment, and in general contributing to an expanding level of total output. There isn't necessarily a conflict between the

two targets of economic efficiency and growth, but such a conflict may arise. There's always the danger that extensive and indiscriminate attacks on seller concentration *per se* might dull profit incentives and thus might have the bad side effect of slowing technological progress and growth.

The regulation of seller concentration is also used to pursue goals other than economic ones, goals which are political, social, or ethical. A frequently mentioned aim is to try, by eliminating excessive monopoly profits, to achieve a distribution of income that is compatible with an egalitarian and democratic society. Another goal, related to this one, is to maintain a distribution of economic power that is politically and socially acceptable. Many proponents of strong antitrust laws say that regulation of seller concentration should be used to prevent a firm from establishing a position of market dominance that would permit it to exploit consumers or unfairly coerce its rivals. They also say that the government must see to it that the small businessman and the newcomer have a fair chance. They say this because they believe that this policy reflects the ideals of the founders of the U.S. and also because they feel that small businessmen contribute strongly to the successful functioning of a democratic society. One last note: For many people, competition is a desirable end in itself.

U.S. ANTITRUST POLICY

Antitrust policy in the United States is based on laws that have been subject to over half a century of judicial review and interpretation. Thus the current interpretation of these laws has evolved not only from the changing attitudes of the courts, but also from the way in which successive attorney generals have tried to enforce these laws and the types of violations they have chosen to prosecute. We cannot hope, in a few pages, to describe current policy in detail. The most we can do is to comment briefly on the major aspects of this policy: the prohibition of collusion that restrains trade, the prohibition of monopolization, and the prohibition of those business practices which promote monopolization.

The Prohibition of Collusion

Federal antitrust activity began with passage of the Sherman Act in 1890. Section 1 of this act bans collusion. It states:

Every contract, combination in the form of trust or otherwise, or conspiracy, in restraint of trade or commerce among the several States or with foreign nations, is hereby declared to be illegal.

To enforce this section of the law, the attorney general may institute either criminal or civil actions against alleged violators. If a criminal conviction is obtained, jail sentences of up to one year and fines of up to $50,000 may be imposed on each guilty firm or person. If a civil conviction is obtained, the court may issue an order enjoining the defendants from continuing their illegal activities. Since the fines resulting from a criminal conviction are too small to have much deterrent power, and since jail sentences have almost never been imposed, the real bite of the Sherman Act is the attorney general's power to bring civil suits and to obtain court injunctions against continued collusion.

It's hard to say just how successful Section I of the Sherman Act has been in regulating collusion. The courts have consistently said that Section 1 prohibits *all* agreements that restrain trade, and they have established no rule to distinguish reasonable (and therefore permissible) agreements from unreasonable (and therefore illegal) ones. Section 1 thus forced an end to overt collusion on the American business scene, and by so doing it ruled out European-type cartels in American industry. The Sherman Act has forced collusion to assume a covert form, and this in itself may be regarded as a benefit, since covert collusion is unlikely to be adequate for perfect cooperation and coordination among rival firms.

On the other hand, the fact that collusion must be covert presents a problem when it comes to enforcement of antitrust laws. To prosecute for covert collusion, the Department of Justice must establish its existence by inference, and it's hard to do that. Consider for example price leadership, a fairly common form of covert collusion. The only overt evidence that price leadership need leave behind is a pattern of suspiciously parallel prices (parallel in the sense that the prices have gone up and down together in a matching pattern). Even this kind of evidence can be tampered with if the colluding firms consciously ripple price, and if they shift the role of price leader from one firm to another. Although one could conceivably view the mere existence of parallel prices as adequate evidence that collusion exists, the courts have not not been willing to do so. They have inferred the existence of collusion only when there has been parallelism *plus* overt acts that pointed to collusion.

Thus Section 1 of the Sherman Act has been useful in policing collusion in industries in which producers are so numerous that collusion is difficult to maintain without creating overt evidence of its existence. But it has been of little use as a deterrent to collusion in oligopolistic industries, because (1) rival producers are so few that tacit collusion can be maintained without generating such overt evidence, and (2) in such industries, collusion may consist of nothing more palpable than the recognition by rival sellers that their prices and profits are mutually dependent. To the extent that this is the case, there isn't any injunction that the courts could issue that would force these rivals to behave independently. In effect the only way to reduce tacit collusion in highly oligopolistic markets is to apply a structural remedy: dissolution or dismemberment of the offending firms.

The Prohibition of Monopolization

Section 2 of the Sherman Act bans monopolization. It states:

Every person who shall monopolize, or attempt to monopolize, or combine or conspire with any other person or persons to monopolize any part of the trade or commerce among the several States, or with foreign nations, shall be deemed guilty of a misdemeanor. . . .

To enforce this section of the law, the attorney general may again resort to either criminal or civil suits. The criminal penalties that may be imposed for Section 2 violations, like those for Section 1 violations, have little deterrent power. Therefore the real teeth of the act are the attorney general's power to bring civil suits and the courts' power to issue remedial orders when violations are found.

In any discussion of Section 2 of the Sherman Act, the question arises: What does *monopolize* mean? One answer is that "to monopolize" means to exercise a monopoly or near-monopoly over the supply of some commodity; thus "monopolize" is a structural concept. This interpretation, however, has not been accepted by the courts, as evidenced by their unwillingness to find that the near-monopolies exercised by Eastman Kodak and other companies in their respective industries constitute violations of Section 2.

Historically the courts have interpreted monopolization to mean a successful attempt by one firm (or by several firms acting jointly) to establish or maintain a monopoly when such an attempt was accompanied by "unreasonable" restraint of trade, that is, by collusion or by exclusionary or predatory tactics. Since the courts' rule of reason leaves the creation and maintenance of monopoly through normal and prudent business practices in the realm of legal acts, it sharply limits the breadth of regulation that may be undertaken under Section 2.

In this respect, however, the 1945 Alcoa case may have been an important turning point: The courts found that Alcoa's near-monopoly over the supply of primary aluminum and its pursuit of certain normal and prudent business practices designed to exclude competition (e.g., the expansion of capacity in excess of demand and the preemptive buying of inputs) constituted monopolization and thus violated Section 2.

When the courts have found violations of Section 2, they have taken a variety of remedial actions. In many instances they have issued orders enjoining the guilty firms from continuing certain illegal activities, such as collusion or the practice of predatory or exclusionary tactics. They have also issued orders requiring that guilty firms henceforth act in ways designed to promote competition within their industry. For example, in cases in which firms have become monopolies by virtue of their ownership of certain patents, the courts have ordered offending firms to license at no cost, or at a minimal cost, all firms desiring to use this patent.

Remedial orders of this sort, like those imposed on Section 1 violators, are obviously designed primarily to modify the behavior of sellers in an industry, but not to modify the structure of that industry. In a few cases, however, when the tactics used by firms to create or defend their monopoly positions have been particularly vicious or objectionable, the courts have dissolved the offending firms. For example, Standard Oil and American Tobacco were both broken up in 1911. In general, however, the courts have been loath to impose such a drastic remedy. Thus in 1946, when the courts decided that tacit collusion among the three largest U.S. cigarette producers constituted a violation of Section 2, they issued no remedial order, nor could they conceive of any. This was so because they were unwilling to dissolve these firms; and no conceivable court injunction could have forced these firms to behave independently.

Because of the courts' narrow interpretation of the meaning of monopolization and their unwillingness to resort to structural remedies, the usefulness of Section 2 of the Sherman Act in attacking business concentration has been limited. This act has not been effective in preventing mergers that substantially lessened competition, because the courts have viewed mergers as "reasonable" if they produced benefits such as increased efficiency in production. Also, as indicated above, Section 2 has been powerless to prevent the creation or maintenance by normal business practices of monopoly or highly concentrated oligopoly. The courts' tendency to view the existence of a few undisturbed competitors in an industry dominated by one large firm (or several of them) as proof that these dominant firms are not trying to monopolize the industry has encouraged a live-and-let-live attitude that may have actually weakened competition in some industries.

The Clayton Act

Dissatisfaction with the Sherman Act, whose impact fell far short of the hopes of its original supporters, led to the passage in 1914 of the Clayton Act. This act was designed to prohibit certain business practices that would substantially lessen competition, and is enforceable either by the Federal Trade Commission, which can issue cease-and-desist orders, or by the Department of Justice, which can bring civil suits to obtain a court injunction requiring that the defendants cease their illegal activities.

Section 2 of the Clayton Act bans various forms of price discrimination. This ban, especially in its amended form (the Robinson-Patman Act of 1936), was designed to protect the little fellow, but it may do more to restrain than to promote competition. We shall discuss this in Chapter 25.

Section 3 of the Clayton Act prohibits *tying agreements* and *exclusive-dealing contracts* whenever such agreements would "substantially lessen competition." A tying agreement is one in which a seller agrees to supply a given product only on the condition that the buyer also purchase other goods from him. An exclusive-dealing arrangement requires that a buyer of one seller's goods agree not to purchase or deal in the outputs of rival sellers.

Both tying and exclusive-dealing contracts are common, particularly in distribution. Such agreements constitute a significant barrier to entry and thus to competition in a number of industries, including the automobile industry. In interpreting the Clayton Act ban on exclusive dealing and tying arrangements, however, the courts have held that such agreements "substantially lessen competition" and are thus illegal *only* when one of the firms which practices them also holds a dominant position in the market in question. This interpretation has limited the range of situations to which Section 2 of the Clayton Act is applicable.

Section 7 of the Clayton Act prohibits mergers that would substantially lessen competition. Because of a technicality this prohibition was easily circumvented until it was amended in 1950 by the Celler-Kefauver Act. Since then antimerger actions by the Department of Justice and the Federal Trade Commission have become an important part of antitrust policy. In ruling on such actions the courts have generally taken the stand that a merger between any group of firms whose combined market share exceeded 15% would substantially lessen competition and should therefore not be permitted. Successful enforcement of this part of the Clayton Act could play an important role in maintaining the competitive character of those U.S. industries that are not already characterized by a high degree of seller concentration.

The Federal Trade Commission Act

The final major piece of Federal antitrust legislation is the Federal Trade Commission Act. The purpose of this act, which was passed in 1914, is to establish standards for fair, ethical, nondeceptive competition in business. Thus many Federal Trade Commission (FTC) actions have to do with protecting the consumer from business practices that are misleading or injurious. For example, in recent action the FTC has tried to get producers of consumer goods to end "cents-off" and "bonus-pack" advertising on the grounds that such offers are often made for so long that "there's no regular price and alleged reductions of the regular price are false and misleading." The FTC has also promoted curbs on cigarette advertising and wants such advertising to carry warnings of the health hazards associated with smoking.

The FTC Act was not intended to be an antitrust act, but the courts have interpreted its prohibition of "unfair" competition as a prohibition of agreements that restrain trade. On the basis of this interpretation, the FTC has actively entered the antitrust field (the Clorox case mentioned below resulted from an FTC challenge).

Conglomerates and Antitrust Policy

Prior to World War II most mergers were either *horizontal** (a horizontal merger occurs when one firm buys out another that produces an identical or complementary output) or *vertical* (a vertical merger occurs when one firm buys out another that supplies its inputs or buys its outputs). Since World War II, however, the *conglomerate* merger (a merger between firms producing totally unrelated products) has become increasingly prevalent.

Sometimes conglomerate mergers are undertaken to reduce seasonal, cyclical, and other risks associated with the principal operations of the acquiring firm. (For example, a capital goods producer might attempt to even out the cyclical bumps in his traditional business by diversifying into a noncyclical line. It may sound improbable, but Buckeye Steel Castings, a producer of railroad equipment, went into the production of plastic baby goods for precisely this reason!) More often conglomerate mergers are undertaken simply because they are a profitable investment for the acquiring firm. This is especially likely when the acquiring firm is—as often happens—a large one which through infusions of capital and managerial skills can dramatically improve the profitability of the smaller firms it acquires.

Conglomerates today are large, powerful, and profitable, and are growing at an unprecedented pace. Naturally their intrusion into the economic scene and their rapid growth raises antitrust questions. Should the government oppose the expansion of this free-form type of business organization or should it allow conglomerates to grow so long as they stay diversified and do not attempt to monopolize any one field?

The answer presumably hinges on whether conglomerate mergers subtract from or add to competition. Conglomerates, in order to make sure that they do not run afoul of antitrusters, usually avoid buying out firms that are leaders in their industry. Instead they buy out second- and third-rung firms and then attempt—by providing these firms with capital, engineering skills, and managerial talent—to make them into first-rung, highly profitable firms. To the extent that this occurs, however, conglomerate mergers are likely to increase, not decrease, competition.

The Department of Justice has yet to pronounce policy on conglomerate mergers. The government has, however, opposed several conglomerate mergers which seemed to threaten either competition or the public interest. The FTC, in a precedent-setting case, opposed the acquisition of Clorox (a maker of household bleach) by Proctor and Gamble, even though P and G had no bleach line of its own. The FTC contended, and the courts accepted the thesis, that the acquisition of Clorox by P and G would substantially les-

---

* Horizontal, vertical, and conglomerate mergers were discussed at the end of Chapter 11. If you skipped this chapter, you may at this point find it useful to turn back and read pages 182–184, which deal with mergers.

sen competition in the bleach industry for two reasons: First, P and G was a large firm which, given its product line, might logically have gone into bleach production on its own. Second, P and G, because it was one of the nation's large advertisers, would have been able through promotional activities to create a consumer preference for Clorox that would have dissuaded new entrants into the bleach industry, and that would have discouraged active competition from companies already in the industry.

A second key instance in which the government has opposed a large conglomerate merger was the proposed merger of the American Broadcasting Company into the International Telephone and Telegraph Company. Here one important issue raised by the Department of Justice was whether or not ABC, if it were to become part of a large conglomerate firm, would be able to or be permitted to preserve its independence and its integrity, especially as a broadcaster of news.

PROBLEMS

1 In early 1967 Bristol-Myers was producing three different toothpastes, three different headache remedies, and a host of competing deodorants in spray, mist, and roll-on form. Why do you think that Bristol-Myers and many other companies find it profitable to introduce new products that compete directly with products they already sell? Would a perfect competitor ever find it useful to do so?

2 "Product differentiation turns out to be a profitable tactic for the firms that pursue it only because consumers are ignorant and susceptible to the persuasive appeals of individual sellers." Discuss.

3 "Patents and copyrights, since they establish monopolies, conflict directly with the procompetitive goals of antitrust policy and should therefore be abolished." Discuss this proposition. Is there something "unfair" about giving an author a temporary monopoly over his output? Do you think that granting patents and copyright monopolies sometimes stimulates creative activities and thus adds to society's total output? In other words, is it possible that market imperfections may add to rather than subtract from total output? If so, does the proposition that an optimal allocation of resources must be an efficient one need qualification?

4 Verify that the area of the shaded rectangle in Fig. 24.3 represents the loss incurred by the firm in producing the output q'. For this to be true, must AC be average variable cost or average total cost?

5 It is sometimes claimed that advertising stimulates the economy. Yet advertising, insofar as it contributes to product differentiation, may also be a source of inefficiency. Are these two effects of advertising necessarily inconsistent?

6 In the text we discussed various types of *seller* regulation intended to improve economic efficiency. Since much inefficiency arises as the result of downward-

sloping demand curves facing individual producers, it seems that it might be possible to employ *buyer* regulation instead.

a) Can you think of any ways in which this might be done? [*Hint:* Which side of the market is directly affected by a price ceiling?]

b) Do such forms of buyer regulation as age limits on tobacco purchases and insurance requirements for car ownership improve or lessen economic efficiency?

7   In the text we stated that a pattern of parallel prices in an industry might be viewed as evidence of collusion. However, we also know that all producers in a perfectly competitive industry will charge the same price. What qualification must be made (and was made implicitly in the text) if parallel pricing is to be used as conclusive evidence of collusion?

8   Discuss the following dialog between Senator Kefauver and Mr. Roger Blough, who heads the giant U.S. Steel.

SENATOR KEFAUVER: ". . . if the prices [charged by different steel companies for the same product] are different, that is not competition?"

MR. BLOUGH: "I would say that the buyer in that situation has this choice. He chooses to buy from one company at $5 higher . . . he chooses to buy from our company at $5 lower. Now if you call that competition and a desirable form of competition, you may have it your way. I say that the buyer has more choice when the other fellow's price matches our price . . ."

(Hearings before the Subcommittee on Antitrust and Monopoly of the Committee on the Judiciary, U.S. Senate, 85th Congress, pages 312–313.)

9   Comment on the reasoning behind, and the effects you would expect to follow from, the following Supreme Court decision: "In a 6-to-2 decision, the High Court said national companies that cut prices selectively in local or regional markets may be held liable in private antitrust actions even if a smaller company continues to hold the dominant position in the market." (*Wall Street Journal,* April 25, 1967)

10   Often the costs a company incurs in defending itself in antitrust violation suits are many times higher than the fine it would have to pay if it were found guilty. What impact do you think this has on the effectiveness of antitrust laws?

CHAPTER 25

THE REGULATION OF
COMPETITION

In Chapter 24 we discussed government policies to limit seller concentration and promote competition. Despite its generally procompetitive orientation, the government, surprisingly enough, also has policies that restrain competition, although their stated purpose may be something else. They are generally set up to cope with situations in which government policy makers deem competition "unworkable" or "excessive," or in which society feels that the incomes and economic bargaining power of certain groups should be protected and strengthened.

To analyze the kinds of anticompetitive policies the government has pursued, we shall examine government regulation in three areas: public utilities, the distributive trades, and agriculture.

THE REGULATION OF PUBLIC UTILITIES

Natural Monopolies and Oligopolies

In certain industries, limiting seller concentration is not a satisfactory way to protect the public interest. In these industries, efficient production requires high seller concentration; in some cases it even requires monopoly. Industries in which efficient production requires high seller concentration are known as *natural monopolies* or *oligopolies*.

In any local market the provision of water, gas, electricity, and telephone services are all natural monopolies, because economies of scale are high in the production of such services and because competition between rival producers would result in an irritating and wasteful duplication of facilities. No consumer wants the telephones of five competing companies lined up in his living room or three sets of electric wires running into his house. Examples of natural oligopolies are provided by competing forms of public transportation (e.g., trains, buses, and airlines) and by competing radio or television stations.

The Need for Regulation

Natural monopolies and oligopolies could of course be allowed to operate in complete freedom, but experience suggests that this would be unsatisfactory for a number of reasons: (1) It would expose the consumer to exploitation through monopoly pricing. (2) It would not guarantee that vital services such as water and electricity would be provided to consumers on the continuing and broad basis that public interest demands. (3) In most of the industries in question, fixed costs are high relative to variable costs, and therefore price competition would prove unworkable unless producers were numerous.

For these and other reasons, many natural monopolies and oligopolies have been designated *public utilities* and subjected to public regulation. Such regulation usually follows a fairly definite pattern. First, only a single firm (or several firms) are franchised to produce and sell a certain service or commodity. In exchange for this monopoly or near-monopoly, the firm or firms must submit to continued regulation by a government-appointed commission. Utilities that serve intrastate markets are usually regulated by state public-utility commissions, while utilities that serve interstate markets are regulated by Federal commissions. The principal Federal regulatory commissions are always making news, so their names are probably familiar to you. Their functions, however, may not be. The Federal Communications Commission (FCC) is responsible for regulating companies that provide interstate telephone and telegraph services. The Interstate Commerce Commission (ICC) regulates interstate railroads and truckers. The Civil Aeronautics Board (CAB) regulates domestic airlines. And the Federal Power Commission (FPC) regulates the interstate sale of electricity and the interstate pipelines through which natural gas is transmitted.

Pitfalls and Problems in Utility Regulation

Whenever a state or federal commission regulates an industry, its goal should be to ensure that the industry operates in the public interest; that is, that it operates at minimum cost, that it engages in marginal cost pricing, that it expands capacity as rapidly as needed, and that it constantly tries to improve the services it provides.

The idea of regulating natural monopolies and oligopolies so that they serve the public interest is a simple and an appealing one, but it turns out to raise a lot of problems. One problem is that regulatory commissions are fully effective only if they have an adequate-sized staff, composed of dedicated people whose skills and knowledge match those of the personnel of the regulated companies. Unfortunately, staffs of this size and caliber cost much more than most states are willing to spend. As a result, relations between regulatory commissions and regulated industries are usually an uneven struggle, in which all the advantages that money can buy (including top-flight people) are stacked on the side of the regulated industries.

A second factor that restricts the effectiveness of public-utility commissions is the fact that their powers are limited. About all a commission can do is to control the prices charged by the companies it regulates. It is supposed to set the prices high enough so that the companies can earn a "reasonable" rate of return (often interpreted as being 6 to 8%) on their invested capital.

This means, of course, that the revenues received by regulated firms tend to be calculated on a cost-plus basis, and as a result regulated firms lack the incentives that nonregulated firms have to minimize costs. Also, if regulated companies, because they lack such incentives, adopt inefficient high-cost methods of production, there is little that a public-utility commission can do to force them to switch to more efficient ones.

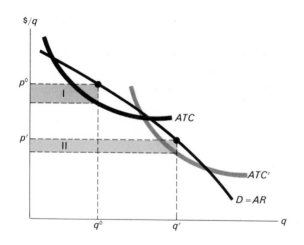

25|1

Regulation, to be effective, would require a regulated monopolist to expand investment, lower price, and raise output.

Another cross that a public-utility commission has to bear is that it cannot control the investments made by the firms it regulates. Let us consider a simple example: The cost and revenue curves in Fig. 25.1 are those of a regulated natural monopolist. Initially this firm produces the output q^0, charges the price p^0, and earns profits represented by the shaded rectangle labeled I. By substantially increasing its investment in plant and equipment this firm could lower its average total cost curve from ATC to ATC'.* If it operated on the curve ATC', it could—by producing the output q'—earn profits represented by the shaded rectangle labeled II. Suppose that these profits were enough to yield the regulated firm the same "reasonable" return

---

* As we saw in Chapter 10, when a firm invests in additional plant and equipment, its short-run cost curves will shift rightward and perhaps downward.

on invested capital that it earned by producing q^0. Then the proposed expansion would serve the public interest without harming those of the firm. But management in the regulated firm might fail to undertake the needed expansion because of inertia or fear of risk. In that case, the commission responsible for regulating this firm, given its own limited powers, could only accept the firm's decision to follow an investment policy that would keep price undesirably high and output undesirably low.

Problems in the Regulation of Natural Oligopolies

Public-utility commissions often have to regulate not a single monopolist, but a group of rival oligopolists. This is a complicated task because, when more than one firm produces an industry's output, the regulatory commission cannot assure that this output will be produced at minimum cost simply by requiring each producer to adopt the most efficient (i.e., lowest-cost) methods of production possible. The commission also must make sure that (1) all firms in the industry incur identical marginal costs,* and (2) the number of firms in the industry is adjusted so that each produces just enough output to realize full economies of scale in production.

Oligopolists in a regulated industry often produce outputs that are substitutes for outputs produced by firms in other industries. For example, airlines produce transportation services that are substitutes for those produced by railroads, long-haul truckers, and even ocean shippers. Whenever rival *oligopolies*† produce substitute services, it is important that each of these services be priced at marginal cost. If some are not, resources will be allocated inefficiently. To take a case in point, if airline prices are set above marginal cost, while railroad prices are set below marginal cost, too many shippers will use trains, too few will use planes, and society will end up devoting more resources to railroads and fewer to air transport than it should. As we have already noted, in the U.S. different modes of transportation are regulated by different commissions (e.g., the railroads and long-haul truckers are regulated by the ICC, the airlines by the CAB, the gas pipelines by the FCC, and so forth). This condition is an unfortunate one because it almost guarantees that dissimilar policies will be used to price competitive transportation services, and society's allocation of resources to transportation will therefore be inefficient.

The regulation of competing oligopolies is difficult enough under normal conditions, but it poses especially tough problems whenever sweeping technological changes occur. To illustrate: Suppose that producers in a regulated industry face the demand curve D shown in Fig. 25.2, that they price

---

* Recall that we showed in Fig. 22.2 that to minimize *joint* costs rival oligopolists must equate their marginal costs.

† That is, oligopolistic industries.

their output at p^0, and that they earn "reasonable" profits equal to the area of the shaded rectangle drawn between the curves AC and D. Now suppose that a technological change occurs which permits producers in a second related industry to provide a new service that would compete directly with the service produced by these firms; this new service, let us say, is introduced and priced at marginal cost. Then demand for the service produced by firms in the first industry would drop from D to D', that is, to a level at which these firms would no longer be able to operate profitably. The public-utility commission responsible for regulating the two industries can either (a) require the innovating producers to price their new service at marginal cost, which will thus doom firms in the first industry to a rapid demise, or (b) seek out some alternative solution that will permit the continued survival of firms in both industries.

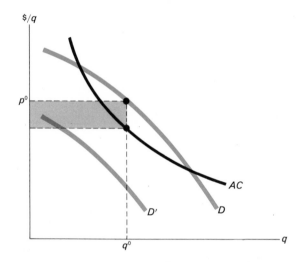

25|2

Introduction of a new, low-cost, competing product lowers demand for the output of the firm whose AC curve is shown here.

Unfortunately for some utilities, but fortunately for consumers, the problem is far from theoretical; in fact, it happens all the time. For example, just a few years ago most experts thought that synchronous satellites would be useful for communication only in the distant future. Then in 1965 Comsat orbited Early Bird, a synchronous satellite that provided 240 overseas circuits. This capacity alone represented a 20% increase in the total number of circuits connecting the U.S. with overseas points, and soon Comsat will be orbiting 1200-circuit satellites!

What is exciting to the consumer and disturbing to some producers about communications satellites is not just that they work, but that they provide overseas circuits at a fraction of the cost that undersea cables do. In fact, satellite circuits are so cheap relative to cable circuits that, if Comsat were to price its services at marginal cost, the international record carriers who specialize in data transmission by ocean cable would be out of business overnight. Simultaneously AT&T and the European telephone companies would find the profitability of their expensive transatlantic cables severely threatened. Also Americans vacationing in Europe would find that it was a lot cheaper to call home these days than it used to be.

The pricing policy that Comsat and the communications companies that compete with and complement it will follow depends not only on what the FCC decides but also on the attitudes adopted by European governments, which, after all, operate the phones at the other end of the overseas circuits that Comsat would like to open up.

Comsat with its new low-cost technology raises questions not only about the price that should be charged for international communication services, but also about the prices that should be charged for domestic data transmission and telephone calls. It also tells us something about the American approach to regulation: whenever a regulatory commission sets the profits a firm may earn as a percent of the firm's total invested capital, it may discourage this firm from making *capital-saving* innovations. Thus, for example, the FCC's recent ruling that AT&T's profits on interstate services should be limited to $7\frac{1}{2}\%$ of invested capital may be partly responsible for the less-than-enthusiastic way in which AT&T has gone about exploring the possibilities of using capital-saving satellites to provide domestic communication services.

REGULATION OF DISTRIBUTION

In our discussion of government regulation of natural monopolies and oligopolies, we focused on government intervention in industries, in which technology requires high seller concentration. The government, however, has also intervened in areas of economic activity in which technology is consistent with seller manyness and in which sellers are many. One such area is the distributive trades. Congress and the state legislatures have enacted many measures designed to limit competition in the distributive trades. Why was such legislation called for? What ends has it served? Is it satisfactory?

The Initial Problem

Let's look at the problems that such legislation sought to solve. After World War I the distributive trades began to undergo a structural evolution. There emerged a new breed of distributors who, by introducing mass distribution techniques, achieved large and hitherto unexploited economies of scale. Frequently these new-breed distributors—and new-style retailers—established chains of stores in different areas. They often did their own wholesaling also (i.e., they *vertically integrated* retailing and wholesaling). Some (notably the large chains) even began to produce a portion of the goods they sold (i.e., they vertically integrated manufacturing, wholesaling, and retailing under a single corporate roof). The new-breed distributors, by introducing self-service stores and eliminating credit and delivery, also created streamlined, low-cost services that competed with the more elaborate, high-cost services that the established independents had been offering for years.

As mass distribution techniques and new low-cost services were introduced into retailing, the large stores grabbed an increasing share of the total market for distribution services, and many small, formerly prosperous independents felt the pinch in their profits. If these small firms had responded to change by moving rapidly into other lines, there would have been no problem. Many, however, were unwilling or unable to do so, and as a result they suffered chronically depressed earnings.

These firms—as any student of human nature could have predicted—attributed their problems not the the fact that they were being displaced by a superior form of business organization, but to the fact that large sellers enjoyed "unfair" advantages and engaged in unfair practices, and that competition in the industry was "excessive." To cure this situation the small retailers organized and lobbied for protection.

Legislative Remedies

As the depression of the 1930's deepened, the retailers' pleas for aid increased. Congress and the state legislatures finally responded by passing certain measures whose principal, if unavowed, purpose was to restrict competition in the distributive trades and in particular to restrict the growth of large integrated distributors.

Chain-store taxes. One means by which state legislatures sought to aid independent retailers was to impose special taxes on chain stores. These taxes, despite their discriminatory character, did little to stem the growth of chain stores. Today they remain on the books in relatively few states.

Fair-trade laws. A second means was to adopt state "fair-trade" laws. The typical state fair-trade law had two principal features: (1) It permitted a manufacturer to enter into resale-price agreements with retailers, stipulating that the retailer could not sell the product at a price below the one specified in the agreement. (2) It provided that, so long as some retailers signed such an agreement, all other retailers were bound to abide by the terms of this agreement. In effect fair-trade laws set up a mechanism by which individual manufacturers, acting together with a small minority of retailers, could engage in extensive price fixing at the retail level.

On paper the fair-trade laws of the 1930's were potent. In practice, however, their impact has been limited, for several reasons: (1) Fair trade has proved workable only in lines in which products are sharply differentiated in the consumer's mind. Thus fair trade has been widely practiced in the sale of drugs, liquor, and appliances, which consumers frequently buy by brand, but not in the sale of food and clothing, where brand names are less important. (2) Chain stores have circumvented fair-trade laws by selling at discount prices goods produced to their own specifications and marketed under their own private labels. (3) The states themselves have not assumed the enforcement of fair-trade prices but have left this up to the manufacturers of fair-traded products. (4) The courts in a number of states have in recent years declared fair-trade laws or parts of them unconstitutional. In fact, fair trade laws are today fully effective in fewer than 20 states.

The Robinson-Patman Act. On the Federal level, the most important legislation to limit competition in distribution is the Robinson-Patman Act, passed in 1936 as an amendment to the Clayton Act. Its most important provision forbids manufacturers to sell to large buyers at lower prices than to small buyers, unless they can prove that it costs them more to fill orders to small buyers than to large buyers. This provision was designed to prevent large chain stores from using their extra bargaining strength (*monopsony* power in the jargon of Chapter 21) to extract discriminatory price concessions from sellers. The Robinson-Patman Act also forbids manufacturers to grant brokerage allowances to large buyers, even when cost differences justify such allowances. This provision is more difficult to justify than the first, since it actively discriminates against large buyers.

Although Robinson-Patman is still on the books, it has been widely circumvented by the large buyers and chain stores against which it was directed. Chain stores frequently order specially designed, private-label products from manufacturers, and on such products they are free to bargain for the best price they can get. Also many chains have purchased or set up production facilities and actually manufacture private-label merchandise.

The Record of Regulation

The effectiveness of much of the legislation designed to limit competition in distribution, as we have pointed out, has been lessened by the fact that it was easily circumvented, and thus its success in curbing the growth of large retailers has also been vitiated. The desirability of even its limited results can be questioned, because much of this legislation was misguided, for two reasons: (1) It failed to recognize that the real root of the distress suffered by small retailers was neither excessive competition nor the monopsony power of large retailers, but the laggard pace at which redundant sellers were leaving the industry (i.e., in the immobility of the resources engaged in retailing). (2) It was set up to stem the introduction of mass distribution techniques that promised to increase consumer welfare both by reducing the cost of distribution and by increasing the consumer's range of choice.

GOVERNMENT POLICY IN AGRICULTURE

A second area of economic activity in which the government has intervened to limit competition is agriculture. The means the government has used are both extensive in scope and very much in the public eye. Few citizens have ever heard of Robinson-Patman, but everybody knows that the U.S. has a farm policy, and everybody debates its pros and cons!

The government's policy toward agriculture, unlike its policy toward the distributive trades, does not just restrict what market participants can do. It calls for the government to intervene in agricultural markets as a buyer and to engage in other costly programs to aid farmers. Thus this program imposes on consumers and taxpayers not only "invisible" costs in the form of an induced misallocation of resources, but also very visible costs in the form of high government expenditures. Currently direct government payments to farmers average out to about $1,000 per farmer, and total Department of Agriculture expenditures run over $3 billion a year! Large as it is, this figure still understates total government spending on agriculture, since farm-oriented programs such as soil conservation are carried out and financed by departments other than the Department of Agriculture.

Why has the government intervened extensively in agricultural markets? What have its policies accomplished? Should these policies be modified?

Causes of Agricultural Distress

When we think of the increases in productivity that have occurred in the past few years, we usually think first of the startling increases in productivity in industry. But productivity has also risen dramatically in agriculture. Figure 25.3 shows that, since 1929, total farm employment has been halved, while total farm output has almost doubled.

Although productivity has risen rapidly, consumer demand for agricultural products has grown at a relatively slow pace, for two reasons: (1) Demand for agricultural products is notoriously inelastic with respect to price,* and therefore price decreases induced by rising productivity have not significantly increased the demand for agricultural products. (2) The amount that people spend on food (recall Fig. 4.2) does not rise proportionately with their incomes (in the jargon of economists, the income elasticity† of consumer demand for agricultural products is low). Therefore the demand for agricultural products increases more slowly than national income does.

---

* Recall the data on price elasticities in Table 4.1.

† The consumer's income elasticity (ϵ_y) is a first cousin to his price elasticity. It is given by the expression

$$\epsilon_y = \left| \frac{\text{percentage change in quantity}}{\text{percentage change in income}} \right|.$$

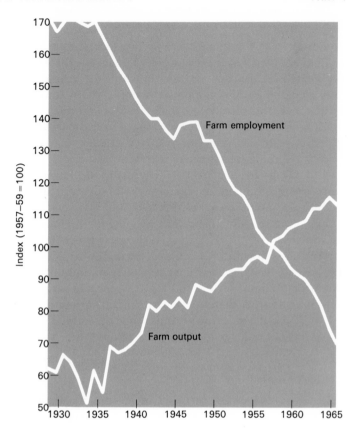

25|3

In agriculture, employment is on the decline but output is rising.
(Source: U.S. Department of Agriculture)

The fact that productivity increases have outstripped demand increases has meant that the quantity of resources—especially farmers and farm laborers—required to meet the country's food needs has declined. As indicated by Fig. 25.3, this decline has to some extent been matched by an exodus of farmers from agriculture, but this exodus has not been as rapid as the decline in the need for them. Consequently, since the end of World War I, there has been a chronic tendency toward overproduction in agriculture, and the returns earned by farmers and farm laborers have been depressed compared with those earned by workers in industry. Today farmers and farm workers earn roughly half what their counterparts in industry do.*

* Recall the data on income according to occupation in Table 15.1.

Policies to Raise Farm Prices and Farm Income

Because of the low incomes in agriculture and the distress that they created, especially during the 1930's, the government felt compelled to act. The apparent cause of low farm incomes was (at least to the untrained eye) low farm prices. Therefore the government began by emphasizing, and has continued to emphasize, programs to raise farm prices.

Over the 30-odd years that it has intervened in agricultural markets, the government has employed a variety of price-support programs. Many of them share certain key elements in common: in particular the concept of *parity prices.* Over time the prices that farmers have had to pay for *industry*'s products have been rising. If the prices that farmers get for *their* products were to rise just as fast, then the real value (i.e., purchasing power) of a "bushel" of farm output would remain constant over time. The level of farm prices that would be required to bring about this happy circumstance is known as the parity level. Parity prices are generally calculated on the basis of the average prices that prevailed during the period 1910–14. So since industrial prices have roughly tripled since 1910–14, prices for wheat, cotton and other crops would have to have risen to approximately 3 times their 1910–14 level to be at parity.

Programs to raise farm prices to parity. One easy way for the government to maintain farm prices at parity would have been simply to legislate minimum prices for agricultural products.* If the government had done so, however, supply would have exceeded demand at support prices, and some farmers would have been unable to sell their crops at the support price, or at any other price for that matter.

To illustrate: Suppose the curves in Fig. 25.4(a) represent supply and demand in the wheat market. Then the price p^0, which is the price that equates the supply of and demand for wheat, is the price that would be established in a free market. Suppose, however, that the government, instead of allowing the price p^0 to be established, requires that all wheat be sold at p', the high parity price for wheat. Then consumers will demand only q' of wheat, farms will supply q'', and excess supply equal to $(q'' - q')$ will emerge.

One attractive (at least from the farmer's point of view) way for the government to deal with this excess supply is to buy it up. This is what the government has frequently done. It has often pegged agricultural prices— sometimes at 100% of parity, generally at levels well below this figure—by buying up all excess supply that emerges at the support prices it sets.

If the government used crop purchases to establish the support price p' in the market shown in Fig. 25.4(a), then (as you can verify) it would incur

---

* As we saw in Chapter 15, the government, by setting a minimum wage, has in effect legislated a minimum price for unskilled labor.

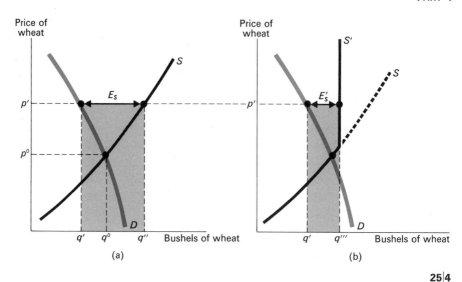

25|4

Alternative price-support programs in the wheat market.
a) No limit is imposed on the supply of wheat.   b) The supply of wheat is limited to S'.

total costs equal to $p'(q'' - q')$, that is, equal to the area of the shaded rectangle shown in the figure. This example thus shows that the use of crop purchases to prop agricultural prices can be extremely expensive for the government, especially if high support prices elicit big increases in supply.

Since high government expenditures lead to high taxes, which of course are unpopular with voters, the government has naturally tried to keep the cost of its agricultural support programs as low as possible. One way it has attempted to do so is by restricting the number of acres that individual farmers may devote to corn, wheat, and other key crops. To show how such restrictions can reduce the cost of the government's price-support program, let's return to our wheat-market example. Suppose that the government restricts the total number of acres that farmers can devote to wheat. Then the supply curve of wheat (see Fig. 25.4b) will shift from S to S'. This shift reduces excess supply at the support prices from E_s to E'_s, and the cost of the government's price-propping falls from $p'(q'' - q')$ to the much smaller figure $p'(q''' - q')$.

Although the reduction of supply through acreage restriction costs the government nothing, the government has adopted other programs aimed at supply reduction that *do* mean spending money: It has paid farmers to hold land idle (i.e., to "deposit" acres in what it calls the Soil Bank), it has subsidized the transfer of farmland back to forest, and it has even undertaken programs to help farmers convert excess farm acres into money-making recreation areas.

Another way the government uses to decrease the cost of its price supports is expansion of demand. To expand demand for U.S. farm products, the government subsidizes cheap school lunches, gives away surplus commodities to the poor, and sells food stamps to them at a discount. It also subsidizes the export of certain crops, such as cotton, whose domestic support prices are high relative to world prices. In addition, under Public Law 480 the government sells for local currencies or long-term credits wheat, cotton, and other surplus commodities to food-short underdeveloped countries, such as India, Pakistan, and (in pre-Suez-1967 days at least) Egypt. Since the proceeds realized by the government under PL 480 sales are of limited usefulness, such sales come close to being foreign-aid gifts.

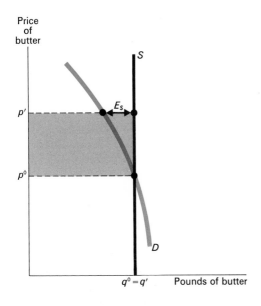

25|5

If the government uses a direct subsidy program, supporting the price of butter at p' will cost it an amount equal to $(p' - p^0)q'$, the area of the shaded rectangle.

Subsidy programs. So far we have considered programs that aid the farmer by raising farm prices above the level that would equate supply and demand. The government, however, can also aid the farmer in a different way. It can let farm prices fall to their equilibrium level and pay the farmer a subsidy equal to the difference between the equilibrium price established by supply and demand and the parity price (or some lower "support" price).

To illustrate: Consider the market for butter. If this market were left to its own devices, then, as indicated in Fig. 25.5, the price p^0 would be established for butter, dairy farmers would produce q^0 pounds of butter, and consumers would eat this amount of it. Suppose, however, that the government were to decide that p^0 represented an inadequate return for dairy farmers and that it wanted them to receive the higher price p'. Then it might establish the price p' in the marketplace by buying up whatever excess supply,

E_s, of butter that emerged at the support price p'. Alternatively, however, it could let the price of butter fall to the market-clearing level p^0 and pay farmers a subsidy equal to $(p' - p^0)$ for each pound of butter they sold. If it did this, it would incur total costs equal to $(p' - p^0)q'$. In Fig. 25.5 this amount is represented by the area of the shaded rectangle.

If we assume that under either approach the government would restrict to q^0 the amount of butter that farmers were permitted to supply at the price p', i.e., if we assume that under either program q' will equal q^0, then both programs would yield farmers the same total revenue $p'q'$. Therefore farmers ought to be indifferent between the two approaches. In actual practice they may not be, because so long as the government supports price by buying up excess supply, it looks to the farmer and to the taxpayer as if the farmer were really "earning" all the revenue he receives. Under the subsidy program, however, it is clear that part of the farmer's total revenue is a dole, the amount of which is painfully easy to calculate.

Consumers are likely to prefer the subsidy program to the crop-purchase program for several reasons. One is that the subsidy program makes farm products available to consumers at low market-clearing prices. The crop-purchase program, on the other hand, raises the prices consumers must pay. In other words, it is equivalent to a hidden tax on consumer incomes. Furthermore this "tax" is a socially undesirable one. Reason: Low-income consumers spend a higher percentage of their income on food than high-income consumers do (recall Fig. 4.2), so the "tax" created by artificially high farm prices hits low-income consumers harder than high-income ones.* In the jargon of the economist, it is a *regressive* tax.

A second advantage to the consumer of a subsidy program is that under such a program all output is actually consumed, while under a crop-purchase program some output is likely to be wasted. As an illustration, let's look again at the butter market. Under a subsidy program, consumers will eat all the q^0 pounds of butter dairymen produce, and none will be wasted. But under a crop-purchase program, the government will buy up E_s of butter, store it till it turns rancid, and then throw it out. Thus under such a program E_s of butter will probably be wasted. If you've already started to worry about your cholesterol count, you may think that wasting E_s of butter isn't so bad. Maybe it will reduce the incidence of heart disease! But note that the *scarce* resources devoted to producing this butter could have been used to produce something that's "safe" and that we'd all like to eat more more of.

We have talked about the preferences of consumers and farmers. Now let us ask which program is the best from the government's point of view. When the government buys up crops, it could of course just bury or burn

---

* If you're poor John Smith and spend 30% of your income on food, a program that raises farm prices by 20% is equivalent to slapping a 6% tax on your income. On the other hand, if you're rich John Rockerfull and spend only 1% of your income on food, the same program will be equivalent to only a 0.2% tax on your income.

them. But it doesn't or at least it hasn't since the 1930's. Instead it stores them, in the hope that in some future period demand will be so high or supply so low that the equilibrium prices of these commodities will rise above support levels. If this happens the government, by selling off stored commodities, can get its own money back and at the same time help out consumers by holding farm prices down to support levels. Unfortunately things rarely work out this way. One reason, as we saw in the case of butter, is that some price-supported commodities are too perishable to be stored for long. Another is that the government usually sets support prices so high that excess demand rarely occurs at the support prices. Thus when the government uses crop purchases to raise the price of a nonperishable commodity like wheat, it is likely to end up owning and storing immense quantities of this commodity (unless of course it severely restricts output). Thus from the government's point of view a subsidy program has one obvious advantage over a crop-purchase program: It eliminates the possibility that the government might have to store billions of dollars' worth of surplus farm commodities.

To determine which approach will cost the government more money, let us again consider the butter market. So long as the government restricts butter output to q', dairy farmers will get the same revenue $p'q'$, regardless of which program the government uses. In order to guarantee farmers the total revenue $p'q'$, the government under either program will have to pay farmers the difference between $p'q'$ and the total amount that consumers spend on butter. Thus the program that will be cheapest for the government is the one that leads consumers to spend the most on butter. Which program this is depends of course on the now-familiar concept of elasticity of demand.* If demand for butter is *inelastic*, consumers will respond to a rise in the price of butter from p^0 to p' by spending more on butter, and a crop-purchase program will cost the government less than a subsidy one. On the other hand, if demand for butter is elastic, the opposite will occur.

The elasticity of consumer demand for most farm products is, as we have seen, quite low. Thus for most crops the direct cost of a purchase-and-storage program would probably be smaller than that of a subsidy program. This may go a long way toward explaining why direct subsidies have played a relatively minor role in U.S. farm programs.

The Record of Regulation

Government farm programs can be faulted on a number of counts. For one thing, the idea that farm prices should be maintained at parity is a misguided one. Parity pricing is supposed to maintain the incomes of farm laborers on a par with those of factory laborers. To attain this goal, however, the government should not freeze the relationship between farm and factory

---

* We first introduced it back in Chapter 4.

prices, but permit this relationship to fluctuate over time in a way that re-flects whatever differences there are in the relative rates at which productivity is rising in the two sectors. Thus, for example, if productivity is rising more rapidly in industry than on the farm, the government should let farm prices rise relative to factory prices so that labor in both sectors will earn the same real wage. On the other hand, if productivity is rising faster on the farm than in the factory, farm prices should fall relative to factory prices.

If this last alternative seems unfair to farmers, consider the plight of AT&T. In 1915 AT&T charged $20.70 for a 3-minute station-to-station call from New York to San Francisco. Since then prices of things in general have roughly tripled. So, on a parity basis, AT&T today ought to get $62.10 for the same call. Instead it gets only $1.00 (at evening rates). Does this mean that workers and capital employed in the telephone business earn abysmally low returns? Not at all. It means that the telephone company's productivity has risen so fast that labor and capital employed there would earn supernormal returns if telephone prices had not fallen over time.

A second problem with current farm programs is that the big fellows get the lion's share. These programs do much to help large farmers who have big outputs and high incomes, but little to help small farmers who have small outputs and low incomes. Figure 25.6 gives some idea of just how unequally the benefits of government farm programs are distributed among farmers. It shows that the 15% of farmers whose average gross sales run over $20,000 per year receive almost 45% of the total payments made under government farm programs. On the other hand, the 55% of farmers whose average gross sales run under $5,000 per year receive less than 18%.

A third problem with government farm programs is that they fail to attack the two major roots of the farm problem: (1) Many farmers and farm

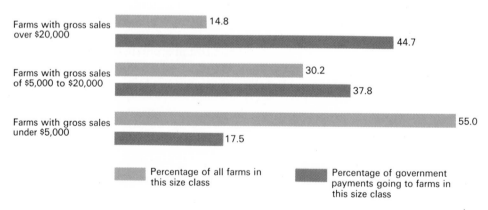

25|6

Payments made under government farm programs do most to aid farmers who have high cash receipts. (Source: *Food, Fiber, and the Future*; Washington, D.C.: Report of the National Advisory Commission on Food and Fiber, July 1967, page 192)

laborers who could and ought to move out of agriculture are slow to do so. (2) In the agricultural sector there are many small farmers and laborers who, because they lack education and skills, are doomed to subsist in poverty unless they are helped.

PROBLEMS

1   It is easy enough to see how there is monopolistic restriction of output in a market controlled by a *single* monopolist. But how can it exist in a monopolistically competitive market in which sellers are *numerous?* [*Hint:* Compare the equilibrium of a perfect competitor with that of a monopolistic competitor.]

2   Arguments on the side of fair-trade laws and attempts by retailers to organize state that the average small merchant has about the same level of skill and earns about the same level of income as a skilled worker in industry; therefore small merchants should be permitted to organize just as skilled workers do.

Do you agree with this argument? What do you think about its applicability to small farmers? In answering these questions consider the structures of the markets in which skilled workers, merchants, and farmers sell their services and outputs.

3   Suppose that the *XYD* Corporation, an American-based outfit, in good faith and at a cost of $10 million, lays an underwater telephone cable between the fabled island of Atlantis and Hawaii. (The cable runs, of course, through the Suez Canal.) Initially the profit prospects on this cable seem good, but then someone discovers that a single $1 million flying saucer placed over the Suez Canal will do exactly the same job, and the variable costs of running the saucer will be only half those of running the cable! Obviously a conflict of interests has arisen between *XYD* and Flying Saucers, Inc.

Suppose that you were responsible for regulating these two utility companies. How would you price their services? How would your decision affect the efficiency of world resource allocation? Would it be "fair" to consumers in Atlantis and Hawaii? To investors in *XYD?* To investors in Flying Saucers, Inc.?

Does a normal free market economy offer "fair" protection to investors against technological change? Against changes in consumer tastes? Against other sorts of change? Would you expect that a world in which the "fair" interests of investors were protected against change would grow faster or slower, would change more or less rapidly, than one in which the interests of investors were unprotected from change? Defend your answer, since the question at hand can be argued both ways.

4   Currently the cost of long-distance television distribution within the U.S. is about $65 million a year, but estimates suggest that, if synchronous satellites were used, a $19 billion saving could be achieved. American Telephone and Telegraph, the major domestic distributor of TV programs, argues that such savings should be passed along to all users of its long-distance facilities, which means of course that the projected cost savings wouldn't result in a significant rate reduction for anyone. The TV networks naturally enough argue that all the savings should be passed on directly to them. Finally McGeorge Bundy, of

the Ford Foundation, argues that most of the projected savings should be used as a "social dividend" to provide free channels to educational and institutional TV. Bundy's proposition is of course equivalent to imposing a whopping tax on the networks; but he argues that, because the networks have been given without charge a scarce and valuable national asset—the right to broadcast on part of the frequency spectrum—then logic and justice favor taxing them to finance noncommercial TV.

Suppose that you were on the Federal Communications Commission, and so had to rule on all these conflicting proposals. What position would you take? Does each of these proposals have some merit? When you are answering this question, bear in mind the fact that the U.S. is currently the only major country without a noncommercial TV network.

5   "Home delivery of milk by several different companies in the same local area causes needless duplication of facilities and is inefficient. Therefore milk delivery should be turned into a local, regulated monopoly." Discuss.

6   "Frequently regulated monopolists enjoy economies of scale over very extensive ranges of output. Therefore if we want public-utility commissions to enforce marginal cost pricing, we ought to give them the power to require utility firms to operate at a loss and the means to subsidize such losses." Comment. [*Hint:* Refer to Fig. 24.3.]

7   In Chapters 21 and 22 we noted that price discrimination, if practicable, is frequently profitable for monopolists, and for groups of colluding oligopolists, so it isn't surprising that many regulated companies want to practice price discrimination. Generally speaking they are permitted to do so, and on an extensive scale. (For example, what electricity costs you depends not just on how much you use, but on whether you are a home owner, on whether you use electricity for lighting or for heating water, etc.). Do you think that public-utility commissions should permit and even encourage regulated companies to engage in price discrimination? Are there pros and cons to both sides of this argument? If so, which side do you think carries more weight?

8   Airlines currently engage in what the bus industry has called a ridiculous "mishmash" of promotional fares (i.e., in extensive price discrimination). Bus lines have attacked in particular the special discount fares which the airlines grant to large families traveling together and to college-age youths. According to bus lines, such fares are unjust to other air travelers because they contribute to the high level of general air fares; they are also unjust to bus companies because they are aimed specifically at people who would normally travel by bus.

To end these unjust forms of price discrimination, the bus lines challenged their legality in court. If you had been the judge, how would you have ruled? [The New Orleans judge who actually did have to rule on this in 1967 ordered the Civil Aeronautics Board to consider fully the bus lines' request that the fares in question be declared illegal.]

9   The following startling quote appeared in a U.S. Department of Agriculture bulletin: "In 1965 the total farm value of potatoes was $840 million, the highest in three decades, due to an unusually *small* crop." Can you explain this state-

ment, using our old friend elasticity of demand? Or do you think it was probably just a misprint?

10 "If the demand for farm products is extremely inelastic, the government can significantly raise farm income simply by restricting the quantity of output that farmers are permitted to produce." Right or wrong? Defend your answer with pen, paper, and an appropriate diagram.

11 i) A recent study suggests that an adequate-sized farm will need $123,000 of capital investment by 1980; that is double the amount of capital investment needed today. Reason for the big increase is partly that farms will increase in size and partly that capital will continue to be substituted for labor.

ii) Between 1964 and 1966 the percent of U.S. canning tomatoes picked by machine rose from under 3% to over 50%. Mechanical harvesters are now being developed for almost all crops except strawberries.

iii) Some conglomerate (i.e., multi-product-line) firms have, according to the *Wall Street Journal*, discovered that by engaging in commercial farming operations they can reap profits "well above the average on invested capital." Recall that we noted back in Chapter 11 that Textron, a leading conglomerate, is—in addition to being a producer of rocket engines and golf carts—also one of the nation's leading chicken farmers!

What do these randomly selected observations suggest to you about trends in farming? About the need for a U.S. agricultural policy? About the form that such a policy ought to take in future years?

12 "Between 1950 and 1965 the price of farm land rose 110%. Given the rising price of farm land, the fair thing to do is to raise farm prices to compensate farmers for their higher costs." Comment. [*Hint:* Does Figure 15.1, which deals with the relationship between the price of cranberries and the price of bogs, have any relevance here?]

13 The entrance of large-scale and even corporate producers into agriculture has tended to lower the prices of some agricultural products, such as broilers, which can be raised using mass-production methods. Thus the advent of the corporate farmer promises to benefit the consumer in the long run.

Independent farmers and their trade organizations contend, however, that any price decreases will be only temporary. They argue that if the trend to corporate farming continues, eventually a few giants will control the farming industry, curtailing competition. "Whoever heard of reduced competition lowering price?" asks a lobbyist for one farm group. (*Wall Street Journal*, Aug. 9, 1967)

Discuss this quote. Do you think that agriculture is likely to be monopolized or oligopolized in the foreseeable future? How do you expect the advent of corporate farmers to affect farm prices over the long run? Why?

14 The government sets minimum prices both for farm products and for labor. It buys up the resulting excess supply in agricultural markets, but not the resulting excess supply in the labor market. Can you think of any theoretical, practical, or ethical justification for this distinction?

Part 5
FINANCIAL MARKETS

CHAPTER 26

FUNDS FLOWS AND
FINANCIAL ASSETS

In Parts 3 and 4 we talked mainly about markets in which producers and consumers trade *real* outputs (i.e., goods and services) and *real* inputs, such as labor and land. There is another important class of markets. These are the markets in which financial assets*—ranging from gilt-edge bonds to speculative stocks—are created and traded.

To most people *financial markets* are an exciting topic, because the workings of these markets are unfamiliar to them and because of the heady aura of Wall Street and high finance that surrounds these markets. Financial markets are extremely important. The funds flows which take place through these markets play a significant role in financing the expenditures made by both consumers and investors, and the efficiency with which these markets allocate funds among alternative uses, and in particular among alternative investment projects, influences both the rate and direction of the economy's growth.

WHY DO FINANCIAL ASSETS EXIST?

Financial assets are the stock-in-trade of financial markets. Why do financial assets exist? Before we answer this question, we need to make a few preliminary observations.

Whenever a consumer provides productive inputs (land, labor, or capital) to the business sector, he earns income, i.e., purchasing power. In contrast, whenever he buys goods and services, he uses up purchasing power. In the jargon of economists, *generalized purchasing power is referred to as "funds."* Thus, whenever a consumer earns income he receives funds, and whenever he buys goods and services he uses up funds. Take Jones and his wife, for example. Jones works for the Nuclear Orbit Company, and each week he receives $290 in wages (in funds). Jones's wife doesn't work. Instead she spends a lot of time buying goods and services. And each time she makes a purchase, she uses up some of the income (funds) Jones earns.

---

* We defined these back in Chapter 2.

Funds Deficits and Funds Surpluses

Jones and his wife might spend on goods and services the precise amount of funds they receive from current income. If they did, their funds budget would be in *balance*. (In other words, they would use up on purchases of goods and services the precise quantity of purchasing power they receive from current income.) On the other hand, Jones and his wife might devote more funds to goods and services than they receive in current income. In this case they would incur a *funds deficit*. Finally Jones and his wife might spend fewer funds on goods and services than they receive from current income. Then they would have a *funds surplus*.

Presumably the taxes Jones pays to the government are a payment for the goods and services (roads, schools, beaches, and so forth) that the government provides for Jones and other consumers. Thus, if you recall the income statement we set up for Jones in Table 2.1, you might think that the funds surplus (or deficit) that Jones incurs during the current period must equal his current period saving (or dissaving), that is, the difference between his after-tax income and his current consumption expenditures.

This, however, is not the case. Why? Table 2.2, which presents Jones's balance sheet, gives us a clue. It reminds us that during the current period Jones and his wife, in addition to buying goods and services for current consumption, might also buy capital goods (i.e., physical assets), such as a house or a new car. To purchase capital goods, the Joneses must of course use funds, just as they do when they purchase consumption goods. Thus during the current period:

The funds deficit or funds surplus that a consumer incurs equals the difference between the funds he receives from current income and the funds he spends on taxes, current consumption, and capital goods.

Firms, like consumers, also receive funds and use up funds. A firm is said to incur a funds *deficit* whenever the total funds it spends on goods, services, and taxes exceeds the total funds it has received from the sale of current output. Similarly a firm is said to incur a funds *surplus* whenever the funds it spends on goods, services, and taxes are less than the total funds it has received from the sale of current output.

To illustrate this, consider our old friend, Tectronics, Inc. They're the new firm that sells folding light bulbs; we looked at their income statement and balance sheet back in Chapter 6. Whenever Tectronics sells output, they receive revenue (funds). Most of these funds are used in buying up the productive inputs (goods and services) that Tectronics needs to produce their folding bulbs. Some also go to pay for taxes and some are used to pay out dividends (i.e., a return to the input equity capital). Whatever funds are left over after these expenses have been paid represent—as we pointed out in Chapter 6—Tectronics' period saving. Tectronics' period savings do not, however, represent its funds deficit or surplus for the current period, any more than Jones's savings represents his, because Tectronics, like Jones, might also decide to buy some new capital equipment (a bulb-folding machine) during the current period. And if they do, this will cost them funds. Thus during the current period:

The funds deficit or funds surplus that a firm incurs equals the difference between the funds it receives from the sale of current output and the funds it spends on productive inputs, taxes, and capital goods.

Whenever a producer or consumer incurs a funds deficit, he has to obtain external financing (i.e., demand funds from outside sources) in order to cover his total needs for funds. Suppose that Jones, whose income equals $290 a week, decides that next week he'd like to buy $190 worth of goods for current consumption plus a $700 sailboat. This means that he'll have to get $600 of funds from some outside source (maybe a bank loan),* because the $290 of funds he gets from his current income won't suffice to cover the $890 of expenditures he wants to make during the week.

Funds deficits have to be covered by external financing. What about funds surpluses? Whenever a producer or consumer incurs a funds surplus, he has to furnish external financing (i.e., supply funds to outside sources) in order to absorb the excess funds this surplus creates. For example, if Jones and his wife decide to forgo buying that new sailboat, they'll have $100 of funds from current income that they do not need to spend on goods and services. If they don't use up these funds themselves (remember funds are purchasing power, *not* money), they'll have to dispose of them by supplying them (perhaps via a loan) to some other spending units. You may object that no one *makes* Jones do anything with his excess funds. He could, if he chose to, simply hold them in the form of cash or a bank deposit. You are right, but so are we; because in a modern economy, money (including bank deposits) is created through "debt monetization," and for this reason a surplus unit which accumulates cash in effect supplies funds to deficit units.†

The Creation of Financial Assets

Let us now return to our original question: Why do financial assets exist? Well, in any society in which circumstances do not force all consumers and producers to have balanced funds budgets, the number of consumers and producers who do so during any period is likely to be small. Many con-

---

* On this page and the next we want to focus on the way financial assets are *created*, not on the way they are traded and extinguished. So we shall ignore for the moment situations in which a *spending unit* (see page 10) obtains external financing by selling a previously acquired financial asset, or supplies external financing by paying off a previously incurred liability.

† This idea, and debt monetization, are tricky points, to be explained in Chapter 28.

sumers and producers have funds surpluses, while many others incur funds deficits. Such surpluses and deficits have to be covered, however, by transfers of funds from surplus to deficit units. When such a transfer occurs, a financial *instrument* will be created to give evidence of the debt or equity claims which the funds supplier, by right of this transfer, has obtained against the funds receiver. This financial instrument, regardless of form, will constitute a financial *asset* to the surplus unit that receives it. Thus we see that financial assets are created when funds-surplus units supply external financing to deficit units. (Jones uses his $100 funds surplus to buy a bond that Tectronics issues to cover its $100 funds deficit. This bond gives Jones a claim against Tectronics; so from Tectronics' point of view the transaction creates a liability, but from Jones's point of view it creates a financial asset.)

Although financial assets all arise in connection with the transfer of funds between surplus and deficit units, they differ widely in form. Thus a spending unit with a funds surplus might trade off its surplus for bonds, for stock, for bonds convertible into stock, for mortgages, or for a variety of other financial assets. These assets vary in certain fundamental ways. Some financial assets—as we'll see in later chapters—incorporate claims redeemable in the short run, while others establish claims redeemable only in the long run. Some entitle the holder to interest or dividends; others do not. Some expose the *holder* to risk, while still others expose the *issuer* to risk.

Financial assets are heterogeneous because, as indicated by Chapters 5 and 11, the needs and preferences of both individual investors and individual borrowers differ widely. Funds-surplus units have varied savings goals, and their preferences with respect to asset characteristics such as return, risk, and liquidity are dissimilar. Therefore no one security, no matter how cleverly contrived, could possibly appeal equally to all of them. Individual funds-deficit units also pursue different goals, finance different types of expenditures, and differ in their willingness to assume risk. Therefore no one security could be issued with equal appropriateness by all of them. Thus the diverse collection of financial assets which investors demand is willingly supplied by borrowers and equity issuers; and the heterogeneity of financial assets turns out to be a natural outcome of the diversity of people's psychology and needs.

FLOW-OF-FUNDS ACCOUNTS

The fact that during every income period all consumers and all firms receive and dispense funds means that for each such spending unit we could set up a flow-of-funds account.

A spending unit's flow-of-funds account lists for a given period of time the sources of all funds it receives and the uses to which it puts these funds.

Flow-of-funds accounts are extremely useful in a discussion of financial markets,* because they provide information that we cannot get from the income statements or the balance sheets of consumers and producers about the direction and volume of funds that are flowing between these spending units.

The Consumer's Flow-of-Funds Account

Table 26.1 shows a flow-of-funds account for John Jones for the year 1970. As you will recall, a consumer's income represents a source of funds, while tax payments and expenditures on current consumption represent uses of funds. Therefore we are tempted to record Jones's savings for the year as a source of funds. Some of Jones's consumption expenditures, however, represent depreciation; and depreciation doesn't call for funds outlays. It just records the fact that, as Jones uses his house and car, they wear out and lose value. So what we want to record as a source of funds on Jones's 1970 flow-of-funds account is not Jones's *net* saving *in*cluding depreciation, but his *gross* saving *ex*cluding depreciation. For Jones this latter figure turns out to be $1,700, since $600 of his 1970 consumption was depreciation. (Turn back to Table 2.1 and you'll see that Jones's 1970 net as opposed to gross savings equaled only $1,100.)

Look at the fourth entry on Jones's flow-of-funds account: In 1970 Jones used $10,000 of funds to add a new wing to his house. Certainly his gross saving of $1,700 did not cover this expense. So where did he get the money

TABLE 26|1

Flow-of-Funds Account: John Jones, January 1, 1970–December 31, 1970

	Uses	Sources
Gross saving	$ 0	$1,700
Cash	100	0
Bank deposits	− 2,000	0
Purchase and sale of capital goods		
Addition to own home	10,000	0
Corporate stocks	− 1,000	0
Bonds	500	0
Short-term debt	0	− 200
Long-term debt (mortgage)	0	6,100
Total sources and uses of funds	$7,600	$7,600

---

* Flow-of-funds accounts are a relatively recent development. They were pioneered by Morris Copeland in *A Study of Money Flows in the United States;* New York: National Bureau of Economic Research, 1952.

to finance this? Part of the answer lies in the last entry on Jones's flow-of-funds account. It tells us that Jones got $6,100 of funds by increasing the mortgage on his house.

But this is still not enough to finance that new wing. Where did he get the rest? The *negative* use entries in his flow-of-funds account give us the answer. The first negative use entry tells us that Jones got $2,000 by dipping into his bank account; the second tells us that he got another $1,000 by selling corporate stock. (Blue Sky Uranium Hunters, Inc., was doing awfully well, but Jones thought it had probably hit a peak.)

Now we know the additional transactions Jones went through to get the extra funds he needed. But why do we call them negative uses? Wouldn't it be clearer to record them as positive sources? Yes; but if we did we might lose information. Jones might lend funds as well as borrow them. So if we used only positive source and use entries, a positive source of funds resulting from a change in Jones's short-term debt position might indicate either that Jones had got money from a new loan granted to him or that he had got it because someone he had loaned money to paid him back. To avoid confusion of this sort, the flow-of-funds accountant has the following convention:

All changes in assets are recorded as uses; all changes in liabilities are recorded as sources.

According to this convention, if Jones loans $200, that's a positive use. If he gets paid back $200, that's a negative use. On the other hand, if Jones borrows $500, that's a positive source, but if he pays back a $500 debt, that's a negative source.

There are still three entries on Jones's flow-of-funds account that we have not mentioned. One is the $100 use entry for cash, which means that Jones wound up at the end of the year with $100 more cash in his pocket than he had at the beginning of the year (i.e., he used $100 of funds to build up his cash balance).

Another is the $500 use entry for bonds. This tells us that Jones, at the same time he was getting out of Blue Sky, decided in a conservative moment to buy $500 of Tectronics' gilt-edge bonds. Finally the −$200 source entry recorded under short-term debt reflects the fact that Jones began the year owing the local department store $200 but ended the year—miraculously enough—owing them nothing. (Mrs. Jones broke her leg Thanksgiving week and couldn't get out to do any Christmas shopping.)

When we look over Jones's flow-of-funds account, we notice that his total sources of funds during 1970 just equaled his total uses of funds during 1970. Is this equality coincidental or does it have to hold?

The key to answering this question lies in the fact that *every economic transaction a consumer makes involves simultaneously both a source and a use of funds*. That is, every source of funds must be immediately matched by an equivalent use of funds, and vice versa.

The reason for this is that funds (as we have observed) are purchasing power, and there is no such thing as pure purchasing power. Therefore whenever the consumer receives funds, he has to accept them in some concrete form, and the moment he does so he uses funds. For example, Jones's weekly salary of $290 represents a source of funds. Jones's boss, however, can't give Jones just plain funds. He has to pay Jones in some concrete medium; for example, cash. Then Jones's cash balance will rise by $290, and his $290 source of funds from income will be precisely offset by a $290 use of funds to acquire cash. Or perhaps Jones's boss simply writes Jones a check, and Jones deposits it in his bank account. Then Jones's $290 source of funds from income will be precisely offset by a $290 use of funds to acquire additional bank deposits. Taking your cue from the argument we have just presented, you can readily show why a use of funds has to be offset by an equal source of funds.

With all this in mind, we can easily see that at the end of any income period a consumer's flow-of-funds account has to be in balance. In this respect the consumer's flow-of-funds account resembles his balance sheet, which, as we saw in Chapter 2, also always has to balance.

A Firm's Flow-of-Funds Account

The firm's flow-of-funds account is similar to the consumer's. Table 26.2 gives Tectronics' flow-of-funds account for 1970. Most of the entries are self-explanatory. The $17,000 *gross* saving entry is the sum of the $8,000

TABLE 26|2

Flow-of-Funds Account: Tectronics Corporation, January 1, 1970–December 31, 1970

	Uses	Sources
Gross saving	$	$17,000
Cash and bank deposits	3,000	0
Accounts receivable and accounts payable	5,000	2,000
Inventories	2,000	0
Purchases and sale of fixed assets		
New $50,000		
Used − 20,000		
	30,000	0
Notes payable	0	− 2,000
Government and other securities	1,000	0
Bonds payable	0	6,000
Mortgages payable	0	18,000
Total sources and uses of funds	$41,000	$41,000

of profits that Tectronics retained during 1970 plus the $9,000 of depreciation it incurred. The next entries tell us that Tectronics used $5,000 to extend credit to buyers of its bulbs (i.e., to increase its accounts receivable) and that it got $2,000 by running up unpaid bills (accounts payable) at suppliers. Tectronics also used $2,000 to finance an increase in its inventories. In addition it made a $50,000 investment in new plant and equipment, which it financed largely by selling off $20,000 of used plant and equipment, by incurring a $18,000 mortgage, and by selling $6,000 worth of bonds. Finally, this account shows that during 1970 Tectronics decreased its notes payable by $2,000 and increased its holding of government securities by $1,000.

The last line shows that Tectronics' total sources of funds during 1970 just equaled its total use of funds, which is only to be expected, because, by the same argument we used to show that a consumer's flow-of-funds account must always be in balance, a firm's flow-of-funds account must always balance too.

THE SIZE AND DIRECTION OF EXTERNAL FUNDS FLOWS

We have said that funds deficits have to be covered and funds surpluses absorbed by transfers of funds from surplus to deficit units. As a result in every sector of the economy there are spending units that supply external finance and others that demand it. However, in some sectors, spending units supply and demand much larger amounts of external financing than in others. Also in some sectors surplus units predominate, while in others deficit units do.

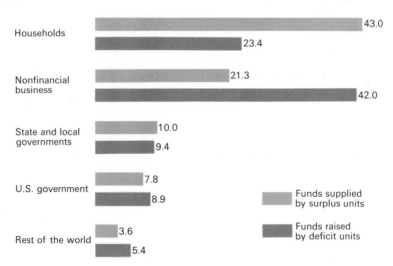

26|1

Total funds raised and supplied by deficit and surplus units in different sectors, 1966 (billions of dollars). (Source: *Federal Reserve Bulletin*)

To keep track of the situation, the Federal Reserve Board (people who are on a first-name basis with it are fond of calling it "the Fed") has set up, for broad sectors of the economy, flow-of-funds accounts like those we set up for Jones the consumer and Tectronics the firm. Figure 26.1 records data taken from these accounts, which show that in 1966 consumers as a group (i.e., the household sector) supplied $43.0 billion and raised $23.4 billion. Thus the net surplus of this sector was a king-size $20 billion. Where were the deficit units that absorbed these funds? The remaining figures in Fig. 26.1 show that the state-and-local government sector, the U.S. government sector, and the rest-of-the-world sector (i.e., foreigners) all supplied and raised about equal amounts of funds. So the $20 billion of funds that households supplied went to cover the $20 billion net deficit which nonfinancial business firms (i.e., firms that produce goods and nonfinancial services) incurred.

In this respect 1966 was not an atypical year. Generally in any growing economy consumers transfer to the business sector funds this sector needs to finance its increasing investment in plant, equipment, and other forms of capital stock.

PROBLEMS

1   Did John Jones (see Table 26.1) have a deficit or a surplus of funds during 1970? If he did, how much was it? How do you calculate it?

2   Calculate your own flow-of-funds account for last month. Did it balance? If not, why not?

3   Bert Brown is a bachelor. He likes to dress well so every week he spends about $40 on new clothes. He spends even more on eating out ($50 a week) because he hasn't yet figured out how to boil an egg. During 1969 he earned $10,000. He had to pay $1,000 in income taxes and he spent, all told, $9,900 on current consumption. He also bought a used car for $1,100 and ten shares of Ford Motor Company stock at $50 apiece. About November New York began to look so bleak to him that he flew to Hawaii. He went on a fly-now-pay-later plan, and as a result he now owes the airline $500. All in all it was an expensive year for poor Brown, and his bank account shows it. At the end of the year it was $2,000 lower than at the beginning. Draw up Brown's 1969 flow-of-funds account. (There were no other changes on his balance sheet during 1969.)

4   On Dec. 31, 1971, most people are out celebrating New Year's Eve, but not James Phibete. He's a star downhill skier and never smokes, drinks, or stays up late. James does have his peculiarities, however. He's hipped on numbers. So while most people are out seeing the New Year in, James is sitting in the the college library setting up his flow-of-funds account for 1971. At 11 P.M. he gets this account into precise balance, and on that happy note he hops into his car and starts home. Unfortunately, halfway back to the dorm, James fails

to negotiate an important curve and totally wrecks his $1,000 car. He does not get hurt, but he is terribly upset because he doesn't know how to handle the loss of his car in his flow-of-funds account. Can you help him out? What difference would it make whether or not his car was insured for $1,000?

5   Did Tectronics have a deficit or a surplus of funds during 1970? If so, how much did it total?

6   In 1980 the economy in general slumped, but this turned out to be a great year for the Nuclear Orbit Corporation. They earned total profits of $50,000 and retained $15,000. This buoyant record raised their expectations about the future, and so they decided to invest in $100,000 of new plant and equipment. The All American Life Insurance Co. granted them a mortgage that paid for most of this ($80,000 to be precise). However, the trend in their capital stock wasn't just uphill; during the year their existing capital stock depreciated by $5,000.

There were also a few other changes in Nuclear Orbit's balance sheet during 1980. Their inventories went up $1,000, their notes payable went up by a like amount, they paid off $10,000 of bonds that came due, they sold off $2,000 of government securities, they ran down their bank account by $4,000, and they increased their accounts payable by another $4,000.

What was Nuclear Orbit's funds deficit or funds surplus during 1980? Set up their 1980 flow-of-funds account.

7   In Table 26.2 we recorded Tectronics' 1970 flow-of-funds account. How would this account have been altered if, during 1970, the following events had taken place:
    a) Tectronics had used another $1,000 of its cash balances to pay out dividends to shareholders?
    b) Tectronics had withdrawn $2,000 from its bank account to finance additional inventories?
    c) Tectronics had rented a $30,000 filament-curling machine and used $2,000 of cash to pay the first year's rental?

8   Usually in a money economy financial assets are created and traded in exchange for money. (If you borrow from a bank to cover a funds deficit, you get money from them. If you buy a share of IBM, you have to pay money.) Does this mean that financial assets could not exist in a barter economy (i.e., in an economy in which producers and consumers traded goods for goods and used no money)? [*Hint:* Could a consumer or producer in a barter economy run a funds deficit or a funds surplus?]

9   "Every use a consumer makes of funds has to be offset by an equivalent source of funds." Prove or disprove.

10 According to Fig. 26.1 the household sector is simultaneously a principal supplier and user of external finance. How can this be?

CHAPTER 27

THE ROLE OF FINANCIAL INTERMEDIARIES

In Chapter 26 we pointed out that funds surpluses and deficits incurred by individual spending units have to be offset by transfers of funds from surplus to deficit units. Sometimes such funds flows occur *directly* between ultimate funds-deficit and ultimate funds-surplus units. For example, corporations often finance funds deficits by selling new issues of stocks and bonds, some of which go directly into the hands of ultimate funds-surplus units in the consumer sector. (Tectronics, as we saw in Chapter 26, covered part of its 1970 funds deficit by issuing and selling new bonds directly to Jones and other consumers.) Also the federal government covers its frequent funds deficits by selling bonds, some of which are bought directly by funds-surplus units in the consumer and nonfinancial business sectors.

THE ROLE OF FINANCIAL INTERMEDIARIES*

The quantities of funds that flow *directly* between surplus and deficit units are large. However, most funds transferred from surplus to deficit units pass through the hands of financial *middlemen*. Jones may decide to use his surplus funds to buy, not stock in Tectronics, but shares in an investment company, the Ever-Upward Mutual Fund. Ever-Upward then uses the funds it obtains from Jones and other investors to buy stock in Tectronics and other companies, such as IBM, Ford, duPont, and so forth. In addition to buying mutual fund shares, Jones deposits some of his surplus funds in commercial banks. The banks in turn pass on these funds, by means of bank loans, to deficit units, such as business firms in need of inventory financing, consumers wanting mortgages, and students wanting tuition loans.

---

* The pioneering work on a theory of financial intermediaries was done by John G. Gurley and Edward S. Shaw. For reference see: *Money in a Theory of Finance*, Washington, D.C.: The Brookings Institution, 1960.

The middlemen—they are called *financial intermediaries*—who inter-mediate between ultimate funds-surplus and ultimate funds-deficit units differ widely in character, but all play essentially the same role. A financial intermediary is not (as the name might imply) merely a wholesaler who buys financial assets in bulk and resells them in smaller quantities. A financial intermediary solicits funds from surplus units in exchange for debt or equity claims that it issues against itself; it then passes these funds to deficit units in exchange for debt or equity claims that *they* issue against *them*selves. (The Ever-Upward Fund sells equity claims against itself to Jones and other consumers and uses the funds it obtains to buy debt and equity claims against other nonfinancial business firms.) A financial intermediary thus functions as a dealer, "buying" funds from surplus units in exchange for its own *indirect* securities and "selling" funds to deficit units in exchange for their *primary* securities.

The distinction between a financial intermediary and an ordinary wholesaler is an important one. Contrast the way an investment banker operates with the way a savings bank does. When a corporation raises funds by issuing new stock or bonds, it usually sells its newly issued bonds or stock in a single large block to an investment banking firm, which then resells them in smaller lots at a slight markup. Thus an investment banker is not very different from the operator of a corner grocery store who buys Camp-bell's soup by the case and resells it at a slight markup by the can.* In con-trast to investment bankers and grocery stores, a savings bank deals in quite different assets. The bank accepts deposits (i.e., sells short-term, highly liquid claims against itself) and then uses the funds it has obtained to buy long-term, highly illiquid assets such as mortgages.

Because financial intermediaries sell claims against themselves and buy claims against others, they enter intimately into the process by which funds are transferred from surplus to deficit units, and in doing so, they create a big proportion of the total financial assets (including money!) held by con-sumers and nonfinancial business firms.

These financial intermediaries include the Federal Reserve banks, com-mercial banks, mutual savings banks, savings and loan associations, life insurance companies, pension funds, and mutual funds. In addition, non-financial business firms, the government, and even consumers sometimes act as financial intermediaries. For example, when government (state, local, or federal) collects and invests funds earmarked for pension or other special purposes, it acts as a financial intermediary. When a consumer borrows from his bank or his broker in order to buy financial assets, he too is acting

---

* We should perhaps qualify this statement by noting that investment bankers frequently serve as financial advisors to the firms whose stock and bonds they distribute, while grocery stores presumably provide no such services to food manufacturers.

as a financial intermediary. But such activities are small compared with those of financial business firms. Therefore we shall reserve the term "financial intermediary" to describe business firms whose principal function is to act as middlemen in funds transfers.

THE IMPORTANCE OF FINANCIAL INTERMEDIARIES

At the beginning of this chapter we said that most of the funds that flow between funds-deficit and funds-surplus units pass through the hands of financial intermediaries. Let us be more specific, and divide the funds flows that occur between surplus and deficit units into (a) those that travel a direct route from surplus to deficit units and (b) those that travel an indirect route via financial intermediaries.

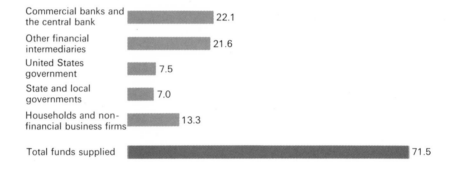

27|1

Funds supplied to funds-deficit units, by source, 1966 (billions of dollars).
(Source: *Federal Reserve Bulletin*)

Figure 27.1 does just this. It shows that of the $71.5 billion of external finance that funds-deficit units obtained during 1966, almost $44 billion came from banks and other financial intermediaries, and that the U.S. government and state and local governments supplied over $14 billion. Much of this represented funds held by the government in pension, social security, and other trust funds or funds borrowed by government agencies to finance loans to special classes of borrowers, such as home builders and small business firms. As we said above, whenever the government invests such special-purpose funds, it is in effect acting as a financial intermediary, so we might well class the $14 billion of external finance supplied by government as funds supplied by financial intermediaries. This leaves us with a net flow of $13.3 billion that went directly from ultimate surplus units in the household and nonfinancial business sectors to ultimate deficit units. This $13.3 billion figure was much larger in 1966 than in most years, because during 1966 the interest rates yielded by primary securities reached record highs, and many investors who would normally have put their funds in financial institutions bought primary securities instead.

The data in Fig. 27.1 indicate that (depending on how we classify funds supplied by the government sector) roughly 60 to 80% of total external financing is provided by financial intermediaries. Thus, by any measure we choose, the role of financial intermediaries in our economy is an extremely important one.

Intermediaries' Share in the External Finance of Individual Sectors

Let us now consider the role of financial intermediaries in each of the principal sectors of the economy. (Note how often we use the word "sector." It is another old-reliable in the jargon of the economist, meaning "a distinctive part of the economy.")

The household sector, as we have already pointed out, is the economy's principal supplier of external finance. In 1966, roughly 80% of the surplus funds which this sector supplied to the economy were "deposited" with financial intermediaries. These funds were used to build up the cash balances, time deposits, life insurance reserves, and pension fund reserves held by (or in custody for) private individuals. Thus the household sector relies mostly on financial intermediaries to handle its surplus funds. It also relies heavily on financial intermediaries for external financing, as witness the fact that the debts incurred by households consist mostly of consumer credit loans and mortgage loans, both of which are supplied by financial intermediaries.

The nonfinancial business sector gives a somewhat different picture. Relative to the consumer sector, this sector is not an important supplier of external finance to others, either directly or indirectly. It is, however, an important *user* of external finance. Its principal sources of external funds are (a) bank loans, (b) mortgages, and (c) the sale of bonds, in that order. Since financial intermediaries are the only important holders of mortgages on corporate property, and since they also purchase the bulk of new corporate bonds, they supply almost all the external financing obtained by nonfinancial businesses, even though the ultimate source of these funds is the household sector.*

---

* We are speaking here of the external financing that the business sector receives from other sectors. For many firms in the business sector, *trade credit* (i.e., credit extended by one nonfinancial business firm to another) is an important source of external finance.

State and local governments, like nonfinancial businesses, often have funds deficits, and to cover them they sell debt obligations. Financial intermediaries currently hold about one-half of all outstanding state and local bonds; they also buy most of the new bonds issued by state and local governments.

The federal government incurs funds deficits too, and it also covers them by selling debt obligations. Currently financial intermediaries hold about one-half of the outstanding federal debt; they are also large purchasers of new issues of government securities.

WHY DO FINANCIAL INTERMEDIARIES EXIST?

The services of financial intermediaries obviously don't come free. Yet surplus units, particularly those in the consumer sector, often dispose of their surplus funds by buying *indirect* securities issued by financial intermediaries. Why doesn't each surplus unit assemble a portfolio of *primary* securities that—given its preferences with respect to risk, liquidity, and return—would be optimal for it? The reason is that financial intermediaries can create indirect securities which—judged in terms of price stability, liquidity and return—are more appealing to many investors than the primary securities they replace.*

How can intermediaries do this? That is, how can they make a profit themselves and still keep the investor happy?

One reason is that do-it-yourself assembling of optimal portfolios is not without cost for the investor. If he is to succeed, he must collect and digest vast quantities of information on available financial assets. Consider poor Jones. If he decides to assemble his own portfolio, he'll face the gargantuan task of weighing the merits of the over 4000 stocks and bonds currently traded on organized exchanges, and the even larger number of stocks that are traded over the counter.† Jones will also have to consider a variety of other primary securities from home mortgages to commercial paper that he, as an optimizing investor, might choose to hold. Mind you, he has to do all this *and* hold down his job and eat and sleep. Clearly he's going to need a secretary, a statistical analyst, and a computer.

So too will an institutional investor, since such a firm will face the same dismaying range of choice that Jones does. *But* economies of scale operate

---

* At the beginning of the chapter we distinguished between *indirect* securities issued by financial intermediaries and *primary* securities issued by ultimate funds deficit units.

† Some stocks are traded on organized exchanges, the two largest of which are the New York Stock Exchange and the American Stock Exchange. Many others are traded in a less formal way between dealers and brokers in what is known as the *over-the-counter market.* We'll talk about this market and the exchanges in Chapter 32.

here, and they favor the big institutional investor who has a lot of money to invest.* The reason is that, when you are designing a portfolio, the investment decisions that you have to make when you're investing $1 million can just as well be used as a basis for investing $100 million. Therefore a large institution, even though its absolute costs of portfolio selection are certain to be high, will incur lower portfolio-selection costs per dollar invested than a small investor does.

A second cost to the investor of assembling his portfolio are the actual costs of buying securities. Although securities are purchased under varying circumstances, broker-dealers usually experience economies of scale on large sales. (It probably doesn't cost a broker any more to execute Rich Smith's order for 1000 shares of Nuclear Orbit, Inc., than it does for him to execute Shoestring Jones's order for 5 shares.) Generally brokers' fees or markup margins reflect at least a part of these economies of scale. So the transactions costs incurred by large institutions are lower, per dollar invested, than those incurred by small investors.

The cost of investing in primary securities is not the only reason why financial intermediaries are able to create appealing indirect securities. As we pointed out in Chapter 5, any investor who is a risk averter wants to *diversify* his portfolio in order to reduce risk. Many financial assets, however, are available only in large indivisible units. Some stocks cost three or four hundred dollars per share, and in Europe you can find stocks that cost $10,000 per share. (If you're shopping in that price range, that is.) For this reason the small investor often has a hard time diversifying. A large financial intermediary, on the other hand, does not, and thus it can issue indirect securities which, because they are backed by a diversified portfolio, represent in the eyes of the small investor a substitute for the diversified portfolio he cannot assemble on his own.

The reasons we have given for the existence of financial intermediaries —that knowledge and transactions are not without cost and that financial assets are not divisible—concern what we might call "market imperfections." But even aside from such imperfections, there is justification for financial intermediaries, for several reasons.

1) In an uncertain world the task of investing calls for judgment and foresight. Naturally investors are not equally endowed with these two virtues. Therefore many investors, instead of managing their own portfolios, entrust their funds to some person who by nature is innately better suited to assume the role of portfolio manager.

---

* To say that a firm experiences economies of scale means that its average costs go down as its scale of operation goes up.

2) So long as different people receive and spend their incomes at different times, any institution which offers to accept deposits from individuals who are looking for a safe place to "store" short-term money balances will find that the total quantity of funds deposited with it never falls to zero, but instead fluctuates within a relatively narrow range around some positive average level.* Therefore such an institution can invest at least some of the funds deposited with it in income-bearing *primary* securities. The moment it does so, however, it becomes a financial intermediary. (This, as we shall see in Chapter 28, explains the genesis of banks.)

3) In an uncertain world, consumers like Jones and firms like Tectronics face contingencies, ranging from fire to theft to hurricanes, against which they want to protect themselves. If the probability that such a contingency will occur in any one firm or household is independent of the probability that it will occur in some other firm or household (e.g., if the probability that Smith's house will burn down is independent of the probability that Jones's, Johnson's, or anybody else's will burn down), then people who face a common contingency can protect themselves against it by pooling their risks. They all contribute small amounts to a single fund whose proceeds are used to compensate the losses of contributors who are unfortunate enough to suffer the contingency protected against.

Because there is such a need for facilities to pool independent risks, many casualty insurance companies have come into being. At first glance one would think that there wouldn't be any basis for such firms to act as financial intermediaries, because ideally they could operate each year by collecting just enough premiums to cover the total claims (losses) they would have to pay out plus their costs of operation. In actual practice, however, things don't work out this way. Casualty insurance companies can't predict what their actual losses will be in a given year; also the incidence of some sorts of contingencies varies from one year to the next. So such companies often accumulate large reserves to protect themselves against years when losses are high (years when there's a big hurricane, a wave of looting, or a big city riot). Naturally these companies invest their reserves, and when they do they act as financial intermediaries between insurance-policy holders and funds-deficit units. Life insurance companies also do the same thing, but, as we shall see, many life insurance policies combine protection with savings. So a life insurance company in effect accepts "savings deposits" and thus functions much more like a typical intermediary than other sorts of insurance companies do.

---

* Problem 3 at the end of this chapter illustrates this point.

PROBLEMS

1   Suppose that you had $10 of surplus funds. How would you invest them? What if you had $1,000 of surplus funds? $100,000? $1,000,000?

     When you answer this question, specify whether you would buy indirect securities issued by financial intermediaries or primary securities issued by ultimate deficit units (i.e., whether you would invest in savings deposits, common stock, mutual fund shares, corporate bonds, life insurance policies, or other securities). What considerations would influence your choice? Would they vary depending on the amount of money you had to invest? Do your answers shed any light on why financial intermediaries play an important role in transferring funds from ultimate surplus to ultimate deficit units?

2   Do you think that an investment company such as the Ever-Upward Mutual Fund might exist even in a world in which knowledge and transactions were without cost and in which all financial assets were divisible into very small units? Explain your answer.

3   Wildcat is a little bank with no branch offices. It's located in a pretty small town, and it doesn't have many depositors. In fact it has only three, Smith, Brown, and Jones. At the beginning of the month, these three depositors hold balances at Wildcat equal to $300, $200, and $100, respectively. During a typical month (which we assume for simplicity starts out on Monday and has 28 days) the receipts and expenditures of each of these depositors follow a definite pattern. Smith always deposits a $200 paycheck on the 15th and another on the 26th. And he regularly withdraws $30 a day during the first half of the month and $10 a day thereafter, 5 days a week. Jones deposits his paychecks on Fridays; they run a sort of irregular pattern, $175 the first Friday, $50 the second, $125 the third and $50 the fourth. Also Jones shops only on Tuesdays; he always spends exactly $100; and he withdraws the $100 Tuesday afternoon just before he goes shopping. Brown, the poorest of all, deposits an $80 check every Friday at Wildcat, but he's back on Monday morning to withdraw $75.

     What amount of the dollars that Smith, Brown, and Jones deposit at Wildcat can Wildcat lend out during the first week of the month without running the risk that one of these depositors will come in and demand cash that it doesn't have? What about the other three weeks of the month? Does your answer suggest anything about why banks can profitably exist?

*Appendix to Chapter 27

FINANCIAL INTERMEDIARIES AS PROFIT-MAXIMIZING FIRMS

Financial intermediaries, as we shall see, are extremely diverse. They issue very different types of indirect securities, acquire very different types of primary securities, and have very different ratios of debt to equity capital. Given this diversity, can we develop a single theory that will explain the behavior of all?

Yes. Financial intermediaries, whatever their differences may be, all† pursue the same fundamental goal that nonfinancial business firms do: They want to maximize current and future profits. The chief difference between intermediaries and goods-producing firms is not their aim, but the nature of the inputs they use, the sort of production function they have, and the kinds of output they produce. Therefore we can apply to financial intermediaries the same theory of profit maximization developed in Part 2 for goods-producing firms (with a few obvious modifications of course).

Let us try to develop a general description or model of the intermediary as a profit-maximizing firm: The principal *inputs* an intermediary uses, naturally, are the funds it gets from depositors (or shareholders or policy-holders) in exchange for the indirect securities it issues. Its *output* consists of the investments it makes with these funds. Thus an intermediary's main cost is the return it pays on "borrowed" funds, while its sole income is the return it gets on invested funds. The size of its profits depends on the volume of funds it borrows and invests, on the spread between its borrowing and lending rates, and on the size of its administrative costs.

Consider the Backwater Branch Bank. They get funds by soliciting savings deposits. Then they lend these funds to consumers who want to buy

---

* Students who have not yet read Part 2 should omit this starred appendix.

† Mutual (i.e., "depositor"-owned) institutions are a possible exception. Even for such institutions, however, there are good grounds for thinking that management will behave as if profit maximization were its goal.

cars, remodel kitchens, or send Junior to college. Backwater charges a higher rate on the funds it lends out than it pays on the savings deposits it accepts. The margin between Backwater's borrowing and lending rates isn't all profit, however. Backwater's loan officer and secretaries have to be paid. And then there are local realty taxes, lighting, heating, and depreciation on the bank building. Once these administrative costs are paid, there is still usually a margin left between Backwater's costs and receipts. This margin equals their profits.

To describe the equilibrium of a profit-maximizing intermediary is a complex task. Let us begin by assuming that our intermediary, Backwater, deals only in one-year securities, and that it has a pretty good idea of what is going to happen in the current year. (This assumption eliminates the problem of uncertainty.) Each year Backwater's profits equal its total loans times the spread between its borrowing and lending rates (i.e., its gross income from investment) minus its fixed or administrative costs. Therefore whenever Backwater increases its total loans, its profits will rise. To increase its loans, however, Backwater will have to raise its borrowing rate, lower its lending rate, or both; in other words, it will have to reduce its rate spread, and in doing so it will lower profits. For this reason, to maximize profits Backwater should increase its loans up to (but *not* beyond) the point at which the profit increase associated with a small rise in loan volume just equals the profit decrease associated with the resulting reduction in rate spread. In terms of the analysis in Chapter 9, Backwater (or any intermediary) will maximize profits by increasing loan volume up to the point at which the *marginal cost* it incurs in soliciting an additional deposit dollar just equals the *marginal revenue* it obtains by investing that dollar.

That pretty much sums up profit-maximization for an intermediary if the character of the indirect security it issues is fixed. The typical intermediary, however, can vary not only the *return* it pays on its security, but also some of the other characteristics of this security. Backwater might decide to pay full interest on deposits received up to the 10th of the month. Or they might offer free in-town parking to depositors. A different demand curve will be associated with each indirect security (i.e., set of terms) that Backwater might offer savers. So the quantity of deposits Backwater attracts will depend not only on the *total* deposit rate (i.e., *nominal* deposit rate plus the cost of extra features) it pays, but also on the design of its security. Therefore an intermediary will earn the maximum possible profits only if it offers the indirect security that creates the most favorable possible relationship between the deposit rate it pays and the quantity of deposits it attracts. Thus to maximize profits an intermediary must practice *"security differentiation"* in soliciting funds inputs, just as goods producers practice *product* differentiation in selling their outputs.*

---

* See Chapter 23.

The Effect of Uncertainty on the Operations of an Intermediary

We have been talking about firms that deal only in one-period securities and don't have any uncertainties about the future. Obviously this doesn't apply to most intermediaries. Life insurance companies, for example, issue policies of indefinite duration and buy bonds that won't mature for decades.

When it decides what securities to issue and acquire, an intermediary that deals in multi-period securities has to consider the way its decisions affect not only current profits, but also future profits. This brings the intermediary smack up against the familiar problem of uncertainty. In an uncertain world, an intermediary like Backwater that makes loans faces the danger that some of these loans won't be repaid, i.e., *there's the risk of capital loss.* If an intermediary issues a *fixed*-price security* (like Backwater's savings deposits), and if the "sale" of this security is its only source of funds, then if the intermediary suffers even a small capital loss (e.g., *one* unpaid loan in excess of current earnings), it will end up having more deposit liabilities than assets (i.e., it will end up being insolvent). But if an intermediary has some equity funds, then if it suffers a small capital loss in excess of current earnings, this loss will reduce its net worth (i.e., the equity interest of its owners), but it won't render the intermediary insolvent.

Since equity capital offers protection against capital losses, Backwater and other intermediaries that issue fixed-price securities respond to uncertainty by soliciting equity capital. Presumably the riskier the loans an intermediary makes, the more equity capital it will want to hold relative to its total liabilities, or (what is the same thing) the more equity capital it will want to hold relative to its total assets.

For a good example, compare finance companies (like the Ezee Credit Company) with commercial banks like Backwater. The Ezee Credit Company says, in foot-high neon letters, "You can get up to $500 on your signature alone." Finance companies make riskier loans than ordinary commercial banks do. Their average capital losses for each $100 of loans they extend are 6 to 7 times greater than those of commercial banks. Thus we would expect (and the data in Problem 10 show) that at every asset level finance companies have a higher ratio of equity capital to total assets than commercial banks do.†

---

* In Chapter 5 we distinguished between *variable*-price assets—such as common stock and bonds—and *fixed*-price assets—such as cash and bank deposits.

† The fact that finance companies, commercial banks, and other intermediaries regularly suffer capital losses in connection with the loans they extend doesn't mean that they always have negative profits (i.e., losses). Such companies maintain a wide enough spread between their borrowing and lending rates to cover their expenses *plus* their anticipated capital losses. Thus what is likely to cause losses and solvency problems is not anticipated capital losses, but large *un*anticipated ones.

Financial intermediaries that operate under uncertainty also often face *the risk of illiquidity*. Backwater Branch Bank can't predict for sure in just which period depositors will withdraw funds, so whenever it uses funds deposited with it to make *multi*-period investments, it runs the risk that sometime soon depositors might just demand more cash than the bank has on hand. To protect against this risk, intermediaries keep some of the funds they receive in cash, and in liquid assets such as government bonds, which, unlike customer loans and mortgages, can be rapidly converted into cash.

The acuteness with which an intermediary feels the risk of illiquidity depends on the variability of the deposits it receives. Take the case of multi-branch versus single-branch (i.e., unit) banks. If a bank like Backwater has a lot of branches, then deposits will probably be increasing at some branches at the same time they are decreasing at others, so the bank's total deposits won't show as much variability as its deposits at any one branch do. Therefore a multibranch bank is likely to experience less variability in its total deposits than a unit bank does, and for this reason we would expect (and the data in Problem 4 show) that the average multibranch bank holds a lower ratio of liquid to total assets than the average unit bank of similar size.

A financial intermediary that operates under uncertainty faces choices similar to but more complex than those faced by an intermediary that operates under certainty. It has to make the same volume-versus-spread and security-design decisions as an intermediary that operates under certainty. In addition, it has to decide what proportion of equity to debt capital to maintain (i.e., what amount of debt leverage to use); and it has to select the maturity of the indirect securities it issues, and the maturities of the primary securities it buys. When it makes these decisions, it has to keep in mind the effect these decisions have, not just on the *profits* it earns, but also on the *risk* of insolvency and illiquidity that it incurs.

Since a firm that operates under certainty has just one objective—maximizing profits—we can identify *its* equilibrium position. But the equilibrium position of an intermediary that operates under uncertainty (and real ones all do*) is harder to pin down. In Chapter 11 we said that any entrepreneur who operates under uncertainty will have well-defined risk preferences and that, when he chooses among the alternative investment-financing options open to his firm, he will always select the one that ranks highest in terms of these risk preferences. So, in studying the way that an intermediary attains equilibrium, we assume the following: (1) The entrepreneur who runs the intermediary has definite risk preferences. (2) He will always adjust the composition of the intermediary's asset portfolio, the

---

* See the footnote on page 160 for an explanation of the reason for this certainty–uncertainty comparison.

design of its indirect security, and the size of its debt–equity ratio so that this firm attains *the* feasible investment-financing option that ranks highest from the standpoint of his risk preferences.

Debt Structure: An Example

The above two assumptions about the behavior of intermediaries can be used to develop a model that will explain the way intermediaries operating under different circumstances attain equilibrium. To illustrate, let us work through an example about the debt structure of such firms. (Two other examples are presented in Problems 4 and 5.)

Recall that in the appendix to Chapter 11 we showed that, if an entrepreneur has definite risk preferences, he can rank different pairs of assets and liabilities.* His attitude toward different pairs of assets and liabilities can be represented by a *preference map*.

Any entrepreneur naturally prefers having few liabilities to having many. Thus his indifference curves between different liabilities slope downward; *higher* indifference curves correspond to *lower* levels of satisfaction. Also, since intermediaries often incur not just one sort but many different sorts of liabilities, the typical entrepreneur's indifference curves between different liabilities must be *concave* to the origin, like those in Fig. 27.2.†

Now consider two intermediaries, both of whom borrow funds from funds-surplus units and lend them out to consumers who have funds deficits. The first, the Ezee Credit Company, does a lively business. Consumer demand for its loans is quite steady. The second, Instant Money, Inc., finds that demand for its loans fluctuates considerably over time.

This difference affects the debt preferences of these two firms. Ezee Credit is quite sure that it can keep all the funds it borrows loaned out, so long-term debt doesn't look risky to it. Instant Money, on the other hand, *isn't* so sure, and therefore it views long-term debt as a risky proposition. Thus—all other things constant—Ezee Credit would be more willing to substitute long-term for short-term debt than Instant Money would. In other words, if short-term debt were measured along the vertical axis and long-term debt along the horizontal axis, Ezee Credit would have *flatter* indifference curves between long- and short-term debt than Instant Money would.

This difference in the preferences of the two firms exerts a systematic influence on the proportions of long- to short-term debt that they incur. Sup-

---

* Recall that we also showed in Chapter 5 that the consumer's risk preferences enable him to rank different pairs of assets and liabilities. (See Figs. 5.1 and 5.3 and the related discussion.)

† The reasoning here is like the reasoning we used in Part 2 to establish the shape of the consumer's indifference map. See Problem 3 at the end of this appendix.

pose that each wants to borrow $500,000. Then each will have to attain equilibrium somewhere along the budget line in Fig. 27.2 (note that this line contains all debt combinations that total $500,000).* Curve I in Fig. 27.2 represents one curve from Ezee Credit's preference map between short- and long-term debt. Thus Ezee Credit will obviously attain equilibrium at point A, and it will combine short- and long-term debt in the proportion $(S/L)_I$. Curve II represents an indifference curve from Instant Money's preference map. Since this curve is steeper than curve I, Instant Money can't attain equilibrium at point A, but at point B, where a second one of its indifference curves, II', is just tangent to the budget line gg.

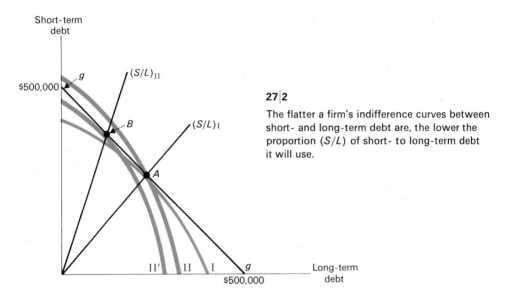

27|2

The flatter a firm's indifference curves between short- and long-term debt are, the lower the proportion (S/L) of short- to long-term debt it will use.

By comparing points A and B, we see that Instant Money will use a higher proportion of short-term to long-term debt than Ezee Credit will. Thus our theory predicts that if two intermediaries operate under roughly similar circumstances, but one experiences much more volatile loan demand than the other, then the first will tend to use a higher proportion of short- to long-term debt than the second.

To test this prediction, let us compare the debt structure of sales finance and consumer finance companies. Both sorts of companies obtain funds by selling short-term notes and long-term bonds. However, consumer finance companies lend directly to consumers, while sales finance companies lend to consumers indirectly by buying up the installment-credit contracts that

---

* In drawing up the budget line gg, we have assumed for simplicity that (1) both firms sell debt instruments at face value, and (2) any differences in the interest costs of different liabilities will be reflected in the shape of the firm's preferences between these liabilities.

consumers who buy durable goods sign. Sales of consumer durables vary greatly from year to year. So sales finance companies experience a much more volatile demand for loans than consumer finance companies do. Therefore our theory predicts that (all other things equal) sales finance companies will have a higher ratio of short- to long-term debt than consumer finance companies do. Figure 27.3 shows that this prediction is borne out by the facts.

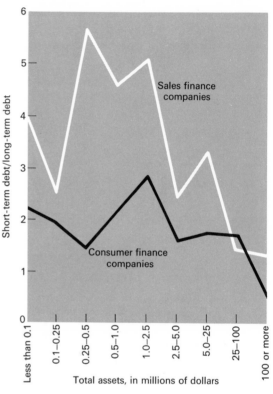

27|3

Sales finance companies use a higher proportion of short- to long-term debt than consumer finance companies of comparable asset size do. (Source: *Federal Reserve Bulletin*, April 1967)

PROBLEMS

1 In November 1965 Detroit's Bank of the Commonwealth set off a local checking account war by offering free checking accounts to depositors with a minimum balance of $194 instead of the usual $300. During the ensuing months competing banks retaliated by shaving their minimum balance requirements even lower. Finally in 1967 the Bank of the Commonwealth offered a free no-minimum-deposit checking account to any depositor willing to keep $500 in a savings account at the bank. This escalating battle of the banks, besides benefiting Detroit check writers, provides an interesting example of competition via security differentiation. Can you think of any instances from your own experiences in which rival financial intermediaries have engaged in competitive security differentiation?

2 According to the *Wall Street Journal* (June 22, 1967) a large Indianapolis bank charges its best customers \$3.50 annually per \$100 on auto loans. For riskier auto loans it scales the charge upward at 50-cent intervals to \$5.50 per \$100. Would you characterize this practice as price discrimination in the sense we used this term in Chapter 20? [*Hint:* A loan is a loan is a loan—or is it?] Explain your answer.

*3 In the text we said that the typical entrepreneur who runs a financial intermediary will have concave, downward-sloping indifference curves between any two liabilities. Let L_1 and L_2 denote two different kinds of liabilities:

   a) Show, using an appropriate diagram, that the entrepreneur's indifference curves between L_1 and L_2 will slope downward.

   b) Show also that higher indifference curves will correspond to lower levels of satisfaction.

   c) Show that if the entrepreneur's indifference curves are convex, he will never incur both types of liabilities simultaneously.

   Note: In problems 7 and 8 below, we assume that the intermediaries in question are risk averters in the sense that they have convex indifference curves between any two assets.

*4 Consider two banks A and B that are identical in all respects except that A experiences much more variability in its deposits than B does. Presumably this will make A less willing than B to substitute loans for liquid assets. Thus if we measure liquid assets along the vertical axis and loans along the horizontal axis, A will have flatter indifference curves than B. Draw an appropriate diagram, and investigate what effect this difference in asset preferences will have on the proportions in which A and B allocate their investable funds between loans and liquid assets. Check whether or not your conclusion jibes with our comments in the text on the behavior of branch banks versus unit banks. The relevant statistics are presented below.

Total Loans as a Percent of Loans Plus Liquid Assets

Deposit size, in thousands of dollars	Less than 5,000	5,000– 25,000	25,000– 100,000	100,000– 500,000	Over 500,000
Unit banks:					
less than 25% time deposits	44.17	45.63	53.63	61.27	66.06
25–50% time deposits	47.53	48.60	50.25	52.01	—
over 50% time deposits	51.44	50.77	46.00	—	—
Branch banks:					
less than 25% time deposits	—	58.59	55.90	61.30	68.59
25–50% time deposits	—	56.97	54.71	57.74	62.79
over 50% time deposits	—	57.78	57.38	60.48	—

Source: P. M. Horvitz: "Economies of Scale in Banking," in *Private Financial Institutions*, by the Commission on Money and Credit; Englewood Cliffs, N.J.: Prentice Hall, 1963. In the table, liquid assets do not include required reserves.

* These problems are based on results derived in Chapter 11.

*5 Assume that the Backwater Branch Bank invests in liquid assets and in a single kind of loan. Also assume that Backwater is a price taker in the loan market and that it always makes loans at a discount; that is, it pays the borrower only the discounted value of the loan. (The discounted value of a one-year loan equals $[1/(1 + r)] \cdot P$, where r is the interest rate and P is the amount of the loan). Show that there are good reasons to believe that Backwater's supply curve of loans, $s = s(r)$, slopes upward. [*Hint:* Draw an appropriate indifference map for Backwater, in which you measure loans along the vertical axis and liquid assets along the horizontal axis. Then show that, as you move to the right along any horizontal line on this indifference map, the indifference curves you cross ought to become flatter and flatter.]

*6 Consider the following statistics. They show that financial intermediaries tend to decrease their ratio of equity capital to total assets (i.e., to increase their debt/equity ratio) as their total assets increase. If you look back on the data in Problem 17 of Chapter 11, you will see that manufacturing firms behave in exactly the opposite way. What reasons can you think of that might explain this contrast?

Equity/Total Asset Ratios for Commercial Banks and Finance Companies

Asset size, in thousands of dollars	Less than 100	100– 500	500– 1,000	1,000– 2,500	2,500– 5,000	5,000– 25,000	25,000– 100,000	More than or equal to 100,000
Commercial banks: equity/total assets	0.53	0.33	0.18	0.11	0.10	0.08	0.08	0.08
Finance companies: equity/total assets	0.70	0.47	0.33	0.28	0.18	0.22	0.15	0.13

Source: U.S. Department of the Treasury and the Board of Governors of the Federal Reserve System. Data are for 1963–64.

CHAPTER 28

MONEY AND BANKS

Traditionally economists have distinguished between banks on the one hand and financial intermediaries on the other. As we examine a bank closely, however, we shall find that its operations consist in accepting funds deposits (i.e., in borrowing funds) at one interest rate and in making investments (i.e., in loaning out funds) at another, higher interest rate. We find also that it is the spread between the bank's borrowing and lending rates that permits it to cover costs and to glean some profits from its operations. Thus a bank is as much a financial intermediary as a life insurance company, a savings and loan association, or a pension fund.

Banks are the oldest kind of financial intermediary, and remain the single most important one. The feature that distinguishes banks from other intermediaries and that endows them with special prominence is this:

Banks, in the course of their operations, create liabilities (i.e., indirect securities) which serve as money.

Among financial intermediaries, banks and banks alone have this power.

MONEY

We have distinguished banks from other financial intermediaries by the fact that they issue indirect securities that serve as money. How shall we define money? What things do we use as money?

What Is Money?

To define money, let us first analyze the functions that textbooks usually claim money fulfills.

1) *Money provides a unit of account,* in terms of which the prices of all commodities are quoted. Imagine a barter economy in which sellers quoted prices in terms of a variety of commodities. The quoted price of a cow might be half a horse, the price of a horse 40 chickens, and the price of a

chicken—well, just a fraction of a cow! *Noncommensurable prices* of this sort would create confusion, and make it difficult for any trader to keep track of his receipts and outlays. These difficulties, however, could be overcome if traders agreed to quote all prices in terms of a single commodity, or unit of account. This unit of account could be any arbitrarily selected commodity (for example, chickens); or it could be some *nonexistent* object. The traders—although they live in an economy in which *no* dollars exist—could easily introduce the dollar as a unit of account! To do so, they would only need to set the price of some arbitrarily selected commodity, say chickens, equal to $1. Then by using the ratios at which chickens and other commodities exchange, they could calculate dollar prices for these commodities. If the price of chickens were set equal to $1, the prices of horses and cows would be $40 and $20, respectively. It may sound farfetched to say that traders could use nonexistent dollars for a unit of account, but historical and anthropological studies indicate that many primitive societies adopted nonexistent objects as units of account. Examples can be found close to home: Posh British shops quote prices in guineas instead of pounds and shillings, yet the British government stopped minting guineas in 1813.

2) *Money serves as a medium of exchange.* A medium of exchange is any object or commodity that is acceptable to sellers, not because it is desired for its own sake (although it may be), but because it can readily be exchanged for other goods. Consider again the barter economy described above. This economy has no medium of exchange, so a trader who wants to exchange a horse for chickens can trade only if the chicken seller either needs a horse or knows that he can buy something he needs with a horse. Since such a coincidence of wants seldom occurs, an impasse may result. Traders could presumably overcome impasses of this sort by roundabout trades involving numerous commodities and traders, but their lives would be simplified if they agreed to make and receive all payments in terms of a single commodity; in other words, if they designated one commodity as their *medium of exchange.*

In a modern economy money represents a claim against some sort of institution. Thus it is a financial asset just like a stock or a bond, and one way spending units can absorb their funds surpluses (i.e., store up their purchasing power over time) is by building up their money balances. Thus we come to the third function of money.

3) *Money provides a store of value.*

The fourth and final function of money is that

4) *Money serves as a standard of deferred payment.* That is, it serves as the unit of account, in terms of which future payments (e.g., those associated with the repayment of currently contracted debts) are stipulated.

Let's now return to our original question: What is money? Perhaps, in light of the above points, we could say that money is any object that simultaneously fulfills all four functions of money. That won't quite do as a definition, though, because the functions of money have not, in every economy, been fulfilled by a single object. In the Middle Ages, for example, metal coins of small denominations were used for trading while other fictitious coins—frequently of higher demoninations—were used as units of account. Recently gold has often served as a standard of deferred payment in countries in which paper currency was the common medium of exchange. Gold and paper currency have also competed side by side as media of exchange. They did so in the U.S. until gold coins were withdrawn from circulation after Congress passed the Gold Reserve Act in 1934. Therefore the definition of money proposed above is too restrictive, and we shall define money simply as follows:

Money is any object that functions widely as a medium of exchange.

Money in the U.S. Today

Let us now use our definition of money to list the things that serve as money in the U.S. today. Certainly *coins* and *currency* will be at the top of our list, since these are the media of payment that we use in our small everyday transactions. In addition, however, we also make many payments (especially large ones) by check. Thus checks, like coins and currency, are an important medium of exchange, and *checking account balances* must therefore be included in our money supply.

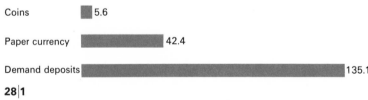

28|1

The U.S. money supply, June 31, 1967. (Source: *Federal Reserve Bulletin*)

The current composition of the U.S. money supply is shown in Fig. 28.1. There we see that coins and paper currency—which we are so accustomed to think of as money—actually constitute less than one-fourth of our total money supply. Checking account balances, or *demand deposits* as they are more properly known, account for the remaining three-fourths.

The principal elements of our money supply have varied origins. Coins are minted by the Treasury, which sells them at face value to the banks, which in turn supply them to customers. The face value of each type of coin currently minted by the Treasury exceeds by a considerable amount the market value of the metals it contains. Therefore the Treasury earns a profit, referred to as *seigniorage,* on its minting activities. Its rate of production, however, is not dictated by the profit motive; the Treasury is supposed to mint whatever quantity of coin the public needs. However, it has not always been able to meet this goal. During the early 1960's, its inability to expand production fast enough to meet demand resulted in a severe coin shortage, which left supermarkets literally wondering where their next nickel was coming from, and which even drove a few of them to make change with wooden nickels of their own manufacture!

Of the over $40 billion of paper notes currently in circulation in the U.S., only a small fraction were printed and put into circulation by the Treasury. All the rest, as we shall see when we discuss the Federal Reserve System, were issued by, and are thus liabilities of, the central bank.

Treasury coins, Treasury notes, and Federal Reserve notes are, like all modern currencies, *fiat money.* That is, by government fiat they have been made *legal tender,* and *the public is required to accept them at face value,* despite the fact that their face value exceeds by a wide margin their negligible *intrinsic worth.*

Demand deposits, which constitute the final and most important element of our money supply, are issued by neither the federal government nor its designated monetary authority. They are the liabilities of private commercial banks, and are created by the banks in the normal course of their operations.

THE GENESIS OF BANKS

Bank-created money, which we shall refer to as *inside money,* has always been a substitute for, and competitive with, *money produced outside the banking system,* that is, *outside money.**

How did money-creating banks arise in societies which already had outside money? Banks probably began when people who held large amounts of *outside money* (which might have been gold coin, silver bullion, or even some form of fiat money) discovered that it was more convenient to deposit their money with an institution that specialized in safeguarding money than to store it themselves. Since such institutions eventually developed into

---

* In the theoretical literature of economics, "inside money" usually refers to money created through the monetization of *private* debt and "outside money" to money created through the monetization of *public* debt (or money backed by gold). We have modified this definition slightly because the distinction that is important for this chapter and the next is the distinction between money that private banks create and money that originates from other sources.

banks, we shall here, for simplicity, begin to refer to them as banks (although technically they did not become banks until, in addition to accepting deposits, they also began to extend loans).

When a depositor put money in a bank, he obtained a claim against the bank for that amount of money, and he would naturally demand some tangible evidence of this claim. One way the bank gave such evidence was by recording the amount of the deposit on its ledger and promising the depositor that he could withdraw an equivalent amount of money *on demand*. In other words, the bank would credit the depositor with what we would today call a *demand deposit*.

A depositor who wanted to use some of his money to pay a bill could always go to his bank, withdraw the precise amount he needed, and pass this money on to his creditor. A simpler approach—and one that became increasingly popular, first in commercial circles and later with the general populace—was for the depositor who wanted to pay a bill to request in writing that his bank "pay to the order of" his creditor a specified sum of money.

When the creditor got this check, he might present it directly to the bank and demand payment in cash; the bank would pay out a sum equal to the amount of the check, and simultaneously debit the depositor's account by (i.e., deduct from the depositor's account) an equal sum.

Alternatively, the check receiver might deposit the check in *his* bank account. If he happened to deposit the check at the bank against which it was drawn, this bank could effect the required payment simply by crediting (adding to) his account and debiting the check writer's account. If he did not, the bank receiving the check would have to present the check for payment to the bank against which it was drawn. Once such payment was effected, appropriate debits and credits would be made in the accounts of the check writer and the check depositor by their respective banks.

Since *bank liabilities* in the form of deposit money were obviously safer and in many ways more convenient to hold and to use than *outside money,* and since their convertibility into outside money was guaranteed by the banks, they naturally came to compete with outside money as a medium of exchange. Depositors chose to withdraw outside money from the banks less and less frequently. Individual banks, of course, would lose outside money whenever checks written against them were deposited with other banks. But such losses would generally be matched by the gains that resulted whenever checks written against other banks were deposited with them. Thus the typical banker found that, although he could (in theory at least) be called on at any moment to convert all his bank's deposit liabilities into outside money, in practice his bank's *net* losses or gains of outside money during any period were never more than a fraction of the amount it held on deposit.

After bankers realized this, they also realized that, without impairing their commitment to convert deposit liabilities into money on demand, *they could issue (create) demand deposits not only in exchange for deposits of outside money, but also in exchange for income-bearing debt instruments.* In other words, they found that, within limits, they could safely extend loans simply by crediting demand deposits to borrowers. Bankers eagerly seized on this opportunity, since they could earn income on each loan extended.

The important thing about all this is not that the institutions that initially specialized in storing outside money began to extend loans, but that —by exchanging deposit liabilities which functioned as money for private debt claims which did not—they began to *create money,* that is, they began to *monetize private debt.* When they did so, they became banks in the modern sense of the word.

An Example of Money Creation

Here's an example of the way a bank creates money by monetizing debt. So that it will approximate as closely as possible the setup under which American banks operate, let's assume that cash (i.e., coin and currency) functions as outside money.

Suppose that Mammon Smith deposits $100 of cash (i.e., outside money) in the Wampum National Bank in exchange for a demand deposit of equal size. By accepting this deposit, Wampum National receives a $100 asset in the form of cash and incurs a $100 liability in the form of demand deposit claims against itself. By making this deposit, Smith gives up $100 of cash and receives $100 of deposit money. These balance-sheet *changes* are recorded in Table 28.1.

TABLE 28|1

The bank (Wampum National)		The depositor (Smith)	
Assets	Liabilities	Assets	Liabilities
+$100 cash	+$100 demand deposits	−$100 cash +$100 demand deposits	

Working from this table, let's see what happens to the money supply as a result of this deposit. Since demand deposits—like coin and currency— are money, when Smith puts his cash into Wampum National, he simply exchanges one form of money for another, more convenient, form: demand deposits. The transaction has no effect whatever on the quantity of money he holds. It does, of course, increase the quantity of cash Wampum National holds, but, since Wampum knows that this cash is a reserve against the claims (liabilities) it has incurred in accepting a cash deposit, this cash has in effect been withdrawn from circulation and thus should not be counted as part of the money supply. Therefore the deposit of cash in a bank *per se* has no effect on the money supply.

Now suppose that Wampum National loans Scanty Brown $80. If it pays out this loan by crediting Brown's deposit account with $80, then the bank's debt claims against borrowers (an asset) and its deposit liabilities will both rise by $80. These balance-sheet *changes* are recorded in Table 28.2.

TABLE 28|2

The bank (Wampum National)		The depositor (Brown)	
Assets	Liabilities	Assets	Liabilities
+$80 loan	+$80 demand deposits	+$80 demand deposits	+$80 loan

Table 28.2 shows the effect that the loan extended by Wampum National has on the money supply: The quantity of deposit money Brown holds has risen by $80, and at the same time the quantity of other forms of money in circulation has not declined. Therefore Wampum National, by extending the $80 loan, has increased the money supply by $80. In other words, *the bank, by exchanging a deposit liability against itself for an $80 debt claim, has monetized that claim and thereby created $80 of money.*

So a bank loan does increase the money supply. But that's not the end of our money-creation story, because Wampum is likely to lose cash when it extends a loan. The reason is that Brown presumably contracts the loan in order to finance immediate expenditures, and thus he does not maintain the deposit balance he has as a result of the loan. He buys the goods he wants and pays for them by writing checks against his deposit account. If Wampum National is just one small bank among many, most of Brown's checks will be deposited at other banks, each of which will immediately present any check (drawn against Wampum National but deposited with it) to Wampum National for payment in *cash,* and Wampum National will lose a sum of cash equal to (or almost equal to*) the amount of the loan it has made.

---

* We say *almost* because some of the checks Brown writes might be deposited by their recipients in Wampum National, and—to the extent that this occurs—Wampum National will lose less cash.

Thus when Wampum National accepts a $100 deposit and extends an $80 loan, it might, as the loan's proceeds are spent, easily lose $80 of cash through check collections. If so, the net changes in its balance sheet would assume the form recorded in Table 28.3.

TABLE 28|3

The bank (Wampum National)	
Assets	Liabilities
+$20 cash +$80 loan	+$100 demand deposits

What happened to the $80 of money Wampum National created when it extended a loan? Brown "used up" this deposit money by writing checks against it, but he did not destroy it. He simply initiated a process by which this deposit money was transferred from Wampum National to the other banks in which his checks were deposited. Thus even after Wampum National loses the deposits it has created by extending a loan, the money it has created remains in existence, and will continue in existence until the loan is repaid.

Banks as Financial Intermediaries

Whenever banks create money, they are also acting as *financial intermediaries,* as we defined them on page 411.

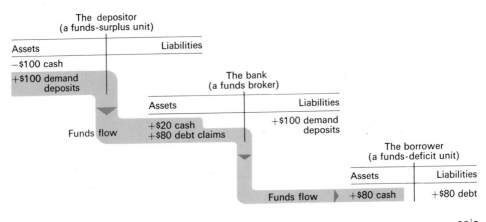

28|2

When a bank accepts deposits and makes loans, it acts as a financial intermediary.

Let us again consider the simple $100-deposit, $80-loan example given above. Only this time—to show the funds flows involved in these transactions—let us assume that Wampum National Bank pays out *cash* rather than deposit balances to the borrower. Then the changes which occur on the balance sheets of the depositor, the bank, and the borrower will be those recorded in Fig. 28.2. Here we see that the bank, when it accepts a $100 deposit and makes an $80 loan, not only creates $80 of money, but also acts as a funds broker, passing on to a funds-deficit unit $80 of funds deposited with it by a funds-surplus unit.

THE DETERMINANTS OF BANK GROWTH

We have been talking about *how* banks create money. An equally important question is: What determines *how much* money banks create?*

Reserves and the Risk of Illiquidity

Since it tends to lose cash each time it makes a loan, a bank—by extending loans—impairs its ability to meet depositor demands for cash. The more loans it extends, the greater the impairment. Thus a banker who wants both profit and safety is inevitably forced into adopting a compromise rule of thumb, to the effect that his bank may continue to loan out money until its cash reserves (i.e., holdings of outside money) as a percentage of its total deposit liabilities have declined to some specified limit. This limit represents the point at which the increasing risk associated with declining reserves begins to outweigh, in the banker's mind, the increasing profits that are also associated with declining reserves.

The height of the *reserve ratio* (i.e., the ratio of cash reserves to deposit liabilities) the banker decides to maintain depends on a number of factors: (1) The greater the variability of the deposits he accepts, the more he will want liquidity and the higher the reserve ratio he will want to maintain. (2) The more illiquid the loans he makes (i.e., the longer it would take him to turn them into cash), the higher the reserve ratio he will want to maintain. On the other hand, (3) the stronger the demand for bank loans, the more profitable such loans will be, and the lower the reserve ratio he will be tempted to maintain.

The above three factors are all objective, measurable ones, but there is one other factor, less measurable but no less important, that influences the banker's decision about how high a reserve ratio to maintain: the banker's risk preferences. After he has taken objective factors into account, his de-

---

* Some of the points discussed here were first raised in the appendix at the end of Chapter 26, where we discussed the way financial intermediaries maximize profits.

cision will always reduce to a choice between risk and profits. The banker can resolve such a choice only on the basis of his own willingness to incur risk in the pursuit of profit.

Since entrepreneurial risk preference (as we noted in Chapter 11) is a personal subjective characteristic, different bankers make quite different choices as to the height of the reserve ratios they would like to maintain. Also, since the objective factors such as deposit variability and loan profitability change over time, the decision a banker makes as to his reserve ratio changes from year to year, as conditions change.

The fact that bankers commit themselves to holding reserves equal to a specified fraction of their total deposits means that their ability to extend loans, and thus to create deposit money, depends on the quantity of outside money deposited with them. The amount of outside money banks receive in deposit depends on two factors: (1) The total quantity of outside money in circulation. The more there is, the greater the flow into banks' coffers. (2) The asset preferences of money holders (i.e., of consumers and firms). Do these spending units prefer to hold deposit money or outside money? The stronger their preferences for deposit money, the greater the quantity of outside money they deposit with banks.

Thus the four factors that determine the amount of money banks can create are:

1) The demand for bank loans
2) The risk preferences of individual bankers
3) The asset preferences of money holders
4) The quantity of outside money in circulation

When any one of these factors changes, the quantity of money that the banks can create also changes. If bankers become more daring (i.e., if a shift in their risk preferences makes them willing to assume greater risks), they lower their target reserve ratio, extend more loans, and create more money. If the quantity of outside money deposited with banks increases (either because more outside money is put into circulation or because the asset preferences of money holders shift in favor of deposit money), the banks' reserve ratio will rise and they will increase the quantity of loans they extend and thus the quantity of deposit money they create.

Multiple Deposit Creation: An Example

Now we come to a rather surprising anomaly. If someone were to ask you, you'd probably hazard a guess that for every dollar of outside money deposited with banks, the banks would be able to create one dollar of deposit money (or maybe less, since a bank always holds reserves equal to some fraction of its total deposits). But that estimate would be wrong. Whenever banks receive a dollar of outside money in deposit, they can *as a group* create 2, 3, or some other multiple number of deposit dollars.

Example: Suppose for simplicity that all banks decide to hold reserves equal to 20% of their total deposits and that all money holders decide to hold any increases in their money balances in the form of deposit money (i.e., that they don't respond to an increase in their money balances by withdrawing outside money from the banks). What is the *maximum* amount of new deposit money that the banks could create if one of them (the Wampum National Bank) received a cash (i.e., outside money) deposit of $10,000?

Well now, Wampum National will certainly be able to loan out more money, since the deposit will increase its cash reserves and its deposit liabilities by *equal* amounts. But it is only one bank among many, and thus any loan it makes will result in an equal, or almost equal, reduction in its reserves. Therefore it cannot safely expand its loans (and investments) by more than $8,000. The reason is that, if it did so, its reserves might fall below 20% of its deposits.

So that's how much deposit money a *single* bank can create on the basis of a $10,000 increase in reserves. Now let's think about how much money *the banking system as a whole* can create on the basis of a $10,000 increase in reserves.

Let's suppose that the Wampum National Bank loans $8,000 to Scanty Brown; it pays out the loan by crediting $8,000 to Brown's deposit account. Brown uses the money to finance the purchase of some pneumatic trash-mashing equipment which he can mount on the back of his truck. He pays for this equipment by writing an $8,000 check to the manufacturer of this equipment, "Smasher" Jones.

Now "Smasher" Jones happens to deposit this check in another bank, the Sanity National Bank. As soon as Sanity National presents this check to Wampum National for payment, Wampum's reserves will fall by $8,000. And, as we see in Table 28.4, Wampum will have regained equilibrium, in the sense that its reserves again equal precisely one-fifth of its deposits.

TABLE 28|4

Step 1 in the Money-Creation Process

The Wampum National Bank receives a $10,000 cash deposit		The Wampum National Bank regains equilibrium by making an $8,000 loan	
Assets	Liabilities	Assets	Liabilities
+$10,000 cash	+$10,000 demand deposits	+$2,000 cash +$8,000 loans	+$10,000 demand deposits

The plot thickens: Sanity National, whose deposits and reserves have both risen by $8,000, is now in disequilibrium. To regain equilibrium, Sanity National (assuming that it *also* tries to maintain a reserve ratio of 1 to 5) will have to make loans totaling $6,400. Suppose now that the proceeds of these loans are all deposited in a third bank, the Paycheck Trust Company. Then Sanity National's reserves will fall by $6,400 and (as indicated by Table 28.5) it will have regained equilibrium.

TABLE 28|5

Step 2 in the Money-Creation Process

The Sanity National Bank receives an $8,000 cash deposit		The Sanity National Bank regains equilibrium by making loans totaling $6,400	
Assets	Liabilities	Assets	Liabilities
+$8,000 cash	+$8,000 demand deposits	+$1,600 cash +$6,400 loans	+$8,000 demand deposits

The Paycheck Trust Company has gained the $6,400 of reserves lost by the Sanity National Bank and for this reason it is now in disequilibrium. To regain equilibrium it must increase its loans and investments by $5,120. Now if the proceeds of these loans are deposited in some fourth bank, the Furthermore National, then Paycheck Trust will have lost its "excess" reserves and, as shown in Table 28.6, will have restored its reserve–deposit ratio to the 1-to-5 level. Furthermore National, on the other hand, will now be in disequilibrium!

TABLE 28|6

Step 3 in the Money-Creation Process

The Paycheck Trust Company receives a $6,400 cash deposit		The Paycheck Trust Company regains equilibrium by making loans totaling $5,120	
Assets	Liabilities	Assets	Liabilities
+$6,400 cash	+$6,400 demand deposits	+$1,280 cash +$1,520 loans	+$6,400 demand deposits

So you can see that the money-creation story is a process that involves an infinite number of steps. How could it end? It can't, so long as every bank maintains a reserve ratio *less than 1* and every check receiver exchanges his checks for deposit money, not cash.

Assuming that the money-creation process set in motion by a deposit of additional reserves in the banking system is an infinite one, does this mean that the amount of money the banks can create is also infinite? No, because although the money-creation process results in an infinite number of additions to the money supply, each successive addition is smaller; so much smaller that the sum of all the additions approaches a *finite* limit. We can figure out this limit by means of mathematics.

To illustrate, let's calculate the maximum amount of money the banking system we have been discussing can create on the basis of $10,000 of extra reserves. Suppose that every bank in this system attempts to maintain a reserve ratio of 1 to 5. Then, when someone deposits $10,000 cash in the Wampum National Bank, the total quantity of *deposit money* created will equal the original $10,000 demand deposit extended by Wampum National, plus the $8,000 that Wampum National creates by expanding its loans, plus the $6,400 created by the Sanity National Bank, plus the $5,120 created by the Paycheck Trust Company, plus the money created by Furthermore National, and so on and so forth *ad infinitum*. The total expansion of deposit money created by that original $10,000 deposit can be represented by the expression

$$\$10,000 \left[1 + \tfrac{4}{5} + (\tfrac{4}{5})^2 + (\tfrac{4}{5})^3 + \cdots \right].$$

If we now apply to this expression the simple algebraic rule that

$$1 + r + r^2 + r^3 + \cdots = 1/(1 - r), \text{ for all } r < 1,$$

we can easily show that the total expansion of deposit money by the banking system will equal, in the long run,

$$\$10,000 \left(\frac{1}{1 - \tfrac{4}{5}} \right) \qquad \text{or} \qquad \$50,000.*$$

Our example shows that a banking system in which all banks maintain reserves equal to only 20% of deposits can create $5 of deposit money for each $1 of increase in reserves. This is true even though each individual bank in the system is unwilling to lend out more than a fraction (four-fifths, to be precise) of the funds it receives through new deposits.

---

* Note that this result refers to banks' creation of *deposit money*. If the cash originally deposited in Wampum National (and consequently withdrawn from circulation) initially constituted part of the money supply, then the creation of $50,000 of deposit money by the banks would correspond to only a $40,000 increase in the *total money supply*, i.e., in cash plus deposit money.

Our example also brings to light a fact that will be important in the next chapter, when we discuss central banking, and later on when we discuss monetary theory:

Any fractional-reserve banking system (i.e., any system in which all banks maintain reserve ratios less than 1) *can engage in a multiple expansion of deposit money each time its reserves are increased.*

We want to know the extent of this multiple expansion. As our example suggests, the *coefficient of expansion* in a fractional-reserve system can be represented by the expression $1/(1 - r)$, in which $(1 - r)$ equals the reserve ratio maintained by all banks in the system. Note that this coefficient is based on the assumption that money holders, throughout the money-creation process, refrain from withdrawing outside money from the banks. If money holders instead respond to increases in their deposit-money balances by demanding additional outside money, the relevant coefficient of expansion will be significantly *smaller* than $1/(1 - r)$. [Check the reason for this statement.]

Equity Capital and the Risk of Capital Loss

Whenever a bank extends loans, it runs—as we have said—the risk of illiquidity. It also runs a second risk: that loans won't be repaid, and that as a result the bank will suffer a capital loss.

If a bank's only source of funds is the deposits it accepts, then even a small capital loss (one in excess of current earnings) would leave it with liabilities greater than assets; in other words, even a small capital loss would render the bank insolvent. To protect against this risk, the banker usually invests some equity capital in his bank or solicits equity investments from outside sources. If he does, and if his bank is then unfortunate enough to suffer capital losses, the value of the bank's equity capital (i.e., its net worth) will fall by an amount equal to these losses and the funds that depositors have placed with the bank will be protected against loss.

Every dollar of equity capital protects the bank and its depositors against just one dollar of capital loss. So the banker has to decide, not only *whether* to provide his bank with equity capital, but also *how much*. In other words, he has to decide how much protection he should buy for his bank and its depositors.

A bank which utilizes equity capital will of course have to divide its profits among all suppliers of equity dollars. Therefore as a bank increases its ratio of equity dollars to deposit dollars in order to reduce the risk of capital loss, it sooner or later has to divide its earnings pie into more slices. So the risk of capital loss, like the risk of illiquidity, forces the banker who wants both profits and safety to adopt a compromise rule of thumb, to the effect that his bank must hold equity capital equal to some fixed ratio of his total deposits or his total loans.

The height of this equity ratio will depend partly on objective factors such as the riskiness of the loans he makes and the cost of equity capital, but also (like the height of the reserve ratio) on the banker's own risk preferences. Therefore it follows that equity–deposit ratios vary from bank to bank, and that this ratio changes over time as conditions and thus objective risks under which banks operate change.

AMERICAN COMMERCIAL BANKS

We have been talking about the theory of banks. Let us now examine the way commercial banks actually operate in the U.S. economy.

Sources of Commercial Bank Funds

Commercial banks issue two basic sorts of indirect securities: (1) *demand deposits* (i.e., checking-account money) and (2) *time deposits.* Demand deposits (as the name implies) are withdrawable on demand. Banks are not permitted to pay interest on them, and in fact most banks impose service charges on them. Banks issue many forms of time deposits: (a) The type most common and the most familiar to the man in the street is the savings deposit. Each time John Jones makes a deposit, it is registered in his passbook. Technically such deposits can be withdrawn only after a 30-day waiting period, but in practice they are withdrawable on demand; they are not negotiable. (b) Many commercial banks also issue savings certificates, or certificates of deposit, which are redeemable only at maturity. Although commercial banks pay interest on all the time deposits they issue, rates vary from bank to bank and from one instrument (i.e., type of savings security) to another. Generally banks located in financial centers pay the highest rates, and they pay them on nonredeemable securities of high denomination and long maturity.

The variety of deposit instruments that different banks offer and the variety of rates that they pay on time deposits reflect the dissimilar environments (including differing competitive conditions) in which individual banks operate. For example, big banks in financial centers offer large-denomination certificates of deposit paying high rates of return because they compete for corporate funds which might otherwise be invested in Treasury bills or other high-yielding money-market instruments.* The country cousins of money-market banks offer low-denomination certificates of deposit paying low rates of return because they compete for the funds of small local

---

* We shall discuss the money market and the instruments traded in it in Chapter 31.

depositors who don't have the opportunity to invest in money-market instruments.

As indicated in Fig. 28.3, the amount of money commercial banks get from demand deposits and the amount they get from time deposits are roughly equal. Since about two-thirds of banks' demand and time deposits are held by individuals, the consumer sector is the banks' principal supplier of funds. The nonfinancial business sector ranks next in importance; it holds about one-third of commercial banks' demand deposits and a somewhat smaller percentage of their time deposits.

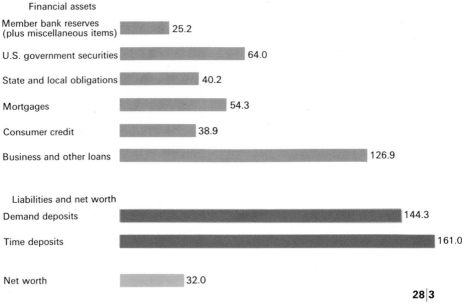

28|3

Principal assets and liabilities of U.S. commercial banks, Jan. 1, 1967 (billions of dollars). (Source: *Federal Reserve Bulletin*)

Uses of Commercial Bank Funds

When we were discussing the theory of banks, we said that banks accept deposits from funds-surplus units and *pass the money along to funds-deficit units* by means of direct loans. Another way that banks perform this function is by buying income-bearing financial assets issued by deficit units. Thus the asset side of a bank's balance sheet shows not only loans and cash, but also a variety of securities.

Because banks buy securities, they have a much wider range of choice about how to use the money people deposit with them than one would gather from our theoretical discussion. However, in making this choice, they are not completely free. They have to operate under a number of constraints, the most important of which is that they must deposit, in a non-interest-bearing account at the central bank,* reserves equal to a specified percentage of the total funds deposited with them.†

Commercial banks also have to adhere to rules laid down by the various state and federal authorities which regulate their activities. These rules do the following:

1) They prevent banks from investing in certain classes of assets, such as common stock and nonmarketable corporate debt issues.
2) They control, somewhat, the kinds of loans that banks may extend. For example, they limit the length and loan-value ratios of mortgage loans.
3) They force banks into a degree of diversification, by limiting the quantity of funds a bank may lend to a single firm or person.

Despite these constraints on its freedom, when a commercial bank designs its asset portfolio it can still choose among a wide range of assets that differ not only as to type, but as to maturity and rate of return. In making its choice, the bank is naturally influenced by the rates of return, the liquidity, and the risk of capital loss associated with the different assets available to it.

Look again at Fig. 28.3. It shows that commercial banks, after they have met nondiscretionary reserve requirements, allocate their funds between two kinds of investments: debt securities and direct loans. Apparently the various influences which affect the asset choices made by banks lead them to adopt a compromise investment policy. They split their free funds between:

1) negotiable debt instruments, which offer high liquidity and negligible risk, but relatively low earnings, and
2) direct loans, which offer relatively high returns, but zero liquidity and a certain degree of risk.

THE REGULATION OF COMMERCIAL BANKS

As we have seen, there are several agencies which regulate commercial banks. These agencies set up rules as to the types of indirect securities banks may issue and the kinds of investments they may make. All banks are subject to regulation by the authority (state or national) which charters them. Banks that are members of the Federal Reserve System are also subject to regulation by it. And all banks whose deposits are insured by the FDIC (Federal Deposit Insurance Corporation) are subject to regulation by *it*. Why should banks be singled out for so much special regulation?

---

* We shall talk about the central bank in the next chapter.

† Under current regulations any cash a bank holds in its vault also counts toward its required reserves. U.S. banks, however, don't usually choose to hold much vault cash.

There are several reasons: In a modern economy most payments are made with money, and therefore any disruption of the payments mechanism would paralyze economic life. Banks—to the extent that they accept deposits of payments media (i.e., money) and transfer title to these media—act as *guardians of the payments mechanism*.* Therefore economic stability demands that banks remain solvent.

Historically, however, when banks have been left to their own devices, they haven't been able to stay solvent. Until recent times individual bank failures, and even waves of bank failures, were distressingly common. The inevitable result of this poor record was that banks were subjected to a variety of regulations, the principal purpose of which was to protect bank solvency.

PROBLEMS

1   Are coins, currency, and checks (i.e., demand deposits) equally acceptable for all purposes as media of exchange? Can you think of any situations in which one or more of the three would not be an acceptable means of payments?

2   As we pointed out in the text, during the coin shortage of the early 1960's some grocery stores couldn't find enough coins to make change. So they resorted to handing out wooden nickels, quarters, and other coins of their own manufacture. The shopper who accepted this odd "currency" could bring it back to the store and spend it there any time he chose to, but he couldn't spend it anywhere else. Were such wooden coins money, according to our definition? Did passing them out enable the grocery store to obtain interest-free loans from its customers? Explain your answer.

3   "When you go window shopping, you are using money in a very real sense, even if you don't have any cash in your pocket and even if your bank account shows a zero balance." Explain. What function does money serve when you are window shopping? Or to put it another way: Why does the window shopper bother to look at prices?

4   Throughout history an amazing variety of commodities have been used as money. In colonial America, for example, gold and silver coins were the official media of exchange, but the supply was inadequate to meet people's needs. So the colonialists also used as money such varied objects as rum, tobacco, corn, cattle, wampum, and even "musket balls of full bore." Since so many commodities have functioned as a medium of exchange, you'd probably guess (and you'd be right) that some commodities fulfill this function more efficiently than others. What characteristics should a commodity have in order to func-

---

* To separate in your mind a bank's two principal roles, (1) *financial intermediary* and (2) *guardian of the payments mechanism*, note that if a bank were required to hold 100% reserves against its deposits (a requirement often proposed), it couldn't function as an intermediary, but it *could* keep on functioning as guardian of the payments mechanism.

tion successfully as a medium of exchange? Is a commodity that is a good medium of exchange necessarily a good store of value, and vice versa?

5 a) It's easy to acquire the notion that the use of money develops naturally with civilization, and that the more advanced a civilization is, the more extensive will be its use of money. Yet in two highly developed civilizations, ancient Egypt and the realm of the Incas, money was almost unknown and unused. What reasons can you suggest to explain this?

   b) It has been suggested that someday the U.S. will be a "moneyless" society. The authors of such statements maintain that someday everybody's paychecks will automatically be deposited directly in their bank accounts and all the expenditures they make will automatically be charged against their bank accounts, so people won't have to carry around any cash or write checks to effect transactions. Would such a society really be moneyless, by our definition of money? Explain your answer.

6 Show that a bank creates deposit money when it purchases a bond just as it creates deposit money when it extends a loan.

7 When we talked about the way a banker responds to the risk of illiquidity, we assumed that he could invest funds deposited with his bank in only one way: by making loans. U.S. banks, as we have seen, can also invest funds deposited with them in highly liquid debt securities such as short-term government bonds. How do you think the freedom to do so affects a banker's preferences concerning the reserve ratio he would like to maintain?

8 Assume that all banks hold reserves equal to 25% of their deposits. Assume also that all banks are "loaned up," i.e., that they have no excess reserves. How would a $100,000 withdrawal of cash (i.e., of outside money) from the banks affect the total quantity of deposit money the banks could create? Would it result in a contraction in total deposit money? In a multiple contraction? Defend your answer by working through the first steps in the chain of events that such a withdrawal would set in motion.

9 The dividing line between financial assets that are money and those that aren't is not always easy to draw. For example, in defining the U.S. money supply, we included demand deposits, but *ex*cluded time deposits; other people often include time deposits. What reasons can you think of for including (or for excluding) time deposits from the money supply? What about deposits in savings and loan associations? Deposits at mutual savings banks?

10 Suppose that Smith decides to withdraw $1,000 from his savings account and deposit these funds in his checking account. How would his decision affect the total quantity of deposit money the banks could create:

   a) If banks maintained reserve ratios equal to 1 to 5 for both time and demand deposits?

   b) If banks maintained reserve ratios equal to 1 to 10 for time deposits and 1 to 5 for demand deposits.

Assume that the banks are initially fully loaned up and that they remain so; also state how you define the money supply.

11   One convenient way to analyze the way banks create deposit money is to think
      of the banking system as composed, not of many independent banks, but of a
      single *monopoly* bank which—like the independent banks we talked about
      before—always strives to keep reserves equal to some fraction, $1/r$, of total
      deposits.

      Suppose that this monopoly bank gets a \$10,000 deposit of outside money,
      and that it knows that people won't respond to increases in their deposit
      balances by withdrawing outside money from it. What is the maximum
      amount of deposit money that this bank could create in response to this
      deposit and still maintain reserves equal to $1/r$ of total deposits? [*Hint:* Does
      this monopoly bank have to worry about losing reserves through check clear-
      ings the way the independent banks in our money-creation example had to?]

12   In the text we presented proof that a fractional-reserve banking system can
      engage in a multiple expansion of its deposit liabilities. Can you verify this
      result by means of the aggregate balance sheet for U.S. banks in Fig. 28.3?
      Explain your answer.

CHAPTER 29

THE CENTRAL BANK

In the preceding chapter we talked about private commercial banks. There is also, in every modern economy, another type of banking institution: the central bank. National central banks differ as to the circumstances under which they operate and the specific tools they use, but their principal function is always the same.

Central banks control the quantity and quality of the money supply.

In most countries they also act as bankers to the national government, and often they are charged with maintaining the exchange rate (i.e., the price) at which domestic money is traded for foreign money in the open market.

THE FEDERAL RESERVE SYSTEM

The Federal Reserve System, which today functions as the central bank of the U.S., was established by an act of Congress in 1913. The act divided the country into twelve Federal Reserve districts and established a *Federal Reserve bank* to serve each of them. Under this act, all nationally chartered banks must join the Federal Reserve system and all state-chartered banks are invited to do so. The 6000-plus banks that are members of the Federal Reserve System account for 80% of commercial bank assets and over 80% of the deposits held by commercial banks.

Every private bank that joins the Federal Reserve System has to contribute to the capital stock of the Federal Reserve bank in its district an amount equal to 3% of its own capital and surplus. Therefore a Federal Reserve bank is in effect *owned by* the member banks in its district. The private ownership of the Federal Reserve banks is, however, only nominal; the purpose of these banks is to serve the interests of the public as a whole, and not just those of the commercial banks, which own them.*

---

* Member banks receive a cumulative, statutory dividend of 6% on their Federal Reserve bank stock; all other profits earned by the system are paid to the U.S. Treasury.

The Board of Governors of the Federal Reserve System formulates Federal Reserve policy and also supervises and coordinates the activities of the individual Federal Reserve banks. This board, located in Washington, is composed of 7 members; each is appointed by the President to serve a 14-year term.

As we shall see when we discuss the operations of the Federal Reserve System, purchases and sales of government securities constitute one of the most powerful tools available to the Fed* for implementing the policies laid out by the board of governors. Therefore there's a special committee, called the *Open Market Committee,* to supervise the system's operations in the government bond market. This committee has 12 members; they include all 7 members of the board of governors of the Federal Reserve System, the president of the New York Federal Reserve Bank, and the presidents of four of the remaining Federal Reserve banks. The reason that the president of the New York Federal Reserve Bank has a permanent seat is that the New York Fed, given its location at the center of the nation's financial markets, is naturally responsible for interpreting and carrying out the policy directives laid down by the Open Market Committee.

CONTROLLING THE QUALITY OF THE MONEY SUPPLY

We have said that one of the most important functions of any central bank is to maintain and improve the *quality* of the money supply. The reason that it is necessary for a nation to set up a special institution to carry out this function is that most transactions in a modern economic society demand the use of money as a medium of exchange. Thus, if economic life is to flow smoothly, the money a society uses must be a convenient, inexpensive, and nondisruptive means of effecting payments. Unfortunately these desirable qualities are not natural attributes of money, nor are they necessary ones. So central banks work hard to achieve them.

Check Clearing

We have stressed the fact that a nation's money supply must function efficiently as a medium of exchange. In countries like the United States, demand deposits (i.e., checking accounts) form the single largest component of the money supply.† Therefore demand deposits of necessity must be a fast, cheap means of effecting payments, which they can be only if banks can collect quickly and inexpensively on checks that are deposited with them but that are drawn against other banks.

---

* Since we shall be discussing the Federal Reserve System so much, we might as well get used to its nickname, the Fed.

† Look back at Fig. 28.1 to see the composition of the U.S. money supply.

In Chapter 28, we said that, whenever a bank receives in deposit a check drawn against another bank, it collects on this check by presenting it to the bank against which it is drawn and demanding payment in cash. From our discussion you perhaps gathered that banks do their own check collecting. They don't. In actual practice, they usually delegate this task to a *clearing house*.

A clearing house is an organization formed by a number of banks in order to make check collection among themselves as rapid, convenient, and cheap as possible.

Member banks present to the clearing house each day all checks deposited with them but drawn against other clearing-house banks. The clearing house (1) calculates the total amount of all checks presented for collection both *by* and *against* each member bank. (2) Then, for each member bank, it nets the first total against the second. (3) Finally it *demands from* or *pays to* each member bank a sum equal to that bank's *net cash loss* or *gain* through check collections on that day. The obvious virtue of a clearing house is that most checks presented to the clearing house for collection cancel each other out. As a result, the number of interbank cash payments that must be made in connection with check clearing is sharply reduced. After the clearing house has done its work, it returns each check presented to it for collection to the bank against which this check was drawn, so that the check writer's account can be appropriately debited.

Most private clearing houses in the U.S. are so set up that they can clear checks between local banks quickly. However, banks continually have to deal with checks drawn against distant banks. New York banks get checks drawn against California ones, Minnesota banks get checks drawn against Florida ones, and so forth. Such checks are cleared through the Fed, which acts as a central clearing house for member banks throughout the country. The Fed is able to do this because:

The Federal Reserve System acts as a banker to banks.

The Fed accepts deposits of cash and checks from member banks, and in return it grants them deposit balances against which they can withdraw cash and write checks. Suppose that the Paycheck Trust Company and the Furthermore National are both members of the Federal Reserve System. The Paycheck Trust Company gets a check for $500 drawn against the Furthermore National. It is easy (in theory at least) for the Fed to collect on this check for the Paycheck Trust Company. The Fed simply credits Paycheck Trust's account with $500 and simultaneously debits Furthermore National's account by $500. Sounds simple. But of course the Fed's job as the nation's chief check collector isn't all that easy. Americans write a fantastic number of checks: In 1966 the Fed cleared more than 5.7 billion of them, representing a total of over $2 trillion!

A Uniform Elastic Currency

In order for a nation's money supply to function as an effective means of payment, its cash component* must have a number of important characteristics.

1) *Currency must be uniform.*

Every dollar must be like (i.e., equal in value to) every other dollar. Today this condition is met in the U.S.; it hasn't always been, however. In the years just before the Civil War the currency of the U.S. was composed of a chaotic collection of notes, issued by more than a thousand different state banks, and ranging in value all the way from zero to face value. During those years it obviously made a lot of difference to people what kind of dollars they received and what kind they paid out, and people spent a lot of effort checking the value of currency before they would accept it.

2) *Currency must be elastic.*

Figure 29.1 indicates that as an economy grows, and as people make more transactions, they demand more currency. So the currency component of the money supply has to grow with national output. Figure 29.1 also suggests that demand for currency is seasonal. In the U.S. people want to have a lot of cash in their pockets around Christmas when they are shopping, but during the rest of the year, they are content to hold less.

Probably the most important step the Fed has taken to improve the quality of the U.S. money supply was to create a uniform elastic currency. It did this by issuing and putting into circulation note liabilities against itself. Today these notes, known as *Federal Reserve notes,* constitute the bulk of our currency, and (as indicated by Fig. 29.1) the total quantity of them in circulation is roughly $40 billion.

Fed dollars are uniform because they are all identical liabilities of a single institution. They are elastic in supply because the Fed—although it does attempt to limit the size of the total money supply—makes no attempt to control the way people divide their money balances between currency and bank deposits. It supplies people with whatever amount of currency they choose to hold, given the size of their overall money balances (i.e., given the size of the total money supply).

Naturally there are contractions and expansions in the quantity of Fed currency in circulation. If people want to hold more currency, they demand (withdraw) it from the commercial banks. If the banks don't happen to have on hand as much currency as people demand, there is no cause for

---

* In the United States, the cash component equals roughly one-fourth of the money supply (see Fig. 28.1).

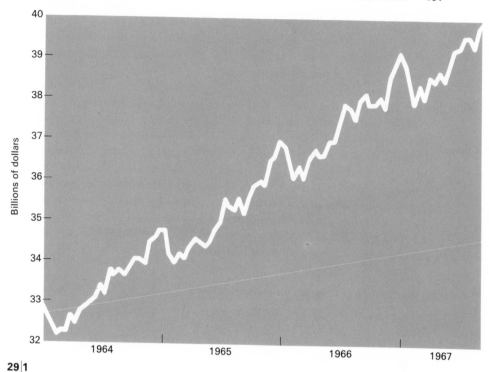

29|1

Currency in circulation in the U.S. The total quantity of currency that people demand fluctuates up and down seasonally, but the long-term trend is upward. (Source: *Federal Reserve Bulletin*)

alarm. A commercial bank can always order whatever quantity of currency it needs from the Fed; the amount of this purchase is charged against its deposit account at the Fed.* If people decide that they want to hold *less* currency, this process is reversed. People deposit their excess currency with commercial banks; when the banks acquire more currency than they choose to hold in their vaults, they deposit *their* excess with the Fed. Thus the public, via the commercial banks, can obtain without delay whatever quantity of currency it chooses to hold. In addition to distributing its own note liabilities, the Fed also distributes coins, which it buys from Treasury mints at face value and sells to member banks, again at face value.

---

* This doesn't mean that banks, because of the existence of the Fed, face no liquidity problem, but only that, under the U.S. system, banks don't have to hold all their liquid funds (reserves) in the form of vault cash. They can hold part of them in the safer and more convenient medium of deposits at a Federal Reserve bank. This point will become clearer to you when you read the next section.

CONTROLLING THE QUANTITY OF MONEY

We have seen that one important function of a central bank is to control the quality of the money supply. Another is to control the quantity of deposit money that private banks create.

Central banks like the Fed work hard to control the quantity of money that commercial banks create because, as we shall see in Part 6, by doing so they can alter the cost and availability of credit to private borrowers. Such alterations influence consumers' and firms' expenditures, which in turn affects the economy's level of output and the prices at which this output is sold. Thus central banks strive to regulate the creation of money so that they can promote important policy objectives, such as full employment and price stability. The use of central bank powers to promote such objectives is known as *monetary policy,* and we shall discuss it in Chapter 39. For the moment we shall focus on the way one central bank, the Fed, controls deposit creation by private commercial banks.

The Fed's Control Over Deposit Creation

In Chapter 28 we defined *inside money* as money created by commercial banks.

Outside money is money created by some institution other than commercial banks.

Cash (i.e., coin minted by the Treasury and currency issued by the Fed) is one form of outside money. For John Q. Public, cash is the only form of outside money (or at least the only form *he* can hold). This does not hold true for a commercial bank. As we have seen, a commercial bank can hold deposit balances at the Fed, balances which can be converted on demand into cash. Therefore, from the point of view of the banks that hold them, these balances constitute a second form of outside money.

In Chapter 28 we saw that the amount of deposit money commercial banks can create largely depends on two variables:

1) *the quantity of outside money they hold (i.e., the level of bank reserves),*
2) *the ratio of outside money to demand deposits (i.e., the reserve ratio) they maintain.*

The Fed has the power to influence the values of both of these variables, and thus it can regulate the quantity of deposit money that banks create.

Member Bank Reserve Requirements

The Fed establishes the minimum reserve ratios that all member banks in the Federal Reserve system must maintain. A bank's deposits at the Fed and its vault cash count as reserves. As of November 1967, the minimum reserve ratios which the Fed required member banks to maintain against *demand* deposits equaled 16½% for Federal Reserve city banks and 12% for other banks. The minimum it required member banks to maintain against *time* deposits equaled 3% on their first $5 million (of time deposits) and 6% on their time deposits in excess of $5 million.

Within specified limits the Fed can change the reserve ratios it requires member banks to maintain. When it does so, it alters the commercial banks' ability to create deposit money. For example, if the Fed were to lower required reserves from, say, 20% to 10% of deposits, it would double the amount of deposit money that the banks could create. If it were to *raise* reserve requirements from 20% to 25% of deposits, it would cut by one-fifth the amount of deposit money that the banks could create.*

One important observation to make about *required* reserves is that the true function of such reserves is not to ensure the safety of the banks that hold them but to restrict the ability of these banks to create deposit money. The reason that required reserves don't add to a bank's safety is that the moment a bank draws on its required reserves to meet depositor demand for cash, it violates the reserve requirement it is supposed to respect, and so threatens its solvency. Thus required reserves are not reserves at all!

Note that we are not suggesting that, because required reserves are not really reserves, commercial banks hold no reserves at all. Sometimes they hold reserves in excess of what is required. Also, as we pointed out in Chapter 28, the bonds that commercial banks hold provide them with an important source of liquidity, and so too does the Fed's discount window. (We'll come to that presently.)

The Level of Member Bank Reserves

We have said that banks hold most of their required reserves in the form of deposits at the Fed, i.e., in the form of Federal Reserve deposit liabilities. Banks are practically the only holders of such liabilities. So whenever the Fed increases its outstanding deposit liabilities, it expands the reserves of member banks. And whenever it decreases its outstanding deposit liabilities, it contracts the reserves of member banks.

The Fed alters the size of its deposit liabilities largely by buying and selling debt securities. Suppose that the Fed buys $100,000 of government bonds from the Wampum National Bank and pays for them with a check drawn against itself. Wampum National collects on this check by depositing it in its reserve account at the Fed. The result (see Table 29.1) is a $100,000

---

* To prove these statements, use the multiple expansion formula derived in Chapter 28 to show that the quantity of deposit money that the banks could create for each $1 of reserves held by them would be $5 if they maintained 20% reserves against deposits, $10 if they maintained 10% reserves, and $4 if they maintained 25% reserves.

TABLE 29|1

The Fed Creates Member Bank Reserves by
Purchasing Government Securities from a Member Bank

The Fed		The Wampum National Bank	
Assets	Liabilities	Assets	Liabilities
+$100,000 government securities	+$100,000 member bank reserves	+$100,000 reserves −$100,000 government securities	

increase in Wampum National's reserves. Thus the Fed, simply by exchanging its own deposit liabilities for debt securities, can create reserve
deposits and thereby increase bank reserves. It can decrease the reserves of
member banks simply by reversing this transaction: that is, by selling bonds.
To prove this, trace out the changes that would occur on the balance sheets
of the Fed and the member banks as a result of the sale by the Fed to the
commercial banks of $100,000 of government bonds.

Due to charter restrictions on the types of securities the Fed may acquire, historical precedent, and simple convenience, the Fed, when it expands and contracts bank reserves, limits itself to two types of transactions:

1) The purchase and sale of government securities,
2) The discounting of short-term commercial debt instruments held by
   member banks.

TABLE 29|2

The Fed Creates Member Bank Reserves by
Purchasing Government Securities from a Bank Depositor

The Fed		The Wampum National Bank	
Assets	Liabilities	Assets	Liabilities
+$50,000 government securities	+$50,000 member bank reserves	+$50,000 reserves	+$50,000 demand deposits

Jones	
Assets	Liabilities
−$50,000 government securities +$50,000 demand deposits	

Open-Market Operations

The Fed's purchase and sale of government securities are known as *open-market operations,* since it buys and sells them mostly in the open market. The Fed undertakes open-market operations at its own initiative, its main purpose being to adjust the level of reserves of member banks. As Table 29.1 shows, the Fed can increase the reserves of member banks directly by buying bonds from member banks. It can also increase the reserves of member banks indirectly by buying bonds from *nonbank* sellers. Suppose that J. Wunderbar Jones, who does his banking at the Wampum National Bank, inherits a nice packet of money from his grandfather; $50,000 of it happens to be in bonds, which Jones puts up for sale. The Fed buys the bonds from Jones, and pays for them by check. Jones deposits the Fed's check in his account at Wampum National. Wampum National exchanges the Fed's check for a credit to *its* reserve account. Thus the Fed's purchase sets in motion a series of transactions, the end result of which (see Table 29.2) is to increase the reserves of member banks.

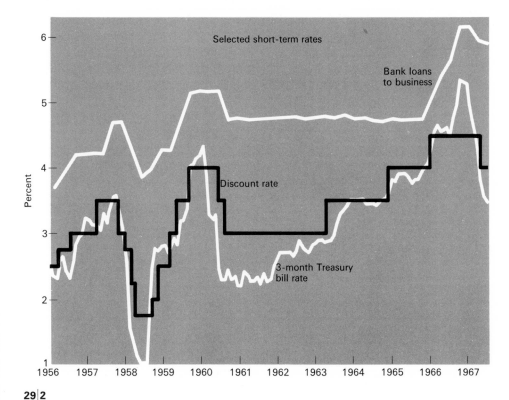

29|2

The Fed usually sets the discount rate to follow other short-term rates, such as the rates on short-term government bonds (Treasury bills) and on bank loans to business.
(Source: *Federal Reserve Bulletin*)

Discounting Short-Term Commercial Debt Instruments

A second way the Fed adds to bank reserves is by *discounting* (i.e., by buying at a discount) short-term commercial debt instruments offered to it by member banks. Discounting takes place *at the initiative of the member banks;* its purpose is to enable member banks to meet temporary reserve deficiencies by "borrowing" from the Fed. Since discounts add to the reserves of member banks, the Fed, in order to keep control of the money supply, has to see to it that banks don't use this measure too often. The Fed could discourage excessive borrowing by member banks by setting its *discount rate* above other short-term rates. But the Fed, as you can see by Fig. 29.2, sets its discount rate to follow other short-term rates. To keep banks from over-using the discount window, the Fed has said that the use of the discount facility by member banks is not a right, but a privilege, one to be used sparingly and only on a temporary basis.

The Government Debt and the Money Supply

The fact that the Fed makes discounting a privilege and uses open-market purchases of government securities as its principal means of expanding the reserves of member banks is reflected in the consolidated balance sheet of the 12 Federal Reserve banks, as recorded in Table 29.3. At the beginning of 1967 the Fed held only $0.4 billion of discounts and other loans, but $44.3 billion of government securities.

TABLE 29|3

Consolidated Balance Sheet of the 12 Federal Reserve
Banks, Jan. 1, 1967 (Billions of Dollars) (Source: *Federal Reserve Bulletin*)

Assets		Liabilities	
Gold certificates	$ 12.7	Federal Reserve notes	$ 39.3
Discounts, advances, and		Deposits	
acceptances	0.4	Member bank reserves	19.8
U.S. government securities	44.3	U.S. Treasury and foreign	
Cash items in process of		central banks	1.2
collection	7.9	Other liabilities	5.6
Other assets	1.8	*Net Worth*	1.2
Total	67.1	*Total*	67.1

One important implication of the Fed's reliance on open-market operations rather than discounting to expand bank reserves is that outside money is created largely through the monetization* of *public,* not private, debt.

---

* Recall that we talked in Chapter 28 about the way commercial banks create deposit money by *monetizing* private debt.

Therefore the public debt plays an important role as the ultimate basis, or backing, of our money supply! The reason is as follows: The Fed, if given a completely free hand, could create bank reserves by monetizing anything from soybeans to common stock. However, if its open-market operations are to be reasonably smooth, it has to deal in an asset which is (a) *available in extremely large quantities,* (b) *homogeneous,* and (c) *which has an active secondary (resale) market.* Government bonds are about the only financial asset that fills this bill. Thus they have been singled out for this important role. However, if the government should ever do anything as "unfortunate" as paying off the national debt, changes would certainly have to be made so that some other asset could take the place of government bonds in the Fed's portfolio.

Selective Credit Controls and Moral Suasion

In addition to using the tools we have already discussed, the Fed has some-times influenced deposit creation and the availability of credit by imposing selective controls on credit. It has done this by announcing what it thinks banks ought and ought not to do.

Margin requirements were the first selective credit control applied by the Fed, and the only one now in force. These requirements limit the amount of credit that banks and other regulated lenders may extend to people who want to use the money to buy common stocks. For example, in November 1963 the Fed set the margin requirements at 70%. This means that if a person wants to buy $10,000 worth of common stock *on the margin* (i.e., on credit), he will have to put up $7,000 of his own money, since $3,000 is the maximum amount that a bank, his broker, or any other regu-lated lender can legally lend him. It was the Securities Exchange Act, passed by Congress in 1934, that gave the Fed the authority to set these margin requirements. The purpose of such regulation is to prevent credit-financed speculative excesses of the sort that preceded the 1929 stock market crash.

Consumer installment credit is another area in which the Fed has applied selective controls. During World War II, the period 1948–49, and the Korean War, the Fed—acting under temporary authority granted by Con-gress—established minimum down payments and maximum loan maturities permissible in installment sales contracts for autos, appliances, and other so-called consumer durables.* The purpose of such regulation was to put the brakes on consumption during periods in which the aggregate demands

---

* "Consumer durables" is economists' jargon for large, rather expensive items which last a long time and which you can put off buying if you have to.

for goods and services made by consumers, business, and government were straining the economy's productive capacity and thus exerting a strong upward pressure on prices.

During the Korean War Congress gave the Fed the authority to institute limits on the maximum loan–value ratios and maximum maturities permissible on home mortgages. This temporarily slowed the rate of home construction by limiting the supply of mortgage money available to prospective buyers.

Moral suasion is another tool the Fed uses to control credit. The Fed tries to control the volume and direction of credit flows by asking banks to adopt certain policies which it believes would serve the public interest. The effectiveness of such measures is of course limited, but moral suasion often gets better results than one might expect. Banks know that public opinion is probably on the side of the Fed, that the Fed controls access to the discount window, and that the Fed has the option of replacing an ignored "suggestion" with a stronger measure. For example, in the fall of 1966 the Fed asked commercial banks to slow down the rate at which they were expanding business loans. Simultaneously the Fed let it be known that, if the banks did not cooperate, it might feel called on to lower the maximum rate payable on large-denomination certificates of deposit and thus cut off this important source of bank deposits.

BANKER TO THE FEDERAL GOVERNMENT

We have said that two important functions of the central bank are to control the quantity and quality of the money supply. A third is to act as banker to the national government. Therefore, in the United States, the Federal Reserve Bank is special banker to the U.S. Treasury.

You may think that the U.S. Treasury doesn't need a special banker, since it writes and receives checks just like any other bank depositor. There is, however, one important difference between the Treasury and other bank depositors. Treasury tax receipts and disbursements are measured not in thousands or even millions of dollars, but in billions of dollars. Also Treasury disbursements and receipts tend to bunch, for example, around tax dates. If nothing were done to offset them, Treasury receipts and disbursements, because of their size and "bunchiness," would cause sharp fluctuations in commercial bank reserves and thus in the size of the money supply and the availability of credit. It's the Fed's job, as banker to the Treasury, to carry out various financial maneuvers designed to see that this does not happen.

The Fed participates actively in the government bond market, not only occasionally when it wants to make long-term increases or decreases in the reserves of its member banks, but constantly. The Fed uses day-to-day open-

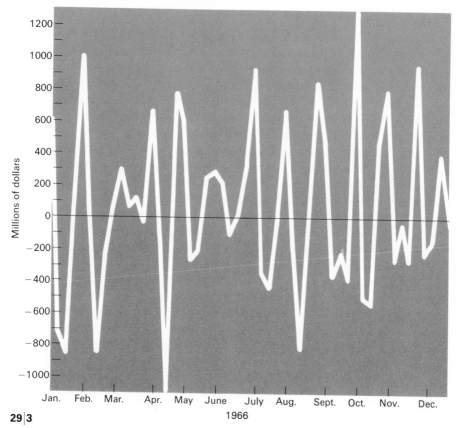

29|3

Week-to-week changes in the Fed's holdings of government securities.
(Source: *Federal Reserve Bulletin*)

market operations to offset the destabilizing changes that occur in the
reserves of its member banks on account of fluctuations in Treasury balances
and other short-term phenomena, such as (a) seasonal changes in the public's desire to hold currency and (b) random changes in the size of the *float*.*
The data plotted in Fig. 29.3 give some idea of how large-scale the Fed's
short-term operations in the government bond market are, and they also indicate how widely the Fed's holdings of government bonds fluctuate from
week to week.

---

* Thumbnail definition: *Float* is composed of checks for which the Fed has given member
banks credit but on which it hasn't yet collected; that is, checks that are outstanding and
in process of collection. Even with airmail transportation and modern check-handling
practices, there can be a variation in any month of between ¼ and ½ billion dollars of
float outstanding!

GOLD AND THE FED

It is the duty of the Federal Reserve System to regulate the size of the money supply in the public interest. Thus you would think that any restrictions the government might impose on the Fed's ability to create or destroy outside money would be undesirable, since such restrictions could only hinder the Fed in doing its duty. At the time the Fed was created, however, domestic bank liabilities were convertible on demand into gold, and so were all major currencies. Therefore the framers of the Federal Reserve Act made Fed dollars convertible into gold, too, and also required the Fed *to fractionally back all its liabilities with gold.* This reserve requirement limited the Fed's ability to create outside money, just as the reserve requirements imposed by the Fed on commercial banks limit their ability to create inside money. Thus the original Federal Reserve Act put the Fed in a position analogous to that of the commercial banks. There was only one difference: For commercial banks, deposits at the Fed were outside money, while for the Fed, gold played the role of outside money.

During the crisis years of the early 1930's, the government changed both the monetary role and the dollar price of gold. In 1933 the government made it unlawful for private citizens and private banks to hold gold. Then in 1934 Congress passed the Gold Reserve Act, which authorized the President to *devalue* the dollar, i.e., to raise the dollar price of gold. On January 31, 1934, this price was raised from $20.67 to $35.00 per ounce.*

So that the Treasury alone should "profit" from devaluation, the title to all gold owned by the Federal Reserve banks was transferred to the Treasury before devaluation. Thus on the day of devaluation, the Treasury was the only legal and only substantial holder of gold in the U.S.

This would have been the logical time to cut the tie between the domestic money supply and the national gold stock by abolishing the gold-reserve requirement imposed on the Fed. But sentiment in favor of a currency backed by gold won out over logic, and the gold-reserve requirement continued in force. Since 1934 the Fed has not held gold itself, but *gold certificates,* which the Treasury issues against its gold holdings and deposits with the Fed. (Gold certificates are a Treasury liability, but a Fed asset.) The reserve requirements imposed on the Fed have been altered each time they

---

* If you think back on our discussion of supply and demand in Chapter 13, you may wonder how Congress could legislate the price of gold. Actually, it couldn't. What it did was to peg the price of gold in terms of dollars by requiring the Treasury to stand ready to sell (to foreign buyers) and to buy (from domestic *or* foreign sellers) unlimited amounts of gold at $35 an ounce. Since the Treasury's buying price considerably exceeded gold's going market price, the Treasury—when it pegged the price of gold—in effect established a *commodity support program* for gold, like the federal government's support programs for agricultural products (see Chapter 25), except that the Treasury tries to support the *world* price of gold, while the Department of Agriculture supports only the *domestic* prices of farm products. (We'll return to gold, dollars, and international payments in Chapters 46 and 47.)

threatened to limit the Fed's freedom of action. Thus, even though these requirements exist, their power to restrict the Fed's money-creating capabilities has never been more than nominal. The most recent alteration in these reserve requirements happened in 1965, when Congress abolished the requirement that the Fed hold gold reserves equal to 25% of its deposit liabilities, although the Fed must still hold gold reserves equal to 25% of its *note* liabilities. This requirement, too, will probably be changed soon.*

The distinction currently made by Congress between the Fed's deposit liabilities and its note liabilities is an illogical one, since member banks can, as we have seen, freely convert Federal Reserve deposit liabilities into Federal Reserve notes, and vice versa. Federal Reserve notes do of course carry the written promise that the U.S. will pay the bearer "lawful money" on demand (read the fine print on a ten-dollar bill and see), but the best exchange that a person holding a Federal Reserve note can hope to make with the Fed would be to trade a tattered bill for a crisp new one. The Fed's promise to pay "lawful money" is nothing but a memento of the days when Fed dollars were convertible into gold dollars; that is, of the days when Federal Reserve notes were a liability of the Fed in the sense that they constituted a claim against the Fed's gold stock.

THE FED AS A FINANCIAL INTERMEDIARY

People seldom think of Federal Reserve banks as financial intermediaries. Nevertheless, in the course of their operations Federal Reserve banks do transmit funds from surplus to deficit units and thus function as funds brokers. There is one important difference, however, between the Fed and other intermediaries: The principal objective of the Fed is not to maximize profits, but rather, by means of an effective use of monetary policy, to promote national economic goals. Despite its orientation, the Fed does earn substantial profits, but these are incidental to its operations.

The Fed issues two principal types of indirect securities: Federal Reserve notes and deposit claims. Federal Reserve notes may be held by anyone, but deposit claims against the Fed may be held only by member banks, the Treasury, and foreign central banks.

Table 29.3 shows that two-thirds of the Fed's outstanding liabilities are in the form of Federal Reserve notes, while most of the remaining one-third are in the form of member-bank reserve deposits. It also shows that the Fed holds two principal assets: gold certificates and government securities.

Today the Fed's gold holdings are declining,† and increases in assets are almost exclusively in the form of increases in its holdings of government

---

* As we go to press (March 1968), Congress abolished the requirement that Federal Reserve notes be backed by gold. Thus it cut the last gold fetter on the Fed's money-creating power.

† This reflects the U.S. balance-of-payments deficit, which we shall discuss in Chapter 47.

securities. Thus the Fed, in its role of financial intermediary, functions largely as a conduit through which funds flow from member banks and from holders of Federal Reserve notes to the federal government.

FEDERAL DEPOSIT INSURANCE

Until recently bank panics were common in this country. A typical panic began when the public, alarmed by some event such as the failure of a prominent bank or the outbreak of war, would make sudden, massive demands on the banks to convert bank liabilities into outside money. (In the early years this outside money was gold coin; later it was central bank notes.) Banks held reserves equal to only a fraction of their total deposit liabilities, so they could meet such demands only to the extent that they succeeded in converting their income-bearing assets into cash. A single bank acting alone can always trade its assets for cash, but the banking system as a whole cannot liquidate its assets on balance unless it finds buyers outside the system. This was difficult (if not impossible) during a panic, since money was scarce, interest rates high, and security prices low. Therefore bank panics caused many banks to stop paying out cash and also led to widespread bank failures. Both results disrupted the affairs of individual bank depositors and the economic life of the country as a whole. Therefore people realized that the government had to figure out a way to stop bank panics.

There were two ways to achieve this: (1) taking the power of money creation away from banks that accepted deposits by requiring them to hold 100% reserves, (2) establishing an institution that, by monetizing bank assets, could create the additional reserves needed by the banks during a crisis. In other words, the government could stop bank panics either by eliminating financial intermediation as a bank function or by providing banks with a lender of last resort.

When it set up the Federal Reserve system, the United States took the second approach, since the Fed, as we have seen, has the power to monetize both public and private debt and is thus in a position to serve as a lender of last resort. The creation of the Federal Reserve system should have stopped mass bank failures, but it didn't. During the early 1930's, unprecedented waves of failures swept the U.S. banking system. They came about not because the Fed didn't have the power to aid the banks during a crisis, but because it failed to assume its responsibility for doing so.

One consequence of this bad experience was the creation in 1934 of the Federal Deposit Insurance Corporation (FDIC), whose purpose is to provide federal insurance of bank deposits. The FDIC collects from each bank whose deposits it insures a premium equal to a small percentage of the bank's total deposits; in return it insures these deposits up to a maximum of $15,000 per depositor. All banks that are members of the Federal Reserve system are required to join the FDIC and most nonmember banks have chosen to join.

Deposit insurance protects depositors in failed banks, but its chief benefit has proved to be that it has significantly reduced the contingency insured against: bank failures. Deposit insurance accomplishes this by reason of the fact that it makes a deposit in a failed bank as good as one in a solvent bank, and as a result the fears that once set off bank panics have ceased to exist. Of course poorly or dishonestly managed banks do still occasionally fail. But when this happens, the FDIC can often effect a rapid merger between the insolvent bank and a solvent one. The failed bank's doors never close, and an unobservant depositor might not even notice that anything untoward had occurred at his bank.

PROBLEMS

1   a) Suppose that the Fed were to sell $100,000 of government bonds to a commercial bank. What changes would occur in the balance sheets of the Fed and the commercial bank?

   b) Suppose that the Fed were to sell $100,000 of government bonds to John Jones, and that Jones paid for these bonds with a check drawn against his bank. What changes would occur in the balance sheets of the Fed, Jones, and Jones's bank?

2   Before the Treasury-Fed accord in March 1951, the Fed was committed to support the prices of Treasury bonds (i.e., the Fed was supposed to buy up Treasury bonds whenever their prices threatened to fall below par). Would such a commitment restrict the Fed's ability to regulate the creation of deposit money? If so, why?

3   "If moral suasion is effective, then the assumption that banks seek to maximize profits must be incorrect." Comment.

4   Federal Reserve banks typically earn much larger profits than the 6% dividend they pay to stockholding member banks (see the footnote on page 447). What does the information in Table 29.3 indicate about the reason why the Fed is able to earn such a big profit?

5   Representative Patman, chairman of the House Banking Committee, has said that the government should borrow not by selling high-interest-rate bonds to the "money kings" of the private banking system, but by selling bonds bearing a 1% interest rate (i.e., a rate just high enough to cover administrative costs) to the Federal Reserve banks. Patman claims that his proposal would put an end to the "interest taxation" that the government has to pay on funds it borrows to put up public works and to finance other useful projects.

   a) If this proposal were adopted, how would it affect the Fed's ability to regulate deposit creation by private banks?

   b) Would the Treasury gain anything by paying a low interest rate on bonds held by the Fed? [*Hint:* See footnote on page 447.]

c) Does our discussion in Chapter 18 suggest any good reason why the government ought to pay the same interest rate that other borrowers do on the funds it obtains from lenders?

6   A possible alternative to our current banking system would be to set up one under which (1) the central bank alone monetized debt and was responsible for creating money and (2) the commercial banks were required to hold 100% reserves and were thus responsible only for regulating the payments mechanism. Describe in detail how such a system might work and contrast its operation with that of our present system. Comment in particular on how such a system would affect the costs incurred by bank depositors and the sources of loanable funds available to the government and to private borrowers. What advantages and disadvantages might such a system offer?

7   Suppose that the government paid off all its debt. Then there would be no government bonds outstanding and the Fed couldn't create outside money by monetizing public debt. The Fed might then have to create outside money by monetizing common stock. What would be the pros and cons of such an eventuality? Would it matter if the Fed lost money? Could the Fed ever be insolvent in the usual (or in any meaningful) sense of the term? How would the public be likely to react to a Fed that lost money? (Note that so far the Fed has generally been a money maker.)

8   Most of the gold owned by the U.S. Treasury is stored in Fort Knox. Suppose that an enterprising band of crooks succeeded in doing what James Bond's opponent, Goldfinger, didn't manage to do: ferret away all that gold. Then our money wouldn't be backed by gold any more. Would this mean that U.S. dollars would immediately lose all value? Explain your answer.

   Suppose that the fellows who run Fort Knox are poor at bookkeeping, and one morning they discover that the government has twice as much gold buried there as they thought it had. How would this discovery affect the value of the dollars in your pocket?

9   In 1965 the requirement that the Fed hold gold reserves against its deposit liabilities was removed, so that the gold losses the U.S. was experiencing as a result of its balance-of-payments deficit would not force a contraction in the domestic money supply. Could the Fed, alternatively, have averted such an eventuality by lowering the reserve requirements of member banks? Would this other approach have lessened the flexibility of Fed operations designed to control the creation of deposit money? Explain your answer.

CHAPTER 30

*NONBANK INTERMEDIARIES

In Chapters 28 and 29 we looked at two kinds of financial intermediaries: commercial banks and the central bank. In addition, there are a number of nonbank intermediaries: mutual savings banks, savings and loan associations, life insurance companies, noninsured pension funds, finance companies, and mutual funds. In this chapter we shall briefly survey the operations of each.

THE RELATIVE IMPORTANCE OF DIFFERENT INTERMEDIARIES

Look at Table 30.1, and you will see statistics that indicate the relative importance of the above intermediaries. When you compare the rates at which different intermediaries are acquiring assets, it gives you an idea of the relative rates at which they are growing. The year 1966, however, was an unusual one with respect to financial markets: Interest rates soared while stock prices fell. Therefore the figures in column one of Table 30.1 are somewhat misleading. For one thing, rising interest rates led many investors who would usually have put their surplus funds in savings banks and savings and loan associations to buy primary debt securities which were yielding record rates of return. Thus the growth rates of savings banks and savings and loan associations were abnormally low during 1966. But noninsured pension funds, which collect funds largely through contractual savings plans, grew faster than ever. Also the financial assets of mutual funds decreased, because of the decline in stock prices.

The data in the second column of Table 30.1 show how dissimilar different financial intermediaries are in size and importance. Nonbank financial intermediaries play a more prominent role as funds brokers than banks do, but banks remain the single most important intermediary, with insurance

---

* The reader may omit this starred chapter without losing continuity.

TABLE 30|1

Financial Assets of *Principal* U.S. Financial Intermediaries (1966)

Financial intermediary	Net financial assets acquired during 1966*	Total financial assets held at the end of 1966*
Federal Reserve system	4.2	67.3
Commercial banks	20.9	357.0
All nonbank intermediaries	30.1	572.8
Mutual savings banks	2.8	61.0
Savings and loan associations	4.4	133.9
Life insurance companies	8.4	160.9
Noninsured pension funds	5.9	70.6
Finance companies	3.2	45.0
Mutual funds	−1.5	34.3
Other	6.9	67.1

*In billions of dollars. Source: *Federal Reserve Bulletin.*

companies and savings and loan associations coming next in line. However, this ranking can change. As economic conditions change, as institutional arrangements in capital markets evolve, and as the needs and preferences of surplus and deficit units are altered, some financial intermediaries increase in relative importance, while others decline.

Let us now look at nonbank financial intermediaries one by one.

MUTUAL SAVINGS BANKS

Mutual savings banks are a special class of banks authorized by the laws of certain northern and eastern states. As the name mutual implies, these banks have neither stockholders nor outstanding stock. They are owned by their depositors, and their principal objective is to maximize profits for their owner-depositors.

Mutual savings banks obtain funds by accepting two sorts of time deposits: regular savings accounts and special-notice accounts. They pay higher rates on notice accounts than on regular ones, but there's a catch. When you put money in a regular account, you can withdraw it on demand. You can withdraw money from a notice account only after you have given the bank advance notice. Regular savings accounts appeal to the small saver who wants liquidity. Special-notice accounts, since they emphasize yield at the expense of liquidity, appeal to the large saver who has many investment opportunities and to whom yield is more important than liquidity.

When mutual savings banks invest funds deposited with them, they have to obey various restrictions laid down by state regulatory authorities.

These restrictions prevent them from investing more than a given fraction of their total assets in certain kinds of securities, such as corporate stocks, and bonds; they also control the kinds of investments banks may make within these categories. For example, a mutual savings bank may invest only in bonds issued by corporations that meet various requirements with respect to size, earnings, capital structure, and so forth.

In addition to staying within the limits set by these restrictions, a mutual savings bank, when it selects its asset portfolio, is influenced by a number of factors. (1) It wants to earn, and to pass on to its depositors, the highest rates of return possible. (2) The fixed-price nature of the indirect security it issues (i.e., of the time deposits it accepts) predisposes it to buy low-risk assets. (3) It needs liquidity, for the same reasons that a commercial bank does: It must be prepared at all times to convert its *deposit* liabilities into cash. However, since it accepts only *time* (as opposed to *demand*) deposits, a mutual savings bank's need for liquidity is somewhat less than that of a commercial bank.

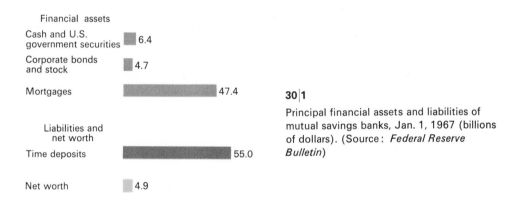

30|1

Principal financial assets and liabilities of mutual savings banks, Jan. 1, 1967 (billions of dollars). (Source: *Federal Reserve Bulletin*)

Mutual savings banks attain these varied goals by adopting a compromise like that adopted by commercial banks: They hold one class of assets (government securities) for liquidity and a second class of assets (mortgages) for return (see Fig. 30.1). They also hold some corporate bonds and stock, but the quantities involved are small, largely because of the above-mentioned restrictions imposed by regulatory authorities. Incidentally, in view of the fact that mutual savings banks have no shareholders, you may be surprised to find "net worth" listed in Fig. 30.1. The reason is that the law requires mutual savings banks to retain some of their earnings in order to build up reserves, so that they can meet any capital losses they might incur in the future and so that their overall financial position will be strengthened.

The government has not created any special lender of last resort for mutual savings banks, but in a time of crisis, the Fed would presumably come to their aid; also mutual saving banks can become members of the Federal Home Loan bank system, of which more later.

SAVINGS AND LOAN ASSOCIATIONS

Savings and loan associations are local thrift institutions that specialize in home financing. Most of them are mutual, but some savings and loan associations (in particular the large, aggressive California associations) are investor-owned corporations. There have been savings and loan associations in the United States for over 100 years, but only since the end of World War II have they emerged as major financial institutions. Their growth is a consequence of the postwar housing boom.

To obtain funds, savings and loan associations issue a single sort of indirect security, *share accounts*. These accounts are similar to time deposits at commercial or mutual savings banks, and, like bank deposits, they are insured by a federally sponsored agency, the Federal Savings and Loan Insurance Corporation. A savings and loan association usually solicits funds only on a local basis, but aggressive associations in high-interest areas such as California actively solicit funds on a national basis by means of advertising, premium give-aways, and brokers. Most of the funds that savings and loan associations have at their disposal come from share deposits, as Fig. 30.2 shows.

When savings and loan associations invest the money people deposit with them, they have to operate under quite strict regulations. The charters granted to such institutions usually specify that most of their funds must be

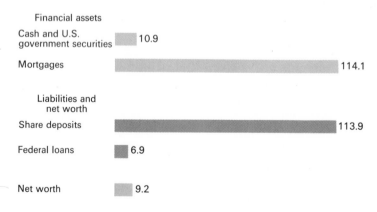

30|2

Principal financial assets and liabilities of savings and loan associations, Jan. 1, 1967 (billions of dollars). (Source: *Federal Reserve Bulletin*)

invested in first mortgages, that their investments in nonmortgage financial assets must be limited in scope, and that most of their mortgage loans must be on local properties. All these restrictions leave them with very little freedom of choice as to investments, and thus the bulk of their funds are invested in mortgages (see Fig. 30.2). Since mortgages are extremely illiquid, savings and loan associations (like commercial banks and mutual savings banks) need some liquidity to meet possible depositor demands for cash. Therefore savings and loan associations, in addition to holding mortgages, also hold cash and government securities specifically for liquidity.

Savings and loan associations, like banks, also need a lender of last resort if they are to weather the crises that might come their way, so the government during the 1930's sponsored the creation of the *Federal Home Loan banks,* which are, to savings and loan associations, what the Federal Reserve banks are to commercial banks.

In addition to being a lender of last resort, the Federal Home Loan banks also provide savings and loan associations with funds to meet seasonal and other temporary imbalances in the rate at which they receive deposits and lend out funds. Such loans are reflected in the $6.9 billion "Federal loan" figure in Fig. 30.2.

LIFE INSURANCE COMPANIES

Life insurance companies specialize in insuring the lives of individuals. An insurance policy is a contract between the insured and the insurer under which the insurer, in exchange for a fee (or premium) promises that, if the insured should die during the contract period, it will pay his beneficiaries an amount equal to the face value of the policy issued to him. Since the face amount of this policy is usually many times larger than the premium paid, you would think that such policies would expose the insurer to great risk. Not so. An insurance company insures the lives of so many people that it can predict its average losses per policy, and it sets its premiums high enough to cover these predictable losses. In other words, the principal function of an insurance company is not to assume policyholder risks but to *pool* them.

Some life insurance policies provide protection only, but others combine protection with savings.* This kind of policy is more expensive. Under this kind of a contract, the insurance company agrees, in exchange for a relatively high annual premium, to pay out the face value of the policy if the insured dies while the policy is in force *and* to pay out a gradually increasing cash value if the insured surrenders his policy before he dies. The

---

* See the footnote on page 66, in which we distinguished between a *term insurance* policy, which incorporates no savings element, and a *straight life insurance* policy, which combines savings with protection.

policy's cash value thus represents the insured's accumulated savings under the policy.

Most cash-value policies are sold to individuals, but some are sold to *insured pension funds*. Under an insured pension program, a cash-value policy is purchased on the life of each person for whom a pension must be provided. If he dies before he retires, his beneficiaries receive the face value of his policy. If he lives to retirement, the accumulated cash value of his policy supplies the money for the pension that is coming to him.

When life insurance companies choose the way to invest the funds "deposited" with them by buyers of cash-value insurance, they have to abide by state regulations as to both the quality of the assets they may acquire and the percent of their total assets they may invest in certain types of assets.

Despite these regulations, however, insurance companies still have considerable freedom in choosing their asset portfolios, much more than savings and loan associations do. When they make their selections, life insurance companies are influenced by a number of factors: (1) Whether they are investor-owned or mutual, they want to earn a high rate of return on their assets. (2) The fixed-price nature of the "securities" they issue inclines them to buy low-risk assets. (3) They need liquidity to meet death claims, policy redemptions, and other cash needs.

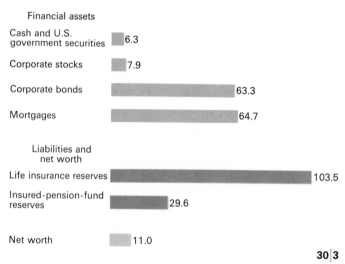

30|3

Principal financial assets and liabilities of life insurance companies, Jan. 1, 1967 (billions of dollars).
(Source : *Federal Reserve Bulletin*)

To attain these varied goals, life insurance companies put their money in different assets for different purposes (see Fig. 30.3): a few government securities and cash (for liquidity), and most of the rest in high-yielding mortgages and corporate bonds.

Life insurance companies hold little corporate stock, but since many insurance companies now offer *variable annuities* (i.e., policies whose return is based on the market value and return paid by the assets that back them), the common-stock holdings of insurance companies may well increase in the future.

Private or *noninsured pension funds,* which are subject to less regulation and are often less conservatively managed than insurance companies, invest much more heavily in common stocks. At the end of 1965, for example, insurance companies held only about 6% of their funds in common stock, but noninsured pension funds held close to 60%.

MUTUAL FUNDS

As we pointed out in Chapter 27 and earlier in Chapter 5, any single investor who tackles the job of assembling a diversified investment portfolio learns that asset indivisibilities and information costs (in terms of both money and time) constitute real barriers. A mutual fund enables the small investor to escape these difficulties; it gives him a chance to participate in a diversified, professionally managed investment portfolio. A mutual fund solicits funds from investors through the sale, usually on a *continuous* basis, of its own variable-price *equity shares.* These funds are pooled and invested, with the aid of professional counsel, in a diversified portfolio of securities.

Mutual fund shareholders participate in this portfolio in two senses: (1) They receive periodic distributions of dividends and realized capital gains. (2) The value of each share they hold depends on the portfolio's market value, because a mutual fund will redeem its outstanding shares on demand, at *net asset value;* that is, at a value equal to the fund's net assets per share.*

When mutual funds decide how to invest funds "deposited" with them, they don't have to take into account many of the considerations that are so important to other intermediaries. A mutual fund doesn't have to worry about liquidity, since it can always get cash by selling off securities. If its shareholders choose to redeem their shares for cash during periods when security prices are depressed, the capital losses will be borne not by the fund itself, but by those shareholders who insist on cashing in their shares at such an unpropitious moment. A mutual fund doesn't issue a fixed-price security

---

* Most mutual funds continuously solicit new funds through the sale of additional shares; they are *open-end investment companies.* There also exist *closed-end investment companies,* which neither solicit new funds through the sale of additional shares nor offer to redeem their outstanding shares. The stock of a closed-end investment company is traded in stock exchanges and over the counter. Although closed-end investment companies are much less important than open-end ones if measured in terms of total assets, they too give individual investors a chance to participate in a diversified, professionally managed portfolio.

and doesn't promise shareholders a fixed return, so it doesn't have to worry about the possibility that an ill-fated investment policy might render it incapable of fulfilling its obligations to "depositors." It does, however, have to be concerned about the possibility that a poor investment record might cause "depositors" to shift their funds out of *its* shares and into those of some better-performing investment company.

30|4

Financial assets and liabilities of mutual funds, Jan. 1, 1967 (billions of dollars). (Source: *Federal Reserve Bulletin*)

When the management of a mutual fund decides what sort of portfolio to assemble with the funds placed under its stewardship, it usually adopts some stated objective—such as income, growth, or security—which appeals to a wide group of potential investors, and tries to invest in securities whose characteristics are consistent with this goal. Mutual funds display considerable diversity in their *professed* objectives, but as a group they invest almost exclusively in corporate stocks (see Fig. 30.4), presumably because stocks, despite temporary setbacks, have risen almost steadily since World War II.

FINANCE COMPANIES

There are three principal types of finance companies: consumer finance companies, sales finance companies, and business finance companies.

Consumer finance companies specialize in making small installment loans, so that people can buy consumer durables (including automobiles), so that they can repair and modernize their homes, or so that they can do other things such as consolidating and refinancing outstanding debt. Because the loans they extend are small and because the credit rating of their typical borrower is not the best, small loan companies incur such high costs that they couldn't operate profitably without charging interest rates that exceed those charged by competing lenders such as banks. Therefore consumer finance companies all operate under enabling small-loan acts. The provisions of these acts vary from state to state, but generally they permit companies that make small, short-duration installment loans to charge interest rates considerably above the limits set by state usury laws. You might think that small-loan acts discriminate against the small borrower who can't qualify for lower-rate bank loans. However, their purpose is not to permit exploitation of him but to protect him from loan sharks by providing him with a legitimate, if expensive, source of borrowed funds.

Sales finance companies also specialize in lending to consumers, but they don't do so directly. They do so *indirectly,* by buying up installment credit contracts that result when retailers of durable goods sell to consumers "on time." ("Only $50 down and 36 months to pay!")

Business finance companies. Some of these companies, known as *commercial factors,* specialize in financing business accounts receivable, others in financing the sale of commercial, industrial, and farm equipment.

Finance companies are investor-owned and so have some *equity capital;* their principal source of funds, however, is debt. As we can see from Fig. 30.5, *short-term bank loans* are an important source of credit to finance companies. They also get money by selling their own short-term notes, or *paper,* as it is called in the money market. The large, better-known finance companies get money by selling bonds to various buyers, including insurance companies, pension funds, and investment companies.

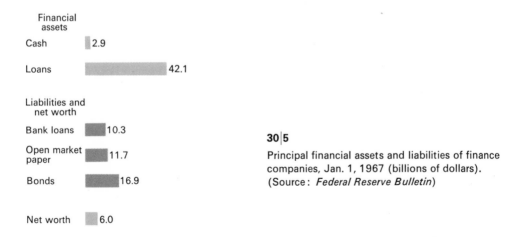

30|5
Principal financial assets and liabilities of finance companies, Jan. 1, 1967 (billions of dollars). (Source: *Federal Reserve Bulletin*)

Since finance companies—unlike the other financial intermediaries we have considered—often obtain funds not from ultimate surplus units, but from other intermediaries, they are often called *secondary intermediaries.*

PROBLEMS

1   On Jan. 1, 1967, savings and loan associations and mutual savings banks held cash reserves of $1.1 billion and $2.3 billion, respectively. If you compare these figures with other figures on their balance sheets (see Figs. 30.1 and 30.2), you will see that their cash reserves constitute only a small fraction of their total deposits. Does this mean that these institutions, like commercial banks, can engage in a multiple expansion of their deposit liabilities? [*Hint:* See Problem 12 at the end of Chapter 28.] Explain your answer.

2   Currently commercial banks are forbidden to pay interest on demand deposits. They are permitted to pay interest on time deposits, but the Fed imposes ceilings on the rates. Under regulations in force in November 1967, commercial banks could pay no more than 4% on regular passbook savings accounts, 5% on certificates of deposit in denominations of less than $100,000, and 5.5% on certificates of deposit in larger denominations.

a) Does the authority to limit the deposit rates banks can pay add anything to the Fed's ability to control the creation of deposit money? [*Hint:* Will such limits affect the quantity of currency people choose to hold ? The way people allocate their total surplus funds between time and demand deposits at banks? The way people allocate their surplus funds between banks and nonbank intermediaries? If so, how would this factor affect the ability of the banks to create deposit money?]

b) Does the authority to limit the deposit rates commercial banks pay enable the Fed to control the terms on which banks compete with nonbank intermediaries? Can you think of any situation in which it would be important for the Fed to have such power? [*Hint:* Look at the assets held by commercial banks (Fig. 28.3), by savings and loan associations (Fig. 30.2), and by mutual savings banks (Fig. 30.1). During a period of rising interest rates, which of these institutions would be able to most quickly raise the rate of return it earns on its investments and thus the deposit rates it pays? What would happen to savings and loan associations and mutual savings banks if commercial banks suddenly started to pay 1% more than *they* could pay on savings deposits?]

3   In the U.S., financial institutions make long-term mortgage loans at fixed interest rates with no provision for raising the rates borrowers pay if interest rates rise (or for lowering them if interest rates fall). An alternative to this system would be one under which rates on outstanding mortgage loans were tied to current market rates.

    Discuss the pros and cons of these two systems, taking into account the interests of the homeowners who borrow, the institutions which lend, and the depositors who supply funds to these institutions. Also consider the impact that the two policies would have on the competitive positions of different financial intermediaries (a) when interest rates were falling and (b) when interest rates were rising.

4   A mutual fund is managed by an advisory firm which, in return for its services, receives an annual fee equal to a fixed percent (often 1%) of the fund's assets. Do you think that the interests of the fund's shareholders and those of the ad-

visory firm might ever conflict? The Securities and Exchange Commission (SEC) which regulates mutual funds thinks they can. Here's a situation: A mutual fund is offered a discount by its broker on big purchases and sales. The fund could accept this discount itself (i.e., it could pay the broker a smaller fee). Or it could pay the broker the *full* fee and direct him to pay out ("give up" in the jargon of Wall Street) the amount of the discount to some other broker whom the fund wanted to reward (perhaps because he had sold a lot of the fund's shares). Which course of action is in the interests of the fund's shareholders? Which is in the interests of the advisory service? If you were a member of the SEC, would you be concerned if you found that "give-ups" were common?

5   a) A levered mutual fund is one that invests not only equity funds obtained by selling shares but also debt capital. What advantages and what risks would be associated with holding shares in a levered as opposed to a non-levered fund? [*Hint:* Recall our discussion of debt leverage at the beginning of Chapter 11.]

    b) Some funds emphasize growth; others emphasize current income. Which do you think would find leverage more attractive?

6   The data presented below show that, at each level of assets, savings and loan associations have a lower ratio of equity capital to total assets than commercial banks do. What reasons can you give to explain this? [*Hint:* Consider the kinds of investments each institution makes.] When a savings and loan association decides on the appropriate equity–total-asset ratio, do you think it matters whether or not it is owned by stockholders or organized as a mutual savings association?

Savings and Loan Associations (Asset Size in Thousands of Dollars)

	Less than 100	100– 500	500– 1,000	1,000– 2,500	2,500– 5,000	5,000– 25,000	25,000– 100,000	More than or equal to 100,000
Equity/total assets	0.13	0.13	0.17	0.09	0.07	0.07	0.06	0.05

Note: Similar data for commercial banks are given in Problem 9 of Chapter 27. (Source: The U.S. Treasury Department. Data are for 1963–64.)

*7   The Federal Home Loan banks (FHLB) provide a source of liquidity to savings and loan associations just as the Fed provides a source of liquidity to commercial banks. How do you think that the rate that the FHLB charges savings and loan associations on the loans it makes to them would influence the preferences of the typical savings and loan association for mortgages versus liquid assets? Use your answer to predict the way that a rise in the rate charged by the FHLB would affect the ratio of liquid assets to total assets held by the average savings and loan association.

---

* A starred problem is one that is unusually difficult.

CHAPTER 31

THE MONEY MARKET

We have discussed financial intermediaries and the way they operate. Now let us go back to the main topic of this part of the book: financial markets.

THE STOCK IN TRADE OF FINANCIAL MARKETS

As we have said, the stock in trade of financial markets is financial assets: debt securities and equities. Table 31.1 shows the principal ones outstanding at the end of 1966. The first entry, *U.S. government securities,* refers only to *negotiable* securities, and therefore it understates total federal debt by about $100 billion.* The four subentries under that divide U.S. government securities according to maturity. Of these securities, bills have the shortest maturity, bonds the longest.

The next four entries in Table 31.1 are self-explanatory; but look at the two that follow: *commercial paper* and *bankers' acceptances.* We'll say more about these later. For now, let's just say that these entries refer to short-term commercial debt obligations that are sold in the open market. *Negotiable certificates of deposit,* as we pointed out earlier, are a special form of time deposit issued by commercial banks.

The term *security loans* refers to bank loans against stocks and bonds. About 40% of such loans are used to finance the security inventories of brokers and dealers. The rest represent loans granted to individuals and firms against security collateral. *Bank loans to business* are also included in Table 31.1 because, for business borrowers, bank loans compete as a source of funds with the sale of negotiable debt instruments. The final entry in Table 31.1 is the only one that does not refer to a debt-type obligation: *corporate stocks.*

---

* This $100 billion of nonnegotiable securities takes the form of savings bonds sold to individuals and special nonnegotiable securities held by government trust funds.

TABLE 31|1

Money-Market and Other Financial-Market Obligations Outstanding (End of 1966)*

Type of security		Billions of dollars
Negotiable U.S. government securities		218.0
Bills	64.7	
Certificates	5.9	
Notes	48.3	
Bonds and other	99.1	
State and local obligations		105.9
Corporate and foreign bonds		135.9
Mortgages on 1- to 4-family houses		225.3
Other mortgages		94.1
Commercial paper		13.3
Bankers' acceptances		3.6
Negotiable certificates of deposit in denominations over $100,000		15.6
Security loans		17.0
Bank loans to business		113.3
Corporate stocks		666.3

*Source: *Federal Reserve Bulletin.*

THE MONEY MARKET

Most of the debt and equity instruments in Table 31.1 originate and are traded in four financial markets: (1) the money market, (2) the bond market, (3) the mortgage market, and (4) the stock market. In this chapter we shall discuss the money market; in Chapter 32 we shall get to the other three.

The money market stands out in many ways as the most interesting and perhaps the most important of the financial markets, not only because the instruments which constitute the stock in trade of this market are traded in tremendous volume and under extremely volatile conditions, but also because it is primarily through the purchase and sale of these money-market instruments that the Fed regulates the level of member-bank reserves.

To the uninitiated, the term "money market" may be misleading, because it suggests a place in which people exchange money for money; an obviously pointless operation. Actually:

The term "money market" refers simply to the market in which short-term debt instruments are bought and sold for money.

To put it another way, the money market is the market in which debt instruments only slightly less liquid than money are traded for money.

The money market's stock in trade consists of many actively traded securities, each of which has its own degree of liquidity. This market enables market participants to make continuous, precise adjustments in their liquidity; it gives them a chance to cover temporary deficits by selling their own short-term debt instruments for money, and to work off temporary surpluses by buying short-term income-bearing debt instruments with money.

The principal participants in the money market are: the Treasury, which finances part of the federal debt through the sale of money-market instruments; the Fed, which conducts most of its open-market operations in the money market; the commercial banks, which continuously adjust their individual reserve positions through money-market transactions; large nonbank financial intermediaries, such as big insurance and finance companies, large nonfinancial corporations, government credit agencies, state treasurers, and foreign central banks that hold substantial dollar deposits in New York.

The principal items the money market deals in are: (1) Treasury bills and other U.S. government securities of short maturity, (2) Federal funds, (3) bankers' acceptances, (4) commercial paper, (5) large-denomination certificates of deposit, (6) short-term obligations of federal agencies, and (7) short-term obligations of state and local governments.

As the length of this list suggests, the money market is not really *a* market, but *a set of* interdependent markets, in which a variety of debt instruments—all in some sense *substitutes* for each other—are traded. Let us now discuss the principal sectors of the money market one by one.

Federal Funds

Whenever a money-market instrument is traded, the seller gets a check for one of two sorts of money: *today's* money or *tomorrow's*. The distinction between the two can be explained as follows: When a bank that is a member of the Federal Reserve system (let's say it's the Paycheck Trust Company) receives a check, it deposits this check for a credit in its reserve account at the Fed.* Now if the deposited check happens to be drawn against *another* member bank (the Wampum National Bank), collection on the check will take at least one to two days, and the Fed thus waits one to two days before it gives Paycheck Trust credit for its check. However, if the deposited check is drawn against the Fed itself (that is, against Wampum National's reserve account at the Fed), the Fed grants Paycheck Trust immediate credit for its check. Thus checks drawn against the Fed—or *Federal funds,* as they are called—represent today's money, while checks drawn against ordinary commercial banks represent tomorrow's.

Since World War II, interest rates have risen, and Federal funds have increasingly displaced ordinary money (i.e., checks drawn against commer-

---

* It may do this by presenting the check for collection either to a local clearing house or directly to the Fed.

cial banks) as the method of payment in money-market transactions. Treasury bills are traded only for Federal funds, and most other money-market instruments also specify payment in Federal funds.

The Federal Funds Market

Federal funds are used not just as a means of payment. They are also actively borrowed and lent, so much so that the Federal funds market is one of the dominant sectors of the money market.

Transactions in the Federal funds market are referred to, in the jargon of the trade, as purchases and sales, but these transactions actually involve the borrowing and lending of Federal funds. Most loans of Federal funds are made at a rate at or below the discount rate, and on an overnight (i.e., one-day) basis. This means of course that the *percentage* rate of return yielded by the average Federal-funds loan is miniscule. Lenders of Federal funds, however, generally deal in such large sums that the *absolute* amounts of interest they earn on individual transactions are certainly nothing to sneeze at.*

Like most sectors of the money market, the market for Federal funds is a national one, centered in New York, but situated in no single place or exchange. It's an over-the-counter market in which lenders and borrowers are brought together by means of brokers and "accommodating" banks. The principal brokers in this market continuously (via telephone and telegraph) get bids and offers for Federal funds. On the basis of these bids and offers, they quote going market rates and match buyers and sellers. They do not, however, take a position in Federal funds themselves (i.e., they don't hold inventories of them). A number of large city banks also buy and sell Federal funds, primarily as an accommodation to the country banks for whom they act as correspondents.† For this reason they are known as *accommodating banks*.

The main participants in the market which brokers and accommodating banks "make" for Federal funds are commercial banks, which sell funds whenever they have reserve surpluses and buy them whenever they have reserve deficits. A variety of nonbank participants are also active in the Federal-funds market: nonbank buyers, sellers, or dealers in Treasury bills and other money-market instruments that are traded for Federal funds.

---

* Example: Suppose that the Federal funds rate stood at 4.50% per annum; then a large money-market bank which held a temporary reserve surplus of $4 million could earn $500 by lending out its surplus reserves for one night.

† *Correspondent banks* are large city banks that accept deposits from country banks and that, in exchange for these deposits, provide services such as collecting checks; buying, selling, and safeguarding securities; helping the country banks carry out foreign transactions; providing bank wire facilities; and so forth.

The Government Securities Market

The U.S. Treasury is responsible for financing over $300 billion of federal debt. To do so, it sells various negotiable and nonnegotiable debt instruments. The four main types of negotiable securities it sells are: (1) bills, (2) certificates, (3) notes, and (4) bonds. *Treasury bills* have a maturity of 3 months to a year. They pay no interest, and are sold at a *discount;* their yield depends on the spread between the price at which they are sold and their face value at maturity. Treasury *certificates of indebtedness, notes, and bonds* are all fixed-interest securities customarily issued at par (face value). Maturities run up to a year for certificates, from 1 to 7 years for notes, and over 5 years for bonds.

Any government security with a short maturity can be classified as a money-market instrument, but the key government security traded in the money market is the Treasury bill. The reason that Treasury bills are so in demand is that they are a short-term, actively traded, essentially riskless security, and therefore their price varies little and their liquidity is high. Large investors often hold Treasury bills both to meet their continuing needs for liquidity and to absorb any temporary surpluses of funds they might have. Another reason why Treasury bills are so sought-after is that the Fed, throughout the 1950's and early 1960's, carried out most of its open-market operations in Treasury bills.

Treasury bills are issued on a weekly basis by means of sealed-bid auctions managed jointly by the Treasury and the Fed. Participants in the average weekly auction usually include the Fed—which may choose to "roll over" the maturing bills it holds (i.e., replace them with bills that will mature at a later date)—a number of commercial banks, and all the principal dealers in government securities.*

About 20 large banks and nonbank *dealers* are active in the government securities market. Each one stands ready to buy and sell a variety of government securities at the bid and asked prices he quotes; by doing so he *makes a market,* as it is called, in these securities. Dealers in government securities absorb only about one-fifth of new issues of Treasury bills and a smaller fraction of new issues of bills that have longer maturities. However, these dealers constitute the heart of the government securities market, since almost all trading in outstanding issues takes place in over-the-counter, dealer-made markets. (Some government bonds are quoted and sold on the New York Stock Exchange, but the trading done there is small in volume.)

The chief actors in the government securities market are the commercial banks that buy and sell these securities in order to adjust the liquidity of

---

* A dealer is a *risk taker* who trades for his own account and whose overall profits are determined by his trading profits and losses. By contrast, a broker takes no position in (i.e., doesn't buy for himself) the securities he trades.

their investment portfolios. Nonbank financial intermediaries also hold these securities for liquidity, and this makes them important participants too. In addition, corporations and private individuals buy and sell government securities, and so does the New York Fed, which handles all purchases and sales for the open-market account of the Federal Reserve system as a whole.

The Commercial Paper Market

Some large business firms not only borrow directly from financial institutions such as banks, but they also borrow by selling unsecured, non-interest-bearing, short-term promissory notes in the open market. Such notes are called *commercial paper*. Today sales finance companies* are the dominant borrowers in the commercial-paper market. A few nonfinancial corporations, all with top credit ratings, also borrow in the commercial-paper market, especially to meet seasonal needs for financing.

About half the borrowing in this market is done through dealers, who usually buy paper directly from the issuer at a small discount and then resell it to their retail customers at an even smaller discount. Customers of commercial-paper dealers are mainly small-to-medium-size banks and nonfinancial business corporations. Nonbank intermediaries also participate in this market, though to a lesser extent.

A few of the largest and best-known sales finance companies (whose individual needs for short-term financing may run as high as $1 billion!) bypass the commercial-paper dealers and place their paper directly with large investors. Direct placement gives the investor a chance to obtain notes whose face value and maturity are tailored to meet his needs, and also enables the borrower to obtain funds at a slightly lower rate than he would have had to pay if he had sold his notes through a dealer.

Bankers' Acceptances

Firms often finance goods they buy for cash and goods they sell on credit, either by direct bank loans or by the sale of commercial paper. There is also a third method: *bankers' acceptances*. The use of this method of financing falls somewhere in between bank loans and commercial paper. In effect it involves the sale in the open market of a bill whose redemption at maturity is guaranteed by the borrower's bank, which, in the jargon of the trade, *accepts* the bill.

---

* As we pointed out in Chapter 30, a sales finance company is a financial intermediary that uses borrowed funds to buy up the installment sales contracts which consumers who buy durable goods "on time" must sign. An example of a large sales finance company is the General Motors Acceptance Corporation, which uses funds obtained through the sale of commercial paper to buy up the installment sales contracts originated by G.M. dealers.

Bankers' acceptances (look back at Table 31.1) are a much less important instrument in the money market than commercial paper, although their use has increased considerably in the past few years. Due to their special characteristics and to the regulation under which accepting banks must operate, bankers' acceptances are used almost exclusively to finance the importing, exporting, and storing abroad of goods.

Acceptances offer foreign banks certain tax advantages, and foreign banks are more familiar with this device than American investors are. Therefore foreign central banks that hold large dollar balances in New York are important investors in the dollar acceptance market. The only other sizable investors in this market are the large money-market banks.

Commercial Bank Loans

Commercial banks make a lot of different types of short-term loans, but in a discussion of the money market, we need be concerned with only three of them: (1) loans to government securities dealers, (2) loans to brokers and dealers in nongovernment securities, and (3) loans to large corporations. The first two types clearly lie within the precincts of the money market; the third, strictly speaking, does not. However, since—for large corporations at least—borrowing from banks is an alternative to the sale of money-market instruments as a source of funds, we ought to talk about these loans when we are discussing the money market.

Loans to government securities dealers. Most of the money-market banks in (and outside of) New York make *call loans** to dealers in government securities. Call loans are overnight loans which dealers use to finance part of the large inventories of securities they carry. Lending banks usually view call loans to dealers as a means of making day-to-day adjustments in their reserve positions. For this reason the banks change the rates they charge on such loans daily, or even oftener.

Loans to brokers and dealers in nongovernment securities. Brokers have to finance the margin accounts† of their customers, and dealers in nongovernment securities have to finance their security inventories. So they borrow from money-market banks. The lending banks view such loans as a source of liquidity. Therefore they rarely "call" such loans, and seldom change the rate they charge for them. Usually this rate lies at or near the *prime rate* (i.e., the rate charged by the banks to top-quality borrowers). The rate on loans to dealers in government securities is generally somewhat lower.

---

* A call loan is one that is payable on demand of either party.

† An investor who buys securities *on the margin* puts up only part of the purchase price; the rest is covered by a loan from his broker.

Loans to large business corporations. The other money-market instruments we have studied were all "standardized products" sold in competitive markets. However, bank loans to customers that are large business corporations are highly individualized products "sold" in a quite imperfect market. Every bank loan extended to a large business firm is a custom-made instrument whose terms, including rate and maturity, are settled through negotiation between the banker and borrower. Prudence and regulatory authorities both set limits on the amount that a single bank can loan to any one customer. Thus many large business borrowers are not able to satisfy all their legitimate needs for short-term funds with a single or even several bank loans, and for this reason they turn to the commercial-paper market to obtain some or all of the short-term funds they need.

*PRICE DETERMINATION IN THE MONEY MARKET

Competitive Conditions in the Money Market

The easiest way to explain how the prices of the various securities sold in the money market are determined is to seek out, among the various market models derived in Parts 3 and 4, the one that most closely resembles competitive conditions in the money market. Therefore let us begin by considering the structure of the different sectors that comprise the money market. This structure can be described in terms of three principal characteristics.

1) *The different securities sold in each sector of the money market are either homogeneous or near homogeneous.*

For example, all Treasury bills of a given issue are identical with respect to risk, maturity, and other characteristics that interest the rational investor. Even commercial paper, although it is issued by approximately 300 different companies, is (within any given maturity range) a near-homogeneous product, since it is standard in form and uniformly low in risk.

2) *All buyers and sellers in each sector of the money market have access to full and immediate information about market price.*

The brokers and dealers, who figuratively stand at the center of the money market, constantly receive and search out bids and offers from buyers and sellers throughout the country. Their activities have created a web of communications that binds each sector of the money market into a single national market. Because of this web, all investors who buy and sell money-market securities have constant access via telephone and telegraph to information about the current market prices of these securities.

---

* Students who have not read Parts 3 and 4 may omit the remainder of this chapter without losing continuity.

3) *Buyers and sellers are so numerous that most of them can't influence price.*

A *few* investors are large enough to occasionally exert a perceptible influence on market price, either by means of their purchases or their sales, but this influence is only slight and transitory.*

The above three observations indicate that the competitive conditions in the different sectors of the money market are most closely represented by the perfectly competitive model. Thus we can analyze price determination in each sector of this market simply by applying the tools of supply and demand. We can conclude that the price of—or more properly the rate of return yielded by—every security is determined by the intersection of a downward-sloping demand curve that represents buyers' market behavior with an upward-sloping supply curve that represents sellers' market behavior.

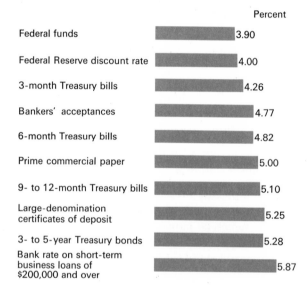

Percent

Federal funds — 3.90

Federal Reserve discount rate — 4.00

3-month Treasury bills — 4.26

Bankers' acceptances — 4.77

6-month Treasury bills — 4.82

Prime commercial paper — 5.00

9- to 12-month Treasury bills — 5.10

Large-denomination certificates of deposit — 5.25

3- to 5-year Treasury bonds — 5.28

Bank rate on short-term business loans of $200,000 and over — 5.87

31|1

Selected money-market rates, end of August 1967.
(Source: *Federal Reserve Bulletin*)

Links Between Prices in the Money Market

If money-market instruments had identical characteristics, they would yield identical rates of return, but they differ as to maturity, risk, and liquidity. Therefore no single rate of return ever rules throughout the money market. "Price" in this market assumes the form of a range of rates like that in Fig. 31.1. The relationships between the rates of return on different money-market instruments always reflect various special circumstances, but those in Fig. 31.1 are typical.

---

* The Fed, of course, is an exception; but since its purchases and sales are not dictated by the profit motive, this exception need not trouble us.

Let us analyze the way these typical money-market rates are determined. First: Investors and borrowers view money-market instruments as close substitutes for each other, which means that the individual sectors of this market comprise a set of highly *interrelated* markets. Therefore, as we said in our discussion of general equilibrium in Chapter 16, the price in one sector of the money market is influenced by the prices in other sectors of it. Second: All other things being constant, investors always prefer more-liquid to less-liquid assets, and riskless to risky ones. Therefore it stands to reason that low-risk, highly liquid assets will be at the bottom when it comes to yield, and higher-risk, less-liquid assets at the top. This relationship is illustrated by Fig. 31.1, in which we see that, at the end of August 1967, low-risk, highly liquid loans of Federal funds yielded a significantly lower rate of return than higher-risk, less-liquid commercial paper. Note also that Treasury bills of short maturity (i.e., of high liquidity) yielded lower rates of return than Treasury bills of longer maturity.

Our description of the way the structure of money-market yields is determined suggests that the rate of return yielded by any one instrument can fluctuate only within a relatively narrow range, whose upper and lower limits are determined by the rates of return yielded by money-market instruments of similar risk and liquidity.

To illustrate this point, let us investigate the way the rate of return on commercial paper sold in the open market is influenced by other money-market rates. Firms that borrow in the commercial-paper market all have high credit ratings. Therefore they can borrow on favorable terms from banks, and the amount they borrow in the commercial-paper market depends on how high the rate there is compared with the rate banks charge on large short-term loans to business firms. If the rate on commercial paper were to rise as high as the bank-loan rate, firms would borrow very little in the commercial-paper market. But if the commercial-paper rate were to fall below the bank-loan rate, firms would shift some of their borrowing away from the banks and into the commercial-paper market. Therefore the demand-for-funds curve in the commercial-paper market must slope downward (see Fig. 31.2) and intersect the vertical axis in the vicinity of the bank rate on large loans.

To an investor, the money-market security closest to commercial paper, in terms of risk and liquidity, is the banker's acceptance. Commercial paper and bankers' acceptances are both short-term liabilities of firms with high credit ratings, but bankers' acceptances are less risky than commercial paper because they've been guaranteed (i.e., accepted) by a bank. Therefore the willingness of investors to supply funds in the commercial-paper market depends on how high the rate on commercial paper is compared with the rate on bankers' acceptances. If the rate on commercial paper were to fall below that on bankers' acceptances, then the amount of money investors would put into commercial paper would be negligible. But if the rate on

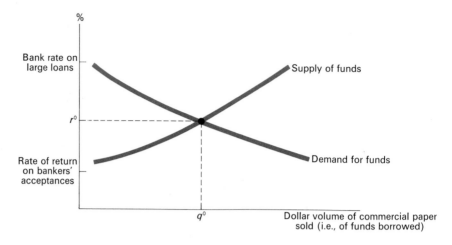

31|2

In equilibrium, the commercial-paper rate, r^0, will lie between the bank rate on large loans and the rate of return on bankers' acceptances.

commercial paper were to rise above that on bankers' acceptances, investors would shift their funds out of bankers' acceptances and into commercial paper. Therefore the supply-of-funds curve in the commercial-paper market must slope upward (look again at Fig. 31.2), and intersect the vertical axis in the vicinity of the bankers'-acceptance rate.

We have seen that potential borrowers in the commercial-paper market can turn to alternative sources of credit (banks) and potential lenders can invest in alternative instruments (bankers' acceptances). Therefore we would expect the rate of return established in this market to always fall (as Fig. 31.2 shows) within a relatively narrow range whose bounds are determined by the bank rate on large loans and the yield on bankers' acceptances. Figure 31.3 bears out this prediction.

The Effect of Change on Money-Market Yields

Since prices in different sectors of the money market are so closely linked, a shift in supply or demand in any one sector of it affects rates of return (or yields) in the whole market. Example: Suppose that a sharp rise in consumer installment buying causes an equally sharp rise in the number of installment sales contracts offered to sales finance companies. And suppose that this in turn causes a marked increase in the amount of money finance companies borrow in the commercial-paper market (i.e., an upward shift in the demand-for-funds curve in this market). The first consequence will be an increase in the yield on commercial paper. This increase will cause inves-

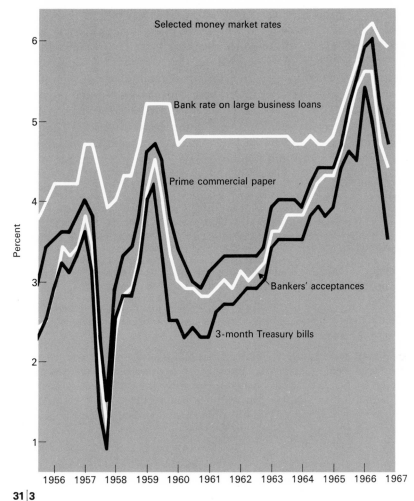

31 | 3
Over time, money-market rates move up and down together.
(Source : *Federal Reserve Bulletin*)

tors to shift funds out of other sectors of the money market into the commercial-paper market, and as a result the supply-of-funds curves in other sectors
will shift to the left and the rates of return in these other sectors will rise.
At the same time deficit units will begin to stop borrowing in the commercial-paper market because of the rate rise there, and will shift their borrowing to the banks. As a result the bank-loan rate may also rise. Thus, because
of the reactions of both investors and borrowers, the rate rise in the commercial-paper market will be transmitted immediately to all other sectors of
the money market.

This, however, is not the end of the story. As you should verify, the rate rises induced in other sectors of the money market by the rate rise in the commercial-paper market will reinforce the rate rise in the commercial-paper market. And this in turn will reinforce the rate rises in all other sectors of the money market! Our example thus suggests that any change in the supply of or demand for funds in one sector of the money market will not only alter the price in that market, but also set off a chain reaction whose effect will be to nudge all other money-market rates in the same direction.* For this reason we would expect money-market rates to move, roughly speaking, in unison, and Fig. 31.3 shows that indeed they do.

PROBLEMS

1   "The existence of the Federal funds market makes it possible for banks to utilize more efficiently the aggregate reserves that the Fed makes available to them." Discuss.

2   How might an increase in the discount rate affect the rate on Federal funds? What about a hike in the Treasury bill rate?

3   How would an increase in the supply of Treasury bills (i.e., a rightward shift in the supply curve of Treasury bills) affect the rate of return on commercial paper? Illustrate your answer with a diagram.

4   In the text we talked about the effect of risk and liquidity on the rates of return yielded by different money-market instruments. Another factor we did not mention is investors' expectations about the direction in which interest rates will move in the future. Suppose that investors believe that during the next few months interest rates will fall. How would this affect the relationship between the rates of return on Treasury bills of different maturities (e.g., on 3-month, 6-month, and 9-month bills)?

5   Suppose that a spurt in corporate investment leads to a big increase in the supply of long-term corporate bonds. How would this affect interest rates in the money market? Explain your answer.

6   A certain bank buys and sells government bonds for its own portfolio; and it is willing, as a convenience to depositors, to buy and sell long-term government bonds for them. The bank also buys and sells Treasury bills for its own portfolio, but it won't help out depositors by buying and selling bills for them. What considerations might explain this profit-maximizing institution's asymmetric attitude toward bills and bonds?

7   Look up in the *Wall Street Journal* (or any paper with a good financial section) the rates that Treasury bills of different maturities (say a bill with a 3-month

---

* Recall our discussion in Chapter 16 of the repercussions that a price change in one competitive market has on the prices in related competitive markets. See in particular Fig. 16.1.

maturity, one with a 6-month maturity and one with a 9-month maturity) are currently yielding.

a) What differences exist in the rates of return on these securities? Can you explain these differences in terms of differences in their relative liquidity? In terms of investors' expectations as to future interest rates?

b) For a week or two collect and plot data on the rates of return on the securities you have picked to study. Do the resulting time series appear to be related? If so, is the relationship what you expect? Explain your answer.

8   "Federal funds are inside money to the Fed, outside money to the commercial banks, and not money at all to the average citizen." Discuss.

9   On Jan. 11, 1967, a page-2 headline in the *Wall Street Journal* read:

"Prime" Rate Is Cut to 5¾% by Small Bank in
Minneapolis, Flabbergasting the Industry

What does this headline indicate to you about the competitive structure of the banking industry?

CHAPTER 32

OTHER FINANCIAL MARKETS

THE BOND MARKET

The difference between the bond* market and the money market is that the bond market deals in *long*-term as opposed to *short*-term debt securities. This distinction is easy enough to make on paper but not so easy to make in practice. The dividing line between what is short term and what is long term is nebulous. Also the distinction between long-term and short-term debt instruments is based on *current* maturity. Therefore a long-term bond, as its current maturity declines, passes from the long-term into the short-term market.

For convenience, let us divide what is sold on the bond market into three broad categories: (1) U.S. government securities, (2) state and local obligations, and (3) corporate and foreign bonds. Table 31.1 showed that the securities outstanding in each at the end of 1966 totaled roughly $93 billion, $106 billion, and $136 billion, respectively. As we might expect, the figure for corporate and foreign bonds is a conglomerate: About 80% represents bonds issued by nonfinancial corporations (that is, manufacturing and utility firms such as U.S. Steel and AT&T), about 12% the long-term obligations of finance companies, and about 8% foreign bonds (that is, bonds issued by foreign governments such as Denmark, Japan, and Australia).

These diverse borrowers are brought to the market by a variety of needs. The U.S. government sells bonds in order to cover its general operating deficit. State and local governments and nonfinancial corporations sell bonds to finance specific capital expenditures. Sales finance companies sell bonds so they can get money to lend out.

---

* For a quick rundown on the difference between stocks and bonds, see pages 87–89. When you buy a share of stock in a company, you own a fraction of that company. If a company issues bonds (say they cost $1000 apiece) and you buy one of them, you are simply loaning that company $1000.

Issuing Techniques

A bond issue may be distributed in several ways; the manner depends on who the borrower is. U.S. Government bonds (as opposed to bills) are offered directly to the public by the Treasury at a *fixed price* (which usually equals their par or face value) and at a *fixed coupon rate.** State and local government bonds and many new corporate ones are distributed by means of *investment banking firms.* An investment banking firm doesn't have to be a bank; in fact, most of them aren't. An investment banking firm is a firm that specializes in buying up new issues of bonds and stocks "wholesale" from the issuer and reselling them at a slight markup to the investing public (including financial institutions).

A lot of new corporate bonds are still being publicly offered, but in the past few years it has become increasingly common for corporations to place their bonds with large investors (primarily life insurance companies) through direct negotiation. This saves distribution costs and permits both lender and borrower to tailor the terms of the issue to meet their needs. The borrower can get an advance financing commitment from the lender, and also negotiate for an extended pay-out period in cases in which all the funds to be borrowed don't have to be spent simultaneously. Since the direct lender wants to protect the borrower's solvency and thus the value of the loan extended to him, the direct lender often keeps in close touch with the borrower's operations and acts as a financial adviser to him. Thus a bond issue placed directly with an insurance company may in reality be more akin to a bank loan than to a publicly distributed bond issue.

The Secondary Market for Bonds

The market for bonds is all one market, actually, but economists use two words to describe two different aspects of it. The *new-issue market* is the market for brand-new bonds that have just been issued by some company or government. The *secondary market* is the market for bonds that are being sold for the second (or third, or tenth) time, to new owners. (One could think of it as the used-bond market, or perhaps the secondhand bond market.)

Many bonds are listed and traded on the New York Stock Exchange, but the secondary market for bonds is mainly an over-the-counter one. The heart of this market is the dealers, who quote bid-and-asked prices for individual issues and thus *"make"* markets in them. The number of bond issues runs into thousands, so no one dealer makes markets in all of them. Each dealer specializes in a certain number of active issues.

---

* *Coupon rate* in this case means interest rate. Bonds carry coupons which the bondholder clips and mails in to the issuing corporation to get his interest.

Strange to say, only a small volume of trading takes place in the secondary bond market. The sparse (or *thin,* as economists say) nature of this market reflects the distribution of bond ownership between investor classes. You would expect bonds held by individuals to be actively traded. But Fig. 32.1 shows that only a small fraction of bonds are held by individuals (i.e., households). The remainder are held largely by financial intermediaries and pension funds, that is, by institutions that are likely to be hold-until-maturity investors.

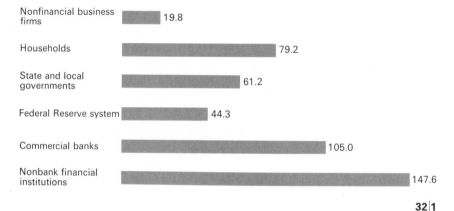

32│1

Distribution of bond ownership among investor groups, December 1966 (billions of dollars). Household figure excludes nonnegotiable U.S. government savings bonds. (Source: *Federal Reserve Bulletin*)

Price Determination in the Bond Market

Because the secondary markets for individual bond issues are so thin, you might think that they would be very imperfect. But no. The dealer-made secondary markets in which investors trade bonds for cash are—despite certain imperfections—basically competitive. Price there is determined not by individual buyers and sellers but by demand and supply. This is so because the bonds traded there are—within any maturity and risk class—close substitutes for each other and, for this reason, the price of a security is determined not by demand and supply for that security alone, but by demand and supply for all the securities which resemble it in risk and maturity.

You might also think that the new-issues market would have serious imperfections, since every new bond issue is an individualized product, differentiated from all others by the credit-worthiness of the issuer, by its own special terms, and by its maturity. In addition every new issue, initially at least, is under the monopoly control either of the issuer or the investment banker into whose hands it has passed, and is offered at an administered rather than a market-determined price. Sounds like a monopoly market rather than a competitive market; but actually there isn't much monopoly power exercised in this market. Reason: Bonds of a given class and quality are, as we just said, close substitutes for each other. Therefore the demand curve for a security is a highly elastic (i.e., almost horizontal) curve that intersects the price axis at the *going market price* for bonds that are similar to it. Thus a bond issuer's optimal offering price is usually a competitively established market price that reflects the preferences, needs, and liquidity of all the borrowers and lenders in the bond market.

THE MORTGAGE MARKET

As we saw in Table 31.1, the volume of mortgages is about three times that of corporate bonds, about twice that of state and local obligations, and about equal to the negotiable portion of the national debt. Thus from the point of view of volume, the mortgage market is the most important market in which debt securities are created and sold.

Three-fourths of the money borrowed in the mortgage market goes to buy 1-to-4-family homes. The other one-fourth is used to finance apartment buildings, shopping centers, and other business properties. Figure 32.2 shows that most mortgage lending is done by financial intermediaries, especially commercial banks, savings and loan associations, mutual savings banks, and life insurance companies. Savings and loan associations dominate the residential mortgage market; insurance companies are the largest lenders in the market for other mortgages.

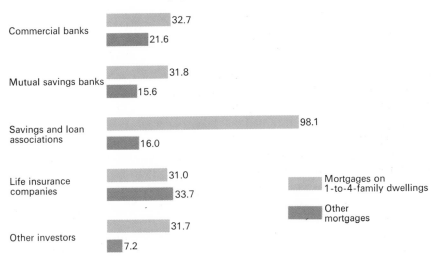

32|2

Distribution of mortgage ownership among investor groups, December 1966 (billions of dollars). (Source: *Federal Reserve Bulletin*)

Local Mortgage Markets

Most mortgage money is borrowed from intermediaries close to the scene, so to speak, of the mortgage. Mortgage money doesn't flow very readily from one region to another, for the following reasons: (1) The average small-to-medium size mortgage must be originated and serviced on the spot. (2) Lenders who deal in nonlocal mortgages risk getting involved—at faraway places—in foreclosing on delinquent mortgages and then disposing of the mortgaged properties, which is time-consuming and costly. (3) Some institutional lenders are restricted as to the types and quantities of out-of-state and even out-of-local-area mortgages they may acquire.

Because of these impediments to the flow of funds from one region to another, the mortgage market is mostly a set of loosely connected *local* markets, in which the borrowers are builders and buyers of homes and of small business properties, and the lenders are local commercial banks, savings and loan associations, and savings banks. Because there are so few suppliers in the average local mortgage market, it is often strongly oligopolistic, so the going mortgage rate is an administered price. The sellers set the rate, and change it only infrequently.

The National Mortgage Market

In order for a fragmented mortgage market to allocate resources efficiently, the relationship between the demand for and supply of funds must be about the same in every sector of the market. In the United States, however, shifts of industry and population from one region to another have created a problem: The local demand for mortgage money relative to the local supply is much higher in some regions than in others, so mortgage rates differ from region to region. Naturally this creates an incentive for lenders in low-rate areas to move their funds into high-rate areas, and for borrowers in high-rate areas to try to get money in low-rate areas. As a result, a national mortgage market, of sorts, has emerged.

Two main types of transactions take place in this market: (1) Big commercial and industrial properties are financed by *large* banks and insurance companies whose lending is national in scope. (2) In high-rate areas, such as the rapidly expanding Southwest, home mortgages are granted by middlemen (known as *mortgage companies*) and then resold to outside investors, particularly large life insurance companies. Sometimes commercial banks and savings and loan associations also sell to outside investors mortgages they have originated. Mortgages sold to outside investors continue to be serviced by the originator, who receives a fee for this service. Because of the risks incurred by investors in nonlocal mortgages, the only mortgages sold to outside investors are those that have been insured by the Federal Housing Administration or the Veterans' Administration.

Since many borrowers and lenders are active in the national mortgage market, price determination there is more competitive than it is in the average local mortgage market, where supply is in the hands of a few lenders and price is inflexible. Nevertheless, the national mortgage market is characterized by real and important imperfections, particularly because of the extreme heterogeneity of the debt instruments "sold" there.

The Secondary Market for Mortgages

The secondary market for mortgages is practically nonexistent, except for a few sales that take place through *mortgage brokers;* this despite the fact that the federal government in 1938 set up the Federal National Mortgage Association (familiarly known as "Fanny May") specifically to provide federal mortgage insurance and to create a broad secondary market for federally insured mortgages. Fanny May failed to do this for two reasons: (1) Even government-insured mortgages are too heterogeneous a commodity to be traded about like Treasury bills. (2) During the postwar period of rising interest rates, Fanny May decided to support price* in the mortgage market, so it bought mortgages but practically never sold them.

The fact that the secondary market for mortgages is practically nonexistent, except for special-purchase programs of Fanny May, means that mortgages are an *illiquid* asset. Most institutional investors, however, hold mortgages until maturity, and they hold other assets for liquidity; so this isn't usually a serious problem to them. But suppose there were to be another serious depression or an extended run by depositors on savings institutions. Then these investors might need a lender of last resort who could protect their solvency by monetizing their mortgage portfolios. Under present regulations, the Fed isn't set up to do this, and neither is Fanny May.

THE STOCK MARKET

The main thing that goes on in the stock market is the distribution of new stocks (economists call them *equity shares* or *equities*) and the trading of outstanding (i.e., "used") ones. These activities take place in (1) *organized exchanges* and (2) *over-the-counter* markets. The most important of the organized exchanges is the New York Stock Exchange (NYSE) which accounts for about 85% of the dollar volume on all exchanges. Next comes the American Stock Exchange (ASE), which accounts for about 7 of the remaining 15%. And then there are some small regional exchanges whose aggregate dollar volume is about equal to that of the ASE. The over-the-counter market in stocks is "made" by many dealers and brokers, most of whom are also active in other securities markets.

---

* Here price refers to the price at which outstanding mortgages are resold by one investor to another.

People usually think of the major function of the stock market as being a market in which business firms can raise additional equity capital through the sale of stock. But in point of fact new issues account for only a fraction of total stock-market volume. The stock market is thus mostly a *secondary* market. Here are some figures: During 1965 the total volume on all organized stock exchanges was $89 billion, but the volume of new issues was only $2.3 billion, and much of this represented not new issues proper, but firms "going public."*

The fact that business firms raise relatively little money through the sale of new stock and bonds reflects the fact that many firms rely heavily on retained earnings as a source of long-term capital, though not all of them do. Some make frequent "trips" to both the bond market and the stock market to obtain new capital. Public utilities do, for example. The reason is that public utilities are subject to so many price and profit regulations that they have a hard time accumulating enough retained earnings to finance the large investments they are continually having to make.

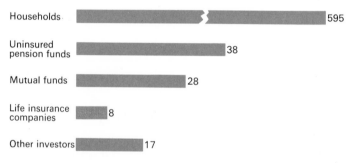

Households   595

Uninsured
pension funds   38

Mutual funds   28

Life insurance   8
companies

Other investors   17

32|3
Distribution of stock ownership among investor groups, December 1966 (billions of dollars).
(Source: *Federal Reserve Bulletin*)

Currently Americans hold close to $700 billion of stock, mostly in domestic corporations. The lion's share of this stock is owned by private citizens (see Fig. 32.3), although mutual funds and uninsured pension funds also have significant holdings.

The New-Issues Market for Stocks

Like new bond issues, new stock issues are often distributed through investment bankers. Investment bankers also handle sales of large blocks of stock

---

* When shares in a previously closely held corporation are offered for public sale, one says that the firm is "going public."

held by single people or institutions (these are known as *secondary offerings*). You can easily understand why an investment banker is needed to sell the stock of a new or relatively unknown company. But you may wonder why they're needed to sell new issues or secondary offerings of well-known stocks. Answer: The market for almost any stock—even an actively traded one—is too *thin* (i.e., too low in volume) to absorb large increases in supply without price drops. In such a situation the function of an investment banker is to seek out enough buyers (i.e., to drum up enough *demand*) so that a new issue or secondary offering can be sold off at the going market price instead of at a lower, temporarily depressed one.

Instead of turning to an investment banker, an established firm may also drum up demand for a new stock issue by distributing to its shareholders "rights" which entitle them to buy certain quantities of the newly issued stock at a price a bit below the stock's going market price. Since these rights are negotiable, they are actively traded from the time they are issued until they expire, and a stockholder who doesn't choose to exercise his rights can sell them to another investor who will.

The Secondary Market in Stocks

The outstanding stocks of most big companies in the U.S. are traded on organized exchanges. In order to be listed on the pace-setting New York Stock Exchange, a company must fulfill stringent requirements as to size, profitability, distribution of stock ownership, and so forth. Companies listed on the American Stock Exchange must also fulfill various requirements, though somewhat less stringent ones. Most stocks listed exclusively on regional exchanges are those of relatively small local companies. Regional exchanges also list and carry out trades in stocks listed on the two New York exchanges.

In setting up the rules under which they operate, the two New York exchanges have tried to create for each stock they list a market that meets two conditions: (1) Trades may be effected at any time during the day, and (2) price is to display reasonable continuity from trade to trade. These goals would not be hard to achieve in a market in which volume was consistently high, but they cannot be achieved in the thin markets that exist for many listed stocks unless there is professional intervention. This intervention is provided by *specialists* who operate on the floors of both exchanges. Each specialist is responsible for one or more stocks, and he plays a dual role *vis-à-vis* these stocks: (1) He acts as a *broker,* holding and executing buy and sell orders in these stocks. (2) To promote continuous trading and price continuity in these stocks, he acts as a *dealer;* he continuously quotes bid-and-asked prices in his specialty stocks, and he stands ready to buy or sell reasonable quantities of them at the prices he quotes.

The over-the-counter market in stocks functions much as the other dealer-made markets we have examined do. Many stocks traded over the counter are those of small, relatively unknown companies. However, the stocks of certain large, profitable firms (including many big banks and insurance companies) are also traded this way. Also big institutional investors, such as mutual funds, sometimes buy and sell in the over-the-counter market stocks, such as IBM and AT&T, which are listed on the organized exchanges.

Price Determination in the Stock Market

Even though the markets in which individual stocks are traded are thin ones which require the intervention of specialists if price is to be maintained, the market model that most accurately describes the way the prices of stocks are determined is not, as you might expect, an imperfectly competitive one, but the *perfectly competitive* one. To show this, let us recall the traits of a perfectly competitive market and see to what extent the market for stocks fits these requirements.

1) *The product sold in a perfectly competitive market must be homogeneous.*

Is this condition met in stock markets? Yes. Every one of a firm's outstanding shares conveys identical rights and privileges.* If John Q. Public buys 10 shares of IBM, he doesn't care *which* of the firm's 55 million outstanding shares he buys, because he knows that all these shares are indistinguishable, one from another.

2) *All participants in a perfectly competitive market must have full and immediate knowledge of current prices.*

The markets for stocks do meet this requirement approximately, if not perfectly, since information on prices is quickly and widely disseminated in several ways. The New York Stock Exchange has a ticker tape that flashes out to almost 4000 brokerage offices across the country price and volume data on individual trades as they take place. Ticker-tape data are also used to compile NYSE stock tables, which appear in more than 500 daily newspapers; ASE stock tables also appear in many newspapers. Data on market volume are not available for stocks traded over the counter, but the National Association of Securities Dealers does publish each day the bid and asked prices posted by dealers who make markets in such stocks.

---

* Of course, a firm may have more than one class of stock outstanding (such as Class A, Class B, etc.), but we don't need to worry about this, since different classes of stock in the same firm sell at different prices and can be thought of as being traded in different markets.

3) *Buyers and sellers, because they are so numerous, must regard market price as given.*

This condition may not hold for the occasional seller of a large block of stock, but it certainly holds for the rank-and-file investors who buy a little of this and sell a few shares of that. But where, you may ask, does the price-manipulating specialist fit into the picture? The answer is that *if he functions properly,* he does not contravene the forces of supply and demand which determine the going price of his specialty stocks. He simply enables the market mechanism to function more smoothly than it would in his absence. Specifically, by absorbing (through purchases and sales on his own account) those temporary imbalances between supply and demand which result from the uneven flow of buy and sell orders, he minimizes the transient influences which even a small investor might otherwise exercise on market price.

The Regulation of Securities Markets

As an aftermath of the stock market's momentous plunge in 1929, Congress in 1932 staged an investigation of banking practices and securities markets, which uncovered a host of flagrant abuses. Many of these abuses had magnified the sweeping losses that investors took during the crash.

Shocked by these discoveries, Congress passed a number of statutes: Two of the most important were the Securities Act of 1933 and the Securities Exchange Act of 1934. These laws require that any corporation whose stock is listed on an exchange must file periodic reports on its operations with an independent government agency, known as the Securities and Exchange Commission (SEC). Furthermore the SEC requires any issuer of new stock or bonds to disclose publicly all the facts investors need to evaluate the risks and prospects of these securities. The SEC is also responsible for preventing the manipulation of prices of securities in both the over-the-counter market and organized exchanges.

These Federal securities laws contain other important provisions: (1) They forbid commercial banks to underwrite new corporate security issues. (2) They impose on mutual funds and other investment companies requirements designed to up the chances that these companies will be operated in the interests of their shareholders rather than of their management. (3) They set forth measures aimed at the breakup of large holding companies.*

---

*Thumbnail definition: A *holding company* is a company that doesn't engage in any productive activities on its own, but controls a number of other firms that do. It does this by acquiring enough stock in these other firms so that it can select their directors and executives and thus determine their policies.

PROBLEMS

1   Some people say that if bond yields and other interest rates go up, stock prices are likely to decline. Can you think of any reasons why this should be so?

2   Look back at the data we gave in Chapter 30 on the composition of the assets held by different intermediaries. Do these data tell you anything about why yields in the mortgage and bond markets might be interrelated?

3   Suppose that an active secondary market for mortgages were to develop. What effect do you think this might have on mortgage rates? How do you think it would affect the operations of intermediaries, such as savings and loan associations, commercial banks, and insurance companies, who are active investors in mortgages?

4   Government expenditures go up, and the Treasury announces that it will have to borrow an extra $10 billion. This doesn't affect the size of the interest payments yielded by outstanding bonds (Treasury and corporate), but it's likely to depress their prices. Explain why.

5   Over a period of time, the fluctuations in the prices of outstanding bonds for two established corporations, say AT&T and Sperry Rand, are likely to maintain a similar pattern. But chances are the prices of their common stocks will not fluctuate similarly. Why the contrast?

6   Today more and more people are putting their personal savings into financial institutions like insurance companies, pension funds, and mutual funds, which invest heavily in corporate stocks and bonds. Given the scale and continuity of their investment operations, we assume that these institutions are more sophisticated investors than any John Q. Public who buys stocks and bonds. What pressures might such an increase in investor sophistication put on corporate management? What change might it portend for the quality of corporate management? Can you think of any desirable (or undesirable) aspects of such a change?

7   In the text we said that, because Fanny May decided during the postwar period of *rising* interest rates to support the prices at which outstanding mortgages were resold by one investor to another, they ended up always buying but rarely selling mortgages. Explain why Fanny May's decision had this effect. [*Hint:* How do you think a rise in interest rates would affect the resale value of outstanding mortgages?]

*Appendix to Chapter 32

FUNDS FLOWS AND RESOURCE ALLOCATION

In this chapter and Chapter 31, we have talked about how funds flow through financial markets from deficit units to surplus units. Now let us talk about the flow of funds from the standpoint of the efficiency of resource allocation.

Obviously people are better off if they can trade one kind of real good for another (e.g., apples for oranges). But it is less obvious why people are better off if they can trade funds for financial assets. How do such trades contribute to welfare? Well, consider the consumer. As we said in Chapter 3, Mr. Average Consumer is strongly motivated to save in some periods and dissave in others; i.e., to arrange his expenditure time path in a way that differs from his income time path (see Fig. 3.2). To do so, he may have to incur funds deficits in some periods and funds surpluses in others. The opportunity to trade funds for financial assets, and vice versa (i.e., to incur funds deficits and funds surpluses) thus contributes to his welfare because it increases his freedom to choose the way he allocates his consumption expenditures among different periods of his life.

Take the case of Lukewarm Smith. He has no chance to, or doesn't want to, invest in real productive assets; that is, he is a consumer who, like many of us, isn't interested in being a capital-using entrepreneur on the side. If Smith couldn't store up funds (i.e., generalized purchasing power) in the form of financial assets, the only way he could save would be to accumulate stocks of consumer goods. Barrels of flour, sides of beef, crates of soap— the list is endless. Holding such stocks would be expensive and troublesome (even his front hallway would have cartons of beans clear to the ceiling) and the goods would probably deteriorate over time, so that Smith would earn

---

* Students who have not yet read Parts 3 and 4 should omit this appendix.

a negative return on his stockpile, i.e., the goods he held would be worth less and less as time passed.

It's not just the opportunity to accumulate financial *assets* that increases Lukewarm Smith's range of choice in allocating his resources; the chance to incur financial *liabilities* does too. The fact that Smith can get money by borrowing means that if he wants to make a productive investment (in his own education, say, or in a house), he can do so whenever it's most appropriate in terms of his own needs and the opportunities open to him. He won't have to wait until he has saved enough money to pay for this asset. Also the fact that he can borrow means that, if he has unanticipated needs (sickness, a sudden move, falling in love and getting married, or some other unforeseen event), and if he doesn't have enough assets to cover this need, he won't necessarily suffer. He can obtain resources to meet his current needs by giving up claims against future goods.

The possibility of funds transfers also makes *firms* better off, for several reasons. (1) The fact that firms can obtain funds by issuing debt and equity claims against themselves means that they can invest in productive assets that they could not have financed if they had had to rely solely on their own resources. Thus the fact that firms can incur funds deficits increases the pace at which they can invest, and this in turn increases their capability, and the capability of the economy as a whole, of producing output in the future. (2) The possibility of funds transfers is also important to firms because it increases demand for their products. Smith, Jones, Brown, and lots of other consumers are able to buy new cars, boats, washing machines, and houses only because they can borrow money to pay for them. If they couldn't, they'd either have to do without these goods or settle for models that were less expensive. (If Smith couldn't get his Bearcub convertible financed at the bank, he might have to make do with a cheaper foreign-made car. And where would Detroit be then?)

Finally we should mention that the free flow of funds from surplus to deficit units promotes the mobility of resources, which in turn increases input productivity and raises output.* For example, the fact that mortgage financing is readily available makes houses easier to sell (i.e., more liquid), and this in turn makes it simpler for workers to move from place to place in response to changing job opportunities. So too does the fact that a worker may be able to borrow money to finance his move from one job to another.

An Efficient Allocation of Funds

In Chapter 18 we said that resource allocation is efficient only if there are no unconsummated trades of one *good* for another that would increase one

---

* See pages 282–283, on which we talked about the relationship between the mobility of resources and the efficiency of resource allocation.

person's welfare without simultaneously decreasing another's. If we now allow for the possibility that people and firms can trade not only goods, but also *funds,* this implies the following additional condition:

Resource allocation is efficient only if there are no unconsummated trades of funds for financial assets that would increase one person's welfare without simultaneously decreasing another's. *

The above condition for efficiency in funds allocation is a stringent one. It would, however, hold if all financial markets were perfectly competitive; that is: (1) If the potential buyers and sellers of every type of security were numerous. (2) If these potential buyers and sellers all had perfect knowledge of market opportunities. (3) If there were no impediments to the free flow of funds in response to market prices. (4) If the assets traded were homogeneous and divisible into small units.†

The Promotion of Funds Flows by Intermediaries

In everyday financial markets these conditions are not universally or even generally met. In some markets, there are few participants, in others the channeling of information to participants is imperfect, in still others there are impediments to the free flow of funds from deficit to surplus units (especially when the flow is from one region to another).

Because they keep people from making welfare-increasing trades of funds for financial assets, the imperfections of financial markets reduce the efficiency with which funds are allocated. Financial intermediaries, however, create additional channels through which funds can flow, thereby promoting such trades and contributing to the efficiency of resource allocation.

Intermediaries operate on a large scale. Therefore they can promote, indirectly, transfers of funds that might otherwise have been prevented by the following factors:

1) *Asset indivisibilities.* (Jones can scrape up $100 to buy a life insurance policy, but he hasn't got $1,000 to buy one of the Nuclear Orbit Corporation's bonds.)
2) *High transaction costs.*
3) *Inadequate knowledge on the part of either the borrower or the lender.* (Jones wouldn't buy one of Nuclear Orbit's bonds even if he did have the money, because he never reads the financial pages and he hasn't ever heard of the company.)

---

* Note that here we are talking about the efficiency of resource allocation measured in terms of people's preferences and expectations *at the time they trade,* i.e., about efficiency in an *ex ante* sense.

† If you assume that all consumers and firms are risk averters, you can show this by using an argument similar to the one we used in the Appendix to Chapter 18.

Financial intermediaries solicit funds in one area and lend them out in another. By such means they can circumvent, somewhat, the various legal, institutional, and geographic barriers that impede the free flow of funds between surplus and deficit units located in different regions. (Jones's insurance company uses the money it collects from Jones in Vermont to make a mortgage loan on the Smiths' house in Arizona.) Financial intermediaries also facilitate indirect trades of funds between deficit and surplus units by substituting for the heterogeneous and often illiquid obligations issued by deficit units their own homogeneous and more liquid securities. (Bert Brown is content to keep his money in the Sanity National Bank; he *knows* what bank deposits are. But he'd be leery of putting his money into commercial paper issued by Nuclear Orbit or some other firm—"Who are *they*, anyway?" —and he certainly wouldn't put his money into anything as illiquid as the Smiths' mortgage. What if Mrs. Brown smashed up the car next week? Brown might need cash in a hurry.)

The Evolution of Financial Intermediaries

At any point in time, the assets that intermediaries as a group hold and the indirect securities they issue depend on (1) the asset preferences of surplus units and (2) the volume and character of the credit needs of deficit units. These factors naturally change as economic conditions change. So to retain their importance in the allocation process, intermediaries have to continually alter the mix of the indirect securities they issue and the primary securities they buy.

Since different economic climates favor different intermediaries, it stands to reason that this alteration in mix would mean a concomitant evolution of individual intermediaries, and that, during each period, each intermediary would diversify in the direction most favored by economic conditions during that period. To some extent such diversification does occur. (Examples: Savings banks are trying to get into the lucrative consumer-credit business; commercial banks want to initiate mutual funds.) However, the tendency for different intermediaries to evolve into conglomerate firms—each offering a wide range of indirect securities and investing in a wide range of primary securities—is thwarted by (a) the strict charters and enabling laws under which most intermediaries operate, and by (b) tax laws, which often favor existing forms of intermediation and penalize innovations.

Because different intermediaries maintain their individual identities over time, their relative prominence continually changes in response to changing economic conditions. When housing booms, savings and loan associations, which specialize in mortgage financing, grow faster than other intermediaries. When the prices of goods rise, mutual funds spurt in growth, since they offer a hedge against inflation. As the relative prominence of different intermediaries changes over time, the mix of securities issued and bought by these institutions *as a group* evolves in response to the changing needs of the times. Therefore intermediaries, despite their individual difficulties in adjusting to change, can as a group maintain their importance in the allocation process, and keep on contributing to the efficiency of resource allocation.

PROBLEMS

1   Can a consumer save without having a funds surplus? What about the relationship between dissaving and a funds deficit? Is such a relationship a consistent one?

2   Suppose that you were charged with setting ceilings on the deposit rates paid by commercial banks, mutual savings banks, and savings and loan associations. In the interests of an efficient allocation of resources, what general guidelines would you follow? (For example: Would you impose the same ceiling on the same kind of deposit in different institutions or would you distinguish between institutions? Would you impose different ceilings on different types of deposits? Would you distinguish between institutions in fast-growing and those in slow-growing areas?) Might you decide to simply abolish all deposit-rate ceilings and let supply and demand determine these "prices"?

3   "The government ought to insure demand deposits at commercial banks [it does; recall the FDIC we talked about in Chapter 29] because commercial banks are guardians of the payments mechanism. But it shouldn't insure deposits at savings and loan associations, because such insurance decreases the efficiency of resource allocation by reducing the incentive of depositors to keep an eye on the investment policies of these institutions." Comment. [*Hint:* Try looking at the income statement and balance sheet of your local bank and savings and loan association, and see what you can find out about how sound their investment policies are.]

Part 6
MACRO MODELS AND
MACRO POLICY

CHAPTER 33

MACRO MODELS AND MACRO POLICY

In Parts 3 and 4 we studied the way perfectly and imperfectly competitive goods markets operate, and in Part 5 we discussed financial markets. In Part 6 we have two goals: (1) To develop a macroeconomic model that combines both goods and financial markets and thus ties together the three preceding parts. (2) To analyze how and to what extent the government sector, given the policy tools at its disposal, can attain the macroeconomic objectives that it sets for itself.

MACRO MODELS

A macroeconomic model is one that represents the behavior of the economy as a whole. We could try to build a model made up of many variables, like the general equilibrium model in Chapter 16. Such a model, however, would be difficult to construct, and too general and unwieldy to be useful as a tool for analyzing the behavior of the economy as a whole. Therefore we shall develop here an aggregative model, in which the key variables are national income, total investment, total consumption, total government expenditure, and other economic aggregates.

We shall use our macroeconomic model to analyze the way an economy such as that of the United States behaves, and to discuss the factors that determine the level of national income and employment, the price level, and the rate at which the economy grows.

Any country's level of employment, and the factors that determine it, are extremely important. Recent history has shown that unemployment in a modern economy often reaches troubling levels. When it does, a gap opens between the level of output actually produced and the level of output the economy could have produced if there had been full employment. This point is illustrated in Fig. 33.1, which shows actual and potential output for the U.S. during the decade 1956–66. A gap between actual and potential

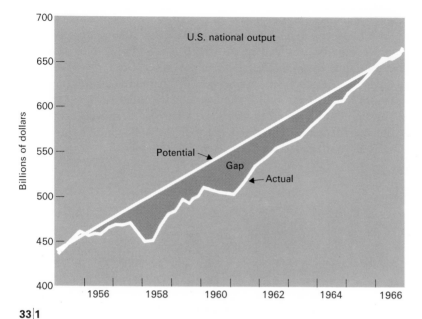

33|1

During the decade 1956–1966, unemployment created a gap between actual and potential output in the U.S. (Source: *Economic Report of the President, 1967*, page 43)

output is socially undesirable because it represents a wasted opportunity to satisfy people's needs. This waste can assume serious proportions: The gap pictured in Fig. 33.1 totaled roughly $300 billion over the decade. That is, it was larger than the total expenditures that state and local governments made for education during this period, and almost as large as the total investments made by business in durable equipment!

Although today we recognize that the question of what determines the level of employment and output is very important, this question received little attention before the 1930's, because before this time many economists espoused the *classical theory of employment.* According to this theory, the economy, through price and wage adjustments, would automatically tend to full employment. Proponents of the theory, on the basis of this reasoning, were apt to dismiss depressions as temporary, self-correcting aberrations of the economic system.

The classical position that unemployment was impossible in theory and therefore relatively unimportant in practice could be sustained as long as the periods of unemployment that did occur were short. In the 1930's, however, the world economy was rocked by the Great Depression. The country hit hardest was the U.S., where unemployment rose to 24.9% in 1933 and remained at high levels until the end of the decade (see Fig. 33.2).

A theory that offered an alternative to the classical system, and one that explained how continued unemployment—like that during the 1930's—could occur, was finally proposed by the English economist John Maynard Keynes, in his famous *General Theory of Employment, Interest, and Money,* published in 1936. Keynes' ideas have been much modified and amplified during the more than 30 years since they were first presented, but they still constitute the foundation on which most macroeconomic models are based. Certainly the macro model that we present in the following chapters can be described as *Keynesian,* and we shall refer to it that way.

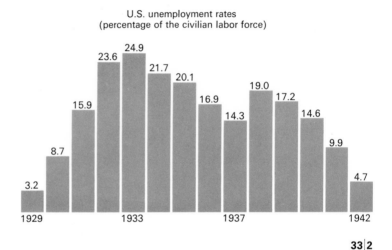

U.S. unemployment rates
(percentage of the civilian labor force)

33|2

The Great Depression led, in the U.S., to a severe and long-lived rise in unemployment.
(Source: U.S. Department of Commerce)

Although the Keynesian model is helpful in explaining fluctuations in employment and income, this is not the only use to which it can be put. We shall use this model as a starting point for our analysis of a number of problems, such as what causes changes in the price level and what determines the rate at which the economy grows.

MACROECONOMIC POLICY

Our second goal in Part 6 is to discuss the *objectives* and *instruments* of macroeconomic policy. Most governments these days recognize that they have a responsibility to improve the performance of the national economy. But there are many ways of measuring an economy's performance, and different nations face different economic problems. Therefore it isn't surprising that the list of macroeconomic goals that a government might have is long and that not all governments have the same ones.

Let us now list the principal macroeconomic targets of the U.S. government:

1) *Full employment.*

Under the 1946 Employment Act, full employment was made an officially sanctioned objective of public policy. In this act, Congress declared that

". . . it is the continuing policy and responsibility of the Federal Government to use all practicable means consistent with its needs and obligations . . . to coordinate and utilize all its plans, functions, and resources for the purpose of creating and maintaining . . . conditions under which there will be afforded useful employment opportunities . . . for those able, willing, and seeking work, and to promote maximum employment, production, and purchasing power."

Full employment is an important target not only because unemployment wastes potential output, but also because of the loss of social standing and self-respect which is the lot of the unemployed worker.

2) *The maintenance of price stability.*

This objective is an important one, since inflation hurts those with fixed incomes, distorts economic incentives (including the incentive to save), and impairs a nation's competitive position in world markets.

3) *Rapid economic growth.*

Growth is an important objective because in a dynamic economy, in which technology is constantly improving and the labor force constantly expanding, output must grow if unemployment is to be prevented. Growth is also important because the extra output it provides can be used to meet the unsatisfied wants of the population for better housing, better recreation facilities, better schools, and so forth.

4) *The maintenance of balance-of-payments equilibrium.*

If the U.S. were to have a continuing balance-of-payments deficit, eventually it would have to either devalue the dollar or impose direct controls that, by distorting trade patterns and international flows of capital, would limit not only the freedom, but also the real income of its citizens.

5) *An adequate supply of collectively consumed goods,* such as police protection, national defense, highways, schools, and so forth.

To achieve its various macroeconomic goals, the government has a variety of policy instruments. It can (a) impose taxes, (b) make expenditures, (c) impose direct controls such as price and wage ceilings, and (d) influence, through the central bank, the cost and availability of capital.

The government needs so many policy instruments in order to achieve the goals it sets for itself because each instrument may suffice to achieve only one goal, and—to the extent that this is the case—the government will need at least one instrument for every target it sets. Suppose that the government sets up two goals: price stability and maximum possible growth. If both are to be accomplished simultaneously, the government will have to encourage investment and at the same time restrict consumption. To encourage investment, the government could lower interest rates, but this policy would certainly not lower consumption. It might even raise it. Therefore the government would have to employ some other instrument—for example, a high tax on wages—to decrease consumption.

Whatever the government's objectives, its choice of instruments is influenced by the *efficiency, selectivity,* and *flexibility* of the instruments available to it.

An instrument is efficient if it produces a large impact when it is changed by a small amount.

Example: Changes in the interest rate are an efficient instrument for controlling the borrowing of state and local governments but an inefficient one for controlling the borrowing of speculators in the stock market. The reason is that stock-market speculators hope for a large gain over a short period, and therefore are fairly insensitive to changes in interest rates.*

An instrument is selective if it has great impact on one objective but little impact on others.

Selectivity is important because if a government did not have selective instruments, it might, for example, find itself in the awkward position of being unable to promote full employment without inadvertently creating a balance-of-payments deficit, and of therefore being forced to choose between two goals. This possibility is not just theoretical; the U.S. has been faced with precisely such a problem throughout the 1960's.

An instrument is flexible if it can be put into operation quickly and reversed quickly, as need arises.

Economic conditions change rapidly. So in many situations a government needs instruments that can be initiated rapidly, that will produce their impact without delay, and that can be quickly reversed. Changes in the availability of credit are a good example of a flexible instrument: The central bank can make day-to-day alterations in the level of commercial bank re-

---

* Recall that in Chapter 29 we said that the Fed has slapped stock buyers with a margin requirement of 70% cash (see page 457) in order to control speculation. One reason for this rule is that hiking interest rates was not effective enough as a curb to speculation.

serves. An example of an *inflexible* instrument is public works. It takes a long time for public works to get started, and once started they are irreversible, in the sense that they are useless unless completed.

A SUMMARY OF WHAT IS TO COME

In Chapter 34, we shall discuss the meaning of national income, and how it is measured. In Chapter 35 we shall analyze the way the equilibrium level of national income is determined. The following five chapters describe the government sector, analyze the factors that determine whether the economy is performing well or badly, and point out what the government can do—given the instruments at its disposal—to improve this performance.

PROBLEMS

1　Do you think the federal government should pursue a conscious macroeconomic policy? If so, what goals do you think it should set? Why?

2　If there were to be a conflict between any of these goals, which would you consider the most important for the government to achieve? For example, if you were a government policy-maker and had to make a choice between full employment and price stability, which would you consider more important? Why?

3　To what extent is the government currently achieving the goals it has set for itself? The goals you think it ought to set ?

CHAPTER 34

THE NATIONAL
INCOME ACCOUNTS

DEFINING NATIONAL INCOME

National income refers to the total income earned and received by a nation during a given year. In Chapter 1 we said that any spending unit's income equals the payments or purchasing power it obtains by supplying inputs to producers.* So we could define national income as *the sum of the income payments* (wages, rents, interest, and profits) *earned by all spending units in the economy.*

There's also another way to define it. When we talked about the consumer we distinguished between his *money* income (i.e., the total money payments he receives for the inputs he supplies to producers) and his *real* income, that is, the market basket of goods and services he could buy with his money income. This second way of looking at income suggests that an alternative way to define national income is: *the sum of all goods and services produced by business firms in the economy.*

Intermediate Goods

To make this second definition precise, we'll have to add several qualifications. For one thing, there is the problem posed by *intermediate* goods, that is, goods produced by one firm and used as productive inputs by another. Tectronics, Inc., sells its folding light bulbs, not only to consumers, but also to other producers who use them as inputs. The Nuclear Orbit Corporation, for example, buys bulbs from Tectronics and installs them in a special folding lamp it sells to consumers. This means that if, when we were summing

---

* Later in this chapter it may help you to keep in mind the following point: Since the economist defines income as payments received for productive services, speculative profits (Jones buys IBM for $300 and sells it for $600) *don't count as income;* they are capital gains.

up the economy's total output of goods, we were to add all the bulbs Tectronics produces to all the lamps Nuclear Orbit produces, we'd end up counting the light bulbs Tectronics sells to Nuclear Orbit *twice:* Once when Tectronics sells them to Nuclear Orbit and once again when Nuclear Orbit sells its lamps (bulb included) to consumers. To avoid the danger of counting a single output twice (or three times or even more), we must rephrase our second definition of national income as follows: National income equals the sum of all *final outputs* produced in the economy; that is, total output minus intermediate goods.

Capital Goods

Now we hit a snag: The dividing line between intermediate and final goods is difficult to draw. Shall we treat *capital* goods produced during the current period as intermediate or as final goods?

Take Tectronics, for example. They buy a new $50,000 bulb-folding machine this year. Should we include this machine in final output or treat it as an intermediate good? On the one hand it can be argued that this bulb-folding machine—and all other capital goods as well—are used to produce other goods. Thus they are intermediate goods and should be excluded from final output.

On the other hand, it can be argued that capital goods produce services over many periods (Tectronics expects its bulb-folding machine to last 15 years), and that their creation thus enhances the nation's ability to produce output in the future. Hence our definition of national income ought to be widened to include not only currently consumed goods but also capital goods.

We can reconcile these apparently conflicting points of view by adding into each year's final output the *net* addition made to the nation's capital stock by investment during that year. That is, we include in each year's final output the *gross* investment the economy has made in capital goods during that year, and we subtract all depreciation of capital goods that occurs in connection with the production of this output. With this approach to capital goods, we have to rephrase our second definition still more precisely: National income during any period equals the economy's *net* final output during that period.

National Income Is Evaluated at Market Price

So long as we stick to our first definition of national income as the sum of the income payments earned by all spending units in the economy, we can readily figure out national income, since most of the factor payments we have to add will be designated in dollars. However, if we try to apply our second definition of national income as the sum of the economy's net final outputs, we're going to encounter an apples-and-oranges problem of addition. How can we sum up Smith's new Bearcub convertible, Tectronics' bulb-folding machine, and Jones's platter of steak to get a measure of national income? The national income accountant has an answer. He says, "Presumably goods are worth to people at least what they pay for them. So we'll evaluate all the goods and services that enter into national income at their current market prices. Then we'll add the resulting figures to get a dollar measure of the economy's net final output."

Total Factor* Incomes Equal Net Final Output

We have proposed two definitions of national income:

1) *National income is the sum of all factor incomes (including profits) generated through the production of final output.*

2) *National income is the economy's net final output evaluated at current market prices.*

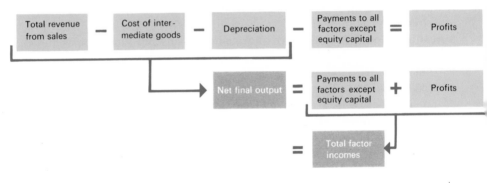

34|1

Our two measures of national income, net final output and total factor incomes, are equal.

These two definitions amount to the same thing. To see why, we first recall from Chapter 6 that a firm's profits are defined as its total revenue minus its total cost. (See the income statement for Tectronics on page 92.) This definition tells us that the profits earned by all firms in the economy must equal the total revenue these firms get from the sale of all goods (i.e., consumption goods, capital goods, and intermediate goods) *minus* the costs they incur for intermediate goods, for depreciation, and for all factors of production except equity capital. (See the top line of Fig. 34.1.) Next we

---

* *Factor* here means factors of production, such as labor, land, and other inputs. "Factor incomes" is econ-English for the incomes that these factors earn.

observe that the total revenue that firms get from the sale of all goods minus the costs they incur for intermediate goods and for depreciation equals the value of the economy's net final output. (See the left side of Fig. 34.1.)

Now if we put this observation and the preceding one together, we see that the economy's net final output equals the sum of (1) the incomes paid out by producers to all factors of production except equity capital plus (2) the profits earned by all producers. (See the middle line of Fig. 34.1.) Profits, however (like interest, wages, and rent), are the income of a factor of production: equity capital. So the economy's net final output equals the sum of all factor incomes generated through the production of this output, and thus our two definitions of national income come to the same thing. Figure 34.1 shows this schematically.

The Government Sector

To keep things simple, we have implicitly dealt in our discussion so far with an economy in which there was no government. Let us now see what happens if we take the government into account.

The basic function of government is to produce goods and services. A lot of these goods and services (especially those that benefit consumers) ought to be classed as final output, but some (including many that benefit firms) are really intermediate goods. The national income accountant agrees with this point of view, but he throws up his hands at the thought of trying to untangle the government's intermediate outputs from its final outputs. So *he simply treats all government output as final goods.*

Goods and services produced by the government aren't usually sold, so —unlike goods and services produced by private firms—they can't be evaluated at market price. This poses a problem: How can government output be added into the economy's net final output? The income accountant has a simple answer. Always an optimist, he says: "Government output must be worth at least what it costs, so we'll add it into the economy's net final output at cost."

According to this approach, net final output in an economy that has a government sector equals the sum of all net final outputs devoted to consumption and net investment *plus* all expenditures made by government (1) on goods and services (i.e., on electric typewriters, jet fighters, and so forth), and (2) on factors of production (e.g., senators, secretaries, and other civil servants).

It's easy to show that this new twist in the definition of the economy's net final output doesn't alter the equality between national income measured according to the net-final-output approach and national income measured according to the total-factor-incomes approach. But to keep things simple, let us take this point on faith here and prove it in the appendix that follows.

SETTING UP A NATIONAL INCOME AND PRODUCT ACCOUNT

If he wanted to, the national income accountant could simply use his definition of net final output to calculate a figure for national income and let it go at that. But generally he is more ambitious. He wants to set up a *national income and product account* to describe (1) the way the economy's net final output is allocated among different uses (consumption, investment, and government expenditures) and (2) the way the total money income generated through the production of this output is allocated among different income categories (rent, profits, wages, and so forth).

To set up such an account, the income accountant collects data on the total profits, wages, rents, and other types of income factors earn. He also collects data on the total goods people consume, on the net investment in physical assets that firms make, and on the total output that the government produces. Then he records all the data he has collected in an income and product account, whose left-hand side lists product uses and whose right-hand side lists factor incomes. If the income accountant hasn't erred in his calculations and if he lives in a *closed* economy (that is, one that doesn't trade with other countries), the left-hand side of his account will measure net final output, the right-hand side will measure total factor incomes, and the two sides will be precisely equal. If the accountant lives in an *open* economy, however, things will turn out to be a little more complex: Some of the goods produced by the economy will be exported and some of the goods consumed by the economy will be imported. So to get the product-uses side of his account to represent net final output, the accountant will have to add an additional entry, "exports minus imports." And he will end up with an account that has the general structure shown in Table 34.1.

THE U.S. NATIONAL INCOME ACCOUNTS

Table 34.2 shows the U.S. income and product account for 1966. The basic structure of this table is similar to that of Table 34.1. Table 34.2 is longer, however, because it has subentries under the headings for consumption, investment, government, and net exports; it gives more information that way.

There is another structural difference between Table 34.2 and Table 34.1. Table 34.2 records both investment and final output on a *gross* rather than a *net* basis (and it adds depreciation to the income-sources side of the account to keep both sides in balance). The reason for this is that the accuracy of depreciation estimates is questionable, at best. So the U.S. Department of Commerce, which sets up the U.S. income and product account, chooses to stress the gross rather than the net side of the picture.

Look now at the entries under "gross private domestic investment." In Chapter 2 we said that consumer purchases of durable goods were a form of investment, so you may be surprised that consumer durables are omitted from gross investment. The reason is that the Department of Commerce

TABLE 34|1

A National Income and Product Account

Product uses	Income sources	
Consumption	Wages	
Net investment	Dividends	
Government	Retained profits	
Exports minus imports		
Net final output =	Total factor incomes =	National income

TABLE 34|2

The U.S. National Income and Product Account for 1966 (Billions of Dollars) *

Product uses			Income sources		
Personal consumption		$464.9	Compensation of employees		$433.3
Durable goods	$ 69.3		Proprietors' income		57.8
Nondurable goods	206.2		Rental income of persons		18.9
Services	189.4		Net interest		20.0
Gross private domestic			Corporate profits and in-		
investment		117.0	ventory valuation adj.		80.2
Residential structures	25.7		Corporate profits taxes	33.9	
Business plant and			Dividends	20.9	
equipment	79.2		Retained profits	27.5	
Business inventories	12.1		Inventory valuation		
			adjustment	−2.1	
Government purchases of			National income		610.2
goods and services		153.0			
Federal	76.8		Indirect business taxes		65.5
State and local	76.2		Statistical discrepancy plus		
Net exports of goods and			adjustments		.9
services		4.8			
Exports	42.7		Net national product		676.6
Less: Imports	−37.9		Depreciation		63.1
Gross national product		739.7	Gross national product		739.7

*Source: U.S. Department of Commerce

treats all purchases of consumer durables (except houses) as current consumption, not because the purchase of durable goods doesn't constitute investment, but because depreciation on consumer durables is so hard to estimate.

The final entry on the product-uses side of Table 34.2 represents the gross output of final goods and services allocated during the year to consumption, *gross* investment, government, and net exports. This total is called the *gross national product,* or *GNP.* You can't pick up a newspaper these days without running smack into a discussion of gross national product. Well, there it is, and now you know how the national income accountant arrives at his figures!

The first set of entries on the income-sources side of Table 34.2 breaks down consumer- and business-sector income into its major parts. "Compensation of employees" means wages and salaries. "Proprietors' income" means the profits of unincorporated businesses. "Rental income of persons" includes not only rents paid to private persons by tenants, but also *imputed* rents which homeowners are thought of as paying to themselves. The national income accountant adds imputed rents into national income because homeowners do provide housing services to themselves, just as landlords provide housing services to their tenants, and services of both sorts contribute equally to national income.

Table 34.2 shows total corporate profits as a single figure and then divides this into taxes, dividends, and retained profits. The corporate profits figure includes not only profits proper, but also capital gains and losses due to changes in the prices at which corporations value their inventories. Such capital gains and losses aren't factor incomes and aren't part of national income. So, to cancel them out, the income accountant adds an offsetting entry which he calls "inventory-valuation adjustment."

In Department of Commerce parlance, the total factor incomes and the corporate profits generated through the production of national output are referred to as *national income*. National income is smaller than GNP because the latter figure includes depreciation. Also because GNP is calculated by adding the market value of goods sold, GNP contains indirect business taxes (i.e., excise and sales taxes) that are not included in national income.

The sum of national income and indirect business taxes is referred to as the economy's *net national product* (*NNP*). This important statistic represents the economy's total output of final goods and services, minus whatever capital-stock depreciation has occurred in connection with its production. In its concept, NNP is a truer measure of the economy's output than GNP, but GNP figures are more widely quoted. There are several reasons for this: One (as suggested above) is that the depreciation figure recorded in the national income accounts is questionable. Another is that it is *gross*, not net, investment that creates employment in capital-goods industries.

Other Income Concepts

National income measures the total factor incomes generated through the production of national output. It is not, however, a very good measure of the funds that consumers actually receive to put in their pockets and dispose of as they please. To obtain a measure of consumers' *disposable income,* we must add and subtract several things. First, we must subtract from national income the following items: corporate profits taxes, the inventory valuation adjustment, and retained corporate profits. None of these accrue to consumers. Second, we must subtract all contributions which employers and employees make for social insurance (i.e., social security payments). Third, we must add all *government transfer payments*—such as interest on the government debt, social security benefits, and veterans' pensions—made to individuals. These items may be viewed as income by their recipients, but they do not represent payments for current productive services. For this reason they are excluded both from the government-expenditures entry on the product-uses side of the national income account and from the factor-incomes entries on the sources side.

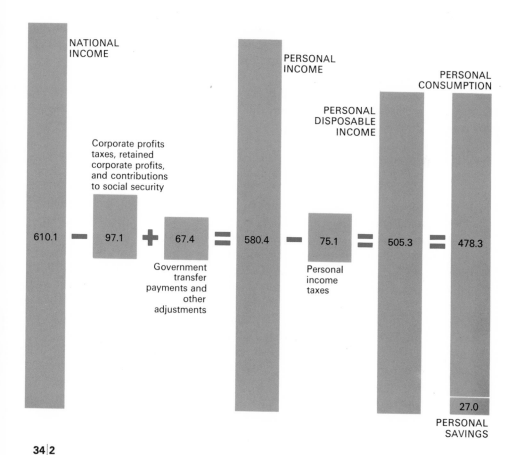

34|2

U.S. national income, personal income, and disposable income during 1966 (billions of dollars). (Source: U.S. Department of Commerce)

After we have done the above adding and subtracting, we obtain a figure known as *personal income*. Now we subtract from this figure all income taxes (and certain other taxes) that people have to pay. This leaves us with *personal disposable income*. This figure can itself be subdivided into two further categories: *personal consumption* and *personal savings*.

The rather complex relationship between the different national income concepts we have described is shown in Fig. 34.2.

Current Prices, Constant Prices, and Changes in the Price Level

One important way that people want to use the national income accounts is to study how the size and composition of national income changes over time. But there's a problem: Year-to-year changes in national income reflect not only changes in *real* output, but also changes in output *prices*. This is so because the national income accountant evaluates each year's output at the market prices prevailing in that year; and the general level of prices often changes from one year to the next. Thus when prices rise, year-to-year changes in GNP, reflecting this price change, overstate the real rate of growth of national output; when prices fall, the opposite occurs.

The obvious way to get around this problem would be to evaluate each year's GNP at some *constant* set of prices instead of at *current* prices. The economy's final output, however, consists of such a vast number of different products that this procedure, although simple enough in concept, would involve tremendously long and complex calculations, and would be a nearly endless chore.

The national income accountant has another way out of this dilemma. He calculates the major components of each year's GNP in current prices and then uses *price indexes* to deflate them. A price index is simply a number which records the average price of some group of commodities during one period as a percentage of the average price of these same commodities in some other *base* period. Any year's price index thus tells us the average amount by which the prices of certain commodities have risen or fallen since the base period. Example: The consumer price index stood at 115 at the end of 1966. This means that the average prices paid by consumers rose 15% between the period 1957–59 (this is the *base period* currently used by the Department of Commerce) and 1966. Similarly, the wholesale price index stood at 106 at the end of 1966. This means that, over the same period, wholesale prices rose only 6%.

The use of price deflators makes a big difference in GNP comparisons over time. To illustrate: Between 1958 and 1966—a period characterized by generally mild price increases—GNP in current prices rose $292 billion, while GNP in constant (i.e., 1958) prices rose only $200 billion!

PROBLEMS

1   Zee is a quaint little country. It has only two producers: One makes widgets, the other gizmos. Some widgets are used to make gizmos and some gizmos are used to make widgets. But mostly widgets and gizmos are bought by consumers. There aren't any capital goods in Zee.

    During 1970 Widgets, Inc., sold $1,000 words of widgets. It spent $150 on gizmo inputs, $550 on labor inputs, and $100 on capital inputs. Also it paid out $100 in dividends. Gizmos are more popular than widgets. In fact Gizmos, Unlimited, sold $2,000 worth of them during 1970. They also spent $200 on widget inputs, $1600 on labor inputs, and $100 on capital inputs; but they didn't pay out any dividends.

    a) Set up income statements (like the one in Table 6.6 on page 92), for Widgets, Incorporated, and Gizmos, Unlimited.

    b) Calculate the value of the total *final* output produced in Zee during 1970.

    c) Calculate the total factor incomes (including profits) generated through the production of this output.

    d) Are these two measures of national income equal? Should they be? Why or why not?

2   Name some goods and services that the government provides and that you think ought to be classified as final outputs. Name some that you think ought to be classified as intermediate goods. Does the government produce some goods and services that are hard to classify as either one or the other?

3   In a closed economy consumption plus net investment plus government expenditures equals: (1) the total quantity of final output *consumed* by the economy as a whole, and (2) the total quantity of final output *produced* by the economy as a whole. What does this sum equal in an open economy? What does your answer tell you about why an "exports-minus-imports" entry has to be included in the income and product account of an open economy?

4   The following figures are taken from the United States income and product account for the year 2000: Personal consumption, $2700 billion; corporate profits, $390 billion; gross private domestic investment, $580 billion; indirect business taxes, $350 billion; exports, $220 billion; depreciation, $290 billion; government purchases of goods and services, $710 billion; and imports, $160 billion.

    Do you have enough information to calculate gross national product? Net national product? National income? If so, what are they?

5   Suppose that, in figuring national income, we were to add up the beef cattle that farmers sell to meat packers, the sides of beef that packing houses sell to supermarkets, and the cuts of meat that these markets sell retail to housewives. Would we be overstating the economy's total output of final goods? Explain your answer.

6   Why do you think the Commerce Department includes residential structures, but not washing machines, in gross private domestic investment?

*Appendix to Chapter 34

SETTING UP A NATIONAL INCOME AND PRODUCT ACCOUNT

We have set up various accounts for both consumers and firms. Is there some way that we could add these accounts to come up with a national income and product account?

Here's a possibility: Suppose that we were to set up, for every spending unit in the economy, a flow-of-funds account that showed its income as a source of funds and its purchases of consumer and capital goods as uses of funds. Then we could add the flow-of-funds accounts of individual consumers and producers to obtain sector accounts, and the sector accounts to obtain a single national account. Suppose that, as we added, we carefully *netted out* (i.e., canceled out) all sources and uses of funds arising from (1) trades in existing physical assets (Brown sells a used car to Adams), (2) trades in existing financial assets (Jones sells a share of IBM to Smith), and (3) all

TABLE 34|3

Setting Up a Flow-of-Funds Account for the Consumer Sector

Smith				Jones		
Uses			Sources	Uses		Sources
Consumption	$14	Wages	$10	Consumption $20	Wages	$20
Loans to		Rent	5			
business	1					

➕

---

* The purpose of this appendix is to give you some feel for the process of aggregation which underlies not only the national income accounts, but also our whole discussion of macroeconomics. Pay especial attention to the tables, which are in the form of giant equations; they give the picture clearly.

trades that create financial assets (Tectronics sells newly issued bonds to Hanson).† Then we'd obtain a national account which would record, on the sources side, all payments received by different factors of production, and, on the uses side, all the uses to which the net final output was put.

A Two-Sector Model

Let us test this approach by setting up a national income and product account for a simple economy in which there are just two sorts of spending units: consumers and producers.

First we set up flow-of-funds accounts for each spending unit. As you'll recall, when we set up consumer John Jones's flow-of-funds account in Table 26.1, we did not record either his income or his consumption expenditures. We recorded his year's saving as a source of funds: a simple approach, which corresponds to the format that the Federal Reserve Board uses in publishing flow-of-funds data for U.S. spending units. For present purposes, however, we want a flow-of-funds statement that records both the consumer's income and his consumption expenditures. Therefore we shall record his total income, not his savings, as a source of funds, and his consumption expenditures as a use of funds. This procedure is illustrated in the flow-of-funds account in Table 34.3, across the bottoms of these two pages.

When we set up Tectronics' flow-of-funds account back in Table 26.2, we recorded its *gross* investment in capital goods as a use of funds. For present purposes, however, we need a flow-of-funds statement that records the firm's *net* investment (i.e., gross investment minus current depreciation) as a use of funds. To obtain such a flow-of-funds statement, we proceed as we did when we set up Table 26.2, except that now we deduct current depreciation from the gross-investment entry on the uses side of the account; and—

Brown					Consumer sector			
Uses		Sources			Uses		Sources	
Consumption	$10	Wages	$5		Consumption	$44	Wages	$35
Loans to		Dividends	7		Loans to		Rent	5
business	2				business	3	Dividends	7

† The reason that we want to net out all sources and uses of funds that result from such trades is that these trades (although admittedly they are important) fail to generate either income or output; and these are the two things that the account we are setting up is supposed to record.

TABLE 34|4

Setting Up a National Income and Product Account

Consumer sector				Business sector			
Uses		Sources		Uses		Sources	
Consumption	$90	Wages	$91	*Gross* investment	$15	Retained	
Loans to		Dividends	4	Less depreciation	4	profits	$6
business	5			*Net* investment	$11	Loans to	
						business	5

to keep the account in balance—we deduct current depreciation from the gross-savings entry on the sources side as well. A firm's gross savings minus its current depreciation equals its retained profits; so this procedure gives us a flow-of-funds account like the business-sector one in Table 34.4, which you see spread across the tops of these two pages.

Setting up flow-of-funds accounts for consumers and producers is the first step in deriving a national income and product account. The second is adding the accounts of all consumers to get a single consumer-sector account, and adding the accounts of all firms to get a single business-sector account. This addition procedure is illustrated in Table 34.3. *There we consolidate flow-of-funds accounts for three consumers—Smith, Jones, and Brown—to obtain a flow-of-funds account for the consumer sector.* Note that, to get the $35 source entry, wages, in the consumer-sector account, we add the $10, $20, and $5 of wages that Smith, Jones, and Brown received. (We've used very small amounts in our figures, in order to simplify things. You can mentally multiply by 10, or 100, or 1000, if you wish.) Similarly, to get the $3 use entry for loans to business, in the consumer-sector account, we add the $1, $0, and $2 of loans that Smith, Jones, and Brown made to the business sector. If the individual flow-of-funds accounts of all consumers balance, so must the consumer-sector account obtained by adding them. Check this relationship to make sure it holds in Table 34.3.

We can do the same thing for the business sector. By adding just the way we did when we obtained a flow-of-funds account for the consumer sector, we can obtain the business sector's flow-of-funds account. Once we have both sectors' flow-of-funds accounts, we can set up the national income and product account by adding the two. Example: Suppose that consumers and producers in our economy make the following transactions: Consumers supply labor and equity capital to business, and in return receive $91 in wages and $4 in dividends. They spend $90 of their income on consumption goods and lend the remaining $5 to business firms. Business firms, in addition to the $90 of final output they sell to consumers, sell $15 of capital goods

The national income and product account			
Uses		**Sources**	
Consumption	$90	Wages	$91
Net investment	11	Dividends	4
		Retained profits	6
National income	$101	*National income*	$101

to other firms (i.e., business firms buy $15 worth of the business sector's final output). Also, besides the $91 of wages they pay out, business firms incur $4 of depreciation, distribute $4 of dividends, and retain profits equal to $6. The sources and uses of funds which result from these transactions are summarized in the consumer-sector and business-sector accounts in Table 34.4.

Let us now add these two accounts. And, as we do so, let us net out (or cancel out) all source and use entries that result from transactions that have to do with either the sale of existing financial assets or the creation of new ones. (In the present context this means that we must net out the source and use entries associated with consumer loans to business.) Then we shall obtain the national income and product account shown in Table 34.4. Note that this is precisely the sort of account we set out to obtain: The left-hand side records the way national income measured in terms of net final output was allocated between consumption and investment, while the right-hand side records the way national income measured in terms of the total income payments generated through production of this output was allocated between wages, dividends, and retained earnings. Note also that the measures of national income on the two sides of the account are equal, as we said that they should be.

Adding a Government Sector

So far we've been working with an economy that had only two sectors: consumers and businesses. Now let's get a bit more complicated—and closer to conditions that actually prevail—and add a government sector.

Whenever the government buys goods and pays wages, it uses funds. And whenever it receives taxes and incurs debt it receives funds. So we can set up a flow-of-funds account for the government sector just as we do for any other spending unit. It will look like the one in Table 34.5 (see pages 528–529).

To obtain an income and product account for an economy that includes a government sector, we simply add up (i.e., aggregate) the flow-of-funds

TABLE 34|5

Setting Up a National Income and Product Account that Includes Government

Consumer sector				Business sector			
Uses		Sources		Uses		Sources	
Consumption	$85	Wages	$96	Net investment	$11	Retained	
Taxes	6	Dividends	4			profits	$6
Loans to						Loans to	
business	5					business	5
Loans to							
government	4						

accounts of the consumer, business, and government sectors. Doing so is easy if we follow two simple conventions. First, following the lead of the national income accountant, we treat all the goods and services government produces as final output, and we value them at cost. Second, as we aggregate sector accounts, we treat the income taxes and the profits taxes that the government collects and the debt it incurs as strictly financial transactions and net them out (i.e., cancel them out).

Keeping these remarks in mind, let us now go ahead and add a government sector to the two-sector model we've been using. Suppose that this government sector buys $5 of inputs from the consumer sector and $5 of output from the business sector, that it levies $6 of taxes on the consumer sector, and that it borrows $4 from (i.e., sells $4 of bonds to) the consumer sector. Suppose also that consumers respond to these changes by reducing their consumption by $5. Then the flow-of-funds accounts of the consumer, business, and government sectors will be those shown in Table 34.5. If we add these three, we get the income and product account in Table 34.5. *Note:* This account must balance because every government source of funds cancels out an equivalent consumer- or business-sector use of funds.

TABLE 34|6

Setting Up a National Income and Product Account for an Open Economy

Consumer sector				Business sector			
Uses		Sources		Uses		Sources	
Consumption	$85	Wages	$91	Net		Retained	
Loans to		Dividends	4	investment	$11	profits	$6
business	5					Loans to	
Loans to						business	5
foreigners	5						

+

Government sector		
Uses	Sources	
Goods purchases $5	Taxes	$6
Wages 5	Loans to government	4

=

National income and product account			
Uses		Sources	
Consumption	$85	Wages	$96
Net investment	11	Dividends	4
Government	10	Retained profits	6
National income	$106	*National income*	$106

Adding a Foreign-Trade Sector

Both the examples we have presented so far concern a *closed* economy; that is, an economy that does not trade with the rest of the world. But economies these days are *open* economies. They import some of the goods they consume, and they export some of the goods they produce.

To set up a national income and product account for an open economy, we first construct flow-of-funds accounts for each domestic sector of the economy and for the rest-of-the-world sector as well. Then we add these sector accounts to get a single national income and product account.

In illustrating this procedure, we can cut corners if we simply add a foreign-trade sector to the two-sector model in Table 34.4. To do so, we make the following assumptions: (1) Domestic business firms export $10 worth of goods to the rest of the world. (2) Domestic consumers decrease their consumption of domestically produced goods by $10 and simultaneously increase their consumption of imported goods from zero to $5.

+

Rest-of-the-world sector			
Uses		Sources	
Exports $10	Imports	$5	
	Loans to		
	foreigners	5	

=

National income and product account			
Uses		Sources	
Consumption	$85	Wages	$91
Net investment	11	Dividends	4
Exports *minus*		Retained	
imports	5	profits	6
National income	$101	*National income*	$101

(3) Domestic consumers use the extra $5 they now save to extend loans to foreigners. These assumptions imply that the flow-of-funds accounts for consumers, business firms, and the rest-of-the-world sector will be those shown in Table 34.6. If we now add these three sector accounts, we shall obtain (check the figures yourself) the income and product account in Table 34.6. The only aspect of this income and product account that calls for special comment is that the account shows imports not as a positive source, but as a negative use. We do this because we want the uses side of this account to record the net amount of domestic final output absorbed by the rest of the world. This net·figure equals exports of domestic goods minus imports of foreign goods.

An Income and Product Account for a Four-Sector Account

Now that we have worked through these three examples, we know that we can construct a national income and product account for an actual economy that has a government sector and that engages in foreign trade by: (1) setting up flow-of-funds accounts for the consumer, business, government, and rest-of-the-world sectors, and (2) adding these sector accounts. The result, of course, will be an account like the one we presented earlier in Table 34.1.

PROBLEMS

1   When we were constructing the consumer-sector flow-of-funds account in Table 34.1, we assumed to keep things simple that Smith, Jones, and Brown did not trade any physical or financial assets with each other. What if we drop this assumption?

a) Suppose that Smith, in addition to the transactions recorded on his flow-of-funds account in Table 34.1, also sells two shares of IBM stock to Jones for $1200 in cash. How would this transaction affect the flow-of-funds accounts of Smith and Jones? Show that, in setting up the consumer-sector flow-of-funds account, we can net out this financial transaction without destroying the balance of the resulting account. Suppose that you want to use the consumer-sector flow-of-funds account to set up a national income and product account. Should you net out this transaction? [Hint: Does either side of this transaction have anything to do with either of the two measures we have proposed for national income?]

b) Repeat part (a) of the question, but this time assume that Brown sells Smith a used car in exchange for a $1,000 IOU.

2   Assume that the following transactions occur in a two-sector economy:

Consumers receive wages and salaries totaling $950, plus dividends of $35 on corporate stock. They use this income to buy $850 worth of goods and services from the business sector and $135 worth of newly issued corporate stock and bonds.

Business firms, in addition to selling goods and services to consumers and floating new stock and bonds, also invest in $300 of fixed capital, incur $60 of depreciation on fixed capital and run down their inventories by $15.

a) Show that the business sector's retained profits equal $90.

b) Construct flow-of-funds accounts for the consumer and business sectors.

c) Use these accounts to set up a national income and product account.

3   Repeat Problem 2, this time assuming that business firms accumulate $15 of inventories. Show that in this situation national income will be $30 greater than it was in Problem 2.

4   At the end of 1980, the national income accountant in Zee calculates the following flow-of-funds accounts for the consumer, business, government, and rest-of-the-world sectors. Use these accounts to set up a 1980 national income and product account for Zee.

Consumer sector

Uses		Sources	
Consumption	$100	Wages	$100
Taxes	20	Dividends	30
Loans to business	15	Loans from foreigners	10
Loans to government	5		

Business sector

Uses		Sources	
Gross investment	$65	Retained profits	$40
Less: depreciation	10	Loans to business	15
Net investment	$55		

Rest-of-the-world sector

Uses		Sources	
Exports	$10	Imports	$20
Loans from foreigners	10		

Government sector

Uses		Sources	
Goods purchases	$15	Taxes	$20
Wages	10	Loans to government	5

5   Suppose that a government sector is added to the economy in Problem 2. The
     government receives $40 in taxes from consumers, $30 in corporate profits taxes
     from businesses, and $50 in loans from consumers. It uses these funds to make
     factor payments of $70 to consumers and to buy $50 worth of goods from
     businesses. Consumers respond by decreasing their consumption by $20. Busi-
     ness profits do not change, since the increase in taxes and decrease in sales to
     consumers are exactly offset by the increase in sales to the government.

     a) Construct flow-of-funds accounts for the consumer, business, and government
        sectors.

     b) Use these accounts to construct a national income and product account.

CHAPTER 35

INCOME DETERMINATION:
A SHORT-RUN MODEL

In some years a country's economy rolls along at full steam. Investment booms, workers all have jobs, consumption is high, and the economy's actual output matches its potential output. But in other years (recall Fig. 33.1), the economy chugs along far below full employment. Investment slumps, workers can't find jobs, and a wasteful gap emerges between the economy's actual and its potential output.

Since high national output = prosperity and plenty, while low national output = deprivation and misery, we naturally want to find out what makes the economy tick the way it does: why it booms in one period and slumps in another. Economists who have studied these questions have found that the key to answering them lies in the relationships of savings and investment to national income. Therefore we shall begin our study of why the economy stagnates in some periods and grows exuberantly in others by examining these relationships. Then we shall use what we learn to set up a simple model that shows how the level of output produced by the economy is determined during any short-run period.

To keep things simple, we shall talk at first about an economy that has *no* government sector and *no* foreign trade. Also we shall hold to three assumptions throughout our discussion: (1) interest rates are maintained at a constant level by the central bank, (2) prices remain constant so long as the economy is at or below full employment, and (3) all savings occur in the consumer sector. Our no-government assumption implies that national income will equal the economy's net final output. So in this chapter we shall use the terms "national income" and "national output" interchangeably.

THE AGGREGATE CONSUMPTION FUNCTION

In Chapter 3 we surveyed a consumer's motives for (a) saving and (b) consumption. We said that a typical consumer would dissave at low levels of income, save at high levels of income, and that, once he passed his break-even (income-equal-to-consumption) point, the higher his income the more he would save. We also showed that if he behaved this way, the relationship between his income and his planned (or desired) expenditure on consumption could be represented by a *consumption function* shaped like the one in Fig. 3.6 (see page 26).

Every consumer has a consumption function. So by adding the consumption functions of all consumers, we should be able to obtain an *aggregate consumption function.*

An aggregate consumption function is a schedule that tells us how much consumers as a group would *desire* or *plan* to spend on consumption at each level of national income that might exist.

Such an addition process is possible. However, different people have different consumption functions. (Jones might spend half again as much as Smith at every income level. Or Jones and Smith might both have the same break-even points, but Jones might spend 90¢ of every extra dollar of income he gets while Smith spends only 80¢.) This tells us that at any income level, the total amount that consumers plan to spend depends not only on how big national income is but also on *who gets it* (i.e., on the distribution of income). This means that, when we add the consumption functions of individual consumers to get the aggregate consumption function, we have to take the distribution of income into account.

The reason we want an aggregate consumption function is to predict how consumption would change in response to changes in national income. But suppose that each time national income were to change the income distribution were also to change. Then the aggregate consumption function would *shift* each time income changed, and we wouldn't be able to use it to predict changes in consumption. Fortunately the possibility of a constantly shifting consumption function needn't worry us too much. Reason: The distribution of income is quite stable over the short run, and it's the short run we're concerned with here. Also (see Problems 10–12) even fair-sized changes in the distribution of income may cause only small shifts in the aggregate consumption function.

Let us denote total consumption by C and national income by Y. Then we can represent the aggregate consumption function by the expression

$$C = C(Y).$$

When we plot the curve $C = C(Y)$, we can be pretty sure that it will turn out to be shaped like the consumption function of the average consumer. After all, the aggregate consumption function is derived by adding the consumption functions of individual consumers; so it ought to have the general shape of the curve in Fig. 35.1.

When you look at this figure, recall from Chapter 3 that at any point above the 45° line consumption exceeds income, while at any point below the 45° line income exceeds consumption. Hence the intersection of the consumption function with the 45° line indicates the point at which consumers as a group break even: Their consumption expenditures just equal their income. Pay attention to something else here: The fact that the consumption function begins above the 45° line and then falls below it indicates that consumers as a group will dissave (i.e., spend more than they earn) when national income is low, but save when it is high.

The slope of the consumption function equals the ratio between the change in total consumption, ΔC, induced by a small change in national income, ΔY, and the change in income itself. This ratio, $\Delta C/\Delta Y$, is known as the *marginal propensity to consume* (MPC).

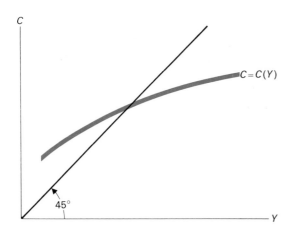

35|1

The aggregate consumption function, $C = C(Y)$, represents the short-run relationship between national income Y and aggregate consumption C.

The consumption function in Fig. 35.1 slopes upward but cuts the 45° line from above. This tells us that the MPC must be positive but less than 1.* That's as it should be. An MPC of less than 1 means that consumers as a group respond to a rise in national income by increasing their consumption by a somewhat smaller amount, and back in Chapter 3 we argued that that's just how Mr. Typical Consumer behaves.

THE AGGREGATE INVESTMENT SCHEDULE

In Chapters 10 and 11, when we were talking about the firm's investment decision, we showed that two of the most important factors on which the size of the firm's investment expenditures depend are (1) the entrepreneur's expectations as to what demand for his firm's output will be in the future and (2) the availability and current cost of capital. The entrepreneur's

---

* This is easy to verify because the slope of the 45° line equals 1.

expectations as to future demand for his output largely depend on current
demand for it, and this in turn depends on the level of current consumption.
But current consumption depends on current national income, so current
national income inevitably plays a big part in forming the entrepreneur's
expectations. Current national income also, because of its effect on demand
for the firm's output and thus on the firm's profits, influences both the cost
of capital and its availability to the firm. The stronger the demand for the
firm's output, the more profits it can earn; the more profits the firm earns,
the higher the price it will be able to get for newly issued stock, the lower
the rate at which it will be able to borrow, and (probably) the more it will
be able to borrow.* Because high national income bolsters the entrepreneur's expectations as to future demand for his output and decreases the
cost and availability of capital, a firm will usually respond to an increase in
national income by raising its expenditures for investment and to a decrease
in national income by lowering them.

Investments made by the firm in response to changes in the level of
national income are called *induced investments*. A firm may also make
many investments that aren't influenced by (i.e., that are fairly independent
of) the current level of national income. Such investments are called *autonomous investments*. These include investments made because an innovation
has rendered existing plant and equipment obsolete (oxygen-injection fur-
naces have done this in the steel industry), investments made because an invention has made possible the production of a new output (transistors and
lasers did just this), and investments in housing made because population is
expanding or migrating into new regions.

Our observations about induced and autonomous investment suggest
that we could set up for each firm an investment schedule that would show
how much this firm would *plan* or *desire* to invest at each level of national
income that might exist. By adding the investment schedules of all firms in
the economy, we could obtain an aggregate investment schedule:

$$I = I(Y).$$

An aggregate investment schedule tells us how much business firms as a
group would *plan* or *desire* to spend on net investment at each level of
national income that might exist.

The shape of the aggregate investment schedule will depend on the following: Since some of the investments that firms make are induced by rising
national income, total investment will rise as income rises. In other words,
the aggregate investment schedule will slope upward. And since some of the

---

* Also, if we allow for the possibility of business saving, the more profits a firm earns, the
more profits it is likely to retain (i.e., the more it is likely to save), and the more it saves,
the more internal funds it will have available for financing current investment.

35|2

The aggregate investment schedule, $I = I(Y)$, shows the relationship between aggregate net investment I and national income Y.

investments that firms make are autonomous (i.e., independent of the level of national income), the curve describing aggregate investment will start at a point well above the origin. Therefore this schedule ought to have the general shape of the one in Fig. 35.2.

A SIMPLE MODEL OF INCOME DETERMINATION

Consumption and investment both represent demand for final output. Therefore if we add the consumption and investment schedules we have just derived, we obtain an *aggregate demand schedule for national output* (see Fig. 35.3).

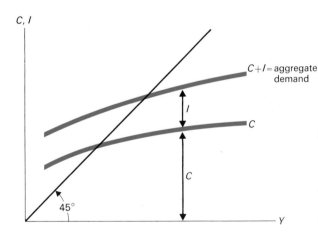

35|3

When we add the consumption and investment schedules, we obtain an aggregate demand schedule, $C + I$, that summarizes the relationship between output demanded and output produced.

The aggregate demand schedule for national output summarizes the relationship between the goods and services demanded by consumers and investors and the quantity of output produced (i.e., the level of national income).

Once we have the aggregate demand schedule in hand, we can readily answer the question we posed at the beginning of this chapter: What determines the level of output that the economy will produce during any period? We can show that during each period the behavior of savers and investors tends to establish a *unique* level of output (or—what is the same thing—income). Moreover, once this income—which economists refer to as the economy's *equilibrium income*—is established, it tends to endure so long as aggregate demand for output (i.e., the behavior of consumers and investors) remains constant.

To illustrate: Look at Fig. 35.4 and try to identify the equilibrium income of the economy whose aggregate demand schedule is shown there. Finding this point depends on one key observation:

At any point along the 45° line, the final output demanded by consumers and investors precisely equals the total final output produced. (Output demanded is measured along the vertical axis, output produced along the horizontal one.)

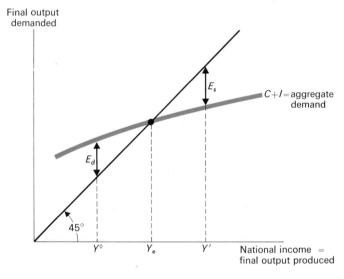

35|4

At the income level Y_e, total output demanded by consumers and investors equals total output produced. Thus Y_e represents the economy's equilibrium income.

From this observation it follows that the income level, Y_e, at which the aggregate demand schedule intersects the 45° line, must be an equilibrium income for the economy. The reason is that, at the income level Y_e, suppliers will be able to sell all the goods they produce, demanders will be able to buy all the goods they demand, and there will be no dissatisfied persons who, through their attempts to make increased purchases or sales, would force a change in the level of income and output.

We have now proved that the income level Y_e is an equilibrium income. Is there any income lower than Y_e that could *also* be an equilibrium income? Suppose that the income Y^0 were established: At that income, the amount of goods and services demanded (by consumers and investors) would exceed output produced by the amount E_d. Producers would find their inventories depleted, their shelves bare, and their customers unsatisfied. They would respond by producing more output, and as they did, national income would rise. And it would continue to rise until the excess demand for goods had been eliminated, that is, until the level Y_e had been attained. So neither Y^0 nor any other level of income below Y_e could be an equilibrium one.

What about an income level higher than Y_e? Suppose that the income Y' were established. At that income, the amount of output produced would exceed the amount of goods demanded by E_s. Producers would accumulate large inventories of unsold goods, which they would like to sell but for which they couldn't find buyers. To correct this situation, they would produce less output, and as they did, national income would fall. And it would continue to fall until the level Y_e was established. Therefore it's obvious that neither Y' nor any other income level above Y_e could be an equilibrium one.

SAVING AND INVESTMENT

Our conclusion that the economy will have a unique equilibrium income, one that equates output demanded with output produced, is a crucial one. Let's examine it now from a slightly different point of view: saving and investment.

Since a person's saving equals the difference between his income and his consumption, and since the 45° line shows all points at which his income and consumption would be equal, the vertical distance at any income level between his consumption function and the 45° line equals his saving at that income level. Therefore, by using a person's consumption function, we can set up a *saving schedule* that shows the relationship between his income and his *planned* saving, just as his consumption schedule shows the relationship between his income and his *planned* consumption (see Fig. 35.5).

To make sure you understand the relationship between a person's consumption and his saving schedules, prove the following statements: (1) At every income level at which his consumption function lies above the 45° line, his saving schedule must lie below the income axis. (2) At every income level at which his consumption function lies below the 45° line, his saving schedule must lie above the income axis. (3) At the break-even income level at which his consumption function crosses the 45° line, his saving schedule must cross the income axis.

35|5

We can use a person's consumption
function to derive his saving
schedule.

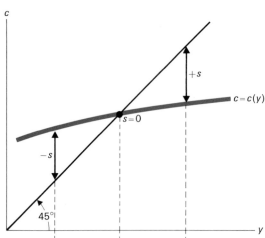

a) A person's consumption schedule.

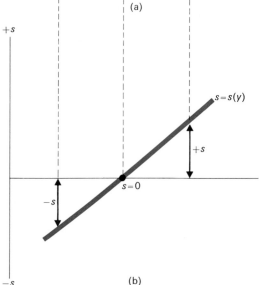

b) The same person's saving
schedule.

Now that's the saving schedule of just one person. If we add the saving
schedules of all people (just as we added their consumption schedules), we
obtain an *aggregate saving schedule,*

$$S = S(Y).$$

An aggregate saving schedule tells us how much consumers as a group would
plan to save at every level of national income that might exist.

This aggregate saving schedule should resemble in shape the individual
saving schedules from which it is derived, as the one in Fig. 35.6 does.

Suppose now that we plot the aggregate saving and investment schedules together (Fig. 35.6). Let's see whether, on the basis of the information contained in these two curves, we can locate the economy's equilibrium income. To do so, we must begin by taking a closer look at just what aggregate saving is. Since the savings of any one consumer equals his income minus his consumption, the aggregate saving of all consumers must equal national income minus total consumption expenditures. However, national income, as we have seen, equals national output. So aggregate savings must equal *that portion of total output which consumers abstain from consuming.*

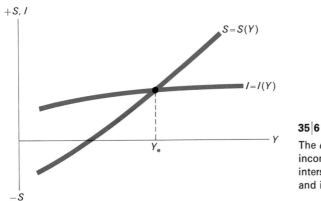

35|6

The *equilibrium* level of national income Y_e is indicated by the intersection of the aggregate saving and investment schedules.

When we used the $C + I$ approach to locating the economy's equilibrium income, we found that the economy attains equilibrium at the income level at which output demanded just equals output produced. Therefore, since saving represents output produced *but not demanded for consumption,* the only level of income at which the economy can attain equilibrium is one at which the amount of output that consumers abstain from demanding just equals the amount of output that *investors* demand. Figure 35.6 shows that this level is the level Y_e at which the savings and investment schedules intersect.

If you understand the reasoning behind this result, you can readily see that any income level smaller than Y_e (i.e., any level at which planned investment exceeds planned saving) can't be an equilibrium one. If such an income level *were* established, output demanded would exceed output produced, and national income would rise. Similarly, any income level larger than Y_e (i.e., any level at which planned investment is less than planned saving) can't be an equilibrium one. If such an income level *were* established, output produced would exceed output demanded, and national income would fall.

35|7
Some not-so-obvious results of our theory of income determination.

a) If people try to save more—as evidenced by a shift in the savings schedule from S to S'—income will fall and so will aggregate savings.

b) If people try to save less—as evidenced by a shift in the savings schedule from S to S'—income will rise and so will aggregate savings.

c) If investment spending rises—as evidenced by a shift in the investment schedule from I to I'—income will rise and will savings.

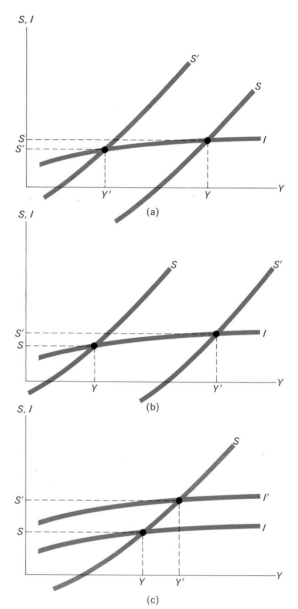

(a)

(b)

(c)

Our two approaches to income determination thus prove that an economy does have a unique equilibrium income, and that we can characterize it either as:

1) *The income level at which goods demanded just equal goods produced,* or as

2) *The income level at which planned savings just equal planned investment.*

These two equilibrium conditions are identical, because planned-savings-equal-to-planned-investment   implies   goods-demanded-equal-to-goods-produced, and vice versa.

Savings and Investment: Some Not-So-Obvious Results

The above savings–investment model is useful not only because it helps us to understand how income is determined, but also because we can use it to make some interesting and not-so-obvious points.

The first is known as *the paradox of thrift*. Suppose that events lead people to fear that a recession is about to hit the country. They will probably react to such a threat by trying to *increase* their current savings. Will this attempt, which makes the aggregate saving schedule shift to the left, succeed? Surprisingly enough, no. Figure 35.7(a) shows that, as people try to increase their current savings, they will cause national income to decline from Y to Y', and as a result their realized savings will *fall*, not rise!

Figure 35.7(b) shows our second not-so-obvious result: If consumers as a group try to save *less* (i.e., if the saving schedule shifts to the right), savings will actually *increase!* Third, Fig. 35.7(c) shows that if investment spending shifts upward (i.e., if the community as a whole tries to spend *more*), the result will be a *rise* in savings!

These three results appear to defy common sense. However, if you have been following and understanding our step-by-step analysis, you can explain why each is true.

EQUILIBRIUM INCOME VERSUS FULL-EMPLOYMENT INCOME

We said in Chapter 33 that full employment is a key target of a government's macroeconomic policy. Does an economy's equilibrium income Y_e necessarily correspond to its full-employment income Y_f? Figure 35.8 shows that these two levels are identical only when the aggregate demand schedule happens to intersect the 45° line at the economy's full-employment income. This, however, doesn't always occur, so the answer is unfortunately no.

A Deflationary Gap

Whenever an economy's aggregate demand schedule intersects the 45° line below its full-employment income, the demand for goods and services will be insufficient to bring the economy up to its full-employment income. The amount of this insufficiency is called the *deflationary gap:* Figure 35.8 (a) shows that it equals the vertical distance between the aggregate demand schedule and the point on the 45° line that corresponds to the full-employment income.

35|8

The economy's equilibrium income doesn't necessarily correspond to its full-employment income.

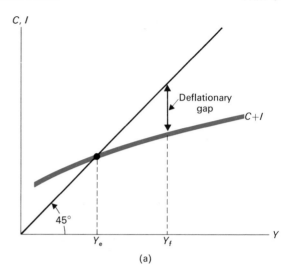

a) If equilibrium income Y_e is less than full-employment income Y_f, a *deflationary gap* exists.

(a)

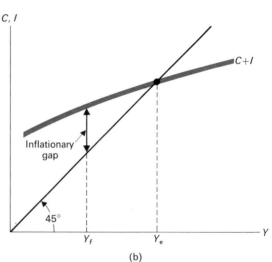

b) If equilibrium income Y_e exceeds full-employment income Y_f, an *inflationary gap* exists.

(b)

Once the economy attains its equilibrium level of income, it tends to maintain this level so long as nothing happens to alter the behavior of consumers or investors. So in an economy plagued by a deflationary gap, there is the danger that unemployment, once established, may persist for a number of years. Why don't the attempts of unemployed workers to find jobs result in a bidding-down of the wage rate to a level sufficiently low to restore balance between the supply of and demand for labor? In a perfectly competitive economy, such a bidding-down presumably *would* occur. But in an imperfectly competitive economy like ours, it doesn't. Union wage contracts, minimum wage laws, and other factors combine to create a situation which practically rules out drops in the wage rate.*

An Inflationary Gap

Whenever an economy's aggregate demand schedule intersects the 45° line at an income level that is greater than its full-employment income, its "equilibrium" income exceeds its full-employment output. The amount by which aggregate demand exceeds aggregate output at the economy's full-employment income is called the *inflationary gap.*

   This "equilibrium" income (Fig. 35.8b) is clearly unattainable, since consumers and investors cannot consume more goods than the economy is capable of producing. However, there's nothing to stop them from trying, and when they do, too many dollars pursue too few goods, with the result that prices rise. Inflationary tendencies are the inevitable result of "excess" aggregate demand.

THE MULTIPLIER

We have said [and Fig. 35.7 (b) and (c) show clearly] that whenever aggregate spending rises—either because investors invest more or because consumers save less—national income rises. By how much? Well, let's work out a simple numerical example and then use it as a basis for a general conclusion.

A Numerical Example

Let us assume that investment does not increase with income (i.e., that the investment schedule is horizontal), and that the marginal propensity to consume† equals 0.8. Suppose that there is a $1 billion increase in autonomous investment. How much would national income rise as a result? You might say, right off the bat, that it would rise by $1 billion, because after all the production of an additional $1 billion of investment goods would generate an additional $1 billion of factor income. But this answer is incomplete. Those consumers who get that extra $1 billion in income won't save all of it. We're assuming, remember, that the marginal propensity to consume equals 0.8; therefore those people will spend an extra $800 million on consumption. By doing so they will generate an additional $800 million of national income. (Are you beginning to get the picture?) The receivers of *this* income will in

---

* In Chapter 15 we showed that if an inflexible price floor were imposed on the labor market, this would result in involuntary unemployment whenever the price floor was set above the equilibrium wage rate.

† Recall that we defined this on page 535 as the slope, $\Delta C/\Delta Y$, of the consumption function.

turn increase *their* consumption by $640 million (i.e., by 0.8 times $800 million), and in doing so *they* will generate an extra $640 million of national income. This $640 million will also accrue to consumers, and these people will increase *their* consumption and thereby generate a still further increase in national income.

And so on. And so on. And so on. . . .

So you can see that an autonomous increase in investment sets off a *chain reaction,* at each step of which there will be a new addition to national income. Each successive addition will be smaller than the one that preceded it, so that the total increase in income will approach a finite and easily defined limit.

Now let's find an equation that will help us determine this limit: The total income that a $1 billion increase in investment will induce can be represented by the following expression:*

$$Y = [\$1 \text{ billion}] \cdot [1 + (0.8) + (0.8)^2 + (0.8)^3 + \cdots].$$

If we now apply to this expression the algebraic rule that

$$(1 + r + r^2 + r^3 + \cdots) = 1/(1 - r) \qquad \text{for all } r < 1,$$

we can show that the total increase in income, ΔY, generated by the $1 billion increase in investment will equal [$1 billion]·[1/(1 − 0.8)] or $5 billion.

We can prove the result we have just obtained algebraically by means of a diagram. But first, this message: Since any change in national income, ΔY, must be fully allocated between a change in consumption, ΔC, and a change in savings, ΔS,† the slope of the savings schedule, $\Delta S/\Delta Y$, *plus* the slope of the consumption function, $\Delta C/\Delta Y$, must equal 1. Therefore if the slope of the consumption function equals 0.8, the slope of the savings schedule must equal 0.2.

Now look at Fig. 35.9. It shows that, if the savings schedule has a slope equal to 0.2, a $1 billion increase in investment will increase national income by $5 billion!

A General Result

Our numerical example shows us that, whenever autonomous investment rises by ΔI, national income will rise by some multiple of this increase, i.e., that

$$\Delta Y = m \cdot \Delta I,$$

---

* Perhaps you've noticed (we hope you have) that the explanation here is identical to the explanation of money creation by commercial banks (Chapter 28).

† In other words, since $\Delta Y = \Delta C + \Delta S$ by definition.

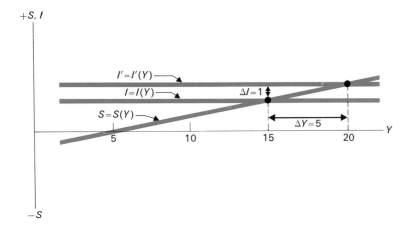

35|9
If the slope of the savings schedule is 0.2, a $1 billion increase in autonomous investment will raise national income by $5 billion.

in which m is a positive constant known as *the multiplier*. How big will m be? Our example suggests, and it can easily be proved,* that the multiplier will equal

$$m = 1/(1 - \text{MPC})$$

(remember that MPC stands for the *marginal propensity to consume*).

Since the sum of the slopes of the saving and consumption functions equals 1 by definition, the multiplier can also be written in the form

$$m = 1/\text{MPS},$$

in which MPS represents the slope of the saving schedule, or the *marginal propensity to save,* as it is known.

---

* *Proof:* Assume that consumption is a linear function of national income, and represent it by the expression $C = a + \text{MPC} \cdot Y$, in which a is a positive constant. Assume that investment is fixed, and represent it by the expression $I = \bar{I}$. Then substitute the expressions for C and I into the definitional equation, $Y \equiv C + I$, to obtain the relationship $Y = a + \text{MPC} \cdot Y + \bar{I}$. Finally solve this relationship for Y and rewrite it as follows:

$$Y = a/(1 - \text{MPC}) + 1/(1 - \text{MPC}) \cdot \bar{I}.$$

From this expression we see that, if investment changes by an amount ΔI, then since a is a constant the resulting change in income, ΔY, will be given by the expression $\Delta Y = 1/(1 - \text{MPC}) \cdot \Delta I$. If we now substitute this expression for ΔY into the equation $Y = m \cdot \Delta I$ that we gave above for the multiplier, it follows that $m = 1/(1 - \text{MPC})$, which is the result we set out to prove.

PROBLEMS

1   In the text we called the $C + I$ function the aggregate demand schedule for national output. What is the aggregate supply schedule for national output?

2   Bert Brown's consumption function is given by the expression

$$c = \$1500 + 0.9y,$$

in which y and c represent his income and his consumption expenditures, respectively. What is Bert's savings schedule? Plot both schedules the way the schedules in Fig. 35.5 are plotted. Verify that statements (1), (2), and (3) on page 539 hold true.

3   "In an economy in which there was no investment, the equilibrium level of income would always be at the break-even level of consumers as a group. This suggests that it's possible for some people to save only if other people are willing to invest." Discuss.

*4   Our description of the way the economy attains its equilibrium level of income (business firms find that their inventories are rising or falling unexpectedly so they adjust output, this changes income, and so forth) indicates that *it may take some time* for the economy to attain equilibrium. If it does, then during those periods when the economy is working its way toward equilibrium, the level of output established in the economy may not be an equilibrium one, i.e., it may not be one at which *planned* savings equal *planned* investment. Nevertheless, at the end of such a period, *measured* savings will equal *measured* investment. We know the latter is true because the definitions of national income Y and aggregate savings S as

$$Y \equiv C + I \qquad \text{and} \qquad S \equiv Y - C$$

imply that in a two-sector economy of the sort we have considered,

$$S \equiv I.$$

How is it possible for measured savings to equal measured investment at the end of a period in which planned investment did not equal planned savings? [*Hint:* If consumers planned to save more than investors wanted to invest, might some *un*planned investment occur in business inventories? What if firms planned to invest more than consumers wanted to save?]

5   a) The "paradox of thrift" states that if consumers as a group try to save more they will end up by saving less. What will happen to the *percentage* of their income that they save?

   b) By definition, consumers must spend on consumption goods that part of their incomes which they do not save. Does this mean that the thrifty consumers in the paradox of thrift will end up by consuming more as a result of their decision to consume less (i.e., save more)? Why or why not?

6   Under what circumstances might the aggregate demand schedule *not* intersect the 45° line at any positive level of national income? Do you think such a situation is likely? If it were to occur, how would the economy behave?

7   Aggregate consumption, C, depends on national income, Y. Suppose specifically that

$$C = \$100 \text{ billion} + 0.75Y.$$

Suppose also that investment is a constant $10 billion at all levels of national income.

a) What is the equilibrium level of national income?

b) Suppose that the full-employment level of national income were $600 billion. Would there be an inflationary or a deflationary gap in the economy? How big would it be?

c) Suppose that investment were to shift autonomously upward from $10 billion to $30 billion a year. Use the formula for the multiplier to calculate how much national income would rise.

d) Verify the result you obtained in (c) by means of a diagram.

*8   Prove that if the investment schedule slopes upward, the multiplier m will be given by the expression

$$m = \frac{1}{\text{MPS} - \text{MPI}}$$

where MPS is the slope of the saving schedule and MPI is the slope of the investment schedule.

*9   Let us drop the assumption that consumers are the only savers in the economy and allow for the possibility that firms save too (i.e., that firms retain profits). But let us keep the assumption that interest rates are fixed. What do Problems 11–14 in the appendix to Chapter 11 tell us about why the aggregate investment schedule is likely to slope upward?

PROBLEMS ON AGGREGATION

*10   Let y stand for the income and c for the consumption expenditures of an individual consumer. Then the following equations represent the consumption functions of three consumers, u, v, and w:

$$c_u = \$10 + 0.90y_u, \qquad c_v = \$12 + 0.92y_v, \qquad c_w = \$9 + 0.96y_w.$$

Assume that national income Y is distributed among these three consumers as follows:

$$y_u = \left(\tfrac{1}{3}\right)Y, \qquad y_v = \left(\tfrac{1}{4}\right)Y, \qquad y_w = \left(\tfrac{5}{12}\right)Y.$$

a) Show that the aggregate consumption function which shows the relationship between total consumption C and national income Y will be given by the expression $C = 31 + 0.93Y$.

b) What is the break-even level of income for these three consumers as a group?

---

* Starred problems are problems that are unusually difficult.

*11 Suppose that the distribution of national income Y among our three consumers, u, v, and w, is given by the equations

$$y_u = \alpha Y, \qquad y_v = \beta Y, \qquad \text{and} \qquad y_w = \gamma Y,$$

where $\alpha + \beta + \gamma = 1$. Suppose also that you know that the aggregate consumption function is given by the expression $C = \$31 + 0.93Y$.

a) Show that many values of α, β, and γ will produce this aggregate consumption function. [*Hint:* You already know from Problem 12 that $\alpha = \frac{1}{3}$, $\beta = \frac{1}{4}$, and $\gamma = \frac{5}{12}$ will do the trick.]

b) What does your conclusion that many values of α, β, and γ will produce the same aggregate consumption function tell you about how sensitive the shape and position of the aggregate consumption function is likely to be to changes in the distribution of income?

*12 Suppose that national income equals $\$10,000$, that consumer u receives $\$3,000$, that consumer v receives $\$4,000$, and that consumer w receives $\$3,000$.

a) Show that aggregate consumption will equal $\$9,291$.

b) Suppose now that national income rises by $\$10$ in the following way: consumer w loses $\$200$ of income, consumer u gets an additional $\$200$ of income, and consumer v gets an additional $\$10$ of income. What will the marginal propensity to consume $(\Delta C/\Delta Y)$ associated with these changes be?

c) "The aggregate consumption function obtained by adding the consumption functions of individual consumers will accurately predict how consumption would be altered by a rise or fall in national income only if changes in the *level* of national income do not significantly alter the *distribution* of income." Comment.

CHAPTER 36

SHORT-RUN FLUCTUATIONS IN NATIONAL INCOME AND OUTPUT

Since Chapter 35 laid so much stress on locating the economy's equilibrium level of income, you may have got the impression that, once an economy attained an equilibrium level of income, it would continue at that level for years. However, economic activity is seldom that stable. On the contrary, in a dynamic economy like ours, there are continual changes in autonomous investment opportunities, business expectations, the tastes of consumers, the kinds of goods available, and all the other factors that underlie investment and consumption. As such changes occur, the aggregate investment and consumption schedules shift, and of course so does the aggregate demand schedule for national output, and thus the equilibrium level of national income and output.

Figure 36.1 gives some idea of the variability of national output over time. It shows that, although U.S. industrial output has often changed in an erratic or random manner, it has also displayed two fairly regular characteristics: (1) Industrial output has *grown* steadily, with only one serious interruption (caused by the depression of the 1930's). (2) Industrial output seems to have moved in *cycles* around its long-term upward trend.

The cycles that appear to occur so regularly in industrial activity (and also in national output as a whole) bring with them many socially undesirable consequences: Inflation often becomes a problem at the top of the cycle, while investment slumps and unemployment reaches serious proportions at the low point of the cycle. For these reasons, strong cyclical movements in national income and output are incompatible with the goals of full employment, price stability, and steady growth. Therefore modern governments try to eradicate—or at least mitigate—the cycle.

How successful a government is in trying to temper the cycle depends partly on how well economists can answer two fundamental questions: (1) Why do income and output fluctuate in a cyclical pattern over time? (2) How can one know where in the cycle the economy stands at any given moment? These two questions are tough ones, and thus the theories that

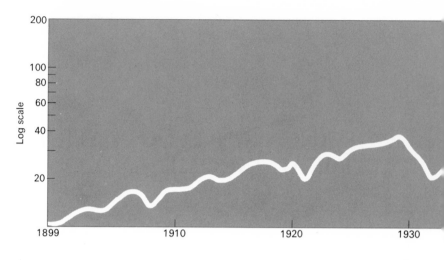

36|1

economists have so far proposed—despite the considerable time and thought devoted to formulating them—do not fully explain the whys and wherefores of cycles. They do, however, offer some useful insights.

THE BUSINESS CYCLE

When we say that an economy is subject to business cycles over time, what we mean is that the economy's level of output seems to fluctuate in a cyclical pattern around its long-term trend. In an expanding economy, this means that national income does not grow at a steady rate. Its growth rate sprints ahead, then comes to a peak, then falls off or even becomes negative, and finally hits bottom. After that the whole pattern begins again.

Figure 36.2 shows the path traced out by such a business cycle in a growing economy: Note that the level of business activity at each successive peak—or each successive trough—is higher than it was at the one that preceded it. In a growing economy the *expansionary* phase of the cycle is likely to be more pronounced (i.e., to lead to a larger change in the level of national income) than the *contractionary* phase. The contractionary phase may involve nothing more than a temporary pause in the long-term growth of national output.

The cycles in Fig. 36.2 have been given a smooth and regular appearance in order to emphasize their wavelike character. But there's nothing smooth about the shape or regular about the duration of actual business cycles. Some are long, while others are short. Some are violent, others mild. All, however, trace out an irregular wavelike pattern over time.

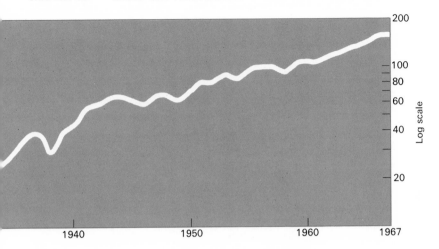

Index of U.S. industrial activity, 1899–1967; (1957–1959 = 100). Figures for 1899–1957 are from AT&T, by special permission; figures for 1957–1967 are from the Federal Reserve Board.

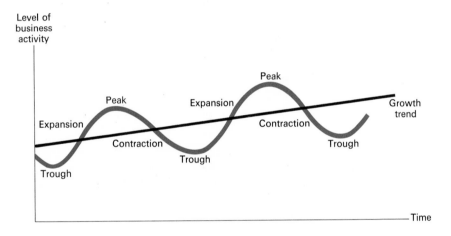

36|2
The path of the business cycle in a growing economy.

The Physiognomy of the Cycle

Since economists speak of "the cycle" and identify definite peaks and troughs in it, you might assume that the cycle affects all sectors of the economy in the same way. That is not the case. Therefore when we sketch a time-profile of the cycle, it describes what happened to the *general* level of business activity, not to the level in each and every sector.

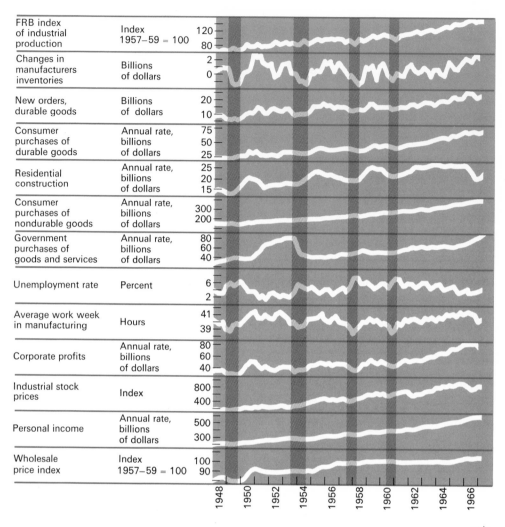

36|3

This diagram, in which shaded areas indicate periods of business contraction and unshaded areas business expansion, shows the evolution of several key economic variables during three recent cycles. (Source: U.S. Department of Commerce)

Figure 36.3 shows just *how* different the impact of the cycle is on different sectors of the economy. It traces the paths of 13 key variables during three recent cycles. The Federal Reserve Board index of industrial production, one of the best indicators of what is happening to the general level of activity throughout the economy, heads the list. This index doesn't tell the whole story of a cycle, but it does show that industrial production dips during recessions and rises during expansions.

The next six categories in Fig. 36.3 all refer to important elements in aggregate demand. Of these the first four—"changes in manufacturers' inventories," "new orders for durable goods," "consumers' purchases of consumer durable goods," and "residential construction"—all refer to different types of investment expenditures, while the last two—"consumer purchases of nondurable goods" and "government purchases of goods and services" refer to noninvestment elements of aggregate demand. Note how unstable the indicators which refer to business and consumer investment are compared with the noninvestment expenditures of consumers and government purchases of goods and services. This suggests that *instability in aggregate investment is a big factor in the cycle,* and that if we want to know the causes of cycles we should try to locate the sources of instability in investment.

The last six categories in Fig. 36.3 offer a cross section of economic indicators. The cycle shows up dramatically in unemployment, in the average length of the work week, in corporate profits, and in stock prices. However, it is barely perceptible in the chart of personal income. This may come as a surprise, but there are reasons: (1) More and more people get annual salaries instead of hourly wages. (2) Many people out of jobs get unemployment compensation. (3) Wages tend to rise even during a recession.

Note that the cycle is also barely perceptible in the wholesale price index, which since 1953 has risen slowly but steadily.

EXPLAINING THE CYCLE

During the last several hundred years many people—philosophers, economists, stockbrokers, and the man in the street—have tried to figure out the causes of business cycles, and have come up with a mixed bag of theories, as you might expect. They have attributed business fluctuations to everything from sunspots to psychology.

Economists have narrowed the range of their theories considerably in recent years, as they have come to understand more about why an economy behaves as it does, but even now there is no one theory about cycles that they all are willing to accept. However, they do recognize that any explanation of cyclical fluctuations must take into account two fundamental facts:

1) Many ups and downs are attributable in part to *outside shocks,* such as wars, droughts, technological innovation, or changes in population.

2) The economy seems to respond to outside shocks by making *cyclical adjustments,* in the sense that it tends to amplify in size, to extend over time, and to eventually reverse the impact which the shock exerted.

We shall now talk about (1) the shocks that are likely to impinge on an economy and (2) the characteristics of an economy's internal structure that lead it to make cyclical adjustments in response to such shocks.

Outside Shocks

When we think back on our discussion of income determination in Chapter 35, we realize that an outside shock that alters the level of national income must do so by changing either (a) the quantity of goods produced in the economy or (b) the quantity of goods demanded from it. A drought that destroyed many crops would be a good example of (a). A change that shifted either the consumption or investment component of aggregate demand would be a good example of (b).

Many outside shocks that impinge on the economy alter the equilibrium level of income by shifting the *autonomous*-investment component of business investment, and thus of aggregate demand.* The kinds of outside shocks that can do this are as varied as the reasons why people invest. Often these shocks are in the form of innovations, which—by opening the door to new markets, raw materials, products, or production processes—create new opportunities for investment in business plant and equipment. Just think of the bursts of autonomous investment triggered by the invention of railroads, electricity, the telephone, and automobiles, in earlier years, and of television, computers, and nuclear power in recent years.

When new sources of raw materials are discovered, their exploitation requires considerable investment in production and refining facilities; therefore these discoveries are another form of outside shock that can increase the level of autonomous investment in an economy. Postwar examples range from uranium strikes in Canada to the discovery of oil and gold under Alaskan offshore waters.

The various shocks which impinge on the economy may dramatically shift not only the investment schedule, but also the consumption function. Shocks which affect the consumption function often do so through their effect on the investment component of consumer expenditures, that is, through their effect on consumer purchases of durable goods. One reason is that durable goods—because they last a long time, because services can be purchased in their place (e.g., laundry services can be purchased in place of a washer-dryer), and because many of them are luxury goods—are a type of expenditure that is easily postponable.

What are some of the outside shocks that bring about variations in the level of purchases of consumer durables? For some products (e.g., automobiles, kitchen stoves) that people buy not just to provide utilitarian services but also to show off how rich they are or what good taste they have, one big

---

* Right here it's important that you remember what we said in Chapter 35 (page 536) about the difference between induced investments and autonomous investments. *Induced investments* are those made in response to changes in the level of national income. *Autonomous investments* are those whose rationale is fairly independent of changes in the income level.

source of outside shocks is the unpredictable shifts which take place in consumer tastes. Example: Auto sales spurt when consumers like a new model (e.g., Ford's Mustang), but sag when consumers tire of an old model or take a strong dislike to a new one. (Does anyone remember the Edsel?)

Shifts in consumer spending on durable goods may also be induced by innovations that lead to the introduction of new consumer durables. For examples of the exhilarating effect that innovations can have on consumer purchases of durable goods, look around you: In the past few years there has been a whole range of products, from sit-down power mowers to dishwashers to color television sets. Finally we might mention that population expansions and migrations are the causes of large-scale investments in both new housing and consumer durables.

The Accelerator

Now that we understand a little about the outside shocks that can strike an economy, let's analyze the characteristics of an economy's internal structure that lead it to make cyclical adjustments in response to these shocks.

Remember that we said, when we were discussing Fig. 36.3, that *instability in aggregate investment is a big factor in the business cycle.* Now we can show one reason why. Whenever an outside shock changes total spending and thus national income, induced investment is also altered. Moreover, increases in income increase induced investment, while decreases lower it. Therefore changes in *induced* investment amplify the impact that *autonomous* shifts in spending have on national income. Also if changes in induced investment occur some time after (i.e., if they lag behind) the shift in autonomous spending that causes them, they will extend its effect over a longer period of time.

Many economists assume that the relationship between induced investment and income is rigid; that is, they assume that firms always want to hold a capital stock equal to some multiple of their current output. From this assumption it follows that:

The amount that business firms as a group invest during any period depends on the change (if any) that occurs in their total output (i.e., in national income) during this period.

This proposition, which is known as the *acceleration principle,* can be stated mathematically as follows:

$$I = k \cdot \Delta Y,$$

where I represents aggregate induced investment, ΔY the change in national income, and k the fixed relationship that firms try to maintain between their

TABLE 36|1

The Acceleration Principle in Action (Millions of Dollars) *

Period	Output	Desired capital stock	Replacement investment	Induced investment	Gross investment
1	100	200	20	0	20
2	110	220	20	20	40
3	130	260	20	40	60
4	150	300	20	40	60
5	160	320	20	20	40
6	160	320	20	0	20
7	150	300	20	−20	0
8	145	290	20	−10	10

*$k = 2$.

capital stock and their output.* The constant k is known both as the *capital coefficient* and the *accelerator*.

To show the way the acceleration principle works, consider a simple example: Assume that the business sector as a whole maintains a capital stock equal to twice its current output (i.e., that $k = 2$). (You can see this in the first two columns of Table 36.1.) Assume also that the current age distribution and size of this capital stock are such that during each period business firms must replace $20 million of it. Finally assume that the business sector is initially in equilibrium, that is, that its current-period output of $100 million just equals its previous-period output, and that it therefore has no need to adjust its $200 million capital stock up or down. In this equilibrium position, which corresponds to line 1 of Table 36.1, the business sector invests in $20 million of replacement equipment, but makes no induced investments.

Now look at the column labeled "output" in Table 36.1. These figures give an idea of how business output might evolve from one time period to another in response to autonomous shifts in consumption and investment.

---

* This argument can be stated more precisely as follows: Suppose that in each period firms adjust their capital stock, K, so that it equals k times their current output, Y. Then the capital stock firms want during time period $t - 1$ can be given by the expression $K_{t-1} = k \cdot Y_{t-1}$, and the capital stock firms want during the succeeding time period t can be given by the expression $K_t = k \cdot Y_t$.

Suppose that firms succeed, during each period, in adjusting their capital stock to the level they want. Then their net investment in period t equals the difference between the capital stock they want during $t - 1$ and the capital stock they want during t; in symbols, $I_t = K_t - K_{t-1}$. If we now substitute into this relationship the expressions given above for K_{t-1} and K_t, it follows that $I_t = k(Y_t - Y_{t-1}) = k \cdot \Delta Y$. This is precisely the result suggested by the intuitive argument presented above.

The effect that this evolution in demand for output will have on business investment is this (follow this across the table): Desired capital stock in each period will equal twice the output produced during the period; replacement investment will equal by assumption a constant $20 million per period; induced investment will equal the capital stock desired during that period minus the capital stock desired during the previous period; and gross investment will equal the sum of the replacement and induced investments made during the period.

Table 36.1 shows that, in an accelerator model of the sort we are working with, the following facts hold true: (1) Changes in induced investment will reinforce autonomous changes in output demand. (2) If the accelerator k exceeds 1, induced changes in investment will be greater than the autonomous changes in demand for output that produce them. (3) Induced investment can be sustained at a *positive* level only so long as demand for output continues to *rise*.

This last observation gives us our first clue as to how an expansion sparked by an autonomous increase in either investment or consumption might be reversed. It suggests that, whenever investment follows an accelerator pattern, a mere leveling-off of the growth of autonomous investment or consumption would bring about a decline in induced investment.

We can apply the acceleration principle not only to business investment in fixed capital, but also to business investment in inventories. We simply make the assumption that inventory managers solve the problem of meeting uncertain future demand by adopting the arbitrary rule that they will always hold inventories equal to some multiple of their current sales. Whenever inventory investment follows an accelerator pattern, the manager's induced investments (i.e., his inventory purchases) will display greater variability than the autonomous changes in demand for his output.

Multiplier–Accelerator Models

Induced investment is not the only characteristic of an economy that amplifies the impact that autonomous shifts in spending have on national income. The multiplier, which we encountered in Chapter 35, does so too. Since the multiplier takes several time periods to work itself out, it will also extend in time the impact that shifts in autonomous spending have on national income.

An autonomous shift in spending sets the multiplier and the accelerator into motion simultaneously. What sort of results are likely to occur when the two are combined? The answer is that an economy in which both operate will—for at least some values of the multiplier and the accelerator—have an internal structure that not only amplifies and extends in time, but also eventually *reverses* the impact that changes in autonomous spending have on national income. In other words, the economy's internal structure will be such that the economy responds to external shocks by making *cyclical* adjustments.

To illustrate: Suppose that the marginal propensity to consume equals 0.5 (i.e., that the multiplier equals 2) and that the accelerator equals 1. Suppose also that sales take place and income accrues at the end of the period so that producers and consumers react in each period to the income or change in income that took place during the preceding period. Suppose finally that during period 1 the economy (which initially is in equilibrium) experiences a $1 billion increase in autonomous investment. (Economists call such a jolt a "disturbance.")

TABLE 36|2

A Multiplier–Accelerator Model in Action (Billions of Dollars)*

Period	Change from the base period in			
	Autonomous investment	Induced investment	Induced consumption	National income and output
1	0.0	0.0	0.0	0.0
2	1.0	0.0	0.0	1.0
3	1.0	1.0	0.5	2.5
4	1.0	1.5	1.3	3.8
5	1.0	1.3	1.9	4.2
6	1.0	0.4	2.1	3.5
7	1.0	−0.7	1.8	2.1
8	1.0	−1.4	1.1	0.7
9	1.0	−1.4	0.4	0.0
10	1.0	−0.7	0.0	0.3
11	1.0	0.3	0.2	1.5
12	1.0	1.2	0.8	3.0
13	1.0	1.5	1.5	4.0
14	1.0	1.0	2.0	4.0
15	1.0	0.0	2.0	3.0
16	1.0	−1.0	1.5	1.5

*Figures are rounded to the nearest tenth of a billion; $k = 2$ and MPC $= 0.5$.

Table 36.2 shows that the first effect of this increase is a $1 billion increase in national income during period 2. As a result, consumption during period 3 rises by $0.5 billion, while induced investment rises by $1 billion. These spending increases mean that during period 3 national income rises by another $1.5 billion. As a result consumption during period 4 rises by an additional $0.8 billion, for a total increase of $1.3 billion, while induced investment rises to $1.5 billion.

At this point it might appear that the $1 billion increase in autonomous investment has launched national income into an ever-increasing upward spiral. But no. By the time we get to period 6, national income begins to *decline,* and continues to decline until period 9.

Why this reverse in direction? The answer is that, with the given values of the multiplier and accelerator, the rate of increase in sales, which is quite high in the periods immediately following the initial disturbance, soon begins to taper off. This reduces the incentive for producers to maintain a high rate of induced investment. So induced investment levels off, and then declines. As it does, so does the consumption supported by income earned in producing investment goods. Thus the interaction of consumption and investment, which initially produces a cumulative and self-reinforcing upward movement, ultimately goes into reverse.

Look now beyond period 9. National income turns up again. But not for good. By period 15 it has turned down again. Thus the increase in autonomous investment assumed in Table 36.2 has set off not an upward spiral in income, but a cyclical movement, which will keep on until some other outside disturbance jolts the system and changes its path.*

It may seem to you that, by combining the multiplier and the accelerator, we have constructed a model that satisfactorily explains why the economy responds to outside shocks by making cyclical adjustments. Actually, we haven't. The first problem with multiplier–accelerator models is that the way they respond to outside disturbances depends on the numerical values assumed by the multiplier and the accelerator. Now we don't know precisely what these values will be in practice (they're likely to vary from place to place, and maybe even from one decade to another). But we do have a good idea of the range of values in which they are likely to fall. If we try out

---

* A general statement of the multiplier-accelerator model illustrated in Table 36.2 is as follows: The relationship between consumption and income in this model incorporates the assumption that current consumption, C_t, equals some positive constant b plus the product of the marginal propensity to consume, c, and income in the preceding period, Y_{t-1}. In symbols, $C_t = c \cdot Y_{t-1} + b$. This model also incorporates the assumption that current investment, I_t, equals autonomous investment, A, plus the product of the accelerator, k, and the change in income during the preceding period. In symbols, $I_t = k(Y_{t-1} - Y_{t-2}) + A$.

If we substitute these expressions for C_t and I_t into the definition $Y_t \equiv C_t + I_t$, we obtain the following expression for current income:

$$Y_t = c \cdot Y_{t-1} + b + k(Y_{t-1} - Y_{t-2}) + A,$$

which we can write more simply as

$$Y_t = (c + k)Y_{t-1} - k \cdot Y_{t-2} + (b + A).$$

This says that, whenever the multiplier and the accelerator operate simultaneously, current income is a lagged function of income during preceding periods; it also indicates that the precise relationship between current and past income depends on the values of the marginal propensity to consume and the accelerator.

different pairs of these likely values, we hit a snag. Some of the multiplier–accelerator models we get would respond to outside disturbances by making cyclical adjustments. But many other equally likely models would respond to outside disturbances by taking off into exponential growth or by plunging into exponential contraction. Thus we can't count on multiplier–accelerator models to produce well-behaved cycles in response to outside disturbances. To overcome this shortcoming, some theorists have tried to build "floors" and "ceilings" into their models, so that explosive contractions and expansions will be reversed and the desired cyclical pattern thereby achieved. This approach has one weakness: It implies that all business cycles resemble each other at both their upper and their lower turning points. They don't, of course.*

A second problem with multiplier–accelerator models is that, even if we are dealing with an economy in which the values of the multiplier and the accelerator are consistent with regular cycles, we can't expect that the economy—once started on a neat cyclical path—will continue on it for any length of time. A multiplier–accelerator model takes into account only three variables: consumption, investment, and income. What about the values of all the other economic variables? Interest rates, wage rates, labor productivity, and other economic variables significantly influence investment and consumption. These may hold still for a short time, but after awhile they begin to change. When they do, the economy will be shifted out of its cyclical path.

Summary

At the beginning of this section we set out to find a theory or model that would provide a foolproof explanation of business cycles. Obviously we haven't succeeded. We have, however, hammered home three points: (1) Autonomous shifts in spending, especially autonomous shifts in investment, play an important part in producing economic fluctuations. (2) Two internal characteristics of the economy—the accelerator and the multiplier—go a long way toward explaining why the economy responds to outside shocks by making cyclical adjustments. (3) The principal source of economic instability is the investment component of consumer and business expenditures.

---

* For example, the popular ceiling-floor models—which claim that upswings will be cut short by full employment, while downswings will be cut short by the fact that gross induced investment can't fall below zero—don't jibe with reality, since several recent U.S. expansions have stopped short of full employment, while all recent U.S. recessions have sustained levels of gross induced investment far above zero.

PROBLEMS OF PREDICTION

We have said that it is very important for government policy-makers to know where in the cycle the economy is, and to be able to predict where it is going. Businessmen, too, are vitally interested in economic forecasts, since the profitability of their investments will largely depend on future changes in the level of economic activity. Stock market speculators, commodity traders, and others with irons in the Wall Street fire also need to know where national income and output are going.

If business cycles always traced out the same pattern, or if economists had a theory that completely explained them, it would be no trick to determine the economy's current position in the cycle and to predict the future course of economic activity. But neither condition obtains, and thus forecasting remains a difficult and uncertain endeavor.

Barometric Forecasting

Some forecasters of economic activity take an empirical as opposed to a theoretical approach to the problem, and therefore their work is referred to as *barometric forecasting.* Barometric forecasting is based on the premise that successive business cycles, even if they are not identical in all respects, will display at least a few similarities that are so strong and consistent that the forecaster will be able to identify the pattern and turning points of the current cycle by comparing it with past cycles.

In the U.S. today the most serious work in the field of barometric forecasting is carried out by the National Bureau of Economic Research. This bureau has tried to identify certain economic variables, or *indicators,* which fluctuate over time in a consistent fashion relative to the cycle as a whole, and whose position can thus be used to determine where the economy currently stands in the cycle and what the economic outlook for the near future is.

To find such indicators, the Bureau of Economic Research has compared the time paths traced out by hundreds of economic variables with the time path traced out by the cycle as a whole, and has successfully singled out a number of indicators which tend to consistently lead, move in step with, or lag behind the cycle. The *leading* indicators include industrial stock prices, new orders for durable goods, residential building contracts, and new incorporations. *Roughly coincident* indicators include the rate of unemployment, industrial production, corporate profits, and gross national product. *Lagging* indicators include personal income, consumer installment debt, and manufacturers' inventories.

Using their knowledge of which indicators lead and which lag behind the cycle, economists from the National Bureau, and other forecasters as well, have tried to predict *turning points* in economic activity on the basis of current trends in these indicators. Theoretically this approach ought to work, but in practice it is far from satisfactory, for the following reasons:

1) By the time all the data are collected, recorded, and examined, several months have usually gone by.

This means that the data the forecaster has to work with are always old, not current, and this puts a crimp in his ability to predict where the economy is going before it actually gets there; also his forecasts aren't much use to the businessman or policy-maker who needs to see further than a few months into the future.

2) Indicators are sensitive to factors other than the cycle; they seem to lead a life of their own and have an annoying tendency to give false signals.

Examples are shown in Fig. 36.3: A downturn in new orders for durable goods falsely signaled a recession in 1951. A downturn in stock prices falsely signaled a recession in 1962. In addition to giving premature signals, indicators may also give late signals, or on occasion no signal at all!

3) Indicators cannot take into account the effect of government policy measures on economic activity.

Anyone who uses indicators to read the future, therefore, has to add to them his knowledge of what policy actions the government may be currently undertaking to alter the path on which the economy is about to tread.

Econometric Forecasting

Since barometric forecasts yield only uncertain, short-term forecasts of turning points in business activity, and since they don't indicate the magnitude of the changes they predict, there's a clear need for other types of forecasts. So economists have come up with *econometric forecasts,* that is, statistical forecasts that take as their starting point some sort of theory of aggregate economic behavior.

The methods used to establish econometric forecasts vary widely in character and complexity. Almost all of them today, however, are made within the framework of some sort of Keynesian model,* like the one we presented in Chapter 35. The procedure by which these forecasts are made calls for the forecaster to first estimate the major components of aggregate demand and then to use these estimates as a basis for gauging the remaining components of aggregate demand and national income.

---

* Keynesian models of income determination are based on ideas that the English economist Lord Keynes put forth during the 1930's. These models all resemble the one we presented in Chapter 35. They stress the way the relationship between savings and investment determines the level of national income, and they allow for the possibility that the economy will attain equilibrium at less than full employment.

To illustrate: Suppose that we are (heaven forfend!) government forecasters, and that we want to use a multiplier–accelerator model similar to the one discussed above to construct an econometric forecast of current national income Y_t. As we showed in the footnote on page 561, this model can be summarized by the following equations (subscripts refer to time periods):

$$C_t = cY_{t-1} + b, \tag{1}$$

$$I_t = k(Y_{t-1} - Y_{t-2}) + A, \tag{2}$$

$$Y_t = C_t + I_t. \tag{3}$$

Equation (1) says that current consumption C_t equals the marginal propensity to consume c times income in the preceding period Y_{t-1}, plus a constant, b. Equation (2) says that current investment I_t equals the product of the accelerator k and the change in income that occurred in the preceding period, $(Y_{t-1} - Y_{t-2})$, plus autonomous investment, A. Equation (3) simply defines current income as the sum of current consumption and current investment.

To use this model to predict Y_t, we first collect data on the values assumed during the past by each of the values, C, I, and Y, that appear in the model. Next we use these data to estimate numerical values for all the constants, or *parameters*, of the model: These are c and b in the consumption equation and k in the investment equation. Then, using whatever information we can obtain on rates of technological change and other causal factors, we project autonomous investment A. Then we substitute this figure, along with observed values for Y_{t-1} and Y_{t-2}, into Eq. (2). By doing so we obtain an estimate of current investment, I_t. Next we substitute the observed value of Y_{t-1} into Eq. (1) to obtain an estimate of current consumption, C_t. Finally we substitute our estimates for C_t and I_t into Eq. (3) to obtain an estimate of current income Y_t.

How good is our estimate likely to be? Unfortunately, not very good. One reason why is that we based our estimate on a very simple model that fails to take into account the impact which changes in interest rates, prices, and other variables have on consumption and investment spending. Therefore the relationships which constitute our model will hold over time only in a very inexact fashion. So any estimates we make on the basis of this model will be imprecise ones.

However, a remedy in the form of a computer is now at hand. To avoid imprecision resulting from the omission of key variables, econometricians have, since the advent of electronic computers, developed very complex models which contain many more relationships and variables than the simple model presented above. For example, the Klein-Goldberger model of the U.S. economy incorporates 20 variables to be predicted and 20 relationships, while the Brookings Institute quarterly model contains 65!

Complex models can reduce the uncertainty associated with the forecaster's estimates, but they can't totally eliminate it, for several reasons: (1) Some of the preliminary estimates which the forecaster feeds into his model (e.g., the estimate for autonomous investment in the example above) may prove incorrect. (2) No matter how many variables the model takes into account, the possibility always remains that economic activity will be jolted out of its predicted path by an unpredictable—at least from the forecaster's viewpoint—disturbance. For example, a capricious decision by consumers to dislike this year's auto model might lower national income below the predicted level, while an unanticipated foreign crisis that called for increased military expenditures might increase it above the predicted levels. (3) There is always the possibility that the forecaster's model will give poor results because the structure of the economy has changed since the model was put together or because the model fails to include some important relationship or variable.

Given all these uncertainties, the careful forecaster usually cross-checks his predictions against whatever information about the future he can glean from outside sources. He checks his investment forecast, for example, against the results of the SEC and the McGraw-Hill surveys of business investment intentions, his consumption forecast against the results of the University of Michigan survey of consumer attitudes and the Census Bureau survey of consumer spending intentions, and his forecast of the general trend in national income against the trend in key economic indicators.

Despite all precautions, the final prediction that the forecaster comes up with will still be an uncertain one. Therefore business investors, stock market speculators, and government policy-makers are all forced to operate on the basis of forecasts that are at best well-informed guesses about what the future will bring. This fact of life has important implications for government policy. One is that it puts a premium on the government's ability to act quickly. Another is that it makes control over flexible instrument variables an absolute prerequisite for successful policy.

PROBLEMS

1 Given that economic activity is indeed cyclical, why can't economists predict, say, next year's income by saying that income will rise next year if it fell this year and that it will fall next year if it rose this year?

2 "An outside or *exogenous* factor in an economic theory is really just any factor that the economist can't explain. Thus in a truly complete economic theory nothing would be exogenous." Comment.

3 Continue the computations of the model in Table 36.2 through the thirtieth period. Does the amplitude of the cycle in this case seem to be getting larger, getting smaller, or staying the same over time?

4   In Table 36.1, why does gross investment fluctuate more widely than induced investment? Could induced investment in the situation described in this table ever fall below −$20 million? On what factors does your answer depend? What does it mean that gross investment equals zero, while induced investment equals −$20 million?

5   a) Set up a model similar to that of Table 36.2, but with a marginal propensity to consume of 0.2 instead of 0.5. Calculate the national income for enough periods to make the nature of the cycle evident.

    b) Repeat part (a) with a marginal propensity to consume of 0.8. What seems to be the effect of changes in the value of this constant on the amplitude of the cycle, the length of the cycle, and the tendency of the cycle to converge or diverge over time?

6   Determine the influence of the value of the accelerator on the cycle by setting up models like Table 36.2, but with the accelerator equal to 0.5 in one model and 2.0 in another model.

7   Why do you think that forecasters often use seasonally adjusted data, that is, data from which strictly seasonal fluctuations have been eliminated? [*Hint:* If you were to look at figures for retail sales for November, December, and January, what would you find out if you didn't look at seasonally adjusted data?]

8   On page 563 we listed some of the leading, coincident, and lagging indicators that the National Bureau of Economic Research has identified. Why do you think these particular indicators display the timing they do? What does Fig. 36.3 tell you about how reliable these indicators are likely to be as predictors of where business activity is going?

9   In the text we said that whenever inventory investment follows an accelerator pattern, the inventory manager's induced investments (i.e., his inventory purchases) will display greater variability than the autonomous change in demand for his output. Set up a simple numerical example that shows this.

*10 As we said in the text, the acceleration principle can be applied, not only to business investment in fixed equipment, but also to business investment in inventories. To illustrate this second possibility, consider the following example: There are two firms, a retailer and a wholesaler. The retailer sells to the public and buys only from the wholesaler. The wholesaler sells only to the retailer and buys from a manufacturer. Both the retailer and the wholesaler attempt to keep their current-period inventories equal to a multiple (1.5) of their last-period sales.

At the beginning of period t, the retailer's inventory, $(I_1)_t$, will be given by the expression

$$(I_1)_t = (I_1)_{t-1} + (O_1)_{t-1} - D_{t-1},$$

in which $(I_1)_{t-1}$ represents the retailer's inventory at the beginning of period $t-1$, $(O_1)_{t-1}$ represents the goods he orders from the wholesaler during period $t-1$ and D_{t-1} represents the goods that the public demands from the retailer

---

* Starred problems are problems that are unusually difficult.

during period $t-1$. The quantity of goods which the retailer orders from the wholesaler during each period t will equal the difference between his desired inventory (1.5) D_{t-1}, and his actual inventory, I_t, plus the amount of goods he expects to sell during period t (assume that this equals D_{t-1}). In symbols,

$$(O_1)_t = (1.5D_{t-1} - (I_1)_t) + D_{t-1} = 2.5D_{t-1} - (I_1)_t.$$

Let $(I_2)_t$ represent the wholesaler's inventory at the beginning of period t, and let $(O_2)_t$ represent the quantity of goods he orders from the manufacturer during period t. Then we can write:

$$(I_2)_t = (I_2)_{t-1} + (O_2)_{t-1} - (O_1)_{t-1}, \qquad (O_2)_t = 2.5(O_1)_{t-1} - (I_2)_t.$$

a) In what sense would the following combination of values for the variables in our model represent an equilibrium combination?

$$D_0 = 10; \qquad (I_1)_0 = 15; \qquad (O_1)_0 = 10; \qquad (I_2)_0 = 15; \qquad (O_2)_0 = 10.$$

Would any other combination of values for these variables also represent an equilibrium combination?

b) Starting from the above equilibrium, trace out the effect over time on O_1, I_1, O_2 and I_2 of a permanent one-unit increase in final demand.

c) Suppose that we added another inventory-holding firm to our example (a second wholesaler who sold to our first wholesaler). How do you think that the behavior of O_3 and I_3 would compare with that of O_i and I_i $(i = 1,2)$?

CHAPTER 37

THE PUBLIC SECTOR

In Chapter 2 we introduced the consumer and in Chapter 6 the firm. Both consumers and producers, of course, play key roles in the economy. Now we're coming to a third vital sector: the government.

Actually we're going to focus on the government in the broad sense, as the *public sector*. By this we mean government institutions proper (such as the courts and the Congress) and government enterprises (such as the Post Office) as well.

THE DIMENSIONS OF THE PUBLIC SECTOR

Let's begin by looking at a few statistics. Figure 37.1 shows that since the turn of the century government expenditures in the U.S. have been rising rapidly; so rapidly that their growth has outpaced by a wide margin the growth of the U.S. gross national product!

And it isn't just *federal* government spending that is big, nor federal government expenditures only that have been soaring. In recent years state and local expenditures have been rising more rapidly than total federal expenditures. As we can see by looking at Fig. 37.2, today the total spending of state and local governments equals that of the federal government on nondefense items.

There is an explanation for these surprising figures. Since the end of World War II, the population of the U.S. has expanded greatly (between 1946 and 1966 it rose almost 40%). This increase has of course required new schools, roads, libraries, colleges, sidewalks, sewers, and lots of other goods and services that it is primarily the responsibility of state and local governments to provide. So circumstances have forced state and local governments into the continuous and vigorous expansion of their expenditures that you see reflected in Fig. 37.2.

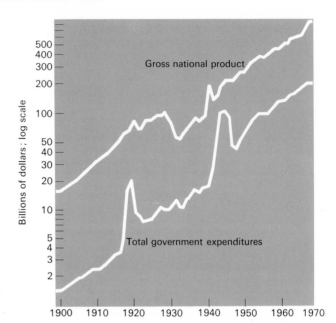

37|1

In the past half century,
government spending in the U.S.
has grown more rapidly than
gross national output. (Source:
U.S. Department
of Commerce)

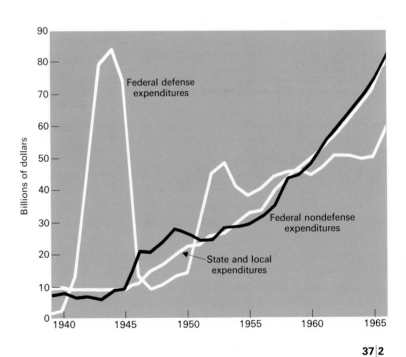

37|2

Since the end of World War II, government nondefense expenditures
at the federal, state, and local levels have soared. (Source: U.S. Department of Commerce)

THE FUNCTIONS OF THE PUBLIC SECTOR

If we lived in an avowed socialist or communist state, we wouldn't be surprised that the public sector was big and getting bigger all the time. But we live in a market economy, and as a nation we continually extol the virtues of private enterprise. Why, in our market economy, is the public sector so big and why does it continue to expand?

Figures 37.3 and 37.4, which break down federal, state, and local government spending according to use, give some clues to the answer. They indicate that much of government spending is for goods and services that private producers in a market economy could not (or would not) provide to consumers at what society would consider a reasonable price. They also show that most of the rest of government spending goes to promote certain social goals which we *as a nation* choose to strive toward, but which our market economy, operating in complete freedom, would not achieve.

Collective Goods

Many services that government provides are services that cannot be split up and sold "by the piece" to individual citizens and business firms. They have to be produced for, and consumed collectively by, all people in a society. One example of such a *collective good* is national defense. Defense can't be consumed by some individuals in a country and not by others. Either everybody is defended against outside attack or nobody is.

Because collective goods can't be supplied to some individuals and not to others, it would be to everybody's advantage to let "the other fellow" pay for such services. Suppose, for a moment, that national defense were paid for by voluntary contributions, and that Fred Jones knew that Smith, Brown, and a lot of other consumers had put up money to buy national defense services. This means that Jones would be protected whether he contributed or not. So why should he? Of course Jones might be patriotic but, in order to contribute his fair share, he would have to give up buying a lot of the good things of life that he'd like to have. So he might decide to sit back and do the rational thing: be a free-loader. Because Jones, and a lot of other rational consumers, wouldn't be willing to pay for collective goods, such goods can't be produced and sold by private, profit-maximizing firms. If society is going to enjoy the benefits of them at all, they will have to be provided by government.

If we look back at Fig. 37.2, we see that in the United States expenditures on a single collective good, national defense, account for almost half of total federal spending and almost one-third of total government spending at all levels. Other collective goods provided by the government range from local police and fire protection to plowing snow off roads in winter. Thus the main reason why government expenditures are so big is the existence, and importance, of collective goods.

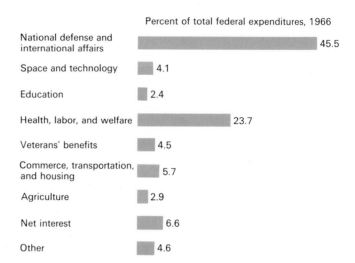

Percent of total federal expenditures, 1966

National defense and international affairs	45.5
Space and technology	4.1
Education	2.4
Health, labor, and welfare	23.7
Veterans' benefits	4.5
Commerce, transportation, and housing	5.7
Agriculture	2.9
Net interest	6.6
Other	4.6

37|3

At the federal level a single item, national defense, accounts for almost half of total expenditures. The next-most-important item is health, labor, and welfare. (Source: U.S. Department of Commerce)

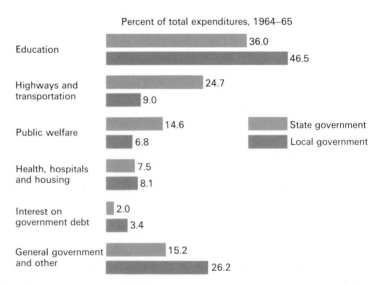

Percent of total expenditures, 1964–65

Education	36.0
	46.5
Highways and transportation	24.7
	9.0
Public welfare	14.6
	6.8
Health, hospitals and housing	7.5
	8.1
Interest on government debt	2.0
	3.4
General government and other	15.2
	26.2

State government
Local government

37|4

At the state and local levels, education, highways, and welfare are the biggest single items in government expenditure. (Source: U.S. Department of Commerce, Bureau of the Census)

Natural Monopolies and Oligopolies

In Chapter 25 we said that in certain industries efficient production requires that producers be few in number, or maybe that there be just one.* However, as we saw in Chapter 24, whenever a service is produced by a single firm or by just a few, these firms, in attempting to maximize profits, are likely to practice monopolistic output restriction, i.e., to charge a price that's too high and so produce an output that's too small to be consistent with an efficient allocation of resources.

For this reason and others the government often designates industries in which efficient production requires high seller concentration as *public utilities,* and it regulates both prices and output in these industries. In addition to this regulation of private producers, the government can set up *government enterprises* to carry out production in such industries. In the U.S. both approaches are common. For example, producers in the telephone, railroad, and air transport industries are all private, but the government regulates them; the post office, though, is a government enterprise. Electric power and garbage collection are services that, in some communities, are produced by natural monopolies that are government-regulated companies. In other communities, the same services are provided by government enterprises (public power companies, in the case of electricity, and public works departments, in the case of garbage collection).

In theory at least, whether a government regulates private companies or whether it runs its own enterprises, the results ought to be similar, given efficiency in both kinds of operations. There isn't any clear-cut dividing line between those natural monopolies that ought to be regulated by the government and those that ought to be run as government enterprises. The choice between these two approaches *does,* however, make a lot of difference in the *size* of the public sector. The prominent role of the government sector in many West European countries reflects the fact that these countries have opted to run as government enterprises many natural oligopolies and monopolies (e.g., the railroads, the airlines, and the telephone company) that are run as regulated public utilities in the U.S.

The fact that there are these natural monopolies and oligopolies is one reason why government enterprises exist. Another reason is that in some industries, the research and development expenses associated with new products are so large that only a government (and a big one at that) can afford to underwrite them. For example, the U.S. government has sponsored the

---

* An industry in which efficient production requires that production be carried out by a single seller is known as a *natural monopoly*. One in which efficient production requires that production be carried out by just a few producers is known as a *natural oligopoly*. The telephone company is a good example of a natural monopoly, the railroads of a natural oligopoly.

development of nuclear power reactors, communications satellites, and a supersonic transport plane; the French and English governments have combined forces to develop a competing supersonic jet.

Social Goals

Even if there were no collective goods and no natural oligopolies or monopolies, government expenditures would still be large, because many government expenditures are made in response to a third factor, society's desire to achieve certain social goals that a market economy operating on its own wouldn't achieve. In the U.S., the biggest single item in this social-goals category—and one of the fastest-growing items in the overall budget of government—is education. As a society we take the position that every individual, whether he can afford it or not, is entitled to an education, at least through high school, and in some states (such as California) this "right" has been extended to cover a free college education. Education, especially at the primary and secondary levels, has been largely removed from the market sphere of the economy and is provided by the government as a free service. Until recently the burden of providing educational services fell almost exclusively on local and state governments. This explains why expenditures for education represent almost 50% of local government expenditures and over 30% of state government expenditures, but less than 3% of federal government expenditures.

Another social goal our society attempts to achieve through government action is a more equitable distribution of income and output than our economy operating on its own would establish. To achieve this goal, the government provides special services to groups of individuals who it feels ought to get such services but who otherwise would not. Examples are school programs such as Operation Head Start and Operation Upward Bound, low-cost housing for the urban poor, job training for the unemployed, and research and advisory services to farmers.

To make the distribution of output more equitable, the government also makes extensive cash payments to people whose income is lower than the government thinks it ought to be. For example, it raises the incomes of the poor by making cash payments to them under welfare programs. It raises the incomes of the handicapped, of widows, and of the elderly by paying out veterans' pensions and Social Security benefits. It raises the incomes of the unemployed by paying out unemployment benefits. And, as we saw in Chapter 25, it raises the incomes of farm workers relative to factory workers by maintaining expensive price-propping programs for many crops.

Whenever the government makes a payment to someone on the basis of his need, the person who gets the check—although he is probably deserving—hasn't provided any productive services in exchange for these funds. So the money he receives doesn't represent income he has earned; it represents a *transfer* to him of income earned by some other person. Economists refer to such payments as *transfer payments*.

Many of the transfer payments which the government makes—such as unemployment benefits and Social Security payments—are made in connection with programs that resemble insurance schemes. Why should the government be in the insurance business? There are two reasons:

(1) Many workers, if left to their own devices, wouldn't (or couldn't) adequately protect themselves and their families against unemployment, disablement, old age, or premature death of the family's wage-earner. So the government has set up programs to make sure that every worker is provided with at least minimum protection against these contingencies.

(2) The government doesn't have to worry about earning a profit the way a private company does. It doesn't even have to worry about breaking even. Therefore it can use what are nominally insurance programs to alter the distribution of income and thus the allocation of resources. Consider the Social Security program. The government makes no pretense of operating this program on an actuarial basis that would limit the benefits a person would receive to the amount of premiums he had paid in during his working years. The limits on current benefit payments are set only by the amount of taxes that Congress is willing to impose on workers who are now paying "premiums." So the Social Security program is not so much an insurance scheme as a device by which the government transfers income from people who are working right now to people who, because of age or infirmity, don't work any more.

HOW MUCH GOVERNMENT EXPENDITURE?

When we were discussing government expenditures, we pointed out several reasons why such expenditures loom large even in a market economy: the existence of collective goods, the existence of natural monopolies, and the fact that the government pursues a variety of social goals. Now let's focus on a second aspect of government expenditures: In a market economy, how large should such expenditures be?

So far as government payments to redistribute income and to accomplish other social goals are concerned, the answer to this question depends on value judgments.* So there isn't much that the economist, speaking as an economist, can say (although he may have plenty of opinions as a citizen, taxpayer, and philosopher). However, for other areas of government activity, the economist can and does offer guidelines as to how much government in a market economy ought to spend.

---

* We mentioned the role of value judgments as a basis for policy formation in the discussion of positive versus normative economics in Chapter 1.

Government Outputs That Are Sold

Let us take an easy case first: If the government operates a natural monopoly or oligopoly as a government enterprise, and if it wants resource allocation to be efficient, it should follow several rules for its expenditures. (1) It should strive to see that government enterprises produce output at minimum cost. (2) In determining how much output these enterprises should produce (i.e., how much they should spend on inputs), the government should require each to expand its output to the point at which the price it gets for the service it produces just equals the marginal cost it incurs in producing this service.*

Here we must remember a point illustrated back in Fig. 24.3: Requiring an enterprise to price at marginal cost may lead it (a) to earn profits, (b) to incur a loss, or (c) to earn no profits at all. Whether an enterprise does one or the other depends on the relationship between its cost curves and the demand for its output. So, if we direct a government enterprise to price at marginal cost, we can't judge its efficiency by the size of its profits or losses.

Government Outputs That Aren't Sold

"Price at marginal cost and satisfy market demand" is a good rule for identifying how much the government ought to spend on providing services that it *sells* to the population. But now let's consider the many collective goods, such as roads and national defense, that government produces but *does not sell* to people. How much should it spend on them?

Whenever the economy is operating at full employment (that is, whenever it is producing and using up all the output it can), the resources it devotes to creating collective goods will be subtracted from those available for producing private goods. So public goods, in addition to bringing benefits to the population, also impose an opportunity cost (see page 93) in the form of forgone private goods. With this in mind, economists and government decision-makers have formulated a rule (called the *benefit-cost principle*) for determining how much the government ought to spend on producing collective goods: *Keep spending on collective goods so long as the marginal benefits they yield exceeds their marginal cost; but stop when marginal benefits have fallen to a level at which they equal marginal cost.*

Resources used to produce one collective good are subtracted from those available for producing some other collective good. For this reason the

---

* The marginal cost of any output equals the extra total cost that a firm would incur if it were to produce one more unit of this output. For example, if handling one extra letter increases the total costs incurred by the post office by 6¢, then the marginal cost of this service is 6¢. In Chapter 18 we showed that an efficient allocation of resources requires that all goods and services be priced at marginal cost; in Chapter 25 we applied this rule to pricing in regulated industries.

benefit-cost principle also tells us that the allocation of government expenditures among different collective goods will be efficient only if the marginal benefits yielded by the last dollars spent on all these goods are equal. For example: The U.S. government is financing research in a number of areas, two of which are nuclear reactors and supersonic transports. How should it allocate its research funds between these two projects? The benefit-cost analyst would say: "Let it divide its research dollars so that the marginal benefits provided by the two projects are equal." The supersonic transport, or SST, excites the imagination, but the proportion of the population that is likely to ever cross any ocean in such a plane is exceedingly small. Breeder reactors, on the other hand, hold out the promise of fantastically cheap power that will benefit everybody:

> Scientists and technicians, in a frustrating search for some way to describe the changes that their work [on breeder reactors] portends, speak glowingly of air-conditioning Africa and heating the subarctic.*

So the benefit-cost analyst would probably say that dollars spent on developing a breeder reactor offer greater potential benefits than those spent on developing an SST; and for this reason the government ought to devote more research dollars to reactors than to the SST. In fact it seems likely that the government will do the opposite. A proponent of the SST might argue that this is as it should be, because in our benefit-cost calculations we have neglected one important factor: the big contribution that a successful SST would make to national prestige.

The fact that government expenditures yield benefits such as prestige and defense that are hard to measure in dollars and cents means that the benefit-cost principle, while easy to spell out in theory, is often difficult to apply in practice. Also it's often impossible in our uncertain world to know what benefits a given expenditure will yield until after it is made. Maybe $3 billion of research will provide a superb breeder reactor. Or maybe it will just prove that the problems associated with developing such a reactor are more intractable than scientists think. Maybe a $5 billion anti-missile system would be a good investment because it would keep us from being attacked. Or maybe it would be a poor investment because we aren't going to be attacked anyway. Who can know until long after the expenditure decision has been made?

Although the benefit-cost principle doesn't offer easy solutions to all the expenditure decisions that the government has to make, it is a useful device because it provides a framework within which such decisions can be analyzed, and it focuses the attention of the decision-maker where it ought to be: on the comparative costs and benefits associated with alternative projects.

---

* *Fortune*, March 1967, "The Next Step is the Breeder Reactor," page 121.

Theory Versus Political Reality

We have been talking about the rules that the government ought to follow in deciding how much to spend, and how to allocate this spending among different projects. In actual practice, of course, the process of deciding on the size and composition of U.S. government expenditures is nowhere near this rational. For one thing the expenditures Congress votes to make depend partly on the pressures which different groups bring to bear on Congress. The needs of well-organized groups such as farmers, veterans, and highway users are likely to be generously met while the needs of other, less-organized groups are met only frugally, if at all. Thus it's possible that while we spend billions on the SST and getting to the moon, we may be simultaneously neglecting other programs that would bring much higher marginal benefits.

And lobbying isn't the only obstacle to rational budgeting. Americans tend, as the editors of *Fortune* have put it, to "use what an accountant would call the LIFO—'last in, first out'—approach" to government budget decisions. That is, lawmakers tend to think of old established programs such as the multi-billion-dollar farm-support program as good programs that can't be cut by more than nominal amounts. On the other hand, they view the latest programs to be proposed as expendable, or at least postponable. So when Congress decides how to allocate expenditures, it doesn't scrutinize the relative merits of all the programs it undertakes, from public works to anti-poverty to space capsules. It views old programs as given and does most of the trimming that has to be done on new ones. One consequence of this attitude is that Congress appears convinced that the expensive Vietnam war means that we can't afford new Great Society programs; yet it never seems to occur to Congress that the same expensive war might mean that we can't afford to continue subsidizing the production of tobacco and cotton we don't want, or that we can't afford to keep subsidizing a domestic merchant marine that is too high-cost to compete with its foreign rivals.

PAYING FOR GOVERNMENT EXPENDITURES

As we have seen, the government even of a free market economy is called on to make large expenditures. How does it obtain funds to pay for them? Principally from three sources: (1) Some government enterprises, such as the post office and the Federal Reserve System, sell the services they produce, and the revenues they get accrue dirctly or indirectly to the government. (2) The government, as we are all painfully aware, imposes a wide variety of taxes. (3) The government often obtains funds by borrowing.

We've already pointed out that the government ought to price the services it produces at marginal cost. Also we talked, in Part 5, about the way the government borrows to cover the funds deficits it so frequently incurs, and in Chapter 38 we shall discuss the impact of the government debt. So in the remainder of this chapter, we can focus on one way the government obtains funds: taxes.

Taxes Take Many Forms

In the U.S. the Federal, state, and local governments impose a variety of taxes: taxes on personal income, taxes on corporate profits, excise taxes (i.e., sales taxes levied on specified commodities such as telephone bills, gasoline, liquor, cigarettes, and plane tickets), general sales taxes levied on all or most goods and services, property taxes (that is, taxes levied on the value of the real assets—particularly land and buildings—and sometimes the financial assets owned by consumers and firms), and general fees such as those charged for drivers' licenses, automobile registration, hunting licenses, and so forth.

In tax discussions a distinction is often made between taxes that are *progressive, regressive,* and *proportional.*

A progressive tax is one that takes an increasing share of a person's income the higher his income is.

The federal personal income tax, which levies higher rates on higher incomes, is a good example of a progressive tax.

A regressive tax is one that takes a decreasing share of a person's income the higher his income is.

As we showed back in Fig. 3.1, the higher a person's income is, the smaller the fraction of income he will devote to consumption. So sales taxes, which are really taxes on consumption, are generally thought to be regressive.

A proportional tax, as its name suggests, is one that takes a constant proportion of a person's income regardless of how high his income rises.

The Social Security tax, which takes a flat 4.4% of all wage income, is a proportional tax, but only up to the income level of $7,800, since that is the maximum amount currently subject to this tax.

Who Taxes What?

Federal, state, and local governments each levy most of the different types of taxes we mentioned above. But the importance of individual taxes as money raisers varies considerably from one level of government to another.

Figure 37.5 shows that for the Federal government, the biggest single revenue raiser is the income tax; the corporate profits tax brings in only half as much. Indirect business taxes (i.e., sales and excise taxes) play a relatively minor role in Federal finances because the government has consistently attempted to avoid heavy reliance on regressive taxes.

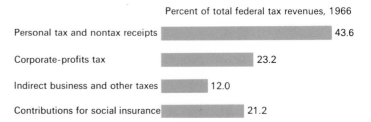

Percent of total federal tax revenues, 1966

Personal tax and nontax receipts   43.6

Corporate-profits tax   23.2

Indirect business and other taxes   12.0

Contributions for social insurance   21.2

37|5

At the federal level the taxes imposed on personal income and corporate profits are the big revenue raisers. (Source: U.S. Department of Commerce)

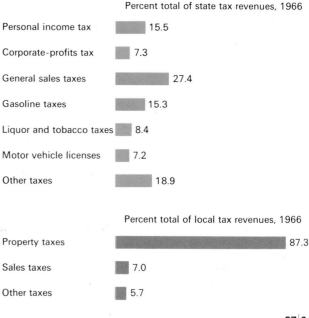

Percent total of state tax revenues, 1966

Personal income tax   15.5

Corporate-profits tax   7.3

General sales taxes   27.4

Gasoline taxes   15.3

Liquor and tobacco taxes   8.4

Motor vehicle licenses   7.2

Other taxes   18.9

Percent total of local tax revenues, 1966

Property taxes   87.3

Sales taxes   7.0

Other taxes   5.7

37|6

State governments rely heavily on sales and excise taxes for revenue, while local governments depend almost exclusively on property taxes. (Source: U.S. Department of Commerce)

At the state level the picture is quite different, as indicated in Fig. 37.6. There the big sources of revenue are general sales taxes and excise taxes on gasoline, liquor, and tobacco. The personal income tax raises only modest revenues, and the corporate profits tax even less.

Figure 37.6 also shows that local governments rely almost solely on a single tax to obtain revenue: the property tax. This reflects not only the fact that it's easy for local authorities to impose this tax, but also the fact that many state governments have imposed limits on the kinds and quantities of taxes that local governments may impose.

Principles of Taxation

The variety of taxes and the differences in the degree to which the several levels of government rely on different taxes raises the question as to what tax structure is a fair one. A number of rules have been proposed, but most of them boil down to two simple propositions.

1) *The benefit principle,* which is that people should be taxed according to the benefits they receive from government expenditures.

2) *The equal-sacrifice principle,* which is that taxes should be allocated so that the sacrifice or burden imposed on every taxpayer is equal to that imposed on every other taxpayer.

This second principle has two important aspects. *First,* it implies that, if people are in similar circumstances (this is generally interpreted to mean "if people have equal incomes"), they ought to pay equal taxes. *Second,* if people have unequal incomes, then those with high incomes should pay more taxes than those with low incomes.

Both the benefit and the equal-sacrifice principles are useful to the policy-maker who has to decide what sorts of taxes to levy. But they don't solve all his problems. Reason: These two principles sometimes conflict. Consider Fruitful Smith, who has five children and a low-paying job. The benefit principle says that Smith ought to be paying high taxes, since the schooling for his children probably costs state and local governments at least $5,000 a year. But the equal-sacrifice principle says that poor Smith shouldn't pay very much in taxes at all.

Because the benefit principle and the equal-sacrifice principle aren't always in accord, the tax structure is likely to reflect a pragmatic compromise between them. The varied taxes imposed by the U.S. federal government reflect just such a compromise. Some federal taxes, such as those imposed on highway users to finance construction of interstate freeways, are clearly consistent with the benefit principle. Others, such as the progressive personal income tax and the inheritance tax, follow the equal-sacrifice principle. But some taxes, like the excise tax on telephone bills, are difficult to reconcile with either principle. In cases like these, you pays yer money, but you doesn't get to take yer choice.

Federal Revenue Sharing: the Next Tax Innovation?

As Harvard's John Kenneth Galbraith and other experts on government finance have suggested, "Prosperity gives the federal government the revenue and the state and local governments the problems."* The reasons for this are explainable as follows: The Federal government relies heavily on the personal income and corporate profits taxes for revenue. Whenever national output grows, personal income and corporate profits grow, and so do federal tax revenues. Economic growth also raises the demand for services provided by the federal government, but on balance prosperity is likely to induce a faster growth of federal revenue than of federal expenditures.

At the state and local level the situation is just the reverse. State and local governments, as Fig. 37.6 shows, rely heavily on property taxes, on sales and excise taxes, and on fixed fees to finance their expenses, so their tax revenues rise slowly as the economy grows. Growth, however, greatly increases the demand for collective goods such as highways, schools, fire stations, libraries, and recreational facilities that state and local governments provide. Thus growth accelerates the spending of state and local governments faster than it adds to their revenue.

To ease this fiscal imbalance, the Federal government has, since the end of World War II, instituted many programs under which it makes grants to state and local governments, to help them finance special categories of expenditures such as highway construction, welfare payments, elementary and secondary education, and housing and community development.

The main advantage of categorical grants-in-aid is that they permit the federal government to single out urgent needs and meet them directly. The main disadvantage is that categorical-aid programs are complex and costly to administer, not only for the Federal government, but also for the state and local governments that benefit from them. This latter weakness has led some students of government finance to argue that the Federal government should deemphasize such aid and provide the states with funds on a no-strings-attached basis. This could be done in various ways. One would be to grant individual taxpayers a credit against their federal income tax liability equal to some portion of the state income taxes they pay. This approach (which would permit the states to indirectly tax the federal government) would encourage more states to enact income taxes, and encourage states that already have them to raise the rates at which they tax income.

There is also another approach that could be used to alleviate the imbalance between federal and state and local finances. Under it the federal government would continue to be the nation's principal collector of taxes on personal income and corporate profits, but it would pass on some of the

---

* Walter W. Heller, *New Dimensions of Political Economy*; New York: W. W. Norton, 1966, page 118.

funds it collects to the states. For example, 5 or 10% of total federal revenues might be earmarked for sharing with the states. A program of this sort was proposed and widely debated prior to the Vietnam war, but the pressures put on the federal budget by this war have temporarily precluded its enactment. However, once the war is ended, proposals for getting money out of the federal tax coffers and into the hands of state and local governments are sure to come to the fore again.

PROBLEMS

1   In the text we said that the government spends large sums on education because it is trying to fulfill a social goal: providing all citizens with the opportunity to become educated. Could it be argued with equal force that the government spends large sums on education because education represents a collective good (i.e., because society as a whole benefits from the fact that the population is literate)?

2   "One fair and feasible way for society to pay for fire protection would be to have the fire department charge people whenever it put out a fire for them." Suggest some pros and cons of this scheme. Would you favor it if you happened to live in a nice wood-frame house next to John Pinchpenny, who would rather see his house burn down than pay the $300 fee charged by the fire department for putting out a house fire? What does this tell you about why fire protection is a collective good? What about public-health measures?

3   In discussing the different reasons why government spending is inevitably large even in a market-oriented economy like ours, we never mentioned government expenditures on courts, law enforcement, the salaries of legislators and other general government items. Would you argue that such expenditures represent collectively consumed goods? If so, why?

*4   When a government makes its tax-expenditure decisions, it has to answer questions such as: Should any groups in society receive transfer payments? If so, who should be taxed to pay for them? How big should these payments be? Could the government answer these questions solely on the basis of the following rule: *Make resource allocation as efficient as possible*? Or would the government have to make some sort of value judgment? Explain your answer. [*Hint:* Might a competitive economy, by means of transfer payments, move from one efficient point to another?]

5   Socialist governments, like governments in market economies, produce collective goods. Should they too follow the marginal-benefit principle in deciding how much to spend on them and how to allocate their expenditures between different collective goods?

6   Contrast the benefit that spending $3 billion a year to put a man on the moon might yield with the benefit that spending an extra $3 billion a year to improve

* This problem refers back to material discussed in Chapter 18.

urban transportation facilities might yield. Do you think that our government's allocation of total expenditures between the space race and urban transportation is in accord with the *marginal-benefit principle?* What are some of the difficulties in answering this question?

7   The Department of Agriculture is spending over $3 million on research to make cigarettes safer. If it succeeds, tobacco growers and smokers will both benefit (growers won't have to worry about what new reports linking death rates to smoking might do to the demand for tobacco, and smokers won't have to worry about what smoking might do to their health). However, making cigarettes safer isn't the only way that the worries of these two groups could be eliminated. Another would be for cigarette smokers to quit smoking and for tobacco growers to switch to another crop.

This second possibility suggests that, if the government wants to maximize the benefits yielded by its expenditure dollars, it ought to ban cigarettes, order farmers to stop growing tobacco, and use the $3 million it is now spending on cigarette research to attack some health problem that can't be traced to such an "easily" eliminated cause. Discuss the issues (including fairness and feasibility) raised by this proposal.

8   Sometimes the dividing line between what ought to be a government expenditure and what ought to be a private expenditure hinges more on the choice of procedure than on the goal. Example: Automobile exhaust creates dangerous air pollution; it's the government's job to see that the situation is remedied. One way the government could do so would be to subsidize the research required to develop an electric auto; in 1967 several senators were pushing for such a subsidy. Another way the government could act would be to establish exhaust control standards and require car manufacturers to meet them at some specified date. This second approach would force the research burden onto the auto manufacturers. Either way, consumers would end up paying the bill for research, either through higher taxes or through higher auto prices. Which approach would you favor? What general issues does this question raise?

9   In the text we noted that a good tax is often thought to be one that taxes "equals" equally. This rule sounds simple enough to apply but it raises a problem: How do we measure equality? Should we use the taxpayer's current income, total assets, net worth, or some measure? Should we permit any deductions from the total income, asset, or other figure we use? If so, why?

CHAPTER 38

FISCAL POLICY

In Chapter 37 we talked about the way the government sector, by means of its expenditure programs, can satisfy society's need for collective goods and attain various social goals that a free market economy operating on its own wouldn't attain. These goals, however, aren't the only ones the government sets for itself. As we pointed out in Chapter 33, the government also pursues certain macroeconomic goals, two of the most important of which are *full employment* and *price stability*. To pursue them, the government can use various measures:

1) The government can alter the size of the expenditures it makes and the quantity of taxes it collects. This is known as *fiscal policy*.
2) The government, acting through the central bank, can make changes in the cost and availability of credit. This is known as *monetary policy*.
3) The government can resort to *direct controls and moral suasion;* for example, in the form of wage–price guideposts.

In this chapter we shall focus on fiscal policy, in Chapter 39 on monetary policy. Then, in Chapter 40, we shall talk about the government's use of guideposts and other *ad hoc* measures to meet the problems of inflation.

ADDING A GOVERNMENT SECTOR TO OUR MACROECONOMIC MODEL

To show how fiscal policy can be used to further full employment and price stability, let us first look at the way government tax receipts and expenditures influence the economy's equilibrium income.

Government Taxes and Aggregate Demand

In a market economy the government can levy taxes on either consumers or firms. If it levies taxes on consumers, it will decrease their disposable in-

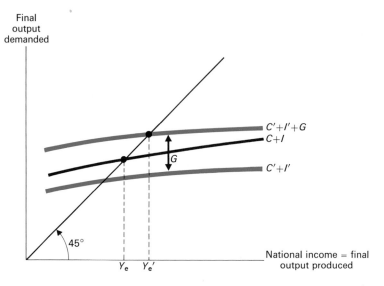

38|1

In the situation pictured here, the government sector has an expansionary impact on the economy's equilibrium income.

come, and this will decrease their demand for goods.* (Remember John Jones, whose income statement we examined back in Table 2.1. If the government imposes taxes on Jones, his disposable income falls. Jones may react to such taxes simply by reducing his saving, but probably he will spend less on consumption too.) Thus:

The taxes that the government imposes on consumers shift the aggregate consumption function downward.

What about the taxes that the government imposes on firms? Well, such taxes have two effects: (1) They lower firms' after-tax profits, which in turn lowers the amount of internal funds firms have available for financing current investment. (2) They lower firms' anticipations as to the future profitability of current investment.

The first effect naturally increases the cost to firms of financing new investments, while the second decreases their demand for new investments. [Take our hypothetical firm, Tectronics, for example (see pages 92–95). They have to decide whether or not to invest in a new bulb-folding machine. If the government taxes corporate profits, Tectronics will have less retained profits to finance this investment with; so, if they do buy it, they'll have to

---

* As we showed in Chapter 3, any person, when he decides how much to save and how much to consume during the current period, must operate within the budget constraint set by his current disposable income.

borrow money and incur the expenses and risks associated with the use of debt capital. Profits taxes also lower the return Tectronics can expect to earn on its machine, and this makes the investment less attractive. Maybe Tectronics will buy its new machine anyway, but chances are that high taxes will lead them to give up at least some of the investments they would otherwise have made.] Therefore we conclude that:

The taxes that the government imposes on firms shift the aggregate investment schedule downward.

Figure 38.1 illustrates the impact of taxes on aggregate demand and on the economy's equilibrium income. In this diagram the imposition of taxes on consumers and business firms shifts the aggregate demand schedule from its initial position at $C + I$ to a lower level $C' + I'$. From this diagram we see that:

Since taxes levied on consumers and firms cut aggregate demand, they lower the economy's equilibrium income.

Government Expenditures and Aggregate Demand

So much for taxes. Let us now focus on government expenditures. When the government buys goods and services, it contributes to aggregate demand. For example, if the government spends an amount equal to G on goods and services (e.g., on typists, senators, typewriters, and jet fighters), then the aggregate demand schedule (which we must now label $C + I + G$) will shift vertically upward by an amount equal to G. A shift of this sort is shown in Fig. 38.1, where the addition of government expenditures to private ones shifts aggregate demand from $C' + I'$ to the higher level $C' + I' + G$. From this diagram we see that:

Since government expenditures add to aggregate demand, they raise the economy's equilibrium income.

In the situation pictured in Fig. 38.1, government expenditures contribute more to aggregate demand than taxes subtract from it; hence the net impact of the government sector on the economy's equilibrium income is to increase it from Y_e to Y'_e. The net impact of the government sector could just as well, however, have been to lower the economy's equilibrium income. Which of these two outcomes occurs depends on several factors. *First,* since taxes lower aggregate demand while government expenditures raise aggregate demand, the greater the government's expenditures G relative to the tax dollars T it collects, the more likely it is that the government sector will have an expansionary impact on income. *Second,* as we have seen, a dollar of taxes is likely to lead consumers to decrease their consumption by less than a dollar, but it may lead firms to reduce investment by more *or* less than a dollar. So what effect the government sector has on the economy's equilibrium income depends not only on the size of G relative to T, but also on how T affects $C + I$.

A FULL-EMPLOYMENT FISCAL POLICY

We have seen that government tax receipts and expenditures influence the level of aggregate demand in the economy, and thus the economy's equilibrium income. Therefore it ought to be possible for the government to shape its tax and expenditure policies in such a way that the economy would continuously attain equilibrium at full employment.

The idea of such a *full-employment fiscal policy* is appealing. Is it feasible from a practical standpoint? That depends on several factors. One factor has to do with something called *output gaps,* and we'd better explain those right here, before you go any further: An output gap refers to the difference between the economy's equilibrium output, Y_e, and its full-employment output, Y_f. Be careful to distinguish it from a *deflationary gap.* A deflationary gap refers to the difference between the level of aggregate demand that would exist at the economy's full employment income and the level of aggregate demand that would be required to bring the economy to equilibrium at full employment. Figure 38.2 shows this distinction.

Now let's get back to the factors that determine the feasibility of a full-employment fiscal policy. Factor 1: *The size of the output gaps the govern-*

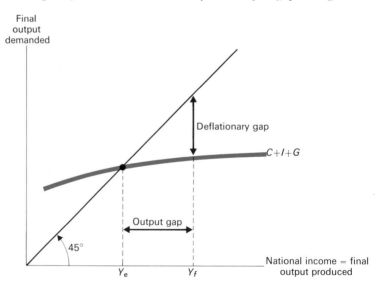

38|2

A deflationary gap and the resulting output gap.

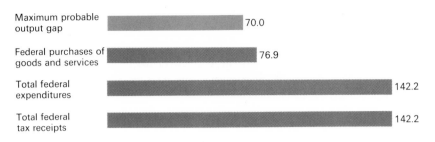

38|3

U.S. federal government expenditures and receipts relative to the maximum probable output gap, 1966 (billions of dollars).

ment encounters relative to the changes it can make in its tax receipts and expenditures. The smaller these gaps and the larger the tax and expenditure changes the government can make, the better its chances of attaining a successful fiscal policy. Factor 2: *The efficiency of changes in taxes and expenditures as instruments for altering national income.** The more efficient they are (i.e., the bigger the change in national income that a given change in taxes or government expenditures induces), the more likely it is that a full-employment fiscal policy will prove feasible.

To illustrate: Consider the case of the United States. During recent years the gaps between the U.S. economy's actual and potential output have not exceeded 10% of the economy's potential output; generally they've been less. (See Fig. 33.1 on page 509.) So at current income levels, we would expect that the U.S. might at worst be confronted with a $70 billion output gap, but probably it wouldn't encounter a gap more than half this size.

How do the changes that the government could make in taxes and expenditures compare with the output gaps it might face? Figure 38.3 shows that U.S. government purchases of goods and services currently run about $77 billion a year, while federal expenditures (including transfer payments) and federal tax receipts currently run over $140 billion a year. These data thus suggest that the U.S. government could make adjustments in its tax receipts and expenditures that would be quite sizable in comparison with any output gap it might encounter.

Whether or not these adjustments would suffice to close such a gap depends not only on their absolute size, but also on the efficiency of tax and expenditure adjustments as instruments for altering the economy's equilibrium income. In recent years, it has been estimated that in the U.S. each $1 of taxes collected by the government lowers the economy's equilibrium in-

---

* Recall from Chapter 33 that an *efficient* policy instrument is one that produces a large effect when it is changed by a small amount.

come by $2 to $3, while each $1 of expenditure made by the government raises the economy's equilibrium income by a similar multiple.* Thus tax and expenditure changes are quite efficient instruments for altering the economy's equilibrium income, and the U.S. government appears to be well equipped to combat, through fiscal policy, any gap between the economy's actual and potential outputs that might emerge as a result of a deflationary gap.

Is it equally well equipped to combat any upward pressure on prices that might emerge from an inflationary gap? Probably yes, since recent inflations have been small in magnitude and short in duration. So far as inflation is concerned, the really tricky problems (as we shall see in Chapter 40) are posed not by inflations that appear when demand is excessive, but by inflations that appear when the economy is at or below full employment.

Problems of Implementation

Forecasts about the direction in which the economy will move in the future are inevitably incomplete and uncertain. Also economic trends are subject to rapid change. Therefore the design and implementation of a discretionary fiscal policy, although it may sound simple in theory, is always fraught with difficulties in practice.

To begin with there is the problem of *timing*. Suppose that the economy appears to be in for a recession. Then the government policy-maker must ask himself whether stimulating measures should be begun today, should be postponed until six weeks from now, or should have been initiated months earlier. The answer is important because, if he acts too late, some degree of recession will be inevitable. If he acts prematurely (i.e., if a temporary pause in the economy's upswing is mistaken for the beginning of a recession), a destabilizing stimulus will be given to aggregate demand and thus to economic activity.

A second important problem connected with a discretionary fiscal policy is deciding *how much* action is called for. Again suppose that the economy seems to be on the verge of a recession and that the policy-maker has concluded that now is the time for a tax cut. Then should taxes be cut by $5 billion, by $10 billion, or by even more? If the policy-maker makes too small a cut, the budding recession will be permitted to gain momentum. But if he makes too big a cut, a destabilizing upswing may result.

Since the policy-maker is human, his decisions as to when and how much may prove wrong. Also sudden and unanticipated changes may always take place in economic trends. Therefore the policy-maker needs flexible instru-

---

* Arthur M. Okun, "Measuring the Impact of the 1964 Tax Reduction," remarks before the American Statistical Association, Philadelphia, Pa., September 10, 1965.

ments, that is, instruments that can be rapidly initiated and that can also be rapidly reversed.

On the count of flexibility, government expenditures on goods and services, and especially on public works, tend to come out poorly. It takes months and sometimes years to get capital projects such as public buildings, roads, and dams from the planning to the construction stage; and such projects—once started—are irreversible, since they represent a waste of resources unless completed. Almost the only flexibility that government expenditures on public works offer is the small leeway that may exist for projects under construction to be slowed or accelerated and for planned projects to be postponed or hastened.

In a country like the U.S., where federal revenues are collected largely through pay-as-you-go taxes on income and on corporate profits, changes in tax rates—in contrast to changes in expenditures—constitute an extremely flexible and effective policy instrument. For this reason, practicing policy-makers such as the President's Council of Economic Advisors have come to agree that the major tool of short-run stabilization policy should be changes in taxes, not in expenditures.

One trouble with this approach is that Congress jealously guards the prerogative to make even small, temporary changes in tax rates, and it acts only very slowly. Therefore there are exasperating delays between the time the policy-maker decides that the country needs a stabilizing change in tax rates and the time this change is actually made. However, very real progress has been made during the 1960's in increasing the flexibility of federal fiscal policy; and this leads one to hope that, as the lessons of the Keynesian revolution become more widely accepted, some means will be found to permit the government to make the kind of rapid changes in tax rates that a successful short-term stabilization policy requires.

AN AUTOMATIC STABILIZATION POLICY

It's always possible that the policy-maker—given the uncertain conditions under which he must operate—will make mistakes in the size and timing of the measures he recommends. Furthermore, there is usually a significant time lag between recommendation and implementation of a discretionary fiscal policy. Would it be possible to set up a fully *automatic* stabilization policy, that is, a policy which—without the aid of any discretionary intervention—would consistently maintain the economy of the country at full employment?

Let's look at a few relevant facts: Under the present tax policies of the U.S. and many other countries, personal income and corporate profits are taxed at fixed rates, but the amount of these taxes depends on the amount earned. Therefore a decline in national income automatically cuts government tax collections, while a rise in national income automatically increases them. As we saw above, however, a tax cut to meet a decline in income and a tax hike to meet an upward spurt in income is precisely what a stabilizing fiscal policy would call for. Therefore the U.S. economy and many others already benefit from some automatic stabilization.

However, this automatic stabilization is incomplete because automatic changes in tax receipts offset only a fraction of the initial change that occurs in national income as a result of a change in aggregate demand. And the portion that is not offset goes on to induce, via the multiplier, further changes in consumption and investment and thus in national income. Example: Suppose that there were to be a sudden decline in autonomous investment in the U.S. Automatic changes in tax receipts would offset less than one-third of the resulting decline in national income. The other two-thirds would be reflected in decreases in consumers' disposable income and in corporations' after-tax profits. These decreases would induce, via the multiplier, still further decreases in consumption and investment expenditures, and thus in national income.

In order for automatic decreases in government tax revenues to fully offset the initial drop in national income resulting from a drop in aggregate demand, it would be necessary—given that marginal tax rates* are well below 100%—to set up a system under which not only the amount of income taxed, but also the rates at which it is taxed would automatically fall whenever income and employment declined. Such a system might be feasible in theory, but in practice it would pose certain difficulties. The same uncertainties about the future that make it hard for the policy-maker to recommend measures that are correct in timing and size also make it hard for the economist to devise automatic stabilizers that would be strong enough to prevent economic downturns but also reliable enough so that they would never give a destabilizing stimulus to the economy.

Since economists have not yet reached the point at which they can design perfect automatic stabilizers, in the U.S. the best system for the present would probably be one under which the President were given stand-by authority, subject to Congressional veto, to make quick reductions or increases in tax rates whenever he and his economic advisors felt that such action was needed to counteract cyclical ups and downs in economic activity. People have proposed legislation to provide such flexibility, but Congress has never yet enacted it.

---

* In economics marginal always means extra. So *marginal tax rates* are the tax rates that people have to pay on the extra (or marginal) dollars they earn. Example: Smith, a bachelor, has a taxable income of $20,000. If he earns an extra dollar (i.e., if he raises his taxable income to $20,001) he will have to pay 48¢ more in federal income taxes. So his marginal tax rate is 48%.

Automatic Stabilization over the Long Run

Our conclusion that taxes on income and profits provide some automatic stabilization is true only so long as we're talking about *short-run* fluctuations in national income. If we talk about the *long run,* it becomes harder to pin the label "stabilizing" or "destabilizing" on such changes. As an economy grows, government tax receipts rise; and, if the tax system is progressive (i.e., higher incomes taxed at higher rates), tax receipts rise *more rapidly* than income.* Now so long as government expenditures increase in step with these increases in tax collections, automatic tax increases will be largely stabilizing. However, if government expenditures fail to increase as fast as tax receipts rise, automatic increases in tax revenues will lower the rate at which aggregate demand grows. Practicing policy-makers have dubbed this phenomenon *fiscal drag.* Whenever it emerges, the remedy is of course simple: Raise government expenditures or make discretionary cuts in tax rates.

DISCRETIONARY FISCAL POLICY: THE RECENT RECORD

Several decades have passed since the Keynesian revolution first made economists aware of the enormous contribution that discretionary fiscal policy could make to economic stability. Even so, the use of this tool in the U.S. today is still at the experimental stage. It is only since the early 1960's that the federal government has committed itself to a bold fiscal policy whose proportions are commensurate with the tasks to be accomplished. The government's record since this attempt was initiated—although short—is encouraging: During the 1960's, fiscal policy moved the economy from stagnation to dynamic full employment.

To obtain some perspective on the accomplishments of the 1960's, look back a few pages to Fig. 33.1. The output gap shown there indicates that, from 1955 on, the U.S. economy turned in a sluggish and disappointing performance. The years 1955–57 saw a general expansion, but even at its peak, unemployment remained over 4%. And in 1958 unemployment rose to over 7%. The expansion that followed the 1958 downturn was both shorter than the one that preceded it and characterized by greater unemployment. Thus the 1960's began inauspiciously, with the economy in recession, unemployment at high levels, and actual national output far below its potential level.

There was a clear need for a strong expansionary fiscal policy that—by stimulating the economy into a vigorous upswing—would lower unemployment and close the gap between actual and potential output. In response, the Kennedy and later the Johnson administration took certain steps during

---

* Currently ordinary rates of growth in national income automatically raise U.S. government tax receipts by roughly $10 billion a year.

the early 1960's which turned what had been an unintentionally restrictive fiscal policy into a consciously expansionary one.

To get down to cases: In 1962 the Kennedy administration issued new depreciation guidelines which permitted firms to write off (i.e., take depreciation allowances on) plant and equipment more rapidly. This postponed their profits-tax liabilities and thus increased the amount of internal funds available to them for financing current investment. The administration also proposed (and Congress passed) an act designed to stimulate investment by granting a tax credit to firms undertaking new investments.

These measures increased investment and thus aggregate demand. However, unemployment remained high, and in 1963 President Kennedy proposed a cut in federal tax rates. The resulting tax bill, passed in early 1964, produced an $11 billion cut in personal income taxes and a $3 billion cut in corporate profits taxes. This was followed in 1965 by enactment of a $4.6 billion reduction in excise taxes, to be carried out in several stages extending through 1969.

Much of the Kennedy–Johnson switch from a restrictive to an expansionary fiscal policy was carried out by means of tax reduction. However, the first half of the 1960's also saw a considerable rise in federal government expenditures on goods and services: These rose from $53.5 billion in 1960 to $66.8 billion in 1965 and to $77.0 billion in 1966.

Figure 38.4 shows the effect that this increasingly expansionary fiscal policy had on the economy: Between 1960 and 1966 the $50-billion output gap with which the economy entered the decade was closed, unemployment was lowered from more than 6% to less than 4%, 8 million new jobs were created, and real GNP (Gross National Product) rose by roughly one-third. And all this was accomplished with price increases that until 1966 were extremely modest.

In 1966 the economy finally achieved the elusive goal of full employment, and as it did the fiscal policy-maker found himself confronted with a new and in many ways more difficult problem. He had to design a policy that would simultaneously maintain the economy at full employment and prevent inflation; in other words, a policy that would simultaneously stimulate the economy just enough to keep it at full employment and *restrain* the economy just enough to prevent price rises.

This was hard to do because from fall 1966 through 1967 the economy gave off mixed signals: Some indicated weakness and possible recession; others indicated strength and continued inflationary pressures. Also the escalating war in Vietnam made unpredictable demands on the economy. So for the policy-maker the period was a difficult one in which to know what action to take. Finally in August 1967 President Johnson requested that a temporary surtax be placed on income taxes and corporate-profits taxes. Since prices rose 3.7% during 1966 and 2.2% during the first 8 months of 1967, this request seems in retrospect to have come months too late. Even

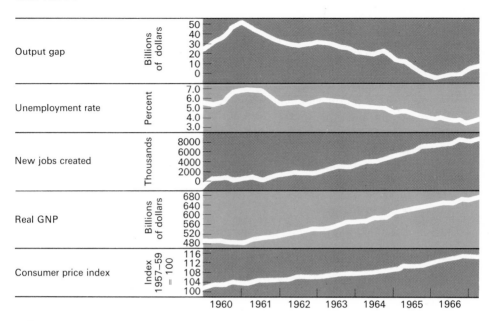

38|4

In the 1960's a bold expansionary fiscal policy closed the output gap, created 7 million jobs, erased excess unemployment, raised real GNP, and resulted in only mild price rises. (Source: U.S. Department of Commerce)

so, Congress greeted the proposed tax hike with scant enthusiasm. Lawmakers who were against the war or against government spending in general argued that the way to take pressure off an overheated economy (i.e., to bring down aggregate demand) was to lower G, not raise T. Others, who were willing to raise T, argued about how the burden of the new taxes should be split between consumers and corporations, between high- and low-income consumers, and between taxpayers who benefit from loopholes (i.e., tax exemptions that some people think are "unjustified") and those who don't. Finally Congress decided to temporarily shelve the president's request for a tax hike, despite the widely recognized need for one. This decision emphasizes a point made earlier in the chapter: If fiscal policy is to be an effective tool for ironing out short-run fluctuations in economic activity, some way has to be found to make it possible for policy-makers to act rapidly in response to changes in economic conditions.

THE NATIONAL DEBT

Whenever aggregate demand is deficient, a government which is trying to follow an active countercyclical fiscal policy should, as we have seen, cut taxes or increase its expenditures. Both these measures, however, will tend to unbalance its budget. So a government faced with insufficient aggregate demand is likely to run a deficit. This deficit will have to be covered by an increase in the national debt. Many people are firmly convinced that any increase in the national debt will inevitably lead to inflation, to the imposition of unfair burdens on future generations, or to some equally dire consequence. So the public views the prospect of an increase in the national debt with anything but equanimity. Because public opposition to debt increases is so deep-seated and so widespread, before we can advocate the use of an active stabilization policy we must answer the following question: Is a growing national debt a threat to, or burden on, an expanding economy?

Inflation and the Debt

Here are the major arguments that are usually voiced against the debt.

Argument 1: *Debt increases are invariably inflationary.*

Fortunately this proposition is invalid. So long as an economy is suffering from a deflationary gap, neither debt-financed government expenditures nor the debt increases associated with them can possibly be inflationary. Their effect will be to put unused resources to work, and perhaps to prevent price declines that would otherwise have occurred.

The public strongly associates debt increases with inflation even though debt-financed expenditures do not always imply inflation because, in the U.S. and in most other countries, the really *big* increases in the public debt have come about, not as a result of countercyclical stabilization policy, but as a result of wars. During a major war, aggregate demand is sure to be excessive, and therefore wartime is a time when an active stabilization policy would call for the government to at least balance its budget and perhaps to run a surplus. However, the level of taxes required to do so would be extremely unpopular and might even dull people's incentives to work. Therefore governments engaged in an all-out war effort invariably run large deficits, despite the fact that in doing so they are sowing the seeds of later inflation.

Servicing the Debt

Argument 2: *The taxes that would have to be levied to service* a growing debt might eventually become so large that they would themselves become a problem.*

There is a grain of truth in this argument, since, in a nondepressed economy, if inflation is to be prevented, interest payments on the debt have

---

* Service = pay interest on.

to be matched by taxes. And *if the debt grows more rapidly than national income,* these taxes might become large enough to dull people's incentives. ("Why should I work hard and earn a raise? I'll only have to give it all to the tax collector.") Or the growth of the debt might interfere with the government's ability to finance other useful projects. Also financing large interest payments by means of tax collections is likely to alter the distribution of income. Just how it would alter it, however, is hard to predict, since *taxes are paid* not only by individuals, but also by financial and nonfinancial businesses, and *government bonds are held* not only by individuals, but also by financial and nonfinancial businesses, government trust funds, and government agencies.

Should the fact that debt service might eventually become a problem keep the government from pursuing an active countercyclical policy during a prolonged depression? No. The apparent dilemma posed by such a situation could be solved simply: The government could finance its expenditures with non-interest-bearing IOU's instead of with interest-bearing ones; in other words, the government could finance its expenditures by printing new money instead of borrowing old money!* Such a course of action would not be inflationary, *so long as aggregate demand lagged behind the economy's ability to produce output.*

Shifting the Burden of the Debt

Argument 3: *Increases in the national debt are unfair because they shift onto future generations the burden of paying for the current generation's expenditures.*

When we evaluate this argument, we must distinguish between an *external* and an *internal* debt.

A country incurs an *external* debt by buying more goods and services from foreigners than it supplies to them. To pay off such a debt, it must in some future period supply more goods and services to foreigners than it buys from them. Therefore an external debt benefits the generation which incurs it by increasing the quantity of resources available to that generation, while it imposes a burden on the future generation that must give up some part of its income to repay this debt.†

---

* Since the Fed is forbidden to buy bonds *directly* from the Treasury, to say that the U.S. government was printing money would imply that the U.S. Treasury was selling bonds in the open market at the same time that the Fed was buying bonds there. Note that the money "printed" here would of course be *deposit* money.

† This observation does not imply that external debts are necessarily undesirable. For example, an underdeveloped country that borrows abroad to obtain the extra resources necessary to invest in capital projects such as roads, schools, or industrial facilities is increasing both its real wealth and its income-producing potential. Therefore the future generation which is required to pay back this debt may on balance benefit from it.

A country incurs an *internal* debt when the government borrows purchasing power from *domestic* spending units. This means that, whenever
the government finances current expenditures by an increase in its internal
debt, resources are transferred from the private to the public sector, but
nothing is added to the total quantity of resources available to the economy.
However, if this is the case, then whenever the government finances current
expenditures by an increase in its internal debt, the current generation pays
for these expenditures by foregoing current opportunities for private consumption and private investment.

Of course debt-financed government expenditures, even if they are in a
real sense "paid for" by the generation that makes them, do leave behind a
residue of increased private-sector claims against the public sector (i.e., of
outstanding government bonds). However, since the public sector can meet
these claims only by taxing the private sector, the private sector's claims
against the public sector in effect constitute claims against itself. Thus a
nation's internal debt is something it owes itself, and for this reason such a
debt cannot impose any net repayment burden on future generations. At
worst its existence might, as we have pointed out, alter the domestic income
distribution in the future.

The distinction between an external and an internal debt is an important one for fiscal policy. An expansionary fiscal policy can be financed by

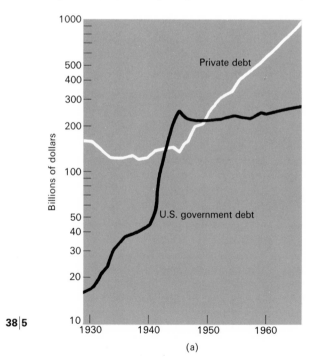

38|5

(a)

increases in *internal* (not external) debt, and for this reason the pursuit of such a policy, regardless of whether or not it led to increases in the national debt, imposes no burden on future generations.

The Positive Side of the Debt

Let us end our discussion of why a growing national debt is not as calamitous as the man in the street might think by noting that a large, slowly growing debt is likely to have some decidedly *beneficial* aspects. Here are the reasons:

(1) In the U.S. and in other countries in which the domestic money supply is created in part by monetizing public debt, the central bank and the commercial banks can increase the money supply to keep pace with the growth of the economy only if the government makes available to them an adequate supply of debt claims against itself.

(2) Government debt securities are riskless and homogeneous. Therefore the existence of a large national debt, such as we have in the U.S., does much to provide needed liquidity for all the financial and nonfinancial businesses that either cannot or would prefer not to maintain their liquidity by holding bank demand or time deposits.

(3) The government debt provides a safe instrument in which the unsophisticated and unwary investor can place his funds.

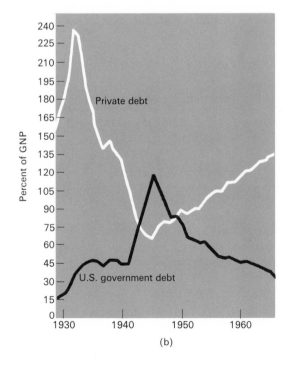

38|5

The U.S. government debt keeps growing, but measured against either private debt or GNP its importance has declined since the end of World War II. (Source: Department of Commerce)

(b)

The United States National Debt

To conclude our discussion of debt and fiscal policy, let's make a few brief comments on the U.S. national debt.

At the end of 1966 the net debt of the federal government and of federal agencies totaled $274.6 billion dollars, a figure so large that it is hard for an ordinary person, who measures his income and debt in thousands of dollars, to comprehend! This figure taken alone would seem to indicate that the government is encumbered by an enormous debt. If we compare the debt with the GNP, however, we find that the government debt equals less than 50% of national income (see Fig. 38.5). Viewed in this perspective, the debt's proportions appear much less awesome. Another way to gain some perspective on the size of the federal debt is to compare it with total private debt. Viewed in these terms, the national debt appears almost diminutive.

Although the U.S. national debt may be quite reasonable in size, there is no denying that it has grown constantly over the last 30 years. Nevertheless its growth rate has been so sluggish since the end of the war that its importance relative to both total GNP and total private debt has steadily declined (see Fig. 38.5).

Most of the U.S. debt was created during wars or periods of prosperity when the government was unable or unwilling to levy enough taxes to cover its expenditures. Therefore we can in no sense view the U.S. debt as a by-product of countercyclical fiscal policy. Also, since almost all the U.S. debt is internally held,* it is a debt that we owe ourselves, and its existence therefore imposes no repayment burden on future generations.

PROBLEMS

1   "A government committed to a full-employment fiscal policy should never levy taxes just because it needs money; it should levy taxes only when it wants to curb aggregate spending, and then it should levy them regardless of whether or not it needs money." Discuss.

2   Transfer payments (Social Security benefits, veterans' pensions, etc.) are usually intended to alter the distribution of income in favor of lower-income groups. We saw in Chapter 3, however, that low-income groups tend to spend a higher percentage of their incomes than do high-income groups. With this in mind, suppose that an increase in transfer payments is exactly matched by an increase in taxes on all consumers, so that total disposable income remains unchanged. Would you expect any change in the economy's equilibrium income to result? If so, what would be the direction of the change?

---

* Currently only about $15 billion of U.S. government debt is held by foreign central banks and other foreign spending units.

3   At the beginning of his presidency, Franklin D. Roosevelt declared:

     Revenue must cover expenditures by one means or another. Any government,
     like any family, can for one year spend a little more than it earns. But you
     and I know that a continuation of that habit means the poorhouse.

     Comment. So far as the government is concerned, what would you take the
     term "poorhouse" to mean in this context?

4   It's often suggested that the government should react to a recession by spend-
     ing more rather than by taxing less. Reason: "Recessions are a good time
     for the government to catch up on needed investments." Comment on this
     statement. What does it imply about how the speaker views the "normal"
     divisions of aggregate investment between the public and private sectors?
     Would you agree?

5   In the text we talked just about the federal government pursuing an active
     fiscal policy. Would it be realistic to expect state and local governments to
     carry out an active full-employment fiscal policy? Can you think of any diffi-
     culties they might face that would not be fully shared by the federal govern-
     ment?

6   a) As we noted in the text, changes in government spending don't provide
        the fiscal policy-maker with a very flexible tool because it's hard to change
        spending on roads, post offices, and other capital projects rapidly. How-
        ever, the government does not spend just on public works. It also makes
        transfer payments, and it could presumably alter the rates at which it makes
        such payments just as rapidly as it alters tax rates. Do you think changes
        in transfer payments would make a good anticyclical device?

     b) If the government increased welfare benefits and pensions during an eco-
        nomic downswing, it would presumably have a hard time cutting them back
        later when the economy got into an upswing. However, there's another way
        the government could increase transfer payments that would not be so hard
        to reverse: It could simply print up a lot of money and pass out X dollars
        per head. Contrast the feasibility of this approach with that of a tax cut.
        Would it be as effective in stimulating economic activity? Would it be as
        fair?

7   "Automatic stabilizers cannot completely stabilize economic activity because
     their effect at best is to pare down the multiplier associated with an automatic
     change in spending." Discuss.

8   a) The imposition of any tax will cause the $C + I$ line in Fig. 38.1 to shift
        downward. However, the nature of this shift depends on the nature of the
        tax. Show that the more progressive the tax, the flatter the after-tax $C + I$
        line is likely to be.

     b) Show that, the flatter the $C + I$ line, the less the change in equilibrium out-
        put induced by a shift in, say, autonomous investment.

     c) Contrast the effectiveness of a progressive income tax with that of a pro-
        portional tax as an automatic stabilizer.

9 A policy which has been followed in some countries at various times has consisted roughly in accepting the autonomous fluctuations that occur in T over time, while keeping a balanced budget by varying G. Theory suggests that such a policy would be *destabilizing*. Can you explain why? [*Hint:* In theory which should be bigger, the multiplier associated with a change in T or one associated with an equivalent change in G?]

10 a) In testifying before the Joint Economic Committee, a representative of the American Bankers' Association (ABA) said:

> Our Federal budget has now become mammoth and threatens to continue to grow at a rapid rate. . . . Even when it is in balance, a budget the size of ours has a net inflationary impact on the economy. . . .

Would you agree with this statement? [*Hint:* Does *expansionary* necessarily = *inflationary?*]

b) Contrast the ABA statement with the following AFL-CIO position:

> The government sector . . . directly accounts for only a small part of total economic activities. . . . The policy of attempting to balance the Federal budget at all costs should be halted.

Who do you think is right? (Both statements are taken from "Employment, Growth, and Price Levels," Hearings Before the Joint Economic Committee, 86th Congress, Washington, 1959.)

11 Use the relationships embodied in the national income and product account to show that whenever a country incurs an external debt it adds to the quantity of resources available to it. Also show that whenever a country pays back an external debt it decreases the quantity of resources available to it.

CHAPTER 39

MONETARY POLICY

As we shall see in this chapter, the Fed, by using the various instruments at its disposal (the purchase and sale of government securities, changes in the reserve requirements of member banks, and changes in the discount rate), can alter the cost and availability of credit. And this in turn alters both aggregate consumption and aggregate investment. Thus the government can pursue the goals of full employment and price stability not only by changing its tax and expenditure policies, but also by consciously regulating, through central-bank action, the cost and availability of credit. This second means of maintaining full employment is known as *monetary policy*.

We could talk, in this chapter, about monetary policy from a general point of view, with only occasional references to the U.S. scene. However, each nation's central bank has its own individual set of powers and prerogatives and each nation's financial markets have their own distinctive arrangements. Therefore a general approach would narrow the scope of our discussion and afford us little opportunity to point to specific illustrations. For this reason we shall focus on the operations of U.S. monetary policy within the context of current U.S. financial and monetary institutions. However, bear in mind that, while the details may apply specifically to the U.S., the principles that underlie our discussion are of general validity.

A RESTRICTIVE MONETARY POLICY

A monetary policy that is designed to *stimulate* aggregate demand is referred to as *expansionary*. One that is designed to *curtail* aggregate demand is referred to as *restrictive*. Let us begin by looking at the way a restrictive monetary policy operates.

Suppose that consumers' demands for goods and services were booming and that there was a boom in business investment too. Figure 39.1 shows what would result: an inflationary gap. Let's say that the Fed responds to this gap by instituting a restrictive monetary policy. It might do this by

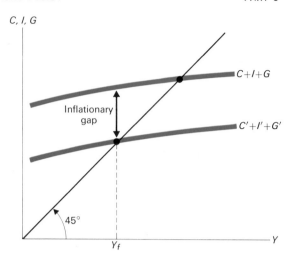

39|1

In the face of an inflationary gap, the task of monetary policy is to lower aggregate demand from $C + I + G$ to $C' + I' + G'$.

selling government securities in the open market, by raising the reserve requirements of member banks, or both. To reinforce and dramatize these measures, the Fed might also up the discount rate.

The Fed's purpose in instituting a restrictive monetary policy is to lower aggregate consumption and aggregate investment by increasing the cost and decreasing the availability of bank loans and also of other forms of credit. Will this policy do the trick? If so, how? To answer these questions, we must follow the whole chain of actions and reactions that the Fed's measures will set in motion, and see what sorts of responses the banks will make to the Fed's actions, how these bank responses will tighten conditions in nonbank sectors of the credit market, and whether or not a general tightening of the credit market will really put the lid on aggregate spending.

BANK RESPONSES TO A RESTRICTIVE MONETARY POLICY

Let us assume that the Fed institutes its restrictive monetary policy by selling government securities in the open market. We recall from Chapter 29 that whenever the Fed does this, the reserves of member banks fall, by the full amount of the securities sold if the banks themselves buy these securities, and by a smaller amount if bank depositors buy them. Thus the initial impact on the banks of the Fed's open-market sales is to lower the banks' excess reserves, or to create reserve deficiencies.

Initial Bank Responses to the Fed's Policy

This upsets the equilibrium of the banks, and to regain it they have to make offsetting changes in their assets, their liabilities, or both. The banks *could* adjust to this decline in their reserves by lowering their total loans to private borrowers, but they aren't likely to do so, because the same in conditions that lead the Fed to institute a restrictive monetary p create a heavy demand for bank loans. Banks, after all, are priv making institutions, and customer loans are a prime source of th So naturally they want to make as many loans as possible. Therefore, as far as possible, banks try to regain equilibrium by adjusting other items on their balance sheets.

1) *Lowering excess reserves.* Excess reserves provide a certain flexibility, especially for banks that aren't active participants in the money market. Thus there are incentives, particularly for small out-of-town banks, to maintain some excess reserves. However, when the demand for bank loans is high relative to the supply of loanable funds available to the banks, the *opportunity cost* incurred by banks that hold excess reserves will rise. And, because of this change, some banks whose excess reserves are decreased by the Fed's action may decide to adjust to this change simply by accepting it.

2) *Borrowing at the discount window.* The Fed's open-market sales force some banks into reserve deficiencies, and of course these banks can't adjust as simply as this; they have to find some means to cover these deficiencies. One way out is to borrow at the Fed's discount window, although generally banks are reluctant to borrow heavily at the discount window because of the Fed's disapproval of continuous and large-scale borrowing there. But, if the Fed, by lowering bank reserves, forces the banks to choose between increased discounts and decreased loans, banks just go ahead and increase their discounts, even though they risk possible Fed disapproval.

3) *Selling off bonds.* Another way banks try to adjust to a decline in their reserves is by selling off some of the Treasury bills and other government securities which they normally hold as secondary reserves. An individual bank can always obtain additional reserves by selling off bonds. But can the banking system *as a whole* do so? In other words, can the banking system add to its total reserves by liquidating its bond holdings? From our discussion in Chapter 29, it's obvious that the answer is *no,* so long as the Fed refuses (as we would expect it to) to buy up any of the bonds proffered by the banks.*

This doesn't mean that there's no way for banks as a group to use bond sales to sustain and perhaps even increase their loans to private borrowers in

---

* This assertion depends on the assumption that investors don't pay for the bonds they buy from the banks with *cash* (i.e., outside money); in other words, it assumes that people won't respond to higher interest rates by depositing some of the cash they hold in the banks. So far as the U.S. is concerned, this assumption is a reasonable one because people hold cash mainly for making transactions, not as a store of value that competes with other financial assets (including government bonds) that they might hold.

the face of a restrictive Fed policy. On the contrary. Banks that have more people wanting to borrow than they have funds available to loan out may sell off bonds to banks that have an inadequate demand for loans. If they do, the resulting shift in the ownership of total bank reserves may just be enough to enable the banks to keep on making loans to private borrowers at the same level as before. Another thing: If banks sell off bonds *to their depositors,* the deposit liabilities of the banking system as a whole will decrease by the amount of these sales, and hence the total amount of reserves that the banks are required to hold will fall. But the total amount of reserves held by the banks *as a group* won't be affected.

4) *Seeking new deposits.* Banks also try to adjust to the fall in their reserves by actively seeking new deposits. They do this by decreasing their service charge on demand deposits (that means checking accounts, remember?), by increasing their rate of interest on time deposits (that means savings accounts, remember?), or by offering special negotiable certificates of deposit designed to appeal to large savers and corporate depositors.

An individual bank can always increase its deposits and thus its reserves by "sweetening" the deposit securities it offers. But can the banking system *as a whole* do so? Our discussion in Chapter 29 tells us that the answer is no, because the only way the reserves of the banking system as a whole can be increased is by the Fed acquiring additional securities.* However, banks, by increasing their interest rates on time deposits, may succeed in shifting the composition of bank deposits away from demand deposits toward time deposits. If they do, their reserve position will improve, because the reserves that banks are required to hold against time deposits are only about one-third as large as the reserves that they are required to hold against demand deposits.

Bank Responses to a Continuing Restrictive Monetary Policy

The above four means, then, constitute banks' initial responses to a reduction in their aggregate reserves. It is evident that the banks may be able to adjust to the Fed's open-market sales without decreasing the size of their loan portfolios.

Thus on the first round at least, the commercial banks may frustrate the Fed's attempt to increase the cost and decrease the availability of bank loans. Does the Fed give up? No. It continues to exert pressure on the banks by selling more securities and perhaps by raising the reserve requirements of member banks or by hiking the discount rate. If the Fed perseveres long enough, it will eventually succeed in forcing the banks to decrease their lending activities.

---

* Here again we are assuming that the quantity of cash people hold doesn't depend on the rate of return they can obtain on other financial assets, including bank deposits.

Why? Well, there are definite upper limits on the extent to which the banks can pursue each of the above forms of adjustment. Here are four stone walls the banks run into when they are trying to adjust their reserves as described above:

1) The quantity of excess reserves the banks hold at the time that the Fed initiates its restrictive monetary policy sets an upper limit on the quantity of excess reserves that the banks can lose.
2) The Fed's disinclination to extend loans sets an upper limit on the quantity of funds the banks can borrow at the discount window.
3) People—and business firms as well—need to keep a fair balance of money on hand (in demand-deposit accounts) to make business transactions with, and this sets an upper limit on the shift that the banks can induce away from demand deposits toward time deposits.
4) The more bonds the banks sell off in their search for liquidity, the less attractive this method of adjustment becomes, because when banks try to sell off their holdings of government bonds, this increases the supply of them offered in the open market (i.e., it shifts the supply curve of government bonds to the right), and as a result the prices they fetch will fall. The more bonds the commercial banks sell, the lower bond prices fall and the larger the *capital losses* the banks would incur if they were to sell off still more. At some point the banks begin to feel *"locked into"* their bond holdings; they become unwilling to make further trades of bonds for liquid funds at the prevailing low prices.

After this happens, and after the banks have exhausted all other means of adjustment, the restrictive monetary policy forces them to curtail their loans to customers. The most direct way they do this is by increasing the rate of interest they charge on loans. Banks, though, don't rely solely on this device to hold would-be borrowers at bay. Every bank fears that, if it were to sharply increase its loan rates whenever money was temporarily tight, it would damage its relationship with customers, and thus lose valuable deposit and loan business in the future. So when money turns tight, banks often resort to nonprice means to ration out their limited supply of loanable funds. They may: (a) request that business borrowers pare down their loan requests, (b) refuse loans to new customers, (c) stiffen the credit standards applied to borrowers, and (d) terminate lines of credit to certain less-favored borrowers, such as finance companies, who are always asking banks for loans but never give them large deposits.

Bank Responses to the Fed's 1963–1966 Tightening of Credit

Lest you think that our discussion of bank responses to a restrictive monetary policy has been just hypothetical or theoretical, let's pause right here and look at a few figures.

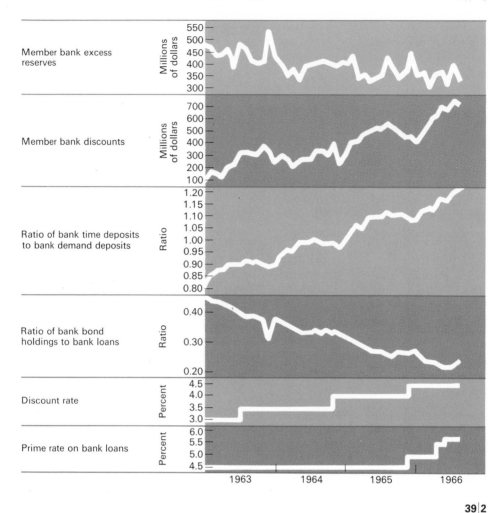

39|2

Commercial bank responses to the Fed's gradual tightening of credit during the period 1963–1966.
(Source: *Federal Reserve Bulletin*)

During the period 1963–1966, the Fed gradually moved from an expansionary to a restrictive monetary policy. Initially it did this because it was concerned over the deteriorating state of the U.S. balance of payments. Later it did so because it was concerned over the danger of domestic inflation. The Fed's policy reached its most restrictive point during 1966 when (as we said in Chapter 38) fiscal policy was probably not restrictive enough. In the fall of 1966, the boom in business investment finally appeared to have been broken, and Fed policy became less restrictive.

Throughout this period 1963–1966, the Fed put pressure on the banks by creating new bank reserves at a rate slower than the rate at which the demand for bank loans was increasing. Figure 39.2 shows that the banks responded to this gradually increasing pressure pretty much the way our observations above would have predicted: As a group they sharply decreased their excess reserves and increased their discounts. Individual banks, trying to attract new deposits, upped the rates they paid on time deposits. As a result the ratio of time deposits to demand deposits rose significantly. Banks sold off bonds to get money to make more loans to customers, and the result was that the ratio of their bond-holding to their outstanding loans declined sharply. Toward the end of the period (and only after the Fed had made several increases in the discount rate) the banks increased the interest rate they charged on loans to prime bank customers.

IMPACT OF A RESTRICTIVE MONETARY POLICY ON OTHER SECTORS OF THE CREDIT MARKET

As we have seen, if the Fed adheres to a restrictive monetary policy long enough and hard enough, it can eventually bring about a significant increase in the cost of—and decrease in the availability of—bank loans. The impact of the Fed's actions is not, however, limited to the market for bank loans. All the banks' varied responses to the Fed's policy in the long run transmit the restrictive effect of the Fed's actions to other sectors of the credit market.

The final effect of the Fed's actions is to tighten not only the market for bank loans, but all other sectors of the credit market as well.

To show just *how* the restrictive effect of the Fed's actions is transmitted to the rest of the credit market, we shall consider three bank responses—the sell-off of bank-held securities, the raising of bank deposit rates, and the raising of bank loan rates—and see how these three moves affect the cost and availability of funds in other parts of the credit market.

1) *The sell-off of bank-held securities.* When banks try to sell off their Treasury bills and longer-term government bonds, this forces a general *fall* in the price and *rise* in the yield of these securities.* Accordingly the yields on corporate short- and long-term debt securities are also forced upward, since investors are willing to buy corporate debt securities only if the yields on them exceed the yields on government bonds by a margin wide enough to compensate for their extra riskiness. Thus when banks sell off govern-

---

* The rate a bond *yields* equals the *fixed* amount of interest the bond pays each year as a percent of the bond's current market price. Example: A $1,000 bond which bears a 5% coupon and which is currently selling for $900 yields $50/$900 or 5.5%. Since a bond's market price is *variable,* so too is its yield.

ment securities, this exerts an upward pressure not only on the yield of government securities, but also on the yields of *all* corporate debt securities, from commercial paper to long-term bonds.*

2) *Increases in bank time deposit rates.* When banks raise the rates they pay on time deposits, and especially when they design special securities to appeal to large-scale investors, they draw funds away from the markets for Treasury bills, commercial paper, and other money-market instruments. Accordingly the availability of loanable funds in these markets decreases, and an *upward* pressure is exerted on yields throughout the money market.

Increases in bank time deposit rates also tend to draw funds out of competing financial institutions, such as mutual savings banks and savings and loan associations. These competing institutions naturally try to match any increase that the commercial banks make in the rates they pay on time deposits. As mutual savings banks and savings and loan associations raise the deposit rates they pay, they also have to make comparable raises in the interest rates they charge on loans.

3) *Increases in the cost and decreases in the availability of bank loans.* If the Fed pursues its restrictive monetary policy far enough to force banks to increase the cost and lessen the availability of bank loans, many would-be borrowers turn to competing financial institutions or to other segments of the credit market. As they do so, the pressure for rate rises in these other sectors of the credit market will be intensified. Here are some examples.

First: People who can't get personal or mortgage loans from commercial banks turn to savings and loan associations, mutual savings banks, or even personal finance companies in their search for funds. This means that the loan demand faced by these institutions will rise, and they will be forced to ration out their loanable funds either by charging higher rates on their loans or by restricting the availability of such loans.

Second: Big nonfinancial business firms, and consumer finance companies too, respond to a rise in the cost and a decrease in the availability of bank loans by increasing their borrowing in the commercial paper market. Accordingly the supply of paper offered in this market increases, and so does the rate yielded by such paper. Business borrowers may also respond to a tightening of the bank credit market by substituting bond issues for long-term bank loans, and this puts additional upward pressure on corporate bond yields.

Third: Most life insurance policies grant the policyholder the right to borrow from the insurance company against the *cash value* of his policy. The rates charged on such loans are *fixed rates,* stipulated in the policy.

---

* If this point is unclear to you, reread the end of Chapter 31, where we discussed the way money-market rates are determined and the way the rates yielded by different money-market instruments are interrelated.

Therefore, when money is tight, these rates usually compare favorably with bank and market rates. For this reason, when the cost of bank credit goes up, a lot of people who need money and who hold life insurance policies take out loans against their policies. To the extent that this occurs, there is a cash drain on insurance companies. If the drain is prolonged, the insurance companies . . . Well, you couldn't say that they run out of money (they never do that); let's just say that they can't maintain their normal pace of investment in mortgages, industrial bonds, and other capital market instruments. As a result an upward pressure is created on the rates of return yielded by these instruments.

Fourth: An increase in bank loan rates leads to an immediate rise in the rates charged by secondary intermediaries, who get their money in part by borrowing from banks. For example, a rise in the rate at which banks lend to brokers means that the rates that brokers charge customers who buy stock on the margin rise equivalently. Similarly, a rise in the rate at which banks lend to consumer finance companies means that the rates these companies charge rise equivalently, provided of course that they aren't already at the legal ceilings.

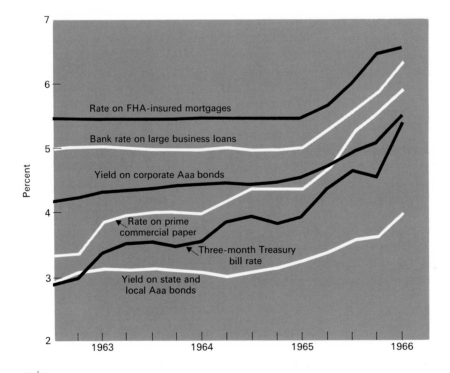

39|3

During the period 1963–1966, when monetary policy turned increasingly restrictive, interest rates rose throughout the credit market. (Source: *Federal Reserve Bulletin*)

The Impact of a Restrictive Monetary Policy on Credit-Market Rates

The observations we have just made all indicate that a restrictive monetary policy not only tightens the market for bank loans, but all other sectors of the credit market as well. Figure 39.3 confirms this conclusion by showing that during the period 1963–1966 the Fed's increasingly restrictive monetary policy raised interest rates not only on bank loans, but throughout the entire credit market.

IMPACT OF A RESTRICTIVE MONETARY POLICY ON INVESTMENT AND CONSUMPTION

If you remember back as far as page 604—and you probably do if you've got this far—you'll recall that the *real* purpose of a restrictive monetary policy is *not* to tighten credit, but to lower aggregate demand. Whether or not a restrictive monetary policy succeeds in doing this depends on how sensitive investment and consumption are to changes in the cost and availability of credit.

Business Investment

Economists have long debated the question of whether or not business investment is sensitive to (i.e., *elastic* with respect to) changes in the interest rate. Naturally no one questions the fact that, *if* changes in the interest rate *do* affect investment, then increases in the interest rate reduce it, while decreases in the interest rate raise it. What many people *do* question is whether or not changes in the general level of interest rates exert a strong influence on the level of investment.*

In an attempt to answer this question, economists have made various statistical studies, usually in the form of questionnaires. In general the studies indicate that the interest elasticity of investment is *low*, but we can't really be sure of this, because most of these studies have built-in biases or other defects which limit their usefulness as a basis for valid generalizations.

Economic theory, however, gives us a clue as to the probable interest elasticity of investment. In Chapter 9 we noted that the smaller the proportion of total costs a given input represents, the lower the elasticity of a firm's demand for that input. Therefore the elasticity of a firm's demand for investment goods (i.e., for input capital) will be lower the smaller the cost of this input relative to the cost of the other inputs the firm uses. The relationship between the cost of the firm's capital inputs and the cost of its other inputs depends in part on the durability of its investment goods. If a firm

---

* In other words, everyone recognizes the fact that the investment demand schedule, like the one in Fig. 10.2, will slope downward. The question is whether this curve will be highly elastic or almost vertical.

uses short-lived investment goods, the interest costs associated with financing this equipment will be small relative to the other costs it incurs, and the interest elasticity of its investments will presumably be small. Real-life firms, as we saw in Chapter 11, operate in an uncertain world, in which even near-term returns are difficult to predict. And for this reason, when firms are evaluating the future profitability of prospective investments, many of them do so on the basis of arbitrarily short pay-off periods. The use of an extremely short pay-off period is, however, equivalent to viewing all investment goods as short-lived. So the widespread use of short pay-off periods suggests that the interest elasticity of business investment as a whole is probably low.

But this doesn't mean that tight conditions in the credit market have little or no impact on the investment expenditures of business firms. After all, a business firm can't finance current investment expenditures with borrowed funds unless it can find a willing lender. And as we pointed out above, whenever money is tight, banks and other lenders may resort to refusing loans and other nonprice means to ration out their limited supplies of loanable funds. Therefore, during periods of tight money, at least some businesses will probably have to call off or postpone investment projects because they can't get money to finance them.

Credit rationing does affect all classes of would-be borrowers to some degree, but certain classes of borrowers are more successful than others in devising ways to get around it. For example, large firms (provided that they are willing to pay high interest charges) can maintain their investment spending in the face of credit rationing by selling additional commercial paper and by floating new bond issues. Small firms which cannot obtain funds by selling their debt obligations in the open market may be able to negotiate broader and/or longer credit terms from their suppliers, and in this way soften the impact of credit rationing on their operations.

There isn't any conclusive answer to the question of how sensitive business investment is to tight money. We can only say that a tight money policy probably exerts an important—but not a crucial—restraining influence on business investment.

Government Investment

Although investment by the business sector runs into the billions every year, this represents only a part of total national investment. Another important part is represented by the roads, schools, dams, and other productive facilities built by federal, state, and local governments.

Investment expenditures made by the *federal* government aren't likely to be sensitive to changes in the cost of borrowed capital because the federal government doesn't use current market rates of interest when it matches the cost of a proposed capital project against its potential benefits.*   The investment decisions of state and local governments, on the other hand, may display a good deal of interest elasticity, because (a) these governments have to worry about the effect that high interest payments will have on the tax rates they must impose, and (b) statutory limits are sometimes imposed on the interest rates that state and local governments are allowed to pay on their debt obligations.

Consumer Spending

You would think that a tight money policy would strongly affect the expenditures of Mr. John Q. Public. In theory at least, an increase in interest rates ought to reduce consumer spending in *two* ways: It ought to encourage some consumers to borrow less and others to save more. Studies indicate, however, that the current savings and short-term borrowings of consumers are actually insensitive to interest-rate changes of the magnitude induced by shifts in monetary policy.

The fact that changes in the interest rate don't affect consumer saving isn't surprising. It shows that the reason why people save is not just to earn interest, but (remember what we said in Chapter 3?) to protect themselves against unforeseeable contingencies and to satisfy foreseeable future needs.

The fact that changes in the interest rate don't affect consumer short-term borrowing probably reflects two things: (1) Finance charges on short-term loans are often so expressed that John Q. Public finds it hard to figure out just *what* interest rate he is paying. (2) A lot of short-term consumer debt is used to finance the purchase of consumer durables; and we all know that consumer durables (belying their name) tend to be short-lived. So people's demand for money to finance the purchase of durable goods—like business firms' demand for funds to finance the purchase of short-lived capital goods—is relatively interest inelastic.

This interest inelasticity doesn't mean that people's spending is totally unaffected by tight money. Like business firms, consumers—when they try to borrow while money is tight—find that institutional lenders have sharpened credit standards, shortened loan maturities, and instituted a number of other credit-rationing devices. Because of such devices, consumers as a group can't borrow as much as they'd like to; as a result they have to curtail their intended purchases of durable *and* nondurable goods.

Also, when money is tight, people who try to get long-term mortgage loans encounter credit rationing that is, if anything, even stiffer than that

---

* During a period in which the Fed was imposing a restrictive *monetary* policy designed to curb aggregate demand, the federal government might of course decide—as part of a restrictive *fiscal* policy—to make discretionary cuts or postponements in its investment expenditures.

encountered by people seeking short-term loans, because, during periods of credit restraint, a number of factors work together to lessen the availability of mortgage financing. These factors include: (1) The ceilings imposed by regulatory authorities on the interest rates that savings institutions may pay to their depositors. (2) The ceiling imposed by law in some areas on the rates that savings banks may charge on mortgage loans. (3) The rate limits imposed on mortgages insured by the Veterans' Administration and the Federal Housing Administration. Therefore a restrictive monetary policy hits residential construction earlier, harder, and longer than it hits any other segment of aggregate spending.

Summary

Now that we've talked about the interest elasticity of business, government, and consumer spending, let's get back to our original problem: the efficacy of a restrictive monetary policy in curbing aggregate demand. All things considered, it would seem that the interest rate increases induced by a restrictive monetary policy are unlikely *per se* to really restrain aggregate spending very much. On the other hand, the credit rationing induced by a restrictive monetary policy does eventually curb aggregate spending markedly. The disadvantage of credit rationing is that it affects some classes of spending units more than others and some types of spending more than others: It has little impact on the investment spending of large corporations, which can always obtain funds by selling their own debt securities in the open market, but considerable impact on the investment spending of small firms and consumers, who can obtain debt capital only by borrowing from banks and other institutional lenders.

PROBLEMS OF IMPLEMENTATION

We have seen that a restrictive monetary policy, applied with sufficient vigor and persistence, eventually tightens conditions throughout the credit market and thereby curbs the aggregate expenditures of both consumers and investors. Nevertheless, the implementation of such a policy poses problems.

The most sophisticated predictions that economic forecasters can come up with are at best well-informed guesses, and economic trends are subject to sharp and unpredictable fluctuations. Therefore the monetary policy-maker—like the fiscal policy-maker—has to make difficult choices with respect to the *timing* and *size* of the measures he undertakes. These are crucial choices, because if the policy-maker waits too long to act, he may permit a nascent inflation or recession to gain momentum. If he acts too soon, he may add destabilizing stimuli to the economy. If he takes actions that are too weak, he will fail to counter the inflationary or deflationary trends he has set out to eliminate. If he takes actions that are too strong, he may bring about a destabilizing shift in the direction of economic activity.

Because it's always possible that the policy-maker's decisions with respect to when and how much will, as events unfold, prove to have been incorrect, and since there may always be sudden shifts in economic trends, the monetary policy-maker—like the fiscal policy-maker—must have *flexible* instruments at his disposal. The principal tools of the monetary policy-maker are: (a) open market operations, (b) changes in the discount rate, and (c) changes in the reserve requirements of member banks. On the count of flexibility, these tools ring up a mixed score. On the plus side is the fact that they can be trotted out in a hurry and just as rapidly reversed, at the discretion of the central bank. On the minus side is the fact that there's usually a lag between the time these tools are put to work and the time at which they significantly alter conditions in the credit market. Just how long this lag is depends on the initial liquidity of the economy, especially on the quantity of the banks' excess reserves and on the size of the inactive deposit balances which the public has and is willing to trade for government and other primary securities.

Other Limitations

There's no question that a restrictive monetary policy can eventually be made to work. But there are definite limits to the *size* of the adjustments it can successfully and smoothly effect. There are four main reasons for this.

First: If the Fed's tightening of credit-market conditions is overly vigorous, investors will anticipate continued increases in interest rates, and this may create a situation in which the flow of loanable funds to the credit market dries up, debt securities cannot be sold, and the credit market practically ceases to function.

Second: A vigorous restrictive monetary policy, by dramatically and swiftly raising interest rates, may threaten the solvency of savings banks and savings and loan associations. These institutions—given the *long-term* nature of their earnings assets—aren't in as good a position as the commercial banks are to rapidly "capture" interest-rate increases. Nevertheless they must—given the *short-term* nature of their deposit liabilities—pay deposit rates that are competitive with those paid by the commercial banks on time deposits.

Third: Because monetary policy has an uneven effect on different types of spending, an overly vigorous monetary policy will bring certain types of spending, such as spending for home construction, to a near halt.

Fourth: A sharply restrictive monetary policy may irreversibly alter the expectations of borrowers and lenders, and may thus create temporarily irreversible changes in credit-market conditions. A policy that leads to a dramatic rise in interest rates may so alter expectations that even after this policy has been abandoned in favor of a more expansionary one, lenders remain unwilling to make long-term loans because they fear that interest rates will soon rise again, while borrowers seek to borrow long-term funds that they do not need immediately because they think that such funds will cost more tomorrow than today.

The above four dangers of a restrictive monetary policy that attempts to accomplish "too much" are far from theoretical. Each of them came true to some degree during the late summer and fall of 1966 when the Fed pursued an exceptionally restrictive monetary policy that (a) brought the capital market to the brink of crisis, (b) caused a dramatic decline in home construction, (c) so threatened the solvency of some intermediaries that the government felt compelled to impose ceilings on the deposit rates that commercial banks and competing savings institutions could pay, and (d) left banks reluctant to grant long-term loans and borrowers scrambling for long-term funds months after the restrictive character of the Fed's policy had clearly been replaced by a more expansionary one.

AN EXPANSIONARY MONETARY POLICY

A restrictive monetary policy is used to overcome an inflationary gap, an *expansionary* monetary policy to overcome a *deflationary* gap.

Suppose that, as a result of a downward shift either in consumer demand for goods and services or in business demand for investment goods, a deflationary gap like that in Fig. 39.4 emerges. The Fed's job would then be to institute an expansionary monetary policy that would *ease* conditions throughout the credit market, and thus induce an *upward* shift in aggregate demand.

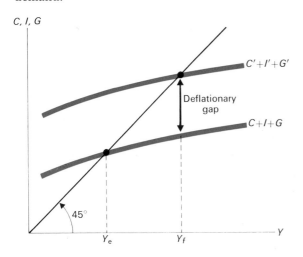

39|4

In the face of a deflationary gap, the Fed's job is to raise aggregate demand from $C + I + G$ to $C' + I' + G'$.

The Fed would start the ball rolling by buying government securities in the open market, lowering the reserve requirements of member banks, or both. In addition it would probably lower the discount rate and perhaps adopt a more liberal attitude toward member bank borrowing.

The banks, profit-maximizers that they are, would respond to the resulting changes in the conditions under which they operate by (1) lowering the rates they charge on bank loans, (2) increasing the availability of loans, and (3) lowering the rates they pay on savings accounts. In addition, since a decrease in their reserve requirements would increase their free reserves, the banks might (4) replenish their holdings of government and corporate securities.

Just as the impact of a restrictive monetary policy is not confined to the market for bank loans, the impact of an expansionary monetary policy isn't either. The above four responses that banks would make to an expansionary monetary policy would work together to ease the conditions under which other institutional lenders operate and to lower interest rates throughout the credit market.

Whether or not a general decrease in the cost, and increase in the availability, of credit will bring about the desired increase in aggregate demand depends on the responses that consumers and investors make to these changes. When we were talking about the probable impact of a restrictive monetary policy on aggregate spending, we noted that the interest elasticity of most types of spending is low, but that the credit rationing eventually brought on by such a policy might significantly curtail aggregate spending. So if an expansionary monetary policy permits a relaxation of the credit rationing induced by a prior restrictive monetary policy, it may stimulate aggregate spending quite a bit. On the other hand, since the lowering of interest rates that results from an expansionary monetary policy does little, by itself, to stimulate either consumption or investment spending, an expansionary monetary policy is less effective than an expansionary fiscal policy as an instrument for dealing with the problems posed by a severe or persistent deflationary gap.

PROBLEMS

1   Suppose that a bank reacts to a decrease in its excess reserves (as we suggested on page 605 that it might) by just accepting this decrease. What can you say about the bank's equilibrium position *before* its reserves were cut?

2   Trace what happens when a bank sells bonds to bank depositors. Show that:
    a) The reserves held by the banking system as a whole will not change.
    b) The deposit liabilities of the banking system will fall by the amount of the sale.

c) The banking system as a whole will be in a position to extend new loans equal in amount to the market value of the bonds sold.

3   Will a rise in the discount rate *per se* do anything to tighten credit? (Does your answer depend in any way on the relationship between the level of the discount rate and that of other short-term rates?)

4   Trace in detail the way an increase in the reserve requirements of member banks would work to tighten credit. Are there any significant differences between the impact that such a policy would have and the impact that open-market sales would have?

5   The *"net free reserves"* of member banks equal their total excess reserves *minus* their borrowing at the Fed. Some students of monetary policy say that, when you want to find out how tight money is, you should look at the size of "net free reserves." The bigger the *negative* figure you see there, the tighter money is. Others, however, observe that the banks borrow from the Fed to finance new loans, which in turn create new money. So a big negative net reserve figure doesn't indicate that money is tight; it just shows that the banks can make money by borrowing from the Fed and lending it out to others. These monetary mavericks claim that the thing to look at is the rate at which the money supply (usually taken to be cash plus demand deposits) is growing. If the growth of the money supply has been significantly slowed, then money is tight. Which point of view do you think is right? Or do you think both might have their virtues, depending on the situation?

6   Why do you think that the stock market often reacts to a rise in the discount rate by taking a fall? [*Hint:* How is tight money likely to affect the rate of growth of business activity and that of corporate profits?]

7   Banks usually advertise to attract customers for loans. But in the late summer and fall of 1966, when money was extraordinarily tight, many banks stopped such advertising almost completely. What does this tell you about the competitive character of the market for bank loans? About how banks go about rationing out credit?

8   William McChesney Martin, Jr., Chairman of the Board of Governors of the Federal Reserve System and a rather controversial figure on the Washington scene, often describes the Fed's job as "leaning against the [economic] wind." Does this phrase aptly describe what monetary policy can do? Discuss.

9   Suppose that the economy falls into a slump. To get it moving again the Federal government increases spending, cuts taxes, and runs a big deficit. To cover this deficit, the Treasury sells large quantities of bonds. These bond sales of course tighten money and that dampens business activity. Does this mean that an expansionary fiscal policy that calls for a big deficit will inevitably be self-defeating? [*Hint:* What is the proper role of monetary policy here?]

10 Suppose that the government runs a surplus during a period when aggregate demand is excessive and the Fed is trying to implement a restrictive monetary policy. Would coordination of Treasury and Fed policies call for the Treasury

to pay off government bonds as soon as it had cash available to do so, or would it, instead, call for the Treasury to build up its deposit balances? If the latter, should the Treasury build up its balances at the Fed or at the commercial banks? Explain your answer.

11   Why do you think that the idea that an economic downturn is in the wind usually lowers stock prices but raises bond prices? [*Hint:* How is the Fed likely to respond to a downswing in economic activity?]

12   Since the government can use fiscal policy to attain full employment, why should it want or need the tools of monetary policy in addition? [*Hint:* Suppose that the government wanted to achieve full employment plus a maximum rate of growth (i.e., full employment plus high investment). Could it achieve this combination of goals by means of an expansionary fiscal policy alone? By means of a restrictive fiscal policy alone? What if it combined a restrictive fiscal policy with an expansionary monetary policy?]

*13   As we said in the footnote on page 481, the General Motors Acceptance Corporation uses funds obtained through the sale of commercial paper to buy up installment sales contracts originated by GM dealers. Studies show that consumer demand for auto loans is interest inelastic. What does this tell you about the interest elasticity of GMAC's supply curve of commercial paper? [*Hint:* First figure out the relationship between the demand-for-funds curve of auto buyers and GMAC's demand-for-funds curve. Then figure out the relationship between this latter curve and GMAC's supply curve for commercial paper.]

---

* This problem depends on material presented in Parts 2 and 3.

CHAPTER 40

CONTEMPORARY ECONOMIC PROBLEMS

In this chapter we shall talk about some of the pressing unsolved economic problems of the day: the apparent conflict between full employment and price stability; structural unemployment and the persistence of poverty.

PRICE STABILITY VERSUS FULL EMPLOYMENT

Our discussion of fiscal and monetary policy was based on the assumption that price stability and full employment would not conflict and could thus be attained simultaneously. Right here and now we'd better say what we *mean* by "full employment." In a market economy, people are free to work or not work, so we could say that:

The economy has attained full employment when every individual who wants to work at the going wage rate established for the kind of service he has to offer can find a job at that wage rate.

This definition does not imply that the economy will attain full employment only if there aren't any people out looking for jobs, that is, only if involuntary unemployment is zero. In a free dynamic economy, there's always a certain amount of what is called *frictional unemployment.* Changes in the composition of final output, in technology, and in the geographic location of industry mean that the *kinds* of labor that producers demand constantly shifts. (Demand may be going down for steelworkers but up for garage mechanics, or may be going down for textile workers in the North but up for textile workers in the South.) Whenever there are shifts in the kinds of labor that producers demand, workers have to move from one job to another, perhaps from one location to another. All this takes time. Thus at any moment a certain number of people are between jobs, and these are referred to as frictionally unemployed. Many people have jobs that are seasonal, which means that they're idle during part of the year. (Construction workers and farmhands have little to do in the winter, while ski instructors—unless they are also adept at water skiing—face a similar fate in the summer.) Workers who are seasonally unemployed are also referred to as frictionally unemployed. Finally new entrants into the labor force, who have yet to find a niche for themselves, are likewise classified as frictionally unemployed.

Because of frictional unemployment, then, the term "full employment" cannot be taken to mean *no* unemployment. It is estimated that, under normal conditions, frictional unemployment runs from about 3% to a maximum of 4% of the total work force. Thus when the government sets out to achieve full employment, it really only wants to reduce unemployment to an acceptable level of 3 or 4%.

The Record

Can full employment be achieved without inflation? The postwar experience of the U.S. and a number of West European countries as well indicates that the answer may well be no. Evidently inflation—at least of the creeping or mild variety—is likely to become a problem even before full employment is reached.

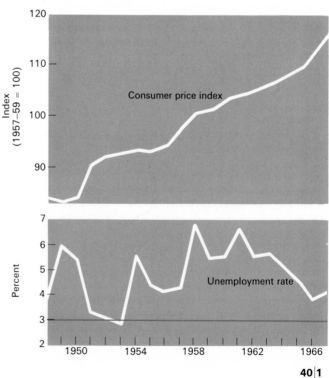

40|1

Unemployment rate and consumer price index in the U.S. since World War II.
(Source: U.S. Department of Commerce)

Figure 40.1 presents evidence marshaled from U.S. experience to support this proposition. It shows that during the postwar period unemployment in excess of normal frictional levels has been a persistent problem for the U.S. During the same period, however, the prices paid by U.S. consumers for goods and services have risen almost steadily. Also consumer prices have risen most rapidly when the rate of unemployment was lowest.

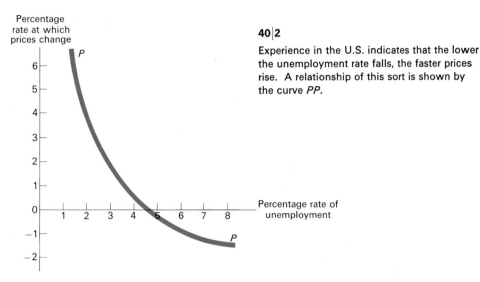

40|2

Experience in the U.S. indicates that the lower the unemployment rate falls, the faster prices rise. A relationship of this sort is shown by the curve *PP*.

In our economy, the relationship between the unemployment rate and the rate at which prices change seems to resemble the curve in Fig. 40.2. Whenever we get unemployment whittled down to acceptable levels, some degree of inflation results; the more successful we are in eliminating non-frictional unemployment, the more serious the degree of inflation.

Conflicting Goals and a Possible Trade-Off

The possibility that our economy may be unable to achieve full employment *and* price stability simultaneously indicates that the government may have to choose one or the other. And any such choice is certain to be a painful one, since economists and John Q. Citizen alike want both.

Full employment is so important because, in a modern industrial society like ours, the rewards and much of the status a person has are derived from his job. Thus a person who can't find work suffers not only economic hardship, but he also loses his place in society, and eventually even his self respect. Another bad consequence of unemployment is that it results, as we pointed out in Chapter 33, in a gap between the economy's actual and potential output and thus in an irretrievable loss in output. Given the many pressing and unfilled wants of our economy (ranging from aiding the poor to improving transportation facilities) such a loss is clearly unacceptable. Thus our economy cannot be judged successful unless it consistently attains full employment.

Stable prices are just as important as full employment, though for different reasons. The inflation in the U.S. since the early 1950's has been mostly of the creeping variety, that is, inflation within the range of 2, 3 or 4% a year. Although creeping inflation does gradually diminish the value of money and fixed-price assets, it does not seriously disrupt economic activity. People can live with creeping inflation, and even prosper in the face of it. In South American countries, there has been rapid inflation. But even a rapid inflation, as much as 10% or even 20% a year, can be lived with. If so, why is so much importance attached to eliminating even mild inflation?

The answer is that many people fear that even a mild inflation, if it continues unchecked for long, will have dire consequences. Many would argue that a creeping inflation will eventually destroy the incentive to save. This contention is, however, open to question. As we noted in Chapter 3, people save in order to meet real needs, and these are in no way diminished (in fact, they may even be strengthened) by creeping inflation. (A college education is going to cost more 10 years hence if there is creeping inflation than if there is not, and the fact that most children plan to go to college is one reason why families save.) Thus it seems likely that creeping inflation will lead people not to stop saving, but to alter the way they hold their savings. People who would normally hold fixed-price debt securities switch to variable-price equities, the value of which will presumably rise at least in step with changes in the overall price level. (For instance, people may take their money out of savings banks and put it into speculative growth stocks.)

A second consequence of even a mild inflation is that over time it diminishes the real incomes of, and thus impose hardships on, people whose income is either fixed or likely to rise more slowly than that of other groups. Retired people who live on fixed pensions or the income from fixed-price securities obviously fall in the first category, while government workers and teachers fall in the second.

Another threat posed by a mild but chronic inflation is that it will eventually imperil a nation's competitive position in world markets and thus create a serious disequilibrium in its balance of payments. (You pay your steel workers a little more this year and a little more next year, and pretty soon the price of steel, and the price of the things made with steel, is so high that you can't sell them in world markets in competition with steel products from other countries where the prices are still low.) We shall talk about this threat and its consequences in Chapter 47.

People also fear creeping inflation because they think that the government might eventually respond to continued price hikes by instituting price and wage controls, the long-run consequences of which might be even more undesirable than those of inflation itself.

Finally: Some people are scared of even a mild inflation because they fear that, if a mild inflation continues uncontrolled for long, it will eventually turn into a *hyperinflation*. In a hyperinflation, prices rise so fast that eventually a point is reached at which no one is willing to receive or hold money. Once such a "flight" away from money occurs, money ceases to function as a medium of exchange (during the hyperinflation in Germany in 1923 paper marks were used for wallpaper), and barter reasserts itself as the principal method of trade. Barter works well enough for farmers in primitive societies, but it's totally unworkable for industrial firms that have to buy raw materials and pay workers with the proceeds received from the sale of their output. Therefore hyperinflation paralyzes economic life. Also it renders worthless not only money, but all fixed-price assets, and in doing so it wipes out the savings of much of the population, particularly the middle class.

A crucial question, then, is: *What are the chances that a mild inflation will build into a hyperinflation?* We go back to the drawing board for our answer. In an economy in which inputs and outputs are exchanged for money, the total value of all goods sold during any period must match the total quantity of money spent during that period. Specifically, the total transactions in physical goods, T, that occur during any period multiplied by the average price, P, at which they occur must equal the total money supply, M, times V, the average number of times that the money supply turns over (i.e., changes hands) during the period.

This relationship, which can be summarized by the expression

$$MV \equiv PT,$$

is of course simply an identity, that is, a relationship that holds by definition. Nevertheless it can tell us something about the sources of hyperinflation. We know that if the economy is at full employment, then total physical transactions T will be a constant. We also know that there are limits on the extent to which the money supply can be utilized more efficiently and thus on the extent to which velocity V can be increased. Therefore it will be possible for the price level P to rise phenomenally only if the money supply M rises at an equally phenomenal rate.

Thus in actual practice hyperinflations are not accidental occurrences that happened to follow a long mild inflation. Hyperinflations are invariably the result of an *enormous* expansion in the money supply. This expansion is always the result of an attempt by the government to finance large-scale expenditures by simply printing money. Only a government demoralized by war or other difficulties would resort to such an obviously disastrous course of action; so hyperinflation isn't usually a threat during normal times.

The last real hyperinflation in the U.S. took place during the Revolution, when the Continental Congress printed up so many notes to finance

Washington's army that the value of these notes fell literally to zero. When this happened, the only way that the Continental Congress could get its currency accepted was to threaten to cut off the ears of anyone who dared to refuse it! (An enduring memento of this episode is the expression, "Not worth a Continental.")

THEORIES OF INFLATION

In Chapter 35 we presented one explanation of why inflation occurs. We showed that whenever aggregate demand exceeds aggregate supply at the economy's full-employment income, an inflationary gap, like the one in Fig. 35.8(b), opens up, and prices are forced into an upward spiral. This *demand-pull inflation* is a kind of inflation that is always a threat when an economy is operating at full employment, but not when it is operating below full employment. To explain why inflation occurs when the economy operates *below* full employment, we must turn to other theories of inflation.

Cost-Push Inflation

The most widely accepted theory of why inflation occurs in an economy that is operating under full employment is the *cost-push* theory. This theory explains creeping inflation in terms of the monopoly power exercised by labor and by business.

The cost-push theory has been propounded in a variety of forms, but the general argument usually runs as follows: Labor unions want to increase both the absolute wage of labor and the share of national income that accrues to labor, so they consistently demand from business wage increases that exceed the increases that occur in labor's productivity as a result of improvements in technology and the increased use of capital equipment. The unions get their way, and the workers get more money per hour. Producers accept the "exorbitant" wage demands made by labor because, by increasing prices, they can pass their cost increases on to consumers. But when they do so, producers lower the real wage gain achieved by labor and thwart labor's attempt to increase its share of national income. Because gradually the prices of goods and services go up, and the worker has to make his paycheck stretch to fit the higher prices. Therefore at the next round of bargaining, labor again demands wage increases that exceed the increase in labor's productivity. Producers again accede to this demand, and they again increase prices. When they do this, they set the stage for still another round of wage-price increases.

And so on. And so on. And so on.

The cost-push price spiral we have just described depends on several assumptions. The first is that organized labor, when it bargains for continually higher wages, is either (1) unconcerned about the reduction in total employment that these wage increases might bring about or (2) believes that the government, by means of monetary and fiscal measures, will act to eliminate any unemployment that might rear its ugly head. The second assumption is that business must believe that the public's demand for its output is so inelastic that if business raises prices because it has to cover wage hikes, the public will keep right on buying, and neither sales nor profits will be seriously diminished.

These assumptions may hold sometimes, but not all the time. Therefore we can't expect the cost-push theory of inflation alone to explain all inflationary episodes that occur when the economy is operating below full employment. Nevertheless the cost-push theory is useful because it often gives important insights into the inflationary process.

Bottleneck or Demand-Shift Inflation

A second theory that explains why inflation occurs in an economy that is operating under full employment is what is called the *bottleneck* or *demand-shift* theory of inflation.

Demand-shift theorists make two observations: (1) The composition of aggregate demand often changes more rapidly than the allocation of resources can be altered. (2) Whenever such demand shifts occur, unemployment results in some sectors, while a demand-pull type of inflation results in others. These two observations offer a plausible description of how *one-shot* price increases often take place in individual industries or sectors of the economy.

Demand-shift theorists broaden this description into an explanation of how creeping inflation happens in the economy as a whole. To do so they make the additional assumption that wages and prices, once they rise, never fall (in the jargon of economists, they are *sticky downward*). This assumption means that, whenever the composition of aggregate demand shifts, the prices of those goods for which demand increases will rise, but the prices of those goods for which demand decreases won't fall (e.g., if demand shifts away from consumer durables onto capital goods, the prices of capital goods will rise, but the prices of consumer durables won't fall). The assumption that prices are sticky downward thus guarantees that every time a demand shift raises the prices of *some* goods, the general level of prices will also rise.

Inflation Theories and Recent U.S. Experience

Since World War II, inflation in the U.S. has taken place in fairly distinct episodes, some of which have followed patterns like the inflation theories presented above. A good illustration of demand-shift inflation is the U.S.

economy during the period 1945–1946. When World War II ended, aggregate demand shifted dramatically from war goods to private goods. Resources couldn't be transferred fast enough to meet this shift. Thus real output declined, while the prices of goods spiraled upward. Another example of a demand-shift inflation is the inflation in 1955–1957. During this period a shift in the composition of aggregate demand away from consumer goods to investment goods pushed up the prices of investment goods, but led to no fall in the prices of consumer goods.

A much-talked-about example of cost-push inflation is the postwar wage-price spiral in steel. After the war steelworkers demanded—and got—a series of wage increases that greatly exceeded the increases in their productivity. This raised the costs of steel producers; they responded by raising steel prices. So we had a cost-push wage-price spiral in steel. This spiral contributed significantly to the inflationary pressures of the period, not only because steel is widely used as an input in the production of other goods, but also because steel wages set the pattern for wage bargains in many other industries.

Remedies for Inflation

We have seen that the government can curb an inflation of the generalized demand-pull sort (i.e., one caused by an inflationary gap) by slapping on a restrictive fiscal or monetary policy that lowers aggregate demand to a level consistent with price stability and full employment. It cannot, however, deal in the same way with demand-shift and cost-push inflations that occur when the economy is at or under full employment. Reason: A restrictive monetary–fiscal policy that lowered aggregate demand enough to eliminate either a demand-shift or a cost-push inflation would also bring on unemployment.

So we come to the problem of how the government can cope with demand-shift and cost-push inflations. Take demand-shift inflation, to start with. The demand-shift theory of inflation rests on the assumption that wages and prices are "sticky downward." Since in a competitive market prices would never be inflexible, this stickiness must reflect the exercise of monopoly power by unions and producers. Therefore one way to eliminate demand-pull inflation would be to institute an antitrust, anti-union policy that restored competition to both the labor market and goods markets. Such a policy, however, wouldn't be feasible from a political point of view. Also it might have a number of drawbacks from an economic point of view. Certainly it would call for a degree of government interference in, and regulation of, the market economy, that most people would find unacceptable.

A second way the government might deal with demand-shift inflation would be to use selective tax changes, selective credit controls, and changes in the composition of government expenditures to lower demand in those sectors in which it is excessive. This policy would, however, bring about certain practical difficulties, especially the familiar problem of timing. Demand shifts happen fast and are often short-lived. The policy-maker who has demand-shift inflation to deal with has to institute his policies in a hurry and at the right moment. But to do so, he has to be able to predict with reasonable accuracy what the near future will bring and he must also have considerable freedom of action. Unfortunately the combination of these two conditions is hard to come by.

Cost-push inflation, like demand-shift inflation, is a tough nut for the government policy-maker to crack. He might begin by using various *ad hoc* measures to combat price increases in specific industries. For example, suppose that producers of a key commodity threatened to raise their prices. The government might respond by threatening (1) to switch its purchases of this commodity from domestic to foreign suppliers, (2) to sell off any excess stocks of this commodity that it has on hand, or by (3) lowering or at least refusing to raise tariffs on imports of this commodity. The U.S. government, in fighting cost-push inflation, has at different times resorted to all these tactics. When aluminum producers in 1965 raised prices even though the administration put pressure on them to hold the line, the government threatened to sell off excess aluminum from its defense stockpile. The government has also consistently refused to raise tariffs on steel, despite the flood of steel imports that rising steel prices in the U.S. have triggered in recent years.

If *ad hoc* measures are inadequate to control cost-push inflation, a government determined to maintain stable prices might decide to impose direct controls on wages, prices, and credit. This forceful approach has one important advantage: When it is applied firmly, it *works*. However, it also has offsetting disadvantages: (1) Direct controls interfere with the working of the free market economy. (2) Direct controls are difficult to administer. (3) Direct controls are invariably interpreted at least some of the time in an unfair and arbitrary fashion. (4) Direct controls create incentives for citizens to set up black markets, to make undercover payments, and to engage in other evasionary tactics. For these reasons direct controls are generally viewed as acceptable only in times of national emergency, such as a war.

Because direct controls are so odious, the U.S. government has in recent years tried to cope with resurgent inflation by issuing "voluntary" wage–price *guideposts*. These say that wages in general should rise no faster than the rate at which labor productivity is rising in the economy as a whole (this rate currently runs around 3% per year). They also say that industries in which the rate of gain of labor productivity is only average should hold prices constant, that industries in which the rate of gain of labor productivity is above average should lower prices, and that industries in which the rate of gain of labor productivity is below average may raise prices. If everybody cooperated and followed the government's guideposts, this would effectively halt cost-push inflation. These guideposts therefore look like an attractive solution to this brand of inflation. However, it has been the experience of the U.S. government that guideposts are unpopular with business (which regards them as a threat to its autonomy and its profits) and also with labor (which regards them as a threat to its goal of increasing the share of national income that labor gets). Guideposts are likely to be widely disregarded whenever strong demand for output leads business and labor to believe that wage increases can easily be passed on to the consumers by means of higher prices on output. Certainly this was the case in 1966 and 1967, when the government's guideposts were badly battered on a number of fronts.

Our remarks on inflation remedies indicate that the government has yet to devise acceptable and successful policies for dealing either with demand-shift or cost-push inflation. This failure is evidenced by the fact that the creeping inflation which re-emerged as a problem in 1966 has continued unabated despite the strenuous efforts the government has made to curb it.

STRUCTURAL UNEMPLOYMENT

Earlier in this chapter we introduced the concept of *frictional* unemployment, which refers to the unavoidable, but *temporary,* unemployment that arises in a dynamic economy because (a) workers change jobs, (b) the composition of final output alters, or (c) technology evolves. Economists and policy-makers often speak of another sort of unemployment: *structural* unemployment. By this they mean *long-term* unemployment that comes about because (a) labor's skills do not match those that industry demands, (b) labor is immobile, or (c) rigidities prevent the wage rate from moving to a level that would equate demand and supply for labor.

Causes and Prevalence of Structural Unemployment

During the late 1950's, a period of rapid technological progress, many students of the labor market concluded that automation was raising the demand for skilled workers and professionals, decreasing the demand for clerical and blue-collar workers, and thus creating a situation in which the skills and ability of the labor force no longer matched those demanded by industry. They argued that the high rates of unemployment experienced in the U.S. after 1953 were the result, not of inadequate aggregate demand, but of structural unemployment created by automation. They also argued that, as time went by, structural unemployment due to automation was going to get steadily worse. This argument had a persuasive ring, especially when unemployment was high, but it doubtless exaggerated automation's capacity for creating structural unemployment. Especially did it ignore several reasons why cost-minimizing firms were not about to make sudden and large-scale substitutions of computers and robots for workers: (1) It's very hard to design (and very expensive to build) machines to do the sort of manipulative-sensatory tasks that most blue-collar workers do. (2) Using computers to control production processes directly not only poses problems that are expensive to solve, but also requires that production processes be thoroughly understood and that historical data exist for all relevant variables. These last two conditions are met for surprisingly few processes these days. The automation argument also underestimated producers' ability to substitute one grade of labor for another, either by altering job routines or by offering workers on-the-job training. And it underestimated the ability of workers to move, by means of retraining and education, from one sector of the labor market to another.

Whatever validity the automation argument may have had or still has, the economic upswing of the early 1960's demonstrated that the high unemployment rates during the late 1950's were more a matter of inadequate demand than of structural unemployment.

Although it seems unlikely that automation is going to raise unemployment to any great heights, there are in the economy today, just as in the past, large pockets of unemployment that cannot be attributed to inadequate aggregate demand. The data in Fig. 40.3 show that unemployment remains high among teenagers and nonwhite (chiefly Negro) men even when aggregate demand has been raised to a level that eliminates all but frictional unemployment among the population at large. Also regional data on unemployment show that pronounced pockets of unemployment exist in areas in which local industry has either moved out or reduced its labor requirement through automation.

Much unemployment that isn't due to inadequate aggregate demand can be traced to labor immobility. Labor may be immobile in two ways: (1) Workers may be unwilling or unable to move from one place to another in response to changing job opportunities, or (2) they may be unable or unwilling to move from industry to industry.

Geographic immobility is easy to explain. Most people just don't hear about job openings in other regions. They are often attached by family and other ties to the areas in which they live. And they know that moving would be troublesome, risky, and expensive.

Interindustry immobility is less easy to explain. In single-industry areas, interindustry immobility may result simply from geographic immobility. In multi-industry areas, however, other factors are at work: For semiskilled workers, an important cause of interindustry immobility is the fact that the job skills acquired by semiskilled workers have little transfer value, and

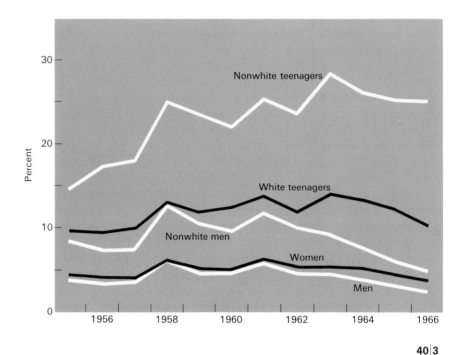

40|3

Selected unemployment rates. (Source: Economic Report of the President, 1967)

semiskilled workers can therefore find employment in a new industry only if they are willing to take a substantial (sometimes as high as 40%) cut in pay. (The skills possessed by a meat cutter who has lost his job because of automation will do him little good when he looks for a job in a steel mill.)

In a dynamic economy in which technology, the mix of final output, and the geographic location of industry are constantly changing, labor immobility (whatever its cause) always creates pockets of unemployment. Examples: The unemployment in West Virginia that came about when the coal mines mechanized and the unemployment in New England that came about when the textile mills moved South. In addition, part of the unemployment among nonwhites can be attributed to the fact that it is hard for them to move out of ghettos where jobs are scarce into prosperous areas where jobs are more plentiful.

Structural unemployment is also created when market imperfections limit the freedom of the wage rates in different sectors of the labor market to adjust to levels that would equate supply and demand. For example, federal and state minimum-wage laws, although they have the laudable intention of raising the incomes of low-wage groups, also tend to create unemployment among teenagers, workers with little education, and older workers who, because they lack experience, have few skills, or have disabilities, may not be worth the minimum wage to prospective employers.

Finally we should mention discrimination. The discrimination both by employers and unions against nonwhites is a big cause of the high level of unemployment among this group. And Negroes aren't the only group against which discrimination is practiced. Older workers are often discriminated against because (a) it's hard to teach them new skills, (b) the cost of training them is high relative to the number of years they are likely to remain on the job, and (c) the pension costs one runs into when one employs an older worker may be pretty steep.

Strategies Against Structural Unemployment

Eliminating structural unemployment calls for a two-pronged effort. (1) The government must make sure that aggregate demand is high enough to eliminate all nonstructural unemployment; this is important because unemployment caused by inadequate aggregate demand can look deceptively like structural unemployment. (2) It must undertake special programs that attack the causes of structural unemployment.

Structural unemployment in depressed areas. One way the government can combat structural unemployment of this sort is by putting through programs designed to create new jobs in depressed areas, either by attracting industry or by developing in other ways the economic potential of these areas. Such programs (like the special redevelopment program established for Appalachia) might include: building new roads, strengthening local health and educational facilities, developing tourist facilities, retraining workers, and extending technical assistance and low-interest loans to new commercial and industrial enterprises.

Development programs are appropriate for depressed regions that have adequate resources to support a prosperous local economy. Some depressed areas, however, do not. In such areas the only answer to structural unemployment is to take steps that will encourage unemployed workers to migrate out of the area into high-employment areas. Such measures might include counseling to help unemployed workers learn about jobs in other areas and relocation allowances that would pay for their moving expenses. Recently the Department of Labor has experimented with programs of both sorts.

Structural unemployment due to inadequate or outdated skills. The best way to attack such unemployment is by means of special manpower-retraining programs. Currently the Federal government is running many such programs, designed to meet the needs of special groups, such as workers displaced by technological change, the illiterate, the young, and the disadvantaged.

Structural unemployment due to discrimination. The Federal government has prohibited discrimination in Federal employment and in companies which handle federal contracts. Also it has sought to enlist voluntary cooperation from unions and business firms in opening up union membership and new job opportunities to nonwhites.

Structural unemployment due to wage restrictions. Continued hikes in the minimum wage are certain to increase structural unemployment among the least-skilled workers in society. In the long run the most effective way to raise the wages of such workers is not to raise the minimum wage, but to give them job training that will raise their value to prospective employers.

THE POVERTY PROBLEM

Many people in our economy suffer from long-term unemployment, receive little or no nonlabor income, and must therefore live in poverty. The presence of poverty in the U.S. seems paradoxical, because we think of the U.S. as being such a rich country. But when we look at income and population figures, we realize that perhaps the U.S. is not as rich as we think, or at least not as rich as the typical filmland portrait of the American family—complete with new home, two-door fastback sedan, stylish clothes, vacation trips, and a pedigreed pooch thrown in for good measure—would suggest. In 1966, for example, Americans received $580 billion in personal income. This sounds like a lot, but on a per capita basis it amounted to less than $3,000 a year, or less than $57 a week.

Inequalities in the Distribution of Income

Although a per capita income of $57 a week is hardly princely, it is enough to secure for a person the necessities of life and to leave him outside the bounds of poverty. Why then does poverty persist in the U.S.? One answer: Income is distributed in an extremely unequal way among the Smiths, Joneses, and Astors who make up the population.

Table 40.1, which gives data on the way income is distributed among U.S. families, shows just how uneven income distribution in the U.S. is. Note the sharp contrast between the incomes received by families on the bottom rung of the income ladder and the incomes received by families on the top rung. Currently 9% of all families fall in the income class of less than $2,000 a year and they get only 2% of the total U.S. income. On the other hand 8% of all families fall in the $15,000-and-over income class, and *they* get 27% of the total U.S. income.

The full import of any data is often hard to grasp when they are simply listed in a table. Therefore figures on income distribution are often shown graphically, in what is known as a *Lorentz curve*. To set up a Lorentz curve, we plot data on the percentage of all families in a given income class and

TABLE 40|1

The Distribution of Pretax Income Among U.S. Families, 1965

Annual income	Families in this class, %	Families in this class and lower classes, %	Income received by families in this class, %	Income received by families in this and lower classes, %
Under $2,000	9	9	1	1
$2,000–$2,999	7	16	3	4
$3,000–$3,999	8	24	3	7
$4,000–$4,999	8	32	4	11
$5,000–$5,999	9	41	6	17
$6,000–$6,999	9	50	11	28
$7,000–$9,999	24	74	19	47
$10,000–$14,999	17	91	26	73
$15,000 and over	8	100	27	100

Source: U.S. Bureau of Census, *Statistical Abstract of the United States*, 1967, pages 332–333.

lower classes against data on the percentage of income received by families in a given income class and lower ones. If the distribution of income is equal (i.e., if the lowest 20% of all families in the income distribution receive 20% of all income; if the lowest 40% of all families in the income distribution receive 40% of total income; and so forth), we shall obtain a straight line like the one labeled "curve of equal income distribution" in Fig. 40.4. If, on the other hand, the distribution of income between families

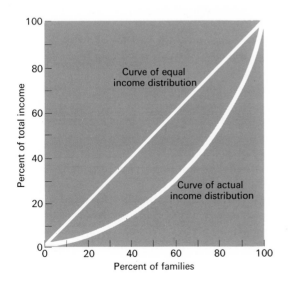

40|4

The bowed-in Lorentz curve shows the way income is distributed among U.S. families.

is unequal, we shall obtain a bowed-in curve like the one labeled "curve of actual income distribution" in Fig. 40.4. This curve, which represents the distribution of income in the U.S., was obtained by plotting the data in the third and fifth columns of Table 40.1. The more unequal the actual distribution of income, the more the curve of actual income distribution will bow in. Thus the deviation between the straight-line curve of equal income distribution and the bowed-in curve of actual income distribution gives us a graphic measure of the degree of inequality that characterizes the actual income distribution.

How Many People Are Poor?

In general terms a family can be said to be poor when it is unable to satisfy its minimum needs for food, clothing, shelter, and other necessities. To measure the number of families living in poverty, we have to adopt some sort of arbitrary measure to separate families that can meet such minimum needs from those that can't. Most families meet their needs primarily out of current income, and since the best data we have on family resources are income data, we usually define poverty in terms of current income. It's hard to settle on an income level to use to divide the poor from the prosperous, since families' needs vary with their size, with their age distribution (babies don't eat much but teenage boys do), with their geographic location (Southern boys can go barefoot in January, but Northern boys need boots), their health, and many other factors. A definition of poverty based on current income is not only hard to establish, but it can also be misleading, because many families receive significant amounts of nonmoney income (farm families raise their own vegetables, and homeowners provide themselves with housing services). Another thing: Some families who can't meet their minimum needs from current income are able to do so by dipping into assets acquired through previous savings (people save not just for their children's college education but also for their own retirement).

Despite the obvious pitfalls that await anyone who sets out to define a poverty boundary in terms of current income, there have been a number of attempts to do so. They indicate that an annual income of $3,000 before taxes proves a rough but reasonable dividing line between families that live in poverty and those that don't.

If we apply this definition of poverty to 1965, the latest year for which we have data, we find that approximately 8 million U.S. families are living in poverty. That's slightly more than 16% of all the families in the U.S., a disturbingly high percentage. However, Fig. 40.5 shows that poverty in the U.S. is on the decline. Right after World War II, more than 11 million families (i.e., 30% of all the families in the U.S.) lived in poverty. Even as recently as the early 1960's 9 million families (i.e., more than 20%) lived in poverty.

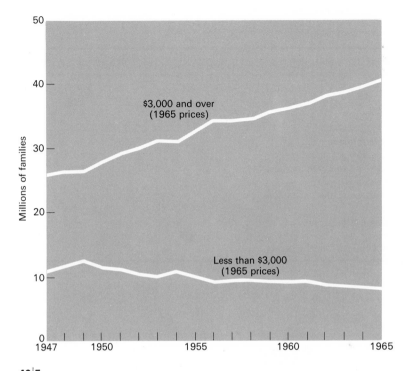

40|5

Over the postwar period the number of U.S. families living in poverty has slowly but steadily declined. (Source: U.S. Department of Commerce)

The progress that has been made in eliminating poverty is due to the rising level of U.S. real income, not to a great shift in the distribution of this income. In fact, the distribution of income in the U.S. has changed surprisingly little since the war. The one-fifth of all families with the lowest incomes still receive today the same 5% of the total U.S. income that they received in 1947.

Who Are the Poor and Why Are They Poor?

Even though the poor are dwindling in number, they are still very much a part of the American scene. Let's take a look at who they are and why they are poor. Table 40.2 shows that in poor families, the head of the household is often someone who is unemployed or who works in a low-paying job. Figure 40.6 gives a few clues as to why they are unemployed or are unable to get better-paying jobs. It shows that a disproportionately large share of poor families are headed by nonwhites, by people with less than 8 years of education, by people who are under 25 years old or over 65 years old, and by fe-

TABLE 40|2

Incidence of Poverty, by Occupation of Family Head, 1964*

Occupation of family head	Incidence of poverty, %
Unemployed	27.6
Employed	10.3
Domestic workers	62.0
Farm laborers or foremen	60.1
Farmers or farm managers	44.8
Laborers, except farm and mine	20.4
Service workers other than domestic	17.4
Operative workers	8.4
Managers, officials, and proprietors	6.5
Sales workers	5.5
Clerical workers	4.9
Craftsmen	4.2
Professional and technical workers	2.5

*Source: U.S. Department of Commerce

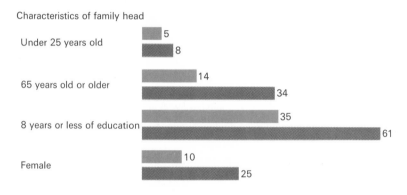

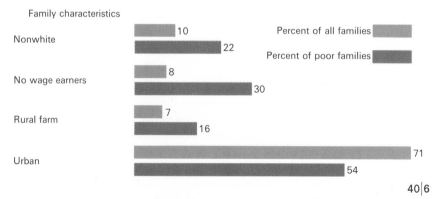

40|6

Characteristics of poor families compared with all families.
(Source: U.S. Department of Commerce. Data are for 1962.)

males. It also shows that a disproportionately large share of poor families live on farms.

Earlier in this chapter we pointed out that it is precisely the nonwhites, the undereducated, the very young, and the very old who are most likely to suffer from structural unemployment or to be shunted—because of discrimination or because of their lack of skills—into low-paying, low-skill occupations. Also, many women who head poor families cannot work because they have small children to care for; and many older workers are unemployable because age or poor health prevents them from holding a steady job. Finally, the incidence of poverty is high among farmers and farm laborers because of a problem we mentioned back in Chapter 15. The rapid increase in farm productivity, coupled with the slow growth of demand for farm output, means that large numbers of agricultural workers must be transferred from farm to industry. Many farm workers, however, are loath to leave the farm because they prefer rural life, because they are unaware of job opportunities in the city, because their skills or educational level do not fit them for most city jobs, or because of the high cost and high risks associated with such a move. This transfer has not taken place as rapidly as it should have, and therefore the incomes of farm workers have dropped below those of workers in industry.

Programs to Eliminate Poverty

Government efforts to eliminate poverty fall into two categories: (1) Measures that attack the causes of poverty. (2) Relief measures that raise the incomes of the poor. Let's talk first about measures that attack the causes of poverty.

We know that two main causes of poverty are long-term unemployment and employment in low-wage occupations. The proper strategies for attacking these causes are those we discussed when we talked about the way the government seeks to eliminate structural unemployment: area development programs, job training, measures to increase the geographic mobility of workers, and measures to end discrimination in employment.

Today fully a third of all poor persons are children. Therefore another important strategy for attacking the causes of poverty is improving the educational facilities open to disadvantaged children.

Most relief measures designed to raise the incomes of the poor take the form of cash payments. Some are made under the Social Security program (not all Social Security payments go to the poor, but many do), and some are made under public assistance (welfare) programs.

Under existing relief programs, money is paid out to the poor not simply because they're poor, but because they suffer from some sort of handicap: e.g., they are old; they are disabled; or, in the case of women heads of households, they have dependent children. Recently a radical departure from this tradition of payments to the handicapped poor has been proposed. Proponents of this new approach want to replace all existing welfare programs and other poverty-fighting schemes with a single program, the *negative income tax.** Proposals vary as to the precise form such a "tax" should take. However, all share certain common characteristics: People with high incomes would have a positive tax liability which they'd have to pay just as they do under our present tax system; but—and here's the innovation—people with low incomes would have a negative tax liability, i.e., they would automatically be granted a subsidy designed to lift them out of the poverty band. They would get this subsidy regardless of *why* they happened to be poor.

Proponents of the negative income tax argue that their program would provide the poor with what they really need: cash. They also contend that a negative income tax would cost *less* than the existing catchall of antipoverty programs. This contention may well be true, but the negative income tax does have one disadvantage: It does nothing to attack the *causes* of poverty; it just alleviates the *symptoms.* Despite this disadvantage, the simpleness and directness of the negative income tax give it an appeal that ensures that people will continue to debate it in the years to come, even if it is not enacted into law.

PROBLEMS

1   In Norway, the United States and a number of other countries, the central bank, although it is permitted to buy government bonds in the open market, is forbidden to buy them directly from the government.

   a) What danger do you think this prohibition is designed to guard against? [*Hint:* In the U.S., when the Federal Reserve System buys government bonds directly from the Treasury, this is equivalent to a situation in which the Treasury simply prints dollar bills to pay for its expenditures.]

   b) If the central bank is committed to promoting stable prices, do you think that this prohibition is (i) important? (ii) superfluous? or (iii) an undesirable constraint on the central bank's freedom?

2   What measures a government ought to take to combat inflation depends in part on what sort of inflation it has to deal with. So it's important for a government to be able to distinguish one type of inflation from another. Suppose that you were a government policy-maker faced with an inflationary economy. What would you look at to determine whether the economy was experiencing cost-push, demand-pull, or demand-shift inflation? Do you think that you would necessarily come up with a clear-cut answer?

---

* The idea of a negative income tax was originated by Milton Friedman of the University of Chicago.

3 "If the demand-shift explanation of creeping inflation did not incorporate the assumption that all price increases were 'permanent,' it would end up explaining, not why the price level moves up over time, but why individual prices fluctuate up and down." Comment.

4 In the fall of 1967, the Johnson administration asked Congress for a 10% tax hike (surtax) to curb what is referred to as demand-push inflation. During the hearing which the tax-writing House Ways and Means Committee conducted over this proposal, Chairman Wilbur Mills seemed to take the position that a tax hike was a good way to deal with a demand-pull inflation but a poor way to deal with a cost-push one. He reasoned that a tax hike might intensify the upward push that rising labor and materials costs were giving to output prices. Discuss the logic of this position.

5 During the hearings mentioned in Problem 4, the following exchange occurred between Mr. Mills, who was unenthusiastic about the tax hike, and Federal Reserve Board Chairman William McChesney Martin, who was for it:

MR. MARTIN: . . . I think that your line of questioning, as I said before, indicates clearly that it [the economy] is not too boomy at the moment.
MR. MILLS: . . . Not too boomy. It is just not booming.
MR. MARTIN: . . . All right, it is not booming. But the point I want to make is . . . that demand pressures are too much for the general economy. We are trying to do too much too fast, in too many areas.*

Would you recommend a tax hike as a good way to fight inflation in a "not-too-boomy" economy? Why or why not?

6 At the beginning of 1967, it was expected that the 3% hike in living costs that occurred during 1966 would be repeated during 1967. This meant that, if the wage increase received by workers during 1967 had been limited to the average annual increase in their productivity (roughly 3%), workers' real income would not have risen at all during the year. To prevent this from happening, should the Council of Economic Advisors have adjusted the 1967 guidepost for wages to recognize in some way the increasing cost of living?

7 During 1967 the minimum wage advanced from $1.25 to $1.40 an hour. This 11% hike, which clearly violated the government's own wage guideline, raises the question: Should the government-imposed minimum wage be exempted from the government-set wage guideline? The Council of Economic Advisers thought that it should, but they may have been wrong or this may have been the only position that it was politically feasible for them to take. What is your answer?

8 In the text we suggested that union contracts which push wages above the level that would equate the supply of and demand for labor are likely to create unemployment. Union leaders, however, claim that wage hikes are a good way to *combat*, not increase, unemployment. They reason that workers will imme-

* *Wall Street Journal,* December 11, 1967.

diately spend any additional income they receive and that this spending will stimulate aggregate demand and raise national output. Contrast these two points of view. [*Hint:* When you analyze the position taken by union leaders, ask yourself: How are higher wages likely to affect business profits, business investment, dividend pay-outs, output prices and other key economic variables?]

9   In Chapter 38 we said that, if a government faced with a big deflationary gap were to run a large deficit to counter this gap, and if it were to cover this deficit by printing up money, this wouldn't be inflationary. Does this remark contradict what we said on pages 625–628 of this chapter?

10   In Brazil during the period 1958–1965 the government had a series of king-sized deficits. Simultaneously the money supply rose from 353 billion cruzeiros to over 9 trillion cruzeiros, and the consumer price index rose from 100 to 2048! What connection do you think these different events had with each other?

11   a) Show that the more unequal the actual distribution of income, the more the Lorentz curve of actual income distribution will bow in.

   b) Is it possible for the Lorentz curve to lie *above* the curve of equal income distribution?

12   Figure 40.4 shows a curve which represents absolute equality in the distribution of income. Can you sketch into this diagram a curve which represents *absolute inequality* in the distribution of income (i.e., a situation in which one consumer gets all the income and nobody else gets any)?

13   As a citizen, humanitarian, and potential taxpayer, what do you think of the idea of replacing present welfare schemes with a negative income tax?

CHAPTER 41

ECONOMIC GROWTH

Strictly speaking, the term "economic growth" refers to any situation in which national output increases. However, since the appeal of growth lies largely in the possibilities it offers for raising people's living standards, economists and the man in the street often use the term in a narrower sense to refer to increases in per capita output. In this chapter, when we use the word growth we usually mean growth in this latter sense.

WHY GROWTH?

Today in almost every country—rich or poor, capitalist or communist—growth ranks high among the goals of government policy. That the poor countries of the world should give top priority to growth is hardly surprising, because the only way they can provide their populations with the rising standard of living to which they aspire is by increasing per capita output. But what about the rich, developed countries, the United States and most of the nations of Western Europe? Why are they great growth watchers, always anxious to speed up their growth rate and to make sure that it at least meets the pace set by other developed countries?

The case of the United States offers some answers. One compelling reason why we accord great importance to growth is the continuing war—hot and cold—between the communist and noncommunist countries of the world. Because of this struggle, we have to provide for national defense, and our ability to do so depends on our capacity to produce output. The East-West struggle also compels us to compete with the communist countries for the allegiance of the underdeveloped countries, and in this competition one factor that counts heavily is how well our market economy performs compared with their planned economies. Of course an economy's performance has many dimensions, but the underdeveloped countries, because of their poverty, are preoccupied with a single one of them: How fast it grows.

Another reason why the United States worries about growth is that significant segments of our population still live in poverty. And, as we saw in Chapter 40, rising national income is a potent force in doing away with these pockets of poverty.

A third reason why growth is important for the United States is that, when we have allocated resources between the public and private sectors, we have too often lavished our growing output on private needs but stinted on public-sector expenditures. So we have high-powered cars (a private good), but end up driving them bumper-to-bumper on inadequate roads (a public good). We have sailboats and motorboats, but the lakes and rivers we would like to use them on are often polluted. Stinting on the public sector doesn't inconvenience the consumer alone. Business firms rely on the public sector to provide them with many vital services, and if it doesn't, the ability of these firms to produce output is impaired. For example, airlines now find that the New York–Boston run takes longer in their newest jets than it used to take in their old piston-engine planes because airport congestion has been raising runway queue-time faster than jet engines have been cutting in-flight air time. In the language of Chapter 37, this means that as a society we are allocating our expenditure dollars between public and private goods so that dollars spent on private goods yield a smaller marginal benefit than dollars spent on public goods. We could of course redress this imbalance simply by shifting resources from the private to the public sector. But people don't like to give up goods they have become accustomed to consuming. So an easier way to meet our needs for more public goods is to accelerate our growth rate and use the resulting extra output to build more schools, parks, airports, roads and other public goods.

INCREASES IN PRODUCTIVE CAPACITY

Now that we've seen why nations value growth, let's talk about the way growth takes place. Suppose that an economy starts out at full employment and that it utilizes its resources efficiently. What conditions must this economy meet in order to produce more output?

The first condition for growth is that *the economy's productive capacity has to increase.* Such an increase might take place either because the amount of resources available to the economy increases or because advances in technology raise the productivity of existing inputs.

Increases in Raw Materials

One way in which the economy's productive resources may increase is through a rise in the supply of natural resources available to the economy. Sometimes this happens, as it has so often happened in the past, because of the discovery of new resources. (A prospector finds gold. Or a drilling crew strikes oil.) Today, however, increases in natural resources are more often tied up with advances in technology. (The development of nuclear power has made uranium a valuable mineral. Changing technology has made it possible to bring up oil from under the sea. The day is coming when people will know how to turn salty sea water into fresh drinking water at low cost. And now people are even talking about opening up undersea mines and farming the oceans.)

Increases in Labor Inputs

Increases in population, and thus in the work force, are another important way the economy's supply of productive inputs can rise.* However, increases in population *per se* are a poor way for the economy to grow if they aren't accompanied by increases in other inputs. If population increases aren't accompanied by increases in a nation's capital stock, each additional worker who enters the labor force will have less and less plant and equipment to work with, and consequently the extra output he yields will probably decline (i.e., diminishing returns with respect to labor are likely to set in). Thus increases in output generated solely by means of increases in population pose the threat of declining per capita output and a declining living standard.

Increases in Capital Inputs

To grow in a way that will bring about large increases in per capita output, and thus in living standards, an economy must increase its capital stock. If its labor supply is increasing, it will have to increase its capital stock faster than it increases its labor supply. Capital, of course, is not a charmed input that is somehow immune to diminishing returns. If an economy increases its capital stock a great deal but doesn't increase its labor supply much, diminishing returns will set in with respect to capital (i.e., each extra unit of capital added to the production process will yield less extra output). How far an economy can go in increasing its capital stock per worker before it experiences diminishing returns with respect to capital depends on the nature of the production functions in its different industries.† If these pro-

---

* The relationship between the size of the population and the size of the work force is, of course, a complex one that depends on varied factors: the age distribution of the population, the length of time people stay in school, and what proportion of wives take outside jobs. But usually increases in population mean increases in the labor force, and vice versa.

† Recall that in Chapter 7 we said that the *production function* faced by producers in any industry is a technical (i.e., engineering) relationship that tells them the maximum levels of output they can obtain by employing various input combinations, or alternatively what minimum input combinations they must use to produce a specified level of output.

duction functions offer many chances to substitute capital for labor, then a great deal of "capital deepening" can occur before the marginal productivity of capital (that's the extra output producers get by employing an extra unit of capital) declines significantly.

Technological Change

Whenever an existing production function is altered or a new one is created, we call that *technological change*. In a modern economy technological change assumes a variety of forms: introduction of new products, improvement in existing products, and changes in the relationship between inputs applied and output produced. Technological changes of this last sort—that is, changes that permit producers to obtain more output with fewer inputs—obviously increase the total output that the economy can produce with its available inputs.

A technological change that opens up new ways for producers to combine inputs to produce output also affects the ease with which they can substitute one input for another. This possibility suggests that we ought to distinguish between (a) technological changes that are *labor-saving* and (b) those that are *capital-saving*.

By a labor-saving (capital-using) innovation, we mean one that alters production functions in such a way that increased quantities of capital can be substituted for labor without decreasing capital's marginal productivity. Example: computers. The invention of computers has opened up large-scale opportunities for substituting capital in the form of complex machines for labor in the form of clerks.

By a capital-saving innovation, we mean one that alters production functions in such a way that producers can decrease the capital inputs they employ per unit of labor without decreasing labor's marginal productivity. Example: communications satellites (recall Chapter 25). Communications satellites offer a way to get messages from one point to another with a lot less capital and no more labor than old methods (e.g., under-sea and over-land cables) required.

Growth in the U.S. Economy

Figure 41.1 presents data on how inputs and output have grown in the U.S. economy over time. It shows that since 1900 the U.S. work force has more than doubled, while the U.S. capital stock has roughly quadrupled. It also shows that U.S. net national output, measured in constant prices, is nine times as large today as it was in 1900.

How was the economy's output able to increase so much faster than its labor and capital inputs? It's just possible that, during the period in ques-

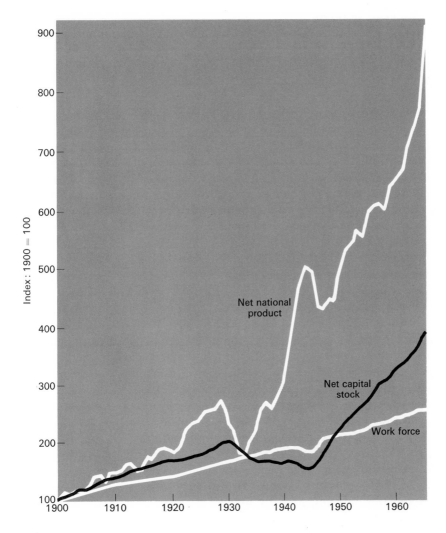

41|1

Growth of inputs and output in the U.S. economy. (Net national product and net capital stock are measured in 1958 dollars.) (Source: U.S. Department of Commerce)

tion, the available supply of natural resources grew so fast that its growth increased the productivity of capital and labor. But it's hard to determine whether or not this happened. For instance: Since 1900 erosion has decreased the supply of some kinds of farmland, but irrigation has increased the supply of others. Iron-ore reserves have been depleted, but known oil reserves have risen. Technological change has decreased the need for coal, but it has made uranium a useful mineral. Thus if we look at how natural resources have changed since 1900, we find a lot of pluses and minuses, and there's no way to figure out the total. We get the feeling, however, that since 1900 natural resources probably didn't grow, or anyway didn't grow much. But if they didn't, then changes in the supply of natural resources— instead of explaining the big increase in the productivity of capital and labor—may actually have worked to hold it down.* There is no pat answer to the question of what did happen. However, many economists think that changes in the supply of natural resources probably had a *neutral* effect on (i.e., neither raised nor lowered) the productivity of capital and labor. They reason that the slow growth of natural resources was offset by the following factors: (1) During the last half century the U.S. has become a big net importer of nonrenewable resources such as minerals. (2) U.S. producers have learned to use resources more efficiently (producing a kilowatt of electric power today takes only a fraction of the coal it used to). (3) U.S. producers have learned to substitute synthetic products such as plastics for nonrenewable minerals such as iron and aluminum.

Although changes in natural resources don't seem to explain the big gap between the growth rates of labor and capital inputs and the growth rate of net output, several other factors perhaps do. Here are some of these probable factors: (1) The way that data on the economy's net capital stock and its net output are calculated. In most countries, including the U.S., the national income accountant treats education as a consumption item. And some education probably is. However, a lot of education—such as the training of engineers, teachers, and typists—is an *investment* that increases labor's skills and thus its productivity. So we really ought to include much of the economy's education expenditures under the heading of investment. If we did that, then our estimates of the economy's net capital stock would be much higher and rising much faster.

(2) As the outputs of individual industries have increased, producers in these industries have undoubtedly been able to organize production more efficiently, and thus get more output out of a given batch of inputs. Recall Fig. 7.1 on page 102. It shows that this phenomenon, which is known as "increasing returns to scale," is still common in a wide range of manufacturing industries.

It would be hard to estimate how much education and increasing returns to scale have contributed to the gap between the rates at which the economy's labor and capital inputs have risen and the rate at which its net output has risen. However, studies made by E. F. Denison and J. W. Kendrick indicate

---

* The fixed supply of natural resources may have brought on diminishing returns with respect to capital and labor both.

that if we tried to correct our input and output series for these factors, we would still be left with a significant gap in growth rates.*

Thus we conclude that in our economy over the last half century technological change has been a potent force in expanding productive capacity.

UTILIZING RESOURCES EFFICIENTLY

We have been talking about the fact that an increase in resources or an advance in technology that increases input productivities increases the economy's capacity to produce output. However, an increase in an economy's *capacity* doesn't guarantee that the output it actually produces will rise by a like amount. In order for that to happen, several other conditions must hold. One is that the economy must utilize the new resources and the new technology efficiently. Although this condition sounds easy to meet, in practice it often poses difficulties. Let's look at some of the reasons.

Opposition to Utilizing Technological Innovations

First take the matter of technological innovation. You might think that producers and workers would always want to adopt technological innovations that would increase the productivity of labor and capital. But not always. Technological advances may promise benefits to some people, but threaten the interests of others: They may eliminate the jobs of certain workers, or they may render the capital stocks of some firms obsolete. Therefore technological innovations are often opposed by workers, business firms, or both. Examples: Automation has made it possible to run subway shuttle trains without a motorman, but in New York City the union insists that a motorman be aboard each train anyway. Synchronous satellites make possible direct station-to-home broadcasting over long distances, but local television stations and cable operators who stand to lose from such an arrangement oppose this new method.

The Need for Labor Mobility

Despite the fact that workers and business firms often oppose changes in the status quo, as an economy grows, the *kinds* of output it produces and the

---

* E. F. Denison, *The Sources of Economic Growth in the United States and the Alternatives Before Us,* Committee for Economic Development, New York, 1962; and J. W. Kendrick, *Productivity Trends in the United States,* National Bureau of Economic Research, Princeton, N.J., 1961. For a further discussion of this point, consult Chapter II in Robert Solow's *Capital Theory and the Rate of Return,* North Holland Publishing Company, Amsterdam, 1963.

way these outputs are produced change. For this reason, labor and capital *must be mobile* if they are to remain fully and efficiently employed. Let us look at the implications of this.

Economic growth changes the composition of producers' demand for labor for several reasons. One has to do with income elasticities of demand. Recall Fig. 4.2 (page 36). It shows that, as income rises, people spend a higher percentage of their consumption dollars on clothing and education, but a lower percentage on food and shelter. The economist sums up this situation by saying that the *income elasticity** of consumer demand is high for some goods (clothing and education), but low for others (food and shelter). Because income elasticity differs from good to good, the *relative* importance of different sectors of the economy inevitably shifts as national and per capita incomes grow. To illustrate this point, consider agriculture and services. The income elasticity of demand is low for farm products but high for education, health care, and other services. So, over time, as income per capita rises, farm output grows more slowly than that of the service industries, and the importance of the agricultural sector relative to that of the service sector declines.

Shifts in the relative importance of the different sectors of the economy naturally creates offsetting shifts in the composition of the demand for labor. Farms need relatively fewer workers; manufacturing firms and service enterprises need more. We can get some idea of the magnitude that these shifts may assume by looking at what has happened to the composition of the U.S. labor force in the last 100 years. Figure 41.2 shows that since 1870 there has been a startling decrease (from 50% to less than 10%) in the percentage of the total U.S. work force employed in agriculture,† and that this decline has been offset by a rapid rise in the proportion of the work force employed in trade, finance, and services, and by slower increases in the proportion employed in manufacturing and government.

A second reason why growth alters the composition of the demand for labor is that, as the economy grows, technological innovations such as the introduction of new products and the development of new modes of transportation, together with differences in the income elasticity of demand for different products, all work to change the composition of the outputs of *individual* sectors and the location of individual industries. Examples: Because of technological innovation and the development of new products, consumers today demand a host of products, from color television sets to home freezers, that were unknown a generation or two ago. Improvements

---

* For a precise definition of this term, see the footnote on page 387.

† This decrease reflects not only the fact that farm output represents a declining proportion of national output, but also the fact that labor productivity has been rising more rapidly on the farm than in the factory. (Recall Fig. 25.3 on page 388.)

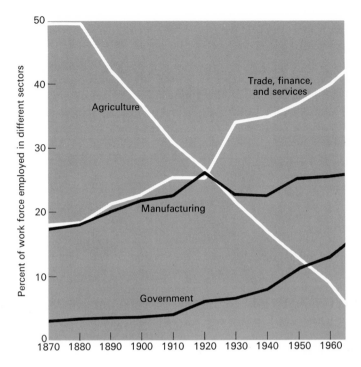

41|2

Over the last century the composition of the work force has shifted dramatically.
(Source: U.S. Department of Commerce)

in transportation, ranging from refrigerated cars to air freight, have made it possible for California and Florida to supply New York with fresh fruit and vegetables. New means of extracting oil from oil-bearing shale promise an expansion of the oil industry to states in which it hasn't previously been strong. Differences in the income elasticity of consumer demand (it's high for meat but low for wheat) mean that the resources devoted to meat production are growing compared with those devoted to wheat production. Whenever there are changes in the outputs and location of individual industries, there are also changes in the composition of the demand for labor. Therefore as the economy grows, the changes that occur in the demand for labor are likely to be even greater than the shifts shown in Fig. 41.2 would indicate.

There's another way that growth shifts the composition of demand for labor: Growth *decreases* the importance of unskilled workers, *increases* the importance of skilled ones, and shifts workers from blue-collar to white-collar and professional jobs. It promotes the emergence of giant corporations, plays down the role of the small independent entrepreneur, and thus increases the proportion of people who are employees rather than employers. The labor force has to shift gears to keep up.

Unless it does, economic growth—by altering the composition of the demand for labor—will create pockets of structural unemployment like the ones discussed in Chapter 40. And, if this happens, a gap will emerge between the economy's actual and potential output. Thus if an economy is going to realize its full growth potential (i.e., increase output as much as possible), it has to have a *mobile labor force,* one that is willing to shift from industry to industry, to move from region to region, to alter its skills, and to accept new responsibilities.

The Need for Capital Mobility

In a growing economy, the same structural changes that shift the composition of the demand for labor also shift the composition of the demand for *capital*. The reason is that growth-induced changes in the structure of the economy naturally alter the productivity of capital in different uses. Therefore if capital doesn't move from use to use in response to shifts in demand for it, its actual productivity will fall below its potential productivity, and a gap will open up between the economy's actual and potential output. So *capital too must be mobile.*

The idea that capital can be mobile may appear impractical: After all, one can't transform a New England textile mill into a Texas oil-drilling rig. In what sense, then, can capital move around?

1) The fact that as capital is used over a period of time it depreciates due to wear and tear and therefore has to be replaced (recall Chapter 6) means that capital can be mobile between industries or between regions in the sense that resources that would have been used to replace depreciated plant and equipment in one industry or place can be used to produce them in some other industry or place. Example: Capital in the textile industry can move from the North to the South if resources that would have been used to replace depreciated equipment in Northern mills is used instead to build up Southern mills. Similarly, capital in the transportation sector can move from railroads to airlines if resources that would have been used to replace worn-out railroad cars are used instead to build jet aircraft.

2) Whenever new funds—either from business saving (i.e., retained profits) or consumer savings—are devoted to investment, these additions to the nation's capital stock can be made in new industries, new types of equipment, or new regions instead of traditional ones. This sort of capital mobility takes place all the time. Today millions of dollars of current savings are

being invested in plant and equipment destined to produce outputs, such as color television sets and tape recorders, that didn't exist a few years ago; to buy capital equipment, such as nuclear power plants and jet airplanes, that were only dreams 30 years ago; and to establish industries in growing regions, such as California and Florida, which used to be mostly palm trees and tourist hotels.

It is patently obvious that capital will be mobile only if business firms are alert to changing investment opportunities. However, this isn't enough. In a modern economy a great deal of saving is done by consumers, but most investing (in *real capital stock*) is done by business firms. Therefore, in order for large net investments in real capital stock to occur, savers have to transfer their excess funds to investors. Savers, however, don't usually know much about the investment opportunities open to different firms. So they can seldom judge which of the many would-be investors who seek their funds have projects that would yield high returns. For their part, would-be investors don't usually know who savers are, or how to solicit their funds. These conditions pose difficulties for the flow of funds between savers and investors; and as the economy grows, these difficulties worsen for several reasons: (1) Economic growth diminishes the role of the small entrepreneur and thus accentuates the division between savers and investors. (2) Economic growth accelerates the rate of change of production techniques and final output, and this makes it harder for savers to evaluate alternative investment opportunities.

The fact that, in a growing economy, various factors impede the free flow of capital from savers to investors means that, in such an economy, capital will be mobile only if there are channels to funnel funds from savers to investors. Generally, as an economy develops, two kinds of channels emerge: *financial markets* and *financial intermediaries*.

WILL DEMAND KEEP PACE WITH CAPACITY?

In addition to resource mobility, there's another condition that has to be met if an increase in capacity is to result in an equivalent increase in output. Rising demand has to keep pace with rising capacity.

As we pointed out in Chapter 35, because wages and prices in many industries are "sticky downward," the economy's equilibrium income Y_e may lie below its full-employment income Y_f. This possibility means that, when the economy's productive capacity increases, its output won't necessarily rise equivalently. In order for that to happen, aggregate demand must also shift upward. This point is illustrated in Fig. 41.3: Initially the economy shown there is in equilibrium at the full-employment output, Y_f. Then

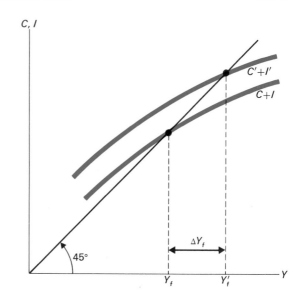

41|3

In order for an increase in capacity, ΔY_f, to be utilized, aggregate demand must shift upward.

advancing technology and increases in resources raise the economy's full-employment income from Y_f to Y'_f. In order for actual output to rise by an equivalent amount, aggregate demand has to shift upward from $C + I$ to $C' + I'$.

The experience of the 1930's, when a deflationary gap persisted year after year, led many economists to fear that private investment and consumption would never be able to rise as fast as investment was raising capacity. Therefore they were afraid that there would be an ever-widening gap between the economy's capacity to produce output and the quantity of output demanded by consumers and investors. They foresaw chronic unemployment and business stagnation, and many of them spoke in dire terms of the threat of *secular* stagnation*. One of the chief proponents of the secular-stagnation thesis was Harvard's Alvin Hansen. He argued that the slowdown in population growth, the closing of the frontier, and the shift in technological change—away from innovations such as railroads, electric power, and autos, whose exploitation required big additions to the nation's capital stock—spelled an end to the investment opportunities that had made it possible, during the previous century of rapid growth, for $C + I$ to keep pace with the economy's constantly rising capacity. Today, however, few economists worry about secular stagnation, partially because economists are confident that secular stagnation, if it materialized, could be dealt with through appropriate fiscal and monetary measures, and also because it's

---

* "Secular" here does not mean secular-as-opposed-to-religious. It means occurring over a long period of time.

hard to worry about secular stagnation when the real question of the day seems to be: How can capacity expand fast enough to keep pace with the rising demands of consumers, investors, and government?

GOVERNMENT POLICIES FOR GROWTH

As we have seen, growth ranks high as an objective of government policy. But growth, pure and simple, is a rather nebulous goal. So most countries translate their desire for growth into some more clearly defined objective, such as a target growth rate for national output. Generally the target rates chosen by growth-minded countries run about 4 or 5% a year, but a few ambitious countries like Japan hope to hit growth rates as high as 8 or 9% a year.

All this growthmanship leads us to ask: What policies can a government pursue to promote growth? Think back to our discussion of the way an economy grows. It indicates that a government program designed to promote growth is likely to have three aspects: (1) increasing the economy's productive capacity, (2) promoting an efficient allocation of resources, and (3) keeping the economy at full employment.

Since we have already talked about government policies to promote full employment, let us now focus on what the government can do to increase output capacity and promote an efficient use of resources.

Promoting an Efficient Allocation of Resources

As we have seen, in a dynamic economy the allocation of resources is efficient only if resources are mobile. Thus one way the government can promote efficiency is by increasing the mobility of capital and labor.

We already mentioned, in Chapter 40, some of the measures that a government can use to promote *labor* mobility: job training programs, employment offices to enable workers in one area to find out about job opportunities in other areas, relocation allowances to workers in areas in which structural unemployment is high, special area redevelopment programs (like the one for Appalachia) and so forth.

A government can also do a lot to promote *capital* mobility. By regulating securities markets and especially by guarding against fraud, the government can smooth the operation of these markets, reduce the risk to investors, and promote the flow of funds from savers to investors. By regulating the activities of financial intermediaries, by insuring the deposits accepted by these institutions, and by providing them with a lender of last resort, the government can enhance the attractiveness of the indirect securities they issue and thus promote the role of these institutions as funnels through which money can flow from savers to investors.

Of course resources may be allocated inefficiently for reasons other than just immobility of capital and labor. Other flies in the ointment are:

1) Restrictions or requirements as to the way that factors may be used. [Example: Union rules that either require firms to employ unneeded workers (featherbedding) or prohibit firms from introducing labor-saving equipment clearly decrease the efficiency with which the economy's work force is utilized.]

2) Imperfections in product markets. [For an example, recall Chapter 24. There we showed that price leadership, which is common in product markets characterized by seller fewness, may lead to a situation* in which efficient low-cost producers operate at output levels that are too small for them to attain minimum cost, while inefficient, high-cost producers, who should have been eliminated by competition, are preserved.]

All this of course indicates that a government can promote growth by attacking market structures that perpetuate existing inefficiencies in resource allocation and by breaking down barriers-to-change that promise to create new inefficiencies.

Finally we should mention that since the government provides postal services, highways, schooling of prospective employees, and a lot of other goods and services that private producers need in order to produce and market their outputs, it's important that government investment grow in step with private investment and output. If it doesn't, the efficiency with which inputs in the private sector can be utilized will decline and output growth will be slowed.

The maxim, "keep government investment in step with private-sector investment" is vague. Can we make it more precise? Well, if an extra dollar is going to be invested in the economy, and if the government wants to maximize the rate at which the economy is growing, it ought to see to it that this dollar is invested in the area in which it will make the greatest contribution to future output, i.e., in the area in which the rate of return it yields over time will be greatest. Therefore the government ought to push public-sector investment to the point at which the marginal rate of return on such investment just equals that on private investment.†

---

* See the discussion of the bread industry on pages 365–367.

† In econ-English, "marginal" always means "extra." So the marginal rate of return is the return yielded by the last or extra dollar invested. As we showed in Chapter 10, the marginal rate of return yielded by any investment is likely to be a decreasing function of the size of that investment.

Policies to Increase Capacity

We said above that the government can stimulate growth not only by taking steps to increase the efficiency with which existing resources are utilized (i.e., by getting the economy to utilize its productive capacity more fully), but also by promoting an increase in the economy's productive capacity.

The government can prod an economy's productive capacity in two ways: (1) by encouraging the growth of productive resources, and (2) by encouraging technological innovations.

Since the key resource in any economy is its *work force,* the government might increase resources by encouraging population growth. However, population growth, even though it might increase total output, probably wouldn't increase per capita output. Also, a government population policy would impinge on individual freedom. So population is one variable that the government isn't likely to tinker with. However, the government might attempt to increase the productivity of the work force by providing people with health care and educational opportunities.

A second productive resource available to an economy is its mineral deposits, waters, land, and other *natural resources.* To encourage the preservation and growth of these, the government can take a variety of steps: (1) It can impose restrictions on the rates at which such resources are used and on the ways in which they are used. (2) It can use tax incentives and subsidies to encourage private producers to practice conservation and to prospect for new resources. (3) It can promote the development of new technologies that will increase the uses to which existing resources can be put. Examples of these policies in the U.S.: The government controls the way resources found on federal lands may be used. It uses subsidies to encourage farmers to practice conservation. And a lot of the research it undertakes, including the plan to find new ways to utilize the resources of the seas, have increased or promise to increase the usefulness of existing natural resources.

A third key resource in an economy is its *capital stock.* The government can promote the growth of the economy's capital stock by increasing its own investment in public capital goods and by encouraging firms to buy more private capital goods. There are several ways the government can encourage them to do this. *First,* it can keep the economy at full employment. This encourages private investment because full employment makes the investment opportunities open to private producers look a lot more attractive. *Second,* if full employment doesn't bring about the desired level of private investment, the government can apply stronger medicine: It can use a restrictive fiscal policy to reduce consumption, while it encourages investment by permitting accelerated depreciation, by granting tax credits for new investment, and by lowering interest rates.

In addition to encouraging the *growth* of resources as a means to increase the economy's productive capacity, the government can also encourage technological innovations that raise input *productivities*. The government might do this by using tax rebates and subsidies to encourage private research, by carrying out some research on its own (especially basic research that would benefit producers in many fields but that wouldn't be worth while for any one producer to undertake) and by financing some vital applied projects that would increase the economy's growth potential but that would be too expensive for private producers.

The activities of the U.S. government give ample evidence of all these policies. The government subsidizes private research on nuclear reactors; it carries out millions of dollars' worth of agricultural research; its National Science Foundation pays for giant cyclotrons that do basic research in physics; and on the more applied level it is financing the development of a supersonic transport plane, which private aircraft manufacturers don't have the resources to do on their own.

THE U.S. RECORD

Since a rapid rate of growth is so important to a country, let us conclude our discussion of economic growth by asking: How are we doing? How does the U.S. growth rate compare with that of other countries?

U.S. Growth Rates

Table 41.1 gives a few answers to the first question. It shows that over the last century, the average annual rate of growth of the U.S. gross national product (GNP) has fallen from slightly over 4% to slightly over 3%. This trend looks unfavorable, but the first column of Table 41.1 shows that it can

TABLE 41|1

U.S. Growth Rates for Population, GNP, and GNP per Capita, 1840–1960*

Period	Average annual rate of growth		
	Population	GNP	GNP per capita
1840–1880	2.73	4.03	1.26
1880–1920	1.88	3.52	1.61
1920–1960	1.31	3.15	1.81
1840–1960	1.97	3.56	1.56

*Source: Simon Kuznets, "Notes on the Pattern of U.S. Economic Growth," in The Nation's Economic Objectives, Edgar O. Edwards, editor, Rice University Semicentennial Publications (Chicago: University of Chicago Press, 1964), page 16.

be explained largely by the sharp fall in the rate of growth of the population. During the early 1800's and early 1900's, the U.S. population grew at an extraordinary rate, reflecting the terrific influx of immigrants during this period.

So far as the U.S. growth record is concerned, the third column in Table 41.1 is the one that tells the really important story. It shows that over the last century, the average annual rate of growth in GNP *per capita* has risen by almost a half. Thus today's Americans are not only richer than their ancestors, but they are also getting richer faster.

International Comparisons

Table 41.2 compares the U.S. growth record with that of several other developed countries. It shows that as a result of immigration from both east and west, population grew over the last hundred years at a much faster pace in the U.S. than it did in any of these other countries. Given the rapid rate of increase in U.S. population, we aren't surprised to see that the U.S. rate of output growth outstripped the rate of output growth of most of these other countries by a wide margin. The one exception is Japan. Japan's high rate of output growth, over 4% per year, reflects the rapidity with which its population grew, the low income level from which it started its growth spurt, and the fact that its late industrialization enabled it to adopt

TABLE 41|2

Comparative Growth Rates for Population, Output, and
Output per Capita in Selected Countries*

| Country and period | Average annual rate of growth | | |
	Population	Output	Output per capita
France 1841–50 to 1958–60	0.24	1.80	1.55
West Germany 1851–55 to 1958–60	1.01	2.45	1.43
United Kingdom 1841 to 1957–59	0.86	2.07	1.20
United States 1840 to 1960	1.97	3.56	1.56
U.S.S.R. 1860 to 1958	0.99	2.87	1.86
Japan 1878–82 to 1958–60	1.21	4.05	2.81

*Source: op. cit., pages 18–19.

quickly technological advances that European countries took many decades to develop.

Column 3 of Table 41.2 compares national rates of growth in output per capita. It is hard to calculate the rate of growth in output per capita for one country, and even harder to calculate comparable rates for several different countries. Therefore the figures in this column are rather rough estimates, and the most we can conclude from them is that output per capita probably has risen at roughly similar rates in the U.S. and in the principal European countries. If so, then the reason why the U.S. standard of living today is materially higher than Western Europe's is not that income per capita has grown during the last century more rapidly here than there, but that a century ago income per capita was already higher in the U.S. than in Western Europe.

PROBLEMS

1   How do you think the U.S. farm program affects the efficiency with which the economy's resources are utilized? How do you think that it affects the U.S. growth rate? [*Hint:* Take a careful look at Fig. 41.2.]

2   John Kenneth Galbraith* has suggested that one reason why Americans stint on public wants but lavish resources on private wants is that billions of advertising dollars are spent every year to convince people that they ought to consume new cars, cosmetics, and cake mixes. But very little, if anything, is spent to convince people that they ought to provide themselves with better schools, roads, public libraries, and so forth.

   Do you think that Galbraith has a point? If not, why not? If so, what do you think ought to be done?

3   Figure 41.2 shows how the composition of the U.S. labor force has shifted as the economy has grown and developed. Would you expect to observe a similar pattern of change in other growing countries? Why or why not?

4   How do you think that minimum-wage laws, featherbedding, and restrictive work rules that prevent the introduction of labor-saving capital equipment or production techniques affect the productivity of labor and the growth rate of the economy? Do you think that there are considerations that justify these practices?

5   a) What are some of the things that the U.S. government does that might be said to increase the mobility of capital?
   b) Does your list include the setting up of the Fed as a lender of last resort? If so, why? [*Hint:* If bank panics† were common, how do you think this would affect savers' feelings about what they would like to do with their surplus funds?]

---

* John Kenneth Galbraith, *The Affluent Society,* Boston: Houghton Mifflin, 1958.
† See page 462.

6 For the past 15 years the Japanese people have been devoting over 14% of their disposable income to savings, and their economy has been growing at an amazing 9% a year. Smith and Brown, who have just finished an introductory course in economics, are discussing the situation. Smith claims that the Japanese have been lucky to grow so fast because with all that saving it's hard to see how demand was able to rise fast enough to keep existing capacity fully employed, and to create opportunities for additional investment as well. Brown argues that Smith has the picture all wrong. The high rate of Japanese savings, far from impeding growth, was a prerequisite for it. All that saving was needed to finance the investment which made it possible for the Japanese economy's productive capacity to grow at such a phenomenal rate.

Who is right, or are they both?

7 a) Show that the consumption function shown in Fig. 35.1 implies that consumers will save an increasing proportion of their disposable income (i.e., that S/Y will rise) as their total disposable income increases.

b) Data for the U.S. indicate that over the last century the savings ratio (S/Y) has remained almost constant except during abnormal periods such as the Great Depression and World War II. Show that these data imply that the short-run consumption function (see Fig. 35.1) must have shifted constantly upward over time. [*Hint:* Work this one out with a diagram.]

8 As we showed in Fig. 41.3, if output is to grow, it isn't enough that capacity increase. In addition, demand must also increase. One way this may happen is through continued upward shifts in the consumption schedule. In the preceding problem we suggested that such upward shifts have in fact occurred. What factors might explain why they have occurred? Here are some hints:

a) In Table 41.1 we show that U.S. population has risen steadily over time. Show that an increase in population shifts the aggregate consumption schedule upward.

b) Yale's James Tobin thinks that, as a person's wealth increases, his consumption function is likely to shift upward. Show that in an economy in which income per capita was rising this would tend to shift the aggregate consumption function upward.

c) Harvard's James Dusenberry argues that over the long run an individual's savings ratio will depend not so much on the absolute amount of disposable income he receives as on his standing in the income distribution. The higher his standing, the higher his savings ratio will be. Show that this hypothesis implies that the aggregate consumption function will shift upward as people's incomes rise.

Can you think of any reasons why people should behave as Dusenberry argues they do? Here is one possibility: People's consumption functions are interdependent; the sort of car Brown wants depends on what sort of car Smith is driving. The man in the street refers to this sort of behavior as "keeping up with the Joneses."

Part 7
INTERNATIONAL
ECONOMICS

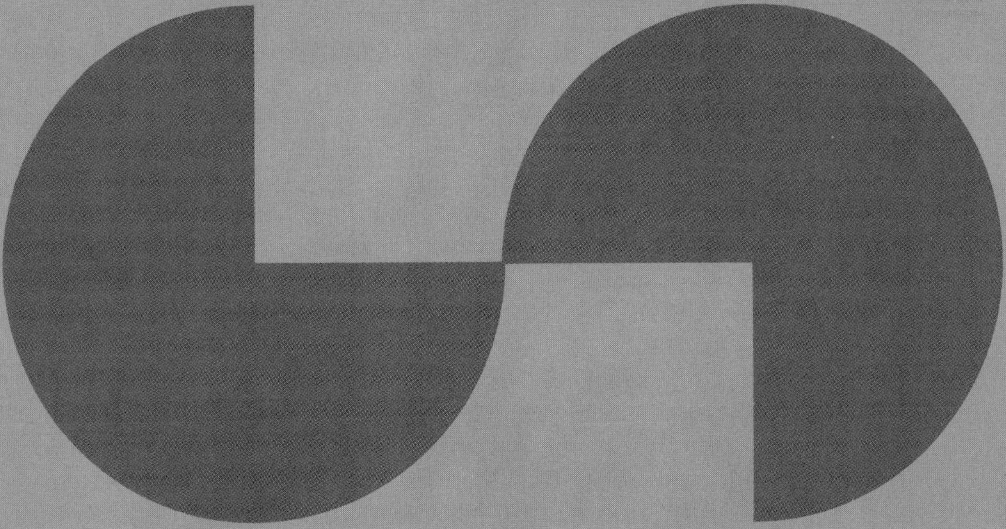

CHAPTER 42

INTRODUCTION TO INTERNATIONAL ECONOMICS

In the jargon of economists, an *open* economy is one that has economic relationships with the rest of the world. A *closed* economy is one that doesn't. When we were talking about the way goods and financial markets operate (Parts 3, 4, 5) and about the way an aggregate economy composed of many such markets operates, we implicitly assumed, to keep things simple, that we were dealing with a closed economy. Now in this part we shall drop this assumption and talk about the relations that an open economy has with the rest of the world.

INTERNATIONAL TRADE FLOWS

As we shift our focus from the domestic to the international scene, the first thing that strikes our attention is the intricate pattern of trade in goods and services that links the different countries and regions of the world. Americans eat bananas from Panama and shrimp from the Mediterranean; they drink tea from India and wine from France; they build bridges with German steel and haul oil in Japanese-built tankers. Of course, international trade isn't all in one direction. Americans sell tobacco to the British, frozen chickens to the Germans, computers to the French, and a host of other agricultural and industrial products throughout the world.

Figure 42.1 represents the web of world trade that results from such transactions. It shows that trading ties link all the major regions of the world, but the direction and strength of these ties vary from region to region. Developed areas like the United States and Western Europe trade heavily with each other, and there is also much trade between the developed and less-developed areas. On the other hand, trade flows between less-developed areas (for example, between Latin America and Africa) are generally small. Trade flows between the Communist-bloc countries and other regions of the world are also small relative to the area and trading potential of these countries.

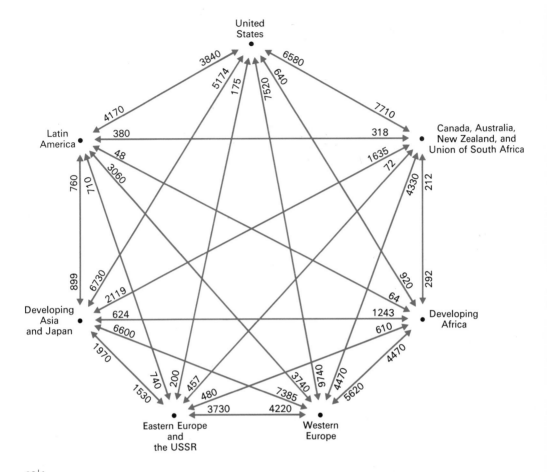

42|1

The web of world commodity trade (1966, millions of dollars).
(Source: United Nations *Monthly Bulletin of Statistics*)

INTERNATIONAL CAPITAL MOVEMENTS

Trade flows are not the only kind of economic relationship that link the nations of the world. Nations are also linked by *capital movements.*

Private citizens and financial institutions in the U.S. buy bonds issued by the World Bank,* which uses the money it gets from bond sales to finance development projects in Latin America, Africa, and other parts of the world. General Electric invests tens of millions of dollars in Machines Bull, a French computer maker. Ford expands its British subsidiary to produce

---

* We shall talk about the World Bank in Chapter 48.

more cars for the British and European markets. Japanese industrialists set up plants in Alaska to produce food and raw materials ranging from fish to timber, largely for export to Japan. These transactions seem at first glance to have a disparate character, but a more careful inspection shows that they have one important characteristic in common: All involve international capital movements, that is, the use of funds supplied by investors in one country to finance investments in another.

International capital movements are often broken into two categories, direct and other. A *direct* investment is one in which a firm uses funds from a domestic source to set up or expand a foreign business enterprise over which it exercises some degree of ownership (equity) control. If IBM were to use U.S. dollars to set up a European subsidiary, that would be a direct investment. Similarly, if Volkswagen were to use German marks to set up an American subsidiary, that would be a direct investment too, but in the opposite direction. "Nondirect" investments are those in which an investor in one country lends to a foreign borrower over whom he exercises no *ownership* control. For example, if a U.S. investor were to buy bonds issued by a Brazilian corporation or a European government, that would be a nondirect investment. Similarly, if a U.S. bank were to lend out funds to a foreign firm, that too would be a nondirect investment.

Data on international capital flows are a lot harder to track down than those on trade flows. So we can't set up a comprehensive multilateral picture of capital flows like the one we set up for trade flows. We can, however, set up a figure which shows the amounts and direction of the capital flows that link the U.S. to other regions of the world.

Figure 42.2 shows that the U.S. is a heavy investor in the rest of the world and that most U.S. investments abroad take the form of direct investments. It also shows that U.S. investors make the bulk of their foreign investments in two areas, Canada and Western Europe. Of course, foreign investment isn't a one-way street; most of the areas we invest in also invest in the United States. But on balance the U.S. is, and has been throughout the postwar period, a sizable net exporter of capital to the rest of the world.*

Why Trade and Capital Flows?

Even a brief perusal of the trade patterns and capital flows in Figs. 42.1 and 42.2 raises questions: What determines which goods a country imports and which it exports? Why does capital move between nations? Do trade and capital flows benefit the countries that make and receive them? In today's

---

* As you study Fig. 42.2, the —$125 million figure on the "U.S.-to-other" arrow may puzzle you. It simply means that during 1966 these countries paid back more money than the U.S. lent them.

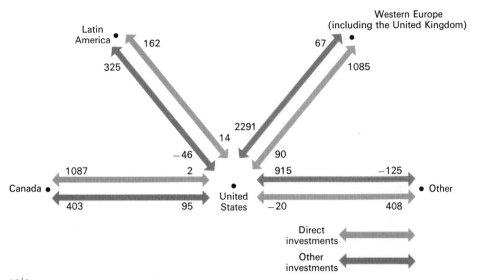

42|2

Capital inflows and outflows link the U.S. to the rest of the world. Figures are for 1966 (millions of dollars). (Source: U.S. Department of Commerce)

ever-narrowing world, these questions are more important than ever. So we shall begin our study of international economics by taking a careful look at the whys and wherefores of international trade and capital movements.

INTERNATIONAL PAYMENTS

The trade flows and capital movements which take place between different countries make necessary vast numbers of payments between people and firms located in different countries. The Japanese firm that wants to put up a timber mill in Alaska needs to pay out dollars to get its mill. The American oil company that wants to buy a tanker in Japan needs to get hold of yen to pay the shipbuilder. To expand its French plant, IBM has to obtain francs to pay for the bricks and mortar, while a Frenchman who wants to buy a stretched-out Detroit auto instead of a compact French one has to use dollars to make this purchase.

Most payments between firms and people in different countries are effected through the exchange of one national currency for another in what is called the *foreign exchange market.* Example: The Frenchman who wants dollars trades francs for dollars in the foreign exchange market, while Americans who hold dollars but want francs make trades of the opposite sort in this same market. There are a great many buyers and sellers in the foreign exchange market; so, if this market were left to its own devices, the exchange rates established there would be determined by supply and demand. And there would be little else to say about international payments. However, exchange rates are not generally permitted to vary by wide amounts. Governments, for reasons we shall discuss later, usually hold these rates at fixed levels (i.e., they "peg" them).

Pegged exchange rates raise the possibility—in fact, the probability— that individual countries will periodically run deficits and surpluses in their balance of payments. As we shall see, a persistent balance-of-payments deficit is something that a country can't live with indefinitely. So we are led to ask: How do balance-of-payments deficits and surpluses come about? Are they likely to be long-lived? If so, how can a country cure them?

Chapters 46 and 47 deal with these questions, and they really end our discussion of international economics. However, there are two more chapters in this part. The first, Chapter 48, deals with economic development. We have waited until the end of our text to discuss this topic because international trade and capital movements often play a vital role in the growth of underdeveloped countries. Our final chapter deals briefly with one alternative to a market economy: the command economies of the socialist and communist states.

PROBLEMS

1   Look at the kinds of international trade transactions mentioned on page 664. What do they suggest to you about why nations trade with one another?

2   Venture some guesses as to why trade is heavy between developed countries, but light between underdeveloped areas.

3   You plan to go to Florida for spring vacation. But you switch and go to Bermuda instead. How will this affect U.S. trade in *goods and services* with the rest of the world?

4   It's easy to think of direct investments that U.S. firms have made in foreign countries. Can you think of any direct investments that foreign firms have made in U.S. industry?

5   Offhand, why do you think that U.S. private capital outflows go largely to two areas, Canada and Western Europe?

CHAPTER 43

THE BALANCE-OF-PAYMENTS ACCOUNT

SETTING UP A BALANCE-OF-PAYMENTS ACCOUNT

In an open economy consumers, producers, and the government usually carry on a wide range of economic transactions with the rest of the world. Seen from the point of view of the domestic economy, some of these transactions (buying imports and lending abroad) *use up* funds; others (selling exports and borrowing abroad) are *sources* of funds.

In Chapter 26 we set up a flow-of-funds account which recorded all sources and uses of funds that a person, John Jones, had as a result of his transactions with other spending units. We also set up a flow-of-funds account for a business firm, Tectronics. Following the same approach we used in these two accounts, we can set up a flow-of-funds account for a country as a whole. This account, which lists all sources and uses of funds that result from transactions between domestic and foreign spending units, is called a country's *balance of payments.*

TABLE 43|1

A Simplified Balance-of-Payments Account

Uses (= debits)	Sources (= credits)
Imports	Exports
Loans to foreigners	Loans from foreigners

Since exports and loans obtained from foreigners are sources of funds, while imports and loans granted to foreigners are uses of funds, a nation's balance-of-payments account will have a general structure like that shown in Table 43.1. As the headings in this table indicate, sources of funds are referred to in balance-of-payments jargon as *credits,* while uses of funds are referred to as *debits.* However, this terminology can be confusing, so in our discussion we shall stick to *sources* and *uses.*

THE U.S. BALANCE-OF-PAYMENTS ACCOUNT

Now let us turn to the United States balance-of-payments account in Table 43.2. This account is similar in structure to the account in Table 43.1, but it contains many more source and use entries. The reason, of course, is that it gives more information this way.

TABLE 43|2

The United States Balance-of-Payments Account, 1966* (Millions of Dollars)

Uses (= debits)		Sources (= credits)	
I. CURRENT ACCOUNT			
Merchandise imports	25,507	Merchandise exports	29,180
Military expenditures	3,649	Military sales	908
Transportation	2,903	Transportation	22,585
Travel	2,623	Travel	1,417
Investment income	1,868	Investment income	6,180
Other services	1,064	Other services	2,640
Imports of goods and services	37,614	*Exports of goods and services*	42,910
Remittances and pensions	992		
II. CAPITAL ACCOUNT			
Direct investment	3,363	Long-term claims and equity	
Long-term claims	213	investments	1,777
Short-term claims	−2,095	Short-term claims	256
U.S. private capital outflow, net	1,481	*Foreign private capital inflow, net*	1,433
U.S. gov't grants and net capital		Long-term claims	735
outflow	3,396	Short-term claims	−1,574
Errors and omissions	589	*Foreign official capital inflow, net*	−839
		Official U.S. gold exports and sales	
		of convertible currencies	568

*Source: Adapted from U.S. Department of Commerce figures.

In studying the U.S. account, note that it is divided into two principal parts: the *current account* and the *capital account*.

The current account records all sources and uses of funds associated with international transactions that yield or use up national income.

The capital account records all sources and uses of funds associated with changes in the foreign assets and liabilities (real and financial) of domestic spending units.

The Current Account

In Table 43.2 the first entry on the sources side of the current account records U.S. private exports of goods, the second U.S. government exports of military equipment. The "transportation," "travel," and "other services" entries all record services (or "invisibles" as they are called) provided by U.S. firms to foreigners. Finally the entry "investment income" records the profits yielded by U.S. direct investments abroad (i.e., by the foreign production facilities of U.S. firms) and interest income yielded by the debt claims that U.S. citizens and the U.S. government hold against foreign firms and foreign governments.

The entries listed on the uses side of the current account are largely self-explanatory. The first entry refers to imports of goods. "Military expenditures" are purchases of foreign goods and services made by U.S. military forces; in 1966 these were large because of the great number of U.S. troops stationed abroad, and because of the Vietnam war. The fifth entry, "investment income," records dividend and interest payments made by U.S. firms and the U.S. government to foreign investors.

The final entry on the uses side of the current account is "remittances and pensions." It records Social Security and other benefits paid out by Americans to foreigners, and funds transfers from U.S. citizens to foreigners (an immigrant sends money to relatives in the "old country"; another person makes a donation to foreigners in need).

The Capital Account

Whenever foreign capital flows into the U.S.—whether to finance the purchase of physical assets in the U.S., an equity interest in a U.S. firm, or a debt claim against a U.S. spending unit—the result is a *receipt* of funds by the U.S. Therefore the *net* inflow (i.e., gross inflow minus gross outflow) of foreign capital into the U.S. is recorded as a *source* of funds in the capital account of the U.S. balance of payments.

In setting up this account (Table 43.2), we have broken the net inflow of foreign *private* capital into the U.S. into two categories. The first, *long-term claims and equity investments,* refers (1) to foreign private capital used to buy equity interests in U.S. firms (a German buys shares in General Motors) and (2) to foreign private capital used to buy long-term debt claims against U.S. firms or the U.S. government (a Frenchman buys bonds issued by AT&T, or Treasury bonds). The second capital-inflow entry, *short-term claims,* refers (1) to private foreign capital used to buy short-term claims against U.S. firms and the U.S. government (a British citizen buys commercial paper or Treasury bills) and (2) to private foreign capital used to obtain deposit claims against U.S. banks (a Japanese exporter deposits dollars in the Bank of America).

The sources side of the capital account records not only foreign private capital inflows, but also foreign *official* capital inflows. Whenever a central bank increases the debt claims it holds against U.S. spending units, this constitutes an official capital inflow. Most of these claims take the form of U.S. government securities and of deposits in U.S. banks (foreign central banks are heavy investors in Treasury bills and in longer-term government bonds; they also hold large dollar deposits at the big New York banks and at the Fed). The dollar claims of foreign central banks play a key role in international finance because they represent an important part of the foreign exchange reserves of the countries that hold them. We'll talk about the somewhat mysterious subject of foreign exchange reserves and what they are used for in Chapters 46 and 47.

Whenever domestic capital flows out of the U.S.—whether to finance a direct investment, the purchase of debt securities, or the making of bank loans—the result is an expenditure of funds by the United States. So we record the net outflow (i.e., gross outflow minus gross inflow) of domestic capital to the rest of the world on the left-hand side of the U.S. capital account as a use of funds.

We have broken U.S. *private* capital outflows into three parts: those used to finance direct investments (IBM expands its French facilities), those used to purchase long-term debt claims (a U.S. investor buys a bond issued by the World Bank), and those used to obtain short-term claims against foreigners (a U.S. bank lends money to a foreign firm).*

The uses side of Table 43.2, in addition to showing U.S. private capital outflows, also shows the net outflow due to U.S. government grants and loans to other countries. There's a lot of foreign aid and military assistance in this big entry.

Turning back to the sources side of the U.S. capital account, we find one entry we haven't discussed yet: *official U.S. gold exports and sales of convertible currencies.* You may wonder why we don't include gold exports in the current account, along with other merchandise exports. But gold, unlike any other commodity, functions as an international currency; and gold movements are used (we shall discuss this point in Chapter 47) to "balance" the international payments of individual nations. Thus gold has a special role, and for this reason purchases and sales of gold, and of currencies convertible into gold, are segregated into a special capital-account entry.

Because the balance-of-payments account is simply an elaborate flow-of-funds account, and because every transaction recorded in such an account involves both a source and a use of funds, the sources and uses sides of the

---

* The fact that the "short-term claims" entry on the uses side of Table 43.2 is a negative amount means that in 1966 foreigners paid back to U.S. lenders more short-term loans than they obtained from them.

balance-of-payments account should—in theory at least—always balance. But in practice, some source and use entries that ought to be recorded in the balance-of-payments account slip by the national income accountant, while others are recorded inaccurately (tourist spending, for example, has to be estimated). Therefore, to bring the sources and uses sides of the balance-of-payments account into balance, the national income accountant must add a final balancing item, "errors and omissions"; it equals the difference between *recorded* uses and *recorded* sources of funds.

Examples of Transactions

To increase our familiarity with the balance-of-payments account, we shall now work out a few examples of how different transactions would be handled in this account. First let us assume that a commodity is exported from the U.S. to some foreign buyer. This export is recorded as a source of funds in the current account under merchandise exports. What will be the offsetting use entry? The answer depends on how the goods are paid for. Suppose that the exporter is paid in foreign currency and that he exchanges this currency for a deposit at a foreign bank, e.g., for a pound, franc, or mark deposit. Then U.S. short-term claims on foreigners will have risen, and the offsetting entry in the U.S. balance-of-payments account will be a short-term capital outflow.

Suppose instead that the exporter is not paid immediately; he grants the foreign purchaser a three-month credit. In this case, too, U.S. short-term claims on foreigners rise, and the offsetting use entry is a short-term capital outflow.

Finally, suppose that the exporter is a private citizen who sends a gift of food and clothing to a foreign citizen. Then the goods export still shows up in the current account as a source entry, but the offsetting entry is now a "grant." This "grant" must appear on the uses side of the balance-of-payments account because it *uses up funds,* in the sense that it discharges the obligation which the recipient would otherwise have incurred to pay for them, either now or at some future time.

As a second example, let us assume that a foreign country, say India, borrows $1 million for 10 years from the U.S. government.* This transaction increases U.S. claims on foreigners. So we record it on the uses side of the U.S. capital account as a long-term capital outflow. (The specific entry is "U.S. gov't grants and net capital outflow.") The nature of the offsetting entry depends on how the Indians use the funds. If they immediately give the funds to a U.S. exporter in exchange for goods exports, the offsetting

---

* Usually U.S. government loans to foreign countries are "tied" to the purchase of U.S. goods. But for the sake of illustration, let's assume that this loan is a cash one.

entry in the U.S. balance-of-payments account is merchandise exports. Suppose, however, that the Indians don't spend the borrowed funds immediately; they invest them temporarily in, say, Treasury bills. This transaction increases foreign claims on the U.S. So we would record it on the sources side of the capital account as a short-term capital inflow.

PROBLEMS

1   Explain in your own words why, in a country's balance-of-payments account, exports should show up as a source of funds, imports as a use of funds, loans from foreigners as a source of funds, and loans to foreigners as a use of funds. How should loan repayments made to foreigners be recorded? What about loan repayments received from foreigners?* This question sounds simple (and it is), but it's important because, if you can answer it, you have mastered all you need to know about how the balance-of-payments account is put together. And that's usually thought to be a pretty difficult task.

2   A Peruvian firm uses $50 thousand it has on deposit in a New York bank to pay an American firm for machinery it is importing into Peru. What are the resulting entries in the U.S. balance of payments? In the Peruvian balance of payments?

3   The French central bank uses $100 million which it had previously invested in U.S. Treasury bills to buy gold from the U.S. government. What entries would this transaction give rise to in the U.S. balance of payments? What about the French balance of payments?

4   An American tourist in Madrid uses a $50 traveler's check to pay his hotel bill. How does this affect the U.S. balance of payments? The Spanish balance of payments?

5   A foreign central bank sells gold to the U.S. to acquire dollars. How will this show up in the U.S. balance of payments? In the balance of payments of the foreign country?

6   a) The U.S. government grants military assistance to a foreign country by giving it $500,000 worth of American-made military equipment. How will this transaction be recorded in the U.S. balance of payments?

     b) The U.S. government grants a foreign country a *tied* loan; that is, a loan whose proceeds must be used to buy American-made goods. Assume that the borrowing country does use the loan to buy American-made goods. How will the loan affect the U.S. balance of payments?

     c) A lot of the economic and military aid that the U.S. grants to foreign countries takes the form of gifts of American goods or of loans that require the recipient to use the proceeds to buy American goods. Suppose that there is a cut in U.S. government aid to foreign countries. How would such a cut influence the U.S. balance on capital account? On current account?

---

* Recall the convention about negative sources and negative uses of funds that we adopted on page 405.

7   A U.S. firm exports $100,000 worth of machinery to Chile. The transaction is financed by the U.S. Export-Import Bank, which extends a long-term loan to the Chilean importer. How does this transaction show up in the U.S. balance of payments? In the balance of payments of Chile?

8   The U.S. government sends India $5 million of wheat during a famine. The wheat is a gift. How would you record this transaction in the U.S. balance of payments?

9   A U.S. firm pays $1,000 in dividends to a German investor, who uses the money to pay off a loan he has with a U.S. bank. How will these transactions show up in the U.S. balance of payments? In the German balance of payments?

CHAPTER 44

THE THEORY OF
INTERNATIONAL TRADE

THE PRINCIPLE OF COMPARATIVE ADVANTAGE

Why does international trade take place? Is it mutually profitable to the countries that trade? A century and a half ago David Ricardo, a famous English economist, set out to answer these questions. He reached two surprisingly simple conclusions: Trade occurs between two countries whenever one of them enjoys a *comparative (cost) advantage* over the other in the production of certain goods. Trade is mutually profitable to nations because it raises real income, and increased real income = increased welfare.

Absolute Advantage: An Example

To show how Ricardo reached these conclusions, let us work through two simple examples. First consider a world in which there are only two countries, the United States and Germany, and only two goods, wheat and steel. In this rather special world, the only input required for production (besides the natural resources found in each country) is workers. In the U.S. a single worker can produce 0.3 of a ton of wheat or 0.2 of a ton of steel in a day, while in Germany a single worker can produce 0.1 of a ton of wheat or 0.4 of a ton of steel in a day.

If we compare these figures (they are summarized in Table 44.1), we see that U.S. workers have a higher productivity with regard to wheat than German workers, but German workers have a higher productivity with regard to steel than U.S. workers do. This differential means that, in order to produce an extra ton of wheat, the U.S. doesn't have to "spend" as many workers as Germany does (the precise figures are $3\frac{1}{3}$ workers versus 10). In steel, however, the situation is just the reverse. To produce an extra ton of steel, the U.S. has to "spend" more workers than Germany does (here the figures are 5 workers versus $2\frac{1}{2}$). To describe this situation the economist says: The U.S. has an *absolute (cost) advantage* in wheat; Germany has one in steel.

Suppose that the U.S. and Germany were both self-sufficient in wheat and steel; i.e., that each country were producing all the wheat and all the steel it consumed. Then Germany would be producing at high cost wheat that the U.S. could produce at lower cost, while the U.S. would be producing at high cost steel that Germany could produce at lower cost. Common sense suggests that, if the U.S. were to devote *more* of its workers to wheat (economists call this *specializing*) and Germany were to devote *more* of its labor to steel, the two countries could raise their joint outputs of wheat and steel, and thus their real incomes.

TABLE 44|1

The U.S. Has an Absolute
Advantage in Wheat, Germany in Steel

	Output of one laborer working one day	
Country	Tons of wheat	Tons of steel
U.S.	0.3	0.2
Germany	0.1	0.4

Sometimes, however, common sense can be misleading. So let's test our hunch in numbers. Suppose that the U.S. and Germany have labor forces of 100 workers each. Initially these countries don't specialize and trade. Instead, each consumes what it produces, and each devotes *half* its labor force to wheat and half to steel. The input coefficients in Table 44.1 tell us that in this situation the U.S. will be able to produce and consume 15 tons of wheat [that is, (0.3 of a ton of wheat per worker) × (50 workers)] and 10 tons of steel, while Germany will be able to produce and consume 5 tons of wheat and 20 tons of steel. (These figures are summarized in Table 44.2.)

TABLE 44|2

Production and Consumption
Before Trade and Specialization

	Total output produced and consumed	
Country	Tons of wheat	Tons of steel
U.S.	15	10
Germany	5	20
Joint	20	30

Now let's add trade and specialization to the picture and see how things change. Suppose that the U.S. decides to devote 80% of its work force to wheat, but only 20% to steel, while Germany decides to take the opposite tack. Then the U.S. will produce 24 tons of wheat and 4 tons of steel, while Germany will produce 2 tons of wheat and 32 tons of steel. Compare these figures (which are given in Table 44.3) with those in Table 44.2, and you'll see that the U.S. and Germany, *solely by specializing* (i.e., without any increase in their labor forces), have been able to increase their joint output of wheat by 6 tons and of steel by 6 tons.

TABLE 44|3

Production After Specialization

Country	Total output produced	
	Tons of wheat	Tons of steel
U.S.	24	4
Germany	2	32
Joint	26	36

Suppose now that the U.S. and Germany agree to trade with each other. The U.S. offers to give Germany 4 tons of its bountiful wheat supply for 7 tons of German steel, and Germany accepts. Then the U.S. can consume 20 tons of wheat and 11 tons of steel, while Germany can consume 6 tons of wheat and 25 tons of steel. These consumption figures are shown in Table 44.4. Compare them with the production–consumption figures in Table 44.2, and you'll see that after specialization and trade the U.S. and Germany are both able to consume more wheat *and* more steel than they could before. So our supposition was correct: The U.S. and Germany, by combining trade with specialization along lines of absolute advantage, are able to raise their real incomes.

TABLE 44|4

Consumption After Specialization and Trade

Country	Total output consumed	
	Tons of wheat	Tons of steel
U.S.	20	11
Germany	6	25
Joint	26	36

From our two-country, two-commodity example, we can draw the following conclusion:

Whenever countries enjoy absolute advantages in different goods, they can produce more of all goods, and thus enjoy more real income, if each specializes in the goods in which it has an absolute advantage, and imports other goods.

Comparative Advantage: An Example

Ricardo didn't have to figure out the above conclusion himself. His predecessors—including the venerable Adam Smith, also a famous English economist—had already done so. Ricardo tackled a much trickier question: What if one of two countries has an absolute cost advantage in *all* goods; can these two countries still increase their real incomes through trade?

To illustrate, consider again the above situation: two countries, the U.S. and Germany; and two goods, wheat and steel. This time, however, assume that a German worker can produce only 0.1 of a ton of steel per day. Then, as Table 44.5 shows, the U.S. will enjoy an *absolute* advantage not only in wheat but also in steel. In this situation it doesn't look as though trade between the United States and Germany would be mutually beneficial. But Ricardo showed that it would be.

TABLE 44|5

The U.S. Has a Comparative
Advantage in Wheat, Germany in Steel

Country	Output of one laborer working one day	
	Tons of wheat	Tons of steel
U.S.	0.3	0.2
Germany	0.1	0.1

To see why, let's take a look at the *opportunity cost* of producing wheat and steel in the U.S. and Germany. The economist defines the opportunity cost of anything as the amount of something else that has to be given up to get it, that is, in terms of the forgone opportunity.* An increase in steel production means that labor has to be shifted out of wheat production into steel production; so steel has an opportunity cost in terms of wheat. Similarly, wheat has an opportunity cost in terms of steel. The input coefficients

---

* We introduced the concept of opportunity cost on page 93.

in Table 44.5 tell us that to produce a ton of steel the U.S. has to use 5 workers. If these 5 workers were instead put to work producing wheat, they would yield 1.5 tons of wheat. So in the U.S. the opportunity cost of 1 ton of steel is 1.5 tons of wheat; by contrast, the opportunity cost of 1 ton of wheat is 0.66 of a ton of steel. What about the situation in Germany? There, as you can easily figure out, the opportunity cost of a ton of wheat is 1 ton of steel, and vice versa.

These figures show a surprising result. Although the U.S. has an absolute cost advantage over Germany in both wheat and steel, nevertheless, if we measure cost in terms of *opportunity* cost, it turns out that the U.S. has a *comparative (cost) advantage* over Germany *only* in wheat. In steel, Germany has a *comparative (cost) advantage* over the U.S.

TABLE 44|6

Production and Consumption
Before Trade and Specialization

Total output produced and consumed		
Country	Tons of wheat	Tons of steel
U.S.	15	10
Germany	5	5
Joint	20	15

This leads us to another hunch: Perhaps if the U.S. and Germany were to specialize along lines of comparative advantage, the two countries could raise their joint outputs of wheat and steel and thus their real incomes. Let's try this out in numbers. Suppose again that the U.S. and Germany have labor forces of 100 workers each, and that initially they don't specialize and trade. Instead each consumes what it produces, and each devotes half its labor force to wheat and half to steel. Then, according to the figures on labor productivity (Table 44.5), the U.S. can produce and consume 15 tons of wheat and 10 tons of steel, Germany 5 tons of wheat and 5 tons of steel. (These figures are shown in Table 44.6.)

Now let us again add trade and specialization to the picture and see what happens. Suppose that the U.S. decides to devote 70% of its work force to wheat but only 30% to steel, while Germany decides to devote its entire work force to steel. The U.S. will produce 21 tons of wheat and 6 tons of steel, Germany 10 tons of steel and no wheat. By comparing these output figures (see Table 44.7) with the pre-specialization ones in Table 44.6, we see that specialization along lines of comparative advantage permits the U.S. and Germany to increase their joint outputs of both wheat and steel.

TABLE 44|7

Production After Specialization

Country	Total output produced	
	Tons of wheat	Tons of steel
U.S.	21	6
Germany	0	10
Joint	21	16

Specialization of course also leaves the U.S. with a bigger supply of wheat relative to steel than it would probably like to consume, while it leaves Germany with a lot of steel but no wheat. These imbalances can easily be corrected through trade. Suppose that the U.S. gives Germany $5\frac{1}{2}$ tons of wheat in exchange for $4\frac{1}{2}$ tons of steel. Then the U.S. can consume $15\frac{1}{2}$ tons of wheat and $10\frac{1}{2}$ tons of steel, while Germany can consume $5\frac{1}{2}$ tons of wheat and $5\frac{1}{2}$ tons of steel. Now compare these figures (see Table 44.8) with the pre-trade consumption figures in Table 44.6, and you will see that as a result of specialization plus trade, the U.S. and Germany have both managed to increase their consumption of both goods, and thus to raise their real incomes.

TABLE 44|8

Consumption After Specialization and Trade

Country	Total output consumed	
	Tons of wheat	Tons of steel
U.S.	$15\frac{1}{2}$	$10\frac{1}{2}$
Germany	$5\frac{1}{2}$	$5\frac{1}{2}$
Joint	21	16

Our example shows that trade between the U.S. and Germany can be mutually profitable, but it doesn't explain why. You may still be wondering: Since U.S. workers are absolutely more efficient than German workers in *both* steel and wheat, how can the U.S. gain from trading with Germany? To figure this out, look again at Table 44.5. It shows that the productivity of German workers *relative to* that of American workers is higher in steel than in wheat. So when the U.S. trades wheat for German steel, each country specializes in the commodity for which its resources are better suited and imports the commodity for which its resources are less well suited. Thus by encouraging specialization, trade raises the efficiency with which U.S. and German resources are utilized and this in turn raises output and real income in both countries.

The example we have just worked through suggests the following conclusion:

Whenever countries enjoy comparative advantages in different goods, they can produce more of all goods and thus enjoy more real income if each specializes in the good or goods in which it has a comparative advantage, and imports other goods.

This conclusion (known as *the principle of comparative advantage*) was the answer Ricardo came up with 150 years ago when he asked: Can nations profit from trade that isn't based on differences in absolute advantage?

The Terms of Trade

If a country doesn't engage in international trade, then (assuming that markets are competitive) the ratio at which one good is exchanged for another in the *domestic* market will equal the opportunity cost of the first good in terms of the second. Thus to continue our comparative-advantage example: If the U.S. doesn't trade with Germany and if U.S. domestic markets are competitive, 1 ton of steel will exchange for 1.5 tons of wheat in the U.S. But in Germany, a ton of steel won't be worth any more than a ton of wheat.

Whenever one country trades goods with another, it's usually at an exchange ratio that differs from the one that would prevail in its domestic market in the absence of trade. This ratio is known as its *terms of trade*. Thus: If Germany trades steel for wheat with the U.S. at the ratio of 1.22 tons of wheat for 1 ton of steel (that's the ratio at which they traded in our comparative-advantage example), this ratio is Germany's terms of trade.

Right now we'd better stop and explain something before we get in any deeper. So far we've always talked about prices in terms of money prices, so it may bother you that here all of a sudden we start quoting prices in terms of ratios at which goods are exchanged. Actually this switch is more apparent than real. Any pair of money prices always implies an exchange ratio. Example: If apples cost 10¢ apiece and oranges 5¢, the exchange ratio between apples and oranges is 2 oranges for 1 apple. Also the exchange ratio between any pair of goods can always be converted into a pair of money prices. Example: If 1 ton of steel can be exchanged for 1.5 tons of wheat, and if a ton of steel sells for $99, then the dollar price of a ton of wheat must be (check and see) $66. Since money prices and exchange ratios aren't really so different, we could talk about money prices here. But different monies are used in different countries (dollars in the U.S., marks in Germany, and francs in France); thus doing so would just add confusion to an already confusing topic. Therefore, to keep our discussion as simple as possible, we'll stick to a barter-economy way of looking at price, that is, to quoting prices in terms of exchange ratios.

Now, back to the subject. Whenever two countries trade with each other, their terms of trade must lie between the exchange ratios that would prevail in the two countries in the absence of trade. Consider again our example of comparative advantage. If the terms of trade at which Germany and the U.S. exchange wheat and steel were set above 1.5 tons of wheat for 1 ton of steel (i.e., above the exchange ratio that would prevail in the U.S. in the absence of trade), it would pay both the U.S. and Germany to export steel in exchange for wheat, but neither country would be willing to produce wheat. On the other hand, if the terms of trade were set below 1 ton of wheat for 1 ton of steel (i.e., below the exchange ratio that would prevail in Germany in the absence of trade), both countries would want to export wheat in exchange for steel, but neither would want to supply steel. So the only terms of trade at which international exchanges of steel for wheat are feasible are those that lie between 1.5 tons of wheat for 1 ton of steel and 1 ton of wheat for 1 ton of steel, that is, between the ratios that would prevail in the U.S. and Germany in the absence of trade.

Terms of Trade and Gains from Trade

Just where a country's terms of trade settle is important because it determines how much the country will gain from trade. To illustrate: Consider again the position of the U.S. in the above example. The U.S. has 100 workers, each of whom can produce 0.3 of a ton of wheat or 0.2 of a ton of steel per day. So, depending on how the U.S. allocates labor between wheat and steel, it will be able to produce 30 tons of wheat and no steel, 20 tons of steel and no wheat, or some combination of both commodities. Suppose that we plot all the different *maximum* output combinations that the U.S. economy is capable of producing. Then we'll get what is called the economy's *production possibility curve*. We have plotted this curve in Fig. 44.1 and labeled it *PP*. Note that *PP* hits the steel axis at the output 20, which is the maximum amount of steel the U.S. can produce if it devotes all its manpower to steel. It hits the wheat axis at the output 30, which is the maximum amount of wheat that the U.S. can produce if it devotes all its manpower to wheat. Also it has a constant slope of −1.5 because, to produce an extra ton of steel, the U.S. would always have to reduce its wheat production by 1.5 tons.

Since the production possibility curve represents the maximum output combinations the U.S. can produce with its fixed labor supply, the U.S. obviously can't produce any output combination such as *C'*, which lies above this curve. So if the U.S. doesn't trade with any other country, the best it can do is to produce and consume at some point such as *C* which lies along its production possibility curve.

However, if the U.S. does trade with other countries, things change. Suppose that the U.S. can trade wheat for steel with Germany at the terms of trade of 1.25 tons of wheat for 1 ton of steel. Suppose also that the U.S. specializes in wheat (i.e., that it produces 30 tons of wheat and no steel). Then the opportunity cost to the U.S. of imported wheat will be less than that of domestically produced wheat, and the U.S. through trade will be able to consume output combinations, such as *C'*, that it could not produce with its own resources. Let us represent these combinations by a *budget line PP'*. Obviously this line will hit the wheat axis at the point 30. Also since the U.S. has to export 1.25 tons of wheat for each 1 ton of steel it imports from Germany, the slope of this line will be −1.25.

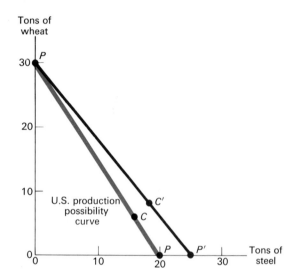

44|1

The more favorable a country's terms of trade, the more it can gain from trade.

By comparing *PP* and *PP'*, we see that the more the slopes of these curves diverge, the more the U.S. can gain from trade. Remember that the slope of *PP* equals the exchange ratio between wheat and steel that would prevail within the U.S. if it *didn't* trade, while the slope of *PP'* equals the international terms of trade. Therefore our observation implies that:

The greater the divergence between the international terms of trade and the exchange ratio that would prevail within a country if it didn't trade, the greater the gain in real income that this country can achieve through trade.

The point at which a country's terms of trade settle depends on the strength of domestic demand for the goods it imports relative to foreign demand for the goods it exports. The stronger a country's demand for *imports,* the higher the price it will have to pay for them, and the less favorable its terms of trade. The stronger the foreign demand for a country's *exports,* the higher the price it will get for them, and the more favorable its terms of trade.

In a country like the U.S., in which foreign trade represents only a small fraction of national income, the height and variability of the terms of trade are not a matter of great importance. In many underdeveloped countries, however, foreign trade is the lifeline, because these countries depend on export earnings to finance both current consumption and vital investments. We shall talk about the problems caused in such countries by fluctuations in their terms of trade—and the devices such countries have used to try to overcome these problems—in Chapter 48.

Multi-Commodity Trade

We developed the principle of comparative advantage in terms of a two-commodity example. Now let us use this principle to explain multi-commodity trade.

TABLE 44|9

Output of one laborer working one day		
Country	Tons of wheat	Tons of machinery	Tons of steel
U.S.	0.3	0.25	0.2
Germany	0.1	0.1	0.1

The main difference between international trade when countries trade in only *two* goods and international trade when they trade in *many* goods is that in the latter case each country is likely to export and import a number of goods. Also, it is generally impossible to determine solely from cost data (i.e., data on input productivities) which goods a country will import and which it will export. To illustrate: Suppose that the U.S. and Germany produce three commodities: wheat, machinery and steel, and that the per diem outputs of German and U.S. workers in these three industries are as shown in Table 44.9. You can see that the U.S. has a comparative advantage in wheat, Germany in steel. So the U.S. will export wheat and Germany steel. But the question of which exports machinery will depend on the strength of the demand in the two countries for each of the three goods they produce. For example, if U.S. demand for steel is great but German demand for wheat is slight, the U.S. may end up exporting both wheat *and* machinery to pay for its steel imports. On the other hand, if German demand for wheat is strong, but U.S. demand for steel is slight, Germany will have to export both steel *and* machinery to pay for its wheat imports.

Multilateral Trade

To keep things simple, we worked out the principle of comparative advantage for a world in which there were only two countries. But this principle can also be used to explain trade in a multi-country world, like the one we live in.

From the standpoint of a single country, trade in a world in which there are many countries does not differ, in essence, from trade in a world in which there are only two countries. Reason: A country's trading partners, no matter how numerous, can always be thought of as a single rest-of-the-world sector. From the standpoint of the world, however, multi-country trade does raise an interesting new possibility: International cost and demand conditions may be such that the countries that trade with each other can realize the full gains available from trade only if they engage in *multilateral trade*. Trade is said to follow a multilateral pattern whenever countries use exports to one area to pay for imports from some other area.

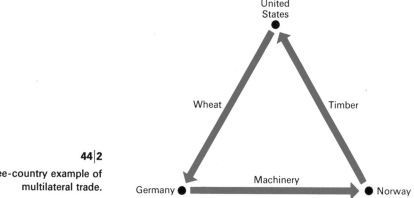

44|2

A three-country example of multilateral trade.

Here's an example of a multilateral trade pattern: Suppose that there are three countries, the United States, Germany, and Norway, and three goods, wheat, machinery, and timber. The U.S. has a comparative advantage in wheat, Germany in machinery, and Norway in timber. Let's say that Germany has a high demand for wheat, Norway for machinery, and the U.S. for timber. Then the pattern of trade that will bring the greatest gains to all three countries is one by which Germany exports machinery to Norway, Norway exports timber to the U.S., and the U.S. exports wheat to Germany. This multilateral trade pattern is pictured in Fig. 44.2.

SOURCES OF COMPARATIVE ADVANTAGE

Differences in comparative advantage are what makes trade profitable. Let us analyze the factors that cause such differences.

Geographic Diversity

One key factor is *geographic diversity,* that is, differences in the climate and natural resources of different regions. Examples: Panama exports bananas because it has a tropical climate. The Congo exports copper because it has large deposits of this scarce ore. Kuwait exports oil because the country literally floats on a vast pool of it.

Because geographic diversity is so important a cause of differences in comparative advantage, international trade plays a bigger role in the economic life of small countries whose resources and climate are homogeneous than in the economic life of large countries that have many geographically diverse regions: Imports equal 41% of national product in Norway, 19% of national product in the United Kingdom, but only 4% of national product in the U.S. (When Norway wants oranges, it has to trade dried codfish with Spain to get them. But New England can get oranges by trading lobsters with California, Florida, or Arizona; and this trade doesn't affect the U.S. balance of payments.)

Differences in Capital–Labor Endowments

Nations differ in *the amounts of capital relative to labor* with which they are endowed. The U.S. and many Western European countries have much capital but little labor. On the other hand, the Orient teems with people but has little capital.

In most industries capital and labor can be used in varying proportions to produce output.* Nevertheless in some industries firms typically use a lot of capital but not much labor, while in others firms typically use a lot of labor but not much capital. Thus, for example, in any country the local oil refinery is likely to use more capital equipment but fewer workers than the local textile mill. The fact that there are *capital-intensive* industries (oil refining) and *labor-intensive* industries (textiles) means (as advanced texts show) that, if one country has a higher capital–labor endowment than another, the opportunity cost of capital-intensive goods will be lower in the first country than in the second, while the opportunity cost of labor-intensive goods will be lower in the second country than in the first. Therefore:

Differences in relative capital–labor endowments are a second source of comparative advantage.

A great deal of the trade between nations can be explained on the basis of differences in relative labor–capital endowments. For example, the

---

* See Chapter 7's discussion of the production function and of the possibilities that exist for substituting one input for another.

Orient's big labor supply is the reason why those countries export textiles, while Western Europe's big capital supply is the reason why this area exports autos, aircraft, and other capital-intensive goods.

Tradition

Sometimes comparative advantage may be largely the result of acquired skills and tradition. People get used to doing a thing and keep on doing it, generation after generation. Examples: The Swiss have a tradition of making watches, the Norwegians of operating a far-flung merchant fleet, and the French—to the delight of gastronomes everywhere—of producing cheeses. Note that each of these traditions is certainly consistent with the resource endowment of the country in question, but it is not an inevitable outcome of it.

OTHER GAINS FROM TRADE

As we have said, international trade based on differences in comparative advantage increases the efficiency with which world resources are used and thus increases the world's real income. But this is not the only gain to be had from international trade. If we allow for market imperfections and for dynamic considerations, trade may yield other gains. Let's look at some of them:

As we saw in Chapter 7, firms often experience *economies of scale*. This means that, as they produce more output, they can utilize inputs more efficiently and thus decrease their average costs of production. In industries in which economies of scale are large and extend over a broad range of output, firms operating in a small national market perhaps can't achieve the high output levels necessary to minimize production costs unless they can export some of their output. In such situations international trade offers an additional gain:

International trade increases the efficiency with which resources are utilized by permitting some firms to take advantage of economies of scale that they couldn't have enjoyed in the absence of trade.

This gain from trade isn't very big for a country like the U.S., which has a large domestic market, but for countries like the Netherlands and Norway, which have small domestic markets, it can be significant.

Whenever the number of producers in a domestic market is small, then (recall Chapter 24) these producers engage in a monopolistic restriction of output. That is, in their quest for maximum profits, they produce too little output for resource allocation to be efficient. One obvious cure is to increase the number of firms selling in the domestic market, and one way to do so is to open up this market to foreign sellers. Thus international trade may offer a third source of gain:

International trade may increase the efficiency with which domestic resources are allocated by decreasing the prevalence and size of monopolistic restrictions on output.

Gains of this sort can be important even when the differences in comparative advantage between trading countries are minimal. Example: One of the biggest sources of gain from intra-European trade in manufactured goods is the fact that such trade breaks down the strong monopolistic restrictions on output that would otherwise persist within the narrow confines of the typical European national market.

A fourth source of gain from trade:

Because international trade exposes domestic producers to foreign competition, it puts pressure on domestic firms to operate as efficiently as possible.

Example: U.S. steel mills are getting competition these days from foreign steel mills, and this puts pressure on U.S. mills to adopt technological advances that were developed abroad and that are already being widely used there.

INTERNATIONAL FACTOR MOVEMENTS

As we have seen, one reason why different countries have different comparative advantages is that some have greater supplies of capital relative to labor than others. In Chapter 7 we said that the *marginal product* of an input (that's the extra output you get by using an extra unit of this input) will fall if increased quantities of this input are employed in a production process in which all other inputs are held constant. This rule, known as the *law of diminishing returns,* can be applied not only to a single firm's production possibilities (that is the way we used it in Chapter 7), but also to the production possibilities of a country as a whole. Used this way, the law of diminishing returns tells us that the marginal product of capital will be lower in countries in which capital is plentiful relative to labor than it is in countries that are capital-poor and labor-rich. So far as the marginal product of labor is concerned, the situation will be precisely the opposite.

In a competitive economy the return an input earns equals the value of its marginal product; so the higher its marginal product, the higher its return. As we have just said, an input's marginal product is higher, the less of it there is relative to other inputs. Therefore under competitive conditions, labor earns a higher rate of return in labor-poor than in labor-rich countries, and the opposite is true for capital. The upshot of this situation is of course that there is an incentive for factors to move from country to country: Labor has an incentive to move from labor-rich, low-wage countries to capital-rich, high-wage countries, and capital has an incentive to move in the opposite direction. The fact that this incentive exists explains why workers from Italy and Yugoslavia take jobs in Northern Europe, and why capital flows from the U.S. and Europe to countries in Latin America, Africa, and Asia.

International factor movements of this sort work to bring each country's capital–labor endowment into line with that of every other country. So factor movements act as a substitute for international trade based on differences in factor endowments. They don't, however, obviate the need for such trade. Language barriers, cultural differences, and strict national immigration laws hamper the free flow of labor between countries. Also the controls that lending and borrowing countries place on capital movements sharply limit the international mobility of capital. Hence international factor movements remain much too small to equalize the relative labor–capital endowments of different countries. Thus differences in comparative advantage persist, and trade based on such differences continues.

International Capital Movements

In today's world tight restrictions are generally placed on the movement of labor from labor-rich to capital-rich countries, but not on movements of capital in the opposite direction. So international capital movements tend to have greater importance than international labor movements.

Capital has been flowing from capital-rich to capital-poor countries for a long time. But the form assumed by such flows has changed considerably from one era to another. During the nineteenth century, which was the heyday of international capital flows, *foreign bonds* were the key instrument by means of which such flows occurred. Governments of capital-poor countries got long-term loans from capital-rich countries by selling bonds—usually to private investors—in London and later in other European financial centers too. World War I, with its attendant disruptions, dealt a severe blow both to the sale of foreign bonds and to the preeminence of the London bond market. During the 1920's the New York bond market grew considerably in importance, and to some extent it assumed the role vacated by London. The ascendancy of the New York bond market was, however, short-lived because the economic collapse of the 1930's, the associated bond defaults, and the resulting restriction on international payments all combined to halt the sale of foreign bonds in the New York market.

Since the end of World War II, the U.S. has reemerged as an important supplier of long-term capital to the rest of the world. Figure 44.3 shows that in the last ten years U.S. private investors have supplied over $47 billion of long-term capital to the rest of the world. Roughly a third of this was in the form of *portfolio investment,* that is, purchases of bonds and other securities. During the early 1960's sales of foreign bonds to U.S. investors spurted ahead at an accelerated pace. Lately, however, they have declined, because the U.S. government began in 1963 to apply an "interest equalization tax" (IET) to foreign bonds purchased by U.S. investors.* The purpose of this tax is to narrow the deficit in the U.S. balance of payments by discouraging long-term outflows of U.S. capital to foreign countries. Because of IET, it's hard to say what will happen to U.S. portfolio investment abroad in future years. Chances are it will remain far below past levels so long as the balance-of-payments deficits persists, and so long as IET remains in force.

Private portfolio investment   12.0

Private direct investment   35.1

Government grants and loans   41.8

44|3

Net long-term capital outflows from the United States to foreign countries, 1956–1966 (billions of dollars). (Source: U.S. Department of Commerce)

Figure 44.3 shows that over the past decade about two-thirds of total U.S. private investment abroad has been in the form of direct investments. Direct investments are those that U.S. firms make in foreign ventures that they either wholly own or own enough of to effectively control. The motives that lead U.S. firms to make direct investments abroad are varied: (1) Capital earns a higher rate of return in foreign, capital-poor countries than it does in the capital-rich U.S. (2) The entrepreneurial expertise, patents, and technical know-how that U.S. firms have give them a special advantage in exploiting foreign investment opportunities. (3) U.S. firms want an assured supply of raw materials, such as oil and ores, that are more readily or more cheaply available in foreign countries than in the U.S.†

At the beginning of 1968 the President announced a drastic clamp-down on U.S. investment abroad, as part of the government's program to curb capital outflows and end the deficit in the U.S. balance of payments. Thus the future of U.S. direct investment abroad, like that of U.S. portfolio investment abroad, is uncertain.

---

* We shall talk about IET in Chapter 47.

† An interesting sidelight on this reason is that currently Japanese investors are making sizable direct investments in Alaska. Reason: The Japanese, who are poor in natural resources, want assured supplies of timber, fish, natural gas, and other products; and they can find them in Alaska.

Private investment is one way that capital flows from the U.S. to the rest of the world; there is also another way. The U.S. government makes grants and loans to foreign countries. Figure 44.3 shows that these grants and loans (not including military assistance) have totaled over $40 billion in the past ten years. These grants and loans to foreign countries cover a host of different programs, from Food for Peace to the Peace Corps. Despite the growing concern over the U.S. deficit, it is unlikely that the U.S. will cut off foreign aid, since much of this aid is tied to the purchase of U.S. goods. Therefore, on balance, foreign aid involves only small outflows of dollars from the U.S. to other countries.

PROBLEMS

1   Zee and Dee are two European countries. They have about the same climate, but the land is better in Dee than in Zee. The result is that in Dee a worker working one day can produce 0.4 of a ton of wheat or 0.2 of a cask of wine, while the same worker working one day in Zee can produce 0.2 of a ton of wheat or 0.1 of a cask of wine. Clearly Dee has an absolute advantage in both wheat and wine. In which product does it have a comparative advantage? Can you think of any circumstances under which it would be mutually profitable for Zee and Dee to trade in wheat and wine?

2   Verify that the productivity figures in Table 44.5 imply that the opportunity cost of 1 ton of wheat is 1 ton of steel in Germany but only 0.66 of a ton of steel in the U.S.

3   Suppose that the productivities of British and Indian workers in steel and textiles are as follows:

Output of one worker working one day		
Country	Tons of steel	Tons of textiles
Britain	1.0	0.9
India	0.8	0.8

a) In which product does Britain have an *absolute* advantage? A *comparative* advantage? What about India?

b) Suppose that India and Britain both have work forces of 100 workers, and suppose that each country allocates half its work force to steel and half to textiles. How much steel and how much textiles will Britain and India produce together?

c) Suppose that India devotes all its work force to the commodity in which it has a comparative advantage, while Britain devotes 80% of its work force to the product in which it has a comparative advantage and 20% to the other commodity. How much steel and how much textiles will Britain and India produce together? What does this tell you about the benefits of international specialization along lines of comparative advantage?

d) Suppose that Britain and India specialize along lines of comparative advantage as assumed in (c), and suppose that Britain trades 41 tons of steel for 38 tons of India's textiles. Show that, as a result of trade and specialization, both Britain and India will be able to consume more of both textiles and steel than they did in the pre-trade situation described under (b) above.

e) If Britain trades 41 tons of steel for 38 tons of textiles, then the international terms of trade must be one ton of steel for how many tons of wheat? Are these feasible terms of trade? [*Hint:* In the absence of trade, a ton of steel could be exchanged for how many tons of textiles in Britain? In India?]

4 a) "The U.S. can gain from trade so long as it is offered any terms of trade that differ from the ratio at which wheat would be exchanged for steel within the U.S. economy in the absence of trade." Right or wrong?

b) Suppose that the U.S. were offered terms of trade of 2 tons of wheat for 1 ton of steel. Would it trade? In what commodity would it specialize? Would these terms of trade be feasible? That is, would Germany be willing to trade with the U.S. at these terms of trade? [Assume that the productivities of U.S. and German workers in wheat and in steel are those shown in Table 44.5.]

5 "A boom in the developed countries is likely to improve the terms of trade of the underdeveloped countries." Discuss.

6 Why do you suppose that the industrial countries, which once exported large quantities of textiles to the underdeveloped countries, today find themselves besieged with textile imports from these very same lands?

CHAPTER 45

TRADE RESTRICTIONS

In Chapter 44 we showed that international trade is mutually profitable for the countries that engage in it, so by all rights countries ought to be anxious to enlarge their foreign trade. In practice, however, things don't always work out that way. Frequently individual nations, far from encouraging international trade, impose restrictions on their imports and sometimes (though less often) on their exports too.

To hamper imports, countries often impose *tariffs* (i.e., taxes) on imported goods, and sometimes they also place *quotas* (i.e., restrictions on quantity sold) on them. Example: The United States imposes tariffs on industrial imports ranging from automobiles to portable television sets; it also has quotas on cheese, crude oil, sugar, and many other imported products. Trade restrictions, of course, aren't one-sided. U.S. goods sold abroad encounter tariffs and quotas. West European countries, for instance, charge tariffs on most manufactured goods they import from the United States. They also have quotas on U.S. agricultural exports, ranging from wheat to frozen chickens. Besides tariffs and quotas, nations frequently use more subtle means to hamper trade. These are known as "invisible tariffs." Some invisible tariffs are applied in the customs shed: delays in clearing imports, the placing of excessive valuations on imports, and the arbitrary application of tariff classifications (the last two ploys can be used to inflate the duty due on imports). Other invisible tariffs take the form of domestic regulations that discriminate against imported goods. France, for example, forbids public advertising of whiskey. (Whiskey is one alcoholic beverage the French don't brew themselves; instead they import it.) The U.S. requires that Japanese mink be labeled "Japanese weasel." (Every woman wants mink, but who dreams of weasel?)

The contrast between our *theoretical* conclusion that trade is mutually profitable and our observation that nations *in practice* often restrict trade raises questions about why trade restrictions are imposed, and how they affect

real income. In situations in which trade restrictions do serve a valid purpose, could they be replaced by other policy instruments that would fulfill
the same purpose without hindering trade and specialization?

*THE ECONOMIC IMPACT OF A TARIFF

To analyze what happens when a tariff is imposed on an imported commodity, we can use the same approach we used in Chapter 14, when we
talked about what happens when a tax is imposed on a domestically produced commodity. This approach relies on supply-and-demand analysis; so
we first set up curves that represent domestic demand and foreign supply of
the imported commodity (let's say it's cheese). At any price domestic demand
for imported cheese (D_m) equals the amount of cheese that domestic consumers demand (D_d) at that price *minus* the amount that domestic firms are
willing to supply (D_s) at that price. So to obtain a curve that represents domestic demand for imported cheese, we subtract the domestic supply curve for it
from the domestic demand curve for it. The domestic demand curve for
cheese will slope downward, while the domestic supply curve will slope
upward. Therefore the domestic demand curve for imported cheese must
slope downward, like the curve D_m in Fig. 45.1. On the other hand, the
foreign supply curve for cheese imports will slope upward like the curve S_m.

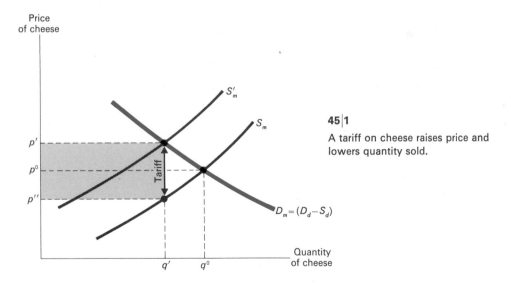

45|1

A tariff on cheese raises price and
lowers quantity sold.

* Students who haven't read Chapter 14 may skip this short section. Just keep in mind
the main conclusion we reach here: *Tariffs reduce international trade and specialization,
and this in turn reduces the world's real income.*

Initially the market for cheese imports (pictured in Fig. 45.1) attains equilibrium at the point (p^0, q^0) at which the market demand curve D_m intersects the market supply curve S_m. Suppose now that a tariff is imposed on this market. Then the market supply curve will shift upward* from S_m to S'_m, and market equilibrium will be shifted from the point (p^0, q^0) to the point (p', q'), at which the new market supply curve S'_m intersects the market demand curve D_m.

By comparing the points (p^0, q^0) and (p', q'), we can learn several things about the impact of the tariff. *First:* The tariff brings in tax revenue to the government. This revenue, which naturally equals the tariff per unit times the quantity sold, is represented in Fig. 45.1 by the area of the shaded rectangle $q'(p' - p'')$. *Second:* The tariff increases the price paid by domestic consumers and received by domestic producers from p^0 to p'. *Third:* It decreases the price received by foreign exporters from p^0 to p''. *Fourth:* It reduces cheese imports from q^0 to q'.

A tariff benefits some and hurts others. Take the case of domestic producers of cheese. Some of the reduction in cheese imports that results from the tariff represents a decrease in domestic consumption of cheese. But some also represents an expansion of domestic production of cheese.† So imposition of the tariff benefits domestic cheese producers in two ways: (a) It raises the price they receive, and (b) it increases the amount they sell. However, domestic consumers lose, because they now consume less cheese, and they have to pay a higher price for it. Also foreign exporters lose because they get a lower price for their cheese, and they sell less of it. It's hard to measure these individual losses and gains against each other. However, we can gauge the impact of the tariff on world welfare in another way. As we saw in Chapter 44, international trade and specialization increase the world's real income. A tariff, however, reduces trade. Therefore, whatever its effects on individual groups of consumers and producers, a tariff reduces the world's real income, and this reduces world welfare.

ARGUMENTS IN FAVOR OF TARIFFS

Now let us look at a few of the arguments in favor of tariffs. In evaluating each of these arguments, we ought to ask ourselves: Is the purpose that the tariff is supposed to serve a valid one? If so, is there some other policy instrument (besides a tariff) that would fulfill this purpose without decreasing world real income and world welfare?

---

* In Chapter 14 we showed that a commodity tax can be represented by an upward shift in the market supply curve. (See Fig. 14.2a on page 225.)

† See Problem 3 at the end of this chapter.

The Immobility of Domestic Factors of Production

If new opportunities to trade exports for imports open up, and if a country takes advantage of them, it will of course have to shift both the composition of its output and the allocation of its resources away from industries that compete with imports into industries that export to foreign markets. So long as a country's resources, especially its workers, are mobile between industries, such a shift won't cause any special problems. As we pointed out in Chapter 40, however, workers are often immobile, either between regions or between industries. So the opening-up of new trade opportunities is likely to threaten some workers not only with the loss of their current jobs, but also with structural unemployment. These workers will naturally react by pleading for tariff protection. As Fig. 45.1 shows, there's no question that a tariff will keep out imports, protect the threatened jobs, and thus prevent the emergence of structural unemployment. But is a tariff the best way to do the job? Our discussion in Chapter 40 suggests that any structural unemployment that might result from expanded foreign trade could be dealt with another way: by means of special programs designed to facilitate the transfer of resources out of industries that compete with imports into other industries in which employment is on the rise. Such programs, unlike tariffs, would not reduce trade and thus real income. Recognizing this point, the U.S. incorporated into the Trade Expansion Act of 1962 (this act provided for general and substantial tariff reductions) provisions which committed the federal government to (1) furnish technical, financial, and tax assistance to domestic firms in import-injured industries, and (2) provide expanded unemployment benefits and training for different kinds of jobs to workers in such industries.

Trade and the Distribution of Income

If the only effect that trade had on a nation's real income were to raise it, international trade would probably be nowhere near as controversial as it is. In practice, however, trade also alters the *distribution* of income. Let's look at the reason why.

Consider the little middle-European country of Philodendron, whose export industries employ a great deal of some input *A* relative to some other input *B*, but whose industries that compete with imports employ much *B* relative to *A*. If Philodendron were to increase its trade with the rest of the world, its export industries would demand more inputs, while its import-competing industries would demand less. And as a result domestic demand for input *A* would rise, while that for input *B* would fall. Thus increased trade would raise the price of *A*, lower the price of *B*, and thereby distribute income away from *A* toward *B*.

In our discussion of comparative advantage, we said that one source of comparative advantage was differences in national endowments of capital relative to labor. Countries with much capital but little labor have a comparative advantage in capital-intensive goods, while countries with much labor but little capital have a comparative advantage in labor-intensive goods. This observation, plus the conclusion we reached in the preceding paragraph, imply the following result: Whenever differences in comparative advantage are based on differences in relative factor endowments, increased international trade tends to redistribute income in favor of those domestic inputs that are in abundant supply and against those that are in scarce supply.

Domestic factors in scarce supply obviously want to prevent this sort of redistribution of income, and the country as a whole may agree that such a redistribution would be undesirable. If so, then the country's government can prevent the undesired redistribution of income by imposing a high tariff on imports in whose production the scarce factor plays an important role (i.e., on imports that would decrease domestic demand for the scarce factor). Countries often seem to design their tariffs so as to protect the income share of the domestic factor that is in scarce supply. For example, a recent study shows that in the United States, where labor is the scarce factor and capital is the abundant one, tariffs are highest on manufactured goods which, it turns out, are also the most labor-intensive commodities that the United States imports.*

Although there is no question that governments can use high tariffs to preserve a distribution of domestic income that free trade would alter, we can ask: Are tariffs the best way to do this? Our discussion in Chapter 37 indicates that the answer is no. There we showed that the government can alter the distribution of income in any way it wants by changing the size and direction of taxes and transfer payments. Moreover, such changes don't have the harmful side effects on international trade and specialization that a tariff does.

Trade and the Level of Employment

From the national income and product account in Table 34.1 on page 519, we can readily figure out that in an open economy (that is, one that trades with the rest of the world), aggregate demand will equal the total amount of output demanded by domestic consumers (C), by domestic investors (I), by the domestic government (G), and by exporters (X), *minus* whatever part of

---

* Beatrice N. Vaccara, *Employment and Output in Protected Manufacturing Industries*, Washington, D.C., Brookings Institute, 1960.

this demand is satisfied by imports (M). In symbols,

$$\text{Aggregate demand} = C + I + G + (X - M).$$

From this expression we see that a *decrease* in imports will *increase* the *net-export* component of aggregate demand [that is, $(X - M)$]. This increase in turn will raise aggregate demand as a whole; and, as we saw in Chapter 35, a rise in aggregate demand will increase the economy's equilibrium income.

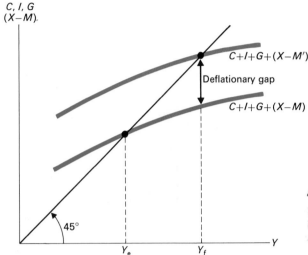

45|2

In an open economy, a decrease in imports raises aggregate demand and equilibrium income.

Suppose that the economy suffers from a deflationary gap. One way the government might overcome this gap would be to pass a bill that put a heavy tariff on imports. The tariff would cut imports; the cut in imports would raise aggregate demand; and the rise in aggregate demand would raise domestic income and employment. This chain of events is illustrated in Fig. 45.2, in which we see that aggregate demand is initially at the level $C + I + G + (X - M)$, and that the economy initially attains equilibrium at the low income level Y_e. Then a tariff is imposed. Imports *fall* from M to M', and aggregate demand shifts *upward* to a new higher level, $C + I + G + (X - M')$. The deflationary gap then disappears and the economy rises to the full-employment income Y_f.

So you can see that tariffs are definitely among the policy instruments that the government can use to achieve full employment. But are tariffs the *best* such instruments available to the government? No, for several reasons. *First:* On purely practical grounds, a tariff designed to raise domestic employment is likely to backfire. Reason: The countries whose commodity exports are cut by the tariff will suffer a fall in income. And as a result they will probably retaliate by raising their own tariffs. If they do, demand for the exports of the country that initially raised its tariffs will drop, and this country will find that all its tariff has done is to cut imports and exports by like amounts, without doing anything to raise domestic output.

Second: Tariffs restrict trade, and this, as we have said, reduces the world's real income. Therefore domestic monetary and fiscal measures of the sort we discussed in Chapters 38 and 39 are always preferable to tariffs as ways to raise domestic income.

Tariffs and the Terms of Trade

As we showed in Chapter 14, imposing a tax on the sale of a commodity leads to a downward shift in the demand curve faced by producers of this commodity.* Thus a tariff (remember a tariff is simply a tax imposed on the sale of imports) shifts downward (i.e., weakens) a country's demand for imports. As we said in Chapter 44, the weaker a country's demand for imports is, the lower the price it must pay for imports (i.e., the more favorable its terms of trade will be). Thus a tariff, by decreasing a country's demand for imports, improves its terms of trade and increases its gain from trade.

Does this mean that it's a good idea for a country to set out to improve its terms of trade by raising its tariffs? Probably no, for several reasons. *First:* The gambit may not work. One country's terms of trade can't improve unless other countries' terms of trade worsen. So any gains that accrue to the tariff-imposing country will be at the expense of other countries. And these other countries are likely to retaliate by hiking their own tariffs. If they do, then the terms-of-trade effect obtained by the country that first raised its tariff will be short-lived and of little value. *Second:* Tariffs imposed to obtain a terms-of-trade effect will, like other tariffs, reduce international trade and specialization, and thus the real income of the world as a whole.

Tariffs for Noneconomic Goals

So far we've discussed *economic* arguments in favor of tariffs. Often, however, tariffs are promoted on *noneconomic* grounds. Of these the most popular is probably national defense. In the United States, for example, we protect our high-cost merchant marine largely on the grounds that we'd need it if we were to fight a long war. We also protect such industries as domestic watchmaking, domestic oil production, and domestic shipbuilding on similar grounds.

---

* See Fig. 14.2(b) on page 225.

The economist, however much he may disapprove of tariffs, has to admit that there may be something to noneconomic arguments for tariffs. But he doesn't have to stop there. He can also talk about the *cost* of such protection. (1) Any noneconomic gains that result from a tariff will have their price: The loss in real income that a tariff imposes on the countries of the world, including the country that imposes it. (2) Any domestic industry that is protected from the rigors of foreign competition may over time become an increasingly inefficient producer and a technical laggard. Example: the U.S. shipbuilding industry. Shipbuilding in the U.S. is strongly protected, and industry spokesmen argue that such protection is needed because shipbuilding calls for so much labor that American shipbuilders, who have to pay high wages, could never survive in open competition with Japanese producers, who can get cheap labor. Yet today it is Japanese, not American, shipbuilders who are developing and applying striking innovations that cut production costs by increasing the productivity of both capital *and* labor. (3) Once the national-defense argument for tariffs is accepted, every domestic industry threatened by imports will tend to fancy itself "vital to national defense."

Tariffs to Protect Infant Industries

A great many industries are characterized by internal or external economies.* In such industries the greater the scale of output, the lower average costs of production are likely to be.

Whenever an industry is characterized by sizable internal or external economies, an established producing nation usually enjoys a cost advantage over a young developing nation. However, this cost advantage need not be based on—and might even be contrary to—the real comparative advantage of the two countries. Think for a moment about this: A high-cost industry in a developing country might be an "infant industry." In economist's jargon that's an industry which, if it were allowed to grow, would (by taking advantage of internal and external economies) gradually move from a position of high-cost comparative disadvantage to one of low-cost comparative advantage. Whenever a country harbors an infant industry, this country, and the world too, will benefit if the infant industry is given an opportunity —through *temporary* tariff protection—to establish itself as an "adult" low-cost producer.

One obvious danger of this infant-industry argument, especially in an underdeveloped country, is that every fledgling industry will demand pro-

---

* *Internal economies* mean that, as an individual producer expands output, his average costs fall; *external economies* mean that, as all producers in the industry expand output, their individual cost curves *shift* downward. (See pages 123–124 and 281–282.)

tection as an infant industry, regardless of where the ultimate comparative advantage of the country lies. And there's another problem: Infant industries are easy enough to talk about in theory. But how can the policy-maker identify them in practice?

*THE ECONOMIC IMPACT OF A QUOTA

As we said earlier, imports are often restricted not only by tariffs, but also by quotas. An import quota sets a limit on the *physical quantity* of a particular commodity that may be imported during a specified time period (e.g., a month or a year). To analyze what happens when a quota is imposed on an imported commodity, we can use the same approach we used to study the impact of a tariff.

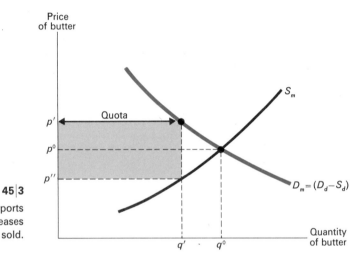

45|3

A quota on butter imports increases price and decreases quantity sold.

Suppose that the curves S_m and D_m in Fig. 45.3 represent the demand for and the supply of butter imports, and suppose that initially no quota is imposed on this market. Then q^0 of butter will be imported, and it will be sold at a price of p^0. Now suppose that the government imposes a quota equal to q' on imported butter. Then the total quantity of imported butter domestic consumers buy will decline from q^0 to q'. As in the case of a tariff, this enforced decline will be matched, partly by a *decline* in domestic consumption and partly by an *increase* in domestic production. Imposition of the quota, since it reduces imports to q', will also raise the price domestic consumers pay for butter from p^0 to p'.

---

* Students who haven't read Chapter 14 can omit this short section on quotas.

A quota, like a tariff, will naturally have a *revenue effect,* i.e., a chance for the government, or someone else, to make some money. This revenue effect is equal to the quantity of goods imported times the difference between the price these goods bring in the domestic market and the price at which they could have been bought in the foreign market. In the situation pictured in Fig. 45.3, this amount, which equals $[q' \cdot (p' - p'')]$, is represented by the shaded rectangle.

A government that imposes a quota can always capture for itself the revenue effect associated with this quota by auctioning off to importers *licenses* that give the bearer the right to bring in goods under the quota. This approach, however—although it has the double advantage of producing revenue for the government and of placing all would-be importers on an equal footing—is rarely used. Instead governments often decide to parcel out import licenses on some arbitrary basis. If the government parcels them out to domestic firms (the U.S. government distributes its crude-oil quota this way), the revenue effect associated with the quota will be captured by the favored domestic importers; and foreign exporters will receive only the price p'' for their goods. If on the other hand the government allocates the quota to foreign exporters (the U.S. government distributes its sugar quota this way), the revenue effect associated with the quota will be captured by the favored foreign exporters, who will receive the price p' on all export sales that come under the quota. It is for this reason that sugar-exporting countries spend a great deal of money lobbying in Washington to get a slice of the U.S. sugar quota. Finally the government may decide that the fairest way to fill a quota is on a first-come-first-served basis. In this case, who gets the revenue effect associated with the quota depends largely on the competitive structure of the market and on whether or not import purchases or export sales are under monopoly or oligopoly control.

Tariffs Versus Quotas

Since the economic impact of a quota is, except for the revenue effect, identical to that of a tariff, you may wonder why a government would ever impose a non-revenue-producing quota when it could get the same results with a revenue-producing tariff. The answer is that in some situations quotas have a distinct advantage over tariffs.

Suppose that the government wants to protect domestic producers against imports. As we have seen, a tariff will generally do the trick. But suppose that foreign supply of the imported commodity is completely *inelastic.* (Canadian farmers have the year's wheat crop all harvested and ready for export.) Then if an importing country (say Germany) hikes its tariff, this hike won't reduce imports and so won't protect domestic producers (German wheat farmers). Instead it will just lower the price received by foreign exporters (Canadian wheat farmers). This possibility is illustrated in Fig. 45.4. Initially this market is in equilibrium at the point at which the market demand curve for imports D_m intersects the market supply curve for imports S_m. At this point domestic consumers buy imports equal to q^0 at the price p^0, and foreign exporters receive the price p^0. Now the government imposes a tariff, which we represent by a *downward* shift in demand from D_m to D'_m. (Recall Fig. 14.2b on page 225.) Then the price received by foreign exporters will fall from p^0 to p''; the price paid by domestic consumers will remain unchanged at p'; the quantity purchased will remain unchanged at q'; and the tariff will exert *no* protective effect whatsoever! Clearly in such a situation the only way the government can protect domestic producers is to impose a quota on imports.

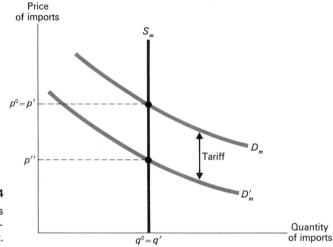

45|4

When the supply of imports is inelastic, a tariff has no protective effect.

Therefore *inelastic foreign supply* is one reason for imposing a quota. A second reason is that *quotas offer a degree of certainty about import quantities* that tariffs do not. A third reason is that, because of treaty agreements, *many countries have lost so much freedom to adjust tariffs* that quotas are the only way they can cut imports.

PRIVATE RESTRICTIONS ON TRADE

So far we have focused on government-imposed restrictions on international trade. There are also *private* restrictions on international trade, in the form of international *cartels*.

An international cartel is a *collusive agreement* set up between sellers in different countries to control world trade in a particular commodity. A cartel agreement may involve the fixing of export prices, the allocation of world markets, the setting up of a patent pool, the imposing of output restrictions, or any one of a number of other features. We discussed collusion and collusive agreements in some detail in Chapter 22 on oligopoly. For an eye-opening description of a cartel in action, reread page 346.

As we said in Chapter 22, collusion functions best when the number of rival sellers is limited. Therefore the most successful cartels have been those that have operated in world markets in which (because of entry barriers of one sort or another) supply was controlled by a small number of oligopolistic rivals. Thus, for example, before World War II cartels controlled world trade in steel, aluminum, magnesium, light bulbs, and many chemicals, all commodities produced by relatively few rival firms.

Since the ultimate purpose of a cartel agreement is to maximize the profits of cartel members, and since profit maximization requires that output be restricted below and price be set above the level that would be established under competitive conditions, cartels—like tariffs and quotas—decrease international trade and specialization and thus reduce the gains from trade.

Prior to World War II cartels were common. They are said to have controlled as much as 30 to 40% of total world trade.* Since the war, however, their role has been much diminished. Their decline is due largely to (a) the decartelization policy pursued in Germany during the allied occupation, (b) the increasingly hostile attitude toward cartels displayed by many West European governments (especially by the Common Market countries, which have a clearly enunciated—if somewhat lenient—anticartel policy), and (c) the prosecution under U.S. antitrust laws of a number of domestic firms which had been a part of international cartels that restricted competition in the U.S. (e.g., du Pont). All this is not to say that cartels are totally a thing of the past. Quite the contrary. The International Air Transport Association, an obvious cartel, still fixes air fares on almost all international flights.

CURRENT COMMERCIAL POLICY AND PROBLEMS

Right after World War II, international trade was severely restricted on all sides by import quotas, state trading agreements, currency regulations, and so forth. This situation was the result of a number of factors: the carry-over of bad habits picked up during the depressed 1930's, the disruptions caused by the war itself, and the prostrate state of Europe at the end of the war.

---

* Fritz Machlup, "The Nature of the International Cartel Problem," in Corwin D. Edwards and others, *A Cartel Policy for the United Nations;* New York: Columbia University Press, 1945, page 11; Edward S. Mason, *Controlling World Trade;* New York: McGraw-Hill, 1946, page 26n.

The General Agreement on Tariffs and Trade (GATT)

Soon after the war, to free international trade from the restrictions that had grown up around it, several steps were taken. One step was the setting up, in 1947, of the *General Agreement on Tariffs and Trade* (GATT), whose purpose was to help nations negotiate reciprocal multilateral reductions in tariffs. Negotiations under the auspices of GATT resulted in tariff reductions in 1947, 1949, 1951, 1956, and again in 1961. The latest series of GATT negotiations, which ran from 1962 to 1967, was widely known as the "Kennedy round" because it was initiated as a result of the Trade Expansion Act passed in 1962 during the Kennedy administration. This act gave U.S. bargainers authority to negotiate tariff cuts of up to 50%, and it resulted in the biggest tariff slashes in the history of GATT. World industrial tariffs were cut by a third, on the average, and world trade in a number of nonagricultural products was also liberalized.

The Organization for European Economic Cooperation (OEEC)

A second step taken soon after the war to free international trade from its bonds was the formation of the *Organization for European Economic Cooperation* (OEEC), part of whose purpose was to liberalize intra-European trade by getting European countries to make mutual reductions in the quotas they imposed on imports from each other.

The OEEC accomplished a great deal, even though it was a loosely organized group whose principal power was that of persuasion. The very fact that it existed, moreover, fanned Europe's long-held hopes for some sort of economic integration among European countries.

The European Coal and Steel Community (ECSC)

The first concrete step toward that integration was the creation, in 1952, of the *European Coal and Steel Community* (ECSC). The purpose of this organization was to establish free trade (no tariffs, no quotas) in coal and steel among the member nations: France, Germany, Italy, Belgium, the Netherlands, and Luxembourg. To do this, these nations had to eliminate all tariffs and quotas on intra-ECSC trade in coal and steel. They had to get rid of discriminatory freight rates that had previously protected domestic coal and steel producers. And they had to gain control of trade-restricting agreements among private producers; this was particularly important, since European coal and steel producers had traditionally used tight cartel agreements to set prices and divide markets.

The objectives of the ECSC were both economic and noneconomic. On the economic plane, the member nations favored the ECSC partly because of the gains that would accrue to them as a result of increased trade and specialization in coal and steel and partly because they knew that intra-ECSC competition would exert pressure on marginal firms to modernize and on submarginal firms (which had formerly been protected by cartels) to close up shop altogether.

The European Economic Community (EEC)

The European Coal and Steel Community was followed by the formation, in 1958, of the *European Economic Community* (EEC), or *Common Market,* as it is more familiarly known. Under the EEC treaty, France, Germany, Italy, Belgium, the Netherlands, and Luxembourg agreed to set up a *customs union:*

When countries set up a customs union, they abolish all restrictions on trade among themselves, and establish a common external tariff on imports from outside countries.

The EEC—by lowering tariff barriers that formerly prevented producers in one EEC country from selling to consumers in another—is greatly increasing competition between producers in different EEC countries. To give EEC producers an opportunity to adjust to this increased competition, the EEC is being established gradually over a transition period; this period began in 1959 and will extend to 1970–1973. Despite initial difficulties and misgivings, the EEC has succeeded so well that member nations have been able to push mutual tariff reduction well ahead of schedule.

On the economic plane the EEC has produced a variety of benefits for member countries: (1) By greatly increasing the intra-community flow of goods, it has enabled member countries to reap new gains from trade, based on differences in comparative advantage. (2) It has enabled producers previously confined to a narrow domestic market to expand their scale of production and thus to take advantage of additional economies of scale. (3) By doing away with the tariffs and quotas that in many industries had made these nations' markets a sheltered haven for domestic producers, it exposed many inefficient firms to a dose of competition that has forced them either to quit altogether or to increase their efficiency by means of new technology and new equipment, or—if they were too small to achieve an efficient scale of operation—by merging with other firms.

A customs union, because it lowers barriers to intra-union trade but not to trade with third countries, in effect discriminates in favor of exporters within the union and against exporters outside the union. Thus there is always a danger that a customs union, by decreasing union trade with third countries, will impose real losses on these countries. So far as the effect of the EEC on the U.S. is concerned, this threat does not seem too great, at least so far as manufactured articles are concerned, for several reasons: (1) The EEC countries, by cutting their external tariffs on several occasions, have displayed a willingness to pursue a liberal trade policy toward nonagricultural imports. (2) Many American firms, representing a wide range of industries and including familiar names such as IBM, General Electric, Ford, International Harvester, Esso, du Pont, and Union Carbide, have set up production facilities within the Common Market itself, and can therefore sell in this market on the same terms as domestic EEC producers.

With respect to agricultural products, the EEC has a trade policy that is considerably less liberal, and that reflects the fact that all EEC countries feel the need to protect their own farmers. The French, in fact, insist that their farmers be given considerable protection. Although the EEC's restrictive policy on food imports will hurt a variety of U.S. agricultural exports, the U.S. is unfortunately in a poor position to argue the merits of free trade in farm products with the Europeans. The reason is that the U.S., despite its comparative advantage in many farm products, has (as we saw in Chapter 25) a wide-ranging program to support farm prices. As part of this program, it imposes tariffs and tight quotas on many farm imports. Some of these controls, like the U.S. quota on cheese imports, are as galling to European farmers as European quotas on imports of U.S. wheat are to American farmers.

The European Free Trade Association (EFTA)

After the Common Market was formed, Great Britain, Sweden, Norway, Denmark, Switzerland, Portugal, and Austria (all countries that did not join the EEC) agreed to set up the *European Free Trade Area* (EFTA).

When countries set up a free-trade area, they abolish all restrictions on trade among themselves, but each country maintains its own set of tariffs and quotas on imports from outside countries.

Like the EEC, EFTA is being formed over a transition period, and so far EFTA tariff reductions have moved along on schedule. Nevertheless, the future of this organization is in doubt, because Britain and several other EFTA countries would like to join the Common Market. Britain has several incentives for doing so. One is the hope voiced by Prime Minister Wilson and others that the increased competition from EEC producers that British firms would have to meet if Britain joined the Common Market would create, in British industry, ". . . a new upsurge in investment and a new concentration on modernization, productivity, and reduced production costs." A second British incentive is the fear that the EFTA market, which is less than half the size of the EEC market, will prove too small to support British industries producing technologically advanced outputs such as nuclear equipment.

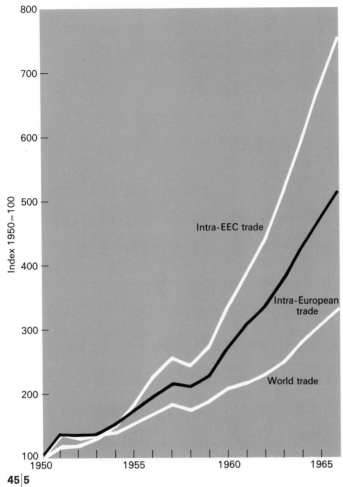

45|5

During the last 14 years, international trade has been growing rapidly.
(Source: United Nations *Monthly Bulletin of Statistics*)

Increasing World Trade

All these trade-promoting organizations that we have described have done
much to eliminate the barriers that hindered international trade during the
first few years after World War II. At the same time other organizations
and programs, some of which we shall discuss in Chapter 46, have done
much to eliminate the restrictions that were imposed on international payments before or during the war.

   As a result of programs of both sorts and of rising real income, trade in
the world at large has tripled since 1950 (see Fig. 45.5) and trade within
Europe, especially within the Common Market, has risen even faster.

PROBLEMS

1   Europeans view the safety standards currently being imposed on all cars sold in the U.S. as an invisible tariff. U.S. tariff negotiators refer to them as a consumer protection measure. Who do you think is right?

2   The French claim that their ban on whiskey advertising is a social measure. How plausible do you think this argument is?

*3 a) Show that, whenever a tariff is imposed on an imported commodity (say butter), the total decline in imports will equal (1) the induced *decrease* in domestic consumption plus (2) the induced *increase* in domestic production of butter.

   b) Show that if domestic demand for butter is elastic, but domestic supply is inelastic, decreased consumption will account for most of the decline in butter imports.

   c) Under what conditions would increased domestic production account for most of the decline in butter imports?

4   West Zee is a small African country. They produce coffee but no tea. People in Zee always drink something after dinner, sometimes coffee and sometimes tea. Currently coffee growers in West Zee are anxiously petitioning the government to impose a heavy tariff on tea imports. Use the general equilibrium analysis presented in Chapter 16 to explain why.

*5 How is it that the tariff graphed in Fig. 45.1 *decreases* the price received by foreign cheese producers, but *increases* the price received by domestic cheese producers?

6   Evaluate each of the pro-tariff points made in the following quote from the Republican Party platform of 1896:

   [The] true American policy taxes foreign products and encourages home industry; it puts the burden of revenue on foreign goods; it secures the American market for the American producer; it upholds the American standard of wages for the American workingman; it puts the factory on the side of the farm, and makes the American farmer less dependent on foreign demand and price; it diffuses general thrift, and founds the strength of all on the strength of each.

7   Tariffs to raise domestic employment are often called "beggar-thy-neighbor" tariffs. Can you explain why?

8   Sometimes countries restrict exports for strategic and other reasons. Using a diagram, show that export restrictions cut domestic income.

9   Import taxes can be imposed on a *specific* (dollars per physical unit) or *ad valorem* (percentage of value) basis. Can you think of any situation in which a specific tax would offer more effective protection than an ad valorem one?

10 "In the situation pictured in Fig. 45.4, a tariff wouldn't reduce imports, but it would improve the terms of trade of the country that imposed it." Discuss.

---

* All starred problems build on material presented in Chapter 14.

11 a) When a country imposes an import quota that cuts down on domestic imports of a particular commodity, what relationship will inevitably exist between the world price for that commodity and the domestic price for it?

    b) What does your answer tell you about why there is a *revenue effect* associated with a quota?

12 Show that if domestic demand for imports is totally inelastic, a tariff will offer domestic producers *no* protection. [*Hint:* Recall from Chapter 14 that a commodity tax can be represented either by a downward shift in demand or by an upward shift in supply.]

13 Do you think that Liechtenstein or Monaco could get much of a terms-of-trade effect by imposing tariffs on key imports? What about the U.S.? Explain your answer.

14 The U.S. applies import quotas much more frequently to agricultural products than to industrial outputs. Why do you think this is the case? [*Hint:* Recall our discussion in Chapter 25 of agriculture and its special problems.]

15 In May 1962 the West German legislature forced Chancellor Adenauer's government to cut in half duties on automobiles imported from other Common Market countries. The objective of this move was to get Volkswagen and other German auto makers to rescind a recent price boost. How effective do you think that such a gambit would be likely to be? Would your answer depend on the competitive structure of the domestic market?

16 Do you think that an across-the-board cut in all tariffs would be a good way to cut domestic inflation? Would your answer depend on the kind of inflation the economy was suffering from? [Recall our discussion in Chapter 40 of the different kinds of inflation.]

17 Can you think of some reasons why cartels are generally considered to be harmful? [*Hint:* Recall our discussion of imperfect competition and economic inefficiency in Chapter 25.]

CHAPTER 46

THE INTERNATIONAL
PAYMENTS MECHANISM

In Chapter 24, when we talked about why international trade takes place, we didn't mention money payments. To keep things simple, we just focused on a barter model of trade; that is, one in which countries trade goods for goods. In actual practice, of course, imports are paid for with money and exports are sold for money. So the existence of international trade—and also of international capital movements—means that large numbers of money payments have to be made between people who live in different countries.

Since there are so many different national currencies, international money payments are possible only because a mechanism for them has been established. There are two ways in which such a mechanism could be set up: (1) People who wanted to effect international payments could do so in foreign currency, which they would get by exchanging their own currency for foreign currency in the open market, at a market-determined rate of exchange. (2) People could make international payments in a special international currency. Because such an international currency could be created in various ways (recall our discussion of banking in Part 6), this second possibility opens up a Pandora's box of possibilities.

The international payments mechanism actually used combines both these approaches. Most international money payments are effected by means of trades of one currency for another in the *foreign exchange market*, but some are effected by means of international money in the form of gold and "reserve currencies." As we shall presently see, the dollar is the world's chief reserve currency today.

THE FOREIGN EXCHANGE MARKET

The foreign exchange market is a market in which many people meet to trade one national currency for another.

712

For example, they trade dollars for marks, marks for francs, or francs for dollars. Thus the national currencies of all countries form the stock in trade of the foreign exchange market.

Who are the participants in this market? From the point of view of any one country, the demanders of *foreign exchange,* that is, of *nondomestic currencies,* include all domestic spending units who want to make payments to foreign spending units. The suppliers of foreign exchange include all foreign spending units who want to make payments to domestic spending units.

This sounds simple, but it opens up many possibilities. Consider, for example, the foreign exchange market from the point of view of the United States. The American importer who wants francs to buy French wine, the American manufacturer who wants lira to put up a plant in Italy, and the American government which wants marks to pay for stationing troops in Germany are all demanders of foreign exchange (that is, they all want to trade dollars for foreign currencies). On the other hand, the Peruvian who wants dollars to buy a U.S. car, the Frenchman who wants dollars to tour the United States, and the Norwegian who wants dollars to invest in IBM (or some other U.S. company) are all suppliers of foreign exchange; that is, they all want to trade foreign currencies for dollars.

As opposed to, say, the New York Stock Exchange, which has a definite abode and fixed trading hours, the foreign exchange market is an over-the-counter market,* one that is confined to no one place, but exists everywhere that people trade one currency for another. Despite its dispersed character, the foreign exchange market does have recognized centers of activity, in which a great volume of trading regularly occurs. These include New York, London, Paris, and other large cities throughout the world.

The New York Foreign Exchange Market

So far as the United States is concerned, the heart of the foreign exchange market, like that of so many other financial markets, is New York City. Not that New Yorkers are the only ones who buy and sell foreign exchange; but the New York market acts as a *clearing house,* balancing the *demands for* and *offers of* foreign exchange made by firms and individuals throughout the country.

Here's the way this balancing-off takes place: Whenever a person or a firm in the U.S. wants to buy or sell foreign exchange (i.e., foreign currencies), they usually turn to their commercial bank. If this bank doesn't happen to

---

* Recall the distinction we made in Chapter 32 between organized exchanges, in which listed stocks are traded, and over-the-counter markets, in which unlisted stocks (and listed ones as well) are traded.

have an active foreign department (and most don't), it meets the foreign exchange needs of its customers by buying foreign exchange from or selling foreign exchange to its correspondent bank.* Since its correspondent or accommodating bank is likely to be in New York, the center of foreign exchange for most people throughout the country is the New York market.

The main domestic participants in the New York foreign exchange market are a score of large New York banks and a handful of out-of-town ones, each of which buys and sells foreign exchange to meet the needs of its customers and correspondents. Sometimes the buy and sell orders received by an exchange-trading bank offset each other (e.g., the supply of pounds offered by an exporter may offset an importer's request for pounds). But naturally this doesn't happen all the time. Therefore a bank that deals in foreign exchange often accumulates unwanted surpluses of some currencies and unintentionally runs down its balances of others. It may get some buy and sell orders that are too large for it to handle with its own resources or it may receive orders for currencies in which it does not normally "take a position" (i.e., hold balances). Then the bank has to look for another bank with whom it can make an offsetting trade. Since it's always possible that, while one New York bank is running low on a certain currency, another is accumulating a surplus in it, such trades often take place between New York exchange-trading banks. Sometimes, however, New York banks *as a group* accumulate an excess supply of (or an excess demand for) a particular currency. When this happens, they have to make an offsetting trade with one of the large foreign banks that constantly bid for and offer foreign exchange in the New York market, or they have to buy and sell foreign exchange directly in a foreign center such as London.

The channels for trading between domestic exchange-trading institutions and foreign-based ones are important. Such trades tie the New York market into the world market, and thus assure that the exchange rates established in New York will be the same as those established in other centers of the foreign exchange market.

Price Determination in the Foreign Exchange Market

The first characteristic that strikes one about the foreign exchange market is that *each currency traded there is a homogeneous product.* Paraphrasing Gertrude Stein, a mark is a mark is a mark, and a franc is a franc is a franc. The second characteristic is that, because all the participants in this market —regardless of where they are based—are bound together by telephone, teletype, and cable, *every trader in the market has almost immediate access to data on the prices at which trades are taking place throughout the market.*

---

* The correspondent relationship between city and country banks was described on page 479.

The third characteristic is that, since all the centers of this market are really interrelated parts of a single wider market, *no one private buyer or seller in the market is large enough to perceptibly influence market price.*

For these three reasons, the structure of the foreign exchange market is competitive. Therefore we can analyze the way price is determined in the various sectors of this market (e.g., the dollar-mark market, the dollar-pound market, and so forth) by using the principle of supply and demand.

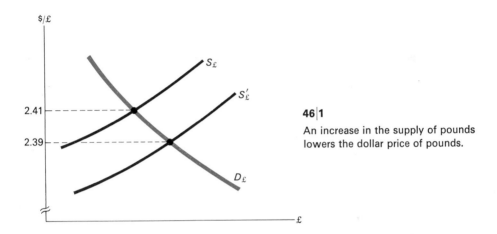

46|1

An increase in the supply of pounds lowers the dollar price of pounds.

Let us start with a simple situation: Suppose that there are only two countries, the U.S. and the U.K., and two currencies, the dollar and the pound. How is the rate at which dollars are exchanged for pounds (i.e., the dollar price of pounds) determined? In the U.S. certain people—importers of British goods, people who are planning trips to the U.K., and American firms who want to pay out dividends and interest to British investors—demand pounds (i.e., supply dollars). How many pounds they demand depends on the number of dollars they have to pay for each pound they buy, i.e., on the dollar price of pounds. Therefore we can represent their behavior by the demand-for-pounds curve $D_£$ in Fig. 46.1. In the U.K. certain other people —importers of U.S. goods, people who are planning trips to the U.S., and people who want to invest in the U.S.—demand dollars (i.e., supply pounds). The amount of pounds they supply depends on the number of dollars they get for each pound they give up, i.e., on the dollar price of pounds. Thus we can represent their behavior by the supply-of-pounds curve $S_£$ in Fig. 46.1. From these two curves, we can readily determine the dollar price that pounds will command in equilibrium. Obviously it has to be $2.41, since this is the only price (i.e., exchange rate) that equates the demand for pounds with the supply of pounds.

In the foreign exchange market, as in any other competitive market, an equilibrium price, once established, is maintained only so long as the conditions that underlie market supply and demand are constant. If these conditions change, then the market supply and demand curves shift, and the market's equilibrium price is altered. To illustrate: Suppose that a shift in tastes leads British consumers to demand more U.S. goods. This would cause British importers to demand more dollars (that is, to offer a larger supply of pounds in exchange for dollars), and as a result the supply curve of pounds would *shift* to the right, and the equilibrium price of pounds would fall. This possibility is illustrated in Fig. 46.1, where a shift to the right in the supply curve of pounds from $S_£$ to $S'_£$ causes the equilibrium exchange rate between dollars and pounds to drop from $2.41 to $2.39.

So far, to keep things simple, we have focused on just two currencies, dollars and pounds. In practice, of course, there are many countries, all of whose currencies are traded in the foreign exchange market. Hence, in addition to the dollar–pound rate, the rates at which dollars are exchanged for marks, pesos, krona, and other currencies are also determined in the foreign exchange market. And also many cross rates (between pounds and marks, between pounds and krona, between krona and marks, and so forth) are determined there, too. The fact that so many exchange rates are determined in the foreign exchange market makes price determination there sound more complex than our first simple example would have led us to believe. But it isn't, really, because each rate is competitively established, so we can think of each as being determined by supply and demand.

Exchange Arbitrage

In a competitive market price is supposed to be the same everywhere. Since the foreign exchange market is a dispersed one, with centers throughout the world, price will be the same everywhere only if the exchange rate established between any two currencies is the same in all centers. Also, since the foreign exchange market deals in many currencies, price will be the same everywhere only if the exchange rates between different currencies are mutually consistent (i.e., if the dollar price of pounds is the same whether we exchange dollars directly for pounds or whether we first exchange dollars for marks and then marks for pounds).

We know that these two conditions will hold, because the moment rates in different centers diverge or cross rates fall out of line, *exchange arbitragers* are brought into action. Exchange arbitragers are individuals who are alert to opportunities to make profits by simultaneously buying and selling foreign exchange in different sectors of the market. Their purchases and sales—by altering supply and demand in these different sectors—tend to bring diverging rates back into line.

Let us look at the way arbitrage works: Consider a case in which the existence of mutually inconsistent cross rates in different centers brings arbitragers into action. Suppose that a price of $0.25 is bid for the German mark in New York, that a price of $0.20 is asked for the Belgian franc in Brussels, and that a price of 0.81 of a mark is bid for the Belgian franc in Dusseldorf. Then a practiced New York trader would recognize that by simultaneously exchanging dollars for francs in Brussels, francs for marks in Dusseldorf, and marks for dollars in New York, he could make a sure profit.

Let's work out the arithmetic of the transaction. Suppose that our alert trader starts out with $10,000. Then at the Brussels asking price of $0.20 per Belgian franc, he will be able (see Fig. 46.2) to buy 50,000 Belgian francs; at the Dusseldorf bid price of 0.81 of a mark per Belgian franc, he will be able to exchange these francs for 40,500 marks; and at the New York bid price of $0.25 per mark, he will be able to exchange his marks for $10,125. Thus our trader, by arbitraging through the Belgian franc, will be able to make a $125 profit—minus, of course, cable and other transaction costs.

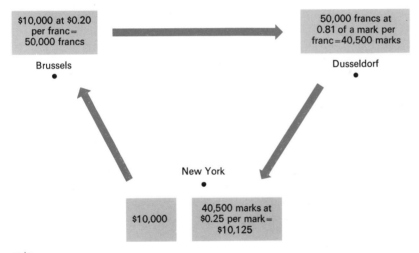

46|2
Arbitrage works to bring divergent cross rates into line.

In interpreting this example, there are two important things to note. *First:* This arbitrage transaction, since it offers a sure profit, is certain to be carried out. *Second:* This transaction—since it simultaneously raises the demand for Belgian francs on the Brussels market, increases the supply of Belgian francs in the Dusseldorf market, and increases the supply of marks in the New York market—works to bring the divergent set of cross rates into line by raising the dollar price of Belgian francs on the Brussels market, lowering the mark price of Belgian francs in the Dusseldorf market, and lowering the dollar price of marks in the New York market. Of course the activities of a single arbitrager won't suffice to bring divergent cross rates into line, but there are many such traders, and the activities of these traders *as a group* guarantee that the foreign exchange market—despite its geographic dispersity—will behave as a single market and establish a single set of mutually consistent exchange rates.

PEGS AND PAR VALUES

If the governments of all nations refrained from taking any actions designed to influence the rates at which national currencies were exchanged for each other, the foreign exchange market, operating in complete freedom, would establish a mutually consistent set of equilibrium exchange rates among all currencies. Also all changes in the demand for and supply of individual currencies—whether they were caused by seasonal variations in trade patterns, by more permanent changes in trade patterns, or by changes in the size or direction of international capital flows—would be immediately accommodated by a change in the equilibrium pattern of exchange rates, with the result that no imbalance between the demand for and supply of any nation's currency would ever exist on more than a momentary basis. In addition, under a system of freely fluctuating exchange rates, every currency would be directly convertible into every other currency, so that the financing of multilateral trade flows of the sort illustrated in Fig. 42.1 would never present a problem.

Threat of Wide Fluctuations in Exchange Rates

Because of their total reliance on the price mechanism, freely fluctuating exchange rates are appealing in theory. However, experience indicates that the elasticities of demand and supply for many currencies are so low that even small shifts in the demand for and supply of these currencies lead to wide fluctuations in exchange rates. Experience also indicates that under a system of freely fluctuating exchange rates, movements in exchange rates elicit *destabilizing,* not stabilizing, speculation. Let's look at what happens when speculation is destabilizing: Suppose that a currency *depreciates* (i.e., falls in exchange value). You might think that speculators would acquire this currency in the expectation that it would subsequently *appreciate* (i.e., rise in exchange value). But no. Speculators try to unload the depreciated currency or even sell it short, in the expectation that it will depreciate still further. When they do this, of course, they decrease the demand for and increase the supply of the depreciated currency, and as a result its price drops still further. Thus destabilizing speculation tends to make small dips in exchange rates into big ones. It also works in the opposite direction; that is, it makes small upswings in exchange rates into big ones.

If wide swings occur in the rates at which different currencies can be exchanged for one another, this disrupts trade flows, distorts long-term capital flows, and creates large price changes in countries that import and export a great many goods. Therefore freely fluctuating exchange rates and the wide swings in exchange rates that they are likely to bring on are regarded as unacceptable.

Par Values Under the IMF

To avoid the disruptive effects of wide fluctuations in exchange rates, the U.S. and a number of other nations committed themselves in 1945 under the Articles of Agreement of the *International Monetary Fund* (IMF) to establish a *par value* (i.e., *official exchange rate*) for their currency in terms of gold or dollars, and to maintain the value of their currency at or near par.

The U.S., under the IMF agreement, set the par value of the dollar at $35 per ounce of gold and committed itself to buy and sell gold in unlimited quantities to foreign central banks at this price. All other IMF participants who have established par values for their currencies have done so by setting up an official exchange rate between their currency and the dollar. To main-

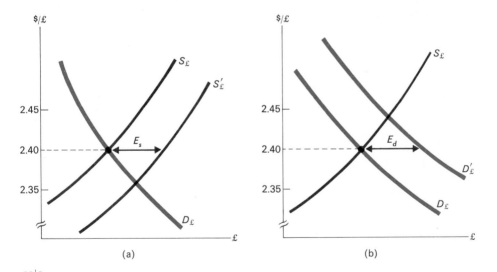

46|3

To maintain the official dollar–pound exchange rate of $2.40, British monetary authorities have to buy up any excess supply of pounds or meet any excess demand for pounds that emerges at this exchange rate.

tain these official exchange rates, each foreign monetary authority intervenes in the foreign exchange market, supplying dollars or domestic currency as need may be in order to bring the market for its currency into equilibrium at or near the official exchange rate.

To illustrate how such intervention works, let us again focus on the pound–dollar market: At the moment the par value of the pound is $2.40. This means that, if the demand and supply curves ruling in the pound–dollar market were those labeled $D_£$ and $S_£$ in Fig. 46.3, British monetary authorities would have no work to do, since the equilibrium exchange rate between dollars and pounds would equal the official exchange rate, or $2.40. However, if the supply of pounds were to increase from $S_£$ to $S'_£$, then (as indicated in Fig. 46.3a) an excess supply of pounds E_s would emerge at the official exchange rate; and, to maintain the pound at *par*, British authorities would have to buy up this excess supply of pounds by supplying dollars to the market. If, on the other hand, the demand for pounds were to increase from $D_£$ to $D'_£$, then in order to maintain the pound at par, British monetary authorities (as indicated in Fig. 46.3b) would have to meet an excess demand for pounds equal to E_d by supplying pounds in exchange for dollars.

TABLE 46|1

Foreign Exchange Rates Quoted in a New York Newspaper (December 27, 1967)

Selling prices for bank transfers in the U.S. for payment abroad, as quoted at 4 p.m. (in dollars)

Country and par value	Wednesday	Previous day
Canada (dollar, 0.925)	0.9250	0.9253
Great Britain (pound, 2.40)	2.4055	2.4020
Belgium (franc, 0.20)	0.020145	0.020150
France (franc, 0.20255)	0.2038	$0.2037\frac{1}{2}$
West Germany (deutschemark, 0.25)	0.2509	0.2510
Argentina ("free" peso)	0.00288	
Brazil ("novo" cruzeiro)	0.3720	
Lebanon (pound, 0.456313)	0.3215	
Hong Kong (HK dollar)	0.1650	
Japan (yen, 0.00277778)	0.002767	
Philippines (peso)	0.2555	

Since exchange rates are all pegged by official intervention in the foreign exchange market, why do newspapers bother to carry exchange-rate quotes like those in Table 46.1? Well, some countries don't try to maintain their currencies at a fixed par value; others that do often let their currency fluctuate within a range running from 1% above to 1% below par. Thus

British authorities do not try to maintain the pound at precisely $2.40; they let it fluctuate between a ceiling slightly above and a floor slightly below $2.40.

How do government pegging operations affect the functioning of the foreign exchange market as we described it earlier? From a purely mechanical point of view, such operations have no effect whatsoever on the functioning of the market, because a government simply enters the market as another buyer or seller of foreign exchange. However, a government exerts a considerable influence on the exchange rate established in this market, both by means of its own purchases and sales and by means of its impact on the expectations and thus the behavior of speculators. For this reason, the foreign exchange market cannot, strictly speaking, be described as perfectly competitive except during periods when it attains equilibrium without official intervention.

Foreign Exchange Reserves

Since exchange-rate pegging calls for the domestic monetary authority to sell domestic currency whenever it appreciates and to sell foreign exchange whenever domestic currency depreciates, the domestic monetary authority can succeed only if (a) *it has access to supplies of domestic currency,* and if (b) *it holds reserves of foreign exchange.* Prior to the 1930's most countries pegged their currencies to gold and held their foreign exchange reserves in the form of gold. Today, though, most countries peg their currencies to the dollar, and hold their foreign exchange reserves partly in gold and partly in dollars and other convertible currencies.

When the International Monetary Fund was set up, people recognized that the member countries would be able to maintain their currencies at par only if they had at their disposal enough foreign exchange to offset any temporary tendency that might arise for their currency to depreciate below par. For the U.S., reserve adequacy was no problem, since it held the bulk of the world's gold: over $20 billion worth. For most European countries, however, reserve adequacy was a real problem, since these countries, as a result of the war, had exhausted their holdings of gold and foreign exchange. To augment the reserves available to these countries, the IMF collected a pool of gold and foreign exchange from member countries, so that it could make loans to member countries that had a temporary need for extra reserves to support their currencies at par. Because of the difficult times in which the IMF was born and the limited resources at its disposal, the results of its initial loans were discouraging. Over time, however, the problems faced by IMF members have assumed more manageable proportions, and the resources available to the IMF have substantially increased. Hence today, for all IMF members, the ability to borrow from the IMF constitutes an important and useful adjunct to their foreign exchange reserves.

PROBLEMS

1   Given that the dollar price of a pound is $2.40, what is the pound price of a dollar? What if the dollar price of a pound were $2.80? What if it were $2.00?

2   Part (a) of Fig. 46.4 shows a market in which people demand and supply pounds in exchange for dollars. When someone who holds dollars demands pounds, he is in effect supplying dollars. Similarly, when someone who holds pounds offers to supply them in exchange for dollars, he is in effect demanding dollars. Thus we could view the market in Fig. 46.4(a) alternatively as a market in which people demand and supply dollars in exchange for pounds. Now, if we know that the demand for pounds equals the supply of pounds at the exchange rate of $2.40 a pound, can we be sure that the demand for dollars will equal the supply of dollars at the equivalent exchange rate of 0.42 of a pound per dollar?

   To figure this out: (1) Use the demand curve for pounds in Fig. 46.4(a) to construct a supply curve for dollars and plot it in Fig. 46.4(b). [*Hint:* The bottom-most dotted point on $D_£$ tells you that if pounds cost $2.00 apiece, people would buy 3 million of them, and to do so they would pay (i.e., supply) 6 million dollars.] (2) Use the supply curve for pounds in Fig. 46.4(a) to construct a demand curve for dollars and plot it in Fig. 46.4(b).

   What equilibrium exchange rate do you come up with in part (b)? Is it equivalent to the one shown in part (a)? Explain why it is or is not.

3   Suppose the dollar price of pounds could fluctuate in response to shifts in demand for and supply of pounds. How would the following affect this rate?

   a) The U.K. joins the Common Market, and this makes U.S. firms want to make more direct investments in the U.K.

   b) British consumers, with the building of their new network of high-speed, dual-carriageway "M" roads, shift tastes and decide to drive U.S. cars.

   c) British short-term interest rates rise to a level several percentage points above U.S. short-term rates.

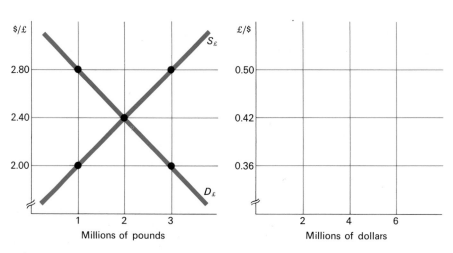

46|4   (a) The market for pounds.   (b) The market for dollars.

d) Prince Charles gets married in Westminster Abbey, and this draws millions of extra U.S. tourists.

4   Analyze the way that each of the events described in Problem 3 would shift the demand for and the supply of dollars, and thus the pound price of dollars. Are the answers you obtain here consistent with those you obtained when you answered Problem 3?

5   Suppose that a price of $0.25 is asked for the mark in New York, that a Belgian franc can be sold for $0.20 in Brussels, and that a Belgian franc costs 0.79 of a mark in Dusseldorf. On what $10,000-arbitrage transaction could you make $120?

6   Currently the French peg the French franc to the dollar at the rate of 1 franc = $0.20. The Germans peg the mark to the dollar at the rate of 1 mark = $0.25. What cross rate between the mark and the franc do these two dollar pegs imply? Will this cross rate be maintained even if the French and German monetary authorities never intervene in the franc-mark market? Explain your answer.

7   The big middle-African country of Gee is a great place for growing wheat and cotton, but it doesn't have much industry. Every spring Gee imports farm equipment, fertilizer, and a lot of other industrial products from cutlery to cars. In the fall, of course, it exports millions of tons of wheat and bales of cotton. Gee has a freely fluctuating exchange rate. What seasonal pattern would you expect this exchange rate to follow? If the world were a stable one, in what sort of seasonal speculation would you expect a profit-maximizing speculator to engage (i.e., in what season would he buy and in what season would he sell Gee's currency)? Would his activities have a stabilizing or a destabilizing influence on Gee's exchange rate?

8   The concept of destabilizing speculation can be applied not just to the foreign exchange market, but to other financial markets and to commodity markets as well. What do you think it would mean for speculation to be destabilizing in the market for a particular stock? Would you expect speculation in the market for, say, AT&T common stock to be stabilizing or destabilizing? What about speculation in the market for some high-flying electronics firm?

9   Whenever a national monetary authority buys or sells foreign exchange in the course of its pegging operations, this transaction shows up as an official capital inflow in the country whose currency was bought and as an official capital outflow in the country whose currency was sold.

a) Suppose that there are just two countries, Philodendron and Petunia. Their total transactions with each other are as follows. Philodendron imports $110,000 worth of goods from Petunia. Petunia imports $100,000 worth of goods from Philodendron, and Petunia's monetary authority acquires $10,000 worth of Philodendron's currency in the course of its pegging operations. Set up Philodendron's balance of payments. Set up Petunia's.

b) Repeat this question, except this time assume that Petunia's monetary authority does nothing, but Philodendron's monetary authority sells $10,000 worth of Petunia's currency in the course of its pegging operations. [Hint: Recall Problem 1 at the end of Chapter 43, and our convention that a decrease in assets is a negative source of funds.]

CHAPTER 47

BALANCE-OF-PAYMENTS ADJUSTMENT

DEFINING BALANCE IN THE BALANCE OF PAYMENTS

People often talk about a country's balance of payments being in *deficit* or *surplus*. But, as we pointed out in Chapter 43, a nation's balance-of-payments account is simply an elaborate flow-of-funds statement, so by definition it must always be in balance. Therefore "balance" in the balance-of-payments account cannot refer to all entries there. It must refer to some *subtotal*. Since one could calculate many different subtotals, how does the national income accountant decide *which* balance-of-payments subtotal to label "balance"? Answer: He designs the "balance" entry so that it tells the government policy-maker something he wants to know.

If the rate at which the domestic currency is exchanged for foreign currencies is pegged, the policy-maker will want to know: *How much foreign exchange* had to be bought or sold during the past year in order to maintain the domestic currency at par?* Answering this question, of course, means measuring the increase or decrease that occurred in the country's foreign exchange reserves. Therefore the measure of balance obtained this way tells the policy-maker not only what happened in the immediate past, but also how capable the country will be of continuing to peg its exchange rate in the future.

Let "current account balance" denote exports of goods and services minus imports; let "net private capital inflows" denote net *in*flows of private foreign capital minus net *out*flows of private domestic capital; and let "domestic official transactions" denote the *net* amount of gold and foreign currencies the domestic monetary authority has had to sell (i.e., total sales minus total purchases) to maintain the domestic currency at par. Then,

---

* When an economist uses the term *foreign exchange,* he means any foreign currencies, plus gold. On the other hand, a nation's foreign exchange *reserves* include only convertible currencies (such as dollars and pounds) and gold.

from our discussion in Chapter 43, it follows that a country's balance-of-payments account (assuming its currency is *not* a reserve currency) can be summed up as follows:

$$\left(\begin{array}{c} \text{Current account balance} \\ + \\ \text{Net } \textit{private} \text{ capital inflows} \\ + \\ \text{Domestic } \textit{official} \text{ transactions} \end{array} \right) \; = \; 0. \qquad (1)$$

Once we have this statement in hand, we can identify the balance-of-payments subtotal that the government policy-maker wants for his accounts. Obviously:

$$\left(\begin{array}{c} \text{Current account balance} \\ + \\ \text{Net } \textit{private} \text{ capital inflows} \end{array} \right) \; = \; \text{BALANCE} \; = \; -(\text{Domestic } \textit{official} \text{ transactions}). \qquad (2)$$

This measure of balance tells us that a country gains gold and foreign exchange (i.e., has a balance-of-payments *surplus*) if exports plus private capital *in*flows exceed imports plus private capital *out*flows. On the other hand, a country loses gold and foreign exchange (i.e., has a balance-of-payments *deficit*) if imports plus private capital outflows exceed exports plus private capital inflows.

Balance for a Key-Currency Country

The above measure of balance is useful, and adequate for many countries, but not for one whose currency is a reserve currency, or *key currency* as it is often called. As we said in Chapter 46, a reserve currency is one in which other countries commonly hold all or part of their foreign exchange reserves. Today the U.S. dollar and the British pound are the world's chief reserve currencies. Thus Kuwait holds part of its foreign exchange reserves in the form of sterling (i.e., pound) balances, while Germany holds part of its reserves in the form of dollar balances.

Whenever the pegging operations* of a country that holds its reserves in a key currency lead it to buy or sell the key currency, its transactions naturally show up in the balance of payments of the key-currency country. So the balance of payments of such a country contains not only the four entries we talked about above, but also a fifth, *foreign official transactions*. (This entry equals the net inflow of foreign official capital.) Therefore, when

---

* We discussed pegging on page 720.

the national income accountant in a key-currency country chooses the way to measure balance in the domestic balance of payments, he has to decide whether to include foreign official transactions in the balance figure he calculates. What he does usually depends on the character he attributes to such transactions.

If the national income accountant views foreign official transactions as *autonomous* capital movement (i.e., capital movement undertaken for reasons independent of the state of the key-currency country's balance of payments), he is inclined to include them in the balance figure, as follows:

$$\begin{pmatrix} \text{Current account balance} \\ + \\ \text{Net } \textit{private} \text{ capital inflows} \\ + \\ \text{Foreign } \textit{official} \text{ transactions} \end{pmatrix} = \text{BALANCE} = -(\text{Domestic } \textit{official} \text{ transactions}). \quad (3)$$

If, on the other hand, the national income accountant views foreign transactions as *accommodating* capital movements (i.e., capital movements designed to help the key-currency country fill a gap between demand and supply for its currency at the peg rate), he will probably exclude them from his balance figure, as follows:

$$\begin{pmatrix} \text{Current account balance} \\ + \\ \text{Net } \textit{private} \text{ capital inflows} \end{pmatrix} = \text{BALANCE} = -\begin{pmatrix} \text{Domestic } \textit{official} \text{ transactions} \\ + \\ \text{Foreign } \textit{official} \text{ transactions} \end{pmatrix}. \quad (4)$$

Balance in the U.S. Balance of Payments

Just after World War II, foreigners were anxious to buy imports from the U.S., but had few goods to export to the U.S. So the demand for dollars exceeded the supply of dollars at the peg rate, and people said that there was a *dollar shortage*. During this period, foreign monetary authorities wanted to build up their dollar balances, and people therefore often thought of "balance" in the U.S. balance of payments in terms of Equation (3) above.

Today, however, things have changed. Now foreign money men are worried about the persistent deficit in the U.S. balance of payments (i.e., about the fact that in recent years the sum of the U.S. current account balance plus net private capital inflows has been negative most of the time), and as a result they have become progressively less anxious to build up their holdings of dollars. So today people usually think of "balance" in the U.S. balance of payments in terms of Equation (4) above or some close variant.

Now look at Table 47.1. Here we have rearranged the U.S. balance-of-payments figures shown in Table 43.2 so that they record what the U.S.

TABLE 47|1

The United States Balance-of-Payments Account, 1966 (Millions of Dollars)*

Exports of goods and services	42,910	*Official U.S. gold exports and*	
Imports of goods and services	−37,614	*sales of convertible currencies*	568
Remittances and grants	− 992	Short-term claims	−1,574
Current account balance	4,304	Long-term claims	735
Foreign private capital inflow, net	1,433	*Foreign official reserve transactions*	− 839
U.S. private capital outflow, net	− 1,481		
U.S. gov't grants and net capital outflow	− 3,396		
Capital account balance	− 3,444		
Errors and omissions	− 589		
OFFICIAL RESERVE TRANSACTIONS BALANCE	271	OFFSETS TO THE OFFICIAL RESERVE TRANSACTIONS BALANCE	− 271

*Adapted from U.S. Department of Commerce figures.

Department of Commerce labels the *official reserve transactions* balance. As you will see, this concept of balance (which means just what it says) is identical to the concept of balance in Equation (4) above. In 1966 the U.S. balance of payments, measured on an official reserve transaction basis, was in slight surplus, largely because the high short-term interest rates prevailing in the U.S. during this year led U.S. commercial banks with overseas operations to repatriate over $2 billion of funds from abroad.* But most of the time in recent years it has been in deficit.

ADJUSTMENT TO BALANCE-OF-PAYMENTS DISEQUILIBRIUM

As we have said, whenever a country has a deficit in its balance of payments, domestic demand for foreign exchange exceeds supply at the peg rate (recall Fig. 46.3b), and the country loses foreign exchange. Obviously if the deficit goes on for a long time it will eventually exhaust the foreign exchange reserves of the country which incurs it; and when this happens, the deficit country will have no choice but to permit its currency to depreciate below par. Therefore a balance-of-payments deficit cannot be permitted to endure indefinitely. If a country is to avoid devaluation, the cause of its balance-of-payments deficit must be cured, or at least the symptoms (i.e., the resulting losses in foreign exchange) must be controlled. We shall consider the second of these two possibilities first.

---

* This naturally resulted in a big short-term capital inflow.

The "No-Adjustment" Solution: Exchange Control

During some eras—the depression of the 1930's, World War II, and the years right after it—economic disruptions were so great that many countries felt that no economic policy would suffice to bring their balance of payments into equilibrium, or at least no policy would do so without creating severe and unwanted side effects such as inflation and unemployment. So they turned to what might be called the "no-adjustment" solution to balance-of-payments disequilibrium: *exchange control.*

Exchange control began quite simply in the 1930's. Some countries that felt they couldn't restore equilibrium to their balance of payments chose to maintain the nominal value of their currencies by imposing direct controls on domestic buyers and sellers of foreign exchange. The government of such a country usually required everyone who received foreign exchange to sell it (at the official rate) to the government. The government then rationed out this foreign exchange among would-be users on the basis of some nonprice criteria. For example, the government might decide to sell foreign exchange to importers of vital raw materials but not to importers of luxury goods or to would-be vacationers on the Riviera.

From these crude beginnings, exchange control grew in many countries into an elaborate, complex set of controls. One prominent aspect of a number of exchange control systems, particularly those currently in use in Latin America, is the application of *multiple exchange rates.* Under a multiple-rate system, different exchange rates are applied to different sorts of transactions. For example, the government may charge importers of food and raw materials a low price for their foreign exchange, but importers of luxury goods a high price for theirs. At the same time the government may pay a low price for the foreign exchange it buys from exporters of goods for which foreign demand is inelastic, but place a high value on foreign exchange it buys from exporters of goods for which foreign demand is highly elastic. A complex system like this enables a government to limit the demand for foreign exchange to the supply available at the peg rate, and also to influence the composition of domestic imports and to maximize the amount of foreign exchange yielded by domestic exports.

Although exchange control can be an effective way of controlling a persistent balance-of-payments deficit, it is an undesirable one, mainly because the artificial exchange rates and limitations on currency convertibility that result from such a system tend to distort the patterns of trade between countries and to prevent multilateral trade flows like those in Fig. 44.3. Thus exchange control prevents trading countries from getting the full benefits available from free multilateral trade. This is the main reason why the International Monetary Fund, from its inception, tried to get its members to abandon exchange control as fast as they could. As a result of the IMF's efforts and because most nations wanted to restore currency convertibility, the major trading nations did give up exchange controls after the war. Many smaller countries, however, still retain elaborate systems of exchange control.

Price Changes as a Means of Adjustment

Suppose that a deficit country eschews the use of direct controls, and tries instead to cure the cause of its deficit by undertaking economic policies that will shift the demand and supply curves for foreign exchange so that demand equals supply at the peg rate. Then two main courses of action are open to it: (1) It can try to lower the general level of domestic prices relative to foreign prices, or (2) it can lower domestic income.

Let us first deal with the first course of action: price changes. Whenever domestic prices fall relative to foreign prices, imports decline and exports rise. Example: Suppose that U.S. prices fall relative to foreign prices. Then Volkswagens become more expensive relative to Ramblers, and German steel more expensive relative to U.S. steel. As this happens, some U.S. car buyers will switch from VW's to Ramblers and some U.S. steel users will switch from German to domestic steel. As a result U.S. imports will decline. Simultaneously foreigners will find that the fall in U.S. prices means that U.S. manufactured goods, farm products, and other exports are now cheaper than they used to be, and so they'll buy more of them.

If U.S. consumers and firms respond to a decrease in U.S. prices by buying fewer imports, they will naturally spend less foreign exchange on imported goods than they used to. The way that the decrease in U.S. prices will affect foreign spending on U.S. goods is less clear-cut. The fact that U.S. prices are now lower will tend to decrease foreign spending on U.S. exports, but the fact that the quantity of U.S. exports foreigners buy is now larger will tend to increase foreign spending on these goods. Which effect wins out in the long run will of course depend on our old friend, elasticity of demand.

How elastic is foreign demand for a country's exports? As we noted in our discussion of tariffs (see Fig. 45.1), a country's demand curve for an imported good equals the downward-sloping domestic demand curve for this good *minus* the upward-sloping domestic supply curve. Therefore a country's demand curve for imports of any good will be more elastic than its overall demand curve for it. Also the fact that a country's exports have to compete in foreign markets with exports from other countries increases the elasticity of foreign demand for them. For these reasons it seems likely that demand for most of a country's exports will be elastic. If it is, then a fall in domestic prices will lead foreigners to increase their spending on domestic goods.

From these observations we see that, if a country can decrease domestic prices relative to foreign prices, the amount of foreign exchange demanded by domestic importers will decrease, while the supply of foreign exchange

earned by domestic exporters will probably increase. So price drops offer a
deficit country one way to achieve balance-of-payments equilibrium, and
price hikes offer a *surplus* country a way to restore balance to its balance of
payments.

Price changes under the gold standard. Economists used to think that under
the gold standard, "equilibrating" price changes of the sort described above
would automatically take place whenever a country had a disequilibrium in
its balance of payments. The reason they expected this to happen lies in the
way the gold standard worked. Basically the gold standard was a set of rules:
(1) Each country was supposed to peg its currency to gold (i.e., to establish an
official exchange rate between its currency and gold). (2) Each country was
supposed to hold gold reserves, and to buy and sell gold as necessary to maintain its currency at the official rate. (3) Each country was supposed to link
the size of its domestic money supply to the size of its gold reserves, so that
an increase in gold reserves would increase its money supply and a decrease
in its gold reserves would decrease its money supply.*

The classical economists who developed the theory of the gold standard
did not think that the economy would ever deviate for any length of time
from full employment. Therefore they took the economy's output as fixed
in the short run. They also assumed that money turns over at a constant
rate. As we pointed out in Chapter 40, if national output and the velocity
of money are constant, then a great increase in the money supply will raise
the price level.† *If* prices are flexible downward, a great decrease in the
money supply will lower the price level. By putting these observations together with what we know about the rules of the gold standard, it's easy to
see how equilibrating price changes were supposed to occur automatically
under the gold standard. According to theory, whenever a gold-standard
country had a balance-of-payments deficit, it would sell gold. The resulting
loss in gold would contract the domestic money supply, and this would
lower domestic prices. As domestic prices fell, equilibrium would be restored
to the country's balance of payments, the outflow of gold would stop, and
domestic prices would stabilize at a new lower level. Whenever a gold-standard country had a balance-of-payments surplus, pretty much the reverse
was supposed to happen. The country would gain gold, its domestic money
supply would expand, its price level would rise, and this would restore
equilibrium to its balance of payments. All this sounds neat and simple. But

---

* This third step could be accomplished in many ways (recall our discussion in Part 5).
One simple way would be to require the central bank to create note and deposit liabilities
equal to a constant multiple of the nation's gold reserve. Under such a system gold reserves would function, as they have in the U.S., as a form of "outside money" for the central
bank.

† Recall that $MV = PT$ (page 625).

it's theory. In practice the gold standard never worked so smoothly. One reason was that national output in gold-standard countries didn't always remain at a constant, full-employment level. Another was that gold-standard countries often disregarded the rules of the game and neutralized the impact which gold flows were supposed to have on the domestic money supply.

Whatever policy priorities there may have been in the heyday of the gold standard, certainly today no nation would try to achieve balance-of-payments equilibrium by inducing *large-scale* changes in its domestic price level. One reason is that price stability is a major target of macroeconomic policy these days. Another is that, once price *in*flation starts, it's hard to stop, whereas price *de*flation, given the inflexibility of prices downward, is almost impossible to start! This doesn't mean, of course, that a nation with a balance-of-payments deficit should ignore what happens to relative prices. On the contrary, a country which has a persistent deficit and which operates— as the U.S. does—in a world in which prices are gradually rising can help its balance-of-payments position over the long run simply by holding its own rate of inflation below the foreign rate of inflation. Conversely, it can harm its balance-of-payments position if it allows its own rate of inflation to get ahead of the foreign rate of inflation.

Income Changes as a Means of Adjustment

In any country some of the inputs and some of the capital goods that domestic producers use are bound to be imported. For example: Japanese textile mills use U.S. cotton, U.S. factories use German machine tools, and Italian oil refineries use Mid-East oil. Also some of the final goods that domestic consumers buy are likely to be imports. U.S. consumers drive French cars, British consumers eat New Zealand lamb, and Norwegians do their wash in automatic washers imported from Italy. Given these facts about imports, it's obvious that whenever national income rises, imports will rise; and whenever national income falls, imports will fall. Figure 47.1 shows this sort of a relationship between U.S. imports and income.

This brings us to the second means by which a country can achieve balance-of-payments equilibrium: income changes. Since decreased income = decreased imports, a country which has a *deficit* in its balance of payments can reduce it by lowering domestic income. Conversely, a country with a *surplus* in its balance of payments can eliminate it by raising income.

Sounds simple enough, doesn't it? But there's a catch. In some situations balance-of-payments equilibrium conflicts with other goals of macroeconomic policy. For example, suppose that a country with a depressed domestic economy has a balance-of-payments deficit. If it lowers income to improve its balance of payments, it will move further away from the goal of

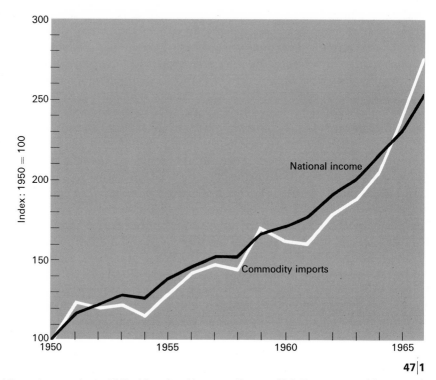

47|1

In the United States imports rise and fall with national income. (Source: U.S. Department of Commerce)

full employment. Or consider the case of a booming economy which is running a balance-of-payments surplus. If it attempts to "raise" income in order to increase imports, it is likely to create an inflationary gap, and the resulting upward spiral of prices will conflict with the goal of price stability. Unfortunately, the possibility that a country may have to choose between balance-of-payments equilibrium and some other important goal such as full employment is far from academic. As we shall see, this sort of painful choice faced both the U.S. and the U.K. during the 1960's.

DEVALUATION*

We have talked about the two principal means (price and income changes) that a country can use to bring its balance of payments into equilibrium while it maintains its currency at par. Sometimes, however, a country whose

---

* To say that a currency is *devalued* (as most people and the press use the term) means that its par value measured in terms of either gold *or* some other currency is lowered. Thus when the British government in November 1967 lowered the official exchange rate between pounds and dollars from $2.80/£ to $2.40/£, the headlines read "Pound Devalued."

balance of payments is in disequilibrium may find that neither of these policies offers it a way to regain equilibrium that is both feasible and acceptable. As we have said, a deficit country may find that it can't use price changes because domestic prices cannot be budged downward, and it may be unwilling to use income changes because lower incomes would result in an intolerable level of unemployment. Faced with such a predicament, there is little that a country committed to free markets (i.e., one that won't use exchange control) can do but devalue its currency.

Some people say that this sums up the spot the U.S. finds itself in today. Certainly it sums up the predicament the British found themselves in in November of 1967. For several years prior to this time, the British had been trying to reverse a persistent balance-of-payments deficit. They couldn't get domestic prices to *fall* (wages were sticky downward; prices of most goods were oligopolistically, not competitively determined; and many vital raw materials and foodstuffs were imported). But they did impose a price–wage freeze to keep domestic prices from *rising*. Simultaneously they applied a restrictive monetary–fiscal policy which, by taking the boom out of the British economy, was supposed to restore its balance of payments to equilibrium. This policy raised unemployment to high levels, and as it dragged out it made the man in the street and many members of the House of Commons, including Wilson's Labourites, increasingly discontent. Nevertheless the deficit persisted, and by the end of November 1967 it was obvious to the British government that it would have to choose between even more deflation and unemployment, or devaluation. It chose devaluation.

The Impact of Devaluation on the Current Account

When a deficit country devalues, it does so to restore equilibrium to its balance of payments. Whether or not devaluation really does the trick depends on the circumstances. Let us look at how devaluation affects the chief components of the devaluing country's balance of payments. Devaluation raises the price of imports* to domestic consumers, so they will buy fewer imports. The fewer imports they buy, the less foreign exchange they will spend on imports. The degree to which devaluation cuts consumers' outlays of foreign exchange on imports depends on the elasticity of their demand for imports. If the country imports a lot of vital raw materials and food it can't do without (as Britain does), its demand for imports will be inelastic and devaluation will cut its foreign-exchange outlays on imports only a little. But if the country's demand for imports is highly elastic (perhaps because close substitutes for most imports can be produced domestically), then devaluation will mean a large cut in the country's outlays of foreign exchange for imports.

---

* The price we are talking about here is price in terms of the domestic currency.

Devaluation's effect on the amount of foreign exchange that the devaluing country earns from exports is more complex. If, after devaluation, domestic exporters just keep their prices at the same level they were before, then (1) their prices (measured in foreign currency) will fall,* and (2) the quantity of goods they sell abroad will increase. The first of these tendencies will reduce the devaluing country's foreign exchange earnings; the second will raise it. Which tendency wins out depends on the elasticity of foreign demand for the devaluing country's exports. If foreign demand is elastic, the devaluing country's export earnings will rise. Since foreign demand for a country's exports (as we said above) usually *is* elastic, devaluation usually boosts the devaluing country's export earnings.

This conclusion, however, depends on one key assumption: that devaluation will lower export prices measured in foreign currency. In other words, that domestic exporters won't respond to devaluation by raising the prices they quote in domestic currency. Sometimes this assumption holds, but not always. (When Britain devalued, the nationalized steel industry, Ford's big British subsidiary, giant Imperial Chemical, and firms in a number of other industries raised the pound prices of the goods they exported by the full amount of the devaluation.) Producers in export industries are likely to raise prices after devaluation for several reasons: (1) The devaluing country may (like Great Britain) import many industrial raw materials. If it does, then devaluation causes an upward shift in the cost curves of domestic producers (including those in export industries), and they respond by raising output prices. (2) Whenever a country devalues, this change will be equivalent, from the point of view of the country's export industries, to an upward shift in demand. As we saw in our study of microeconomics, if demand for an industry's output shifts upward, producers in this industry are likely to respond by raising prices.

Thus we see that the success of devaluation may be threatened by several factors: inelastic foreign demand, inelastic domestic demand, and price rises in export industries. Nevertheless, there is a good chance that devaluation will succeed. Suppose that it does. Can the devaluing country then count its troubles as being over? Unfortunately no, because the gains that devaluation brings may prove short-lived. Whenever a country devalues, the prices domestic consumers have to pay for imports naturally rises. Also, for reasons we have cited, domestic producers often raise prices on their goods, so de-

---

* Example: Suppose that a British exporter of Scotch charges American importers 1 pound per bottle, and suppose that the par value of the pound is $2.80. That means that the dollar price of a bottle of Scotch is $2.80. Now the pound is devalued from $2.80 to $2.40. Then, so long as the British exporter doesn't raise the pound price he charges for Scotch, the dollar price of Scotch will fall from $2.80 to $2.40. But suppose that the British exporter responds to devaluation by raising his price from 1 pound to 1 pound plus 20 pence. Then devaluation will lower the dollar price of Scotch only to $2.60.

valuation brings about higher domestic prices. This rise cuts the real incomes of workers; the workers respond by demanding big wage hikes. If they get them, producers' costs go up, and they have to raise their prices again. Thus there's always the danger that devaluation will set off an inflationary wage-price spiral. If it does, the effect that devaluation had of making domestic goods cheaper relative to foreign goods is wiped out, and any current-account benefits that the devaluing country has reaped from devaluation will vanish.

The Impact of Devaluation on the Capital Account

Devaluation, besides affecting a country's current account (i.e., its exports and imports) also affects its capital account. When a currency is devalued, speculators often take a bearish* point of view. They think that devaluation won't work or that it wasn't big enough. So they believe it will be repeated again soon, and they try to get their money out of the country which has just devalued into some safer haven where they believe that renewed devaluation isn't a threat.

A devaluing country may combat speculative capital outflows by several methods: *It can tighten credit and raise the central bank's discount rate to a high level.* (When Britain devalued, the Bank of England raised its lending rate to a whopping 8%.) Such a policy increases the attractiveness of the domestic money market as a place to put funds by raising the interest rates prevailing there relative to those prevailing in other national money markets. Also, since the classic response of a deficit country determined to maintain its exchange rate is to up the discount rate, such a hike, by showing the government's determination to act, may improve expectations.

A sharp hike in short-term rates, by discouraging short-term capital outflows of domestic funds and encouraging short-term inflows of foreign funds, can dramatically improve a country's balance of payments. Higher interest rates can't, however, be looked on as a third means to long-run adjustment (that is, one in addition to price and income changes). If a hike in domestic interest rates induces a lot of *hot* (i.e., interest-sensitive) money to flow into a country during one period, it can't be expected to repeat this performance in following periods. So the capital-account benefits of a hike in interest rates are likely to be of a one-shot nature. Of course, an interest-rate hike may lead to a long-run improvement in a country's current-account

---

* There's an old proverb about "selling the bearskin before you catch the bear" which is probably the background of the stock-market word *bear:* a person who sells securities or commodities in expectation of a price decline. A *bull,* on the other hand, buys and speculates in anticipation of a price increase. His actions force stock prices up. (Think of a bull tossing something upward on his horns.)

balance. But if it does, it will be by lowering domestic income, so what we are talking about then is not interest-rate changes, but income changes, as a means to long-run adjustment.

Although a hike in short-term interest rates may succeed in preventing a post-devaluation outflow of speculative capital, there's always the danger that it may not. So another measure that a devaluing country might take to strengthen its position is: *It can obtain massive loans of foreign exchange and gold* (or standby credits it can draw on) from the International Monetary Fund or from foreign central banks. (When Britain devalued in 1967, it got $3 billion in fresh credits from the IMF and from foreign central banks to help it support the pound.) Such loans provide the country with sufficient foreign exchange reserves so that it can meet speculative demand for foreign exchange without letting the domestic currency fall below its new par value. The very existence of such loans, if they are big enough (and here "big" is likely to be measured in billions of dollars if we are talking about a key currency), impresses speculators with the size of the resources committed to defending the new pegged rate, and this may convince them that renewed devaluation is not an immediate threat, and thus discourage them from moving funds out of the country.

THE U.S. BALANCE OF PAYMENTS

Figure 47.2 pictures the evolution, from 1946 to the present, of the U.S. balance of payments.* It shows that the U.S. balance of payments has been consistently in deficit ever since the early 1950's. Initially this deficit was regarded as favorable because it gave European countries a much-needed opportunity to build up their foreign exchange reserves by acquiring gold and short-term dollar claims. In 1959, however, the U.S. current account turned from surplus to deficit (see Fig. 47.3), and U.S. gold losses accelerated. With this turn in events, people began to be seriously concerned about the U.S. deficit.

As Fig. 47.3 shows, the U.S. deficit results from the fact that the U.S. incurs too large a deficit in its capital account, given the size of the surplus in its current account. Another way of saying this is that the U.S. has too small a surplus in its current account to finance the large deficit in its capital account. So government efforts to regain balance-of-payments equilibrium have been directed toward two goals: increasing the current-account surplus and decreasing the capital-account deficit.

---

* The balance in Fig. 47.2 is measured on a *liquidity* basis. It includes changes in U.S. liquid liabilities to foreign private investors, and so it differs somewhat from the balance measured on an *official reserve transactions* basis that we talked about earlier.

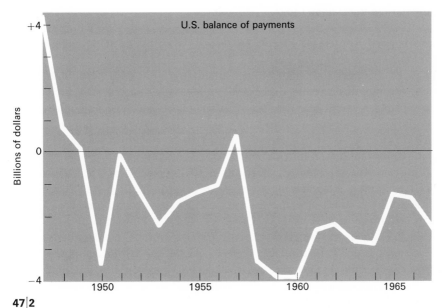

47|2

In recent years the U.S. balance of payments has been persistently in deficit.
(Source: U.S. Department of Commerce)

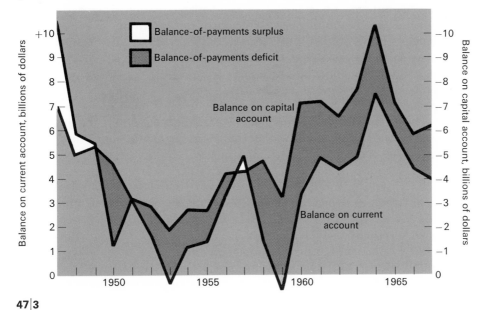

47|3

In most recent years the capital-account deficit has exceeded the current-account surplus.
(Source: U.S. Department of Commerce)

Improving the Balance on Current Accounts

When it tried to increase its current-account surplus, the U.S. government found itself in an awkward position. It couldn't force domestic prices down; thus price changes as a means of adjustment were out of the question. Domestic income was already depressed, so lowering income still further to reduce imports would have produced unacceptable levels of unemployment. Therefore the government didn't try to use price or income changes to improve its current-account balance. Instead it developed a potpourri of *ad hoc* measures and hoped for the best.

One way the government has sought to improve the U.S. balance on current account was by making an effort to keep domestic prices from rising as fast as foreign ones. During the early 1960's this policy worked: Foreign prices rose more rapidly than U.S. prices. As a result the competitive position of U.S. goods in foreign markets improved, while the competitive position of foreign goods in the U.S. market became less favorable. Since 1965, however, government effectiveness in checking inflation has lessened; U.S. prices have spurted upward over 3% a year, and some of the ground gained has undoubtedly been lost.

A second way the U.S. has sought to increase the surplus on its current account has been by requiring foreign recipients of U.S. government grants and loans, military and economic, to spend a large portion of the dollars they get on U.S. goods and services. This practice is known as *tying*. Generally economists frown on tied loans, because the proceeds of a tied loan can't be used to finance multilateral trade flows. Hence tying loans distorts trade patterns away from lines of comparative advantage. Nevertheless tying loans is probably preferable to the alternatives that it is designed to prevent: a stopping of all U.S. foreign aid, or perhaps devaluation of the dollar.

The list of individual items that make up the U.S. current account shows that the two items on which the U.S. rings up a whopping surplus are merchandise trade (close to $4 billion in 1966), and investment income (another $4 billion). Some current-account entries, however, are deficit entries. As of this writing, military expenditures cost the U.S. almost $3 billion a year in foreign exchange, and tourist expenditures add another billion plus to this figure.

To keep down the foreign exchange component of U.S. military spending, the government is constantly prodding our allies to accept a larger share of total defense costs, and to use the dollars they earn from U.S. military spending in their countries to buy jet fighters and other defense hardware from the U.S. Also the U.S. government requires the military to buy goods at home so long as the U.S. price isn't more than 50% above the foreign one.

To stem losses from tourist expenditures, the U.S. government has cut the amount of goods that tourists can bring home duty-free from $500 to

$100. Also it has encouraged foreigners to tour the U.S., and it has suggested to U.S. tourists that they "see America first." Nevertheless U.S. tourists continue to spend more abroad than foreign tourists spend in the U.S., so in 1968 the administration asked Congress to impose a tax on foreign travel.

Measures to Improve the Capital Account

During the early 1960's, the first step the U.S. government took to reduce its deficit on capital account was to raise *short-term* interest rates in the U.S. This step, which increased the attractiveness of the U.S. money market relative to foreign money markets, was designed primarily to discourage short-term outflows of domestic capital. However, it also encouraged foreign central banks who received dollars as a result of the U.S. balance-of-payments deficit to invest these dollars in the U.S. money market instead of cashing them in for gold.

Since the U.S. during the early 1960's was suffering not only from a balance-of-payments deficit but also from unemployment, the government (while it was increasing short-term interest rates) tried to hold down *long-term* interest rates. And it succeeded, at least until the end of 1965, when inflation took the place of unemployment as the compelling problem of the day. Although low long-term interest rates had the desirable effect of encouraging domestic investment, they had the undesirable effect of encouraging foreigners to borrow huge quantities of funds in the U.S. capital market. To counter the resulting capital outflow, the U.S. in 1963 imposed an *interest-equalization tax* (IET) on foreign debt securities sold in the U.S. To discourage U.S. citizens from investing dollars in foreign equities, the interest-equalization tax was applied not only to foreign bonds but also foreign stocks. Finally, to curb capital outflows through direct investment and through bank lending abroad, the Department of Commerce in 1965 set up a program of voluntary restraints on foreign investment by U.S. corporations and banks.

These measures helped to narrow the U.S. deficit in its capital account, but not enough. So at the beginning of 1968 the government tightened the voluntary curbs it had imposed on U.S. bank lending abroad and imposed drastic, mandatory curbs on corporate investment. These forbid U.S. firms to invest in some areas and permit them to make only limited investments in others. Also they require U.S. firms to repatriate (i.e., bring home) a substantial portion of their foreign earnings.

Dollar Devaluation

The various measures to end the U.S. deficit may succeed. But suppose they don't. Should the U.S. then respond by devaluing the dollar, that is, by having the Treasury raise the price it offers to pay for gold from the current $35 an ounce to, say, $50 or even $70 an ounce?

Earlier we pointed out that devaluation will improve the devaluing country's balance on current account provided that (a) foreign demand for domestic exports is elastic, (b) domestic demand for foreign imports is elastic, and (c) devaluation doesn't result in domestic inflation. Presumably the first two of these conditions would be met in the case of a U.S. devaluation. So far as (c) is concerned, we can note that imports today equal roughly 4% of total U.S. output, so devaluation would be much less likely to touch off a big rise in domestic prices in the U.S. than it would in a country like Britain, in which imports loom large relative to domestic output. Thus on balance devaluation would probably substantially raise the U.S. surplus on its current account.

However, the fact that the dollar is a key currency presents some good arguments against devaluation. As we have said, many foreign countries hold a large part of their total foreign exchange reserves in the form of dollar balances and short-term dollar securities. If the U.S. devalued the dollar, these countries would suffer capital losses, since the value of their dollar claims—measured either in gold or in nondollar currencies—would be smaller after devaluation than before.

Such capital losses, besides being unfairly distributed among different countries, might have an added disadvantage: They might discourage foreign countries from holding their reserves in dollars. If this happened, the resulting rush to cash in dollars for gold would deplete U.S. reserves, would do nothing to increase the reserves held by foreign countries, and would thus contract by a sizable amount the total foreign exchange reserves held by all countries. This contraction would occur, moreover, at the very time when the quantity of reserves countries need to hold is going up. Thus dollar devaluation, by weakening confidence in the dollar, might pose a serious problem for world liquidity.

There is also another problem with dollar devaluation. Because the U.S. is a big export customer for many countries and because U.S. exports compete with those of many other countries, if the U.S. were to devalue the dollar, a lot of other countries would undoubtedly respond by devaluing their own currencies. (When Britain devalued the pound, Spain, Denmark, Israel, Hong Kong, Bermuda, and Ireland all followed suit; and observers were surprised that more countries, including the Union of South Africa, did not also.) If devaluation of the dollar triggered devaluation of many other currencies, then devaluation would fail to improve the U.S. balance of payments. It would simply raise the price of gold in terms of most currencies, and leave the U.S. facing the same old deficit.

RESERVE ADEQUACY

In the world today income is rising, and trade is increasing even faster. As trade increases, so does the size of the balance-of-payments deficits that individual countries might run. Thus increased trade means that individual countries need to hold larger reserves. One country can always increase its reserves by running a balance-of-payments surplus. *But how can all countries increase their reserves simultaneously?*

1) *The world's stock of monetary gold could be increased.* This approach, however, has a catch: No such increases are likely to occur. At the current price of gold ($35 an ounce), gold-mining is not very profitable. Every year a few more mines close down. So current world output of gold just about meets current industrial consumption of gold, and net additions to the world's stock of monetary gold are small.

2) *The trading countries could increase their holdings of key currencies.* But there's a catch here too: Countries whose currencies didn't function as a key currency would be able to increase their holdings of the key currency only if the key-currency country incurred a persistent deficit in its balance of payments.* This deficit, however, would eventually weaken the confidence that other countries had in the key currency. They would begin to fear that the key currency might be devalued. If confidence in the key currency were to ebb low enough, a crisis would occur: Countries would try to cash in their holdings of the key currency for gold, the key-currency country wouldn't be able to meet all these demands for gold, and the system would break down. Such a crisis need not, of course, occur. But the threat that it might sets limits on the extent to which a reserve-currency system can be used to produce increased reserves and still remain strong.

3) *The price of gold could be raised.* That is, all currencies could be devalued *vis-à-vis* gold. Such a change would increase the value—measured in dollars, pounds, marks, or any other currency—of the world's existing monetary gold stock. And by so doing it would create an instant increase in world reserves. Increasing the price of gold would also encourage gold mines to increase their output, and as a result the physical size of the world's monetary gold stock might begin to grow again. However, raising the price of gold, like the above other ways to increase reserves, has its drawbacks: (a) The immediate capital gains it would create would be rather unfairly distributed. The U.S., France, and other countries that hold sizable stocks of gold would have big capital gains, while countries that hold their reserves largely in the form of balances of key currencies would have no such gains. (b) Since the world's major gold producers are Russia and the Union of South Africa, raising the price of gold would bestow handsome benefits on two countries which at the moment are hardly in favor in the West. (c) Many people argue that using more of society's scarce resource to dig gold out of one hole—a South African mine—and then bury it in another—a central bank vault—

---

* Here by "balance" we mean: balance on current account + net private capital flows.

would be an unconscionably wasteful way of creating additional reserves, at least in an age in which central bankers know perfectly well how to go about producing "paper gold."

4) *Paper gold could be created.* The idea here would be to transform the International Monetary Fund into a full-fledged *international central bank.* Individual countries would hold their reserves in the form of deposits at this bank; and these deposits would function as international money (i.e., national central banks would use this money in making payments to and receiving payments from each other). This proposed international central bank would create deposit liabilities by accepting deposits of gold *and* by discounting or buying up debt securities, perhaps securities issued by national governments or perhaps securities issued by some international lending institution such as the World Bank, which makes loans to underdeveloped countries. The key part of this setup would be that the international central bank would be able, by *monetizing* debt securities, to create international reserves that would fulfill the function of gold but that would not be backed by gold (or at least backed only fractionally). Money of this sort has been dubbed by many commentators as paper gold.

In 1944 when the IMF was set up, Keynes vigorously advocated the creation of an international central bank capable of creating new international reserves. Today such an institution is again being advocated by Yale's Robert Triffin and other experts who fear that a world liquidity crisis is in the offing. But for the moment, an international central bank seems too radical an innovation to be seriously considered by the major trading nations. These nations have, however, agreed that a world liquidity problem may exist, and to deal with it they have proposed a large-scale expansion in the lending powers of the IMF. Under the proposed scheme, each IMF member would be granted a specified quantity of *Special Drawing Rights* (SDR's). By using its SDR's, a country would be able to borrow from the IMF on terms so liberal (only 30% of the loan would have to be repaid), that the new rights would be more like a new form of money than a new credit facility. Since the quantity of SDR's authorized could be increased in step with the world's rising need for liquidity, SDR's offer one way to stave off world illiquidity.

PROBLEMS

1   a) Suppose that a country exports $200,000 worth of goods and imports $100,000 worth. Suppose also that domestic capital outflows equal $110,000 and that the domestic monetary authority sells $10,000 worth of gold. Using the concept of balance incorporated in Equation (2) on page 725, calculate what the "balance" entry in the country's balance-of-payments account would be.

b) Explain why this balance figure will necessarily be equal in amount but opposite in sign to the entry for "domestic official transactions."

c) Suppose that a country imports $200,000 worth of goods and exports $100,000 worth. Suppose also that the domestic monetary authority buys $10,000 worth of gold. Repeat the questions asked in parts (a) and (b).

2 "If a key-currency country like the U.S. has a deficit (here deficit is measured as the current account balance plus net private capital flows), this must be offset in one of two ways: (1) the key currency country can sell gold, or (2) other countries can acquire increased balances of the key currency." Explain. [*Hint:* Such a deficit means that supply exceeds demand for the key currency at the peg rate. How will each of the alternatives mentioned work to eliminate the excess supply of the key currency?]

3 How does a balance-of-payments deficit or surplus affect a country's ability to peg its currency in future periods? Does your answer give you a clue as to why the continuing U.S. balance-of-payments deficit is being viewed with increasing alarm?

4 Would you want to use the measure of balance incorporated in Equation (2) on page 725 to measure the balance-of-payments position of a country that practiced exchange control? If not, what measure of balance would you think appropriate for such a country?

5 a) "One country's surplus is inevitably another's deficit. Therefore surplus countries, if they value exchange-rate stability, ought to take steps to correct a continuing balance-of-payments surplus." Discuss.

b) Would your answer depend on the circumstances? For example, suppose that *A* was running a surplus because *B* was experiencing a runaway inflation. What should *A* do?

c) A related problem: Suppose that *B* were running a big deficit because *A* was experiencing a prolonged recession. What should *B* do?

6 If a country practices exchange control there is nothing to stop it from setting up a system of multiple exchange rates under which different export transactions take place at different rates. Could such a system be used to improve a country's terms of trade? [*Hint:* Consider this practical case: Demand for coffee is inelastic. The Brazilians, who are big coffee exporters, charge a high price to people who want to buy cruzeiros (that's Brazilian currency) to pay for coffee exports but a much lower price to people who want to buy cruzeiros to pay for exports of other Brazilian goods. What are the Brazilians trying to do?]

7 During the period 1958–1965 the Brazilian money supply rose from over 353 billion cruzeiros to over 9 trillion cruzeiros. Simultaneously the "free rate" on the cruzeiro (i.e., the one at which non-coffee transactions occur) went from 138.5 to 2,220.0 cruzeiros to the dollar. How do you think that these different events were related?

8 At the beginning of 1968 the administration asked Congress to abolish the requirement that the Fed hold gold reserves equal to 25% of its total note

liabilities.* In defending this request, Treasury Secretary Fowler said:

". . . the world knows as a fact that the strength of the dollar depends upon the strength of the U.S. economy rather than upon a legal 25% reserve requirement against Federal Reserve notes, and it is clearly appropriate for this fact now to be recognized in legislation."†

What would you take this statement to mean? Will a strong domestic economy (i.e., one in which employment and output are high) necessarily have a strong currency (i.e., one that tends to appreciate rather than depreciate)? Would it be possible for a country with a weak economy to have a strong currency?

9 During the fall of 1967 the Johnson administration was making a valiant but futile attempt to get Congress to pass a surtax on personal and corporate income taxes. The House Ways and Means Committee, which has to pass on all tax legislation, seemed on the verge of giving the administration a flat no. Then the British devalued the pound and interest in the surtax revived. One Democratic member of the House Ways and Means Committee attempted to explain the change in attitude by saying, "The name of the game now is defending the dollar." What do you think he had in mind? How might raising domestic taxes defend the exchange value of the dollar?

10 In an article on the U.S. balance of payments, the *Wall Street Journal* (Feb. 15, 1968) noted that experts thought that the U.S. balance of payments might well be slated for improvement because of the following favorable developments:

In some key industrial countries, business is picking up steam, and prices are beginning to rise more rapidly than in the U.S.

In the U.S., monetary authorities have recently adopted somewhat more restrictive policies, while many of their foreign counterparts appear to be pursuing policies more likely to bring on price increases.

After a long, steep climb, unit labor costs in the U.S. show signs of leveling off, in contrast to the recent trend in many nations.

Explain how each of these trends might work to improve the U.S. balance of payments.

11 If U.S. exports were to rise by a million dollars, U.S. domestic income would rise by more, perhaps by 2 or even 3 million dollars. Explain why. [*Hint:* Recall our discussion of the multiplier at the end of Chapter 35.]

12 As a solution to the problem of reserve adequacy, what would you think of having all countries switch over to freely fluctuating exchange rates?

13 How well would Triffin's plan for an international central bank or any similar plan work if countries suffered persistent deficits rather than occasional, short-lived ones?

14 "A simple way to solve the problem of reserve adequacy would be for all countries to run balance-of-payments surpluses." Discuss.

---

* We discussed the gold cover requirement imposed on the Fed on pages 460–461.

† Hearings before the House Banking Committee, Jan. 23, 1968.

THE GOLD CRISIS AND THE
FREE MARKET FOR GOLD

In late 1967 and early 1968, there was a lot of talk about gold: Speculators snapped up gold, newspaper headlines talked of a gold crisis, central bankers huddled behind closed doors to discuss gold, and many people in and out of government were convinced that devaluation of the dollar *vis-à-vis* gold was about to be forced on the U.S. What was this gold crisis all about?

As we said in Chapter 46, all the major countries of the West maintain their currencies at par by buying and selling gold and foreign exchange. Thus gold is actively traded among central banks, and throughout the postwar period the price at which it has been traded has been the price at which the dollar is pegged to gold: $35 an ounce. Central bankers, of course, are not the only demanders and suppliers of gold. Dentists, jewelers, and industry demand it too. And private mines throughout the world supply it. In the U.S., private citizens were forbidden to hold gold in 1934, and from that date on the need of private buyers and sellers for a place to trade gold for dollars was met by the U.S. Treasury, which bought gold from domestic producers and sold gold to industrial users at the price of $35 an ounce. Elsewhere in the world the need of private buyers and sellers for a place to trade gold for paper currencies was met by the creation of a free market for gold. For historical reasons and because South Africa sells most of its gold output there, the London market is far and away the largest center of the free market. Producers and industrial users of gold are not the only participants in the London market. Many private speculators from countries in which private hoards of gold are legal, and some from countries in which they aren't, also buy and sell gold in this market.

For a number of years central banks pretty much stayed out of the private market. The result was a *two-tier system,* under which gold traded between central banks at the fixed price of $35 an ounce, and between private traders at a free rate which often exceeded $35 an ounce. This two-tier system was inherently weak in several ways. *First,* there was the danger that, if the free-market price for gold got much above $35 an ounce, small central banks would start up a profitable arbitrage action, buying gold from the U.S. at

$35 an ounce and selling it in the free market at a higher price. *Second,* there was the danger that, if the dollar price of gold in the free market were to rise far above $35 an ounce, confidence in the dollar would be punctured and foreign money men would rush to cash in their dollars for gold.

Despite these dangers, the two-tier market functioned tolerably well for some years. Then in 1960 speculators got the idea that the official price of gold might be raised. Demand for gold soared, and in a single October day the free-market price of gold shot up a spectacular $5 an ounce. The U.S. and the U.K. responded immediately by supplying enough gold to the free market to bring down the price there to the official level.   And in the following year eight nations—the U.S., West Germany, Belgium, the U.K., the Netherlands, Italy, France, and Switzerland—formed the *Gold Pool,* an organization that pegged the free price of gold at the official price by buying and selling gold as needed in the free market. Mostly, thereafter, the Gold Pool sold gold.

So long as the gold losses suffered by the Gold Pool remained at acceptable levels, this stopgap system functioned reasonably well. But in late 1967 and early 1968 this condition ceased to be met. Speculators became convinced that the U.S.—given its persistent balance-of-payments deficit, and given the Federal government's fantastic budget deficits—would have to devalue the dollar.   Also speculators continued to worry about the British pound: Would it be devalued again soon? So they began buying gold in the London market.   And to keep price there at the official price, the Gold Pool had to supply hundreds of tons—billions of dollars' worth—of gold to the free market. Finally in March 1968, the flow of gold from central bank reserves to speculators reached an intolerable level.   Something had to be done. So the U.K. closed the London gold market temporarily, the Fed upped the discount rate, and central bankers from all the Gold-Pool countries (except France which had quit the Pool) rushed to Washington to confer.

To end the crisis, these central bankers could have proposed a number of different measures. The three most talked about were the following: (1) Raise the price of gold *vis-à-vis* all currencies. (2) Devalue the dollar (i.e., raise just the dollar price of gold). (3) Return to a two-tier system, with both an official and a free-market price for gold. The last alternative was the simplest, and it was the one the central bankers took. They took it, however, with a twist. In the statement after their meetings, they declared that henceforth they would refrain not only from *selling* but also from *buying* gold in the free market. They thus removed not only the ceiling, but also the floor they had placed on the free-market price of gold. For the moment a return to the two-tier system has restored calm to the free market for gold. But in order for this system to work well for any length of time, confidence must be restored in the dollar and the pound. To achieve this end, the U.K. has applied strong new measures to close the gap in its balance of payments. But the U.S. has so far shown little enthusiasm for action as opposed to talk, so the future of the dollar remains as uncertain as ever.

CHAPTER 48

ECONOMIC DEVELOPMENT

There are a few rich countries in the world today, and a great many poor ones. Of course this situation is nothing new. It has existed ever since industrialization launched the countries of Western Europe, and later several other countries, onto the path to wealth. What is new, however, is that today people are no longer content to allow this inequity of wealth to persist. People everywhere—and here we're not talking about just economists—feel that the problem of raising income in the poor countries is one of the most challenging of our times.

THE INCOME GAP

To gain some idea of the income gap between the rich and the poor countries of the world, look at Fig. 48.1, which graphs data on income per capita in 23 countries. Comparative data of this sort are inevitably crude and subject to wide margins of error. However, even if we allow for this limitation, two things are obvious: (1) There is a tremendous gap between income per capita in the richest countries of North America, Western Europe, and Oceania and income per capita in the poorest countries of Asia, Africa, and Latin America. (2) Income per capita varies considerably among the different underdeveloped countries. Some, like India, Burma, and the Congo, have very low levels of income per capita. Others, such as Mexico and Greece, have reached an intermediate stage; their income per capita is high relative to that in the poorest countries, but still low relative to that of the richest countries.

Income Growth Versus an Exploding Population

In many poor countries, especially in prominent ones like India, raising the standard of living is a slow task; so slow that one might get the impression that these countries aren't growing at all. But, as column 1 of Table 48.1

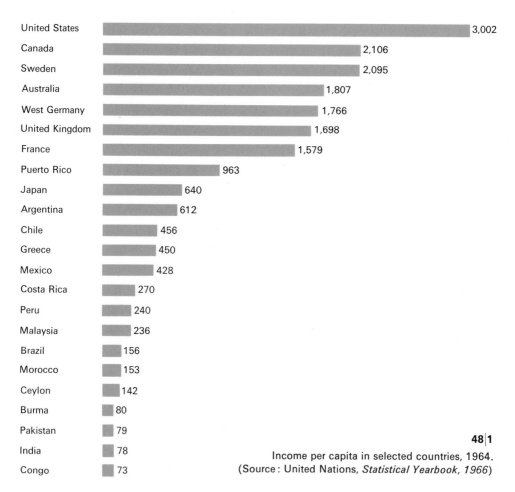

United States   3,002
Canada   2,106
Sweden   2,095
Australia   1,807
West Germany   1,766
United Kingdom   1,698
France   1,579
Puerto Rico   963
Japan   640
Argentina   612
Chile   456
Greece   450
Mexico   428
Costa Rica   270
Peru   240
Malaysia   236
Brazil   156
Morocco   153
Ceylon   142
Burma   80
Pakistan   79
India   78
Congo   73

48|1
Income per capita in selected countries, 1964.
(Source: United Nations, *Statistical Yearbook, 1966*)

shows, this isn't so. In many poor countries national income is growing at rates that compare favorably with those in the high-income countries. And in a few intermediate countries—Japan, Greece, and Puerto Rico—growth rates actually exceed those in the high-income countries.

However, the high rates of growth in total income of many poor countries don't mean that income per capita in these countries is also growing at equally favorable rates. Most poor countries are experiencing explosive rates of population growth. In recent decades DDT, antibiotics, and other health measures have dramatically cut death rates in the low-income areas of the world. But birth rates, despite pills and propaganda, remain as high as ever. The result (see column 3 of Table 48.1) is that in many poor countries population is rising more than 2% and sometimes more than 3% a year. By comparison, in the high-income countries population is growing at much slower rates, in some countries less than 1% a year.

TABLE 48|1

Income and Population Growth in Selected Countries
(Source: United Nations)

| Country | Average annual rate of increase | | Population, 1958–1965 |
| | Gross national product | | |
	Total, 1960–1965	Per capita, 1960–1965	
United States	4.7	3.1	1.5
Sweden	5.0	4.3	0.6
Australia	4.7	2.6	2.1
West Germany	4.9	3.6	1.3
United Kingdom	3.3	2.5	0.7
Puerto Rico	8.4	6.1	2.0
Japan	9.6	8.5	1.0
Chile	4.3	2.0	2.3
Greece	8.5	7.9	0.6
Mexico	6.0	2.5	3.4
Malaysia	6.1	2.8	3.1
Brazil	4.4	1.2	3.0
Morocco	3.4	0.7	2.8
Ceylon	2.2	−0.4	2.6
Burma	4.0	1.9	2.0
Pakistan	5.3	3.2	2.1
India	4.4	1.9	2.3

Because of the population explosion in the poor countries, their income per capita is rising much more slowly than it is in the high-income countries (see column 2 of Table 48.1). As a result the gap between income per capita in the poor and in the rich countries, far from narrowing, is in many instances becoming wider every year.

MEANS TO DEVELOPMENT

Today when economists talk about the poor countries of the world, they almost invariably refer to them as *underdeveloped* countries. By this they generally mean two things: (1) That income per capita in these countries is low relative to what it is in the rich *developed* countries, like the U.S. and the nations of Western Europe, and (2) that these countries have a latent and as yet unrealized potential for growth in income per capita.

How can the underdeveloped countries realize their latent potential for growth? In Chapter 41's discussion of growth, we said that a country can increase income and output by developing new resources, by increasing the quality of its existing resources, by adopting more advanced technology, or by increasing the efficiency with which it utilizes existing resources and technology. Now let us talk about the opportunities for increasing income and output that each of these four possibilities holds for the underdeveloped countries.

Population

Population is a key productive resource in any economy, developed or underdeveloped. But for an underdeveloped country that wants to increase income *per capita,* population growth is more often a liability than an asset. Thus when such a country sets out to increase its human resources, the accent of the measures it takes is more likely to be on improving *quality* than on increasing *quantity.*

In many underdeveloped countries a variety of factors combine to make the quality of the work force much lower than it is in the rich, developed countries. As a result there are usually many things an underdeveloped country can do to upgrade the quality and thus increase the productivity of its work force. To begin with, health measures—especially those aimed at conquering debilitating diseases such as malaria and dysentery—and food programs that counter malnutrition can do a lot to increase the physical stamina of the population and thus to raise its productivity. Education programs which accentuate the three R's or give people new technical skills can make an equally important contribution to raising the productivity of the domestic work force.

Still another way an underdeveloped country can increase the productivity of its work force is by eliminating (or at least lowering) social and institutional barriers that prevent human resources from being utilized efficiently. The typical underdeveloped country has many such barriers: Consideration of class and caste limit the social mobility of labor. Tradition and custom limit the kinds of work that women may do outside the home. Strong family ties, traditional social structures, and ignorance of job opportunities in distant areas all severely limit the geographic mobility of labor.

Adopting Improved Technology

In the underdeveloped countries production is often carried on using primitive technology. Farmers may work the land much as their ancestors centuries ago used to do, and methods of production in industry may be equally primitive. Whenever a country uses backward technology, naturally the productivity of the labor and other inputs it uses is lower than it need be. Thus a second way that the underdeveloped countries can increase output is by adopting improved technology. In this area the underdeveloped countries enjoy a real advantage. They don't have to go through the slow and painful process of technological change and learning that the industrial countries of the West did. They can leapfrog from primitive to modern methods of production simply by copying from the West production methods that it took the West centuries to develop.

Japan is a good example of a country which did just this. Toward the end of the nineteenth century, Japan—which had previously been almost totally isolated from the West and which was ignorant of the industrial methods that the West had developed—set out to industrialize using the Western pattern. She sent out students to learn Western techniques, and she assiduously applied at home the lessons they learned abroad. Simultaneously the government took steps to increase agricultural productivity and to provide the transportation and communication facilities needed by a developing economy. The result was that Japan, despite the handicaps of high population density and a dearth of natural resources, managed in a few decades to turn from a backward country into one firmly launched on the path to industrialization. Today, of course, Japan is one of the world's leading industrial nations.

The chance to import foreign technology offers a real advantage to the underdeveloped countries, but importing such technology also presents problems. The latest production techniques developed in the rich industrial nations, where capital is plentiful and labor is scarce, may have to be adapted before they can be profitably used by the underdeveloped countries, where capital is the scarce input and labor is plentiful. Also, machinery and methods of production imported from abroad may require a degree of sophistication and skill on the part of the work force that laborers in underdeveloped countries usually don't have.

Capital: Uses

A third way the underdeveloped countries can increase output is by adding to their capital stock. This way, of course, is related to the one we just talked about, because the switch to modern technology—be it in agriculture or in industry—often requires big additions to capital stock.

Investment in agriculture. Many underdeveloped countries are short of food. They have to import large quantities of food to feed their populations, and even so their people are inadequately fed and a bad crop year literally threatens famine. Observers often try to "explain" this situation by saying that the underdeveloped countries are overpopulated. Presumably what they mean is that their populations are so large relative to the available supply of land that these countries would never be capable of feeding themselves. The data in Table 48.2 lend some support to this thesis. They show

TABLE 48|2

Population Density in Selected Countries, 1964 (Source: United Nations)

Country	Population per square kilometer	Country	Population per square kilometer
Australia	1	Ceylon	171
Canada	2	India	159
Sweden	17	Japan	265
United States	21	United Kingdom	224
Burma	36	West Germany	229
Malaysia	61	Belgium	310
Pakistan	109		

that some food-short countries, such as India, are densely populated relative to high-income countries such as the U.S., Canada, and Sweden. But Table 48.2 also shows that in several West European countries, in which farm surpluses are more of a problem than food shortages, population density is much greater than in India, Ceylon, or other "overpopulated" countries.

How is it that European farmers do so much better a job of feeding Europe's population than Asian farmers do of feeding theirs? Obviously some land is good for farming, while other land (mountains, desert, and jungle swamp) is not. So we ought to correct the figures in Table 48.2 for differences in the quality of the land available in different countries. Perhaps if we did, we would find that the reason why farmers in India and other densely populated countries in Asia are incapable of feeding the people who live there is that the land available to them is smaller in area and poorer in quality than that available to their European counterparts. However, according to Theodore Schultz of the University of Chicago,* the countries of Western Europe have not only a greater density of population, but also a poorer endowment of farmland than India and the other Asian countries. European countries do a better job of feeding themselves not because the relationship of population to land is more favorable in Europe than in Asia, but because European countries have vastly increased the productivity of both land and labor in agriculture by investing large amounts of capital in the form of: modern farm machinery, new breeds of animals, new strains of crops, and complex plants to produce chemical insecticides and—perhaps most important of all—fertilizer. (Experts estimate that fertilizer alone could increase India's farm output by as much as 50%.)

Schultz's observation is an important one because it emphasizes a point that the underdeveloped countries, who equate high income with industrial-

---

* Theodore W. Schultz, *Transforming Traditional Agriculture,* New Haven: Yale University Press, 1964.

ization, all too often forget: In the typical underdeveloped country agriculture is one of the sectors of the economy in which the productivity of investment is highest. Therefore an underdeveloped country that is bent on increasing its total output ought to make investment in agriculture an important part of its overall development plan.

Natural resources. When people talk about the underdeveloped countries being overpopulated, they mean not only that population in these countries is large relative to the available supply of farm land, but also that population is large relative to the available supply of fuel and mineral resources, so large that these countries are too resource-poor to ever attain a high level of output per capita.

Obviously many underdeveloped countries don't fit this description: The Arabs have oil, the Congo has copper, et cetera. And many underdeveloped countries undoubtedly still contain much hidden mineral wealth. Thus in some underdeveloped countries, natural resources, far from holding back output growth because of their scarcity, may actually encourage it because of their plenitude. Prospecting for and developing mineral and fuel wealth, however, requires large amounts of capital. (Western oil companies, for example, drilled $80 million worth of *dry* holes before they finally managed, in the early 1960's, to add Australia to the world roster of oil-producing countries.) Thus if the underdeveloped countries are going to increase their total output by increasing their outputs of minerals and fuel, they will have to scrape up the capital to make large investments in this sector on their own, or they will have to permit foreign firms to do so.

Manufacturing. Of course not all underdeveloped countries have exploitable mineral and fuel wealth. This doesn't mean, however, that these countries can't raise output per capita to high levels. The experience of a number of countries—England and Japan to name two—indicates that a resource-poor country (just as a factory can) can always earn a living processing imported raw materials and exporting finished goods. But to earn a good living this way, a country has to process a great many raw materials, and to do this it has to have a sizable stock of manufacturing plant and equipment. Thus, to make a living as a processor, a resource-poor country has to invest heavily in manufacturing plant and equipment.

Resource-poor countries aren't the only ones that have to invest in manufacturing. Even in resource-rich countries, population is usually so large relative to the available supply of land and other resources that the average productivity of the work force would be much higher if at least some of the work force were siphoned away from agriculture and mining into manufacturing. Thus, in all the underdeveloped countries, investment in manufacturing has an important role to play in raising per capita output.

Investment in social overhead capital. In all the developed countries, the productivity of land and labor employed in mining, manufacturing, and agriculture has been vastly increased by the fact that the government has provided producers in these sectors with a wide range of collectively consumed capital goods. Underdeveloped countries, on the other hand, usually have few of such goods, and this hampers the growth of their output. Thus, in order to grow, most of the underdeveloped countries need to make continuing, large-scale investments in collective capital goods.

High on the list come roads and other transportation facilities, whose importance in the growth of underdeveloped areas is emphasized by a familiar story: Village X, perched in an inaccessible stretch of mountainous or jungle terrain, could produce more agricultural or handicraft outputs, but it doesn't because it can't get its outputs to market. Then the village, the government, or some foreign-aid program provides the needed road. The village increases output, sells the extra output to city folk, and then uses the proceeds to buy the outputs of other producers elsewhere in the country. In a poor country, what holds production back is often not just a lack of productive facilities, but also a lack of effective *demand*. Specialization and production beyond the subsistence level aren't worth while because extra output can't be gotten to a market where it could be traded for other goods.

Besides roads and transportation facilities, underdeveloped countries also need to invest in many other forms of social-overhead capital. Communications facilities are almost as important as transportation facilities. Also, building up industrial or mining complexes requires not only putting up productive plant and equipment proper, but also providing workers with housing, schools, public health facilities, water mains, sewers, electricity, and so forth.

There is another important form of investment that underdeveloped countries need a lot of: education. It's easy to underestimate the importance —and the cost—of education. Just offhand, education for the small farmer may not seem so important. But if he is going to figure out what crops he ought to grow and what fertilizer he ought to use to get the biggest returns possible, he needs to be able to read, write, and do simple calculations. So must the worker who does even unskilled tasks in industry. And industry, besides needing unskilled workers, needs carpenters, machine operators, typists, and other workers with special skills. To acquire such skills a worker needs special training.

Education and technical training of workers is an expensive kind of investment because it involves two sorts of costs simultaneously: (1) There is the obvious cost of school buildings, equipment, materials, and staff. (2) There is a less obvious opportunity cost: Every hour, week, or year a student spends in school is time that he could have spent doing productive work. So the true cost to society of his education is not just the resources that are devoted to teaching him but also the potential output sacrificed because he is withdrawn from the work force. In the typical underdeveloped country, a high proportion of the total population is of school age, so these two costs together can mount up to a sizable sum.

Capital: Amount Needed

As our list of the kinds of investment that underdeveloped countries need to make indicates, these countries are going to have to sustain very high rates of investment to catch up with the developed countries. Some economists have tried to go further and state just how much investing these countries need to do.

According to W. W. Rostow, economic historian and White House advisor, all the now-developed countries went through a critical 20- or 30-year period during which they saved and invested 10% or more of their total national output, and from which they emerged not only richer but also with an economic structure that lent itself to further growth. Taking their cue from Rostow, a number of economists have concluded that, in order to achieve a high, sustained rate of growth (development economists call this "taking off into sustained growth"), an underdeveloped country will have to make investments of similar magnitude over a similar period of time.

Economists have also come up with the 10% figure by taking a quite different tack. They observe that if an underdeveloped country whose population is growing at the rate of 2% a year wants to raise per capita income by 2% a year, it will have to increase total national output by 4% a year. How much investment a 4% growth rate requires depends on the country's capital–output ratio, that is, on the ratio between the amount of investment that the country makes and the increase in annual income that it obtains. If the country's capital–output ratio equals the quite reasonable figure of 2.5 (that is, if the country has to increase its capital stock by $250 in order to increase its annual output by $100), then the country will have to invest $2.5 \times 4\%$, or 10%, of its current national income in order to keep per capita income rising at the desired rate.

It's probably true that investing 10% of national income is the minimum effort that an underdeveloped country will have to make to "take off." However, it's important not to confuse a necessary condition with a sufficient one. High levels of investment are necessary for rapid growth, but they aren't sufficient. In some underdeveloped countries a given amount of capital will result in a larger increase in output than in others. Just how ready an underdeveloped country is to absorb capital depends on the extent to which it has met the preconditions for growth: (1) How educated the country's population is. (2) How far the country has come in breaking down social and institutional barriers that prevent a rational use of the nation's work force. (3) Whether or not the government is capable of setting up and carrying out a complex development plan. (4) How much investment has already been made in various forms of social-overhead capital.

Capital: Sources

It's easy to say that the underdeveloped countries ought to be investing 10, 15 or some other percent of national output, but in order for them to do so, this amount of resources has to be freed for investment. One obvious way in which this can be done is through domestic saving. Saving, though, comes hard to the typical underdeveloped country for two reasons: (a) Income in these countries is not far above the subsistence level. (b) People in these countries are aware of the standard of living of people in the developed countries and they want to emulate it. As a result the underdeveloped countries devote, on the average, a smaller percentage of their total income to savings and capital formation than the rich, developed countries do. Many developed countries devote 15 or even 20% of their total national output to savings and capital formation. On the other hand the underdeveloped countries, on the average, save perhaps only 5 to 7% of their total output.

According to our estimates of the capital requirements of the underdeveloped countries, this percentage of savings is inadequate to finance the kind of investments that the underdeveloped countries have to make in order to take off. One solution to this problem is inflows of foreign capital. Such inflows permit the underdeveloped countries to import more goods than they export; and this in turn makes it possible for them to devote to current consumption and investment more consumer and capital goods than they could produce on their own.

In days gone by the underdeveloped countries were able to obtain capital from abroad by selling bonds to private investors. However, many factors—including the downfall of the gold standard and the widespread bond defaults during the 1930's—have conspired to kill off the market for foreign bonds. Today it is hard for countries, except rich, developed ones with high credit ratings, to borrow this way.

One way underdeveloped countries obtain foreign capital is by means of *direct investment by foreign firms* (a U.S. company sets up an aluminum plant, a British firm drills for oil, or a German enterprise sets up an assembly plant). Many underdeveloped countries, however, for ideological reasons or because they feel that they have been exploited by foreign investors in the past, follow policies ranging from nationalization to confiscatory taxes that actively discourage rather than encourage foreign investment. The result, as Fig. 48.2 shows, is that the direct investments made by foreign

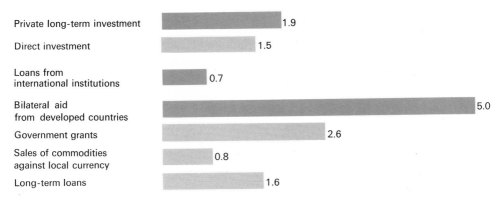

Private long-term investment   1.9

Direct investment   1.5

Loans from
international institutions   0.7

Bilateral aid
from developed countries   5.0

Government grants   2.6

Sales of commodities
against local currency   0.8

Long-term loans   1.6

48|2

Net flow of long-term capital to the underdeveloped countries, annual average 1961–1964 (billions of dollars). (Source: United Nations)

firms in the underdeveloped countries average a meager $1.5 billion dollars a year. (Note that this figure is less than 3% of the total investment that U.S. firms make in domestic plant and equipment during an average year.)*

In addition to getting foreign capital from private investors, underdeveloped countries also obtain *aid and loans from foreign governments.* As early as the 1920's Britain and France began giving economic aid to their colonies. After World War II they were joined by the U.S., which began— for a blend of strategic, military, and humanitarian reasons—to give economic aid to underdeveloped countries throughout the world. In the mid-1950's the Russians and other communist countries also began to make aid commitments. Now, in the 1960's, a number of new countries, including Germany, Italy, and several smaller European countries, have been added to the donor list. As Fig. 48.2 shows, bilateral aid transactions—that is, aid given by the government of one country to that of another—currently runs about $5 billion dollars a year. Much of this aid is in the form of grants and loans (usually the proceeds of bilateral grants and loans are "tied" to the purchase of goods in the aid-giving country). Some bilateral aid takes the form of sales of agricultural commodities for local currencies. (The U.S.

_____

* An interesting sidelight to this situation is that Russia, whose political line has done much to encourage the negative attitude that many underdeveloped countries have toward foreign investment, is currently looking to *private* Japanese investors for help in opening up the vast fuel and mineral resources locked in "underdeveloped" Siberia. Under deals now being negotiated, Japanese firms would provide Russia with as much as $2 billion in capital equipment, which Russia would pay for over an extended period of time by exporting oil, natural gas, timber, and minerals to resource-poor Japan.

sells wheat to India, not for dollars, but for overvalued, inconvertible rupees.*)

A third way the underdeveloped countries get foreign capital is by *borrowing from international institutions,* the most prominent of which is the International Bank for Reconstruction and Development. This institution was set up after World War II to finance reconstruction and to make development loans. The International Bank obtains capital to lend out from two sources: (1) the subscriptions that member countries are required to pay in, and (2) the sale of bonds to private investors. Loans from the International Bank and from similar institutions have financed a variety of useful projects, ranging from power stations to irrigation systems, in the underdeveloped countries. However, as Fig. 48.2 shows, these loans are small in volume. Currently new loans granted average only half a billion dollars a year.

The governments of the underdeveloped countries would like to see much more foreign aid coming their way, especially via the channel of international lending organizations. They contend that the developed countries ought to devote at least 1% of their total income to aiding the underdeveloped countries. And this figure is hardly unrealistic or unattainably high. England in the heyday of its colonial period devoted much more than 1% of its national income to foreign investment. However, the fact that two of the biggest aid givers, the U.S. and Britain, are today suffering severe balance-of-payments difficulties, and the fact that foreign aid, because of the slow results it yields, tends to be misunderstood and unpopular with voters in the aid-giving countries makes it unlikely that the underdeveloped countries are going to see their wish fulfilled, at least during the immediate future.

Since foreign investment doesn't fill the gap between the amount of capital the underdeveloped countries require and the amount they generate through saving, and since this situation seems unlikely to change, the underdeveloped countries—in order to catch up with the developed countries —are going to have to save more and to use what they save more effectively. This is easier said than done, but there are steps that the underdeveloped countries could take to achieve these twin goals. One important one would be to encourage the development of financial markets: a stock market, a bond market, and so forth. A second step would be to encourage the development of financial intermediaries. Financial markets and financial intermediaries may seem like fancy appointments appropriate only to a rich, developed country, but in fact they can serve a very useful function in an underde-

---

* As we noted in Chapter 25, the U.S. uses the sale of agricultural commodities under PL480 to kill two birds with one stone: getting rid of the domestic farm glut and helping out underdeveloped, food-short countries.

veloped country. Reason: In an underdeveloped country, just as in a developed one, the people who save and those who invest in real capital goods (such as machinery and manufacturing plants) often differ; so institutions are needed to channel funds from savers with surplus funds to investors in need of extra funds. In underdeveloped countries there is usually a dearth of such institutions, with the result that savers often invest their surplus funds in unproductive media (they hoard jewelry or tuck gold under the mattress), while producers in need of extra funds have to pay exorbitant rates to obtain even small loans. The emergence of financial intermediaries—that specialize, as many U.S. intermediaries do, in collecting funds from small savers and lending them out to small business firms and households—coupled with the establishment of financial markets would do much to improve this situation.

The Role of Foreign Trade

As a group, the underdeveloped countries are just as active foreign traders as the developed countries are. However, the importance of foreign trade varies greatly from one underdeveloped country to another. Large underdeveloped countries which—because of their size and geographic diversity—are able to produce a wide range of agricultural outputs and a variety of manufactured goods usually rely less heavily on international trade than small countries do. Thus exports and imports represent roughly 40% of total national output in little Jamaica, but only 10% in vast Brazil. The importance of foreign trade in the economic life of an individual underdeveloped country depends not only on its size but also on the kinds and quantities of its natural resources. Some underdeveloped countries have large supplies of exportable resources (Iran has oil and the Congo copper, to name two), and in these countries production for export may run as high as three-fourths of total national output.

The underdeveloped countries as a group export a wide variety of products. Most, however, are primary products: agricultural commodities such as cotton, cocoa, and coffee, and raw materials such as oil and ores. In return for these exports, they import some foodstuffs (e.g., wheat from the U.S. and Canada), and many industrial products: from the simplest consumer goods to the most complex capital equipment, from needles to hydroelectric generators.

The risks of trade. In many underdeveloped countries, especially those that rely heavily on international trade, trade makes economic life risky and precarious. Reason: World supply and demand of many primary products is inelastic. And, as Fig. 48.3 shows, when supply and demand are inelastic, even small shifts in either demand or supply lead to big changes in price. So countries which export sugar, cocoa, coffee, cotton, copper, and other primary products find that the prices of these commodities fluctuate widely from year to year. This situation might not be so bad if the average underdeveloped country exported enough *different* commodities so that the prices of some of its exports would be on the upswing when the prices of some of its other exports were on the downswing. But this isn't the case. An underdeveloped country's exports usually consist almost exclusively of one or two primary products. Examples: Coffee represents more than 60% of the exports of Colombia, bananas more than 40% of the exports of Honduras, sugar more than 80% of the exports of Cuba, cotton more than 50% of the exports of Egypt, rice more than 60% of the exports of Burma, tea more than 60% of the exports of Ceylon, copper more than 50% of the exports of the Congo, tin more than 70% of the exports of Bolivia, and oil more than 90% of the exports of Iraq.

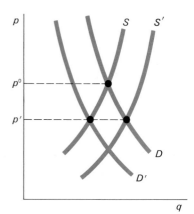

48|3

If supply and demand are inelastic, a small increase in supply or decrease in demand will cause a large fall in price (from p^0 to p').

The fact that the typical underdeveloped country relies heavily on a single export commodity means that fluctuations in the price of this commodity induce big fluctuations in the amount of foreign exchange that the country earns from exports. (A recent U.N. study shows that during the period 1954–1958, year-to-year fluctuations in the export earnings of the underdeveloped countries averaged 9 to 12%.) The underdeveloped country relies on imports both for consumption and for capital goods, and it must of course pay for these imports with foreign exchange. Thus the fluctuations in the prices it gets for its exports make it hard for such a country to maintain a stable standard of living and at the same time to implement long-term investment programs as well.

The underdeveloped countries have tried many schemes to reduce the variability of the prices they receive for their exports; chief among these schemes are *commodity agreements*. A commodity agreement's main object is to keep the price of the commodity in question—be it wheat, tin, coffee, or sugar—at a level that producing countries consider acceptable. If the support price chosen for a given commodity were the commodity's long-run equilibrium price, this support price could be maintained over time by setting up a buffer stock which would absorb excess supply during periods of glut and meet excess demand during times of shortage (providing, of course, that the commodity is nonperishable). Commodity agreements that call for buffer stocks are easy to set up on paper, but they work poorly in practice. One problem with the buffer-stock approach is that, if the buffer stock is financed by the underdeveloped countries, it won't alleviate, and may even worsen, the year-to-year fluctuations in the export earnings of these countries. Another problem is that the support price established for a commodity under such an agreement almost inevitably exceeds the commodity's long-term equilibrium price, and so brings forth permanent excess supply. Because of these and other problems, agreements that raise price by restricting output seem to be a more attractive possibility. However, agreements of this sort don't work out well in practice either. Reason: The actual and potential producers of most primary commodities are so numerous that it is virtually impossible for them to agree on and to effectively police restrictions on output. Therefore price hikes attained through pacts calling for output restriction generally tend to be limited in both size and duration.

The benefits of trade. International trade, although it poses problems for the underdeveloped countries, also brings them real and substantial benefits. Recall our wheat-steel example in Chapter 44. The principle illustrated there applies to the trade of underdeveloped as well as developed countries. According to this principle, the underdeveloped countries, by specializing in the commodities in which they have a comparative advantage and importing other goods in which they have a comparative disadvantage, are able to obtain more consumer and capital goods than they would if they were to produce themselves all the different goods they consume. Thus if the underdeveloped countries were to try to diminish the role of foreign trade in their economic life, they would reduce not only the variability, but also the size of their real income.

To say that the underdeveloped countries benefit from trade with the rest of the world does not, of course, mean that they can't or shouldn't do anything to reduce the risks trade brings. There are, in fact, several steps they can take: (1) They can try to diversify. Perhaps their resources fit them to produce other primary products in addition to those in which they already specialize. (2) They might try to further process some of the raw materials they export. Ghana might export chocolate instead of cocoa; Indonesia might export doormats instead of the coconut fiber used to make them. (3) They might try to add to their exports of primary products more light manufactured goods, such as textiles, T-shirts, or even tennis rackets.

The Role of Government

Many of the underdeveloped countries, although they are in a hurry to grow, distrust the ability of free markets and free enterprise to give them the big push they need to get out of secular stagnation into sustained growth. They usually feel that development, if left in the hands of private investors —foreign *or* domestic—would result in the exploitation of the economy as a whole or at least of large groups in the economy. For these and other reasons, the governments of most underdeveloped countries believe that they must take an active role in promoting and directing economic growth, despite the fact that in almost all the developed countries growth came about as a result of the activities of private investors and consumers, without the benefit of government encouragement or intervention.

In order to stimulate and guide domestic economic growth, most underdeveloped countries have set up *plans* of one sort or another. Such a plan usually covers some fixed time period; five years is a popular figure. The plan sets certain goals for the economy to attain. These goals may be stated in terms of the economy's overall rate of growth, or in terms of the rates of growth of specific commodities such as fertilizer, wheat, steel, and so forth. If the plan is a good one, the goals it sets will be based on a realistic inventory of the resources available to the economy, and will state the way the economy is to attain these goals and the policies that the government intends to use to keep the economy hewing to this line.

The ways that the government may promote and guide the economy are varied. As a minimum, the government will assume responsibility for supplying collective goods such as roads and schools which private producers require but which it's hard for them to supply. The government may also reshape private institutions in a way that helps economic growth. For example, it may encourage the growth of financial markets and financial intermediaries in order to promote savings and to facilitate the flow of funds. In addition, a growth-minded government may try to influence the size and composition of domestic investment by using tax incentives and subsidies to get private producers to invest where it wants them to. Also, it might go a step further and undertake various types of production on its own: It might build its own steel mills, as the Indian government has done, or it might go into mining, light manufacturing, or other areas of economic activity usually reserved, in the developed market economies, for private production.

Planning isn't, of course, a sure-fire cure-all. For one thing, the governments of different underdeveloped countries vary greatly in their ability to actively promote rapid growth. Many underdeveloped countries are split up the middle by geography or by differences in language and religion; and in such countries it may be all that the government can do simply to main-

tain law and order and hold the country together. Many underdeveloped
countries have few trained civil servants at their disposal, and so lack
the human resources necessary to set up and manage a complex development program. In addition government planners, like other people, are
fallible, so they sometimes make mistakes or do foolish things. (They put up
showcase steel mills when they should have invested in more mundane forms
of capital stock like fertilizer plants, or they use scarce resources to set up
grandiose sports stadiums instead of using these resources to acquire productive assets.) Despite these potential drawbacks, planning can and often
does make a real contribution to speeding up a poor country's growth rate.
Thus planning is popular in the underdeveloped countries, and seems sure
to remain so as long as there is such a dismaying gap between the income
levels of the underdeveloped and the developed countries.

PROBLEMS

1   In a 1965 speech President Johnson, who was concerned about the difficulties
that the population explosion in Latin America was creating for development in
this area, remarked that "less than $5 invested in (family planning) is worth
$100 invested in economic growth." Many Latin Americans greeted this none-
too-tactful remark with the retort that: "What we need is more, not fewer people. This will allow us to develop our sparsely settled areas faster." Who is
right, Johnson, who wants to cut population growth, or the Latin Americans,
who are content to let it boom along? Does your answer depend on whether
you define economic growth as growth in national output or as growth in output
per capita? [To gain perspective on this question look back at the figures quoted
in Table 48.1 on annual rates of population growth in different countries.]

2   "To explain much of the trade that occurs between the underdeveloped and
the developed countries, we don't have to invoke the principle of comparative
advantage. The principle of absolute advantage suffices." Discuss.

3   If the underdeveloped countries restrict the output of an export commodity,
they will raise its price but lower the quantity of it they sell. The first effect will
increase their export earnings, *but* the second will decrease them. So why should
the underdeveloped countries expect that, on balance, restricting the output of
an export commodity will raise their export earnings? [*Hint:* Recall our old
friend, elasticity of demand.]

4   In apportioning foreign aid, the U.S. government has been willing to help the
underdeveloped countries invest in areas that are generally reserved for government production in the U.S. (for example, to build dams or set up irrigation
systems), but it has been unwilling to help these countries invest in areas that
are generally reserved for private production in the U.S. (for example, to set
up steel mills or manufacturing plants). Why do you think that the U.S. takes
this position? Do you agree with it?

5   Usually the developed countries impose no tariffs on imports of raw materials, such as copper and cocoa, which the underdeveloped countries export, but they do impose duties on goods made from these raw materials. Do you think that this setup, which "discriminates in favor of the exports of the underdeveloped countries" is actually beneficial to the interests of these countries, or harmful to them? Why?

6   In recent years Brazilians have placed a special tax on exports of "green" (i.e., unprocessed) coffee beans that are used to make instant coffee, but they impose no similar tax on exports of instant coffee. What do you think that the Brazilians are trying to do?

7   The U.S., which taxes imports of chocolate but not of cocoa, claims that the Brazilian export tax on green coffee beans is "discriminatory," and has tried to force the Brazilians to give it up. Do you think that the Brazilian tax on *un*processed beans is any more discriminatory than the U.S. import tax on processed cocoa? Do both taxes have the same purpose?

8   The underdeveloped countries want the developed countries to help them set up commodity agreements and to finance buffer stocks to accompany them. Do you think that this would be a good way for the developed countries to aid the underdeveloped countries? [*Hint:* What does U.S. experience with farm-support programs indicate about what the end result of such a scheme would be likely to be?]

9   The underdeveloped countries are convinced that their growth would get a big boost if the developed countries would agree to impose lower import duties on manufactured goods from underdeveloped countries than on those from developed countries. Do you think that such a *preference system* would really contribute to the growth of the underdeveloped countries? Do you think that it would make a big contribution?

CHAPTER 49

ECONOMIC SYSTEMS:
A COMPARISON

MARKET ECONOMIES AND COMMAND ECONOMIES

Someone once asked the humorist James Thurber, "How's your wife?" Thurber paused a moment, scratched his head, and then replied, "Compared to what?" This story is a reminder that it's always a good idea, in any discussion, to keep in mind the alternatives. So far in this book, we have talked mainly about one method of organizing economic life: the market economy. But there are other methods, of course. In this final chapter, therefore, let us compare the way the market economy works with the way one other method—the command economy—works.

Once a civilization progresses beyond the subsistence stage in which people produce only for their own consumption, some mechanism for organizing and directing economic life is needed. This mechanism has to solve three main problems: (1) What goods the economy is going to produce (bananas or oranges, TV sets or tape recorders), (2) how these goods are to be produced (by combining a lot of capital with a little labor, a lot of labor with a little capital, or some other arrangement?), and (3) in what way these goods are to be distributed among the different consumers in the economy. (Does the steak go to Smith or Jones? And what about the hamburger?)

Let us now compare the way market economies and command economies go about solving these three problems.

Market Economies

We can sum up the most salient features of a *market economy* as follows: (1) Producers are free to decide what goods to produce and how to produce them, and consumers are free to decide what sorts of work to do and what sorts of goods to spend their income on. (2) The decisions consumers and producers make not only reflect their own preferences, tastes, and abilities, but also constitute a response to the prices established for different inputs

765

and outputs. (3) Prices are reasonably free to fluctuate; they depend on the supply of and demand for different goods; and they constitute the chief mechanism by which scarce supply is rationed out among would-be consumers.

There are other characteristics that are often associated with a market economy: (a) *The sovereignty of the consumer.* A typical market economy is responsive to the wishes of the consumer. It produces the goods he wants, and if his tastes change, so does the economy's output. (b) *Private ownership of the means of production.* In a market economy consumers and producers usually own the different inputs that are used to produce the economy's output. (c) *Profits are what motivates producers.* When a firm decides what output to produce and what inputs to use, it considers prices and production possibilities and makes its selection on the basis of where the greatest profit opportunities seem to lie.

Command Economies

To say that an economy is a *command economy* implies, in the most extreme sense of the term, that some person or authority in the society solves the problems of how, what, and for whom by fiat. This authority orders people to supply certain inputs, to produce certain outputs, and to consume certain goods. In a command economy: (a) The consumer by definition is not sovereign. (b) The authority that commands usually owns all nonlabor means of production, such as land and capital stock. (c) Maximizing profit is unlikely to be the guiding motive of productive units.

Mixed Economies

Most economies in the modern world are a mixture of the command and market varieties, with some weighted more heavily in one direction, some more heavily in the other.

The economies of the U.S. and Western Europe are essentially market economies, but they also have strong elements of command. In the U.S., schools, roads, defense, and many other goods and services are provided outside the market sphere. In these areas of economic life, the government decides what outputs are to be produced, how they are to be produced, and who will consume them. In the U.S. the government also influences the decisions of who, what, and for whom that are made by private producers. For example, the government outlaws certain activities such as making book. It also regulates public utilities so that they operate in the public interest; and it tries to keep private producers from doing things—such as polluting streams, setting up shop in the middle of a residential district, and using child labor—that would be against the public interest.

In most West European countries the nonmarket sphere of the economy is, if anything, more extensive than it is in the U.S. Government ownership of the means of production is much more widespread than it is in the U.S. Communications and transportation facilities are owned and run by the government, and sometimes other major industries are too. In Britain, for example, the steel industry jumps disconcertingly back and forth from public to private ownership, depending on whether the Conservative or the Labour party is in power.

In contrast to these predominantly market economies of Western Europe, the economies of Eastern Europe, Russia, and other socialist countries are predominantly command economies. In these countries the government owns almost all means of production; it decides what goods are to be produced, how they are to be produced, and to a certain extent who will consume them. However, in these countries people do receive money wages and they do buy many goods in the marketplace. Thus the socialist economies, like the capitalist economies, are a mixture of market and command.

PROFITS, PRICES, AND PERFORMANCE

How well do the market economies perform as compared with the way the command economies do? Let us look briefly at the pros and cons of each system.

Market Economies

Most market economies are *capitalist,* that is, the means of production within them are owned and controlled by private, profit-maximizing producers. Capitalism as a way of organizing economic activity offers a number of advantages. For one thing, since producers in a capitalist economy are out to maximize profits, they are anxious to produce the goods consumers demand. So output in a capitalist economy is responsive to the ever-changing wants and needs of consumers. Another advantage of a capitalist economy is that production in such an economy is usually carried on with a high degree of efficiency. Reason: Profit-maximizing firms seek to minimize costs, and to do so, they have to utilize inputs as efficiently as possible.

These advantages—and others—notwithstanding, the capitalist economies have during the several centuries of their development also displayed some serious faults. Think back to England during the Industrial Revolution. Workers toiled unbelievably long hours to obtain a meager income on which they could barely subsist. There was a vast gulf between their standard of living and that of the capitalists who owned the factories in which they toiled. And, as if that were not bad enough, the business cycle appeared to make conditions even worse. Periodically waves of depression swept across the capitalist countries, leaving unemployment and misery in their wake. Of course each depression was followed by a new upsurge of prosperity, *but* each period of prosperity was eventually followed by a new depression.

Cyclical insecurity and inequality in the distribution of income weren't the only faults of capitalism. As the capitalist economies grew, monopoly and the exploitation of the consumer grew also. In the U.S. at the turn of the century, the monopolies and trusts seemed to be on the verge of taking over the whole economy. Then thirty years later, in the 1930's, came the Great Depression. The force with which it lowered income and the stubbornness with which it persisted led economic prophets to conclude that something more than cyclical instability was in the wind. They reasoned that the capitalist economies had become victims of secular stagnation. They were stuck on a track that would never turn up.

All these different faults—inequality in the distribution of income, insecurity of income, monopolistic exploitation of the consumer, and the threat of stagnation—add up to a serious indictment of capitalism as a way of organizing economic activity. Yet over time each of these faults has been overcome. With a prod from the progressive income tax, the gap between the rich capitalists and the poor workers has been cut. Modern monetary and fiscal policy has taken much of the sting out of the business cycle. Antitrust policies have curbed the growth of monopolies and robbed them of their power to exploit the consumer. And an unparalleled decade and a half of expansion has dissolved the bugaboo of secular stagnation.

Examining the capitalist countries today, we may conclude that capitalism, tempered with a certain amount of government control, works and works well.

Command Economies

In a command economy all the various outcomes of the economic process can be controlled by fiat. Thus a command economy is, in theory at least, an ideal vehicle for achieving certain economic goals, such as a "fair" distribution of income, a rapid rate of growth, or the elimination of cyclical instability.

In practice, however, a command economy, like a market economy, has its drawbacks. Moreover, although tools have been developed for tempering most of the serious faults of a market economy, the drawbacks of a command economy have proved less tractable.

These difficulties are well illustrated by the experience of the socialist economies which, as we have said, come the closest of any to the command type of economy. In the typical socialist country, the state decides what inputs each productive unit (i.e., firm) will use, what outputs it will produce, and how these outputs will be used. Since an economy of any size is likely to contain thousands of firms, and since these firms are likely to use many thousands of inputs and to produce thousands of different outputs, figuring out a set of commands for all enterprises that are mutually consistent (e.g., a set of commands such that the total amount of steel that steel mills are supposed to produce will equal the total amount of steel that other firms are supposed to use, and so forth) is obviously no simple task.

So a command economy inevitably ends up with a big *bureaucracy,* whose job it is to figure out and administer plans (i.e., sets of commands) that will make it possible for the economy to attain the goals that it has set for itself during the current period and over some longer period, say 5 or 10 years.

In theory there is no reason why a bureaucracy shouldn't do a good job of running a command economy, but in practice it often proves to be a cumbersome and inefficient way to do so. One reason is that the problems that the bureaucracy is supposed to solve frequently exceed in complexity and scope what it is capable of handling. So plans set up by the bureaucracy are incomplete or inconsistent, and the economy doesn't behave as planned: Surpluses of some goods pile up, while acute shortages of other goods emerge. These difficulties are often aggravated by the fact that chains of command within the bureaucracy are so long and complex that decisions can't be made quickly and consequently the economy can't respond rapidly to change.* Finally, the bureaucracy of a command economy sometimes makes the mistake of substituting ideology for rationality as a basis for the decisions that it makes.

The shortcomings of its bureaucracy is only one of the problems likely to plague a command economy. Another is that it's hard for a bureaucracy to set up a plan that induces producers to perform better in one way without inadvertently encouraging them to perform less well in others. The socialist economies provide a good example: Their overriding objective has been to increase total output and in particular to build up heavy industry. Therefore the socialist bureaucracies have set up plans designed to induce producers to raise output as rapidly as possible. Under these plans an output goal is set for each firm, and the firm's performance is measured in terms of how well it meets this goal. Naturally the manager of an enterprise whose performance is measured solely in terms of output produced is going to develop a certain disregard for quality. Also, if he happens to be a manufacturer of consumer goods, he won't have any incentive for caring whether or not the x units of output he produces—be they socks, shoes, or shirts—are of the style and design that consumers want. So output in a socialist economy tends to be poor in quality and not particularly responsive to the needs of consumers.

---

* The last time the Russians revised their price structure, it took them seven years!

The socialist countries, because they put so much emphasis on quantity produced, have also been plagued by another problem. Their producers have no incentive to minimize costs, so they adopt inefficient methods of production:* They use more labor and capital equipment than necessary, they hold excessive inventories, or they combine capital and labor in the wrong proportion (i.e., in a proportion that is inconsistent with an efficient allocation of available inputs).

You might think that the socialist states could solve this problem by simply directing firms to produce efficiently. And to a certain extent they can. For example, a socialist government can direct enterprises to use one worker instead of two (or one machine instead of two), whenever possible. But getting firms to combine inputs in the right proportion is more difficult. Suppose (as is likely to be the case) that some firms have to make more subtle choices: They have to decide whether to use two workers and one machine, or two machines and one worker. What sort of directive can a socialist government issue to ensure that such firms will make the right choice, i.e., one that leads to an efficient allocation of inputs among producers? In a market economy the fact that firms are profit-maximizers and thus cost-minimizers suffices, as we showed in Chapter 18, to ensure that producers will combine capital and labor in the right proportion. So it would seem that a socialist economy ought to be able to achieve the same result by directing all firms to minimize cost. But no. In the typical socialist economy, prices are arbitrarily set by the government without regard to supply and demand. Therefore some inputs are overpriced, while others are underpriced. Thus if the government were to order firms to minimize costs, it might create a situation in which underpriced inputs were in scarce supply, while overpriced ones lay idle. Ordering firms to minimize costs can't be counted on to bring about an efficient use of resources unless the input prices on which producers base their calculations are the "correct" ones, that is, the ones that equate supply and demand.

A socialist planner who wanted to ensure that production would be efficient could, of course, always do so by being careful to establish correct prices before he directed firms to minimize cost. But without the benefit of freely functioning markets, he would be hard put to figure out what these correct prices were. His ideology might also make it hard for him to hit on the correct prices. According to Marxist doctrine, every output derives all its value from the labor used to produce it. So the socialist planner finds it hard to see why capital and land should earn any return at all.

---

* As we said in Chapter 18, *production is efficient* whenever it isn't possible—by rearranging the inputs that different firms use—to increase the output of one firm without decreasing that of another.

Revolution in Eastern Europe

In recent years the leaders of Eastern Europe and Russia have frankly acknowledged that their economic system, whatever its virtues, also has serious faults. Compared with the capitalist system prevailing in Western Europe and the United States, the socialist system just doesn't deliver the goods. And what is worse, the goods it does deliver don't compare in quality with those produced in the West. So economists in the socialist countries have been asking searching questions about what's wrong with their system and what can be done to make it work better.

The rather surprising conclusion that they have come up with is that the socialist system puts too much accent on centralized planning and too little on prices and profits! According to the new brand of socialist thinking, there is nothing inherently wrong with profits so long as the government exercises some control over the conditions under which they are earned and over who pockets them. They have also concluded that the best way to get firms to operate efficiently is to free them from excessive government control and to direct them to maximize profits. Another conclusion: Prices should not be set arbitrarily by the government, but should be free to respond to cost and demand conditions, so that planners can use them to establish priorities and producers can use them to make meaningful profit calculations.

These novel ideas have led the countries of Eastern Europe and Russia to undertake a number of economic "reforms." Plans are underway to free prices partially or wholly from government controls in several of these countries. Firms are being given greater autonomy so that they can manage their own affairs, choose the inputs they use and the output they produce. Managers of state-owned enterprises are being directed to maximize profits. And there's an incentive for them to do so: More and more frequently the bonuses that managers and workers get are being made to depend on the profitability of the enterprises in which they work. Managers of state enterprises are being sent to special schools to learn management techniques. Government planners are talking about opening up the socialist economies to increased competition from the West, largely on the theory that such competition would exert pressure on domestic producers to perform more efficiently.

Of course all this reform doesn't mean that the socialist economies of today will all be capitalist countries by tomorrow. There are a lot of factors —ideological conservatism, vested interests, fear of inflation, fear of unemployment, and a scarcity of good managers—that are making the reformers tread a cautious pace. And the reformers aren't out to ape capitalism in all respects. What they want to bring about is a form of *mixed socialism* that combines what *they* think is the best of the socialist and market systems. Nevertheless, brushing aside ideology and isms, it seems fair to say that the market socialism for which the reformers are shooting resembles in many ways the *mixed capitalism* that moral and legal restrictions on "free" enterprise have created in the market economies. Certainly the two systems, even if they do not become identical, ought to become more compatible, perhaps even capable of peaceful forms of competition and cooperation.

PROBLEMS

1   The U.S. is predominantly a market economy in peacetime, but in time of war we have always switched over to being predominantly a command economy. Why the switch? Is it consistent with our political philosophy?

2   It may be true that a rose is a rose is a rose. But you couldn't say the same about government enterprises. The experience of the U.S. and also of other countries indicates that how well a government enterprise functions depends greatly on the way it is set up. Public corporations, such as the Federal Reserve System, which have a great deal of independence usually operate much more efficiently than enterprises, such as the post office, that are directly under the control of a legislative body. What factors do you think explain this contrast?

3   One of the reforms that Russia and the East European countries have adopted in recent years is charging state enterprises interest on the capital that the state invests in them. Why is this reform necessary in order for resource allocation to be efficient?

4   Yugoslavia has tried to solve the problem of how to get away from private enterprise for reasons of equity and yet remain decentralized for reasons of efficiency by turning over most of the enterprises in the country to the people who work in them. Under the Yugoslav system, each enterprise is managed by a council elected by the workers employed in this enterprise and by a manager hired (and sometimes fired) by this council. The enterprise strives to maximize profits, and at the end of each year all the profits that the firm earns, after an allowance for new investment, are paid out in bonuses to the workers and to the manager of the enterprise.

   a) Can you give reasons why this arrangement stimulates an efficient use of resources?

   b) Why do you think this system has brought about a spurt in the salaries offered to good managers?

   c) How do you think this arrangement is likely to affect the distribution of income between workers and managers? Between workers in different enterprises?

   d) Can you think of any danger that this system might hold for the consumer? [*Hint:* What if a workers' enterprise happened to be a monopoly?]

5   In your opinion, what is the ideal way to organize economic activity?

INDEX